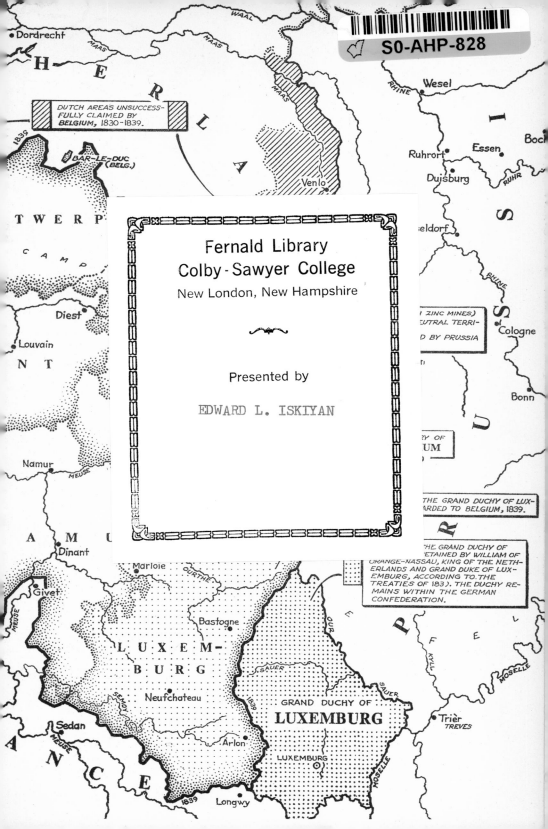

Issues in Contemporary Politics

Historical and Theoretical Perspectives

3

JO NATHAN E. HELMREICH

Belgium and Europe

A Study in Small Power Diplomacy

MOUTON · THE HAGUE · PARIS

Distributed in Belgium by
Librico N. V., Schelle near Antwerp

ISBN: 90–279–7561–2
© 1976, Mouton & Co, The Hague
Jacket design by Françoise Rojare
Printed in Hungary

To my parents
Ernst C. Helmreich
Louise R. Helmreich

Preface

Much has been written about the role of the great powers in the past century and a half, and a fair amount has appeared regarding Belgium and the concept of guaranteed neutrality during the nineteenth century. Yet there has been no long-range study of that small power's diplomatic history from the revolution of 1830 to the post Second World War era. Despite Belgium's key location and involvement in a number of important European affairs, her diplomacy has generally been overlooked amid the power conflicts of greater states. Moreover, much of the literature on specific episodes in Belgian diplomatic history which has appeared since 1945 has been written by participants in the events described; valuable as it is, there seems need for it to be assimilated and examined from a more distant perspective. Finally, there appears to be occasion for a study of Belgium's performance in terms of her actual diplomacy, rather than primarily in the terms of international law and the nature of neutrality.

This last point is of particular interest, for the diplomacy of small states unable to operate from a power base raises problems of diplomatic policy that merit examination in their own right. An investigation of the manner in which one small state has performed and the basic principles to which it holds may be useful at this time when small countries are appearing rapidly and the need of large powers to negotiate with them in a more understanding and effective manner than in the past is increasingly acute.

It should also be noted that the thought, or more accurately the conjecture, has long existed among historians that a careful examination of the diplomacy of small states might produce new information regarding old conundrums and great power diplomacy. While this is less rather than more the rule in Belgium's case, it is true that new insights can be obtained by a review of Belgium's experience, for example with Great Britain prior to the First World War and with France in the interwar period.

This account is intended to speak in varying degrees to these three areas of concern. To the best of my knowledge, it is the first attempt to examine in depth the diplomatic history of Belgium from the present state's inception through the Congo crisis of the 1960s, a span of years that witnessed immense changes both in the political order of Europe and in the ways in which statesmen attempted to create and maintain that order. While Belgium has not always been central to these events, her diplomacy does reveal how a small state responded to the changes and challenges of the international system. Her location and the skills of her leaders have also assured that she has been party to a number of events of significance in Western European affairs.

I have assumed a basic familiarity on the part of the reader with the main stream of European developments so that I may focus as directly as possible on the role and actions of the Belgian statesmen. Partly for reasons of documentation and partly for reasons of perspective, I am most concerned with the years up to 1940; the chapter on the later period is intended to aid the reader's own perspective and to provide some continuity into the present. This is not intended to be a theoretical work, and no attempt has been made to generalize from the actions of one small country principles of diplomatic behavior for all small countries. Such a task must be left to the political scientist who has studies of many small states at his disposal. Yet it is hoped that the diplomatic style of one important small state as it confronted several types of problems has been illuminated while the chief events of its diplomatic history have been discussed explicitly.

I am indebted to the authors of the many fine accounts which provided a foundation for this study. In particular I am indebted to the families of Paul Hymans, Henri Jaspar, and Jules van den Heuvel for permission to consult their papers. Mrs. Dorothy Moore Deflandre, Executive-Secretary of the United States Educational Foundation in Belgium, Mr. Cosemans of the Belgian Archives Générales, and Mr. P. H. Desneux of the Belgian Ministry of Foreign Affairs Service des Archives did much to facilitate my research. The Institute for International Education provided a Fulbright grant which enabled me to work in Brussels.

My sincere thanks go also to President Lawrence L. Pelletier of Allegheny College and to the Allegheny Student Government for research and typing grants. The editors of *French Historical Studies*, *The Historian*, and the *Journal of Modern History* have all kindly granted permission to use portions of my articles which originally appeared in those journals.

Many individuals have helped me along the way. Professor Gordon A. Craig first interested me in the intricacies of small power diplomacy, and Professors Cyril E. Black, Jerome Blum, Arno Mayer, and especially

Professor Jean Stengers of the Free University of Brussels have given advice and encouragement. I am grateful to the late Professor Donald C. McKay for his early guidance which sharpened my concern for France and the Low Countries. Professor Philip M. Benjamin, late Librarian of Allegheny College, was most helpful; Miss Dorothy J. Smith and Mrs. Hedwig McLamb have arranged marvelously many inter-library loans. Professors Paul B. Cares and Jay Luvaas have kept me going when the path did not seem clear. To them and to all of the others – my warm thanks.

I am especially grateful to those persons who have read portions of the manuscript in its various stages of growth: Professors F. Gunther Eyck, S. William Halperin, E. C. Helmreich, Jean Stengers, and my wife, Martha Schaff Helmreich, who has endured much so that this study might be completed. They have saved me from many pitfalls. I am, however, alone responsible for any defects.

Allegheny College
Meadville, Pennsylvania   Jonathan E. Helmreich

Contents

*

1. Introduction

Warriors and diplomats have struggled for centuries over the territories of present-day Belgium. The easiest path between France and Germany and the best avenue for entry of British goods to the Continent, the 'crossroads of Europe' was the bloodstained subject of controversies from before Caesar's Gallic Wars to Napoleon's defeat at Waterloo. It is not surprising that the creation in 1830 of a small, independent state upon the fertile and heavily populated lands was viewed as a bold and most likely foolhardy venture by many observers. In retrospect the step appears all the more fraught with danger because it enhanced rather than reduced the problems posed by Belgium's geographical location. The Dutch were resolved to regain their lost provinces; France and the German Confederation harbored annexationist ambitions. The British, for their part, were determined to prevent any great continental power from controlling Antwerp if the Dutch could not; indeed, they exhibited a marked desire to control the new state's affairs themselves.

The initial crisis was in time surmounted, but the challenge of maintaining Belgium's independence has continued, whether the concern of the moment has been a hostile Germany, an overfriendly France, or an aloof Britain. Because of Belgium's crucial location, the efforts of her diplomats in meeting this challenge are of obvious importance for the history of Western Europe in the nineteenth and twentieth centuries. They also merit attention apart from the particular circumstances of Belgium's place in Europe because they are illustrative of the attitudes and techniques of a small state forced to operate on an international scene characterized by power struggles. An examination from the Belgian viewpoint of incidents heretofore studied primarily in terms of the great nations' policies can also bring forward new information and nuances of interpretation which contribute to a better understanding of European relations in general. Hence the chief purposes of this account: to survey Belgium's foreign affairs since 1830; to consider the nature of a small

1

state's diplomacy in an international political system dominated by great powers; and to examine in detail certain diplomatic crises in which Belgium has played significant roles.

At the risk of belaboring the obvious, it might be well to add a few words concerning the second and third of these objectives, as they are responsible in considerable part for the approach which has been used and for a conscious imbalance in the extent to which various episodes are examined. Many of the problems confronting Belgium are similar to those with which great powers deal. But some are different and most are given changed emphasis and form by the country's small size. Of course there are many factors influencing Belgium's diplomacy, ranging from her geographic location to the relations of the ruling House of Saxe–Coburg, that are not directly connected with the size problem; nevertheless the latter is so pervasive that nearly all Belgium's actions must be interpreted as taking place within its context. Hans J. Morgenthau has pointed out that in international politics, armed strength 'is the most important material factor making for the political power of a nation'.[1] He goes on to say that while reliance solely upon force can not be termed both sage and peaceful, 'no diplomacy that would stake everything on persuasion and compromise deserves to be called intelligent'.[2] Yet in view of Belgium's strictly limited military potential, how far are her diplomats able to go beyond the arts of friendly persuasion and compromise? How have they compensated for the apparent lack of what Morgenthau considers the third essential means of diplomacy, the threat of force?

Because the problems posed by Belgium's size are intriguing in themselves and because a study of the response of the Rue de la loi* to this handicap might be useful in a larger context, an effort will be made to examine in increased detail certain incidents especially revealing of Belgium's diplomacy as a small power. Extra space will also be devoted to matters, such as the reparation and security negotiations after the First World War, in which the Belgian role has not yet been fully explored. Of course this can not always be done because the supply of primary documents is limited, as in the cases of the Congo and of Belgian policy since 1940.

Nor is it possible to comment concerning every aspect of Belgian diplomacy without turning the account into something of a catalogue. Yet it does not seem necessary to do this in order to give an accurate portrayal of the small nation's diplomatic behavior; such a tedious process would merely cloud the outlines of the picture while adding

* The place of the Belgian Government.

material which would meet the needs of only the specialist on a given period of Belgian history. Thus it is that extensive commercial relations with China, Imperial Russia, and other countries, a multitude of colonial tentatives by the first two Leopolds, Belgian relations with the Vatican (more a problem of domestic politics than European diplomacy), and other episodes do not find their way into the narrative. Some matters, such as the Crimean War, albeit they are important for the history of Europe as a whole, will not have great place because they did not involve Belgium deeply. On the other hand, the Congo requires attention even though it did not become a colony until 1908 and even though (or rather, because) the focus of the study is upon Belgium's European diplomacy. Sins both of commission and omission have doubtless occurred. It is nevertheless hoped that the prime intention of providing a general analysis of Belgium's diplomatic history will be achieved.

No study of the foreign policy of a country can be totally divorced from an awareness of developments in domestic affairs. This is especially true for Belgium's history immediately following her revolution and during the troubled period between the two World Wars. The excitability of the populace and the legislative chambers at the time of separation from the Netherlands was natural. When a certain amount of security had been achieved, however, most of the Belgians were content to trust the decisions of their leaders and to unite in loyal support of the actions of their king. The masses paid little attention to international events, and the influential merchant and professional classes were usually more interested in expanding trade and profits than in other matters. Except in times of crisis, it was only when commercial affairs were the issue at hand that the middle classes took a truly active concern in foreign affairs. One of the chief frustrations faced by the king and his ministers before both great wars was the difficulty of making the populace aware of the seriousness of the situation and of the necessity of taking immediate positive steps to meet it.

If during the nineteenth century the people normally spent little time considering foreign affairs, it was in part because their political attention was taken up by other concerns. These primarily were the role of the Roman Catholic Church in education and the extension of the franchise. The union of political groupings which had remained firmly cemented while the revolution was being challenged finally disintegrated in 1847. In its place appeared a government dominated by one party, the Liberals. Their rise to power constituted the first case of party or cabinet government in the western portion of the continent; for the remainder of the century the Belgian governmental process was to become less like the French and resemble more the British model.

The Liberals, led by the brilliant Waltère Frère-Orban, took as one of their main programs the laicization, and on some occasions also the secularization, of the schools. The Catholic party, normally the more conservative, was the advocate of an expanded franchise; its very name indicates the party's position on the school issue. The two parties fought bitterly and exchanged power several times. For the most part the Liberals remained dominant until 1884, when Catholic opposition to the Liberals' bill of 1879 requiring each community to have at least one secular public school brought their downfall. The Catholic majority remained slim until the passage in 1893 of a bill granting universal male suffrage, tempered by a system of plural voting (plural voting was abolished after the First World War, and women finally gained the vote in 1948). Elections in 1894 gave the Catholics a large majority; the Liberals failed even to do as well as the Socialist party, which was participating in its first national election. In later contests the Liberals improved their showing. Nevertheless, by 1914 the Catholics had been in uninterrupted control for thirty years, and the Liberals had become resigned to the role of a constructive opposition.

In the years following the First World War, the Liberals have never been able to gain control of a ministry. They have, however, participated in coalition governments and between the wars exerted considerable influence thanks to the character of their leaders, especially Paul Hymans. The Catholics, on the other hand, usually maintained a clear plurality; though there were really no one-party governments in the inter-war years, nearly all the coalitions were headed by Catholic prime ministers. This same pattern of Catholic party (now called the Social Christian party) dominance has held true since the Second World War, with the exception of the years immediately following the armistice and during a short span in the 1950s.

The expansion of the franchise not only influenced the decline of the Liberals but also had two more direct results which markedly altered the political structure of Belgium. One of these was the growth of the Socialist party as more and more workers gained the vote. Prior to 1914 the Socialists were excluded from all ministries, but during and following the war they were several times members of coalition cabinets. In most cases they were represented at the posts of minister of justice or of foreign affairs by their reknowned leader, Emile Vandervelde. Although Vandervelde once shared leadership of a cabinet, it remained for his young successor, Paul-Henri Spaak, to become in 1938 the first Socialist prime minister with complete powers. From 1945 to 1951, the Socialists played a key role in forcing the abdication of King Leopold III on the grounds that his conduct during the war had been improper and too friendly to the Germans (his decision to remain in Belgium after her defeat is still much debated). The Socialists controlled the cabinet from 1954 to 1958; but since then, except for a show of strength during the strikes of 1960–61, their power has waned. Nevertheless, during the first half of the 1960s the highly respected Spaak kept a firm hold on the foreign ministry portfolio. Differences between the Socialists and the predominant Catholics have frequently been sharp, yet on most issues other than the royal question compromises have usually been worked out. No better example of this can be found than the agreement of 1958 concerning the percentage of the costs of church controlled schools that should be paid by national taxes.

The second of the direct results of universal suffrage requiring mention here is the growth of sharp opposition between the two major linguistic groupings of Belgium. For nearly fourteen centuries the territories of present-day Belgium have been split into two language areas. The border between these has shifted somewhat over the years but has remained remarkably distinct. Today, north of a line running from Maastricht to the North Sea near Dunkirk, the Flemish population speaks a dialect of Dutch. To the south of the line, the population is Walloon, or French-speaking. Brussels is bilingual by law.

Actually, it is not precisely correct to refer to the Walloons and the French-speaking population as synonymous. There is a separate Walloon language which, however, is sufficiently similar to French to be viewed by some as a dialect of that language. Over the past hundred years the speakers of Walloon have decreased in number and their children have adopted French as their language. The small fragment of population in Belgian Luxemburg which speaks German or the Luxemburgish dialect has avoided involvement in the clashes between the two groups, but on occasion has taken advantage of reforms to win certain concessions for themselves.

In 1830 both Flemings and Walloons participated in the revolt, and a Belgian state was established which incorporated both groups. At that time language was as much a matter of political and economic class as ethnic origin. The aristocracy and bourgeoisie of both sections of the country preferred to use the French language. Patriotic and cultural reasons were often cited. Yet pride of class and economic factors were also important, as the textile weaving machinery of the industrial revolution imported from England brought a decline in the Flanders linen industry while the rising demand for coal and iron brought increased prosperity to Wallonia.[3]

The language of business, banking, the law, and politics was French. The former enemy had been Dutch. Thus, despite the presence of a

Flemish-speaking majority, French was the accepted official language following the revolution. Caught up first in the difficulties of obtaining independence and then in the controversies of the religious issue, the major political parties for several decades did not concern themselves greatly with linguistic matters. Only in the 1870s did a Flemish nationalist movement take root and achieve minor alterations in various laws. On the whole, the movement was more one involving pride of language and desire for recognition of the rights of the Flemish in relation to state administrative posts, the army, education, and the courts than a nationalist upsurge demanding separation from French-speaking Belgium. Yet by 1914 extremist groups were calling for administrative autonomy; agitation was widespread for the conversion of one of the four Belgian universities, that at Ghent, from a French to a Flemish-speaking institution.

In the battle for recognition, the Flemings came to oppose anything that would increase the influence of the Walloons and of France, which country was suspected of desiring to annex Belgium. It was to be expected that the Walloons should react in a similar manner, banding together in support of their own interests. During their occupation in the First World War, the Germans did all they could to accentuate the split; when the battles were over, it was clear the Flemings could no longer be denied some of their wishes. Upon his return to Brussels King Albert announced reforms which would improve the position of the Flemish-speaking populace within the nation. Despite the reforms, or perhaps stimulated by them, Flemish demands grew louder. Within the movement two viewpoints gradually emerged, one believing that meaningful reform could be achieved under the existing Belgian political system and the other calling for a major restructuring of that system with Flanders achieving autonomy or even reunion with Holland. Many maximalists, as the latter were termed, left the traditional political parties to join the Front party, an outgrowth of a soldiers' organization formed during the war. Events connected with the Second World War and the second German occupation discredited the Frontist group, but the Flemish movement itself was soon resurgent. It was especially strengthened by the growing preponderance of the Flemish-speaking population, for the birth rate among the devout Roman Catholic Flemish is markedly greater than that of the Walloons.

As linguistic issues have come to dominate elections more and more, the large political parties have been forced to develop wings for each group. The Liberals, who in the 1960s changed their official name to the Party of Liberty and Progress, have best been able to hold together the factions within the party. The Socialists for some time were successful, but a large splinter group left the party and formed the *Mouvement Populaire Walloon* as a result of the strikes of 1960–61. The Flemish have meanwhile been using their votes to put into power Social Christian party members favorable to their demands. Valiant efforts have been made to work out a reasonable solution, but each step has thus far led in the general direction of the division of Belgium into three autonomous administrative districts (Flemish, Walloon, and the Brussels agglomeration), an event which many responsible members of both linguistic groupings have heretofore wished to avoid.

It is against this background of domestic affairs that the Belgian diplomats have performed. At times, as during the later portion of the nineteenth century, these affairs had little specific effect on foreign policy. For those several occasions when they did, an attempt will be made to provide additional information when the crises are discussed individually.

NOTES

1. Morgenthau, *Politics*, p. 29.
2. *Ibid.*, p. 541.
3. Clough, *History of the Flemish movement*, p. 54.

2. Diplomacy of revolution

An opera is an unlikely cause of national disturbance; King William I of the Netherlands therefore saw no reason to ban a performance of *La Muette de Portici* in Brussels on August 25, 1830, even though it had hitherto been prohibited. True, the Belgian populace was restive, but the king had received an encouraging welcome upon his recent visit to a Brussels exhibition of national industry. Moreover, the fireworks scheduled for the twenty-third and the special illuminations in honor of the king's birthday on the following day had been canceled to avoid any gathering of crowds.

William's judgment in this decision, as in many of his regarding the Belgian portion of the Kingdom of the Netherlands, was mistaken. The opera of Scribe and Auber had a subject of appeal to revolutionary sentiments: a Neapolitan uprising against oppressive rule. The passions of the audience in the crowded theater were raised to a patriotic frenzy which passed to the throngs strolling the streets on the summer's evening. The spark was blown to a flame by the political refugees who had made their homes in Brussels. Spurred by knowledge of what had been accomplished in Paris a few weeks earlier, the *Bruxellois* were soon in active rebellion. In a few days volunteers from all over the southern provinces were streaming to their capital. When the Dutch finally overcame their reluctance to use force, William's troops were driven from the city.

Though a good number of battles were to be fought, the Belgians' contest with the Dutch proved more diplomatic than military. While it dragged on until 1839 and beyond, the first years were especially critical. The Dutch had to be resisted and the other powers persuaded to recognize the Belgian revolution. At the same time, it was necessary to establish a government, choose a chief of state, and arrange a myriad of domestic problems. How was the national interest to be defined? How indeed were the wishes of the populace to be determined in the turmoil of revolution, and how could they be translated into diplomatic action in view of the many domestic and international restraints which encumbered the diplomats?

The Belgians, for centuries under the domination of other countries, had little experience on which to rely, especially in diplomatic affairs. Militarily and diplomatically, they were at the mercy of the great powers. This pill the nationalistic revolutionaries found hard to swallow. The years from 1830 to 1833 were therefore a period of reconciliation of ardor and pride to a lack of leverage against the established larger states and to dependence upon the will of others. The vulnerability of the Belgians and the inefficacy of their efforts at diplomacy in these first years was to contrast sharply with the assertive boldness and confidence the Brussels officials were to show once they knew that their state, whether appreciated or not by the other European powers, would continue.

2.1 THE REVOLT

The smoldering fires of resentment at Dutch rule which broke into flame during the opera performance had been fed by years of grievances. The Belgians and the Dutch had been brought together by the diplomats of the great powers sitting at the Congress of Vienna. The Austrian Hapsburgs had no desire to continue their difficult rule in Belgium which had been interrupted by the French Revolution; yet the need of a firm barrier against any future French expansion was unquestionable. Thus when Lord Castlereagh, the British foreign minister, advocated the unification of the Lowlands under William of Nassau-Dietz, the plan was taken up in the major chancelleries.

Although the inhabitants of the southern provinces took little or no part in these discussions, their wishes and welfare were not ignored. Common opposition to Napoleon during the Hundred Days and the linguistic ties between the Dutch and Flemings suggested the two regions might forget their quarrels of past centuries and be willing to cooperate with each other. In any case, the Quadruple Alliance saw unification as necessary because two separate small states could not contain France; even with the added strength of union, the congress required William to build a series of forts through Belgium as a barrier to France. The Eight Articles regulating the union specifically protected Belgian interests. The new state was to be governed by the Dutch Fundamental Law which would first be modified by mutual consent. Religious freedom was to be assured, the Belgian provinces should be represented in the States General in a fitting manner, and Belgian merchants would have access to the markets of Holland and her colonies on an equal footing with the Dutch.

William, who had proclaimed himself King of the Netherlands on March 16, 1815, in response to the threat posed by Napoleon's return from Elba, appointed a select commission of Belgians and Hollanders to consider modification of the Fundamental Law. The commissioners agreed on a government which placed virtually all authority in the hands of the king. Ministers would be responsible only to William; the king would appoint over half of the Senate, and the Second Chamber would reject or approve but not amend legislative proposals. A snag was struck regarding representation in the Chamber, however. The Belgians, whose region possessed 3,400,000 inhabitants compared with Holland's scant 2,000,000, insisted that representation be proportionate to the size of the population.[1] The Dutch would accept no less than equal representation, pointing to their continued independence for two centuries and the colonial peoples over whom they ruled. The southern commissioners were defeated and also forced to accept the religious freedom stipulated by the Eight Articles even though it was opposed by the Belgian Roman Catholic hierarchy.

Disgruntlement over these points led the Belgian notables to reject the modified Fundamental Law decisively. William, however, proclaimed the law accepted; thus the conflict between the king and the Belgians began virtually at the birth of the united state. It was to increase steadily, for the Dutch could not think of Belgium as other than territory annexed to Holland, rather than as an equal part of the state. From the start they made clear their intention of keeping control of most governmental and administrative posts. The home ministry, for example, held 117 Dutch officials compared to 11 from Belgium in 1830; of the army's approximately 2500 officers, less than a fifth were Belgian.[2] Most honorary societies and public establishments were located in the North. The Belgians came to feel they were second class citizens in their own country.

Their annoyance was increased by the knowledge that if Belgian privileges were limited, they bore great responsibilities in paying taxes. The Eight Articles provided that the two regions would share equally their joint debts. But while the former Austrian Netherlands' liabilities amounted to thirty-two million florins, those of Holland amounted to two billion. The Belgians thus found themselves paying taxes to finance a debt which was mostly not of their own creation. Moreover, as the financial situation became more acute, the government successfully imposed the *abbatage* and *mouture*, taxes on butchers' meat and bread. Both were resented as feudal anachronisms, and the *mouture* received particular disapprobation because it weighed on the Belgians far more than the Dutch, who ate more potatoes and less bread than did their southern compatriots. An economic recession and the crop failures experienced in the late 1820s further increased the burden upon the Belgian lower classes, making them all the more ready to join in the upheaval when revolution eventually occurred.

Another aggravation was the king's failure to uphold the sections of the Fundamental Law regarding the independence of judges and the freedom of the press. Instead of a system by which the king would choose judges for life terms from a list presented by the lower chamber or provincial estates, William maintained a provisional arrangement initiated during the war against Napoleon. He thus held complete power in naming judges, who were removable from office at his pleasure. Similarly, there was kept in effect an ordinance published during the Hundred Days against attempts to pervert the loyalty of subjects or to disseminate information injurious to the state. Slightly modified in 1818 and approved by the States General, it nullified the article of the Fundamental Law which provided for freedom of the press. Incidents arising from its strict application were numerous and stimulated Belgian hostility toward the Dutch.

Despite their opposition to the Hollanders' manner of ruling, the Belgians initially were themselves divided. Walloon-Flemish differences, although important, did not yet have a major effect upon political alignments. The clerical question did, as the Catholic party defended the position and authority of the Roman Catholic clergy while the Liberals, under the influence of the principles of the French Revolution, demanded more toleration and less clerical influence. Yet both Catholics and Liberals were Roman Catholics, and in their Catholicism shared a dislike for living under protestant rule. The clericals, resenting being required to give allegiance to a protestant king and opposed to the toleration clause of the Fundamental Law, took only a qualified oath to the constitution. Their intemperate attacks on the regime increased in the years after the union. So acute did the situation become that William negotiated a concordat with the papacy in an attempt to placate the Belgian catholics. All seemed arranged when a change in the Vatican's position made William's efforts go for naught. This breakdown in William's relations with the Catholics did not benefit his position with the Belgian Liberals. Had he been a more skillful politician and more observant of the Belgians' differences, he might have won this group to his side. As it was, he accomplished a more difficult task. By 1828 he had welded the Liberals and Catholics into a united opposition which took as its program freedom of worship, instruction, and the press.

William was an intelligent man, possessing sound training and wide experience. He was also a man obsessed by details, confident in his judgment and ability (which in some areas was considerable), and pride-fully concerned for his untrammeled authority. H. Lytton Bulwer describes him well as 'a ruler who was one of those clever men that constantly do foolish things, and one of those obstinate men that support one bad measure by another worse'.[3]

It was William's failure to recognize the extent of the Belgians' displeas-ure and the growing sense of national identity in their complaints that led him to disregard their protests that the Dutch were running the country solely to their own benefit. His attitude on the language issue is revealing of the lack of communication which existed between him and his new subjects. The king's desire was to build national feeling and unity; to achieve this end, he urged acceptance of Dutch as the national tongue. The language was made official in 1822. The choice was understandable, for the population of all the northern provinces and about half of the southern spoke dialects of the tongue. It was not reasonable. Half the Belgians spoke French or Walloon, and their number included nearly all the professional men and leaders of society. Even though several years of grace for learning the new language were offered, how could Belgian lawyers hope to maintain their positions? How would French-speaking defendants be able to follow the trials? Such problems required scores of years for gradual settlement, but William pressed ahead with impatience. Concessions were made in 1829, but by then a majority of the leading figures of the South, receiving considerable support in Flan-ders as well as in Wallonia, were calling for autonomy from Dutch rule.

By spring of 1830 William's relations with the southern half of his realm were at an impasse. The previous year numerous petitions for re-peal of the *mouture* and *abbatage* had been presented. The king rejected them, although he did make concessions on other taxes, education, and the use of the Dutch language. The angered Belgians thereupon success-fully defeated the proposed ten year ways and means budget and forced the government to settle for a one year budget minus the *mouture*. William in his wrath dismissed six Belgian deputies from their govern-ment posts. The southern press, already bitter in its criticism of the king, became vitriolic. When the monarch finally made significant concessions in June 1830, the time was too late. The fever born of the successful revolution in Paris spread northward with a pernicious influence that Metternich well recognized when he later summarized the causes of the Belgian revolt to his new ambassador to the Netherlands:

This antipathy [between the Belgian people and the Dutch] is founded on the diversity of commercial, agricultural, and other interests between the two parts of the kingdom, and on the opposition between the religious principles of their inhabitants; it has been kept alive by mistakes on the part of the Government as conspicuous as they are to be regretted; but it is none the less probable that had it not been for the recent catastrophe in France, and the action taken by the agents of the revolutionary faction in that country, the occurrences in Belgium would never have assumed the seditious character of an insurrection.[4]

The calm witnessed by William on his visit to Brussels was merely a deceptive lull. Any incident, even as unlikely a one as the performance of an opera, could trigger the mobs into demonstrations. The barricades finally rose the night of August 25.

Although they participated eagerly in the riots, most *Bruxellois* did not at first think in terms of complete separation from Holland. An assembly of notables meeting three days after the outbreak sent a delegation to ask the king to consider Belgium's grievances and to discuss them with the States General. A Committee of Public Safety was formed of which the majority were moderates. Revolutionary groupings did call for a provisional government but, until September 20, in vain. On that day the populace stormed the Brussels *Hôtel de Ville*; the Committee of Public Safety was disbanded as was the citizens' guard that had policed the city. The hold of the moderates was shattered.

Before this occurred, nearly a month had passed in which William could have brought the Belgians into agreement. He failed through a mixture of too little and too much firmness. The first course might have gained the day initially, but the Prince of Orange when sent to negotiate was not empowered to take decisive action to meet their grievances; he merely ordered the royal troops to withdraw from the sectors of Brussels they still controlled. Meant as a conciliatory gesture, it was interpreted as one of weakness. At the same time William dismissed a hated minister and agreed to call the States General for the thirteenth. By then the king was willing to take a stronger line; so were the Belgians, for Charles Rogier had arrived from Liege leading a band of determined revolutionaries. After the extremists seized the town hall, William ordered the show of force that earlier might have succeeded. Since the States General had just voted for administrative separation of the Dutch and Belgian provinces under the king, it was assumed there would be little opposition to the entry of royal troops into Brussels. Nevertheless, the inhabitants did resist, and aided by reinforcements from the countryside, defeated the Dutch in a remarkable battle fought for three days before the Brussels palace. On September 27 the Dutch again withdrew. Following the victory, the Belgians formed a provisional government; most towns in the southern provinces joined the national cause; and Belgians serving in the royal army defected in swarms, leaving William with skeletal formations. The Prince of Orange briefly established himself at Antwerp, but on October 25 he evacuated all but the citadel and two days later subjected the city to a fearful parting bombardment. While the Dutch regrouped their forces, the rebels elected a National Congress which on November 18, 1830, declared Belgium an independent state.

2.2 The London Conference and election of a king

All these events were viewed with something less than equanimity by the great powers of Europe. Revolution was anathema to the conservative eastern courts of Prussia, Russia, and Austria. The July crisis in Paris had been upsetting enough; now it appeared that the contagion was spreading. Worst of all, the Brussels revolt had destroyed the main barrier constructed in 1815 against future French attempts at expansion. Austria and Russia would have liked to intervene, and Tsar Nicholas proposed 60,000 men be mobilized for joint action. But neither country was properly prepared or near enough to Belgium for effective military action, nor did the Prussian king desire Russian troops to march through his territories. Each monarch was disturbed by the unrest plaguing the Tsar in the Polish sections of his empire, unrest which begat revolution by the end of November and thus reduced the possibility of Russian interference in the Belgian crisis. The Prussians, concerned by an outbreak at Aachen and nervous about the fate of their fortress at Luxemburg, did appear committed to action in Belgium when a protest by France halted their preparations.

The position of Louis-Philippe was awkward. The new monarch's hold on the French throne was not secure, and it was evident that while he might partially resist the zealots who urged that France lend military support to the Belgian rebels, he could not ignore them entirely. Yet all of Europe was waiting to chastise him were France to make an overt gesture. Since Prussian invasion of Belgium would bring the domestic overthrow of the July Monarchy in any case, the French foreign minister, Count Molé, warned Berlin that he favored non-intervention in the Belgian affair; if Prussia sent troops, France would also.

It was the generally favorable attitude of Britain which was dominant throughout the Belgians' efforts to challenge the existing order and break into the European system. The Tory Prime Minister at the time of the revolt, the Duke of Wellington, regretted the disruption of the Vienna system. Just the same, he did not want to pledge British military aid to King William I, the weaknesses of whom he readily recognized. England's interests required comfortable relations with France, and when Molé indicated that France wished arrangement of the Belgian matter, the Duke was willing to cooperate.

In The Hague hope was maintained that, given Wellington's past support of the conservative principles of the Vienna settlement and the known sympathies of the eastern courts, an international conference would settle the affair in William's favor. So it was that the king requested the calling of the very conference which in time recognized the Belgian state and proved its best protector from William's grasp. He had assumed the conference would meet at The Hague, but Molé's opposition made London a compromise choice, and it was there that the representatives of the powers assembled on November 4, 1830.

The leading figure throughout the negotiations was the chairman of the conference, Lord Palmerston, who became foreign minister for the Whigs when Wellington's government fell days after the opening session. The change of British governments was a blow to Dutch hopes; it and the Polish Revolution served to turn the conference to a path which it otherwise might not have taken. Chafing, opposing, and sometimes cooperating with Palmerston was the French ambassador, Prince Talleyrand, ancient but still worthy of his reputation as a dextrous and sometimes unscrupulous negotiator. Austria was represented by the hard working but tactless Wessenberg; the Prussian ambassador was the cooperative Heinrich von Bülow, and Russia sent Matuszewic, who was aided (or hindered) by Prince Lieven and his renowned wife. The well liked Baron Falck, later joined by Zuylen van Nyevelt, intended to represent the Dutch in the meetings of the powers; to his sovereign's wrath, however, he was excluded from the conference sessions proper and forced to negotiate on the periphery, as was his young Belgian counterpart, Sylvain Van de Weyer.

Even before Palmerston replaced Wellington, the Belgians made a gain when the conference proposed an armistice based on the borders given Holland by the Treaty of Paris of 1814. Though the powers disclaimed any intention of prejudging the issue, their protocol benefited the Belgians by treating them as recognized belligerents rather than as rebels. Though disgruntled over this 'betrayal' by the powers, William agreed to the armistice as the best means of improving relations throughout all of what he still considered his kingdom. The Belgian reaction was different. The boundaries of 1814 would give Maastricht and the Duchy of Luxemburg to William. The inhabitants of these regions had supported the revolution and were not under Dutch control. Why should they be abandoned? The pro-French faction, angered by European intervention and overconfident of French support and Belgium's own military capabilities, opposed the terms of the armistice. Their sentiments were evident in the congress' November 18 declaration of the independence of the Belgian people 'excepting the relations of Luxemburg with the German

Confederation'. Luxemburg, of which William of Nassau was duke, was a member of the German Confederation, and the Belgians willingly acknowledged that this would necessitate some arrangement; but they also implied that sovereignty in the area belonged to them.

The audacity of the Belgians' declaration would not have borne fruit but for the stubborn behavior of the Dutch king. Having accepted a suspension of arms, he insisted on using Dutch control of the mouth of the Scheldt to close the river, cutting off the trade of Belgium's chief port, Antwerp. The conference, now beginning to adopt increasing powers for itself, resented William's behavior and on December 10 ordered the Scheldt opened. Viewing this as an indication that the conference might be more favorable to them in the future and shrinking before the threat of an international blockade of the Scheldt, the Belgians accepted the armistice. They were, however, still able to indulge their bellicose sentiments, for when William refused to lift his blockade of the river, the rebels resumed their seige of Maastricht. Annoyed by William's disregard for the conference's advice and by his delays, Palmerston seconded the French proposal that Belgium be recognized as independent. Wessenberg, the leader of the eastern court representatives, quickly saw that if the conference were to be maintained, the step was necessary. On December 20 a protocol officially acknowledged Belgium's independence.

The balance of power system had been preserved, as each of the great states recognized that compromises were needed if general warfare were to be avoided. Naturally enough, the two small nations most directly involved had been and would continue to be the least willing to cooperate. This was especially true of the Belgians, who refused to admit compromise settlement for what it was, an advantage for them. It was not their diplomacy nor their military might that gained them their first success, although they persisted in giving these great credit. Rather, it was the stubbornness of the Dutch king and the structure of the international power scene that had aided them. To admit this was nearly impossible for the rebels, as it was William and the order of post-Vienna Europe they were challenging. From their point of view, they were acting positively and boldly outside the existing system; they could not realize that from the different viewpoint of the powers, they were very much within the existing system and that their militant gestures appeared as childish posturing. Thus for many of the succeeding months of negotiation, the Belgians were able sincerely to justify positions that were seemingly indefensible. As Henri Pirenne has commented, they acted 'in their weakness just as had the French Convention at the close of the eighteenth century in its strength'.[5] Eventually the powers, non-plussed by the obstreperousness of the miscreant child they had treated so generously, were to make concessions to Belgium they had originally never contemplated. Almost always this was done in spite of, rather than because of, the rebels' diplomacy.

The immaturity of the Belgians' understanding of their relations with the great powers was revealed in their reception of the Bases of Separation proposed by the conference and the manner in which they chose their new king, two matters which became closely linked. It is not entirely clear how the Bases of Separation were settled upon. Apparently it was Talleyrand who again forced the issue. He did so not out of sympathy for the Belgians but to further his schemes by which France should gain parts of Belgium for herself. There had been calls for this in the French chamber, and it was known that the new French foreign minister, General Horace Sebastiani, would have liked to abandon his sovereign's moderate approach for a more radical policy. But outright annexation could not be accomplished immediately; so Talleyrand on his own initiative proposed that Belgium be made into a federated state. Eventually one of the Walloon divisions might join France. As compensation for England, he suggested that Antwerp and Ostend be maintained as free cities, assuring Britain entry into the Continent for her goods. Such an arrangement met the united opposition of Palmerston and the representatives of the eastern courts. Talleyrand fought fiercely and tried to the last to regain the Philippeville and Marienbourg districts which had been stripped from France after Napoleon's Hundred Days. Eventually the old man was starved into submission at a marathon session.

If the other powers were to reject an arrangement favorable to French expansionism, it was necessary that they have their own program. Championed by Palmerston, it was simple, as stated in a protocol of January 20. Those regions which were not part of the United Provinces in 1790 would belong to Belgium, which state would be neutral. There is much debate over who initiated the neutrality proposal. Matuszewic was one of its earliest supporters; Talleyrand incorporated it in his federation scheme but later firmly opposed it. The economic Bases of Separation were stated in a separate protocol of January 27, which suggested that Belgium should be allowed to trade with Dutch colonies and should pay sixteen thirty-firsts of the existing debt of the Kingdom of the Netherlands.

It was agreed that enclaves created by the terms of the January protocol would be exchanged under the supervision of the five courts. Maastricht and the section of Zeeland through which the Scheldt flowed from Antwerp to the sea went to William, as did the Duchy of Luxemburg by virtue of an exception to the main clause of the arrangement. The right to navigate the Scheldt was guaranteed to the Belgians.

The terms for the most part ran in the favor of King William, who, influenced also by public opinion in Holland, lifted his blockade of the Scheldt. To the Belgians, the Bases seemed more disastrous than the armistice terms, for these were meant to be definitive. The rebels were to be severed from their friends in the Duchy and would lose Venlo and a number of villages on both banks of the Meuse River. Maastricht was given completely to Holland with no compensation for the Belgians, despite their argument that in the past the United Provinces and the Bishop of Liege (whose territorial rights now were attributed to Belgium) had exercised joint authority in the city. Almost as unfortunate was the loss of the left bank of the Scheldt. Although the Flemish-Zeeland region had remained loyal to William the Belgians saw its possession as vital to the insurance of their freedom of movement on the Scheldt and to the protection of Flanders, for the sluices controlling the water outflow from that region were located in the disputed territory. In the opinion which the Belgians communicated to the conference, loss of these lands to the east and north was incompatible with the maintenance of their independence.[6]

This was of course not the case; the Belgians, still intoxicated by the success of their revolt, were in no mood to reason that the powers were being lenient. Compromise on the territorial issue was still psychologically impossible for the rebels. As for the partition of the debt, they thought it unjust; besides paying over half of the debt of the Kingdom of the Netherlands, they would have to finance the same proportion of the large debt incurred by the Dutch before the union.

If the unrealistic territorial aspirations of the Belgians led them to disappointment, so did their initial behavior in the selection of a king. The matter was of critical import to the powers, and the fate of Belgium hung on her choice. The candidate that received the vigorous backing of British Prime Minister Grey and his emissary to Brussels, Lord Ponsonby, was the Prince of Orange. His selection was hardly palatable to the majority of the revolutionaries, and became even less so when William declared he would let his son accept the throne only as his deputy. So ingrained was the Belgians' dislike of their former ruler that far from selecting his son as their monarch, on November 23, 1830, they voted the exclusion of the House of Nassau from Belgium. This step, taken against the advice of several states including France, was a rude gesture to Grey and a direct affront to the Tsar, who was brother-in-law to the Prince.

To the members of the conference, it was a needless expression of vindictiveness which reflected the diplomatic immaturity of the revolutionaries. Yet it was also an expression of the emotional fervor of the revolution which had changed in nature from a rebellion against palpable injustices to something of a national movement. Great sacrifices had been made and blood shed. The original territories of the revolution seemingly had to be retained because, through the participation of their inhabitants in the revolt, the lands had become part of a sacred *patria*. The opponent of the revolt was William of Orange; to accept his son as king would compromise the very Belgian identity of the rebellion. Moreover, the leading revolutionaries were well aware of the Orangist leanings of some of the aristocracy and upper bourgeoisie; they did not wish to allow any chance of a restoration for William.

The Belgians knew the alternatives to their independence were reunion to the Netherlands or partition. As partition would give territory – almost undoubtedly the very territory containing the barrier fortresses – to France, the Belgians boasted they could count on the powers' distrust of France to vitiate the latter alternative.[7] The former they would scotch themselves. They saw the exclusion vote as a gesture of strength and determination, indicating independence of any conference in London which might be trying to control their fate. They were indeed at the mercy of the powers, and some tact might well have been useful. But the possibility of rejecting the prince while not excluding his house required a restraint foreign to the hectic pace of the time and all too uncharacteristic of a revolt.

The group which had worked hardest for the exclusion of Nassau centered about a leading member of the Chamber, Alexandre Gendebien. He and his friends were Francophiles, and Gendebien himself had visited Paris in the fall to sound the possibility of the second son of Louis-Philippe, the Duke of Nemours, ascending the Belgian throne. The French king and his foreign minister played a double game. They knew from Palmerston's warnings that Nemours would never be acceptable to the powers and told the Belgians as much. Yet at the same time they indicated that France would be overjoyed if Nemours could take the Belgian throne.

A further complication was provided by the candidacy of Duke Auguste of Leuchtenberg, the eldest son of Eugene de Beauharnais. If there were a candidate that Louis-Philippe for his own security in France could not allow on the Belgian throne, it was this Bonapartist. Yet the boom for him in the little country was undeniable. Many Belgians, seduced by the magic of the name and by the pleasing thought that they would not be letting the powers dictate their choice, rallied to the Bonapartist banner. Nemours alone could challenge Leuchtenberg; thus when the latter's election appeared imminent French Foreign Minister Sebastiani let it be known he would not support the Bases of Separation so detestable to the Belgians. The revolutionaries quickly made their own interpretations of this gesture and on February 3, 'losing all sense of realities', to use the phrase of Robert Seton-Watson, elected the Duke of Nemours as king.[8]

Palmerston firmly opposed these developments. When Talleyrand attempted to win his acquiscence to the candidacy of Nemours, the Englishman warned of war and proposed that the five powers formally renounce the Belgian throne for their ruling families. Talleyrand squirmed and refused to sign the self-denying protocol of February 1. But the game was up, and once Leuchtenberg was defeated, Louis-Philippe declined the Belgian throne for his son.

By flirting with impossible choices, the Belgians had squandered an opportunity to solidify their position. As long as their government were not fully organized the danger of partition remained real, no matter what the possible difficulties it implied for the European balance of power; and indeed that solution was again mooted in the great capitals. Moreover, the Belgians had opened themselves to considerable humiliation just at the point when mature behavior might have won them concessions from the other powers. Finally, they lost some of the French support which would have been so valuable in such negotiations, for on April 4 that state officially recognized the January protocols. This change of policy was the result of the replacement of the discredited Laffitte as French prime minister by Casimir Périer. Determined to maintain peace, Périer would make what moves he could to improve Franco-British relations.

The election debacle forced the rebels to make changes also. Since a chief of state was a necessity, the elderly Erasme Surlet de Chokier was chosen as regent. He possessed only limited experience and capabilities, had seldom exerted leadership, and was better known for his appreciation of the simple comforts of life than for clear thinking. Yet his friendly and unprepossessing nature won the affection of the people; it was more on this count than on any other that he was first elected president of the National Congress and then regent.[9] As he was an ardent Francophile who defended the election of Nemours despite the powers' obvious distrust of Franco-Belgian ties, it was well the selection of a new prime minister offset the impression made by the choice of a regent.

Joseph Lebeau, although a firm opponent of Orange, was primarily known as the leader of the anti-French party in the congress. He had initially hoped to procure for Belgium a dynasty from the ranks of her own population. His appeal to the Prince de Ligne rejected, he had placed the name of the Duke of Leuchtenberg in candidacy before the congress. The regent would clearly have avoided Lebeau's appointment, but the refusal of Nemours had discredited the Francophiles, and there seemed no alternative to the young lawyer and journalist from Liege.

In the beginning stages of the revolution, Lebeau had been as fiery as most of his compatriots in denouncing the activities of the London Conference, declaring on January 3, 1831, that it must learn that the question of boundaries was within the jurisdiction of the National Congress only.[10] His support of the Bonapartist candidate for the throne had also been unwise. The responsibility of office had a sobering effect, however. Lebeau was acutely aware of the embarrassing position in which the election debacle had placed his country. Further determined to resolve the dynasty question in a manner suitable to his own views before the Francophile party could regain strength, he set out to obtain a monarch as soon as possible.

The first minister was ably aided in his efforts by Sylvain Van de Weyer, the Belgian emissary to London who briefly served Lebeau as foreign minister before returning to the less prominent but critical post to which he was better suited. Van de Weyer proved a mainstay throughout the negotiations, and for the next several decades he continued to be a major influence on Belgian policy. It was indeed fortunate for the Belgians that they had men of his and Lebeau's caliber, not only because of the difficulty of the situation, but also because, like any new state, Belgium lacked a supply of experienced diplomats. Before 1830 only nine of the thirty-nine diplomats of the Netherlands were of Belgian origin. During the first months after the revolution, the Belgians tried upwards to a dozen special commissioners at London in negotiations with Palmerston, the conference, and Prince Leopold. Of them all, Van de Weyer was the most durable and the most successful.

Van de Weyer himself lacked experience, being only twenty-seven years of age at the time of the revolt. Yet he was astute enough to realize that Belgium's future depended on his establishing good relations with Palmerston. France had made clear that she sided with the revolutionaries but would act in their behalf only to the extent this would not alienate the British foreign minister. Upon his arrival in London before the beginning of the conference, Van de Weyer had therefore done all he could to win British friendship. His charming manner and fluent English soon gave him success. He was also amenable to Palmerston's coaching. At one point the Britisher wrote that he had:

persuaded him [Van de Weyer] that the only use of a Plenipotentiary is to disobey his instructions and that a clerk or a messenger would do, if it is only necessary strictly to follow them. I have got him, therefore, to throw overboard most of what he was ordered to do...[11]

Van de Weyer did wish to be accommodating, and this attitude led the great Palmerston to a patronizing tone on occasion, as when he commented that 'our little friend, like Cato's gods, likes to find himself on the side of the victor, and he would not have shifted his ground, had he not felt a strong presentment...' of where victory would lie.[12] Nevertheless, it was Van de Weyer's flexibility and his willingness to support the best settlement that would work, rather than doctrinally to defend unattainable goals, that made him valuable to both the Belgians and the British. Courage he did not lack, for more than once he took positions that conflicted with Belgian public opinion, the wishes of the five powers, or those of his own superiors.

The situation of the Lebeau ministry was awkward, made so by the election fiasco and by the uncompromising stance of previous ministries. Although the Belgians had agreed in late January to a suspension of arms, they had rejected the Bases of Separation; indeed, one of the first acts of the regent was a ringing proclamation to the inhabitants of the Duchy of Luxemburg, bidding them to remain united with their revolutionary brothers in Belgium. It was a deliberate provocation of Europe and, in the view of a later historian, an open invitation to France to invade and annex Belgium and the duchy.[13]

Palmerston, Talleyrand, and Sebastiani, who seldom agreed with each other, were united in their annoyance at the regent's action. When Van de Weyer took the foreign ministry portfolio and in his turn attacked the protocols, he was lectured by the current French emissary in Belgium, General Belliard. Did the Belgian government not realize that in rejecting the protocols the Belgians themselves were weakening those acts of the conference which were most favorable to Belgium, namely those recognizing her independence? Moreover, not only was the regent's proclamation impolitic and dangerous, but it also showed lack of regard for France in that her advice had not been solicited nor had she been forewarned.[14]

These criticisms spotlighted the rebels' dilemma in attempting to modify the protocols. Any questioning of the London Conference would simultaneously cast doubt on Belgium's independence. Any Belgian initiative would be interpreted as ingratitude, if not defiance. The latter issue could be smoothed over once the conditions of the small country's independence had been established; but how to cope with the first while trying to ameliorate the conditions? Lebeau and Van de Weyer became convinced that the only answer was to have a king who could negotiate with the powers for them.

Months earlier the name of Leopold of Saxe-Coburg had been put forward. It received little support for two reasons. Leopold was a protes-

tant and the widower of the late heir to the British crown, Princess Charlotte. True, the prince possessed many of the attributes desired in a monarch – sagacity, political acumen, far reaching connections, natural
dignity, and handsome appearance. So much so, in fact, that he had
earlier been offered the throne of newly independent Greece, which he
had only briefly accepted. Leopold could, of course, change his religious
denomination to accommodate the catholic Belgians, but the link with
England remained a stumbling block. Yet this was just what attracted
Lebeau to Leopold as a candidate. His selection would demonstrate that
the Belgian revolution was a national, rather than a French, one. The
suspicions of the powers would be relaxed and Belgium would presumably gain diplomatic support in Germany and Great Britain.

French opposition to Leopold was to be expected, and so Gendebien
again traveled to Paris. Louis-Philippe would not give his approval but
indicated resignation to the possibility. Sebastiani subsequently proposed
to Palmerston that were Leopold elected, France should gain Marienbourg and Philippeville as compensation. This suggestion even Talleyrand refused to support, and it was repulsed by Palmerston. Despite
Sebastiani's intransigence, and perhaps encouraged by Talleyrand's
shift toward Leopold, Lebeau sent a delegation of notables to contact
the prince.

The delegation was well chosen; Leopold was impressed that two of
Belgium's leading catholics were willing personally to ask him to take
the crown. Having resigned the Greek throne over a question of boundaries, however, he would not accept that of Belgium until such matters
were settled. The protocol of January 20 was irrevocable, he told his
petitioners. Before he could take the crown, the Belgians would have to
accept the protocol in principle; its execution could then be a subject
of negotiation. He would not ascend the throne of a state whose territory was contested by all the powers; moreover it would be of little use
to the Belgians for him so to destroy his relations with the other
courts.[15]

This was not the reply that Lebeau counted on receiving. The situation
deteriorated as Talleyrand again rumored partition, the war parties in
Belgium became vociferous, and the conference grew irritated. On
May 10 what was termed a last protocol inviting the rebels to accept the
January terms was published. Were no acceptance made by June 1, the
powers would break relations with Belgium, approve the German Diet's
plan to send troops into Luxemburg, and automatically oppose Belgium
should she renew hostilities with the Dutch.

Fortunately for the rebels, they had won the sympathy of the British
emissary, Lord Ponsonby. He believed he could not communicate the

May 10 protocol to the Belgians and hastened to London to explain why. Like the Belgians, he saw their claims to Luxemburg and Limburg as justified. He struck a responsive note in Palmerston, who preferred to see Belgium linked with Germany through the Duchy's Confederation connection than tied solely to France. It was not this argument, but Ponsonby's report of the danger of a new revolution if the Belgian government accepted the Bases, that caused the conference to ease its stance. For Ponsonby had vividly depicted the establishment of a republican government, the entry of French volunteers into the Belgian army, an attack on Holland, and the probable spread of war and further revolution throughout all Europe.

Perturbed by Ponsonby's news, the conference took his advice that concessions should be made and that Leopold should quickly be placed on the Belgian throne. A May 21 protocol promised that the powers would again discuss with William the possibility of Belgium retaining some sections of Luxemburg in return for just compensation. This compensation was intended to be territorial in nature, most likely the exchange of sectors of Limburg for portions of Luxemburg. Such an exchange Lebeau would not accept; upon his return to Brussels Ponsonby admitted that any mention of compromise on territorial issues would endanger Leopold's chances of election. Exceeding the authority granted him by the conference, Ponsonby drafted for Lebeau's use in debate a vague letter mentioning the conference's intention to mediate but omitting any reference to territorial compensation. On June 4 Leopold was elected as a result of Lebeau's *tour de force* in the face of considerable opposition. Even so, the militant deputies qualified their vote with the condition that Leopold should not make his acceptance dependent on the abandoning of Luxemburg and Limburg to Holland.

2.3 FURTHER NEGOTIATIONS

It was Lebeau's intention that the sudden election would surprise the conference, cause it to forget its ultimatum, and win the Belgians an influential negotiator. At first it seemed as if his tactic had failed. Ponsonby was recalled following Belgium's failure to accept the Bases by the June 1 deadline, and Belgian relations with the conference were nearly ruptured. The rebels were willing enough to give William compensation for Luxemburg but insisted this had to be in the form of pecuniary indemnity. William and the conference would have none of this, and the delay further irritated the powers. France, Holland, and Prussia were all hoping to partition Belgium, Palmerston commented, 'and these silly Belgians looking only to their half-cunning game are just playing into the hands of their would-be partitioners'.[16]

The justice of Palmerston's warning and the increasing nature of the conference's irritation is evidenced in Talleyrand's note to Sebastiani three weeks later:

If the Belgians...will not yield a single point, if, on the contrary, they continue in their obstinate resistance, it will be impossible to negotiate with them, or to arrive at an arrangement.

After having exhausted every means of persuasion and condescension, and after having gathered so little fruit for all the labour expended, I believe it would really be better to carry out the idea of dividing Belgium...[17]

The obstinacy and cunning to which Palmerston referred were associated with a new approach devised by Jean-Baptiste Nothomb, who with Paul Devaux had recently been appointed special Belgian commissioners to the conference. Through careful examination of maps, Nothomb had found that while the Dutch did indeed control the Venlo area in 1790, by the treaty of that year Belgium possessed several enclaves within present Dutch territories. Could an exchange of these for the Limburg territories be extracted from the conference?

Although British Premier Lord Grey was impressed by the Belgians' claim of joint sovereignty in Maastricht, from the conference's point of view Nothomb's arguments did not have much to recommend them. For the Belgians, they offered a last foothold for continuing negotiation. In consultation with Leopold, the Belgian representatives in London determined to link the enclaves and concession of the left bank of the Scheldt with their demand to pay pecuniary indemnity for Luxemburg. The nature of the Belgians' arguments amused Palmerston but did not anger him, for now also convinced that the Belgian populace would not peaceably accept the January protocols, he wished to alter them without seeming to renounce the previous decisions of the conference. He would not give way on the Luxemburg issue, however, and continued to assert that the only payment that would buy the duchy was land in Limburg.

Eventually Leopold became personally involved in the negotiations, and when the moment was right he played his trump card. The Bases of Separation would have to be altered in a few significant ways, or he would not accept the Belgian throne. The powers hardly wished him to refuse, and even the eastern courts were now convinced that certain clauses of the Bases needed further consideration. The conversion of Baron Bülow to the Belgian views on the enclave and Maastricht issues was decisive. A new version of Bases of Separation contained in eighteen articles drafted at a meeting of Leopold, Palmerston, Nothomb, and Devaux was formally approved by the conference on June 26. The bargaining was exhausting and the Belgians obstinate. During the negotiations the critical Talleyrand wrote his superior:

We have been in conference for the last forty hours, but the [Belgian] Deputies are so little accustomed to such matters as they have now to deal with, and raise so many difficulties, that there is no getting on...[18]

For the Belgians, the virtue of the Eighteen Articles was their vagueness. The revolutionaries were proud that the conference no longer seemed to be imposing conditions on their state. Some disputed points were not specifically settled in Belgium's favor, but at least they were to be the subjects of honorable negotiations. In Luxemburg the *status quo* was to be maintained while Belgium, Holland, and the German Confederation discussed the issue. The right of Belgium to exchange enclave holdings for other territories, perhaps in Limburg, was recognized. It was further agreed that if Belgium could prove the United Provinces did not have exclusive control of Maastricht in 1790, some suitable arrangement would be made. As for the debt, each country was to pay its own debts contracted before the union and divide in just proportion those contracted in common.

Finally, the navigation clauses were revised in Belgium's favor. Ever since the outbreak of the revolution, William had asserted his right to control all traffic on the lower Scheldt. This neither Palmerston nor the representatives of the other powers would allow. The strangulation of Antwerp's trade would force Belgium into such economic depression that she would have to turn to France. Moreover, the Vienna treaty of 1815 had proclaimed freedom of navigation for the Rhine and the Scheldt, and if some clauses of that settlement had fallen, there was no reason others should lose their effect. Balked in their maneuver, the Dutch had insisted freedom of navigation be applicable only to those waterways specifically named in the Vienna treaty. This meant Antwerp would be cut off from the Rhine trade, for the port's connection with the Rhine depended on inland waterways passing through Dutch lands. The Belgian protest was joined by the Rhine states, for William's designation of Antwerp as a Rhine port during the period of union had led these states to develop considerable trade through Antwerp. With British and German support the Belgians persuaded the conference to set aside a strict legal interpretation of the Vienna treaty on this point, and the Eighteen Articles reserved the matter for future negotiation.

Despite these changes, the major outlines of the Bases of Separation remained the same, and there was little Leopold or any other defender of Belgian interests could do about them. Had Leopold been elected at the beginning of the year, he might have performed the miracle Lebeau hoped of him; but, as the king-elect wrote in June, Belgium paid dearly for her Francophile leanings in late 1830; '...it is painful to think what Belgium might have been without the miserable intrigues of that period...'.[19]

When Lebeau surveyed the results of his weeks of tenacious negotiating, he realized he had made progress but achieved no triumph. It was unlikely indeed that the chambers would accept the Eighteen Articles. As he could go no further with the powers, he chose to hoodwink his countrymen into approving the revised Bases. In a magnificent speech he reversed the tide of negative sentiment by implying that the revisions would enable Belgium to obtain her full claims in Luxemburg, Maastricht, and Limburg. The leading Belgian historian of the affair has commented that had events followed a different course, Lebeau might well have been tried for treason; as it was, he deserves credit for saving the country by 'making it adopt the sole solution which allowed Belgium to escape from the impasse in which she had been caught by the intransigence of her first leaders'.[20]

What saved Lebeau's reputation was William's rejection of the articles as too unfavorable to Holland. Even though he knew the powers intended officially to recognize Leopold, the monarch announced that if the prince set foot in Belgium he would treat Leopold as an enemy. Little attention was paid to William's grumblings, and on July 16 Leopold left London on a triumphal journey which culminated in a glorious entry into Brussels three days later. The accolades were everywhere tremendous, and he quickly set about making himself known throughout his realm.

The newly crowned king was in Liege on August 1 when he received notice that the Dutch would attack on August 4. Desirous of upholding their national honor, the Belgians attempted to resist the northern army alone. Their performance in what has come to be called the Ten Days Campaign, though brave, was ineffective. The French, answering a hurried appeal, entered Belgium on the thirteenth, outraced the Prince of Orange to Brussels, and persuaded him to withdraw. Palmerston meanwhile stationed the British fleet off the mouth of the Scheldt and arranged that the French army be considered the mandatory of the conference in upholding the Eighteen Articles. The Belgians, more dependent than ever upon French support, became less tractable to the biddings of the conference. Felix-Armand de Muelenaere, the successor to Lebeau, who had left his post after having obtained Belgium a king, even managed to put the blame on the British. He wrote Van de Weyer: 'The English Ministry by their delays, hesitations, and misplaced fears, have lost for the present all moral influence in Belgium. Whilst in London they were deliberating, they were acting at Paris...'.[21]

The situation deteriorated into a tug-of-war between the French, who were negotiating for territorial compensation for their efforts, and the British, who wished the French to withdraw immediately. By the end of September Palmerston had won his point, and Louis-Philippe ordered his troops home; his compensation was a secret agreement with Leopold that the Belgians would demolish the barrier forts at Charleroi and Tournai, as well as three lesser strongholds.

The failure of the Belgians successfully to defend themselves weakened their bargaining position. The revolutionaries had little reason to expect that the powers would not now try to reach a compromise. The powers had not taken action to uphold strictly the Treaty of Vienna, which had been signed by all the great nations, nor had they moved to support the Bases of Separation, which had been approved by all the countries presently involved save that of the rebels; why should they suddenly ardently defend articles which established members of the European community, the Dutch, had never accepted? As Palmerston commented: 'Is it because the Belgians were unable to defend themselves without foreign aid, that they are to require the five Powers to settle the questions between them and the Dutch entirely according to Belgian demands?'[22]

Leopold, his long time confidant Baron Stockmar, and Van de Weyer labored mightily to prevent changes in the Eighteen Articles. When they found the conference could not be halted on its course, they hindered it. Palmerston grew increasingly vexed by their 'childish discussions about words' and foolish delay.[23] The defeat of the Polish revolutionaries at Warsaw on the eighth of September brought an increase of Russian pressure in support of William and a simultaneous reduction of French willingness to defy the eastern powers. Leopold, who earlier had pleaded to Grey not to 'maltreat this country which really does not deserve it now whatever it might have done before' was reduced to the threat of abdication.[24] The British, who were becoming used to Leopold's despairings, took the king only half-seriously. Palmerston nevertheless wrote letters to soothe Leopold's pride while at the same time warning the Belgian ministers that they would have to give way or risk coercion.

The British foreign minister now wished the rebels to approve Twenty-four Articles agreed upon by the five powers on October 14. These were more beneficial to The Hague than the earlier set, yet they gave consideration to Belgian claims and had the virtue of providing precise formulas concerning issues previously left to future negotiations. About 60 per cent of the Duchy of Luxemburg – the Western section which included some Walloons among its predominantly German speaking populace – was granted to Belgium. In return, William would retain the rest of the duchy, Maastricht, all of the province of Limburg on the right bank of the Meuse, and the region surrounding Venlo; the Dutch enclaves on the left bank of the Meuse were to be surrendered to the rebels. The Belgians had long given up hope of controlling all of Flemish Zeeland and the left bank of the Scheldt to its mouth. These lands, including the strip in which the drainage sluices were located, went to the Dutch, as Palmerston was convinced that they, like Maastricht, were necessary to Holland if she were to form a defense line against France. The Belgians were granted joint fishery, pilotage, and buoyage rights on the Scheldt, the liberty to use that river and the internal waterways leading to the Rhine, and the right of a free connection through the Maastricht appendix. The principle of neutrality and the guarantee of the powers was kept. The debt payment remained high, but it was a smaller share of the national debt than the Belgians had paid before the separation. As Talleyrand claimed, the solution was close to equitable; in any case, in the exchange of territories Belgium was ceding less land and population than was her opponent.

The conference's proposal was a disappointment to the Belgians, who resisted as best they could until Nothomb, returning from a mission in London, persuaded them that unless the Twenty-four Articles were accepted, Belgium lay in grave danger of partition. One last gain was to be made, and Van de Weyer achieved it with the aid of Palmerston. Thus far Britain and France had been the only powers officially to recognize the new state. Were the protocol of the Twenty-four Articles converted into a treaty between Belgium and the five powers, the signatures of the representatives of the three eastern courts would convey, if not the official recognition of those courts, at least an acknowledgement of Belgium's independent status. The plenipotentiaries of the powers were eager to finish their work. Convinced that the establishment of Belgium was necessary for the health of Europe, they signed the accord on November 15, 1831.

Reaction was not long in coming. Metternich was furious that his representatives had signed a treaty with a state not yet recognized by his sovereign. William of Holland, who still hoped that conflict among the powers might produce Belgium's partition, spurned the articles. His opposition gave the eastern courts occasion to delay their ratifications, and all seemed lost when a conflict broke out between Britain and France over which barrier fortresses should be destroyed. France, apparently in the hope that Philippeville and Marienbourg would eventually become French, had recently arranged with Leopold that those fortresses would be spared. Palmerston, learning of this, required Belgium to sign a secret convention on December 14 with all the great powers save France promising destruction of those forts. Sebastiani and Talleyrand finally yielded and on January 31, 1832, Palmerston, Talleyrand, and Van de Weyer exchanged ratifications. Those of the eastern courts came only three months later, after a Russian plea to William to accept the terms was rebuffed. Even then, their ratifications were qualified to the extent they required further negotiation of three articles to which William objected. Van de Weyer, like Lebeau a few months earlier, saw the need for immediate positive action, and on his own authority accepted the qualified ratifications.

For his wise decision, he was ordered to return to Belgium by Foreign Minister De Muelenaere. It was the beginning of a dispute over the extent of Van de Weyer's independent authority which was to appear again in later years. The reason for De Muelenaere's wrath was that acceptance of the qualified ratifications committed the Belgians to further talks with the Dutch before the Antwerp citadel was evacuated. The great powers had viewed the treaty as a guarantee of Belgium's independence, but for the revolutionaries its value was that it presumably had spelled the end of William's hold on Belgian territory.

General Albert Goblet, the chief Belgian negotiator regarding the fortresses, replaced Van de Weyer. On the instructions of De Muelenaere, he announced Belgium would not negotiate until she held the Antwerp citadel herself. As weeks passed, the foreign minister and his supporters veiled their belligerency less carefully until by July of 1832 De Muelenaere was publicly declaring that war against Holland was the only course open to the Belgians. Unlike Van de Weyer and Lebeau, he was convinced that no favorable solution could be obtained from negotiations. Irresolute by nature and lack of experience, although prone to sudden shows of strength, De Muelenaere abdicated foreign policy leadership to the chambers, where hotspurs, unmellowed by the weight of responsibility, called for war.[25]

Fortunately for the Belgians, the main fire of Palmerston's anger was already directed toward William for his rejection of the Twenty-four Articles. Fearing that the marriage of Leopold to Louis-Philippe's eldest daughter, Princess Louise, signified France and Belgium might soon take matters into their own hands, Palmerston in early September made a last effort to reach a settlement acceptable to both Belgium and the Netherlands. This was his 'theme', his personal variation on the Twenty-four Articles. Many of his proposals were identical with those of the treaty, but his version of the articles dealing with the Scheldt, the waterways, and the debt were significantly different.

The theme was designed to be palatable to the Dutch; nevertheless, it did the Belgians some favors. For example, there had been confusion concerning the Scheldt regime. When the powers invoked the Treaty of Vienna to maintain the liberty of navigation on the Scheldt, it was assumed duties would be levied on the shipping on the river. The toll rate was to be that of August 1814. But it was soon discovered that no tolls had, in fact, been in effect at that date. To rectify their error, the powers prescribed in the Twenty-four Articles the same rates set by the Treaty of Mainz for the Rhine. But what was good for the Rhine was not for the Scheldt, for the latter was host to maritime shipping of far greater capacity than that ever found on the Rhine. The Mainz tonnage toll rates would increase freight costs from British and other ports prohibitively.

All this was pointed out to Palmerston by representatives of the Antwerp chamber of commerce and by De Muelenaere, who argued against any tariffs in the hope such an extreme demand would either be successful or be rejected outright by the Dutch. In the former case, the Belgians would make a great gain. In the latter, with further negotiations impossible, the powers would be forced to keep their promise of the November treaty and see that the Antwerp citadel returned to Belgian hands.[26] It was a simple game, and Palmerston was not to be taken in. Choosing as a basis a tariff of one florin per ton, he recommended an annual payment of about 150,000 florins instead of hundreds of individual payments. This sum Belgium could capitalize if she wished. In return for this favorable settlement, the Belgians were to lay aside their demands that William reveal the mysteries of the *syndicat d'amortissement*. This was a commission personally managed by William which, with the intent of reducing the national debt, undertook stock transactions financed by loans from state funds. Its affairs were not in the best of order, and William to the end resisted divulging them to his subjects. The Belgians, of course, harped on the matter both because it caused William embarrassment and because a complete accounting of the *syndicat*'s assets might reduce the amount of debt Belgium would have to pay.

Despite the opportunity of being freed of the Mainz tariff, De Muelenaere would not consider the theme. Instead he continued to insist that the powers enforce the Twenty-four Articles and drive the Dutch from the citadel. The foreign minister was not backed by the king nor by Goblet, Van de Weyer, or Lebeau. Although in June Leopold had advocated an unyielding policy, by the close of the summer he differed sharply with De Muelenaere. Influenced by the appeals of his new father-in-law, the king now believed Belgium would gain more by appearing reasonable and desirous of peace; some conciliatory concessions might be in order if the citadel were evacuated. In London, Goblet reached the decision that it was 'useless and even dangerous' for Belgium to continue importuning the powers and with 'lightness and lack of foresight' to threaten war. The members of the conference, especially Palmerston, who did not want to embarrass the Whig ministry, wished to avoid hostilities. They viewed the evacuation of the citadel more as an eventual result of continued negotiations than as an immediate necessity. Moreover, Goblet warned, if the Belgians did persuade the powers to seize the citadel while the Dutch had not yet refused to continue negotiations, the rebels could expect little support on secondary or future issues.[27]

The arrival of Palmerston's theme, brought by Goblet on September 9, stirred Leopold to action. As was his custom with all Belgian diplomats, he had long been corresponding privately with the emissary, sometimes transmitting instructions which he had not confided to his foreign minister.[28] He knew Goblet believed Belgium should accept the theme, and he therefore threw his support to him. The cabinet resigned, and Leopold persuaded all but De Muelenaere to return to their posts. The new foreign minister was Goblet, who gave Van de Weyer full powers to conclude a treaty on the basis of the theme. In a subsequent letter Goblet made clear his acceptance was stimulated not so much by a liking of the terms as by a desire to shift from Belgium to Holland the onus of any failure to reach a negotiated solution.

In consenting to open direct negotiations, the king has less in view the achievement of an amicable arrangement than the demonstration, in a short delay, of the impossibility of that arrangement. For more than a month, the king of Holland has offered to deal directly with us; and that offer has been considered, rightly or wrongly, as an obstacle to the use of coercive measures. Our goal is to make that obstacle disappear.[29]

The Belgian moderates could not hold out much longer against the prevailing mood of the country. The king was openly exceeding the limits of his constitutional role and could not safely continue doing so. Thus the Belgian acceptance of the theme on September 18 was a true last offer, for it was patent that the moderates would be able to do little more.

It was enough. The Dutch rejected Palmerston's effort out of hand, and the contrast in the actions of the two small countries led Britain and France to intervene. While the eastern courts temporized, French troops laid siege to the Antwerp citadel, which surrendered before Christmas. Although an Anglo-French blockade of the Scheldt had to be maintained until the Dutch acquiesced to their loss, with the prompt release of the citadel to Belgian control by the French, Leopold and his supporters reached the goal the belligerent deputies had asserted could be won only by war. What is more, the citadel had passed into Belgian hands without the rebels relinquishing their hold on those Luxemburg and Limburg territories the Twenty-four Articles had attributed to William of Nassau.

The taking of the citadel did not establish a permanent settlement between the Netherlands and Belgium, and desultory discussions primarily concerning navigation matters continued. The Hague's counter-projects to Palmerston's theme were unsuitable. Some attempt was made to reach provisional arrangements for debt and toll payments which could serve until a definitive settlement were attained. When it became clear that William intended to obtain provisional terms so favorable to himself that he would scarcely be likely to work for a permanent settlement, even the three eastern powers brought pressure on the Dutch ruler to be amenable. Forced to it, the Dutch signed a convention with France and Britain on May 21, 1833, which recognized the *status quo* as the provisional terms on which the disputed issues should rest.

The convention also provided for renewed negotiations. When they finally got under way in July, the Belgian representatives bargained slowly, for they were reluctant to exchange the provisional terms for any that were less favorable, even if permanent. Finally compromising for fear of losing Palmerston's sympathy, they were again saved by William's obstructionism. Despite the passage of several months, he had not yet asked the Diet of the German Confederation and the Agnates of the House of Nassau to approve the territorial division of the Duchy of Luxemburg arranged by the Twenty-four Articles. Moreover, although the Belgians made an important concession on the toll rate, he continued to argue over a quarter of a florin per ton. Angered by the monarch's lack of faith and quibbling attitude, Bülow and Wessenberg declared they could do nothing more to preserve the negotiations. On August 24, 1833, the London Conference adjourned, not to meet again for five years.

2.4 THE DIFFICULTIES OF ADJUSTMENT

The temporary solution was to the advantage of the Belgians, for the May 1833 convention granted them better terms than they would have obtained in a permanent settlement along the lines of the Twenty-four Articles. Until such a settlement was achieved, the Belgians were to remain in possession of those territories of Luxemburg and Limburg which they occupied but were supposed to relinquish according to the treaty of November 15, 1831. On the other hand, the Dutch had been forced to evacuate the Antwerp citadel, although they still held two small forts farther north in Belgian territory. As no agreement had been reached concerning the debt, the Belgians were spared interest payments for the time being. For a similar reason, the rebels avoided the cost of tolls on the Scheldt and other waterways while those same waterways remained open to their traffic.

The Belgians had been fortunate. Few enterprises could be considered more likely than theirs to upset the balance of power in Europe; yet they had successfully undertaken it and used the European balance to maintain that enterprise. Throughout the initial negotiations the rebels had espoused a double standard concerning what might be called the established rules of the diplomatic game. Treaties and promises should be kept, they argued, whenever those promises were favorable to them. When the treaties were disfavorable, the Belgians wished them to be violated. Such an attitude was hardly new in diplomacy; but in a period when the system of international relations was identified by its commitment to order, it marked the diplomats of Belgium as revolutionaries. The ambiguity of their behavior was a natural result of the initial revolutionary act. Only an eventual return to the system of order could preserve the Belgians' new state, yet a premature docility could result in the destruction of their independent existence. Thus the rebels were in the awkward position of first asking that the powers not intervene to support the Vienna treaty and then accepting their intervention because it was the best way to obtain recognition for status as a bona fide belligerent with certain rights as compared to civil rioters. Opposition to enforcement of the Bases of Separation was followed by insistence that the powers stand by verbatim the Eighteen Articles despite the disastrous results of the Ten Days Campaign. Perhaps most peculiar was the chambers' and De Muelenaere's passionate demand for execution of the treaty of November 15 and expulsion of the Dutch from the citadel before negotiations would be continued, when all the available indications were that negotiations would bring the Belgians a more favorable arrangement than that of the Twenty-four Articles.

A parallel to their ambiguous and changing views concerning the enforcement of treaties may be found in the rebels' tendency to mix and sometimes confuse legal and extra-legal means in their diplomacy. For the most part it was not the men who had to deal with the representatives of the other nations who advocated extra-legal means, but the hot bloods of *L'Association nationale* and others sitting in the National Congress. Some ministers of foreign affairs, such as Lebeau and Goblet, were willing to brave the heat of still rebellious passions. To do so took courage; Lebeau's life was several times threatened, and once he and his family fled their dwelling late at night in response to a warning of danger. Others either let themselves be pushed into belligerent attitudes by the irresponsible congress, as did De Muelenaere, or chose to put themselves in a position of leadership of the war movement. Over-confident following their successes in 1830, many Belgians believed a resort to arms would be a panacea for their diplomatic ills. For this to be true, the Belgians would have to be strong enough to win and self-controlled enough not to defeat their opponent so roundly that a great power, such as Prussia, would intervene. This was not the case; ironically it was their northern neighbors who attempted the gambit, although without total success. To quote Sir Charles Webster: 'Small Powers have often defied Great Powers. But there was never a clearer example of the successful use of force by a Small Power in the midst of a negotiation than that employed by William...'[30]

The monarch of the Netherlands was in many ways playing the same sort of game as the Belgians, appealing to the powers when he wished, acting suddenly or delaying immeasurably, and threatening extra-legal measures when his wishes were not heeded. There was a major difference, however, in that William was operating from a position of strength as an established member of the European system, while the Belgians were not. The rebels, as outsiders, were faced with the difficult task of breaking with the established system and rules enough so they could assert their independence, but not so much as to become universally branded as outlaws. This was in part possible because the powers themselves were not adhering to their treaties too strictly. There was a system, but it was not so rigid as is sometimes thought; although the courses followed by the great powers did not go beyond the system's bounds, they were not necessarily fixed or consistent.

The Belgians were treated leniently also because while their revolution destroyed the means by which the Congress of Vienna intended to block French expansion to the north, it did not necessarily demolish the goal the powers had hoped to attain. As long as Lebeau, Van de Weyer, and Goblet were able to show that Belgium viewed herself as an addition to the European system, rather than as an extension of France, then the revolutionaries were not going against the spirit as well as the letter of the 1815 treaties.[31] In this light, the significance of Leopold's election looms large, as does the foolhardiness of the pro-Nemours group.

It is doubtful whether, at the time, all this was clearly visible to the Belgians. They were revolutionaries, and saw events differently than did the diplomats of the established nations. Actions they believed bold and independent were labeled as childish or imprudent by Palmerston and his colleagues. It was particularly difficult to lay aside passions and personal ties of the moment for a longer view or to admit considerable concessions in form even though basic issues might not be affected. This was what Stockmar appealed to De Muelenaere to do, but in vain:

I urge you . . . to prefer the well-being of Belgium to any other personal consideration. A situation, even the most embarrassing, is not without remedy. In the
present case, the capital difficulty is more in form than in substance, and all
that is needed to overcome it is energy.[32]

What annoyed the experienced diplomats most was the Belgians' failure to admit the precariousness of their position and the extent to which they were dependent on the powers for their existence. Thus Palmerston wrote in March of 1831 that 'while the Belgians continue to treat the conference in so unbecoming a manner, and to set up pretensions which place them in a state of moral war, if not actually of physical war, with the four Powers and with all Germany . . . ',[33] he would not enter official relations with the new country. Over a year later, Talleyrand protested the dangerous effect the Belgians' 'foolish bragging' was having on nego-tiations and suggested that France's best course would be 'above all, [to] put down with a strong hand the meddlesome spirit and ridiculous pretensions of the Belgians'.[34] The next day Princess Adelaide, a sister of the French king, wrote the ambassador: 'Truly, the Belgians ought to be very grateful, happy, and satisfied [over French action against the Ant-werp citadel]; but they are not. I must candidly tell you, that I am very angry at their folly and their ingratitude.'[35]

This being the attitude of the Belgians' best supporters, it is not difficult to estimate the opinions of the eastern courts. Part of this annoyance was the natural product of the difficulties involved in any complex negotiation. Much of it stemmed, however, from the immaturity of the Belgians so clearly revealed by their lack of a sense of proportion and by what their critics considered a lack of responsibility.

The challenges to the authority of the conference, the election of Nemours, Surlet de Chokier's provocative promulgation to the citizens of the duchy, the chambers' initial opposition to the Eighteen articles, and the eagerness of De Muelenaere, Gendebien, and others to resume armed hostilities were all out of keeping with what the circumstances seemed to dictate as sensible conduct for the Belgians. The excesses of their behavior occasionally did lead to some successes, as when Ponsonby and the conference became convinced that the January protocols could not be forced on the new state and persuaded the conference to modify its position. But having made their point, the majority of the rebels did not recognize that failure to curb their bellicose statements would worsen their position again. In other instances, such as the exclusion of Nassau, far too much tension was created for the negligible (if any) gain achieved; such tension could only stir designs in Prussia and France contrary to Belgium's best interests. Nor was the lack of proportion and sensitivity for the feelings of other powers limited to the independence issue. In early 1833 Belgium arranged a commercial treaty with the United States that the British had been opposing as a matter of principle. Such crossing of Belgium's greatest benefactor was a foolish result of inexperience; British displeasure soon forced the embarrassed Belgians to ask that the treaty be renegotiated.[36]

Particularly irritating to the powers were the Belgian refusals to entertain compromise, the life-blood of diplomatic negotiation. This above all marked the separation of the rebels from the existing orderly system of the concert of Europe.

Yet it can be said on the rebels' behalf that while their delays and obstinacy were on occasion childish and unnecessarily irritating, the passage of time worked in their favor. As long as the powers did not take action against the revolution, the Belgians were able to strengthen their domestic situation; and talk of possible hostilities against the Dutch no doubt fostered patriotism and feelings of national identity. Moreover, Belgium's continued existence as a political entity distinct from the Netherlands surely served to make even the most conservative powers more accustomed to the idea of the break-up of the 1815 union. In later years, the wise use of time was to become one of the little country's best developed diplomatic skills. Talleyrand himself wondered if the Belgians had some reason for not negotiating more rapidly and admitted they had been encouraged by the condition of Europe and the words of agitators to believe 'that tenacity alone will gain the end they have in view'.[37]

The Belgians, of course, believed that the only way to convince the conference of their intention to remain independent was to resist calls for compromise and remain bellicose. In February of 1832, Leopold wrote his representative in Paris that he was not provoking war, yet he was sure that 'the only way of avoiding one with Holland is to show one's perfect ability to make it'.[38] Although this comment shows Leopold as shrewdly plotting his course, in the initial months of the revolution this approach was not so much a calculated tactic as it was the natural emotional response of a people that had just completed a revolution. Palmerston understood this better than most:

People all say the Belgians are madmen, and there is no use in reasoning with them. I have observed a good deal of method and calculation in their madness, and at all events they are not destitute of that cunning which belongs to insanity. I cannot help thinking therefore that when they find that we are really in earnest, and that they have driven us to the extreme point to which we will go, they will gradually recover their senses, and find out a way to arrange matters somehow or other.[39]

The danger was that the Belgians would not be wise enough to know when to become more amenable. It was fortunate for the nation that Leopold, Lebeau, Nothomb, Van de Weyer, and Goblet were able to brave the passions of the populace and make the necessary accommodations at the proper time. And it was fortunate for them that William of Nassau overplayed his hand and by unsurpassed obduracy enabled the Belgians to emerge from their crisis more successfully than they might well have. It stands as a monument to the increasing maturity of the Belgian diplomats as they gained experience that Goblet, although he was maintaining his policy and the cabinet virtually alone during a period of ministerial crisis and resignations, dared accept Palmerston's theme. He did not like it. He did hope his amenability would win the powers' approval and sympathy if William refused the terms.[40] It was a calculated risk which showed that after nearly two years, the Belgians were beginning to let their minds and not their passions dictate their policy. Goblet was following, as the Belgians were subsequently to do more and more, a line foreshadowed by the Baron d'Hoogvorst in September of 1831 when he notified Metternich of Leopold's accession. The Austrian emissary had explained that the revolution was really the result of William's errors, accidental factors, and the influence of French agitators. Belgium was not revolutionary, but a nation attached to its soil, longing only for repose.[41] By 1833, the Belgians' intention of portraying themselves as part of the European order, rather than an outside entity opposed to it, was being strongly evidenced.

This new posture was the result of changes in the Belgians' concept of their national interest, changes which were influenced both by the continuing success of their revolution and their difficulties in bringing the international relations problems of the revolution to *clôture*. As d'Hoogvorst pointed out, the revolt began more as a demonstration against misrule than as a demonstration of Belgian national identity. The very act of revolt and the unexpected support it received from all classes helped it become, however, something of a national movement. At the end of 1830 one of the most easily defined and initially discernable positive national interests was preservation of the geographic unity of the rebellious territories. It was this goal that first received the chief attention of diplomats and legislators alike. In the heat of the times, many Belgians were prepared to fight for all or nothing.

They failed to note how truly revolutionary their actions were in the view of the established monarchs. Though the Belgians argued as if they were upsetting only the geography of Europe, they were doing far more. Their constitution was the most liberal on the continent, allowing freedom of religion, assembly, and the press. They had a king, it was true; but his power was circumscribed, especially by the requirement that all acts and laws had to be countersigned by ministers responsible to the chambers. In one area alone did he possess full power himself, as com-mander-in-chief of the Belgian armies; but that was only when Belgium was at war. In peacetime the minister of national defense was responsible to parliament for the condition of the armies. In most respects, the king's position could be described as like that of a constitutional monarch in what otherwise might be a republic. In allowing such a constitution and government to continue in their midst, the eastern courts believed they were granting a great deal; the matter of boundaries should not be quib-bled over indefinitely.

Eventually responsible figures in Belgium recognized that a more sophisticated view of the national interest might call for preservation of the new state at the expense of territory. The value of the revolutionaries' enterprise was such that it could not be negated by the loss of portions of Limburg and Luxemburg. Far from all the Belgian politicians and patriots took this view, and as long as the diplomats were responsive to their do-mestic restraints, progress was slow. The tutelage of the powers in time had results, and Lebeau and then Goblet successfully rebelled against their colleagues and were pardoned because they did achieve the goal of national preservation. Continuing existence called for a different set of priorities than did short-range territorial warfare; foremost among them was economic viability. Thus it was that by the third year of negotiations far more was being said about tariffs and shipping rights than about boundaries.

The rebels finally won tolerance, but not acceptance, from the powers. In the last analysis, it was not the Belgians' diplomacy that ensured the continued existence of their state, indeed its initial immaturity and lack of proportion almost provoked partition. It was the conditions, both in international relations and the domestic affairs of other countries, that led Europe to acknowledge the work of the revolutionaries. During the first crucial months the outbreak of the Polish revolt required much of the attention of the eastern courts and helped prevent their intervention in Belgium. Born of a revolution, the July Monarchy in France could not afford to be unsympathetic to the Belgian movement. Yet the sus-picion and hostility directed toward France by the other powers negated the possibility of a partition, in which France would have to share, or of any overt unilateral French support for the rebels. The bombast of the irresponsible Laffitte in time had to give way to the compromising, conciliatory approach of Casimir Périer. Shortly thereafter, the course of affairs in the Near East further militated for a Franco-British *rapprochement*. After such an understanding was accomplished, the Belgians had little hope of altering the course of the London conference by using the threat of French force. Instead, it became necessary to work with, rather than against, the conference, and this is what Leopold did. As Palmerston complained to Granville, much of his difficulties with the Belgians had arisen from 'the double diplomacy, double-dealing, infirmity of purpose, and want of principle in the French government'.[42] Once the politicians in Paris had settled down, those in Brussels had to do so likewise.

Great Britain and Palmerston were, of course, the determining factors. Had Wellington remained in office, the rebels would surely have received short shrift. On the other hand, had the Whigs' position been more secure, Palmerston might have proceeded more leisurely rather than hastening, as he did several times, for fear the cabinet might be forced to resign over the Reform Bill, or other matters, before the negotiations were completed. Palmerston protected and guided the Belgians through the conference because it was in England's best interest that he do so. If an arrangement with Nassau were not possible, then everything should be done to maintain the independence of Belgium. If France or Prussia were to gain control of the territory, the balance in Europe would be upset and untold difficulties stimulated. The maintenance of Antwerp, a major port of entry of British goods into the continent, in the hands of a small power was infinitely preferable to its control by a great nation. For obvious reasons Britain declared for freedom of navigation on the Scheldt and was supported by the German states along the Rhine. It was the diplomacy of these powers, not of Belgium, that kept the Scheldt open.

In the months following their revolution, the Belgians were at the mercy of the powers. Their diplomacy was primarily a matter of reaction, usually negative, to what the powers were doing and saying about them. Indeed, the Belgians had few men with the willingness or ability to take the long-range view needed for the formulation and implementation of a positive diplomatic style. The best Van de Weyer hoped to achieve was to make Palmerston aware of the Belgians' determination to be independent and of their needs for reaching that goal. A small state, much less a revolutionary state, could not challenge Europe without the strong support of a great power. When Lebeau saw such support was not forthcoming from Paris, he recognized that Belgium's collision course with the will of the London conference would have to be altered. He therefore worked at bringing Paris and London into cooperation in favor of Belgium. This was also Leopold's intent. Even before he had officially ascended the Belgian throne, the prince used his personal influence to win the sympathy of all the nations, to balance the French and English against each other, and when that was impossible, to reconcile the two. This surely was the purpose of the diplomatically wise marriage of the prince, with his English connections, to the daughter of Louis-Phillippe.

It is significant that despite the more positive efforts of the Belgians in 1832, the temporary agreement which put on ice the issues still being debated in 1833 was a convention primarily worked out not by the Belgians but by Talleyrand and Palmerston and more or less imposed by them on the Dutch. Similarly, the last military victory of the revolution – the seizure of the Antwerp citadel – had been won by the French; the rebels had been barred from the action so that William could not mistake the European nature of the French intervention or claim an excuse for turning the citadel's guns to the destruction of the Belgian port.

The Belgians had been allowed a niche in the European comity of nations, but it still remained for them to develop their own diplomacy distinct from that provided for them by the other powers. They still had to achieve the leap from being merely tolerated to being truly accepted; from being petitioners of the European order to being contributors to it. The task would require fifteen more years.

2.5 NOTES

1. Edmundson, 'The Low Countries', in *The Cambridge Modern History*, vol. X, p. 521.
2. *Ibid.*, vol. X, p. 525. Waddington, 'L'Insurrection belge', in *Histoire générale du IVe siècle à nos jours*, vol. X, p. 342. See also Bulwer, *The life of Palmerston*, vol. II, p. 18.
3. Bulwer, *The life of Palmerston*, vol. II, p. 10.
4. Metternich, *Memoirs*, vol. V, pp. 35–36: 'Metternich to Wessenberg, Oct. 3, 1830'.
5. Pirenne, *Histoire de Belgique*, vol. IV, p. 11.
6. Juste, *Histoire du Congrès National*, vol. I, p. 163.
7. *Ibid.*, vol. I, pp. 130–131.
8. Seton-Watson, *Britain in Europe, 1789–1914*, p. 159.
9. Pirenne, *Histoire de Belgique*, vol. IV, p. 18.
10. Lebeau, *Souvenirs*, p. 40.
11. Webster, *Foreign policy of Palmerston*, vol. I, p. 111 quotes a Palmerston letter of Nov. 12, 1831.
12. Talleyrand, *Memoirs*, vol. IV, p. 324; 'Palmerston to Talleyrand, July 9, 1831'.

13. Pirenne, *Histoire de Belgique*, vol. IV, p. 19. The text of the proclamation, as well as those of many other declarations and proposed treaties, may be found in Nothomb, *Essai historique*.
14. Juste, *Histoire du Congrès National*, vol. II, p. 57.
15. De Lannoy, *Les origines*, p. 213.
16. 'Palmerston to Ponsonby, June 4, 1831', quoted in Webster, *Foreign policy of Palmerston*, vol. I, p. 136.
17. Talleyrand, *Memoirs*, vol. IV, pp. 151–152: 'Talleyrand to Sebastiani, June 22, 1831'.
18. *Ibid.*, vol. IV, pp. 152–153: 'Talleyrand to Sebastiani, June 24, 1831'.
19. Juste, *Memoirs of Leopold I*, vol. I, p. 131, note: 'Leopold to Le Hon, June 19, 1832'.
20. De Lannoy, *Les origines*, p. 244.
21. Juste, *Memoirs of Leopold I*, vol. I, p. 197; 'De Muelenaere to Van de Weyer, Aug. 16, 1831'.
22. 'Palmerston to Leopold, Oct. 16, 1831', quoted in Webster, *Foreign policy of Palmerston*, vol. I, p. 141.
23. 'Palmerston to Granville, Sept. 16, 1831', quoted in Bulwer, *The life of Palmerston*, vol. II, p. 120.
24. Quoted in Betley, *Belgium and Poland*, pp. 229–230.
25. Goblet, *Mémoires*, vol. I, pp. 111, 115. See also the preface by Armand Freson to Lebeau, *Souvenirs*, pp. 164–165.
26. Bindoff, *The Scheldt question to 1839*, p. 190.
27. Goblet, *Mémoires*, vol. I, pp. 94–108.
28. *Ibid.*, vol. I, pp. 26–27, note.
29. 'Goblet to Van de Weyer, Sept. 25, 1832', quoted in Nothomb, *Essai historique*, vol. I, pp. 302–303, note.
30. Webster, *Foreign policy of Palmerston*, vol. I, p. 141.
31. Nothomb, *Essai historique*, vol. I, p. 38.
32. Goblet, *Mémoires*, vol. I, p. 148: 'Stockmar to Goblet, Aug. 1832'.
33. 'Palmerston to Granville, Mar. 25, 1831', quoted in Bulwer, *The life of Palmerston*, vol II. p. 59.
34. Talleyrand, *Memoirs*, vol. V, p. 45: 'Talleyrand to Duc de Broglie, Dec. 1, 1832'.
35. *Ibid.*, vol. V, p. 47: 'Princess Adelaide to Talleyrand, Dec. 2, 1832'.
36. Laurent, 'Commerce, colonies and claims', p. 551.
37. Talleyrand, *Memoirs*, vol. IV, p. 152: 'Talleyrand to Sebastiani, June 22, 1831'.
38. Juste, *Memoirs of Leopold I*, vol. I, p. 260: 'Leopold to Le Hon, c. Feb. 1832'.
39. 'Palmerston to Granville, May 29, 1831', quoted in Bulwer, *The life of Palmerston*, vol. II, p. 79.
40. Lebeau, *Souvenirs*, pp. 167–168.
41. Metternich, *Memoirs*, vol. V, p. 139: 'Metternich to Trautmansdorff, Sept. 5, 1831'.
42. 'Palmerston to Granville, Mar. 18, 1831', quoted in Bulwer, *The life of Palmerston*, vol. II, p. 56.

3. The problem of acquiring status

Despite the May Convention of 1833, Belgium's position remained uncertain. The climate of international affairs was still inhospitable for such an event as the founding of a revolutionary state. Belgium's survival since August 1830 by no means indicated that the continental nations had ceased to oppose her or had abandoned designs on her territories. The small state's presence was merely tolerated by the powers, and the convention signed at London was at best only a temporary solution. The consensus which it represented and which vouchsafed Belgium's continued existence stemmed not from any real acceptance of the new state but from a recognition by the powers of their mutual differences regarding what should be done with the presumptuous revolutionaries. Paradoxically, Belgium's greatest safety was her greatest danger. What if the alignment of the powers changed, or if new circumstances caused them to agree that the decisions so grudgingly reached in the Twenty-four Articles of 1831 should be disregarded? Clearly Belgium's hopes of becoming truly established and independent depended upon her obtaining an approved place in the European community. Somehow Belgium, the illegitimate child whose unexpected appearance had embarrassed all the chancelleries of Europe, had to prove that her existence should be justified not by the pleasure of the powers but by her own worth and independent sovereign rights.

While the powers were deciding the fate, territorial limits and amount of national debt of the Belgians, Leopold had bitterly commented that 'We are like shuttlecocks among the others'.[1] Like representatives of any new nation, Belgium's diplomats desired not to be viewed with suspicion but dealt with like diplomats of established states. Belgium did not wish to have her internal actions subject to the veto of one or another power nor did she want to feel that she must always cling to some other nation if she were to continue her existence. Her people did not want to belong to a state either ignored by the powers or required by them to behave in a certain manner; they wished to be respected and independent.

The task of gaining status within the body politic of Europe was an arduous one. As a French politician commented ten years later, 'nothing is more difficult in the present condition of Europe than to make a new state live; for my part, I have for a long time thought it impossible...'.[2] Had Belgium been of great size and of some military strength, the problem might have been resolved as soon as a regular government had been established and a monarch set upon the throne. Power has often served as a justification in itself. But Belgium's weakness left her vulnerable to interference and other tactics; these had to be turned aside even while Belgium sought to demonstrate in terms other than military strength her right for recognition. Her leaders had to reassess their views of the national interest and their choice of diplomatic alternatives as their task shifted from establishing the revolution to maintaining a continuing and prosperous state. It was a slow process by which Belgium passed from her position as the problem child and ward of Europe to one of respected citizenship. Nevertheless, by the time the widespread upheavals of 1848 were quelled, Belgium had come close to the achievement of her goal.

3.1 THE FORTRESS AFFAIR

Although the revolutionaries had frequent dealings with the powers before 1833 and had seen their work of 1830 preserved, for the most part they had been bandied about like Leopold's badminton birdies. It was only during later incidents concerning fortress construction and the control of Luxemburg that the Belgians began to develop a distinct diplomatic approach separate from the confusions of war and the diplomacy of the great powers. The challenges made to their country in both cases were accepted with alacrity as opportunities to assert Belgian independence and national rights.

In the spring of 1835, disturbed by William of Holland's continued refusal to accept a definitive settlement and uneasy at the thought that he might again resort to arms, the Belgians made plans to construct a line of fortresses along their northern border from Antwerp to Hasselt. In a letter written to Queen Victoria several years later during another crisis, Leopold stated his view clearly: 'Without, at least, comparative security by means of well regulated measures of defence, no country, be it great or small, can be considered as possessing National Independence'.[3] The defense measures were taken by the Belgians both to prepare for an attack and to gain recognition from the powers. Uppermost in the minds of the Brussels statesmen was the knowledge that the stronger the state became, the more likely it was that the powers would show increased consideration for the Belgian point of view when a definitive settlement was made with the Netherlands.

Most of the three million francs voted by the chambers for the first year of the program were for fortifications along the border. But some were intended for entrenched camps at Beverloo and Diest and for modernization of existing fortifications at Hasselt and Lierre. These plans had hardly been announced when opposition arose from the Prussian Foreign Minister, Johann Ancillon, who argued that construction of the fortresses was a breach of Belgian neutrality. He was especially concerned over the plans for Diest and Hasselt, towns which were almost as close to Germany as to Holland. The Belgian minister at Berlin explained that the fortresses were only for defense and therefore Belgium was fulfilling, not disregarding, the conditions of her neutrality. Ancillon's retort was that the fortresses were a threat to Germany; he would not allow them to be built.[4] Only some months later did the Prussian admit his real worry was that France might declare Belgium's neutrality not accomplished, overrun the small state, and use the fortresses against Prussia.

Neither De Muelenaere, who was again Belgian foreign minister, nor Leopold were inclined to yield. Sylvain van de Weyer commented that Belgium was yet to be convinced that new concessions to Germany, while weakening Belgium's position toward Holland, would win the goodwill of Prussia:

We are always and will be for a long time in a state of suspicion, and despite all our moderation, M. Ancillon in his narrow and impolitic views will not let escape any occasion to give us his claws, even when we ourselves offer a hand.[5]

The inflexible attitude of these men reflected their revolutionary background. Van de Weyer, De Muelenaere, his immediate successor Chevalier Barthélemy de Theux de Meylandt, and other Belgian diplomats had all previously participated in the uprising against the Dutch. They knew and distrusted the unyielding nature of their adversaries and were determined not to grant them an inch. Above all, the revolutionaries dared not reveal any hesitation or weakness, for to do so could lead to domestic crisis, increased demands by their enemies, and the consequent obliteration of independent Belgium.

The plans were therefore not modified even when the Duke of Wellington, while admitting the matter was an internal affair in which Britain should not intervene, indicated he favored postponement of work on the fortifications until negotiations were resumed. Indeed, the small country seemed to want to make clear to the rest of Europe that she had the courage to go against the wishes of a larger power. In a public ceremony in July, General Goblet, now one of the directors of the fortress program, was advanced in rank with a citation praising his work. The gesture angered the Prussians; and, as Ancillon interpreted the British silence as condemnation of the Belgian position, the Belgians were subjected to great pressure. Although he did not threaten use of force, the German stated that if the forts were built, the courts of Austria, Russia, and Prussia would no longer feel bound by the agreement reached in 1831; furthermore, he might withdraw the Prussian legation from Brussels.[6]

The precarious condition of Belgian finances restricted construction to a single entrenchment at Beverloo during the following year. This fact, in combination with Palmerston's eventual support of the Belgian plans, led the Prussians to press the issue less vigorously. The Brussels statesmen, however, had not altered their intentions; the 1837 budget contained appropriations for the fortification of Diest and improvement of works near Hasselt and Lierre. Ancillon repeated his interpretation of Belgian neutrality which implied that Prussia had the right to veto Belgian military measures and again called for the maintenance of the *status quo* of Belgium's defenses. The refusal received was as pre-emptory as those issued earlier, for the new Belgian Foreign Minister, De Theux, was as strong willed as De Muelenaere.

The succession of Baron Heinrich Werther to the Prussian foreign ministry following Ancillon's death did not ease tensions; for while the new minister was not noted for imperious behavior, he had few new ideas and tended to adhere to established policies and the views of his allies, Tsar Nicholas and Metternich. At the beginning of July the Prussians restated their case, this time with the threat that if nothing came of their arguments, relations with Belgium might be reconsidered. The Prussian representative in Brussels, who was about to leave his post, warned it might not be refilled; De Theux replied he was sure Prussia valued its legation in Belgium and would not let it fall from its high state. Continued protests from Berlin were similarly turned aside, and increased Austrian support for Prussia brought more support to Belgium from Palmerston. As time passed, the Prussians agreed to allow a single fort at Diest; Metternich, on the other hand, adhered to the argument of principle that Belgium should not construct any fortresses. De Theux was suspicious of this seeming split between the German courts; fearing that a renunciation of works at Lierre or Hasselt would be turned into an acceptance of the principle upheld by Austria, he remained immovable.

A manner of compromise was reached when Werther accepted Belgian explanations that only defensive measures were being taken at Diest and that the money to be spent on Hasselt and Lierre was for upkeep only and not for new fortifications. Leopold favored complying with Werther's request that the Belgians give a verbal promise they would construct no new fortresses elsewhere than at Diest. But the stubborn De Theux did not wish to do even this, and Palmerston, when asked for advice, agreed with him. Austria and Prussia, unwilling to go to war over the matter, were thus left to back out of their threats as gracefully as they could, stating they realized the Belgian government did not wish to acknowledge before the nationalistic chambers any promises concerning fortress construction.

In winning their diplomatic victory, the Belgians made several gains. Their right to develop their own military system was no longer challenged. Moreover, the Brussels statesmen had indicated that they would have a voice in interpreting the meaning of their own neutrality. At the same time, they had made an initial step toward forcing the European powers to realize that the revolutionaries intended to stay in business and that they should be dealt with as any other government. Finally, the Belgians had increased their own self-confidence and had acquired valuable diplomatic experience.

From the point of view of diplomatic techniques and methods, certain aspects of the Belgian handling of the incident are worthy of note. Military development was undertaken not only for defense, but also as a method of gaining the respect of other powers. Such activities would be expected of a great power; what is remarkable is that a small, newborn state, seemingly handcuffed by the requirements of neutrality, had the audacity to undertake such a venture. Belgium, thanks to Holland's attitude, had reason to act as she did. But without Leopold's relentless insistence on military strength, the fortifications would never have been considered. The importance of adequate military strength for a small power was a contribution of the king to Belgium's approach to foreign policy, and it was to be upheld by his heirs against many parliamentary attacks. The monarch's audacity was matched by the boldness and determination of his ministers, which virtually became stubbornness in the case of De Theux. The minister was obstinate about granting the slightest concession and even refused to build a bridge of vague verbal statements to facilitate the Prussian retreat; similarly, he felt no qualms in calling the bluffs of his opponents almost too loudly. Such tactics and behavior were not what the great German courts expected a minister in a position like his to use, and therefore De Theux may have gained a psychological edge on his adversaries.

Had not Palmerston come to the aid of the Belgian diplomats, the result of the affair could have been different. For it was Britain's support that enabled De Theux to continue his resistance to Prussian pressure when tension increased following the relaxation of 1836. Essential to the Belgian success was the division of opinion among the powers caused by the nature of the affair. Both England and the July Monarchy disapproved of the eastern courts' theories concerning the right of intervention in the internal affairs of smaller states and both wished to protect a fellow constitutional regime; the five powers thus resolved in this instance into two alliance systems advocating different ideologies.

The Belgians were careful to choose a position which could be supported by the British; the threat of Dutch invasion was real, and the forts were always described as defensive measures. Once support was obtained, De Theux used it skillfully, maintaining close touch with Palmerston and continually keeping Werther aware of the British approval of the Belgian position. This technique of playing the powers off against each other had already been essayed by the Belgians in 1831 and 1832. In the period in which the fortress affair occurred, it took on the special form of weakening the consensus and ties which held the European states together. For a small country like Belgium, which could not operate from within the concert of powers, it was necessary to maneuver until a crack could be discerned in the united front presented by the powers, a not too difficult task. This opening had then to be pried as wide as possible by nearly any means, for only thus could the novice nation gain true independence and insert itself into approved status within the body politic of Europe. Caution had to be used not to separate the powers too severely, however, for Belgium's existence was based upon their agreement in 1831.

While giving a good account of themselves throughout the fortress dispute the Brussels statesmen had continued to show a certain lack of self-confidence mixed with brashness and a poorly developed sense of proportion that could be interpreted by more seasoned hands as signs of immaturity. Their reliance upon Palmerston was great and occasionally prevented them from having the courage to follow their own convictions. That they would ask his advice rather frequently may be pardoned, for they were inexperienced and success did depend upon British support and confidence in the Belgians. The citation of General Goblet need not have occurred when it did nor have been done so ostentatiously. Surely De Theux and Leopold were aware of the ceremony; they gravely miscalculated if they thought it would be unnoticed across the border. Furthermore, De Theux's refusal to compromise forced Werther to retreat but also gave him grudges to nurse. Palmerston could afford to offend the Prussians, not so De Theux.

The conduct of the fortress affair had been reasonably satisfactory from the Belgian point of view, and when a new incident arose concerning woodcutting in Luxemburg, De Theux followed the line of approach used previously. Even a brief account of his activities shows that, as in the earlier incident, Belgian diplomacy displayed an audacity and a persistence which were to become characteristic.

William I of Holland, the Grand Duke of Luxemburg, had never recognized the Belgians' claim to his duchy. In October of 1837, even though the May Convention had given Belgium temporary possession and provisional administration of Luxemburg, the duke sent men into the area to cut wood. Belgian rights were violated and De Theux requested that France and Britain protest to Holland; if nothing were done to rectify the matter, Belgium would make use of her legitimate right of defense. The Belgian minister's anger was increased by William's persuasion of the Diet of the German Confederation, of which the duchy was a member and which controlled the Luxemburg fortress, to give the lumbermen any necessary military protection.

By the second week of December, both Britain and France had promised diplomatic aid and sent protests to Holland. Before these *démarches* could bear fruit, however, the commander of the Luxemburg fortress warned against resistance to the lumbering activities and backed his threat by increasing the garrison of the fort. De Theux countered by sending a corps of troops into Luxemburg; his request that France mass troops on her border was judiciously laid aside by that country. The Belgian minister knew from information received by his own representatives and from accounts relayed to him by French diplomats that both Werther and Metternich wished to reach a solution and were anxious that the Belgians not push the matter. He saw the opposition weakening and did all he could to increase pressure and to quicken the pace of developments.[7]

Impressed by British and French notes, Baron Werther soon sent pacific instructions to his representative at Frankfort. Grand Duke William delayed yielding and continued to claim the support of the Diet; in response France assembled 20,000 troops in villages near Luxemburg, and the Austrian president of the Diet succeeded in having that body suspend its earlier actions. By January 12 the Belgian minister at Paris could report that Prussia and Austria had adhered to the *status quo* and that William had withdrawn his lumbermen and privately admitted he was at fault.

In the woodcutting matter, as in the fortress affair, the Belgians had taken advantage of a good diplomatic position. Britain and France were used to counteract the pressures created by Holland and to force Prussia and Austria to withdraw their tacit approval of the Diet's support of

William. Foreign Minister De Theux acted boldly in calling the Diet's bluff by sending troops into the duchy; he remained firm throughout the affair and let it be known that Belgium would not be coerced. Yet by sending troops and pushing the matter, despite Prussian requests that time be allowed to arrange a solution, De Theux again gave Baron Werther a grievance.

Perhaps De Theux hoped for a military clash, thinking that just as the Dutch invasion in 1831 had benefited William's territorial claims, so a spirited Belgian defense of her rights in Luxemburg might aid her claims on the duchy. There is little evidence for this supposition, although no doubt it was thought that the Belgian position in the duchy would be strengthened for the future. De Theux did not press for a sweeping recognition of Belgium's claims to Luxemburg. He rather attempted just one more step beyond the eviction of William's lumbermen by using the affair as a lever to pry the German Confederation into officially recognizing the Convention of 1833; a series of such steps might, with the aid of time, lead Belgium to a goal she could not reach by a single leap. This technique was simple, yet it had aided Belgium in the fortress affair in which approval of one fortress meant tacit acceptance of the entire Belgian defense system. De Theux succeeded in getting Werther to admit the *status quo* in Luxemburg, but the Prussian was still avoiding an actual commitment when another event took all of Europe by surprise.

3.2 THE TREATIES OF 1839

On March 14, 1838, the Dutch ambassador to London informed Lord Palmerston that King William I was ready to sign the Twenty-four Articles of the treaty of November 15, 1831. Apparently the humiliation received for his activities in Luxemburg had caused the autocrat to recognize that he was being out-maneuvered and that the *status quo* was not satisfactory. More important, the Dutch people were discontented and complaining about high taxes, while the States General refused to approve once more a budget burdened with all the debts of the old kingdom. When William learned that receipts from the Indies would be low for the coming year, he decided to end the situation that for eight years had allowed the Belgians to avoid paying either principal or interest on the huge national debt.

The sudden announcement was at first regarded in Belgium as designed to quell discontent in the Dutch parliament; the move would be abandoned following adjournment. De Theux was slow in choosing his course, although he did not differ in this from the diplomats of the other

powers. He needed, however, to act quickly if he were to seize the initiative as in the previous two episodes and thus control the pace of events
in his favor. All his skills and his most carefully constructed techniques
would be called upon. In this contest, both the weak and strong points
of the Belgians' newly developed diplomacy were to be revealed.

De Theux and his countrymen wished to maintain possession of the
Luxemburg and Limburg regions they had provisionally administered
since the revolution. It was hoped that the division of the national debt
would be revised, that payment of arrears on the debt be avoided, and
that a more satisfactory arrangement than the Mainz regime could be
found for the Scheldt and inland waterways. The terms of the Twenty-
four Articles would have to be severely altered; unfortunately for Belgium's hopes, she had given her assent in 1831 to those very articles. Yet
the seven-year delay allowed some room for argument; furthermore, the
great powers themselves were partly responsible for the delay through
their failure to fulfil the clause in the November 15 treaty which stated
they should assure an immediate signing of the treaty by Belgium and
Holland.

The Belgian position was strengthened when Palmerston indicated to
the Dutch that they should not expect the 1831 arrangement to remain
unchanged. As he told Van de Weyer in agreement with the latter's arguments, the five powers 'can not consider as nul and *non avenu* all that has
taken place since October 1831...; the submission of Holland to the
Twenty-four Articles, the sole condition then demanded, will obviously
be insufficient today'.[8] Although Leopold had the friendly support of
Britain and France, it was not known how far this support would be
extended; meanwhile, De Theux's old enemy, Baron Werther, issued
statements concerning the grave consequences if Belgium should try to
maintain the *status quo*.

In contrast to the situations in 1835 and 1837, the present one offered
the Belgians little opportunity to take the offense. The matter at hand
was one on which the five powers had already come to an agreement;
unless a rift could be opened among them, Belgian hopes had small
chance of fruition. De Theux was well aware of this; on March 27 he
wrote Van de Weyer:

Your whole policy should be to act in such a manner as to arouse in the breast
of the conference a divergence of opinion on the reply to be given to the declaration of King William, in a manner so that the latter may easily avail himself of it in order not to follow up his first *démarche*, and so that we may be
able, if necessary, to avail ourselves of the same divergence of opinion in order
not to respond to an invitation which will be addressed to us.[9]

Time was to the advantage of the Belgians, for it could sanction arrangements that conferences could not. Therefore De Theux and Leopold considered how to achieve delay; they thought of refusing to attend the conference and of challenging its competence on the grounds that the Convention of 1833 stipulated further negotiations should be held directly between Belgium and Holland. When these tactics failed to halt the gathering of plenipotentiaries at London, De Theux began a vigorous campaign to persuade the diplomats that all the points previously discussed at the conference, not just those on which no agreement had been reached, should be put on the agenda. The Belgians had earlier admitted the London territorial settlement, but since the Dutch had ruptured those negotiations, all matters should be eligible for consideration.[10]

This view neither the eastern courts nor Palmerston would accept. The British foreign minister declared that the territorial settlement had been accepted by Belgium and the conference powers a long time ago; it could not be altered. Only those points could be examined on which reservations had previously been made: the intermediate waterways and roads, the Scheldt, and the debt. Van de Weyer recognized the hopelessness and the danger of opposing Palmerston and warned De Theux that insistence was unwise.[11]

Once the Belgians agreed to send a delegate to the conference and tacitly seemed to admit the *status quo* could no longer be maintained, Palmerston showed himself favorably disposed toward the new state in most matters other than the territorial issue. This attitude was strained, however, by a series of incidents in various towns in Luxemburg. The most noted of these took place in Strassen on April 22, when the populace celebrated the installation of a new burgomaster by rallying around a tree of liberty and flying a tricolor. The current commander of the Luxemburg fortress, General Dumoulin, took a dim view of such proceedings and sent troops to tear the flag down. The powers all condemned the patriotic statements subsequently made in the Belgian chambers. Belgium's position became more tolerable when Dumoulin went too far in later actions. But whatever had been regained was soon lost when the wildly nationalist representatives in the chamber declared that the nation did not draw back from the consequences of refusing to abandon Limburg and Luxemburg, thus scarcely veiling their willingness to go to war.

The Strassen affair was settled within a month, as a result of the good offices of Britain and of unusual conciliatory attitudes on the parts of both De Theux and Werther. Yet the incident did cost Belgium, for Palmerston became less willing to consider any revision of the Twenty-four Articles. The British minister stated that the Treaty of 1831 was the only claim to independence Belgium had and that to call for its alteration would be to risk her existence. Further incidents might push Belgium into taking foolhardy steps or could provide the German Confederation with an excuse to use its troops. Van de Weyer took these warnings to heart and cautioned his Brussels superiors that perhaps it was time that the populations of the disputed areas heard the harsh language of reality. He, of course, would like Belgium to retain the provinces, but if her propositions were rejected Van de Weyer said, 'I think I should, as a good citizen, resign myself in 1838 as I did in 1831, because that is the price for the independence of the country.'[12]

If the Belgians were dismayed by the firm stand taken by Palmerston, so too were the French, who, though willing to back Belgium in company with Britain, were equally sure they did not wish to defend their opinions alone. Henceforth the diplomats of the July Monarchy, suspecting Palmerston's attitude might be influenced by the fear that France would gain too much from any aid given to Belgium, began to withdraw on to safer ground. Belgian appeals to Foreign Minister Molé were sympathetically received but had little effect until Leopold himself entered into the matter. Molé, upset by the involvement of Louis-Philippe's son-in-law, agreed to support De Theux in the matters of the debt and free navigation of the Scheldt.

With only slight support from France and Britain, De Theux decided to hold to his goals of territorial and debt revision, but not to insist on both of them as *sina qua non* for a settlement. Belgium should, of course, insist on her boundary claims, but the foreign minister personally believed concessions could be made on the territorial issue if debt revisions were obtained. On the other hand, he would pay the entire debt if he could save territory by doing so. As his later tactics revealed, De Theux planned to take advantage of Holland's financial embarrassment and King William's poor relations with the Dutch States General. By having Belgian debt payments reduced, he hoped to force William into bargaining the disputed lands for increased debt payments or ready capital.

The eastern courts were still rejoicing over Palmerston's switch to their point of view when the Englishman dashed their spirits by again supporting the Belgians. De Theux had finally become convinced that unless negotiations soon got under way, the conference when it reconvened might rule that territorial matters could not be discussed at all. He therefore met half-way the Prussian proposal that talks be resumed at the point where they were broken off in 1833. Without admitting the previous territorial settlement to be definitive, the Belgians would commence negotiations with a study of the unsettled financial and navigational problems. Such a compromise was possible because they now saw success in the territorial matter to be predicated upon a huge downward revision of the debt, which issue had not been discussed in 1833. A series of small successes concerning interest rates, debt arrears, and claims on Dutch finances might aid them in obtaining their larger goal. This sign of flexibility was noted by Palmerston, who was now willing to be influenced toward debt revision, although he remained adamant on territorial issues. The arguments used by the Belgians in winning him over were weighty. The debt had been set high in 1831 to bribe William into signing; since he had not, the figure should be revised. More important, Protocol 48 of the Conference allowed for revision if it were shown that the Dutch charts on which the original figure was based were incorrect. This protocol had not been communicated to the Belgians at the time of its drafting, nor had Van de Weyer been allowed to check the veracity of the Dutch tables. Now given the opportunity to review the tables and avail themselves of the protocol, the Belgians believed they could put forward a strong case for reduction of their debt.[13]

The Belgians needed all the help they could get from France; for a variety of reasons, it did not amount to as much as expected. The French cabinet was paralyzed by the thought that its course was becoming separated from Britain's. Upset at Palmerston's dealings with the absolutist courts, the Frenchmen desired whatever negotiating there was to be done to take place in the presence of all the powers. For this reason Molé advocated a formal reconvening of the London Conference. This was the event the Belgians least wished, for they were still playing a delaying game; moreover, additional time was needed for the Belgian Royal Commission to gather material to support its argument concerning the debt. Another example of lack of coordination was Molé's insistence that his ambassador at London, General Sebastiani, obtain assurance from Palmerston that he would approve reconsideration of the debt if the Dutch tables were proved wrong. Van de Weyer had long ago received such a promise and did not wish the British minister to be given a chance to change his mind; the Belgian's appeals to Sebastiani went unanswered, fortunately with no ill effect for the Belgian cause.

The fault of the lack of Franco-Belgian cooperation did not all lie to the south of Leopold's realm. The king himself had reminded De Theux on July 12 that in France 'there have existed certain military pretentions which the Belgian government has ardently battled and over which it has triumphed. The spirit which dictates these pretentions is always present in France...'.[14] It may have been wise to have a cautious attitude toward France; yet at the time there were no special indications of French designs on Belgium, and such suspicion on the part of Leopold and his cabinet could scarcely lead to the frank exchanges of confidence that were necessary if the Belgians and French were to have their way at the conference.

The Belgian commissioners hastily completed their study and concluded that instead of 8,400,000 florins, Belgium should only pay 2,215,000 florins.[15] The Prussian and Russian ambassadors at London categorically refused to admit the debt should be revised and supported Dutch demands for payment of the past eight years' arrears, a sum which totaled over sixty-seven million florins. Palmerston, conscious that King William I had a right to expect the powers to grant him compensation for the loss of territory, disappointed the Belgians by only mildly supporting their demands for a debt reduction. He agreed they might refuse to pay arrears since it was the Dutch, not the Belgians who had failed to sign the treaty. But he saw little virtue in De Theux's argument that the principal of the debt should be cut because the Belgians had been forced by Dutch hostility to spend over 370 million francs for extraordinary defense measures.[16] Eventually, thanks to Palmerston's mediation and skillful use of the *Syndicat d'amortissement* issue to force down Dutch monetary demands, the five powers decided upon a system whereby the Belgians would be granted indirectly what was not granted directly – a reduction in the amount they would have to pay. In place of liquidation of the *Syndicat*, the Belgians were granted a decrease of three million florins per year in their debt. As this was not the total revision the Belgians wished and as the reduction was less than that desired, they continued to argue and succeeded in angering the Prussians by their delaying tactics.

The small nation's diplomats had thus far not achieved their goals and had failed to win many friends. In particular De Theux's long refusal to accept Palmerston's pet proposal for a transactional sum as compensation for non-liquidation of the *Syndicat* proved fruitless and aroused animosities. Even Van de Weyer warned De Theux that he should alter his policy. Yet the foreign minister replied in mid-August that there was nothing to be feared from a dissolution of the conference. A break with the eastern courts would in no way harm the *status quo*. In desperate annoyance with his superior's delaying game, Van de Weyer wrote eleven days later:

It is impossible to maintain the position towards Lord Palmerston in which I have been placed by the system we have followed up until now. The government must take that position – which is also its own – into serious consideration. I have defended it until now with all my ability, but I feel that I can no longer stay on that ground without harming other interests.[17]

On November 13 at the opening of the Belgian chambers a scene took place which further hindered the Belgians' efforts to gain the friendship and respect of the powers. In his opening address Leopold ignored the warning of his foreign minister that the wording of his prepared draft was excessive. His speech was patriotic to high degree; he declared: 'The rights and interest of the country are the only rules of my policy; they will be treated with the care which their importance demands; *they will be defended with perseverance and courage.*'[18] A flood of belligerent speeches and demonstrations broke forth in the chambers. The Senate in its address to the throne a few days later stated it would be 'constantly disposed to support the measures that the defense of territory would render necessary' and promised to review appropriations and military laws. The Chamber of Representatives declared 'we will not draw back before any sacrifice for the defense of the country... The good discipline of our troops, their progress in maneuvers, and the patriotic spirit which animates them prove what we can expect of them in the upholding of our rights.'

The Prussians immediately undertook to have all the powers send a harsh note. Palmerston agreed to join in the protest but did not use the severe form of the indentical notes presented by the absolutist courts; Molé sent no note at all. The affair blew over, but the Belgians had suffered a setback. They were now markedly on the defensive, and Van de Weyer had to devote much of his time to defending past Belgian actions rather than pressing arguments for the alteration of the Twenty-four Articles.

At the beginning of December the conference reconvened after a brief adjournment. Prussia, Russia, and Austria were immovable; there was to be no cession of territory and no further debt reduction. Palmerston, annoyed by news of an unofficial French attempt to persuade the Dutch to exchange some land for an indemnity, was also firm. A protocol was drawn up and presented to Sebastiani on December 6; the old man, allowed no time to send for instructions and fearing a refusal to sign would mean dissolution of the conference and war, gave his signature *ad referendum*.

The powers' exertions were now directed toward obtaining a Belgian signature. Molé wrote that Belgium should acquiesce and that perhaps some land might later be purchased; he would willingly support such an effort. Bonds fell on the Brussels stock exchange and a financial and industrial crisis broke out in the nation. Leopold, perhaps remembering his advice to Princess Victoria that 'good sense must show itself by distinguishing what is and what is not important', convinced his cabinet to raise the amount it would pay to four million florins.[19] This was not the level of payment demanded, and Palmerston threateningly implied that the powers might increase their figure. At this point the revolutionary Louis de Potter called for the formation of a Belgo-Rhinean confederation, and the Belgian cause was further discredited.

One final effort at repurchase of the disputed territories was made by the Belgians, as special envoys were sent to London and Paris. Palmerston met the overture with wrath, excoriated the behavior of the Belgian chambers, and did all he could to hasten the close of the conference.[20] It was clear that Belgium could gain little more except modifications of the Scheldt tolls, and even these hopes quickly fell by the wayside. Further delay would only emphasize the untenability of the Belgians' refusal to fulfill the conditions of a treaty they had long ago accepted and which now their enemy was accepting against his will. Leopold advised, however, that the negotiations not be brought before parliament quite yet. De Theux disregarded the king's advice as the king had earlier disregarded his minister's. The reaction in parliament was the same as two months earlier. Leopold saw the writing on the wall and adjourned the chambers by royal decree. When they learned of De Theux's decision to give in to the powers, three Liberal cabinet members resigned and a full-scale parliamentary crisis was in the making.

Meanwhile France, Prussia, Holland, and Belgium had been mobilizing troops. The conference sent notes to the two small states, and when Belgium was slow to withdraw her troops, she received a harsher warning. The Belgian army contained no division generals with combat experience; to eliminate this deficiency the best combat general available was hired. He was Jan Skrzynecki, the hero of the Polish revolutionaries' victory over the Russians at Ostrolenka. When his presence in the Belgian army was revealed, the autocratic courts waxed indignant. The Belgian foreign minister proclaimed ignorance of the matter and insisted no insult was intended. This protestation did not prevent the Austrian and Prussian ambassadors from demanding their passports. Even at this moment, De Theux clung to what dignity Belgium had left and broke relations with Austria in return, much to Metternich's surprise.

All that remained for De Theux was to collect the pieces and convince the chambers to authorize signature of the treaties. Neither task was pleasant. Assurances concerning the property and religious freedom of the abandoned populations were sought, navigation rules on the Scheldt were discussed, and even some aspects of the debt were again brought up, but the most De Theux could gain was a few small changes encompassed in an interpretive declaration by the powers. The debates in the chambers were furious; Alexandre Gendebien became famous for his thundering, 'No, 380,000 times no for the 380,000 Belgians they sacrifice to fear'.[21] The cabinet survived, however, and was granted authority to sign two treaties, one with the Netherlands and the other with the five powers.

The Austrians would not agree to the treaty unless Skrzynecki were

BELGIUM
1839

30 MI.

30 KM.

VOORNE

MAAS

NE

OVER FLAKKEE

SCHOUWEN

EAST SCHELDT

THOLEN

WALCHEREN

SOUTH BEVELAND

Flushing

WEST SCHELDT

FLEMISH ZEELAND

Terneuzen

SCHELDT

A

ANTWE

Zeebrugge

Ostende

BRUGES

GHENT

E A S T
F L A N D E R S

Lie

Malines
MECHE

Dunkirk

W E S T
F L A N D E R S

SCHELDT

BRUSSELS

B R A B

YSER

Ypres

LYS

Courtrai

SCHELDT

Waterloo

W

1839

Lille

LYS

H
A
I

Tournai

N

A
U

Mons
BERGEN

G
E

Charleroi

F
R
A
N
C
E

> ANTWERP CITADEL, BUT NOT THE CITY, WAS HELD BY THE DUTCH UNTIL SURRENDERED TO FRENCH TROOPS IN 1832; THE CITADEL WAS PLACED UNDER BELGIAN CONTROL IN 1833.

Rotterdam

Quievrain

SAMBRE

1839

BAR-LE-DUC (BELG. CONTROL)

Venlo

Ostend

Bruges

Antwerp

DUTCH-CLAIMED ENCLAVES

Philippe

Ghent

BRUSSELS

Maestricht

Cologne

Ypres

BELGIUM

Liege

Aachen

Mariembour

Lille

Eupen

Mons

Namur

Malmedy

BELGIAN-
CONTROLLED
TERRITORIES
1830 – 1839

ACCORDING TO THE STATUS QUO AGREEMENT OF MAY, 1833

> TERRITORIES ACQUIRED BY THE UNITED NETHERLANDS FROM FRANCE AFTER THE "HUNDRED DAYS", 1815.

GRAND DUCHY
OF
LUXEMBURG
(BELGIAN CONTROL)

Sedan

Luxemburg

> BOUNDARIES OF BELGIUM AND LUXEMBURG 1831

Longwy

> FORTRESS OF LUXEMBURG OCCUPIED BY PRUSSIAN TROOPS FOR THE GERMAN CONFEDERATION.

50 MI.

50 KM.

T. R. MILLER

F

R

1839

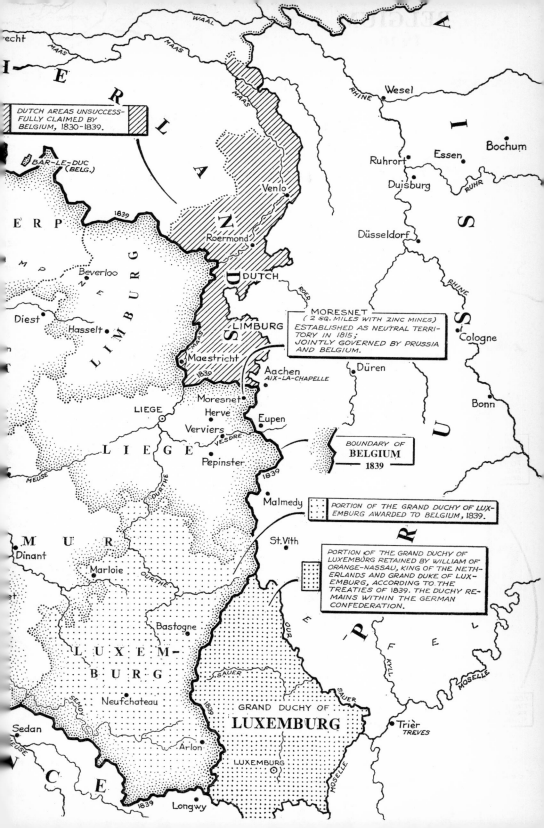

DUTCH AREAS UNSUCCESS-
FULLY CLAIMED BY
BELGIUM, 1830-1839.

MORESNET
(2 SQ. MILES WITH ZINC MINES)
ESTABLISHED AS NEUTRAL TERRI-
TORY IN 1815;
JOINTLY GOVERNED BY PRUSSIA
AND BELGIUM.

BOUNDARY OF
BELGIUM
1839

PORTION OF THE GRAND DUCHY OF LUX-
EMBURG AWARDED TO BELGIUM, 1839.

PORTION OF THE GRAND DUCHY OF
LUXEMBURG RETAINED BY WILLIAM OF
ORANGE-NASSAU, KING OF THE NETH-
ERLANDS AND GRAND DUKE OF LUX-
EMBURG, ACCORDING TO THE
TREATIES OF 1839. THE DUCHY RE-
MAINS WITHIN THE GERMAN
CONFEDERATION.

GRAND DUCHY OF
LUXEMBURG

removed from the Belgian army. Palmerston appealed to Metternich, and in a short time Vienna and Berlin resumed diplomatic relations with Brussels. The treaties were signed at London on April 19, 1839. Many of the articles of November 1831 remained unchanged, including the ones concerning neutrality and territory; those concerning the Scheldt experienced only a few modifications. Belgium had failed to keep all of Limburg and Luxemburg, the debt payments had been only reduced to five million florins per year, and the navigation of the Scheldt was still hindered by annoying laws and tolls. These last had been reduced to 1.5 florins per ton for the main channel of the Scheldt, but the East Scheldt remained under the Mainz tariffs. In the shuffle of negotiations the Belgian right to capitalize the tolls was lost, although gains were made on the issues of pilotage and local fishing traffic. Many details were reserved for study by a Belgo-Dutch commission, whose efforts resulted in a treaty in 1842. The *Syndicat d'amortissement*, while receiving much discussion during negotiations, was not mentioned in the treaties.

The settlement was not to the disadvantage of the Belgians despite their complaints, for setbacks in specific clauses were compensated by the overall confirmation of Belgium's independence. It was surely the losses in Limburg and Luxemburg that most pained the Belgians. The debt figure was admittedly exhorbitant; but a sizeable debt would have had to be paid in any case, and the amount in excess of what the Belgians had willingly accepted was not beyond their ability to meet in time. It was only in connection with the territorial question that financial matters had gained such pressing importance. The issue of the Scheldt was more serious, for Dutch control of access to Antwerp was a blow both to the economy of the new state and its independence. Yet it was possible, as later events proved, that careful negotiations could ameliorate the situation. Control of the Scheldt was really only an aspect of the larger territorial question regarding the fate of Flemish Zeeland. In 1831 the revolutionaries had talked about annexing these lands which had belonged to the United Provinces since the seventeenth century. But the protestant inhabitants of Zeeland had remained loyal to the King of the Netherlands and the Belgians could have little hope of gaining Zeeland in the West while in the east they were basing their claims on the right of self-determination for the populations of Limburg and Luxemburg.

It is not surprising the powers refused to award these last areas and their valuable fortresses to Belgium. The Belgians were notably pro-French, had little physical means of resisting a French invasion, and France herself had still not convinced the other powers that she had abandoned all thought of regaining the glories of the Empire. The new state's continuing existence was granted at the pleasure of the powers, and it did not serve that pleasure for two of the key fortresses in Western Europe to be placed within the easy reach of France. The main obstacle to the exchange of Luxemburg and Limburg for an indemnity was not so much the refusal of King William as it was the opposition of the German Confederation. It was the eastern powers who won Palmerston's support on this issue and choked off the possibility of an exchange even before the Dutch and Belgians had begun serious direct negotiations. Even if William were to give way, the transfer of Confederation territories to Belgium could not have been tolerated by the Diet, for whom German unity was becoming a point of honor. As Henri Pirenne has judged:

If one takes into account the rights of Holland and the German Confederation which it was impossible to violate for the profit of Belgium, it will be agreed that the treaties of 1839 could hardly have been other than what they were.[22]

The result of the London Conference was determined by the attitude of its chairman, Lord Palmerston. The Belgians were correct in addressing their major efforts to winning him to their side. Their task was made difficult by two factors not yet mentioned. The first of these was the weaken ing position of the Melbourne cabinet. It was known that the cabinet would be met with sharp attacks when parliament reconvened, and Palmerston was therefore eager to have the Belgian problem settled as expeditiously as possible. Furthermore, British businessmen and financiers had considerable investments in Holland and would oppose any solution which dealt harshly with the Dutch. There can be little doubt that Palmerston was subject to pressure by his cabinet colleagues to achieve a quick settlement favorable to Holland. The second problem was that presented by Mohammad Ali. By the end of 1838 the Near East was again in crisis. While Britain desired to ally with France in the Belgian affair, Palmerston wished good relations with Russia, Austria, and Prussia because of the eastern question. He had, then, to avoid crossing those powers too sharply at London.

A cabinet crisis and the eastern question had also affected French diplomacy. Public opinion was concerned with the debates over the powers of the king and did not force Molé into more outspoken support of the Belgians. In the months before his January resignation, the premier became disturbed by the tensions in the Orient which were disrupting the July Monarchy's good relations with John Bull. To prevent the breach from widening, Molé frequently gave way to Palmerston on Belgian issues.

These problems, along with the nature of Belgium's task in metamorphosizing an already written treaty, put high hurdles between the Brussels diplomats and their goals. But it was not so much lack of Franco-Belgian coordination in several aspects of the affair or the want of closer

Anglo-French understanding that hurt the Belgian cause. It was the factors which prevented Belgium from using her favorite diplomatic techniques to full advantage and which, above all, prevented her from controlling the pace of the solution of the dispute.

The fortress matter had been a prolonged affair. The point in question was not worthy of a war; furthermore, De Theux was standing up against only one power supported by one other. The longer the fortress building program was allowed to continue, the stronger the Belgian position became and the more fortresses were completed. By combining arguments that the Belgians were not going to build much this year with refusals to submit future Belgian defense measures to foreign control, De Theux won time. Eventually the Prussians let their objections be spoken into empty air. The woodcutting incident was somewhat the reverse; time was in favor of the duke. The longer William was allowed to cut wood in Luxemburg and the longer the fortress commander succeeded in controlling Belgian civil authorities, the weaker the Belgian position became. On this occasion De Theux strove for a hasty conclusion, taking steps such as the sending of troops, a gesture which soon brought the crisis to a head. In both incidents, the Belgians had shown boldness and firmness; more important, by these tactics they succeeded in controlling the pace of events and thus maintained the diplomatic offensive.

Belgium needed time to reach a favorable solution of the dispute with Holland. On June 2, 1835, Leopold wrote Victoria that any changes in Belgium's condition should be effected 'in a very gentle manner'.[23] A year earlier he had written 'it is excessively difficult to *retrace* a false move to get out of a mistake; and there exists very rarely, except in time of war and civil feuds, a necessity for an immediate decision'. This was advice he would have liked to follow in 1838, but time could not be won as easily as in years earlier.

Time might have been obtained if the conference had been postponed and direct negotiations re-established with William. To arrange this, Belgium would have had to face down not just one of the European powers but all of them. She would be challenging both the interests of several individual states and, more important, the principle of order on which the peace of Europe was then founded. The Belgians had successfully done so in 1830; but the task was one they could not want to repeat in detail, even if circumstances permitted. As a result of the negotiations of 1831–33, the Belgians had become shareholders in that principle of order; any dissolution of it could threaten her own existence. The decisions of the great powers' diplomats were motivated more out of self-interest and fear of international war than solicitude for Belgium. Their refusal to let the emotional revolutionaries have their way was nevertheless an indirect acknowledgement that Belgium was considered in some sense within the European system, not standing outside it and subject to the arbitrary actions of any power. Yet if this were to be the case, Belgium would have to pay a price.

The Brussels diplomats could find no lever by which they could sufficiently force the powers apart without carrying the feat so far that Belgium would lose in the ensuing animosity what little security she had. The Belgians also knew that in questioning the competence of the conference they would be offending Palmerston, their main support in previous struggles. Confronted by these difficulties and fearful of making a false move, De Theux was unable to show his former decisiveness; it was his capable minister in London who settled the matter. De Theux soon recovered himself and proved both bold and stubborn in his repeated efforts to have the conference adopt his points of view. Yet from the start, the Belgians were on the defensive. They represented, after all, a militarily weak and diplomatically inexperienced state challenging established powers.

De Theux's defensive posture and his inability to separate the powers and slow the pace of negotiations affected the appearance of his actions once the conference began. Firmness in clinging to his position and audacity in calling for far-reaching revisions of the 1831 settlement no longer were bold maneuvers which took opponents by surprise and forced matters to a favorable conclusion. Rather, they appeared as obstructionism and unreasoned demands. But for the eastern question and ministry difficulties in Paris and London, the Belgians might have been more successful, although their efforts were not totally unrewarded in any case. Unfortunately, the connection of the debt to the territorial settlement was clear to all, and the powers refused to reduce the debt as much as might have been done had De Theux publicly renounced all aspirations to the territories. Such a renunciation was a political impossibility, for De Theux and perhaps even Leopold might have been overthrown by the chauvinistic Belgian populace had such a statement been made. This is the one excuse for De Theux's stubbornness which the Abbé De Lannoy, an authority on early Belgian diplomacy, would accept. He nevertheless could not approve of the foreign minister's policy, which he thought would have had better chances of success were it characterized by 'more moderate language, more flexible conduct, [and] more exact understanding of the exigencies of European politics and diplomatic dealings'.[24] Joseph Lebeau, a Liberal critic of the Catholic De Theux's more conservative views, in his memoirs accused the minister of lack of foresight, a thirst for power, and harboring disastrous illusions. Yet Lebeau's sharpest attack was on those politicians who had not opposed the passions of the chamber as boldly as had Lebeau eight years earlier.[25]

Leopold, De Theux, and Van de Weyer were all aware of the need of keeping Belgium's head high and her dignity unsullied. This was partly why Van de Weyer advised De Theux to be moderate in his opposition to the powers, lest his attitude be interpreted as sullen, impertinent obstinacy. It was also why De Theux insisted on breaking relations with Vienna after Ambassador Rechberg left Brussels. The outbursts of revolutionary fervor in the Belgian parliament were therefore like pigeons coming home to roost on the façade of dignity which De Theux and his friends were attempting to construct.

The Belgian diplomats were claiming that Belgium was an orderly state worthy of respect; meanwhile Belgian politicans were calling for war in disregard of the 1831 treaties and evoking the memory of the glorious revolution, the very heritage that Van de Weyer was attempting to help the powers forget. At one point Palmerston angrily told a Belgian envoy:

Whatever they are, the popular demonstrations, the effervescence of spirits, the general will, the carrying away of the masses, etc., etc..., they are hardly the reasons, the arguments, to oppose to engagements solemnly contracted toward the five powers. If these dangerous principles should be admitted even once, it would be the end of all the treaties and of European public law, and anarchy would take the place of order and justice.[26]

The necessity of Leopold's adjournment of the chambers indicated the small country still had much maturing to do. It was also an example of the important role Leopold played throughout the affair. That the monarch was not innocent of bad judgment is proved by his inflammatory speech to the chambers and his threats of resignation. Nevertheless, he made good use of his family connections, influencing both Louis-Philippe and Queen Victoria in his favor. C. K. Webster described the king's efforts by writing: 'There can be little doubt that Leopold soon realized that it was impossible to get so much and was acting a part. He did it very well, paying a visit to France, writing Palmerston letters...'.[27] Leopold may have been acting, but undoubtedly his pressure on Louis-Philippe and Palmerston did not hurt the Belgian cause.

3.3 CUSTOMS UNION PROPOSALS

The Treaties of 1839 had officially established Belgium among the European powers. Yet her battle to gain respected status did not end immediately. Russian recognition was not obtained until the spring of 1853, and while the 1839 Treaties settled several major issues, there were still others to be resolved before Belgium's position in Europe could be firmly defined.

Some of these issues stemmed from the treaties themselves, which had left a number of details to be worked out directly by Belgium and the Netherlands. The abdication of William I to marry the maid of honor to his first wife facilitated negotiations only slightly. His successor, William II, would not abandon hope that the Orange dynasty would eventually be reaccepted by the Belgians; he therefore reached a final settlement with them more out of pressure from the powers and his own subjects than from a desire to resolve the outstanding differences. By a treaty of November 5, 1842, and a complementary convention of August 8, 1843, several questions of border details, finances, and navigation were regulated.

Another much debated issue, which was only in part related to the recent treaties, concerned Belgium's behavior as a country whose neutrality was both permanent and required. The fortress affair had determined that Belgium had a right to arm herself and that her neutrality gave the powers no authority to interfere in her domestic affairs. On the other hand, the extent to which Belgium might tighten ties with other countries and the larger question of the breadth of Belgium's liberty of action in foreign affairs remained to be determined. The debates over a possible customs union with France did not resolve all aspects of these questions. Yet the eventual result of the customs union proposals did go a long way towards establishing general limitations which the Belgian diplomats would henceforth feel obliged, as neutrals, to observe.

The Treaties of 1839 had dealt a severe blow to Belgian industry. From 1815 to 1830, that industry had been reorganized to meet the needs of the Dutch provinces. Revolution and separation from the Netherlands had therefore been especially disrupting; the loss of the markets of Limburg and Luxemburg nine years later was close to a catastrophe. Capital fled, salaries fell, and depression spread; even the great Cockerill firm was in difficulty. The need for tariff agreements with some neighboring country whose markets would then be available to Belgian producers seemed imperative.

Belgium's plight was not overlooked by the other states; while the Dutch king hoped economic collapse might return his lost provinces to him, the French planned to take their own advantage of the situation. As early as 1836 French Foreign Minister Marshal Soult had proposed a Franco-Belgian customs union; in 1840, the offer was renewed. The reaction of De Theux at that time was similar to that which he had shared with Nothomb on the earlier occasion. Commercial union with France might bring material advantages, but it would also be 'a serious blow to the country's spirit of independence and to the luster of the throne'.[28]

Following the signature of the 1839 Treaties, De Theux's position was weak. Despite the foreign minister's opposition, Leopold had pursued commercial talks with his father-in-law's nation. When De Theux became the scapegoat upon whom the chambers vented their disappointment concerning the treaties, the king chose Lebeau to succeed to the ministry. Anglo-French differences had been growing increasingly sharp over the culminating eastern crisis, and it was Leopold's manifest intention to install a foreign minister who had not been so close to the French as De Theux and who could clearly indicate Belgium's impartiality in the current quarrel between Britain and France. The king, no doubt, was also aware that Lebeau favored a commercial agreement with France.

Within a short time, however, Lebeau had changed his mind. He was probably convinced in part by Van de Weyer's strong opposition. The respected minister in England worried whether France could be trusted and whether she would become mistress of all Belgium's actions. A customs union, he wrote, would deny the development of the national spirit. Belgium's independence would be mocked by others who would say, 'You cannot live without France, it is on her that you must have your eyes constantly fixed, it is she who will regulate your material interests with her laws. You are not a nation yourself, you are something of a subaltern, an accessory...'.[29]

Leopold was himself aware of the danger that France might attempt to turn a commercial union into political dominance. His spokesmen therefore emphasized to Louis-Philippe that any arrangement would be solely commercial; no French customs officials would be allowed on Belgium's northern and eastern boundaries (a privilege for which the French had been fishing). To Lebeau and Van de Weyer's arguments the king replied that a commercial treaty would give Belgium a special advantage. Henceforth, France would be tied to Belgium by a long-term agreement, whereas at present France was bound to Belgium in no specific manner. The complaints of other powers against a Franco-Belgian commercial pact would be vitiated by the avidity with which they themselves were making similar arrangements. He added that the French king had shown considerable goodwill on the matter; it would be improper to break off negotiations after they had been proceeding for several months. For these reasons, Leopold declared the Belgian minister at Paris should be empowered to sign preliminaries for a commerce and tariff treaty.[30]

In mentioning the attitude of the other powers, Leopold acknowledged the growing pressure from those states against the creation of a Franco-Belgian customs union. Concern at first had focused on the difficulty of drawing nearer to France economically while keeping that state at distance politically; indeed, it became the major preoccupation of Belgian diplomats in the next several decades. But now the problem had taken on broader dimensions, and attention centered on Belgium's relations with all the great nations. It was again a case of the Belgian diplomats having to find a posture consonant with their own independence which would simultaneously meet with the approval of the European family. In the minds of most of the Brussels statesmen it was within Belgium's sovereign right to contract a customs agreement with France, despite the arguments of Palmerston and others that such an action would conflict with Belgium's neutrality. Fewer and fewer of the Belgians could disagree, however, with Palmerston's warning that Belgium might be committing political suicide. Even if France did not use the treaty to encroach on Belgium's independence, the Dutch, the *Zollverein*, and possibly also the Austrians and even the British might demand economic privileges in Belgium equal to those granted to France. The Belgians would have to give up all hope of economic independence and with it most of their political independence; at the same time, they would risk seeing their territories divided into quarreling spheres of foreign econommic interests.

While the Near East crisis was at its peak, it was agreed that Franco-Belgian negotiations should be suspended lest the powers think Belgium were siding with France against them. The split within the Belgian government over the policy to be followed grew during the respite. When negotiations resumed in 1841, the Belgians no longer talked of a general customs union but rather of tariff reductions on specific items. By this time, De Muelenaere was again foreign minister; for Lebeau's cabinet, defeated on issues unrelated to foreign policy, had been replaced by one headed by Nothomb.

The French were unwilling to give up a full union, and their reply to the more limited proposal indicated the Belgians' distrust was warranted. France was making great economic sacrifices; her political gain could, therefore, not be veiled but should be 'evident and striking to all the world... The customs union is possible only if executive power regarding tariffs belongs entirely to the French government'.[31] If a treaty were to be concluded, it must grant France control of Belgium's frontiers and customs.

Though it is doubtful the French intended to maintain these harsh demands, such statements caused the Belgians to break off the discussions. This did nothing to solve Belgium's commercial problems, which threatened to become increasingly severe when France announced an intended rise in duties on linen cloth and thread. Were the increase to take place, the major Belgian industry would be crippled and over 138,000 workers left unemployed. Leopold therefore quickly resumed contact with the French, using officers of his own house rather than the appointed-ministers of the government, whom he considered to be less flexible. Despite his appeals and a threat to raise Belgian tariffs on French wines, the linen rates were elevated. The Belgians necessarily had to continue the talks; on July 16, 1842, in return for a lowering of French linen duties, Belgium acquiesced to an entire series of French demands. Many of these, however, were not of major importance, serving mainly to placate vociferous groupings in the French chambers.

Although Lord Aberdeen, the new British foreign minister, had advised against the tariff agreement, and although Metternich had cautioned the Belgians, it was the Prussians who took greatest umbrage. They had warned that reprisals would be taken; when Prussia demanded that she as well as France be granted concessions, the Belgians could do no other than acquiesce, much to the extreme annoyance of Louis-Philippe. The Brussels statesmen were already learning that as part of the delicate European balance of order they could not hope to shift their weight in one direction without making a compensatory move in another. They were also discovering that as a small, neutral nation whose actions could presumably least upset the balance of order, Belgium's independent movements were viewed by others with less, rather than more, indulgence than that granted more dangerous states.

Throughout the negotiations, it had been the Belgians rather than the French who had born the brunt of European opposition to a customs union. This was, no doubt, a result of the belief that newly-created Belgium would be more easily persuaded to back down than France, which country had already given way on the eastern question and would be reluctant to retreat once again. When it was learned in the fall of 1842 that there were plans to transform the tariff agreement into a full-fledged customs union and that Leopold had visited his father-in-law to discuss the matter, pressure on Belgium increased. The Prussians talked of a *casus belli*, and Aberdeen touched on that possibility while underlining his opposition. Only Metternich showed sympathy for the Belgians in their difficult position, yet even he had earlier stated that while Belgium might make individual tariff arrangements, he could not consent to a general customs union. Pressure was brought on France as well, but the wily premier, François Guizot, instructed his ministers to give the impression that it was not France who wished the union, but Belgium.

The Austrians were in particular puzzled by Leopold's behavior. Louis-Philippe was a stubborn man, but the Belgian king was intelligent and well-aware of the powers' opposition. Was he acting in this perverse manner so that he could prove his personal moral independence to his own country? This was not the view of the Austrian minister in London, who reported that 'Leopold affects courage, but timidity is his normal state. He will retire within himself and into that condition when he sees his political existence can be compromised.'[32]

Though it was impossible for Leopold to hold out, his retreat was not marked by any abject surrender. He was most dismayed when Prussia threatened to have a conference called. The king was willing to deal with the powers individually but not collectively. Once a conference had taken a position it would be difficult indeed to sway it, for even those powers which disagreed with the decision would have to adhere to it and punish any Belgian contempt of court. Leopold's anxiety was increased by a letter from his nephew, the British prince consort, warning that the powers' first action might be to withdraw their representatives from Brussels or to demand the demolition of fortresses in southern Belgium which were too easily within Louis-Philippe's reach. In despair, the king commented there was nothing for him to do but abdicate. Apparently he was unaware that Metternich, Aberdeen, and Guizot were also opposed to a conference and that the Prussian tentative proposal had little chance of success.

By the end of 1842, Franco-Belgian talks had been broken off, although Leopold refused to renounce permanently the right to contract a customs union. Prussian Foreign Minister Bülow was not satisfied and campaigned to have the powers send notes to Belgium protesting that a customs union was contrary to Belgium's neutrality. The pace of the controversy had been slowed, however. Given additional months to ponder the matter, Leopold announced the next July that Belgium had ceased to consider a customs union because of the difficulties involved. Belgium nevertheless needed individual trade agreements with her neighbors and would continue to work for them. Metternich was satisfied with the reply; although the Prussians vainly demanded Leopold's statement be put in writing, the incident was closed.

At the time, the European chancelleries ascribed the ending of Franco-Belgian customs talks to their own opposition. More recently it has been suggested that while foreign pressure would eventually have forced some reconsideration, it was opposition within the French chambers that led to the suspension of customs union negotiations.[33] Numerous businessmen and industrialists, particularly from northern France, had been fighting the proposal constantly; domestic opposition was so great that it appears the powers were making a mountain out of what had little chance of becoming a molehill. Resistance in Belgium among governmental circles was also a check which Leopold had far from overcome. For Guizot, who had hopes of building a French-led economic system including Belgium, Holland, and Switzerland, the collapse of the discussions was a severe blow. For Leopold, while it caused him some embarrassment before his government's ministers, the incident had not been entirely unfortunate.

One tangible gain was the limited tariff agreement with France. More important, Leopold had made clear to the diplomats of the other nations that if there were no customs union, Belgium's economic survival depended on obtaining commercial treaties with other nations. The necessity was obvious and the ice had already been broken by the agreements with France and Prussia. Rather than see Belgium forced into closer dependence on France, the Prussians agreed in 1844 to a broader Belgian accord with the *Zollverein*. Satisfactory agreements with France and one with Holland followed in 1845 and 1846. This last treaty was an acknowledgment that the economic abyss into which the Dutch had hoped Belgium would fall had been bridged.

Encouraging also was the conclusion of a treaty with the United States. Since the aborted attempt of 1833, Belgian-American commercial negotiations had experienced increasing difficulties. Conflicts had arisen over Belgium's responsibilities for American losses at Antwerp caused by Dutch shelling of that city in 1830 and over Belgian discussions with the Republic of Texas regarding trade and loan agreements. In a vain effort to win the European terminus of a steamship line to be established by the Americans from New York to Europe, Belgium made important concessions that resulted in ratification of a beneficial trade treaty in 1845. If such pliability was a bit unusual for the little country at the time, it foreshadowed the turn Belgium's diplomacy would take in coming years.[34]

As a result of the customs union affair, Belgium had solidified her position politically as well as economically. The sympathy of Metternich and the European tariff treaties that were signed after the fuss was over indicated this, as did the reluctance of the powers to call a conference on the issue. Belgium was considered no longer a power to be dictated to, but an independent nation to be negotiated with. Even if the French and Prussians might exert considerable pressure on Belgium, she was within the family of European powers. Moreover, the agreements with France and particularly with the *Zollverein* provided the Belgians with opportunities to strengthen ties with their neighbors and win further acceptance. In return for all this, it was understood that Belgium, while she might have the legal right to reach a close *rapport* with any one nation, would refrain from doing so. Her neutrality was not a product of voluntary choice, thus allowing latitude in its implementation; it was required and imposed from without. Henceforth, in order to avoid stimulating suspicions or rivalries, the Belgian diplomats would be circumspect in their dealings with their friends, solicitous of the feelings of possible enemies, and for the most part content to exercise Belgium's freedom of movement in foreign affairs within carefully restrained limits.

3.4 THE ACHIEVEMENT AND ITS DIPLOMACY

On November 3, 1839, Metternich told the Belgian representative at the German Diet:

Without doubt we do not at first love the new-born because they derange and always inquiet the family politic. Yet as soon as we have adopted you, your existence is a part of the *conservative* system to which we are vowed, and we repudiate henceforth as revolutionaries those who would disturb you...[35]

The treaties of 1839 had seen the bastard ward of Europe legitimatized and allowed into the European community, but it was Belgium's continued existence over the years and her survival in 1848 that won her full acceptance and status in the European family of powers. Belgium was no longer considered an artificial creation and a French dependency. The year 1839 brought her political emancipation, which the ensuing years solidified by assuring Belgium's economic stability; her moral emancipation dates from 1848.[36]

The important feature of that year for the Belgians was that no revolution occurred in their country. This is not to say there was no unrest, but prompt action by the new Liberal cabinet and the existing liberal features of the Belgian constitution helped forestall any overt upheaval. A sudden expansion of the franchise and other political and civil service reforms offered significant gains to the lower classes. The strength of the growing metallurgy factories in the south and east helped compensate for unemployment in the textile factories of Flanders; forced loans were levied on the prosperous industries, and public works projects were created to provide jobs and wages.

Even a brief glance at the diplomatic exchanges of the time reveals how interested the other powers were in the strength of Leopold's grip on the throne. Both the king and his foreign minister steadily received praise and thanks for the orderly manner in which the nation and its foreign policy were being conducted. Leopold did waver at one point, and the tension between king and chambers over issues relating to the amount of power the central authority should have was clearly evident. Yet there was no real threat to the monarchy, and indeed there was considerable loyalty. Diplomatic difficulties were experienced; but though foreshadowed during the customs discussions, they were mostly of a different nature than those of the past, as was the Belgian response. When the waves of upheaval had been beaten back throughout Europe and the old regimes were again in control except in France, Belgium was no longer the object of unrelenting suspicion, and she held high standing in the body politic of European nations.

The achievement was the result of painful diplomacy by a handful of men over an extended period. Leopold, by means of his regal appearance, dignity, sagacity, and family connections did much to enhance Belgium in the eyes of his fellow sovereigns. Although his histrionics occasionally annoyed his colleagues, his talents and character were respected by all and led to important friendships, such as those he possessed with Queen Victoria and Prince Metternich. Already allied by marriage to the thrones of England and France, Leopold saw his personal ties to those countries strengthened by the marriage of a nephew to Queen Victoria and a niece to a member of the Orleans family. Other Coburg matches skillfully forwarded by the Belgian king brought ties with the thrones of Portugal and Spain. The respectability of the 'Republican King' and the country over which he reigned could not but profit from these alliances.

Leopold did not hesitate to use his connections to further Belgium's various diplomatic undertakings. To aid him in his activities, he set up a ministry of the royal house which consisted mainly of the king's private secretary, Jules van Praet. The secretary was the intermediary between crown and cabinet. He served as Leopold's instrument in domestic affairs and carried on the king's confidential correspondence with Belgian diplomats abroad, an activity which the foreign office for the most part docilely accepted. Leopold's penchant for negotiating by himself through family channels did sometimes lead to difficulties as in the customs affair. Yet more often the Brussels diplomats were aided by their king's connections, gaining information from London which otherwise might not have been forthcoming. Indeed, Leopold's influence, knowledge, and grasp of affairs was such that an Austrian diplomat in Brussels reported:

The essential point here for a head of a mission is to place himself in such a manner as to know, either directly or through M. Van Praet, the ideas and wishes of His Majesty on all things before inquiring, merely for form, concerning the opinions and views of his ministers. The reason is that, all things being considered, there is in Belgium only King Leopold who is truly a man of politics and who, being up to date on great affairs, knows their meaning and appreciates their importance.[37]

This view may be somewhat exaggerated, for while Leopold's foreign ministers were inexperienced, they were more capable than their critics, and even Leopold, sometimes admitted. It is true that in her diplomatic service Belgium faced a problem familiar to young states, both large and small. That was the scant supply of diplomats of the first order, and the close involvement of those few skilled men in all the affairs of the country. These men, especially in the cases of Van de Weyer and Nothomb, were fully aware of their importance and political weight at home. Van de Weyer, a hero for the role he played in the provisional government, was not afraid of giving his advice freely and of acting on his own. These are virtues rather than vices in a diplomat. Yet there were occasions in the 1830s, and again in 1848, when he visited the exiled Count de Neiully and suggested to Palmerston that the British fleet should demonstrate in the Scheldt, that Van de Weyer flagrantly went beyond his instructions. When criticized, he resigned, forcing Foreign Minister Baron d'Hoffschmidt to take time in the midst of a diplomatic crisis to smooth over their differences in order to get the invaluable minister back on the job.[38]

The Belgians tended to keep their diplomats at the same post. Van de Weyer spent thirty-six years at London as did Nothomb at Berlin, who died at his post in 1881; Count O'Sullivan de Grass de Séovard spent thirty-two years as minister to Austria, and Baron Willmar lived at The Hague for thirteen years. Because of their long terms at one capital, Belgium's representatives acquired positions of respect and honor among the international diplomatic corps in the countries where they were in service. This proved useful when Belgium was gaining status and also in the years following, and it is understandable that Belgium made long use of her most skilled men. But it was also true that the foreign ministers' efforts were sometimes hindered by the faltering ways of the aging representatives; more frequently it would happen that the diplomats would become so acclimated to the foreign state in which they were dwelling that their reports would lose value and their personal opinions and expressions would wander from support of those of their superior in Brussels. Van de Weyer in fact became so anglicized that he retired to an estate near London rather than return to live in Belgium.

The approaches used by the different Belgian foreign ministers in the first two decades of the nation's existence did not vary greatly. D'Hoffschmidt wavered between decisive and cautious actions; most of his predecessors, however, followed De Theux's path, as is indicated by their persistence in tariff discussions with France, despite pressure from abroad and opposition within the countries themselves. It is therefore possible to describe Belgium's diplomacy during the period in which she was battling for status and recognition as bold, persistent, and firm.

The Belgians' willingness to give financial affairs an increasingly central part in their diplomacy over these initial years reflected important changes that were occurring in the small country's economic conditions.

In difficult straits at the time of the revolution, and indeed prodded to revolt in part by economic conditions, the Belgians now possessed perhaps the most advanced industrialized economy on the Continent. Key to this success was the growth of the metallurgy industries, which in turn stimulated production in the rich coal and iron fields of Liege, Charleroi, Mons, and La Louviere. Belgium was the gateway for the industrial revolution into Europe. If the competition of British machinery harmed her textile business, overall compensation was found in the making of engines and machines and especially in the construction of railroads.

The decision of the chambers in 1834 to build a national rail system at a time when even the British experience was limited was a daring demonstration of economic innovation. The task was too large for private investors; the chambers' distrust of a too powerful central government did not deter them from assigning the task to the state. Antwerp and Hal to the south were linked by way of Malines and Brussels, while Ostend and Ans, near Liege, were joined through the major intersection at Malines. The lines soon achieved their purpose, attracting commercial traffic from France and the German states and speeding shipping and travel between Belgium's manufacturing centers and her export areas. The steady demand for metal stimulated Belgium's factories and mines still further and prepared them to sustain an important trade in railway materials with neighboring states as the industrial revolution spread.

As commerce and industry thrived, so did confidence in Belgium's economy. Local and especially foreign investments grew. New banking establishments were founded and old ones expanded their activity, stimulating the growth of family industries into large enterprises; *sociétés anonymes*, which numbered only fifteen in 1830, grew by 151 in the six years from 1833 to 1839. By 1837 shipping tonnage handled at Antwerp was surpassing the best yearly totals reached under the previous regime.[39]

The economic success of the revolutionary state limited the diplomatic alternatives available to Belgium's statesmen while at the same time it provided them with a new bargaining tool. The position of those who called for warfare to maintain Belgium's hold on Luxemburg was weakened. Individuals might advocate an all-or-nothing view, yet Belgium would be risking a great deal if she forced a test of arms. It was apparent now that the small country could survive without the extra territories. A war, even if successful, which was unlikely, would harm the country's economic foundation, including the production facilities and the confidence of international financiers on which hopes for continuation of prosperous survival were based. The interests of the governing French-speaking aristocracy and bourgeoisie were in economic development and peace; both goals, especially the latter, were also consonant with the desires of the peasantry and the growing numbers of factory workers. Already becoming acclimated to a neutral status in international affairs, the majority of Belgian leaders were turning their interests inward, toward political debates and economic development. In time many of them would interpret a prime benefit of neutrality to be the opportunity for exactly this sort of concentration of national interests; they would become irritated when the king would interrupt their domestic discussions with warnings about international conditions and requests for new military bills.

With physical resistance to the will of the powers an unviable alternative, the Brussels diplomats had the choice of maintaining the *status quo* or negotiating the best settlement they could. In trying both avenues, they employed every technique available to them, including the newly acquired possibility of financial compensations.

In all of their efforts, the Belgians were especially concerned with splitting the five powers apart and tried to choose their standpoints accordingly; one of their basic methods was to play groups of powers off against each other. The Brussels statesmen preferred to work by direct dual negotiations during which they could call in the aid of friends to influence the direction of the negotiations or to counter and perhaps nullify unwanted intervention by Werther or Metternich. Van de Weyer has claimed that Belgium might have been able to deal successfully with Holland alone in 1838; it was the interference of Austria and Prussia and their claims to certain lands that prevented Belgium from controlling the outcome of the conference.[40] Certainly the Belgians disliked conferences, for they could not operate as freely as they desired within such a body.

Belgian diplomacy was further characterized by a tendency to fight battles by steps, concentrating on a single goal at a time. When De Theux attempted to gain a blanket revision of the Twenty-four Articles, he was rebuffed; he retreated and worked for his goals one by one, beginning with the debt, and was a bit more successful. The efforts to obtain economic agreements and the woodcutting and fortress affairs revealed similar tactics of working for small, concrete gains rather than for major advances. A good example of this may be found in the first half of the 1840s, when the Prussians' jealousy of France led them to force an economic agreement on the Belgians. The small nation's diplomats soon expanded this opening until the *Zollverein*, conscious of the benefits to be gained by trading through Antwerp, made a treaty which for all intents and purposes ended the economic isolation of Belgium to the east. A few years earlier the Belgians had defended their right to build a few fortresses and did not seek a sweeping formal statement of principle that Belgium should control her own defenses. The result of the limited approach was in this case nearly as effective as a statement of principle. This suggests that after the excesses of the first years the young state's diplomatic outlook was becoming more realistic (although too optimistic in 1838) and concerned with material gains as keys to such less tangible but equally important goals as true independence. *De facto* arrangements were not as good as *de jure* ones, but were much easier to obtain and might later prove useful tools.

Coupled with this approach was a tactic of claiming far more than Belgium could expect to get in hopes that more might be won in the final solution than if she opened with her most moderate bid. It might be argued that this maneuver reflected unrealistic hopes; at times this was so, yet frequently it evidenced shrewd bargaining. The fortress matter moved from permission to build a complete defense system to an argument over the right to build at Diest. Belgium's first claim on the debt was so large that Holland would have had to pay Belgium; later the royal commission put forth a figure which had more chance of being accepted as a base for negotiations, and eventually even this offer was raised by Leopold. One can not help wondering, too, if Leopold persisted in talking of a customs union with France as a means of prodding other nations to be aware of the need to resolve Belgium's economic difficulties by making special treaties. If this were not the intent, at least the effect was achieved.

Like the diplomats of many new nations, the Belgians showed audacity, sometimes in their bluff-calling tactics, sometimes in their persistence, and sometimes in their willingness to include military action among their available tools. Having gained independence by use of arms, they were too eager to resort to them as a cure-all for their problems in international relations. The patriots appeared to believe that if they could demonstrate their feelings clearly and violently enough – and surely the appeal to arms was unmistakable – the powers would relent and give way. Such tactics may have been a mark of independence, but they of course aggravated the hostility of the powers protecting the system of order. To a new state in the 1830s as in the 1950s and 1960s, power seemed equated with military force and independence with the freedom to act as one's wishes dictated. It was only in time that the Belgians became aware that power possessed more than military attributes and that their own interests were frequently best served if they did not push their rights as an independent nation to their logical extremes.

The Brussels diplomats were always ready to enlist the diplomatic and military support of other powers, but they held a definite aversion to becoming too closely attached to any one state. It was difficult to avoid calling upon another power consistently without appearing as its satellite.

This was the one appearance Belgium could not afford if she were to obtain status in the eyes of all other countries. Moreover, it was a problem which she knew she would have to face, in one form or another, for the remainder of her existence. It was partly for this reason and partly because of the terms of the treaties by which their neutrality was guaranteed that the Belgians appeared to take the attitude that it was a duty of the powers to provide Belgium military aid; besides, it was to their interests. As the emergent states of the 1960s expected gratuitous military aid from the powers, so did the Belgians. Indeed, they were annoyed whenever the French or British were slow to reply to a call.

A certain amount of immaturity marked Belgian diplomacy during its first few years. It was constantly evident in the Belgians' hypersensitivity to any development which might possibly cast a shadow of doubt on the fullness of Belgium's independence – again an attitude familiar to present-day newly born states. It underlay also the heavy reliance of De Theux and Van de Weyer upon Palmerston's advice. The public promotion of Goblet and the hiring of Skrzynecki were not wise moves. Yet the greatest evidence of Belgium's immaturity was not so much in her actual diplomacy, or in unfortunate incidents, as in the speeches in parliament. The wild patriotism expressed at home did little to aid the diplomats abroad. Both De Theux and Leopold at times failed to estimate correctly the influence of speeches made within the country upon the attitudes of foreign capitals. This seeming unawareness, which may have been caused by inexperience, disappeared as the result of such warnings as that given by Palmerston. In any case, it is doubtful how much could have been done with the chambers. Palmerston criticized De Theux's handling of the politicians, but had De Theux dealt with them in any other manner (such as keeping them continually informed of the progress of negotiations) the government would have been overthrown in short order.[41]

Belgium was created by a revolution, and the fervor that had brought her forth could not be immediately stifled. It accounted for the rash statements in the chambers and the suspicion of other powers. Surely the bold nature of De Theux's performance showed its influence. The diplomat was an ex-revolutionary and his actions often revealed his aggressive nature; nevertheless occasionally even he would be pushed on by his compatriots. In June of 1838 De Theux personally did not wish to be intransigent with respect to both territory and debt; the belli-cose state of opinion existing within his country forced him to be just that and perhaps prevented him from obtaining a more lucrative compromise than the one he was eventually granted. In the lumbering affair, when he wished to press the pace, the enthusiasm of the populace did not hinder but rather spurred him on; the sending of troops into the duchy benefited rather than harmed the outcome. When he played a delaying game and tried to channel the revolutionary desire for boldness and action into audacity in remaining firm in a position, the results were less satisfactory; such a defensive attitude did not appeal to the revolutionary frame of mind in his country.

The little state's position with respect to the powers also influenced its diplomacy. Belgium's diplomats realized they could not afford a static policy; unless some definite steps forward were attempted, Belgium would slide into the abyss of enfeoffment, if not partition. Why not push against the starched front presented by the powers, and why not accept as much aid as could safely be obtained from any other nation? The best way to avoid being shoved aside was to cling tightly to each gain and then work for another, better foothold.

Belgium's willingness to resort to arms and the audacity and stubbornness of her diplomacy in certain situations reflected not only the diplomatic style of a small state working for recognition but also that of a new revolutionary state determined to make a mark in the world. Belgium's birth by violence in a time when order and stability were watchwords created one of her greatest obstacles, but it helped make dynamism one of the outstanding characteristics of her initial diplomatic style.

3.5 Notes

1. Boulger, *The history of Belgium*, Part II, p. 221.
2. Count Beugnot in the Chamber of Peers, Jan. 25, 1843, during a debate on relations with Belgium, as quoted in Deschamps, *La Belgique devant la France*, p. IX.
.3. *Letters of Queen Victoria*, lst ser., vol. II, p. 459: 'Leopold to Victoria, Mar. 12, 1852'.
4. De Ridder, *La Belgique et la Prusse*, pp. 13, 37: 'Beaulieu to De Muelenaere, Apr. 8, 1835'. De Ridder served for many years as director general and then historical counsellor at the Belgian foreign ministry. He took advantage of his access to the archives to produce scholarly accounts of diplomatic incidents in which Belgium was involved between 1830 and 1854. The greater part of each of his books consists of quotations or paraphrases of Belgian documents; relatively little space is devoted to interpretation.
5. De Ridder, *Ibid.*, pp. 15–18, note: 'Van de Weyer to De Muelenaere, Apr. 28, 1835'.
6. *Ibid.*, p. 24. Palmerston had sent letters supporting the Belgians, but their contents had not yet been communicated to Ancillon when the Goblet promotion took place.
7. *Ibid.*, pp. 119–120.

8. Belgium, M.A.E. Arch., Corr. pol., Leg., G.B., vol. XI, no. 24: 'Van de Weyer to De Theux, Mar. 20, 1838'.
9. Quoted in De Ridder, *Histoire diplomatique du traité*, p. 27.
10. Belgium, M.A.E. Arch., Corr. pol., Leg., G.B., vol. XI, no. 32: 'De Theux to Van de Weyer, Mar. 22, 1838'; no. 53: 'Same to same, Apr. 13, 1838'.
11. *Ibid.*, vol. XI, no. 44: 'Van de Weyer to De Theux, Apr. 2, 1838'; no. 58: 'Same to same, Apr. 18, 1838'. Cf. Webster, *Foreign policy of Palmerston*, vol. I, p. 515.
12. *Ibid.*, vol. XI, no. 72: 'Van de Weyer to De Theux, May 4, 1838'; nos. 92, 93: 'Same to same, May 25, 1838'.
13. *Ibid.*, vol. XI, no. 103: 'De Theux to Van de Weyer, June 2, 1838'; vol. XII, no. 6: 'Same to same, July 7, 1838'. Cf. De Lannoy, *Histoire diplomatique de l'indépendance*, p. 54.
14. De Ridder, *Histoire diplomatique du traité*, p. 105: 'Leopold to De Theux, Aug. 12, 1838'.
15. Of the original debt figure, 6,000,000 florins were payment for commercial rights granted and were not disputed.
16. Belgium, M.A.E. Arch., Corr. pol., Leg. G.B., vol. XII, no. 55: 'Van de Weyer to De Theux, Aug. 10, 1838'.
17. *Ibid.*, no. 87: 'Van de Weyer to De Theux, Aug. 28, 1838'.
18. *Histoire parlementaire*, vol. I, p. XXX. The quotations in the remainder of this paragraph are from the same source, vol. I, pp. XXXIII, XXXVI.
19. *Letters of Queen Victoria*, lst ser., vol. I, p. 47: 'Leopold to Victoria, June 2, 1835'.
20. De Ridder, *Histoire diplomatique du traité*, pp. 265–266.
21. *Histoire parlementaire*, vol. II, p. 368. Texts of De Theux's notes and the powers' reply may be found on pp. 622–639.
22. Pirenne, *Histoire de Belgique*, vol. IV, p. 56.
23. *Letters of Queen Victoria*, lst ser., vol. I, pp. 148–149. The following quotation is from *Ibid.*, p. 92: 'Leopold to Victoria, June 15, 1837'.
24. De Lannoy, *Histoire diplomatique de l'indépendance*, p. 50.
25. Lebeau, *Souvenirs*, pp. 199–201.
26. This comment, made to Count de Gerlache, was reported by Van de Weyer to De Theux, Jan. 15, 1839 (De Ridder, *Histoire diplomatique du traité*, p. 279).
27. Webster, *Foreign policy of Palmerston*, vol. I, p. 517.
28. De Ridder, *Les projets*, p. 12, quotes a message from De Theux to Leopold.
29. De Ridder, *Les projets*, p. 21, quotes a message from Van de Weyer to Le Hon.
30. De Ridder, *Les projets*, pp. 25–27: 'Van Praet and Leopold to De Theux, July 26, 1849'.
31. Dechamps, 'Une page d'histoire', *Revue générale*, vol. I, (1869), pp. 554–555 as quoted in De Ridder, *Les projets*, p. 82.
32. De Ridder, *Les projets*, p. 194: 'Neuman to Metternich, Nov. 12, 1842'.
33. Dechamps, *La Belgique devant la France*, pp. 100–130.
34. Laurent, 'Commerce, colonies and claims', pp. 562–563.

35. Discailles, *Charles Rogier*, vol. III, p. 4.
36. Van de Weyer, 'Histoire des relations extérieures', in *Patria Belgica*, vol. II, p. 345. As Van de Weyer was forced to abandon his writing because of illness, part of the chapter was written by Emile Banning from Van de Weyer's notes.
37. De Ridder, 'Un diplomate autrichien à Bruxelles', p. 134: 'Count Woyna to Metternich, Jan. 13, 1848'.
38. See in De Ridder, *La crise*, vol. I, Exchanges between Van de Weyer and d'Hoffschmidt: pp. 6–8, no. 4: Feb. 27, 1848; pp. 351–352, no. 222: Apr. 6, 1848; pp. 354–356, no. 226: Apr. 8, 1848; pp. 366–369, no. 235: Apr. 11, 1848.
39. Pirenne, *Histoire de Belgique*, vol. IV, p. 53.
40. Van de Weyer, 'Histoire des relations extérieures', p. 330. Carcan-Chanel and Delsemme, *Agents diplomatiques*, pp. 27–28.
41. De Ridder, *Histoire diplomatique du traité*, p. 279, note 2.

4. The challenge of foreign pressure

In the two decades following the revolts of 1848, the Belgian approach to diplomatic problems experienced a transition from the militant diplomacy of a revolutionary nation to the more circumspect attitude of an established state. This transition, the result of a conscious search for a style which could satisfactorily respond to new situations, found significant beginnings during the revolutions but developed only haltingly. By 1871, however, the nature of Belgian diplomacy had been permanently altered. The passing of the old revolutionaries from the scene and the arising of new problems and circumstances led to a gradual disappearance of boldness and tenacity as the outstanding features of Belgium's diplomacy. In their place appeared a flexible, cautious, self-effacing, and clearly defensive attitude. Yet while exhibiting an increased desire to conciliate their enemies and while making small concessions to avoid being forced into larger capitulations, the Belgians reserved a core of toughness which was bared when severe pressure was exercised upon them.

The Europe in which the Belgians were operating between 1848 and 1870 differed markedly from the Europe in which they had struggled to win status. The European concert which had controlled affairs in the earlier period was gravely weakened by the revolutions which removed Metternich from office and replaced the bourgeois monarchy of Louis-Philippe with first the Second Republic and then the Second Empire. What consensus remained was soon disrupted by the Crimean War; and the defeat of Russia meant the Tsardom was now, like France, a revisionist state. Within a brief time the map of Europe experienced significant alterations, as a united Italy and a new North German Confederation under the militant leadership of Prussia appeared. The power relationships of the European states changed also. Russia and Austria lost strength because of their respective defeats in 1856 and 1866, and their influence in external affairs was further decreased by preoccupation with internal events, the emancipation of serfs in Russia and the establishment of a dual system of government for Austria and Hungary. Prussia emerged as the powerful leader of Germany, while Emperor Napoleon III in France revealed his ambition for a position of importance in Europe. England, meanwhile, was retreating into a policy of non-intervention in continental affairs. Europe was in a state of flux.

Such an international condition was not adverse to the expansion and development of national states. But though Belgium had irredentist areas, her main concern as an established country now was to hold on to earlier achievements and to resist pressure exerted on her by other states. The equilibrium of the powers had greatly contributed to the creation of the international consensus allowing Belgium's establishment. With that equilibrium destroyed, how was Belgium's future to be assured; in what manner should Belgium's various interests in economic growth, territorial gain, peaceful withdrawal from the perils of international affairs, and in holding a respected position among the European nations be balanced against each other? How could the thrusts of her main adversary of the period, France, be stayed or turned aside? Would the old diplomatic methods be adequate, or should new ones be developed, and, if so, what? It was in the process of meeting the French challenge that Belgian diplomats tried to answer these questions and Belgian diplomacy underwent its metamorphosis.

4.1 1848

The reaction in Brussels to news of revolution in France on February 24, 1848, was one of shock and foreboding. Metternich had once said that when Paris sneezed, Europe soon caught cold. In view of the close relations between the two capitals, it seemed impossible that the plague of civil rebellion would not spread northward. Long before February the fevers of public unrest had been mounting in the new country. Competition from the developing manufacturing centers in Great Britain had gravely wounded the textile trade of Flanders, and a recent commercial crisis across the channel was forcing several large firms to suspend payments. Unemployment became acute in many sections of Belgium, while nearly the whole of Flanders plunged into deeper impoverishment. As discontent there grew, charges were levied that the Walloon dominated government was derelict in its duties, particularly in its failure to provide remedies for the Flemish economy. Conditions were better in the Southwest than in Flanders and the Borinage, and the continuing operation of the factories there eventually helped to lift Belgium out of her economic reversals.

The rapid rise of industrial capitalism had not been unaccompanied by certain evils. Chief among them was the poverty and misery of the factory and mine workers. Long hours spent laboring in unhealthy conditions for low wages which could purchase only the most meager of diets left many broken in spirit as well as in health. Birth and death rates were high; children were viewed as a source of income and sent to work at tender ages. Prostitution and petty crime were common. Yet the potential for revolt was not great. The workers had only limited awareness of their common needs and no organization. Nor were there many bonds between them and the peasantry, which still made up the large majority of the population. This latter group had a hard life too, but it was one that remained essentially unchanged from that known by their grandfathers. Only in a few scattered areas were voices raised, usually by some member of the middle classes, to the effect that something should be done to relieve the misery of the workers.

The government's capacity for action was limited by lack of funds in the treasury and by the precarious condition of the cabinet's political health. The demise of the political union which had guided Belgium through her first years had long been expected. But this did not mean that when the elections of 1847 finally brought it to an end hostilities would not be aroused. The new Liberal cabinet's difficulties were compounded by the still undeveloped nature of party loyalties which permitted bitter criticisms to be exchanged publicly between members of the government. Most serious of all was the breach which yawned between the king, the cabinet, and the people.

The former consort to the late heir apparent to the British throne had frequently revealed an attitude of martyrdom in assuming the role of constitutional monarch in as 'unmanageable' and 'petty' a state as Belgium. For example, in 1839 he wrote Palmerston:

I tell you honestly, what I never hide from the Belgians, *I do not like to be here*, have these near 8 years led the *most disagreeable* life and only the moral satisfaction of doing *much good* and *preventing much mischief* has reconciled me to the Kingship of this country, one of the *most* difficult and irksome in Europe.[1]

With the crises of the initial years weathered, Leopold's condescension and boredom became increasingly evident, and his plans for extended trips abroad were curtailed only upon the urgings of leading Belgian politicians. By 1848, there were more than a few rumors that Leopold might abdicate.

In the elections of the previous year Leopold had favored the Catholics and did not hesitate to make known his distaste for the politicians suddenly promoted to power. He found them impoverished in ideas and experience; moreover, he was critical of the Liberals' interest in follow-ing a strictly party program. The king preferred a union ministry, perhaps because it allowed him more freedom to act on his own and as a mediator of differences; a party program would weaken his influence. The Liberals and their leader, Charles Rogier, were aware of Leopold's hostility; the result was a series of minor struggles for authority. In two instances, those relating to the appointments of the civil governor of Namur and of Belgium's envoy to the Vatican, Rogier succeeded in replacing individuals who held the king's confidence and support. Leopold eventually acquiesced to the new circumstances. In doing so, he was perhaps wiser and more flexible than some of his fellow sovereigns, whose rigidity and unwillingness to relinquish prerogatives was later to cause them grief. The king may also have benefited from being removed from the heart of the battle over religion and the schools that was so sharply dividing the parties. He avoided having the monarchy tarnished in an argument where there were few winners, becoming more of a symbol of national unity when the parties could agree on little else; in time Leopold even came to have greater freedom in international affairs as the deputies concentrated increasingly on the school crisis.

One of the king's main criticisms of the Liberals in 1847 was that they lacked men of experience and proper maturity to lead the government. Although this view angered Foreign Minister Baron d'Hoffschmidt and Prime Minister Charles Rogier, who had been active in Belgian politics longer than had Leopold, there was some truth to the charge. Despite union governments, since the revolution the care of national affairs had primarily been in the hands of the Catholic faction. Both the French and Austrian ministers could therefore report that of the new ministry, only Rogier and d'Hoffschmidt were men of quality and experience.[2] It was thus all the more ironic that in the first days following the Paris revolt noteworthy leadership was exercised by the Liberals, while the king's behavior suddenly appeared immature.

Accounts vary concerning Leopold's offer to abdicate, made at a cabinet meeting on February 26. Although some authors discredit the story, it is upheld in several different sources and the historian most recently to examine the affair supports its veracity.[3] Apparently shocked by his father-in-law's fate, Leopold briefly gave way to the pessimism and sense of martyrdom to which he was prone. The cabinet rejected the monarch's offer and within a few days Leopold was again his assured and confident self. But even before then Rogier had prodded the govern-ment to several important steps.

On the same day as the cabinet meeting, the chambers were persuaded to pass a law permitting the early collection of eight-twelfths of the annual *contribution foncière.* With the aid of this forced loan, public works could be undertaken to ease unemployment. A week later Rogier appealed to all manufacturers to provide as many jobs as possible for the duration of the crisis. Other tactics were also used to control unrest, as the civic guard was summoned for what proved to be nearly two months' duty.

These measures were only makeshifts, and Rogier decided to tackle a more controversial issue immediately. That was the reduction of the property qualification for the franchise to the constitutional minimum of twenty florins. Many people had been favoring a gradual lowering of the franchise requirement for town dwellers, but uniform and complete reduction was an unexpected step. Rogier chose it for that reason, to stela the radicals' thunder. Although the remaining requirement still kept the franchise significantly restricted, the number of adult males eligible to vote would be doubled. The king lent his support, and in the crisis atmosphere the bill, which incorporated several additional reforms, was quickly passed. In April it was complemented by a stringent civil service reform law. The effect of this legislation was just what Rogier intended. The sting was taken from the economic crisis. The political reforms won the government support among all levels of the populace, support which was evidenced in the Liberals' resounding victory in new elections held in June. The successful completion of these elections, held at the very time that Paris was dissolving into civil war, gave sufficient proof that the government had little to fear from spontaneous domestic uprising. The major problem now would be simultaneously to curtail the activities of agitators sent into Belgium from the south, to prepare for a possible attack by the French Republic, and to maintain amicable relations with that same state.

On the first count there was little to be done unless Belgium's borders were to be closed and a rigorous internal police surveillance system established which would have been repugnant to the great majority of Belgians. The government nevertheless did all it could within reason to counteract the widespread impression that Belgium was a willing host to radicals of all kinds. Karl Marx, who had been writing and organizing the German Workers Union in Brussels, was expelled from Belgium following the February Revolution. A careful watch was kept on all newcomers, and at the frontier special efforts were made in checking passports.

The danger of French attack was considerable. As Van de Weyer commented to Palmerston, 'a republican France was an aggressive and conquering France'.[4] Amid rumors that French troops were moving northward, the Belgian representative in London suggested to Palmerston that 'the pressure of an English fleet in the Scheldt would be a decisive demonstration'.[5] Although Palmerston did not take this approach amiss and merely avoided committing himself, d'Hoffschmidt reprimanded his experienced minister for taking such an initiative.

Throughout the crisis the foreign minister's attitude appears to have been ambivalent. He obviously took pride in Belgium's established status and ability to maintain an independent position in foreign affairs. Yet at the same time he was beset by fear of France. One possible alternative was to call up large numbers of troops and make a clear show of determination to resist any French advances. But such a course would further disrupt the Belgian populace and economy and perhaps provoke the sensibilities of the ambitious new French republic. Another alternative was simply to appear so friendly and innocuous, while at the same time secretly trying to enlist foreign support, that France would not be attracted to expanding her revolution and territories northward.

In general, although there were instances of boldness, caution held the upper hand. Thus it was that d'Hoffschmidt told Van de Weyer that until France became actually aggressive, Belgium 'should abstain with care from every hostile demonstration'.[6] It was only after several incidents, including the interception on March 29 at the Belgian town of Risquons-Tout of a trainload of revolutionaries from France, that the Belgians officially solicited a promise of British support; it was promptly granted by Palmerston.

An episode particularly enlightening regarding Belgian policy concerned the maintenance of diplomatic relations between Brussels and the provisional government in Paris headed by the renowned poet Alphonse de Lamartine. In Brussels, as in other capitals, there was little love for Lamartine, yet there was also concern that he might be replaced by a more radical and aggressive figure. Proximity to France and dynastic connections with the deposed Louis-Philippe made the problem acute for the Belgians. It was for these reasons that the Prince de Ligne, the Belgian representative in Paris, privately visited Lamartine and assured him of Belgian friendship. Shortly thereafter, on February 29, the prince advised d'Hoffschmidt that it was important not to irritate the French; prompt recognition of the provisional government might well forestall invasion.[7] D'Hoffschmidt was apparently of the same opinion, for he replied that *de facto* relations could be established. Should Lamartine inquire if this meant recognition of the provisional government, the answer could be affirmative, on the condition the French officially recognize Belgium's independence and neutrality. Yet before Belgium granted any official recognition, d'Hoffschmidt wished to learn the views of the other powers.[8]

Belgium's relations with the provisional government were indeed a matter of concern for the other chancelleries. Were Belgium to grant official recognition to the men who had deposed Louis-Philippe, the shaky new regime would be on the road to solidifying its position. Hopes for a restoration were dim in any case, but as long as the provisional government was struggling for recognition, so long could the powers use the withholding of recognition as a means of influencing the republicans' policy. Recognition of France by Belgium, which country was the most likely victim of any French aggression, thus had considerable significance for the position taken by the other European states.

Because of Belgium's size, location, and need of peace, d'Hoffschmidt felt required to do just what the other powers were reluctant to do for fear of strengthening the hand of the French. On March 4, the foreign minister informed his emissaries that Belgium was being disturbed by revolutionary propaganda. It was of importance that Belgium stay on peaceful terms with France. Belgium could not stand against a France which so impatiently expected recognition; to do so would be compromising and useless.[9] Apparently d'Hoffschmidt had been won to the views of De Ligne, who the day before had advised his superior that there was no need to demand that Lamartine officially recognize Belgium's independence and neutrality before agreeing to establish contacts. Belgium was already established. She should not have to plead with France to recognize this fact; rather, it was the French government which was pleading for recognition.[10]

A temporary compromise in Franco-Belgian relations was reached with the establishment of unofficial talks between De Ligne and Lamartine on March 5. This was satisfactory to the British, who were now operating on a similar arrangement. But the matter of formal *de facto* recognition had yet to be resolved. What if the French appointed an ambassador to Brussels? In the estimation of the Austrian minister stationed there, a Belgian refusal to receive a French representative would be an open invitation to invasion. Count Woyna felt assured, however, that Belgium 'knew its role as a small power and realized that she was not expected to take any initiative in major international questions'.[11] No decision would be made by the Belgians alone, since their treaties implied, if not required, consultation with the guarantor powers. Similar views were expressed by the British minister, who tried to persuade d'Hoffschmidt to let his actions be governed by the views of the other powers. While the Prussian government did not exert much effort to influence Belgian policy, the Russians, who had not yet even recognized Belgium, were willing to comtemplate a virtual seizure of Belgian policy. The Russian ambassador in London suggested that perhaps the Belgian fortresses should be occupied according to the terms of the secret fortress treaty of December 1831 which provided that the Waterloo coalition could use those forts as a barrier against French aggression. His proposal found no takers.

Despite the hints of the great powers, d'Hoffschmidt let it be known that Belgium would recognize the French government when there was an appropriate opportunity. His rationale was similar to that used in replying to the *caveats* of various foreign representatives. France had recognized the settlement of 1839 and was thus as much an ally of Belgium as were the other powers. Belgium had nothing more to ask of her as long as she abided by the treaty. France's form of government was not Belgium's concern.[12]

As Brison Gooch has pointed out, this was an independent statement.[13] It clearly revealed d'Hoffschmidt's intention to maintain Belgium's identity and control of her own foreign policy. He was supported by his minister at The Hague. Baron Willmar, far from believing the circumstances of Belgium's birth gave the powers an influential voice in Belgian diplomacy, held that Belgium was doubly required to be independent in her decision-making. On March 7 he wrote d'Hoffschmidt:

If from non-recognition the foreign powers should pass to the attack, our neutrality having always been recognized by the other party, our right and our duty will be not to participate in the attack, but to isolate ourselves from the attacking powers. It thus follows that the principle of *isolation*, and by consequence, *isolated action*, is the result of our situation, a situation which the powers created for us.[14]

D'Hoffschmidt's independent behavior and its grumbling acceptance by the other powers had the same significance for Belgium's future foreign affairs as did the fortress affair of 1835 for Belgium's domestic policy. Guaranteed neutrality, as long as Belgium did not violate her founding treaties or openly contradict the sense of their terms, did not give the great powers the right to interfere in Belgium's foreign policy. True, it had never been questioned that as a sovereign state Belgium had the legal right to control her own policy. The powers themselves had never wanted control; but it was frequently implied that they expected to be able to influence Belgian policy in matters affecting all Europe rather easily when they so wished.

D'Hoffschmidt's action could be interpreted as one of firmness and boldness; yet caution and fear were actually the dominating themes. That was the impression of the British minister in Brussels.[15] No doubt the Belgian was in part motivated by a desire to demonstrate his independence; but fear of irritating the French was his primary concern. A refusal to recognize the Republic, or even unintended slights, might bring invasion. To avoid misunderstandings, the foreign minister warned

Belgian diplomatic correspondents to be prudent in their use of language.

Indeed, it seems that d'Hoffschmidt tried as hard as he could to convince himself of the sincerity of Lamartine's promises concerning the integrity of Belgian territory and the Republic's peaceful intentions. After the interception of revolutionaries coming from France at Risquons-Tout and Quiévrain, d'Hoffschmidt demanded a disavowal of revolutionary acts toward Belgium be published by the Paris government. Yet he backed down when Lamartine protested innocence. It was Britain that later forced the disavowal to be printed. Perhaps hoping to convince the French there was no need to invade, d'Hoffschmidt also sent instructions to the Prince de Ligne that he should explain that Belgium was really a republic, except that her president was permanent and hereditary. It scarcely need be mentioned that it is unusual for a state to apologize for its governmental structure to another scarcely born government.[16]

Even more interesting is d'Hoffschmidt's decision a few months later not to take advantage of the offer of the Frankfort Diet to vote, if the Belgians requested it, a guarantee by the German Confederation of Belgian independence and neutrality. The foreign minister believed that should such a *démarche* be made, the Belgian position might be put in doubt and France offended.[17] When the German National Assembly made statements concerning German rights to Maastricht, territory that had been granted to Holland in 1839, d'Hoffschmidt acknowledged the danger for Belgium in any disruption of the treaties or in the presence of German troops in Maastricht. But he did not come to the support of the Dutch, for the reason that Belgium was not directly involved in this test of the 1839 treaties – certainly a timid attitude for a state whose existence depended on the sanctity of those treaties.[18]

As events worked out, d'Hoffschmidt's efforts to regularize relations with France earned him only passing annoyance among the eastern courts and did seem to placate the French. In May, after Lamartine had been succeeded by J. Bastide at the Quai d'Orsay, d'Hoffschmidt recognized the Republic officially. Palmerston inquired why the Belgians did not wait until the French had established a regular government. He was satisfied by the reply that the Prussians, now involved in quelling Polish unrest, had announced their intention shortly to recognize the French Republic anyway. For obvious reasons, Belgium wished to be the first of the major European states to take this action. As d'Hoffschmidt explained to Leopold, there were good economic reasons for the measure. Besides, France would soon have asked for recognition in any case. 'In accepting, we would have lost all the merit of the initiative; a refusal would be equivalent to a rupture' and would bring untold dangers.[19] Thus the Belgian maintained to the end a relatively independent policy in the recognition issue.

Well before the recognition finally took place, d'Hoffschmidt had regained enough confidence to try to reap some advantage from Belgium's plight, as long as in so doing he would not annoy France. At the beginning of March and again after the Risquons-Tout affair, d'Hoffschmidt attempted to extract a loan from the British government, arguing that this was the only way financial stability and continued industrial employment could be maintained in Belgium. Lord Lansdowne, president of the council, soon ruled out the possibility of a direct subsidy. He subsequently reported that the cabinet had rejected another proposal that the sums originally due Leopold by his treaty of marriage to Charlotte be restored to him, although Leopold had renounced them years earlier. The Belgians proved ungraciously stubborn, as after this double refusal Leopold attempted to influence British opinion through the press. When even this had failed, d'Hoffschmidt had the audacity, or *naïveté*, seriously to consider approaching Russia for a loan, a course from which he was dissuaded by Nothomb.[20]

D'Hoffschmidt also hoped to make some gains in his relations with Holland. The Dutch had proved sympathetic throughout the crisis. When they announced troops would be stationed on the Belgo-Dutch border in case of a French move northward, Willmar had protested that this would require Belgium also to put men on the border, so that there would be some truth to the Belgians' claims that they intended to protect all their borders, not just that with France. The Dutch obligingly changed their plans so that Belgium did not have to deprive her southern defenses of needed troops. Now d'Hoffschmidt hoped the Dutch would agree to a reduction in customs on cotton products and coal. Such an agreement, he believed, would not hurt the Dutch and would aid the Belgian industrialists who were talking of the necessity of close relations with France. Moreover, full employment was necessary in Belgium if revolutionary fever were not to seize the workers and spread to Holland. The foreign minister knew the issue was delicate and warned Willmar not to put anything in writing. Yet in two days d'Hoffschmidt became convinced that a gingerly approach was too slow and that the Dutch had to be 'taken by assault'.[21] A diplomatic attack was mounted and was quickly, politely, and firmly repulsed at The Hague.

Action to the north no longer appearing fruitful, the foreign minister turned his energy toward the Grand Duchy of Luxemburg. Recently there had been a decline in commerce and considerable labor unrest in the duchy. D'Hoffschmidt was quick to blame the duchy's connection with the *Zollverein* at the expense of a customs agreement with Belgium. He proposed a treaty moving the *Zollverein* border east and establishing a Belgo-Luxemburg customs union. Again his argument was that without such an economic arrangement, political chaos would result.[22] There was some truth to his claim that the division of Luxemburg in 1839 had damaged the economy of the area and that a customs union was a possible remedy. Politically, however, the proposal belonged in a dream world, not that of reality. Grand Duke William resented the Belgian implication that he was not governing the duchy properly. The Prussian government, which at this time was attempting to induce other German states to join the *Zollverein*, announced that the duchy could not be allowed to leave that customs union. To sidetrack further contemplation of d'Hoffschmidt's proposition, the Prussian minister recommended a Belgo-Dutch customs union.

His attention again deflected, d'Hoffschmidt approached the Dutch, who proved courteous but uninterested. Their faltering colonial commerce could not easily be reconciled with an accord with Belgium. The new Dutch foreign minister, Count Rutger Jan Schimmelpenninck, also expressed the opinion that he did not think that Holland would necessarily fall to French troops even if Belgium did. Baron Willmar wrote in anger and despair that all this 'was a denial of the manifestations of March 1, of the necessity of a good accord, of the spontaneous solidarity proclaimed at The Hague...' by the Dutch king.[23]

Pique over the attitude of Schimmelpenninck's ministry may have contributed to the Belgians' silence a few months later when the German National Assembly cast covetous eyes on Maastricht. Yet d'Hoffschmidt had only himself to blame for the rebuffs he received in the late spring of 1848. He was attempting to use Belgium's smallness and relatively indefensible position against the French as a lever to gain aid from other countries. The British, Prussians, and Dutch all were sympathetic and made concessions or promised aid should conditions worsen. There was, after all, validity to the argument that aid would be needed if Belgium were to maintain the economic stability necessary to forestall revolution. But d'Hoffschmidt pushed his demands too far. Surely the Germans would not allow the Luxemburg clauses of the 1839 treaties, over which they had battled so strongly, to be diluted only nine years later. The other chancelleries, particularly that in The Hague, must have received the impression that Belgium was trying to use the crisis to her own advantage, and it would have been strengthened as it became evident by April that Rogier's legislation was ameliorating the Belgian domestic situation and depriving the foreign minister's pleas of their urgency.

In dealing with the French threat, d'Hoffschmidt was forced to act independently. He demonstrated Belgium's right to conduct her affairs as she wished, but he did so at the price of irritating the northern courts and appearing obsequious to Paris. There was a hint of contradiction in his actions, as he refused advice from the powers on the one hand and expected aid on the other. At times his bold independence could equally well be represented as political *naïveté*, just as his prudence regarding France was correctly interpreted by the British as obsessive fear. But certainly these terms are not mutually exclusive. The situation in 1848 was a confusing one, and the Belgians had to feel their way. None of the other powers were to complain about occasional vagaries in d'Hoffschmidt's behavior. They were thankful that Belgium was proving a bastion immune to the revolutionary germs spreading from Paris. As Queen Victoria commented, Belgium was 'a bright star in the midst of dark clouds'.[24]

4.2 TARIFFS AND THE SCHELDT

Cautious and reticent, or bold and activist, the Belgian state and d'Hoffschmidt survived 1848; but Belgium's problems were not over, for the December 2, 1851, coup by Louis Napoleon and the creation of the Second French Empire provided a source of new dangers. Leopold described the situation to Queen Victoria:

We are here in the awkward position of persons in hot climates, who find themselves in company, for instance in their beds, with a snake; they must *not move, because that irritates* the creature, but they can hardly remain as they are, without a fair chance of [being] bitten...[25]

The description was good; there seemed no easy solution. The search which had hesitantly begun in 1848 for a suitable diplomatic style now moved into full swing.

Napoleon III did not wait long to put pressure upon the small country. The commercial treaty of 1845 concerning tariffs and quotas on linen cloth and thread, wines, and silk was to expire on August 10, 1852. The Rogier cabinet requested that any new treaty be on an expanded basis. Louis Napoleon refused, demanding a halt be put to the Belgian industry of reprinting books that were published in France. (Belgium as yet had not made copyright arrangements with other countries, and her bookmaker's *contrefaction* industry was notorious.) No agreement had been reached when loss in the July 1852 elections forced the Belgian cabinet to resign. Bidden by the king, the Liberals agreed to continue in office temporarily and Rogier requested, to no avail, a continuation of the treaty until a new cabinet could deal with the matter. Although H. J. Walthère Frère-Orban, the minister of public works, refused to condone negotiations which he thought should be left to a future ministry, Rogier and d'Hoffschmidt resumed the discussions.

The course of the talks is reflected in the correspondence between Charles Rogier and his brother Firmin, who was Belgian minister at Paris. On July 23, Charles wrote that continuation of the treaty was not a favor but a necessity. He was amenable to a literature convention, but only if something valuable were gained in return. 'Counterfeiting and coal, *concedo*; counterfeiting and 0, a chimera... Pure and simple prorogation or with stipulations of equal value, those or nothing, understand...'[26] On August 5 he exclaimed, 'They are not seriously dreaming of balancing the *contrefaction* with *Luxemburg* cattle and...hops!' He continued that the Belgians would be 'conciliatory, as much as one would like, but suppliant, no, humble, no, dupe, no'.

Firmin put the situation in the cold light of reality.

If we had at our orders an army of 200,000 men and a fleet of 100 war vessels, we could talk haughtily and present our conditions while saying: take them or leave them. But unfortunately we are not in that situation; we are the less strong. It is necessary then to proceed temperately and strive to obtain not all that we wish, but all that we can.

His letter of August 10 indicated the fate of Charles's hopes and firm resolve: 'The tariff advantages announced for hops, Luxemburg cattle, and cotton cloth are definitely conceded.' He added that there was no use trying for new clauses in the proposed literature convention; 'it is the French ultimatum'.

Belgium's plight as a small state subjected to pressure by a great power is made clear in this incident and in Firmin Rogier's advice to his younger brother. The issue was not serious enough to arouse the concern and intervention of the other powers. Moreover, the international situation did not favor Belgium. England was anxious not to offend the new emperor, and Austria and Prussia were reluctant to become involved at this time. The Belgians had to fend for themselves; and, disturbed by the threats glowered their way, they withdrew onto the defensive.

Within weeks of the earlier dispute, Louis Napoleon raised coal and iron duties; the Belgians, unable to resist, passed a needed press law against attacks on the authority of foreign sovereigns. The tariffs were soon lowered; but the Belgians, so sensitive about their independent rights, had allowed foreign interference to affect domestic lawmaking.[27] They had been blackmailed but had chosen not to put up rigid opposition. Such a course was probably not the one the revolutionary state of the 1830s would have taken, but now new techniques were being used as methods of influencing foreign attitudes toward Belgium, and conciliation and caution were emerging as keynotes in Belgian diplomacy.

During the Crimean War, the Belgians were aware that if formal pressure were not put on them to join the Anglo-Franco-Sardinian alliance, Napoleon III would, nevertheless, appreciate their collaboration. Belgium stuck to her neutrality, although as a result of complaints from the French foreign ministry the Brussels government cautioned private munitions producers of the dangers involved in making any new contracts with belligerents, obviously meaning Russia.

More serious was the Roman question. In January 1855, having learned that Napoleon III planned to reduce the number of French troops protecting the Pope's city, Firmin Rogier made the mistake of inquiring if this would indeed be done. The French immediately asked if Belgium could supply three or four thousand men. Though embarrassed by their minister's initiative, the Belgians declined, saying that to send troops would in essence free French and Piedmontese troops to fight in the Crimea and therefore be a violation of Belgium's neutrality. Perhaps even more influential in the Belgian decision than the official argument of neutrality was the government's fear of becoming involved in the Italian controversy in place of the French: the eventual domestic and international repercussions could only be unfortunate.[28]

If the Belgians were only moderately accommodating to French wishes during the war, shortly thereafter they consciously worked to placate Louis Napoleon. Charles Rogier was again prime minister, having resumed the post he vacated in October 1853. Following Orsini's attempt on the emperor in January of 1858, the Belgian government tried and imprisoned the editors of three Brussels papers for their statements. The prosecution had been initiated at the request of the French minister, as required by Article Three of the 1852 law. It was subsequently decided to abrogate that article so Belgian courts could act on press attacks against neighboring monarchs without waiting for official complaints to be registered from abroad. When Paris continued to complain about Belgian hospitality to French *émigrés*, Minister of Justice Jean-Baptiste Victor Tesch immediately invited several of the leading French republicans to leave Belgium.

This action reflected the flexibility with which Belgian diplomacy was attempting to adapt to new international circumstances. One of the most liberal states in Europe at her birth, Belgium had welcomed *émigrés* from the more conservative states. It was an ideologically satisfying way of identifying Belgium's political stance, and in several instances the newcomers helped to strengthen the newborn country; moreover, the leaders of the revolt had no desire for the strong central administrative and police authority that a firm policy on *émigrés* would require. In 1848 extreme revolutionaries were expelled, but Belgium's general receptiveness was a useful demonstration to the French Republic of the nation's liberality. Now, in an effort to keep the good graces of Napoleon III, Belgian officials tactfully altered their stance, although they avoided setting up a rigid system of surveillance of all foreigners.

Similar concern for the susceptibilities of the French emperor was again shown in 1858 when Leopold, acting upon the advice of a special secret council of defense, urged that fortifications be undertaken at Antwerp. Rogier was willing to ask the chambers for the credits. But, he replied to the king, while the French had accepted earlier Belgian fortifications with only passing ill-will, would they not view new preparations, made at the same time as England was also fortifying, as a continuation on the Continent of England's defensive system and as 'an act of defiance, a demonstration of bad neighborliness'?[29] What if France expressed her displeasure at Belgium's obvious distrust of France's promise to respect treaties and to defend weak countries? Such representations would not be a definitive cause for abandoning the works, 'but would it not be better to avoid such a grave conflict and to conserve the good attitude which we have taken and maintained until now *vis-à-vis* that umbrageous government?'

Rogier cautioned against any 'imprudent demonstration' which would arouse the French serpent but supported the program anyway. He expected the government would be defeated by the parsimonious chambers, and it was. The right opposed what it called 'military exaggerations', while the left split on the issue. The most serious blow was the opposition of the Antwerpians themselves to what they considered half-measures which would waste money and prove disastrous for the well-being of Antwerp. Some Brussels deputies defected because they believed the capital merited more protection, not Antwerp. The cabinet did not resign over the defeat and actually found its normally strong position in the chambers maintained in the elections of 1859. During the Franco-Austrian war of that year, when France was maintaining an army near the Belgian border to protect against a possible Prussian attack, the Belgians again became concerned. After Lord John Russell, the British foreign secretary, indicated that he thought Belgium should quietly improve her defenses, a new bill was proposed. It was passed by a plurality of fifteen, one vote larger than that which had defeated the earlier bill.[30]

Rogier's greatest desire was, however, not so much to avoid conflict with France as to rectify what he considered inequities in the settlement of 1839. In attempting to do this, he met his most notable success and his bitterest defeat.

The possibility of capitalizing the Scheldt tolls had attracted Rogier's attention ever since Belgium was established. To assure the development of Antwerp as a port, the Belgian chambers had voted in June of 1839 to pay the tolls for all ships, foreign and domestic. Debate over whether Dutch ships should be included in this largess was acrid. On the basis of the arguments that a distinction should be made between the commerce of the Dutch and their government, that Dutch ships should be treated in the same manner at all Belgian ports, and that an attempt should be made at reconciliation, it was decided there would be no exceptions in payments. A proviso was inserted, however, calling for a reassessment of the arrangement in 1843. When that date arrived, opinion was so divided that discussion was postponed. The matter had still not been settled when Rogier returned to office in 1857.

The need for capitalization was, by then, great, for almost a million tons of shipping were using the Scheldt annually, costing the Belgians 1,600,000 francs in 1858, more than three times the cost estimated in 1839. Even though the treaty finally signed by the Dutch had not required them to accept a purchase offer for the tolls, the time seemed propitious for negotiating the matter. Relations had been improving and William III was known to want a large sum of money. Moreover, the recent capitalization of some Scandinavian tolls had set a precedent. But Belgium could not hope to pay the entire sum. Other nations would have to contribute, and over the years they had come to expect Belgium would pay the tolls for their ships; many of their commercial treaties with Belgium specifically stipulated this.

When Rogier assumed the foreign ministry portfolio in 1861, he worked furiously at persuading Europe that Belgium should be granted freedom to negotiate a possible capitalization. His efforts were facilitated by the free trade wave then sweeping Europe which occasioned the rewriting of most of Belgium's commercial treaties. An opportunity was thus provided to achieve recognition of Belgium's right to negotiate the matter; Rogier was careful not to jeopardize it by pressing his demands too quickly. The new treaties were used only to gain this limited goal, and no attempt was made to tie in the more difficult point of foreign financial aid for the Belgian project.

In Rogier's step-by-step program, this was the crucial hurdle. It soon became clear that the key to the problem lay in London. If the British could be persuaded to support the plan and to make a large contribution, the Dutch, who initially had been amenable but who were stiffening their terms, would cooperate. Van de Weyer appealed to Chancellor of the Exchequer William E. Gladstone and to Russell; in the early summer of 1862 Rogier personally visited London. His arguments joined with Belgium's announced intention to pay twelve million francs herself proved successful, and the British agreed to pay nine million. The French, meanwhile, responded even more warmly, causing the surprised Firmin Rogier to admit his earlier doubts regarding the enterprise were mistaken. The sudden agreement of Bismarck to Prussian participation, obtained by Nothomb in March of 1863 after much secret negotiation, deprived the Dutch of their last hope of major support. On July 16, 1863, an international treaty was signed at Brussels setting the capitalization of the Scheldt duties at 36,278,566 francs. The prosperity of Antwerp was protected and Belgium spared, for a reasonable figure, the payment of increasingly onerous sums into the indefinite future.[31]

The patience of Rogier's diplomacy in this matter revealed more restraint than might have been expected of the fiery former revolutionary. This was because many of the details were handled by a young secretary in the foreign ministry, François Lambermont, who guided his superior with sage advice. He was made a baron for his pains and played a giant's role in the foreign ministry for the next several decades. Unfortunately for both his and Rogier's dreams, however, their next joint effort to rectify the errors of 1839 proved a failure. Thanks partly to their own earlier diplomacy, the Belgians had moved so far toward a policy of patience and caution that a return to more audacious behavior was no longer palatable to the majority of the cabinet.

4.3 THE LUXEMBURG AFFAIR

Certainly there was one matter in which the Belgians might have been expected to act rashly – the lost sections of Luxemburg. Yet the government, though not Rogier and the king, shrank from chances to retrieve the loss of 1839.

The first such opportunity, if opportunity it was, had come in 1851. The Belgian minister at The Hague was surprised when he was asked by Dutch Foreign Minister Van Sonsbeeck if Belgium might accept overtures concerning the duchy. When d'Hoffschmidt investigated the matter, he was told that Grand Duke William III was against selling but that Van Sonsbeeck remained concerned about his monarch's financial situation and the danger for Holland of possible complications with Germany on account of the duchy. Firmin Rogier was instructed discreetly to inquire what the French attitude would be toward such a transaction. He had not yet found an opportune moment when he was told to postpone his questioning indefinitely, as d'Hoffschmidt feared Louis Napoleon might suspect a coalition was being formed against France. This was a change from the foreign minister's earlier statement that France could not mind Leopold's entrance into the German Confederation as Grand Duke of Luxemburg, for he would be a neutral and a French and British, rather than Prussian, oriented sovereign.[32]

There can be no doubt that d'Hoffschmidt did not press William III for fear of annoying France and perhaps Prussia. It is remarkable, in view of the frequent purchasing attempts of twelve years earlier, that no definite offer was made. A little less caution would not have harmed the Belgian cause and might have brought William to terms.

A few years later an offer was made and accepted; the prospective purchaser was not a Belgian but Emperor of the French. Napoleon III, realizing the Prussian victory at Sadowa in 1866 had dealt his prestige a severe blow, was in ardent pursuit of compensations. In hopes of augmenting French prestige his ambassador at Berlin, Count Vincent Benedetti, proposed in 1866 a secret treaty whereby Prussia would facilitate the cession of Luxemburg to France and would give France military support if she were forced to enter Belgium and were attacked for this by another power. The treaty was never signed, but Bismarck in later interviews indicated he would not oppose French designs in the area of Belgium and Luxemburg.

Although rumors of the treaty quickly reached Brussels, the Belgians had no proof of it until 1870. They were aware that Napoleon III was looking toward their border and were therefore happy when it was announced that the Count of Flanders was to marry Princess Mary of Hohenzollern-Sigmaringen. The linking of Belgian royalty with the ruling family of Prussia was a skillful stroke of royal diplomacy and Napoleon III did not miss its message; henceforth his gaze concentrated on Luxemburg rather than Belgium. Benedetti, however, commented that 'once at Luxemburg, we will be on the road to Brussels; we will arrive there quicker by passing that way'.[33]

The German Confederation, as reorganized after Sadowa, had ceased to include Luxemburg; the duchy still belonged, however, to the *Zollverein*, which it had joined in 1842, and Prussia was still maintaining a garrison in the fortress. Grand Duke William III had failed to elicit a response when he suggested that the Prussians cease garrisoning the fortress. Concerned by the Prussians' attitude, he had his ambassador broach the subject with French Foreign Minister Moustier during the latter part of February 1867. The Frenchman saw his chance and offered to buy the 999 square miles of land. William was reluctant to deal without Prussian approval but agreed when Moustier promised to do the necessary negotiating. Bismarck indicated he would accept the arrangement although he might make a few public protests. The matter should be presented to him as a *fait accompli*; if he were given official notice, things might not go well. Unfortunately, William lost his nerve; on the same day that he agreed to the sale, he officially informed the Prussian ambassador at The Hague of what he was doing.[34]

At this point Bismarck acted, apparently having decided he did not want to abandon Prussian privileges in the duchy without compensation and undoubtedly planning to use the threat of French aggression to force the fearful southern German states into his Confederation. An April 1 interpellation in the *Reichstag*, perhaps instigated by the wily statesman, introduced the affair to the German public; immediate outcries ensued. Bismarck forced postponement of the signing of the documents which would make the sale official. While tempers flared, rumors spread of impending war and the chancelleries of Europe hurriedly sought a solution of the problem.

In Belgium Rogier saw a last opportunity to regain what had been lost nearly thirty years earlier. Were the duchy to be made part of Belgium and declared neutral, France should be satisfied by the evacuation of Prussian troops from the fortress. The strengthening of Belgium and the exclusion of France from Luxemburg would bring the approval of England and Prussia. Attachment to Belgium would assure development of Luxemburg's economy, prevent the area from being a foyer of international intrigue, and encourage the powers to guarantee its security and neurality.[35]

The aging foreign minister, still belonging 'for all his white hair to that audacious generation which had accomplished great things in spite of Europe', set to work to obtain the duchy.[36] Articles presenting 'the Belgian solution' and calling for the annexation of Luxemburg were planted in the press. The author of many of them, Rogier's young protégé Emile Banning, even traveled to Luxemburg equipped with Belgian flags and pamphlets to stir up the inhabitants to act for themselves.[37] Privately, Rogier discreetly suggested his idea to friends in neighboring capitals. It was undoubtedly at his urging that Van de Weyer, an old revolutionary himself, mentioned his personal view to the British premier and foreign minister, Lord Stanley, that 'it might be a satisfactory arrangement for all parties that the territory in dispute should be neutralized and handed over to Belgium, with or without consideration...'.[38]

King Leopold II, who had ascended the throne in 1865, was also active. The acquisition of Luxemburg could give a glorious start to his reign as well as rectify old injustices. During the month of March there had been talk of a plebiscite to determine the wishes of the population of the duchy. Leopold was sure such a vote would be in Belgium's favor, but the negative attitude of the eastern courts toward such a procedure quickly scotched the idea. On April 10, Leopold visited Paris ostensibly to inspect the Belgian display in an exposition, but actually to meet with Napoleon III.

The talks proceeded well and Belgian purchase of the duchy seemed a negotiable possibility when Count Beust, foreign minister for Austria-Hungary, circulated proposals for two compromise solutions. Either Luxemburg would remain under William's control and Prussia would renounce her right to garrison the fortress, or Luxemburg would be reunited to Belgium, which country would return to France the band of territory and fortresses along its border that France had lost in 1815. The Belgian response was prompt. The minister in Vienna did not wait for instructions to declare that Belgium had no intention of sacrificing any part of the country and that she did not search to acquire 'new territories which could only be a source of difficulties and probable dangers for her in the future'.[39] Within a few days similar declarations were made at all the major capitals. As Van de Weyer made clear to Stanley, Belgium had no desire to lose the old Duchy of Bouillon or the 209 communes of the Marienbourg and Philippeville districts. The Belgian constitution declared the inviolability of Belgian lands; new parliamentary elections would be required to alter the constitution, and the Belgian populace would never allow such a territorial transaction.[40]

All this did not mean that Rogier and his friends had abandoned their hopes, but rather that caution had become the controlling policy before the danger of loss of territory and fear of antagonizing avaricious neighbors. When Van de Weyer returned to London after a visit to Brussels, he did not repeat his suggestion of Belgian annexation of the duchy. Although Belgium was disappointed by the loss of 1839, she would make no complaint, wish, or insinuation, he told Stanley. To the Britisher's inquiry if Belgium intended to accept the duchy without offering anything at all, Van de Weyer replied that having asked nothing, Belgium had nothing to offer.[41]

Even though the Brussels statesmen would not give up land, a chance remained that they might obtain the duchy anyway. This may have been the thought behind Van de Weyer's answer to Stanley's question. On April 16, Napoleon III's 'Vice Emperor', Eugène Rouher, wrote that the destruction of the fortress, the evacuation of Prussian troops, and the granting of Luxemburg to Belgium was a solution which had 'a very good chance of success'.[42] A few days later, the emperor himself told British Ambassador Lord Cowley that under no consideration would he accept any augmentation of territory. Rouher made a similar assertion on May 7 and continued:

We are disposed to support it [the return of Luxemburg to Belgium]. But it is not for us to take the initiative: it is for Belgium. Why does Belgium delay?[43]

Fear of appearing too self-seeking and losing the sympathy of the powers at the very time rumors were rife that Bismarck and Napoleon III might have struck a bargain at the expense of Belgium was one reason for Belgian reticence.[44] Another was the attitude of Great Britain. Upon learning of Beust's proposal, Van de Weyer had pressed Stanley for a declaration of England's intention of defending Belgium's neutrality. The foreign minister avoided giving it; instead, he urged the Belgians to arm quickly and quietly. Lord Stanley apparently had some difficulty deciding what policy Great Britain should follow, if any. At first he had viewed the Belgian suggestion favorably, but by the beginning of May, when Van de Weyer again discussed it with him, he was of the opinion that any Belgian initiative would be dangerous and warned against it. This change was no doubt influenced by the views of the experienced Cowley, who, early in April, had advised Sir Edmund Hammond, the permanent undersecretary of the foreign office, 'For heaven's sake do not encourage the idea of giving Luxemburg to Belgium. It would raise a storm here [in Paris] which we shd [*sic*] never allay.'[45]

Queen Victoria, who had been subject to a deluge of letters from her cousin Leopold, held views that were strongly favorable to the Belgian cause. Her influential private secretary, General Grey, was of similar opinion. Together they urged Lord Stanley to support the Belgian solution to the crisis, but without success. The possibility of angering both the French and the Germans, and gratuitously involving Britain in the awkward situation of protecting Belgium in a scuffle over land as remote from the British navy as was the duchy, seemed too great. Indeed, as time passed, Stanley's concern for prudence came to be shared by the queen. On May 6, General Grey wrote Van de Weyer:

I must say it [a letter of Leopold II's] alarms me a little lest he should be *overactive*. You know my opinion... coincides with the queen's, that the simplest and best arrangement would be the transfer of Luxemburg to Belgium and the extension to the former of the neutrality guaranteed to the latter by the great Powers. – But this object will not beadvance d, in my opinion, by any appearance of overeagerness on the part of Belgium to effect it.[46]

Belgium's proximity to Napoleon III's Second Empire and the warnings of her most trusted guarantor were strong recommendations for a cautious policy. Thirty years earlier little heed would have been given them. But now Belgium was an established state; she had gained too much to risk losing the sympathies of the powers.

There were many Belgians who did not favor the forward policy of Leopold and the foreign minister. Jules Devaux, whom Jules van Praet had trained as his successor as secretary to the king, wrote Van de Weyer on May 2 that, 'Rogier is crazier than ever and does and says only stupid-ities. Fortunately he is so completely disavowed by everyone that it will no longer be of consequence.'[47] Devaux's uncle, Van Praet, still served as a minister of the royal house and he, however, apparently supported the king. Van de Weyer vacillated, his energy sapped by illness and age.[48] Leopold Orban, the *Directeur politique* of Rogier's own ministry and brother-in-law of the prime minister, steadfastly opposed the adventure. He believed that should Luxemburg be offered to Belgium, France would consider it only a temporary measure; in such circumstances the gift might eventually prove a source of regret for Belgium.[49]

To a great extent the split was generational. This was especially evi-dent within the cabinet. For years Rogier had led his Liberal party, but now power was shifting to the younger, personable Frère-Orban. Frère-Orban, despite the handicap of not having been born into one of Bel-gium's leading families, had worked his way up in politics until, as a result of cabinet shuffling in the mid-1860s, he had replaced Rogier as prime min-ister. He was known for his brilliance, sharp attacks in debates, and for being a hard man to deal with once he had taken a decision. Frère-Orban personally felt that Belgium should not risk annoying France or Prussia. He was bothered by the extent of the military preparations that the king was recommending, and it may be wondered if Frère-Orban, as a politician and ardent opponent of the Roman Catholic cause, had great interest in adding to the kingdom a population which, in the vast majority, was Roman Catholic.[50]

Rogier could receive only mild public support from the young king. Inexperienced and somewhat frightened of the powers, Leopold II could not ignore the voices calling for caution. He did journey to Paris and Berlin and wrote multitudes of letters to Queen Victoria begging British support in event of war. In private letters of instruction, the king told Van de Weyer to work for Belgian annexation of Luxemburg, but he always advised discretion and reserved behavior.[51] Although officially agreeing with Frère-Orban, he apparently hoped the London settlement would not be definitive, for he also supported Banning's propaganda ac-tivities in the following months.

On May 5, the conflict between Rogier and the moderates was resolved in favor of the latter. On that day, a cabinet meeting was held in the pres-ence of the king for the purpose of drawing up instructions for Van de Weyer, who was to represent Belgium at the London Conference which had met to settle the affair. At issue, however, was the totality of Belgian behavior in foreign affairs; the differences of opinion were evidenced by separate drafts for the instructions presented by Rogier and Frère-Orban. Though the cabinet tactfully combined the two messages, in the meeting it was Frère-Orban's voice and that of the new generation which prevailed.

Van de Weyer was instructed to play a passive role, making no overtures. If the Beust proposals were brought up by another delegate, Van de Weyer was to refuse any cession of territory; if only an indemnity were involved, he might consent *ad referendum*. Frère-Orban later wrote a 'Note on our political situation *vis-à-vis* France' in which he explained that he had thought it best to let the powers take the initiative, for were Belgium to get the duchy without making territorial cessions, 'there would have been only deep humiliation for France and, consequently, sharp resentments for us...'.[52]

These instructions did allow for the possibility the powers might ask Belgium to take over the duchy. Discreet as the language was, Devaux noted there were many Belgian statesmen 'who hold that at no price, even to avoid an immediate war, should Belgium accept Luxemburg'.[53] On the other hand, Van de Weyer was clearly not enfranchised to behave in the manner Rogier suggested in his private letter which accompanied the official instructions:

The statesmen of 1839 who combatted that mutilation of Belgium could today say to their former adversaries: there is your work and here is the moment to correct your errors. You are my dear Minister, of that good race of 1830 which has always kept on its heart the sacrifice... imposed in 1839. The interests of Europe and the maintenance of peace could be involved...[54]

The result of the London Conference was that Prussia relinquished her claims on the garrison and the neutralized duchy remained under the control of Grand Duke William III. Baron Napoleon Eugène Beyens, in his book on the Second Empire, suggests that the Beust proposals were never considered because Bismarck hurried the negotiations so that a discussion of *Zollverein* rights would not arise. Beyens believed that because of the duchy's customs union with Germany, it was just as well Belgium did not get involved.[55] However, no power ever came out against a Belgian solution. It was for this reason that the French statesman Emile Ollivier wrote: 'It is probable that if the Belgian government had supported the matter with resolution, Belgium would have regained the bits torn from her.[56]

Ollivier may have been wrong; yet it is worth noting that the Belgians purposely passed up the opportunity. Great Britain, while obviously reluctant to lend any support, had nothing in principle against the Belgian solution; and Queen Victoria had some sympathy for it. Prussia would have had few objections. No record of the May 5 cabinet meeting has been located, but other sources indicate that consideration of complications with the *Zollverein* played a minor role in the discussion. True, it would have been dangerous to proceed very far in the face of possible French opposition without active British support, but the Belgians did not even fill their trial balloons completely. After seventeen years of being threatened by France, the Brussels officials had allowed their thinking to be dominated by the French bugaboo. Twenty-five years later, the then worldly-wise Leopold II commented bitterly:

In general, we are too timid and we miss our chance to get the good pieces of the cake. It was through fear that in 1869 [*sic*] we did not succeed in getting Luxemburg.[57]

Prudence was a wise policy to follow with respect to the erratic Napoleon III. Nevertheless, the Belgian diplomats let their sensitivity to danger become almost overdeveloped, thus forcing their actions into a pattern of excessive caution and occasional retreat. A self-effacing diplomacy was being constructed in hopes that if Belgium did not annoy Napoleon III or call his attention to her, the emperor might forget any designs he had on Belgian territory.

Other factors also affected the Belgian attitude in foreign affairs. One of the most noticeable of these was the replacement of the old revolutionaries by men of a new generation. This did not occur all at once, but the weakening influence of Charles Rogier was symbolic of what was happening. During the fifteen years before the Franco-Prussian War, Van de Weyer retired from his position at London, as did Firmin Rogier at Paris; Willmar died at The Hague in 1858, and Count de Grass passed away at Vienna seven years later, leaving Nothomb in Berlin as the only revolutionary still at a neighboring court. The replacements for these men did not remember the battles of the 1830s as vividly as did their predecessors; many of them had undergone training in lesser posts and were acquainted with the patience required by the diplomatic profession. Most important, the passing of years had created a new situation; not only were the hotspurs mellowed by time, but also circumstances called for a conservative diplomacy designed to preserve the established state.

Time had furthermore brought a different tenor to domestic affairs in Belgium. The union of the Liberal and Catholic parties had come to an end; the political battles were bitter. The issues were not ones that could be easily solved, for they concerned the role of Roman Catholic religious teachings in schools and Catholic control of cemeteries; the position of convents and nunneries; the need for increased military expenditures; the claims of the growing Flemish movement; and the power dispute between the lower legislative chamber and the Senate. Charles Rogier had generally stood for solutions based on patriotism and not party politics. Not so Frère-Orban, who was an intense partisan and constantly embroiled in controversies. Frère-Orban was not uninterested in foreign affairs, but his primary concern was for other matters. This is not surprising, for while the Belgian boundaries had been settled in 1839, important domestic issues were just now coming to the fore. The absorbing nature of internal politics did not go without effect upon Belgian diplomacy. The vigor formerly directed abroad was used else-where, and when a threat appeared on the horizon, the easiest answer was to conciliate and withdraw.

It should not be thought, however, that the Belgians gave themselves completely over to a policy of timidity, for when Louis Napoleon took his final fling at establishing French influence in Belgium, the Brussels statesmen showed some boldness and considerable stubbornness. The railways affair has been described by Ollivier as a brief 'hallucination', but the Belgians viewed it as a serious matter. In either case, it provides an excellent opportunity to examine the manner in which the small state dealt with a threatening great power.

4.4 THE RAILWAY CRISIS

One of Belgium's prides was her railway system. The first nation in Europe to construct a line, by the 1860s she had an extensive complex which was partly state owned and partly under private control. Unfor-tunately, several of the privately owned lines experienced severe financial difficulties. Especially hard-hit were the *Compagnie du Grand-Luxemburg* and the *Compagnie du Liègeois-Limburgeois*. In the case of the first line, much of the original capital had been dissipated; and dividend payments since 1866 had been irregular.[58]

The situation in Luxemburg was no better; for nearly a decade the *Guillaume-Luxembourg* company had been forced to allot the exploita-tion of its system to the great French *Compagnie de l'Est*. Following the crisis of 1867, the French company decided to solidify its position. On January 21, 1868, an agreement was signed whereby the *Guillaume-Luxembourg* ceded its lines to the French society for forty-five years. In return for an annuity of three million francs per year, *Compagnie de l'Est* gained the operating concession on tracks running from the Swiss border to the city of Luxemburg and on across the Belgian border to Pepinster, near Liege. The sum represented a yearly return of 4,000 francs per kilometer more than what was currently being obtained on these lines. Such losses the French company could not sustain by itself; the imperial government came to its aid with a subsidy.

The Belgians paid little heed to the arrangement made by the Luxemburg company. Frère-Orban and his compatriots were upset, however, when they learned in the closing months of 1868 that the *Compagnie de l'Est* was working out similar arrangements with the Belgian *Compagnie du Grand-Luxembourg* and the *Compagnie du Liègeois-Limburgeois*. The reason for concern was clear. The *Grand-Luxembourg*'s lines ran from Luxemburg to Marloie, there dividing into branches to Brussels and Liege; at the latter city they met the other company's tracks, which continued north to the Dutch border. Since the lines of the *Guillaume-Luxembourg* company, already rented by the French, connected with those of the *Grand-Luxembourg*, a purchase of the right to operate the two Belgian lines would mean that the railroads of the entire region flanking the Rhine from Switzerland to Holland would be under French domination. The Belgians did not desire French trainmen in Brussels and Liege, nor did they wish to have the French set transportation rates for Belgian coal and manufactures.

The situation had not developed without warning. Baron Hirsch, a Jewish financier of German birth who later made profits in railroads in Turkey, was the principal director of the *Compagnie du Liègeois-Limburgeois*. Unlike the lines of the *Grand-Luxembourg*, those of his railway did not connect directly with the *Guillaume-Luxembourg*'s lines but were separated from them by a gap near Liege. In October 1868, he had requested and failed to receive permission to build a spur from his line to Pepinster, thus bridging the gap. As this distance was already covered by a state-owned railway, it should have been clear that Hirsch's purpose was to make his own line more attractive to the French operators of the *Guillaume-Luxembourg* system.

The cabinet was aware that the *Compagnie du Grand Luxembourg* was in trouble. At the beginning of 1868, Victor Tesch, the former minister of justice who was now the chief representative of the company, had told the government his line wished to be purchased by the state or allowed to merge with another line. In the months that followed, Alexandre Jamar, the new minister of public works, made clear that the state would not buy the line and that he did not favor a merger between it and the *Grand-Central* system. Apparently little thought was given by Frère-Orban or Jamar to the possibility of a merger with the *Compagnie de l'Est* until October 29, when the prime minister was informed by Tesch that such negotiations had just begun. Frère-Orban replied that such a cession was impossible and that the government's permission would be necessary.

It is difficult to understand why the government did not act decisively to stop the negotiations. Rogier had resigned as foreign minister soon after the Luxemburg episode, and his successor, Jules van der Stichelen, appears to have left the direction of the incident to Jamar and the prime minister. Perhaps Frère-Orban was engrossed in other matters and felt the whole affair was an effort to force the government into buying the line. It would have been strange if he let deter him Tesch's argument that English investors would resent government interference.[59] On December 11, Jamar stated from the tribune that government authorization was necessary for any sale of railroad rights to a foreign company. The Paris negotiations continued despite this statement, a situation that Frère-Orban found 'very extraordinary'.[60] Perhaps it was not so strange, since by December 12 preliminary agreements had been reached; Jamar's statement was too late.

Baron Eugène Beyens, the Belgian ambassador in Paris, did all he could to convince the companies not to make a deal, but his efforts were vitiated by the reports of his counterpart in Brussels, Viscount La Guéronnière. The Frenchman was scarcely of ministerial caliber; he had won his post for his ardent support of Louis Napoleon in his chauvinistic paper, *La France*. The journalist viewed his job as a stepping-stone to a higher place in the celestial order of the Empire and was determined to accelerate his ascent. An advocate of French annexation of Belgium, he urged his government on, reassuring it that Jamar's speech might be discounted, as Belgian businessmen were in favor of the arrangement. Further encouragement was given the French by Tesch, who told them that Belgium would eventually ratify any accord reached by the railways.[61]

As time passed, the Belgians became sure the French government was involved in the affair, but decided they could do nothing to halt its actions. On February 2, notification was received that the definitive contract ceding the exploitation of the two Belgian railroads to the French *Compagnie de l'Est* for forty-three years had been signed on January 30, 1869. It was learned four days later, however, that a law would have to be passed by the French chambers before the state guarantee (which virtually promised to subsidize the cost to the French company) would be valid.

The Belgians now faced a crisis partly of their own making. Failure to pay attention to what was happening had allowed the railroad negotiations to go too far. The man who might have earliest rung the tocsin was King Leopold II, but he had withdrawn to his château in the Ardennes in grief over the death of his only son. True, once Frère-Orban was informed by Tesch, he hastened to have the matter looked into, but that was in November, not in July when it had originally been decided a committee should undertake that task. Moreover, the committee did not execute its duty, for it obligingly refrained from an investigation of the *Grand-Luxembourg* after Tesch complained that merger negotiations with another society would be jeopardized. The reticence to act in affairs involving another country, which Belgium had developed over the preceding eighteen years, was now not only encouraging Napoleon III in his schemes but also preventing Belgium from taking appropriate measures when they were first necessary.

Existing Belgian laws required government authorization of any railway merger, but they could be easily circumvented. On February 6, it was decided at two emergency cabinet meetings that a new law should be passed; the measure was presented to the chambers the same day, where it received bipartisan support. Before the French government could push the state guarantee through the *Corps législatif*, the Belgians had passed their own law. No cessions, leases, or mergers of railroad lines could be taken without government approval; if this rule were violated, the state could seize and operate the lines for the company.

The French reacted sharply to the Belgian move. The Paris press accused the Belgians of letting their actions be guided by Prussia, a charge which was indignantly denied. The Marquis de La Valette, who had replaced Moustier as French foreign minister, did not protest the Belgians' right to make the law, but expressed his 'sad surprise' that they should undertake a measure so obviously directed against the French government. Beyens attempted to smooth the matter over by insisting that Brussels considered the French government entirely foreign to the affair. Nevertheless, Napoleon III became convinced that he was the object of a challenge which had been planned in concert with Bismarck.[62] On February 19, the emperor wrote to his war minister, Marshal Niel, concerning the possibility of attacking Belgium: 'To be conciliatory and to retreat in the face of a proceeding which injures us is to abdicate, before the face of Europe, all legitimate influence.'[63]

The same day that Napoleon was meditating a possible war, La Guéronnière made a *démarche* at Brussels. The gist of his argument was that the Belgian measure contradicted the principles of the free trade system established by the Franco-Belgian treaty of 1861; the Belgians should examine the railroads' conventions to see how these needed to be modified to assure the development of the commercial interests of both countries. Frère-Orban, although determined not to admit the validity of the railroad agreements, was glad to deal on the economic side of the affair and not bring into daylight the more important political aspect. Were that to be discussed openly, the situation would surely become worse, for negotiations would become entangled in charges that Belgium was interfering in French affairs and rights, and the prestige factor would force the emperor toward increased inflexibility. The premier's response, therefore, was that a commission should be established to study a system of mixed service whereby French economic needs would be cared for and Belgium would retain control of the railroads.[64]

La Guéronnière was disappointed by Frère-Orban's refusal to accept the convention as a basis for future negotiations. Additionally annoyed by Frère-Orban's suggestion that if Belgium were to allow a concession to a French company, she should also give one to a Prussian company in order to be impartial in her neutrality, the minister petulantly declared that Belgium's neutrality 'should be *slightly slanted toward France*'.[65] He seized eagerly, however, the suggestion of mixed service. In Paris the idea was met with less enthusiasm but negotiations continued, centering on what the proposed commission should be authorized to examine. On March 4, the Belgians rejected a French formula because the wording implied Belgian acknowledgement of the agreements made by the railway companies. La Valette's next attempt came closer to Frère-Orban's wishes, as he proposed a commission which would discuss not the conventions themselves, but all economic questions already existing or arising from the conventions. The phrasing was equivocal and Frère-Orban distrusted it. The words could be meant as a bridge for a French retreat or as a ruse.

The prime minister would have continued to resist but for the attitude of the English. The affair was one in which British support could have been expected, but that nation was entertaining a policy of nonintervention. Lord Clarendon, the Liberals' foreign minister, had not taken any immediate action; when he did, his support was half-hearted. He approved resistance to the French claims but criticized Belgium for not buying the railroads and for not finding a course which, although not a capitulation to French demands, would have granted some concessions to the emperor in matters of form. Despite the contrary opinion of his minister in Belgium, John Savile Lumley, Clarendon thought the 'Belgian Govt. has been maladroit thro'out the business...'.[66]

The irritated foreign minister later wrote Queen Victoria that the object of the Belgians was 'to hold out as a menace to their real or supposed enemies that the whole material force of England is at their disposal'.[67] This judgment is too extreme, but that it was not without some foundation is shown by the comment of the Belgian minister at London that 'we ceded because we would not be able to hope for efficacious aid from England in the event our resistance would have brought a French invasion of Belgium'.[68] Clarendon wished to preserve freedom of action, but the Queen thought his course 'so very curiously *guarded*, as to be hardly *straightforward*'.[69] In March, the Englishman was especially upset by a telegram from his minister in Brussels which told him that, 'The King is confident that Your Lordship will let him know whether and when you think he should commence military preparations.'[70]

Clarendon quickly made it clear to the Brussels diplomats that they should deal with France. Frère-Orban would have liked to continue to hold firm but gave way, further influenced by Beyens' urging that some effort at conciliation be shown and by the news that an imminent rupture threatened if Belgium rejected the French proposal. Prodded by Jules van Praet, the aged and wise minister of the royal house, Frère-Orban agreed to the commission as established as 'an evidence of deference to the councils of the English government'.[71]

The premier had no doubt as to who would be the best Belgian to send to Paris, although there were many raised eyebrows when he announced he would go himself. His flaring oratory, stubbornness, and cutting dialectic were fine in the Chamber, but would they serve as well in diplomatic discussions? Frère-Orban, however, liked the idea of a bigger stage for his talents and was not disturbed by the thought of undertaking negotiations in the enemy's camp.

Before Frère-Orban left, La Guérronière did not fail to make a final effort to increase tension. On March 27, he told the secretary general of the Belgian foreign ministry that the growth of Prussia had upset the European balance and that the positions of nations were no longer the same. Belgium 'must henceforth lean towards France'.[72]

The reception Frère-Orban received in Paris was cool but amicable. He was to deal with three men, Foreign Minister La Valette, Minister of Public Works Gressier, and Rouher, the driving force behind the French scheme. Frère-Orban was willing to conciliate the French by working out a system whereby French trains could use Belgian tracks, although the lines would remain in Belgian hands. This solution was not satisfactory to the French, and, after two weeks of negotiations, Rouher still insisted that the contracts be upheld. Hard feelings arose, and Frère-Orban accused the French of behaving toward Belgium in a manner they would not use toward an African tribe. Rouher, exasperated by the way the Belgians had built up the French guarantee to the *Compagnie de l'Est* as an attempt at Belgian independence, offered to withdraw the guarantee.

Matters passed from bad to worse, and it was obvious that the emperor's patience was wearing thin. The Belgian premier had successfully kept the negotiations going by requesting written copies of all French proposals, thus gaining time and avoiding a break over a verbal matter. Nevertheless, by April 20 a rupture seemed inevitable. La Valette alone appeared conciliatory; he tried to convince Frère-Orban to relinquish the *Liègeois-Limburgeoise* line if the *Compagnie de l'Est* abandoned claims on the *Grand-Luxembourg*. Frère-Orban stuck to his principle and made plans to leave Paris. In a last effort, the premier seized upon a suggestion made by Jules Devaux and by Van de Weyer, from his retirement. He hinted that a conference of the countries which had signed the 1839 treaty might be called if Belgium approved or even if she vetoed the change of the railways' ownership. The threat of an appeal to a conference, and, as Frère-Orban noted, more particularly the vagueness of his phrasing, perturbed his listeners. Rouher was sure Prussia was behind the proposal and cried out that France would never attend such a conference, 'rather war than surrender'.[73]

Hitherto the Belgians had scrupulously avoided any intimation that they envisaged Prussian involvement in order not to disturb French susceptibilities. For some time, they had been trying to play the British card against the French without marked success; it therefore seemed worthwhile to risk an extreme French reaction by implying that Belgium might successfully enlist the aid of additional powers.

Fortunately, the emperor's considered opinion was not the same as Rouher's emotional spur-of-the-moment judgment. When Frère-Orban made a final appeal to Napoleon III upon the suggestion of Van Praet, the ruler was surprisingly conciliatory Nothing should be done which would endanger Belgium's autonomy, neutrality, or independence. Perhaps a tariff agreement could be reached.[74] Frère-Orban's hint had come at a psychologically and diplomatically crucial moment for Napoleon III. Disturbed by the news that Frère-Orban was planning to leave Paris, Lord Clarendon had finally indicated that he thought France was being unreasonable in her demands and that Franco-British relations would be harmed if no solution were reached. The emperor knew the temper of British opinion and understood that England, already troubled by difficulties with the United States, was reluctant to become too deeply involved with France; he might, therefore, have discounted the danger of possible British action. But two days later Bismarck had revealed his position, stating he agreed with the English and was willing to enter into talks with them concerning the affair.[75] Frère-Orban's delay of the proceedings had been successful, though just barely.

The Belgian's refusal to give way showed he would be moved only by force. A conference would vote against France; war was the only answer, and Napoleon III shrank from taking this risky step. It was not really in his nature to hold firm against an obstinate opponent. Any war with Belgium, as the emperor himself admitted, would place France in the wrong in the eyes of Europe and might well involve her in a battle with powers much larger than Belgium. Moreover, Frère-Orban had shown himself willing to conciliate by agreeing to come to Paris for discussions. Perhaps the wound given imperial prestige by Belgium's passage of the law blocking the railways transaction was not as noticeable as at first feared, having been covered up by weeks of negotiations. In any case, a mixed service arrangement could give France some concrete economic gains, even if no political advantages were obtained.

On April 27, a protocol was signed in which the French agreed not to execute the conventions concluded by the railway companies and by which a new mixed commission was established to draw up service conventions. Frère-Orban had hoped for a direct entente and not the creation of a second commission, for he feared the January conventions would again be discussed. He yielded, however, and by July 3 all was settled, as arrangements were made for international transit service from Antwerp to Basel and from Antwerp to the Dutch border. Frère-Orban's reception in Brusels was that of a hero. Reticence in acting at the proper moment had allowed Belgium to come dangerously near disaster. The premier's resoluteness and quick thinking at crucial junctures had saved Belgium's railroads, prestige, and perhaps even her independence.

It is doubtful, however, if the premier would have been so successful without the latent threat of Prussian and English intervention. The playing off of the powers against each other was a valuable tool for Belgian diplomacy, and although England's isolationist policy in this period prevented the Brussels diplomats from using it as frequently as they would have liked, it still was of aid. As Clarendon had complained, the Belgians considered themselves to have a special relationship with England which permitted them to expect almost automatic British support in difficult times. This irritated Downing Street, yet Belgium undoubtedly did have a right to call for British aid, for the very creation of the small state had benefited the vital interests of England more than those of any other power. If the habit was occasionally annoying to the British and revealed a certain lack of independence on the part of the Belgians, it nevertheless usually brought the Brussels diplomats what they desired.

4.5 CODA

When the War of 1870 brought the defeat of France and the overthrow of Napoleon III, the Belgians could again breathe freely, though the shadow of the German army was soon to loom dangerously large. There was no doubt they had possessed reason to mistrust France and sincerely did so. Lord Malmesbury wrote on the death of Leopold I that, 'The last years of his life were spent in pertual terror of Louis Napoleon, and he was constantly alarming our Ministers and everybody on the subject.'[76]

This fear, shared by most Belgian diplomats, was reflected in their reluctance to take action and heavy reliance upon caution as the best method of dealing with the serpent keeping them company. They tried to make the creature as little aware of their presence as possible, and when forced to move, did so quickly while lulling it by means of conciliatory measures. These actions may have bolstered Napoleon III's hopes that Belgium would be easy to coerce but avoided wounding the French emperor's pride and prestige. Such a wound would have brought troops to the Belgian borders far more surely than any amount of seeming pliability. Louis Napoleon would have an excuse for aggression; and, given the current attitude of Prussia and Britain, the Belgians recognized that they might have to back their statements alone. The Brussels diplomats had a right to expect strong support from other quarters and in other periods would have received it. As it was, they were deprived of full use of one of their best tools, the technique of playing the powers off against each other.

This loss was partially compensated by the policy of caution and by a practice of making small concessions. The literature convention and press law of 1852 were extorted by Napoleon III, but they served to relieve tension. So did the 1855 law which ruled that attempts made on the life of a foreign sovereign were political crimes for which the culprits could be tried for their lives in Belgian courts. The Belgians gained from their few gestures and, on the whole, passed much less legislation than was demanded. A final example of such minor concessions was Frère-Orban's agreement to discuss the railway affair in Paris and his allowing of some minor service adjustments to mollify the angry French.

The search for a diplomatic style which could soften the threatening attitude of France had led to a cautious, conciliatory approach. It might be said that the Belgians' pride and concern for their dignity became more sophisticated as they learned the necessity of making concessions. They had shown the 'greatest degree of patience in the face of deliberate obstructionism, a diplomatic practice which was then much less common than in recent years'.[77] This same quality had much to do also with the successful capitalization of the Scheldt tolls.

Yet the earlier theme of tenacity and boldness had not vanished. It was merely relegated to a subordinate position and usually reappeared when caution and conciliation failed. In the 1852 tariff discussions, Rogier's desire to oppose France, no matter what, came to the surface; but it was not allowed to control the Belgian attitude in the negotiations. Similarly, revolutionary boldness colored his and Banning's surreptitious actions in Luxemburg in 1867. In the railway affair Frère-Orban showed little desire to give way, although he was willing to make minor concessions. By all time-honored rules, it was unwise for a man untrained in diplomacy to undertake negotiations at a hostile capital. Yet he did this successfully and showed boldness in doing so; undoubtedly he held the Belgian position more firmly than could have most other men.

Especially noticeable was the premier's stubbornness in refusing to have the state buy the railways and in his proposal of an international conference. The latter threat evidenced a change in attitude toward congresses from that of the preceding score of years. The Belgians were still wary of conferences, as their replies to invitations to one in 1863 indicated, but were no longer completely opposed to them, mainly because Belgium would now be allowed to operate as an accepted power within a conference.

There are at least four points which are essential to an understanding of Belgian diplomacy between 1848 and 1870. Belgium had become an established state engrossed in important domestic disputes and therefore was naturally developing a more conservative and reticent approach in foreign affairs. She was also a small state resisting pressure exerted on her by a great power. The international condition of Europe was of additional importance. The revolutionaries stood up to the Prussians and Austrians with relative impunity in the 1830s but could not act similarly toward France in the 1860s. Finally, Belgium was far more dependent upon a rational system of international relations and the main- tenance of European public law than a greater power would be. When these were scrambled and weakened, as by the expansion of Prussia and the British refusal to support the Belgians unequivocally, the small state's diplomats were forced to take a careful attitude. In particular, the tone of their behavior was keyed to the mood of the British foreign office. In the Luxemburg affair, the Belgians were required to adopt a passive attitude, even though a diplomatic offensive might have brought them gain. The railway affair was significantly different in that it did not involve an active effort to improve Belgium's situation, but a defense of the *status quo*. In such a matter the Brussels statesmen were willing to act more vigorously, even if still held back by the tepidness of Britain's concern. Eventually Frère-Orban's daring obstinacy increased the pressure of the crisis and forced Clarendon to lend a hand.

Frequent and continuing appeals for aid annoyed the British, who rightly or wrongly likened them to the boy's cry of 'Wolf!' The Belgians slowly came to realize they could look only to themselves for sure help. Throughout the period when they were neighbors to Napoleon III, caution and the desire to remain bold and unyielding vied with each other in the minds of the Brussels statesmen. The course to be taken was judged separately for each incident, and in nearly all cases caution won out. During the railway affair, the old audacity and stubbornness appeared in Frère-Orban's moves. Yet even he showed willingness to conciliate. An evolution had occurred in Belgian diplomatic style.

A month after young Queen Victoria had ascended the British throne, Leopold I advised her of the great value of discretion:

Humble as it seems, it has often brought about successes in which talent failed and genius did not succeed. Discretion in the great affairs of the world does wonders, and safety depends frequently and is chiefly derived from it...[78]

The relevance of these sentences, written in 1837, to events twenty and thirty years later is obvious. Discretion was at the heart of Belgian diplomacy in the period during which the troops of the Second Empire threatened to innundate the Low Country. Of course, the Belgians were not always discreet; Leopold II's comment to the British minister concerning mobilization was not wise, yet how much did it matter? The sudden passing of the railroad law angered the French, but the Belgians had to act quickly to compensate for their earlier lack of action. Certainly, too, there were points at which the Belgians could be criticized for being excessively cautious toward Louis Napoleon. Despite these weak points in their behavior, the Belgians survived the crisis which for them extended over a score of years; perhaps this fact alone justifies their decisions during the preceding years. Simple as it was, discretion had proved a successful course to safety.

The search for a diplomacy suitable to meet the challenge of pressure from a great power did not progress in a direct-line manner. The themes of boldness and discretion alternated and at times became intertwined; the resolution in favor of the latter developed not as the result of careful orchestration of national policy, but as the result of a series of unplanned *ad hoc* decisions. Behind the particular questions was the more general one concerning the best way to protect the nation's interests as a whole, a problem of which the Brussels officials were always conscious. Gradually, the old habits of boldness and tenacity were discarded as primary approaches, and Belgium's style instead evidenced her diplomats' tendency to be discreet, cautious, and defensive in striving to create a favorable attitude in Paris toward Belgium. Nevertheless, the Belgians reserved a core of toughness for final necessities, and in their dealings with the adversary they were definitely conciliatory, 'but suppliant, no, humble, no, dupe, no'.

4.6 NOTES

1. 'Leopold to Palmerston, Feb. 22, 1839', quoted in Webster, *Foreign policy of Palmerston*, vol. I, p. 519.
2. Gooch, *Belgium and the February revolution*, p. 21. The following few pages owe much to this fine monograph.
3. *Ibid.*, p. 27–28. For a contrary view, see Discailles, *Charles Rogier*, vol. III, p. 235.
4. Gooch, *Belgium and the February revolution*, p. 31.
5. De Ridder, *La crise*, vol. I, pp. 6–8, no. 4: 'Van de Weyer to d'Hoffschmidt, Feb. 27, 1848'.
6. *Ibid.*, vol. I, pp. 32–34, no. 23: 'd'Hoffschmidt to Van de Weyer, Feb. 29, 1848'.
7. Gooch, *Belgium and the February revolution*, pp. 40–41.
8. De Ridder, *La crise*, vol. I, pp. 37–39, no. 27: 'd'Hoffschmidt to de Ligne, Mar. 1, 1848'; p. 53, no. 38: 'Same to same, Mar. 2, 1848'; p. 51, no. 36: 'd'Hoffschmidt to Van de Weyer, Mar. 2, 1848'.
9. *Ibid.*, vol. I, pp. 89–92, no. 59: 'd'Hoffschmidt to legations, Mar. 4, 1848'.
10. *Ibid.*, vol. I, pp. 63–64, no. 45: 'De Ligne to d'Hoffschmidt, Mar. 3, 1848'.
11. Gooch, *Belgium and the February revolution*, p. 44.
12. De Ridder, *La crise*, vol. I, pp. 119–21, no. 74: 'd'Hoffschmidt to legations, Mar. 5, 1848'.
13. Gooch, *Belgium and the February revolution*, p. 48.
14. De Ridder, *La crise*, vol. I, no. 87: pp. 140–142, 'Willmar to d'Hoffschmidt, Mar. 7, 1848'.
15. Gooch, *Belgium and the February revolution*, p. 46.
16. See De Ridder, *La crise*, vol. I, pp. 296–300, 321–328, 332–333, nos. 199, 209, 210, 211, and 214, exchanges between d'Hoffschmidt and de Ligne, Apr. 1 through 4, 1848.
17. The offer was actually made by the Committee of Seventeen, which served as a guiding committee for the Diet legislation (*Ibid.*, vol. II, pp. 23–25, no 271: 'De Rouillé to d'Hoffschmidt, May 9, 1848'; pp. 36–39, no. 281: 'd'Hoffschmidt to Briey, May 15, 1848').
18. *Ibid.*, vol. II, pp. 196–197, 208–209, nos. 398, 410: 'Exchange between Briey and d'Hoffschmidt, Aug. 7 and 11, 1848'; pp. 222–223, no. 418: 'd'Hoffschmidt to legations, Aug. 16, 1848'.
19. *Ibid.*, vol. II, pp. 69–75, no. 306: 'd'Hoffschmidt to Leopold, May 25, 1848'; see also pp. 51–54, no. 292: 'Van de Weyer to d'Hoffschmidt, May 21, 1848'.
20. Gooch, *Belgium and the February revolution*, pp. 71–74, 96–97.
21. De Ridder, *La crise*, vol. I, pp. 207–208, no. 142 bis: 'd'Hoffschmidt to Willmar, Mar. 15, 1848'.
22. *Ibid.*, vol. I, pp. 317–320, no. 207: 'd'Hoffschmidt to Willmar, Apr. 2, 1848'. Gooch, *Belgium and the February revolution*, pp. 91–92.
23. De Ridder, *La crise*, vol. II, p. 21, no. 269: 'Willmar to d'Hoffschmidt, May 8, 1848'.

24. Martin, *Life of the Prince Consort*, vol. II, pp. 29–30, as quoted in Gooch, *Belgium and the February revolution*, p. 84.
25. *Letters of Queen Victoria*, lst ser., vol. II, p. 457: 'Leopold to Victoria, Mar. 5, 1852'.
26. The quotations in this and the following paragraph are taken from documents reproduced on pages 400–410 of Discailles, 'Un diplomate belge'. The monograph is an extensive report of Firmin Rogier's work in Paris, reproducing 525 documents.
27. Belgium had little foreign support. Russia, Austria, and Britain all advised her not to offend France, cf. De Ridder, *Le mariage du roi Léopold II*.
28. Lorette, 'Problèmes de politique étrangère', in *Expansion belge 1831–1865* pp. 568-571.
29. This and the following quotation are from Discailles, *Charles Rogier*, vol. IV, p. 63: 'C. Rogier to Leopold, April 20, 1858'.
30. *Ibid.*, vol. IV, p. 113.
31. The pertinent treaties may be found in Nothomb, *Essai historique*, vol. II, pp. 226–232. See also Discailles, *Charles Rogier*, vol. IV, pp. 165–200.
32. Discailles, 'Un diplomate belge', pp. 357–361: 'd'Hoffschmidt to F. Rogier, Mar. 12, 1851'.
33. Ollivier, *L'Empire libéral*, vol. IX, pp. 168–169.
34. There are several accounts of the affair; one of the most complete may be found in Wampach, *Le Luxembourg*. Emile Banning has written summaries of the affair from the Belgian viewpoint, and some of these are included as appendices to the pertinent chapter in his *Les origines*.
35. Rogier papers, 468, memorandum by Banning: 'Neutralisation du Grand–Duché de Luxembourg. Solution belge.'
36. De Lichtervelde, *Léopold of the Belgians*, p. 64.
37. Discailles, 'Trois dates', pp. 327–329. See also Hymans, *Frére-Orban*, vol. II, pp. 143–144.
38. *Das Staatsarchiv*, vol. XIII (Hamburg, July-Dec. 1867), no. 2774: 'Stanley to Cowley, Apr. 15, 1867'.
39. Rogier papers, no. 468: memorandum.
40. *Das Staatsarchiv*, vol. XIII, no. 2781: 'Stanley to Cowley, Apr. 18, 1867'.
41. Van de Weyer papers, 37: 'Van de Weyer to Rogier, Apr. 17, 1867'. See also Rogier papers, 468: 'Banning memorandum'.
42. Rogier papers, 468.
43. *Ibid.*, letter of May 7 to Rogier signed Dud. Rogier apparently took this information at face value (*Ibid.*: 'Rogier to Van de Weyer, May 9, 1867').
44. After discussion with Stanley, Van de Weyer wrote Rogier on the night of April 17 that it could be held certain that such an arrangement had been made (Van de Weyer papers, 37).
45. 'Cowley to Hammond, Apr. 9, 1867', as quoted in Foot, 'Great Britain', p. 366. Van de Weyer papers, 40: 'Van de Weyer to Devaux, May 2, 1867'; no. 39: 'Van de Weyer to Leopold, May 6, 1867'.
46. Van de Weyer papers, 44.
47. *Ibid.*, 40.

48. Demoulin, 'Léopold II', p. 184.
49. Belgium, M.A.E. Arch., Vols. noirs, Question du Gr.-Duché de Luxembourg, vol. II, part II: 'Orban memorandum, Apr. 11, 1867'.
50. Calmes in his 'Malaise', p. 380, suggests that Frère's concern that addition of new deputies from the duchy would upset his thin majority in the Chamber strengthened his reluctance to work for annexation.
51. Van de Weyer papers, 40.
52. Hymans, *Frère-Orban*, vol. II, p. 145.
53. Beyens, *Le Second Empire*, vol. II, p. 236. The author's father was minister at the court of Napoleon III for several years.
54. Rogier papers, 468: 'Rogier to Van de Weyer, May 5, 1867'.
55. Beyens, *Le Second Empire*, vol. II, p. 243.
56. Ollivier, *L'Empire libéral*, vol. IX, p. 331.
57. Quoted in De Lichtervelde, *Léopold*, p. 68.
58. Craig, 'Great Britain', p. 743.
59. Although this interpretation has been given some credence, Thomas in his 'English investors', pp. 228–243, has demonstrated it has little validity. The most complete account from the Belgian viewpoint may be found in Hymans, *Frère-Orban*, vol. II. See also Rheindorf, 'Der belgische-französiche Eisenbahnkonflikt', pp. 113–136.
60. Beyens, *Le Second Empire*, vol. II, p. 335.
61. France, M.A.E., *Les origines diplomatiques*, vol. XXII, pp. 376–380, no. 7072: 'La Guéronnière to Moustier, Dec. 17, 1868'. Belgium M.A.E. Arch., Corr. pol., Inc. f.-b. 1869–1870, vol. I, no. 20: 'Beyens to Van der Stichelen, Jan. 13, 1869'; no. 29: 'Same to same, Feb. 4, 1869'.
62. Belgium, M.A.E. Arch., Corr. pol., Inc. f.-b., vol. I, no. 37: 'Beyens to Van der Stichelen, Feb. 10, 1869'; no. 62: 'Same to same, Feb. 16, 1869'.
63. Ollivier, *L'Empire libéral*, vol. XI, pp. 375–376.
64. Belgium, M.A.E. Arch., Corr. pol., Inc. f.-b., vol. I, no. 117: 'Van der Stichelen to Beyens, Feb. 20, 1869'; no. 145: 'Note by Frère, Feb. 23, 1869'.
65. *Ibid.*, no. 145: 'Note by Frère, Feb. 23, 1869'.
66. Thomas, 'English investors', p. 230, note. It is interesting to note that similar inattention to a growing problem and hasty false starts once the alarm was rung were again demonstrated by the Belgian cabinet in 1872–73. At that time it appeared that, as a result of complicated financial dealings, the *Grand-Luxembourg* might be purchased by a group of concerns which included significant German interests. Eventually the state was forced to buy some of the lines in question. See G. Kurgan-van Hentenrijk, 'Une étape mouvementée', pp. 395–446.
67. *Letters of Queen Victoria*, 2nd ser., vol. I, p. 590: 'Clarendon to Victoria, Apr. 16, 1868'.
68. Belgium, M.A.E. Arch., Corr. pol., Inc. f.-b., vol. II, no. 179: 'Beaulieu to Van der Stichelen, Apr. 1, 1869'.
69. *Letters of Queen Victoria*, 2nd ser., vol. I, p. 593: 'Note to Gladstone, Apr. 17, 1869'.

70. Quoted in Craig, 'Great Britain', p. 750.
71. Beyens, *Le Second Empire*, vol. II, p. 347. Belgium, M.A.E. Arch., Corr. pol., Inc. f.-b., vol. II, no. 81: 'Beaulieu to Van der Stichelen, Mar. 14, 1869'; no. 84; 'Beyens to Van der Stichelen, Mar. 15, 1869'.
72. Boulger, *The reign of Leopold II, 1865–1909*, vol. I, p. 56.
73. Ollivier, *L'Empire libéral*, vol. XI, p. 384.
74. Belgium, M.A.E. Arch., Corr, pol., Inc. f.-b., vol. III, part I, no. 35: 'Frère to Van der Stichelen, Apr. 23, 1869'. Hymans, *Frère-Orban*, vol. II, p. 274.,
75. France, M.A.E., *Les Origines diplomatiques*, vol. XXIV, pp. 201–202 no. 7412: 'La Tour d'Auvergne to La Valette, Apr. 24, 1869'. Michael in his *Bismarck* suggests Napoleon III's retreat was due to failure to obtain an alliance with Austria.
76. Omond, *Belgium and Luxembourg*, p. 67.
77. Thomas, 'English investors', p. 243.
78. *Letters of Queen Victoria*, 1st ser., vol. I, pp. 112–113: 'Leopold to Victora, July 24, 1837'.

5. Gaining a non-European possession

At the time the defeat of Napoleon III's troops by Prussia in 1870 brought the last major alteration of the map of Western Europe until the First World War, hardly a tenth of the African continent had been colonized. Yet by the turn of the century nearly all of Africa had been claimed as a dependency by some European state. The race for colonies was highly competitive, with Britain, France, and later Germany being the leading contestants; chances seemed slim in such a field for a small nation which had no long-standing claims resulting from explorations in previous centuries and no fleet or army of appreciable size. Nevertheless, despite these obstacles, Belgium entered the race and received a rich prize for her efforts.

More exactly, it was King Leopold II who won the colony, for the government of Belgium had nothing to do with the founding of the Congo Free State and took over control of the colony only in 1908. Properly speaking, then, the acquisition of the Congo in the nineteenth century is not part of the diplomatic history of Belgium. Yet an inquiry into the matter legitimately and necessarily must be included in a discussion of Belgium's diplomacy in Europe. Though the creation of the Congo State was the work of the king, the colony was considered a Belgian enterprise by the European chancelleries, which did not view as very important the distinction between Leopold and the nation of which he was sovereign. Leopold's success, therefore, altered significantly Belgium's relations with the other powers. In the long run, the king's actions were part of Belgian diplomacy and had to be recognized as such, even by the Belgians. His movements were made difficult by many of the same obstacles that hindered his nation's foreign ministry, and in his diplomacy he could never forget the implications of Belgium's small size. The maneuvers he used in obtaining his goal tell much about small power diplomacy and further warrant a brief consideration of this particular episode, which by its size and success is sharply differentiated from the other royal colonial tentatives.

Like his father, Leopold II had his own, somewhat enlarged, private ministry of the royal house. The aged Van Praet had retired to an advisory post upon the death of Leopold I; he was succeeded by his carefully trained nephew, Jules Devaux. Other men, especially Emile Banning and Baron François Lambermont, both high officials in the ministry of foreign affairs, also became invaluable personal agents of the king. That these two, and others in similar positions, saw no conflict in simultaneously acting as officials responsible to parliament and as officials responsible solely to the king, is an indication of the traditional vagueness of the demarcation of Belgian national affairs from strictly royal endeavors. When parliamentary or foreign attacks necessitated, however, the distinction was, of course, clearly drawn indeed.

Of the differences between the royal diplomacy and that of the foreign office, perhaps the most important was that of scope. The correspondence of both Leopolds dealt with matters all over Europe, from Balkan revolts to Spanish and Portuguese royal marriages, while official Belgian diplomacy handled only more proximate concerns, such as tariff and railway agreements with France. Both Leopolds saw their talents as too great to be constrained to the narrow areas of regular diplomacy and did not hesitate to act on their own. In no field was this more true than in colonization. China, Guatemala, the Sudan, and the Congo all felt the touch of Belgian imperialism, despite the little interest and occasional disapproval expressed by Belgian parliaments and cabinets for what they considered wild and far-flung adventures. Quickness of decision was also a hallmark of royal diplomacy; in many instances free of the need to consult political leaders, resolve conflicting views, and build popular support, the monarchs could often act more promptly than could cabinet ministers.

5.1 THE INTERNATIONAL ASSOCIATIONS

The reasons why Leopold II undertook his quest for colonies need only be briefly mentioned. He relished the possibilities of high level diplomacy, adventure, and personal gain. An even more important motive was his belief that only by gaining colonies could Belgium become a truly modern state. The benefits the nation could gain from colonies would be many, he told the Belgian Senate.

You will find there precious outlets for your products, food for your commerce, occupation for all the activities from which we cannot draw a profit at the present time, a useful place for our surplus population, new revenues for the treasury which will perhaps, some day, permit the Government, after the example of the Netherlands, to lower the tax rates in the mother country, and finally, a certain increase in power and a still better position in the center of the great European family.[1]

These were enticing arguments, but how could a small state with no ancient claims establish a dependency? The first step was to find an area in which to work; Leopold's manner of doing this was impulsive. His gaze casted from Japan, Borneo, and the Fiji Islands to the Philippines, Argentina, and West Indies, until he decided 'discreetly to learn if there is anything to do in Africa'.[2] It was natural that Africa attracted him, for news of explorations in that continent had stirred Europe frequently during the previous decade, especially after Henry M. Stanley's famous meeting with the lost Livingston in 1871.

If the wily Leopold were to be successful, it was necessary for him to act quickly; expeditions from other countries were preparing claims. Two Frenchmen had begun exploration of the Congo basin in 1874; a German expedition was also in the field, and at the end of 1875 a British explorer, Lt. V. L. Cameron, announced he had rights to the entire area on the basis of treaties signed with native chiefs. Fortunately for Leopold's future efforts, this claim was disavowed by the British government.

Because of her lack of early activity in Africa, as well as because of her military weakness, Belgium could make no blustering political claims. Were Belgium now to send her own expedition, it would take time, might not meet with success, and certainly would meet with the opposition and suspicions of other nations active in the area. The claims of a Belgian expedition would hold little weight against the prior claims of such expeditions as that of Cameron. An additional difficulty was the general distrust within Belgium and her parliament for expensive and dangerous imperialist ventures; Leopold could legally act on his own, but he still had to be cognizant of public opinion. A Belgian expedition was impracticable.

Leopold therefore took another approach. He had long been building goodwill with geographical societies in various countries; he now tightened his connections with them by means of donations. His plan was to unite these societies into an international organization for scientific exploration and extermination of the slave trade. Such an association could then be used as a tool for Leopold's private endeavors as well as for altruistic international activities. Because of the ruler's past generosity and because his nation apparently had no national interest in the Congo, the confidence of the society leaders in the king's high-minded interests was easily won. After Leopold's proposals had been favorably received by several organizations, invitations to an international conference were extended to philanthropists and geographers of six nations; all were accepted.

Shortly before the conference met, Baron Lambermont, secretary general in the Belgian ministry of foreign affairs, called a meeting of leading Belgians interested in the enterprise. Their purpose in gathering was to agree upon a program which they would later try to persuade the international conference to adopt. Emile Banning, now director of policy in the foreign office, proposed that each power act in different sections of the unknown territory according to its own interests and that an international association be founded reciprocally to support the national agents. Such a plan was opposed by other Belgians, who threatened to withdraw from the enterprise unless it were completely international. The conflict between the expansionists and their more reticent countrymen, which had appeared in the 1860s, had not yet died. When Banning appealed to the king, Leopold replied that he agreed with Banning but that it was necessary to reckon with the state of opinion in Belgium.[3]

The tack which Leopold followed to soothe the suspicions of other nations and of his own subjects was displayed in his opening speech at the conference on September 12, 1876:

The subject which brings us together to-day is one that deserves in the highest degree to engage the attention of the friends of humanity. To open to civilization the only part of the globe where it has not penetrated, to pierce the darkness enshrouding entire populations, that is, if I may venture to say so, a crusade worthy of this century of progress...
Is it necessary for me to say to you that in inviting you to Brussels I have not been guided by egotistical views? No, Gentlemen, if Belgium is small she is happy and satisfied with her lot.[4]

An International Association for the Exploration and Civilization of Central Africa was soon organized. Frequently referred to as the International African Association, it was 'to explore scientifically the unknown parts of Africa, to facilitate the opening of the routes which will enable civilization to penetrate into the interior of the African continent, [and] to discover the means for the suppression of the slave trade...'. An executive committee was formed under the presidency of King Leopold and national committees were founded in most of the member countries.

In a period which stressed progress, an association devoted to scientific exploration, the founding of hospitals and trade outposts, and intent upon extermination of the African slave trade naturally met with approval. National support was another matter. The cost of expeditions was great, and it seemed reasonable that expenses should be defrayed by international cooperation; but in the long run national interests triumphed.

The British refused to join and the enthusiasm in other countries soon waned. Only Germany and Holland contributed over 10,000 francs; Belgium, with the aid of Leopold's purse, contributed over 600,000 francs.[5]

The failure of the African Association in its fund-raising did not lessen its real usefulness to Leopold. It still provided a mask of internationalism behind which the king could operate. Foreign countries could not protest Belgian actions in the Congo if they were under the aegis of an international humanitarian organization. At this stage Leopold's greatest worry may have been the opposition of his subjects to colonial enterprises. But this too had been overcome. Once Leopold had obtained the sanction of internationalism, he assured himself of freedom of action in June 1877 by persuading the first assembly of the International Commission, the governing body of the Association, that the executive committee should have full control of business when the Commission was not in session. A second assembly of the Commission was never called.

Leopold's assertion in his speech to the International Association that he and Belgium were not seeking national gains could scarcely have contrasted more sharply with the intentions the king expressed in private. The following October, Leopold endeavored to enlist the Belgian minister in Madrid, Baron Jules Greindl, in the African venture. Greindl had resisted, for he did not wish to work for a non-Belgian authority but for king and country. He was, however, assured that some national goal would be served and soon became the secretary general of the Association.[6] In a November 17, 1877 letter to Baron Solvyns, Belgian minister in London, the king was even more frank:

According to the circumstances, *I will try to transform these agencies* of the Association *into some sort of Belgian establishment* or into some sort of station ...which will belong to us...
I believe that if at the beginning I clearly charge Stanley to take possession of any region of Africa in my name, the English will stop me... I think I will therefore first entrust to Stanley a task of exploration which will offend no one, and which will provide us some *agencies and staffs of which we will make use as soon as people in Europe and Africa have become accustomed to our claims on the Congo*.[7]

It was Stanley whom Leopold intended to lead the major Association expeditions. In the months following the geographical conference, the Belgian committee sent a not-too-successful expedition to the dark continent but in general displayed little energy. Leopold was waiting for Stanley's return to Europe after his completion in 1877 of the first latitudinal crossing of the Congo region. When Stanley landed at Marseilles in January 1879, he was met by Greindl and Henry S. Sanford, former United States minister in Brussels and Leopold's friend and confidant in African affairs. These two men proposed to Stanley that Leopold 'intended to undertake to do something substantial for Africa'.[8] The explorer was at first uninterested, but after England had declined his proffered services, he was soon in discussion with Leopold.

Considerable time was devoted to arriving at a program which would satisfy Stanley, give the expedition an international flavor, and also serve the personal ambitions of the king. Both men were interested in a venture that would have commercial as well as scientific aspects. Dutch merchants joined the talks and the eventual result was the formation of the *Comité d'études du Haut Congo* in November 1878. This organization intended to support activities, such as the construction of roads, that would be in harmony with the philanthropic and scientific under-takings of the International Association and would also be of commercial use. Stanley was instructed to establish any stations he felt were necessary: 'By lease or purchase, ground enough was to be secured adjoining the stations so as to enable them to be self-sufficient, and . . . land on each side of the route adopted for the traffic was to be purchased or leased, to prevent persons ill-disposed towards us from frustrating the intentions of the Committee. . .'[9] The Committee for Studies of the Upper Congo was a private organization made up of merchants from more than one nation, and, therefore, like the International African Association, was somewhat safe from criticism. Leopold himself was not associated directly with the commercial undertaking, for Colonel Strauch was to be president of the *Comité*. However, Strauch's position as successor to Greindl in the secretary generalship of the Association and presidency of the Belgian national committee indicated how Leopold's agents were assuming control of both the International Association and the *Comité d'études du Haut Congo*.

As chance would have it, the course of events played into Leopold's hands. While Stanley was on route to the Congo, word was received that the group of Dutch merchants forming the *Handels Vereeniging*, which had contributed heavily to the Committee funds, had gone bankrupt. The successors of the company requested that the *Comité* refund the subscriptions made by their predecessors. Sanford advised that the expedition be called back. The king, however, chose another course, having his banker propose that the Committee refund every subscription and that it be dissolved according to Article XIX of the statutes.[10] Leopold himself, in conjunction with any merchants who wished to continue to subscribe, would personally underwrite the expedition. This solution was accepted, and on November 17, 1879, the *Comité* voted itself out of existence.[11] Later, an International Association of the Congo was formed to act as heir to the *Comité*. The interlocking of its directorate with that of the International African Association led, as Leopold probably intended, to a confusion of the two; strictly speaking, later diplomatic negotiations were undertaken in the name of the International Association of the Congo.

Leopold's approach to the problem of gaining a colony was along a devious path. The steps he took were not worked out on a time-table, although in hindsight they fall together neatly enough to suggest they were pre-arranged. The monarch was not sure of the course events would take and therefore established as many avenues for action as possible in hopes that somewhere an opening might be afforded him. When it was, he did not hesitate to act with daring despite the risks involved. The failure of the Dutch company was perhaps the turning point. The African Association allowed Leopold to act on that continent, and the *Comité* had served as a bridge from international altruism to commercial activities. The dissolution of the *Comité* freed him from the clause of its constitution which forbade all political aims. The International Association of the Congo was international only in its name which, in combination with the identity of its personnel with that of the International African Association, permitted it to operate relatively freely. Henceforth, Leopold would be at liberty to achieve his political goals protected by the disguise provided by an international organization. The king was prepared for the opportunity, for he had taken care to have Stanley under contract to him personally as well as to the *Comité*. Now the stations and large tracts of land that Stanley was to acquire for the non-existent Committee would revert to Leopold.

5.2 COMPETITION AND NEGOTIATION

While Stanley was making his trip across Africa, another explorer was also active in the Congo region. He was Count Savorgnan de Brazza, an adventurous Italian who had become an ensign in the French navy. When in 1879 Brazza requested financial aid for a new expedition, Jules Ferry, the great French imperialist who was then minister of education and thus in control of the Office of Scientific Missions, persuaded the French chambers to grant 100,000 francs to the French national committee of the International African Association.

In presenting his bill, Ferry referred to the western portion of the Congo basin as 'essentially a French land' and made it clear that the French did not intend to avoid national gains, although like Leopold they were willing to use the International Association to mask their activities in the Congo.[12] It is believed that about this time a secret arrangement was made between the French committee of the Association and the French government that, instead of the blue and gold flag of the International Association, the tricolor of France would fly over the stations. The pretext for such a change was that only under the flag of an established nation could stations experience security.[13]

The race for the Congo was on when Brazza left France in December 1879. Strauch urged Stanley forward, warning him that Brazza planned to descend the Alima River to its junction with the Congo and to claim the Upper Congo region before Stanley could do so. Stanley refused to hasten, however, preferring to build roads and stations on his way to Stanley Pool. Relations between the explorer and the Belgian national committee became strained; and, in face of the American's obstinate deliberateness and questions concerning the alleged philanthropic nature of the expedition, Leopold occasionally had to relax his pressure.[14]

Thus Belgium and France were already in tacit conflict over the Congo by the end of 1879. The façade of international scientific exploration continued to be employed, but only because both Ferry and Leopold were using it to veil their activities. Brazza reached Stanley Pool in the fall of 1880 well ahead of Stanley, founded a post on the north bank, and then journeyed on down the Congo. He met Stanley, therewith learning that the direct route along the Congo to the sea was pre-empted, and immediately decided to locate a good alternative route to the Atlantic, which route he found to lie in the valleys of the Niari and Kouilou rivers. Leopold, of course, feared French possession of the Stanley Pool area would cut off Belgian access to the deep interior and the richest part of his prospective colony. Belgian representatives of the Association in the Lower Congo were therefore instructed to amputate Brazza's means of access by gaining control of the Atlantic littoral as far north as Loango, including the mouth of the Kouilou River.

Leopold's hopes remained alive, for Brazza failed to complete his discovery by traveling the full length of the Kouilou to the ocean. At the end of 1882 Stanley, who had returned to Europe for rest, was on his way again, this time with instructions to establish stations on both sides of the Congo as well as on the Niari and Kouilou rivers. Apparently in order to make Leopold's actions seem less blatant and perhaps to avoid an incident which might embarrass the king in his own country, it was stipulated that no Belgians should staff the stations on the right bank of the Congo.[15] On December 6, after Leopold had learned of French annexation of certain Congo territories, he wrote:

The goal of the Committee, in establishing itself at the mouth of the Kouilou and on the Niari, is to be able to open a free route on the left bank of the Congo. The concessions on the right bank will serve in the eventual negotiations with the French.[16]

The new acquisitions, then, were intended to be exchanged for the dropping of French claims on the left bank route. There was another possibility, however. If the Portuguese made good their claims on the mouth of the Congo, the Belgians might try to keep control of the Kouilou valley and thus maintain access to Stanley Pool. The incentives were strong, and by May 1883 the Association could evidence its claims on the Niari-Kouilou region with such stations as Baudoinville, Franktown, and Philippeville.

The first overt national act may be attributed to France. During his explorations in the neighborhood of Stanley Pool, Brazza persuaded the chief of the Batékés to sign a treaty giving land to France, 'to whom he cedes his hereditary rights of sovereignty; agreeing, as sign of this cession, to fly the colors of France'.[17] On October 3, 1880, Brazza signed a similar treaty with all the local chiefs of the area. When the treaties were brought before the French chamber at the end of 1882, they were greeted with cheers and approved under a declaration of urgency. Brazza was the hero of the country; the chambers enthusiastically voted 1,275,000 francs for a new expedition.

Leopold and his associates were also busy arranging treaties. For a few pieces of cloth, the chieftains of Vivi ceded their lands and 'all sovereign right'. The extensive nature of the commercial monopolies Leopold obtained was shielded from public view; slowly he was building an impressive commercial empire. If other countries raised questions, Leopold fell back on the protective words 'international' and 'scientific'. In 1882 Portugal, nervous for her vague but age-old claims on the west coast of Africa, demanded explanation of the activities of Brazza and Stanley. Strauch simply replied that, as far as he knew, Brazza 'had a mission from the French Committee of the Association, and grants from the French executive', while 'Stanley, on the contrary, is in the service of the International Committee of Science'.[18]

By fall of that year, however, Leopold realized that a commercial or purely scientific enterprise would be insufficient to counter the French threat. Though the monarch was gaining increasing support from his own subjects, the political implications of Brazza's claims and the awakening of public interest in colonial affairs in France posed dangers. Paul Leroy-Beaulieu, the noted French economist and expansionist, was urging that France act decisively, or otherwise she might descend 'to the

THE BELGIAN CONGO, 1959

FRENCH EQUATORIAL AFRICA

SUDAN (FR.)

Libenge · Eondo ·
Lisala · Aketi · ① Buta · Paulis ·
· Mungbere
PRO·VINCE
ORIENTE·LE · Irumu ①
EQUATEUR
COQUIL-HATVILLE ⊙ STANLEY-VILLE
Boende · Ponthier-ville
COSTER-MANSVILLE ⊙
① Inongo · KIVU · RUANDA
LAKE LEOPOLD · ① Kigali
· Kindu · USUM-BURA ⊙ · ① Kitega
URUNDI
BRAZZA-VILLE ⊙ · Kigoma
LEOPOLD- Port- · Kasongo
LEOPOLD-VILLE ⊙ Kikwit ① Francqui KASAI · Kongolo
· Lusambo · Kabinda ①
CABINDA (PORT.) · Tshela Luebo ① · Albert-ville
· Boma · Thysville LULUA-BOURG ①
· Matadi · Manona
ANGOLA (PORT.) KATANGA · Abercorn
· Kamina ① · Bukama
LAKE MOERO
· Tenke
· Diloto · Kolwezi · Jadot-ville LAKE BANGWEOLO
NORTHERN RHODESIA
· ELISABETH-VILLE ⊙
· Sakania

LAKE ALBERT
LAKE EDWARD
LAKE TANGANIKA

500 MI.
500 KM.

⊕ COLONIAL CAPITALS
⊙ PROVINCIAL CAPITALS
① DISTRICT CAPITALS

FRENCH
· Franktown
EQUATORIAL
· Philippeville AFRICA
· Baudouin-ville
BRAZZA-VILLE ⊙
STANLEY POOL
LEOPOLD-VILLE ⊙
CABINDA (PORT.)
CONGO FREE STATE
CABINDA ①
YELLALA FALLS
· Boma · Matadi
· Banana
LOWER CONGO
ANGOLA (PORT.)
1885

100 MI.
100 KM.

T. R. MILLER

rank of Belgium, but of a Belgium fallen, disquieted, tormented by the splendor of its past and the nullity of its present and its future'.[19] Political claims would trump those of a commercial nature. So it was that in October Leopold ceased to emphasize the latter and gave attention to bolstering the territorial and political aspects of his accords.

The desire of France to strengthen her hold on the stations established by the French national committee of the International Association, and Leopold's own shift of emphasis, partially explain the agreement of November 1882 by which the stations were ceded to the French government. Documentation is scarce, yet it seems reasonable to accept also the suggestion of R. S. Thomson that a bargain was involved.[20] Several weeks before the actual cession occurred, Charles Duclerc, French minister of foreign affairs and head of the government, informed Leopold that:

Following the desire which Your Majesty... expressed to me, it is agreed that no obstacle will be brought to bear upon the relations between the stations established or to be established by the International African Association and the Committee for Studies of the Upper Congo. The passage from one to another of these said stations, through the territory situated between Stanley Pool and the Impila and Djoue rivers, will not be submitted to any change or impediment by us, either in reference to personnel or to articles carried in transit.[21]

The king promptly expressed his satisfaction with the arrangement.

Probably Leopold had agreed to the change of control of the stations in return for the right of passage. In fact, the wording of Duclerc's message suggests that Leopold initiated the talks. The king may have felt that France would take the French committee's stations in any case but would prefer acting with the consent of the Association. Leopold did not yet have control of the Kouilou valley; should the Portuguese succeed in their claims on the Congo mouth, it would be well for the Association to have some assurance of access to the interior. Such entrance could only be to the north of the Congo, and that necessitated good relations with France, which in turn meant some sacrifice.

This apparent bargain between Leopold and Duclerc was followed by a brief attempt to improve relations further, but the contest for the Kouilou brought the effort to a halt. Soon munitions, rifles, and cannon were being shipped from France and Belgium to the Congo. Leopold, hoping to get a strangle-hold on all routes to the interior, instructed his agents to establish control over certain strips of land so that 'it will be impossible to go from Stanley Pool to the sea without crossing the territories [or the Association]...'.[22]

On February 21, 1884, the signing of an Anglo-Portuguese treaty was announced. According to its clauses, Portugal was to have the territory around the mouth of the Congo, while a joint Anglo-Portuguese commission would patrol the river. The outcry from the other powers was instantaneous; opposition developed within the British parliament, and Portugal, unable to withstand the pressure exerted on her, dropped hints that perhaps an international conference should be held. In the end neither the Cortes nor the Commons were to vote on the treaty. It was a close call for Belgium and France, for neither wanted the Congo controlled by a third nation. This is not to say that Leopold was as concerned as were the French, for with the aid of his friend, the Prince of Wales, he had prodded British Foreign Secretary Lord Granville to insert modifications in the treaty which partially protected Association holdings, especially at Vivi.[23]

While Europe debated the Anglo-Portuguese treaty, Brazza was renewing his treaties with Makako at Stanley Pool. By asserting that Makako's control extended to the left bank of the pool and by obtaining the marks of some chieftains who periodically dwelt in that area, Brazza was able to make pretensions on both banks of the pool, whereas earlier he had only claimed the right bank. For France the import of Brazza's achievement was that now France possessed a bargaining tool with which, although it was weak, she might wrest control of the Kouilou valley from the Association.

With France and Belgium at loggerheads and nearly all the nations of Western Europe protesting a treaty which appeared to give that colossus of imperialism, England, an important foothold in a precious colonial area (for Portugal was seen merely as a puppet of perfidious Albion), news of a Franco-Association agreement, which visibly shifted the power arrangement in respect to the Congo, came as a shock to the diplomats of Europe. On April 23, 1884, Strauch, as president of the International Association of the Congo, communicated the following statement to Jules Ferry, now French premier and minister of foreign affairs.

The International Association of the Congo, in the name of the stations and free territories which it has founded in the Congo and in the valley of the Niari-Kouilou, formally declares that it will not cede those possessions to any power, reserving the particular conventions which may be made between France and the Association in order to fix the limits and the conditions of their respective activity. Nevertheless, the Association, desiring to give new proof of its friendly sentiments for France, agrees to give her the right of preference if, by unforeseen circumstances, the Association were led one day to liquidate its possessions.[24]

To the rest of Europe such an arrangement seemed like giving the entire deck of cards to France, for none of Leopold's competitors expected the

International Association to last. Henceforth, France was considered the power to be watched and limited.

Franco-Belgian relations had apparently completed a full circle, from friendship to enmity and back to friendship again. How had this happened and why had this peculiar, internally contradictory document been drafted? To this date little material has been published which sheds light upon these questions. Thomson asserts that France initiated the discussion and that the important second clause of the agreement was added by Leopold after Strauch had completed the reply.[25]

The motivations of Ferry and Leopold are evident, however. Ferry, in his circular to foreign office ministers, explained that the arrangement would facilitate the work of government agents in Africa and would save them from the disruption of competition; furthermore, the danger that a third power might suddenly appear in place of the Association of the Congo was avoided. Ferry expected the agreement would only be the first in a series of negotiations with the Association; and, most important, he was confident the financially embarrassed Association would fail in the near future. Finally, delicate negotiations had been in process since December concerning projects in Indo-China, and a minor factor influencing the premier's decision may have been a wish to avoid a Congo incident which might jeopardize his current strong position before the chambers.

Leopold, however, had no intention of giving way in the Congo. Therefore, surrendering option rights on Association holdings was no great loss. It may be granted he did lose some of his freewheeling liberty of action, but he made considerable gains in return. The king told the German minister that the preference clause, 'had been introduced at our request to prevent Portugal from pursuing us with attacks which could, if she discouraged us, assure her of France as a neighbor...'.[26] The Belgian well knew the small country would not relish such a situation. But Leopold was after bigger game than just Portugal, although he did not admit it. His arrangement on April 23 freed him from competition from Britain and Germany as well as from Portugal. Those countries, which might have profited from, and possibly were working for, a dissolution of the Association, would henceforth rally to its aid in order to prevent Association property from reverting to France. Thus the king was, in a sense, securing his tenure by designating his successor.

The agreement of April 1884 (it was not a treaty and therefore did not have to be ratified) can be viewed as an attempt by two clever diplomatists to outwit each other. Judging it in this light, it is now clear that Leopold was the winner. Yet at the time this was not obvious; all of Europe saw the arrangement as a French triumph.

The day before Strauch sent his note to Paris, the United States granted full recognition to the International Association of the Congo as the government of the Congo. How Leopold achieved this is a story in itself. The king was indebted to the work of Henry S. Sanford and to ignorance on the part of the United States Senate of the facts in the case. Sanford, as a former American minister to Belgium, enjoyed the confidence of the Senate; amidst a confusion of the titles of the *Comité d'études du Haut Congo*, the International African Association, and the International Association of the Congo, he cajoled the senators into passing the measure. They were apparently persuaded by three counts: belief that the independent states to be established in the Congo would eventually become replicas of the Republic of Libera, faith in Leopold's assurances of free trade and suppression of the slave traffic, and pride in the exploits of their fellow American, Stanley. It appears Leopold purposely misled the Americans regarding the monopolistic nature of his Congo treaties; indeed, his *laissez-faire*'ism can be traced to his decision of April 1883 that only by espousing free trade could he hope to win sufficient support in the British Commons to scuttle the Anglo-Portuguese pact.[27]

The recognition proved a precedent and embarrassed Ferry's position. The premier had upheld the view that the Association was not entitled to be treated as a state. It was repeatedly insisted that the Franco-Association notes comprised *arrangements*, not *engagements*, and that they in no way implied recognition of the Association of the Congo. The Frenchman's argument that a private organization should not achieve sovereignty seemed based on firm grounds of international law, but his own actions in dealing with the Association undercut his position. Despite Ferry's efforts to prevent further recognitions, by the end of December 1884 sovereign status had been granted the Association by Germany, Great Britain, Austria-Hungary, and the Netherlands.[28] Thanks to the weakening of the French position due to Ferry's own act of dealing with the Association and to the powers' sudden distrust of France, Leopold's Association was now better situated to dispute with France than it had been for several months.

The opportunity to advocate its claims was given the Association during the Berlin Conference of 1884–85. The initial suggestion of an international congress had come from Portugal in May as a response to the protests over the Anglo-Portuguese treaty. The idea was well received by Bismarck and Ferry, and it was agreed a conference should be called to discuss freedom of commerce and formalities of occupation in the Congo basin.

One of the reasons Bismarck was willing to deal with France was his anger with Britain over Angra-Pequena, a small area in South West

Africa which was claimed by both Germany and England. He suggested to the French ambassador that it might be well for Britain to realize that a Franco-German naval alliance was not an impossibility.[29] The chancellor's relations with Lord Granville improved markedly, however, when in communicating about the proposed conference Bismarck found that England favored free trade along the African coast and on the Congo River. Free trade was to German advantage; Bismarck had called for it in his negotiations with France but had met opposition from Ferry, who desired as much French control as possible in the Congo basin. As a result of his discovery that England also wanted free trade, Bismarck failed to support France as firmly as Ferry had hoped. Though Germany was bound by the negotiations begun with France before the announcement of the April 23 arrangement, Bismarck knew that the Franco-Association of the Congo agreement meant the power to watch was no longer Britain but France. Leopold, aware of Bismarck's concern for free trade in the Congo, urged the establishment of as large a free trade zone as possible. He thus hoped to win generous borders for his state and the support of the German chancellor. Franco-German relations cooled rapidly and on November 8 Bismarck secretly recognized the International Association of the Congo.[30]

The Berlin Conference met the following week. The agreement between France and Germany stipulated that territorial matters would not be taken up. Therefore, the direct results of the meetings were merely conventions dealing with commercial affairs and the protection of the natives. Despite the narrowness of the discussions, it was nevertheless through the conference that the Association finally was established as a sovereign government with its own boundaries. For this Leopold owed thanks to Bismarck. It was the German who insisted that the territorial questions which hovered over the discussions be settled by the end of the conference and who pressured Britain, by threatening her position on the Niger, to recognize Leopold's organization and thus ensure its place before the powers.[31]

Outside the conference, Leopold was experiencing difficulty in his negotiations. Following the April understanding, France had offered exchange of her claims on the left bank of the Congo for possession of the Kouilou valley; talks had broken off when a dispute arose over arbitration procedures. During December the Portuguese, with whom Leopold also had to deal, rejected a settlement which had been proposed by Germany and England at the instigation of the Association. As the year drew to a close, Leopold, in what the French viewed as his last-ditch effort, sent two of his best diplomats, Eugène Pirmez and Emile Banning, to deal with Ferry; Sanford and Lambermont also appeared to plead the cause unofficially. The French, meanwhile, were becoming increasingly sure that the Association would soon founder in its morass of debt and approached the talks with a confident and condescending manner.

The Belgians came to Paris in a difficult position, despite German and American recognition of the Association and the promise of similar action by Britain.[32] France and Portugal were adamant, and the longer they remained firm the more time ran out on the Berlin Conference and the king's dreams and finances. A few years before, Leopold had expected to use his possessions north of the Congo as bargaining tools; when events had proceeded well for him in the Kouilou valley and at Berlin, he briefly hoped to retain permanently some of those areas. Now the ruler reverted to his original plan. He knew he could not continue to rely on Bismarck carrying his load for him; reaching a settlement with France was the Association's own affair and was all the more important because if agreement were obtained, the Association would be finally assured of life. In a state close to desperation, Leopold vowed that if France did not drop her claims on the left bank of the Congo and indemnify the Association for the Niari-Kouilou region, he would order his stations burned and abandon the Congo to the great powers. After learning of a rumor that France and Portugal planned to seize Congo territories at the end of the conference, Leopold wrote Lambermont that were such to occur:

I am irrevocably determined instantly to give leave to all my personnel in Africa after having ordered the destruction of all materials and to withdraw myself completely. I do not believe I have the right, as King of the Belgians, to expose my country to the consequences of a battle which I as an individual would have to wage in Africa against two powers, both friends of Belgium and one a guarantor of her neutrality.[33]

During the first round of the negotiations, Leopold's men made their offer; the Association would cede the entire Niari-Kouilou valley to France for an indemn y of five million francs, which sum obviously was meant to relieve theiAssociation's financial difficulties. Ferry refused to pay the large amount and during the second session offered instead to pay 300,000 francs as purchase price of the Association stations in that area. In addition, he promised to recognize the Association and to take its part in the dispute with Portugal; as a sort of *pourboire* Ferry accepted Pirmez's suggestion of an Association lottery in France to raise funds. The Belgian delegates repaired to Brussels where they easily gained Leopold's consent to the arrangement.[34]

Ferry, however, decided that the Franco-Association agreement would not be signed until Portugal also came to terms. Seeing an opportunity to prolong the strain on the Association, the Frenchman scarcely acted the part of a mediator, much less that of a pro-Association mediator, in the Portuguese-Association parleys. But Leopold's structure refused to collapse and Ferry grew tired of the game. There was opposition in the chambers to his entente with Germany; fighting had broken out in Indo-China. Perhaps what influenced him the most were warnings that it would be better for France to support Leopold than to risk anarchy or perhaps the founding of an independent state like Liberia.[35] Apparently the premier now suspected France might have difficulty in inheriting the Association's holdings. A final factor was Portugal's current attempt to occupy both banks of the Congo.

Negotiations were resumed, and on February 5, 1885, a treaty was signed recognizing the Association of the Congo as a sovereign government. France was granted control of the Kouilou region, boundaries were fixed, and assurances were given that the neutrality of the Association would be respected. Notes were also exchanged indicating French willingness to allow a twenty million franc lottery in France, promising French support of the Association against Portugal, and arranging for a commission to determine the amount France should pay for the ceded stations.

Ferry now proved true to his word; at his instigation the powers put combined pressure on Portugal, and on February 15 the little state gave way. By the treaty of that date the Association kept control of twenty kilometers of coast north of the river and also the ports of Bannana and Boma. Portugal in turn recognized the Association, received most-favored-nation status, and won possession of Malemba and Cabinda north of the Congo and of the left bank of the river as far inland as Noki. Permission was granted the Association to build a railway to the coast over Portuguese land along the left bank.[36]

The International Association of the Congo was recognized by the Belgian chambers on February 23, 1885, and two days later it signed the final Act of the Berlin Conference. By this Act the Association was granted sovereignty over a great portion of the Congo basin and Central Africa as far east as Lake Tanganyika. The Association further gained control of the direct route along the river to the interior as well as the best coastal port. Commercial equality of all nations in the Congo region, free trade for at least twenty years, and free navigation of the river were established; clauses concerning the abolition of the slave trade were also included in the act. In the months after the conference, the Association transformed itself into the Congo Free State. The Belgian parliament, as required by the constitution, granted Leopold permission to assume the sovereignty of the state. The awkwardness of his simultaneous possession of this position and of the Belgian throne was somewhat lessened by the

Congo State's declaration of neutrality in international affairs in August of 1885, in accordance with the opportunity to that effect afforded states of the Congo Basin by Article X of the Berlin Act.

5.3 LEOPOLD'S DIPLOMACY

Despite the odds, Leopold had won a huge colony for himself and for Belgium. This success was based to a considerable extent upon the approach used by the king, and it was his diplomatic style that, above all, aided him in both influencing and tricking the powers into granting him the colony.

The Belgian's approach was imaginative and far reaching, so much so that at one point Bismarck termed Leopold's schemes fantastic. The breadth of his views was almost staggering; for example, he often talked of establishing a colony ranging from Zanzibar to the Nile. This was dreaming, but the point to be noted is that Leopold could conceive such a project and come as close as he eventually did to achieving it. The concept of a Congo State, nominally independent but actually a Belgian colony, and the idea of an International African Association which could be utilized as a mask for national activities were products of an exceptionally fertile mind.

Another indication of the great scope of Leopold's diplomacy was his concern with more than immediate problems. Although Leopold often had to concern himself with detailed matters and had to make temporizing, *ad hoc* decisions, his attention was always directed toward a definite, though distant, goal. His arguments for a colony centered on the rewards Belgium would obtain in years to come, and he was willing to wait out innumerable delays and to make great sacrifices in the present for those gains. This direction of policy toward goals far in the future was an important dimension in Leopold's performance and one that was an innovation in Belgian diplomacy, which heretofore had concentrated on the present in hopes the future would care for itself.

A further characteristic of Leopold's diplomacy illustrative of its scope was his willingness to deal with a problem at all levels and by all avenues. Thus the dimension of depth was joined with the length of view and breadth of the king's diplomatic approach. Leopold did not attack a problem from one angle only, but from all sides at once, encircling it and probing for an opening. He tried international philanthropic associations, commercial expeditions, purely national activities (but the Belgian chambers could not be persuaded to support imperialism), squatter's rights, military activities, and plain negotiation. In his diplomacy Leopold did not limit his field of action, freely dealing both in and out of conferences not only with the powers directly involved in the conflict, but also with such nations as Germany and the United States. The importance of the recognition obtained from the last mentioned country, an event that Ferry apparently had not even considered, is evidence of the value of Leopold's tactic.[37] Nor did the king fail to include among his associates whatever men might be helpful to him; some of his most useful agents were the businessmen in Germany, Britain, and the United States who agitated against the Anglo-Portuguese treaty and stirred support for the supposedly free-trading Association.

Leopold's style was dynamic and active. Knowingly or not, he followed Richelieu's advice that a diplomat should negotiate without ceasing, openly and secretly, and whether or not he could foresee any hopes of his work ever bearing fruit in the present or in the future. Discussions with the French were continually breaking down, yet nearly every break was followed by renewed efforts and an agreement. And while he was negotiating in Paris, the king did not forget to deal in London, Berlin, Washington, or Stanley Pool. If an event occurred which challenged his project, as when his colony's path to the sea was threatened, Leopold did not sit by, but acted swiftly, in this case to get control of the Kouilou valley. The fruits of his activity, for example the some forty-five stations established in the Niari-Kouilou area as compared to France's two or three, were considerable and helped influence United States senators and Bismarck to acknowledge the Association.[38] With Leopold ideas and action marched hand in hand, and the king's determination to achieve his goal, despite whatever obstacle, had much to do with his success.[39]

The Belgian sovereign was always careful to cover his bets. Whenever one gain was made, he quickly moved to ensure its continued safety; this explains his actions in the Kouilou valley and why he allowed the French to take over Association stations in return for a right of passage north of the Congo. Perhaps the best example of this, however, is his prodding of Granville into acknowledging Association rights in the Anglo-Portuguese treaty while at the same time the king secretly stimulated opposition in Britain to that very treaty.[40]

Leopold once wrote:

In colonial matters, policy does not proceed from abstract ideas; it accommodates to the necessities of the moment and modifies itself at the same time as the milieu in which it is applied is being transformed.[41]

This observation concerned Leopold's governing policies in the Congo, but it also describes his diplomacy. Leopold was flexible and opportunistic in his dealings, as is evident from the manner and depth of his approach. The ruler could adapt his imperialism to forms of philanthropy, commercial enterprise, and international diplomacy simultaneously. He was willing and able to change his tack to take advantage of any opening afforded him. Leopold purposely provided himself with alternative approaches so that the chances of a worthwhile opportunity appearing would be increased; when the *Handels Vereeniging* failed, the king saw the possibilities of turning the event to his benefit and did not let himself be influenced by Sanford's cautious advice. Later, he switched rapidly from a monopolistic to a free trade stance in order to improve his project's chance of survival.

Many of the features of Leopold's diplomacy – the sweeping scope, opportunism, activism, and flexibility – indicate that he operated in a bold, daring manner. The king had the courage of his convictions and did not particularly let the risk of financial loss or moral scruples hinder his progress; his evaluation of any action was primarily based on how useful it would be for his purposes. He liked to take the initiative or offensive. This can be seen from his founding of the several associations and from the way he spurred his agents in the Kouilou valley, where a defensive measure was turned into a counter-attack which nearly succeeded in winning permanent possession of lands Leopold originally planned to occupy only briefly for bargaining purposes. One of his favorite techniques was continually to make new moves, thus keeping his opponents off-balance and creating the confused situation in which he could best operate. Thanks to this confusion, the stations established by his own International Association of the Congo were able to fly the blue flag of the International Association for the Exploration and Civilization of Central Africa, an important step in Leopold's taking over of the latter's properties and one that probably did not bother his conscience. Certainly, too, the confusion of associations helped Sanford in gaining United States recognition of Leopold's enterprise.

It should not be thought that because Leopold was imaginative and bold he was not a realist. On the contrary, he never let his ambitions cloud his sight, although they might create magnificent dreams. He knew his limitations but was sly enough not to let his competitors think he did; this was one reason he managed to get so far before the powers took him seriously. He realized his Belgian subjects would not support his ventures, and rather than waste years wooing their permission, he created various organizations which would not offend them. He knew that in the end Belgium would accept the Congo as a colony. Leopold was aware of the opposition he would encounter from the powers in reaching for a colony and therefore was circumspect in picking both his field and manner of action. He yielded in some matters because he believed a few battles might have to be lost if ultimate victory were to be achieved. Thus, concessions to France served to win Belgium the sympathy of the powers while Leopold did not lose too much, for he had earlier compensated for such losses by using the techniques of hedging his bets and demanding far more than he expected to receive at the final settlement.

One of the most interesting aspects of Leopold's diplomacy was the use of international humanitarian organizations. They served him both as a tool and as a costume with which to clothe his activities. The exploration associations were not easily open to criticism and were well fitted to the temper of the times; the idea of progress furthered by scientific investigation and sharpened curiosity concerning the nature of far away lands had caused, for example, the number of geographical societies in France to grow from the single organization of 1871 to the thirteen or more active societies in 1881. In dealing with the powers, Leopold was careful to talk only in terms of what measures would be necessary to further discovery and to eliminate the slave trade. In later years, when the king was obtaining permission from Bismarck to make claims in areas around Lake Tanganyika and the Bahr-el-Ghazel, both men's correspondence referred explicitly only to energetic measures of 'every kind' to suppress the slave trade.[42] This combination of altruism and internationalism was a useful tool of imperialism.

Leopold II has been praised as a king who was more skilled than the professionals in many activities; in no area was his skill more outstanding than in diplomacy. In winning tiny Belgium a colony eight times her size, he succeeded in outwitting the diplomats of all the great powers; even Bismarck was caught in a difficult position. The most remarkable feature of this diplomacy was the manner in which Leopold used Belgium's smallness and weakness to advantage. Certainly far more eyebrows would have been raised in skepticism had the English announced an international foundation which would use funds from every country to explore the Sudan. But Belgium was little, neutral, apparently happy with her lot, and seemed to have only the most honorable and mild intentions; little suspicion was therefore directed toward the Association's executive committee in Brussels. Even after Leopold had long been active in the Congo, only one foreign diplomat, a Portuguese, thought the king planned to set up more than a temporary commercial enterprise.[43] When eventually the king's designs were clear to all, no single power could, in good conscience, or without fear of reprisals from another power or combination of powers, deprive Leopold of too much of his colony. Another advantage, gained from Belgium's newness to imperialism, was that Leopold could at that time concentrate the major portion of his funds and attention in one area, while Ferry had to care for many far spread colonial interests.

By the time the Conference of Berlin had closed, France was particularly aware of how Leopold could and would use Belgium's weakness to enlist the aid of Europe and embarrass his opponents. A few years later, when the French were angry over Leopold's sending of troops north from the Congo into the Nile area, the ministry of colonies had to warn those that called for precipitate action that:

In the eyes of civilized nations we would have little glory and an appearance, certain to be severely interpreted in Europe, of a great power abusing her strength against a little state in pretending to wipe out in one blow the incontestable lead taken by the efforts of King Leopold . . . through admitted sacrifices for a work which, despite its commercial character, has been able to pass itself off in Europe as highly civilizing.[44]

In another situation in 1894, however, the French took care to see that Leopold was 'constrained and forced' to give way.[45]

Leopold's chief triumph was that over Ferry, and his most skillful moves were the agreement of April 1884 and the winning of recognition from the United States and Germany. The United States recognition was clearly the result of lack of suspicion of Leopold, and the arrangement with France took advantage of Ferry's confidence that the Association would soon collapse. By means of the April accord, Leopold obtained the support of Germany, Britain, and the United States in his contest with France, thus making use of the tried and true tactic of playing the powers off against each other. It was a bold move and perhaps did more than anything else to defeat the French. At the outset, Ferry had the advantage and the strength to follow through, but the was fooled into playing the Belgian's game; and, on April 23, 1884, Leopold arranged the rules so that French strength was Ferry's greatest liability and Belgium's weakness was her greatest asset.

Leopold's success in taking what would come to be considered as the prize colony of Africa from beneath the noses of the European diplomats of course affected Belgium's relations with the powers. She had usually been treated kindly, but after the Berlin Conference the large nations no longer showed quite the same solicitude. Comments were made about guarantees outliving their usefulness, and quarrels were to arise over Belgian activities in the Congo. In succeeding years, Belgium saw her special relationship with England weakened and her efforts to establish friendly ties with the French Third Republic fall short of success. The Congo adventure was far from entirely responsible for this, yet it had an influence. Leopold was increasingly forced to take heed that his actions not embarrass Belgium. He could not ignore French threats in 1894 to open 'the Belgian question' or British rumblings in 1905 which suggested his personal activities might cause reconsideration of Belgium's neutral status.[46] While he made some further gains in the Sudan, frequently his propositions were turned down or his successes, such as an agreement with England in 1894, were not allowed to bear fruit. The years following his triumph in 1885 proved bitter for the sovereign of the Congo State. His unique diplomatic style had won the Congo but lost much of its effectiveness as a result of the victory.

The reason for this was that Leopold's best cards, the powers' lack of suspicion and the utilization of international organizations for his own purposes, could be played only once in a generation before losing their trumping quality. Nor could the cry that a great power was using its strength against Belgium unfairly have quite the same effect now Leopold had succeeded in taking one of the richest areas of Africa (and not by entirely scrupulous means at that).

The fact remains that Leopold's diplomacy had won a colony for his small state. It was a diplomacy that was imaginative, creative, active, bold, flexible, utilitarian, and fully developed in all its dimensions, although because of the techniques by which it moved it lost some of its astonishing efficacy with use. The approach and methods Leopold employed were ones that, in many respects, could have been used by almost any small state willing to risk some money; indeed some of them had been successfully essayed by Rogier, De Theux, and other Belgian diplomats. The most important factor in the winning of the Congo Free State for Belgium was, however, not so much any specific technique but the genius of the colony's founder, Leopold II.

5.4 NOTES

1. De Lichtervelde, *Leopold of the Belgians*, p. 33.
2. 'Leopold to Lambermont, Aug. 22, 1875', quoted in Roeykens, 'Les débuts', pp. 95–96.
3. Stengers, 'Textes inédits d'Emile Banning', p. 33.
4. This and the following quotation are from Boulger, *The reign of Leopold II*, vol. I, pp. 129–130.
5. *Mitteilungen der Afrikanischen Gesellschaft in Deutschland*, vol. II (1880–1881), p. 52. An examination of the British position may be found in Anstey, *Britain and the Congo in the Nineteenth Century*.
6. Greindl's letter to Lambermont of Oct. 14, 1876 and the reply of five days later are reproduced in Roeykens, 'Les débuts', pp. 164–167.
7. Quoted in Van Zuylen, *L'Echiquier congolais*, pp. 43–44. While writing his account, Van Zuylen had access to portions of the royal family archives. It is believed, however, that a majority of the most confidential documents on the Congo affair were burned under Leopold's direction.

8. Stanley, *The Congo*, vol. I, p. 2.
9. *Ibid.*, vol. I, p. 27.
10. This article gave the council of the *Comité* the right to dissolve the organization, provided due notice were given, if satisfactory dividends were not obtained and if prospects were poor.
11. The protocol of this meeting is published in 'Aus den Archiven. Zwei bisher unbekannte Dokumente', pp. 305–306.
12. France, *Journal officiel (JORF)*, Aug. 17, 1879, p. 1533.
13. Thomson, *Fondation*, p. 80. News that the French flag would be flown was made public the following August. See report of De Lesseps, including a note by Mizon, in Académie des Sciences, Institut de France, *Comptes rendus*, vol. 91, p. 424. Thomson's book is the best on the subject. Also useful are Masoin, *Histoire de l'Etat indépendant du Congo* and Daye, *Stanley*.
14. Stanley's notes of c. Oct. 1880 questioning Leopold's altruism and the reply of Dec. 31, 1880, indicating the *Comité* no longer insisted Stanley hurry and that a second expedition sent to accelerate Stanley's progress would be recalled, may be found on pp. 1441–1444 of Van Grieken, 'H. M. Stanley au Congo'. Van Grieken's article gives a summary of a catalogue of documents compiled by Notte shortly before the documents themselves were allegedly burned on Leopold's orders.
15. *Ibid.*, pp. 1435–1438: 'Instructions for Stanley, Oct. 30, 1882'.
16. *Ibid.*, p. 1441: '*Comité* to Stanley, Dec. 6, 1882'.
17. From the text of the treaty in France, *JORF*, Nov. 19, 1882, p. 1646.
18. United States Senate, *Senate Report No. 393*, 48th Congress, 1st session, 1884, p. 40.
19. Leroy-Beaulieu, 'La politique continentale'. See also Stengers, 'Léopold II et la rivalité', pp. 439–440.
20. Apparently Leopold learned in June 1882 what the fate of the stations was to be, although they were not ceded until Nov. 28 (Thomson, *Fondation*, p. 92).
21. France, *Livres jaunes (LJ) (1884)*, *Congo*, no. 1: 'Duclerc to Leopold, Oct. 16, 1882'.
22. Van Grieken, 'H. M. Stanley au Congo', p. 1451: 'Leopold to Stanley, July 2, 1883'. See also Vandeplas, 'Quelques measures', pp. 5–13.
23. Crowe, *The Berlin West African Conference*, pp. 78–79. Fitzmaurice, *Life of Lord Granville*, vol. II, pp. 32–33. 'Aus den Archiven. Zur Entstehungsgeschichte, p. 20. Thomson, *Fondation*, p. 141. France, *LJ (1884)*, *Congo*, no. 15: 'Laboulaye to Ferry, Mar. 15, 1884'. Van Zuylen, *L'Echiquier*, pp. 62–63.
24. France, *LJ (1884)*, *Congo*, no. 17: 'Strauch to Ferry, Apr. 23, 1884'.
25. Thomson, *Fondation*, p. 64.
26. 'Aus den Archiven. Zur Entstehungsgeschichte', p. 25.
27. See United States Senate, *Executive Document No. 196*, 49th Congress, 1st session, 1886; also, *Senate Report No. 393*, 48th Congress, 1st session, 1884, and Crowe, *The Berlin West African Conference*, p. 80. Stengers, 'Léopold II et la rivalité', pp. 434, 455–461.

28. France, *Documents diplomatiques français (DDF) (1871–1914)*, 1st ser., vol. V, pp. 415–416, no. 402: 'Ferry to Courcel, Sept. 19, 1884'; pp. 418–422, no. 405: 'Courcel to Ferry, Sept. 21, 1884'; p. 513, no. 485: 'Ferry to Laboulaye, Dec. 13, 1884'.

29. *Ibid.*, 1st ser., vol. V, pp. 423–425, no. 407: 'Courcel to Ferry, Sept. 23, 1884'.

30. Lambermont papers, II, 'Leopold to Lambermont, Nov. 21, 1884'; 'Same to same, Nov. 22, 1884'.

31. Crowe, *The Berlin West African Conference*, p. 147. Lambermont papers, II, 'Lambermont to Leopold, Nov. 19, 1884'. For conflicting interpretations of the Conference and of Bismarck's role, see Power, *Jules Ferry*, pp. 97–115 and Crowe's book cited above.

32. In return for this last it was expected Leopold would back the English on the Niger question, (see Lambermont papers, II, Dec. 4, 1884).

33. *Ibid.*, Dec. 12, 1884.

34. Banning, *Mémoires politiques*, pp. 36–42.

35. France, *DDF (1871–1914)*, 1st ser., vol. V, p. 582–583, no. 554: 'Courcel to Ferry, Feb. 3, 1885'. This private letter did not reach Paris until after Ferry had made his decision. No doubt similar suggestions had been made earlier.

36. The texts of the Association-France and Association-Portugal treaties may be found in France, *LJ (1885)*, *Congo*, pp. 295–321, 327–331, while that of the Berlin Act may be found in United States Senate, *Miscellaneous Document No. 68*, 49th Congress, 1st session, 1886.

37. Ferry's messages to his minister in Washington, Theodore Roustan, were concerned with gaining American support against the Anglo-Portuguese treaty and did not mention U.S. recognition of the Association; Roustan on his part seemed unaware of its implications, and his note that it was being discussed reached Paris only on April 16. Apparently no last minute efforts were made to prevent recognition (France, *DDF (1871–1914)*, 1st ser., vol. V, pp. 245–246, no. 230: 'Roustan to Ferry, Apr. 4, 1884'; p. 248, no. 233 and note: 'Ferry to Roustan, Apr. 10, 1884').

38. 'Aus den Archiven. L'Etat indépendant', pp. 59–91.

39. Thomson, *Fondation*, p. 316.

40. 'Aus den Archiven. Zur Entstehungsgeschichte', pp. 19–20.

41. Stengers, 'Textes inédits', p. 102.

42. Murphy, *The ideology*, p. 5. 'Aus den Archiven. Das Lado- und Bahr el Ghazel-Pachtgebiet', pp. 139–140.

43. 'Aus den Archiven. Zur Entstehungsgeschichte', pp. 30–32.

44. Blanchard, 'Françaises et Belges', p. 16, note.

45. Langer, *The diplomacy*, vol. I, p. 139. Simar, 'Léopold II et le Soudan', pp. 506–528.

46. Collins, *King Leopold*, pp. 40, 230.

6. Implementation of neutrality

In his book concerning early American thought on foreign affairs entitled *To the Farewell Address*, Felix Gilbert notes an attitude prevalent in the colonies which no doubt appeared naïve to diplomats in the Old World. This was the Americans' tendency to view law and legal relationships as separate from, and not to be influenced by, the concerns of power. The two were irreconcilable; a treaty which, rather than striving to establish a situation of Right, reflected a balance of interests of opposing powers was considered improper.[1] Whether the colonists' view was ideally correct or not, it went against centuries of European experience which showed that nearly all aspects of international relations are functions of power concerns and relationships.

In the first decades of Belgium's history as an independent country, her diplomats seemed well aware of the influence power could have on the interpretation of international agreements. Their efforts to turn the Twenty-four Articles of 1831 into a foundation for Belgium's independence more favorable to their wishes rested on their rallying the support of states whose combined strength would balance or outweigh that of the eastern courts. Having upset the legal order of things by revolution, the Belgians for some time accompanied their *démarches* to the European chancelleries with military demonstrations and bold maneuvers not always within the limits of a strict interpretation of the articles. Later, when subject to the designs of Napoleon III, the Belgians recognized that because of the reluctance of other states to become involved Belgium was at a disadvantage. Therefore, in the customs squabble, the Luxemburg affair, and to some extent during the railway crisis, the Brussels statesmen chose not to defend the full limit of their legal rights; instead, they were cautious and willing to make concessions even though their monarch was more daring in his African adventures.

By the turn of the century, the Belgians were becoming increasingly reliant on a legalistic approach and less interested in the realities of their power position. They expected international law and order to defend them but displayed confusion in considering how they in turn would defend international law. There were some who argued that were Belgium's weight thrown into the European power balance, it would make so little difference that a defense system costly in both money and years of men's lives should not be maintained. Others said that for Belgium to develop her defenses was an affront to the powers who had pledged to protect her. The defeat of France in 1870 had removed the previous decades' source of danger, and many Belgians could not bring themselves to distrust the German vanquisher of their recent enemy. Nor were they fully aware of the extent to which the growth of German strength had altered the European equilibrium. No longer was there a balance among several equals, none of whom wished or dared to act without the acquiescence of the others; Europe was dividing into two armed camps with members of each far more solicitous for the needs and views of their friends than for those of other countries, including small neutrals.

Military preparedness was also gravely affected by the complexities of domestic politics. Despite the electoral reform of 1848, only approximately 100,000 Belgians out of a population of over five million could vote in national elections. The pressure for further reform was great, particularly in the Antwerp region. Socialists and radicals pointed out that since the workers could not meet the financial requirements of the franchise, they were being forced to serve without what they believed should be the reciprocal rights of full citizenship. Moreover, military service weighed disproportionately upon the lower classes, who did not have the funds to purchase substitutes to serve for them, as was the custom among the wealthier classes.

Though many of the bourgeoisie did not favor an extension of the franchise, believing the fortunes of the state were best left in the hands of men of property, the anti-militarism of the lower classes struck a sympathetic chord in them. Since 1830, Belgium had been busy enriching herself, building commerce and industry until she had developed an economic and financial power disproportionate to her size. Economic concerns took second place only to the religious controversy. These suggested a cautious policy to avoid risking all that had been gained; furthermore, to the bourgeoisie of Antwerp and elsewhere, expenditure of money and materials on fortifications that should not be used in any case seemed foolish.

Leopold II's urging of reinforcement of Antwerp was therefore strongly opposed in the middle 1860s. The Catholic party soon found that anti-militarism was a fine tool to use against the ruling Liberals. Chief among the anti-militarists was Victor Jacobs of Antwerp, who greatly formulated the right's opposition to the increase in military reserves (from 100,000 to 120,000 men) finally voted in 1869. The Liberals, fearful of being hurt on this issue, resisted royal proposals for action to increase military preparedness despite the king's protests that the constitution made him responsible as commander-in-chief of the armed forces in time of war for the military protection of the country. The nation was currently at peace, and the defense ministers were more concerned with the political position of the cabinet than with the king's warnings. The conflict inherent in the constitution thus became a problem which eventually took on serious proportions.

The small number of legal electors and their division into strongly loyal Liberal and Catholic factions meant that the shift of even a few independent votes could affect the outcome of elections. Aided by the suffrage and anti-militarism issues, the Catholics finally regained office in 1870. The following year they achieved a minor reduction in the franchise requirements for local elections, the effect of which was to give the Catholic party control of many rural communes, especially in Flanders. Confident in the popularity of its program, the cabinet resisted the king's efforts to correct the weaknesses displayed during the mobilization of 1870. Difficulties between king and cabinet grew until in December of 1871 Leopold dismissed the ministers for failure to maintain order in the country after brief disturbances broke out over a minor scandal. The new cabinet did not contain Jacobs, but many Catholic party members were to remember with rancour the king's dismissal of a cabinet that still apparently held the confidence of the chambers; they would further recall that the real issue was not one of order or religion, but concerned the royal views and prerogatives in military affairs.

Suffrage and religious questions were to hold the center of attention over the next decades, but the differences of opinion on military matters were always tacitly present. They emerged again in 1887 when credits were voted for fortifications along the Meuse, but the king's efforts to increase the reserves and institute a system of personal service, rather than purchase of substitutes, were defeated. Only when he was on his deathbed in 1909 was Leopold II able to sign a bill increasing the Belgian forces, an action far too late in coming given the growing tensions in Europe.

In the years after the Franco-Prussian War, Belgium experienced, as far as international affairs were concerned, a sense of well-being and confidence that led to an attitude of complacency. Everyone could point to what was at first called the 'miracle of 1870' but which later was considered the expected course events would take in any future French-German conflict. Respect for Belgium's integrity and their own commitments to international law and the treaties of 1839 would prevent the combatants from violating Belgian territory. Belgium's repeated declarations of neutrality and modest defensive measures would win the trust of the other nations; finally, Great Britain in fulfillment of her obligations would shelter Belgium under her protective wing, threatening intervention against any country which infringed on Belgium's neutrality. The people saw no need to be alarmist; business, crops, and secular control of education seemed more sensible matters to worry about than wars and armies. At patriotic fêtes orators no longer complained of the restrictions forced on Belgium by her neutrality and other clauses of the objectionable treaties of 1839. Instead, the theme was reliance on law and order and the glories of a neutral and loyal Belgium who, by her responsible behavior, would help repress the spectre of war.

Leopold II and his nephew, Albert, who succeeded to the throne in 1909, did not feel so at ease. They constantly warned that Belgium might not again be as fortunate as in 1870. The military, although divided in its views concerning the possible source of any future attack, stressed the need for further toughening of the country's defenses. Yet their case was neither advocated ardently enough nor taken seriously enough for any significant improvements to be made until dangerously late in the crisis leading to the First World War. Even the diplomats did not show much concern until it became patently clear that the international system of the 1870s and 1880s had experienced some important changes.

It was the Moroccan crisis of 1905 that focused the Belgians' attention on the manner in which Europe had slowly divided during the preceding years of imperialistic rivalry. The Kaiser's visit to Tangiers demonstrated the opposition which had grown up between the German dominated Triple Alliance of Germany, Austria-Hungary, and Italy and the Anglo-French Entente newly formed in 1904. The French rightly calculated that the German intention was to destroy the Anglo-French bond and attempted to hold firm. Antagonism between the two enemies reached a dangerous level, and the possibility of war could not be ruled out. As such a conflict would probably be a life or death struggle, it was conceivable that both powers might throw international law and old promises to the wind and use Belgium as a short cut to their opponent's capital.

The problem for the Belgians was how to prevent this from occurring. What course was best? Should they continue to rely upon their neutrality, and, if so, how should they implement their decision? The path selected by the Belgians was not particularly pleasing to either the Alliance or the Entente. The latter group made two efforts to reach an agreement with Belgium for sending aid to the little country if it were attacked. The manner in which the Belgians dealt with these offers and with the final crisis in August 1914 revealed a full development of the cautious style which first appeared in the 1850s and bore also distinct marks of the Belgians' experiences in 1870. The small concessions made in earlier periods were, however, now replaced by a legalism which at one point led the diplomats to a new and rather strained interpretation of Belgium's duties and the intent of the 1839 treaties. This legalism also required the Belgian diplomats to tread a straight and narrow path and to rely upon carefully constructed statements designed to have particular effects upon the other powers. All public pronouncements were carefully weighed and all actions duly circumspect. As the Belgians became increasingly suspicious and more profoundly committed to a legalistic approach, they at the same time grew sensitive regarding the honor and prestige of their country. Considerable pride was developed in the difficult role which the Belgians believed they were playing so well. It was not until the German invasion of August 1914 that they lost confidence in the adequacy of the protection offered by legalism and scrupulous neutrality.

6.1 THE FRANCO-PRUSSIAN WAR

The debate over who bears what degree of responsibility for the origin of the war of 1870 still continues. There is general agreement, however, that following the Prussian defeat of Austria at Sadowa in 1866 and the formation of the North German Confederation considerations of security, power, and prestige were almost irresistibly pressing Bismarck and Napoleon III toward open conflict. In the atmosphere of tension created by the Luxemburg and railway affairs any new crisis was likely to provoke belligerency. This crisis was provided by the declaration in June 1870 of Leopold of Hohenzollern's candidacy for the vacant Spanish throne.

Under Isabella II, Spain had been in close relations with Napoleon III, supporting his pro-catholic policies and providing reliable security at France's back door. In 1868 Isabella was overthrown and replaced by a provisional government the sympathies of which were much less francophile. A new sovereign was needed, and the Spaniards began their search by approaching the ruling family in Portugal, in hopes of fulfilling their dreams of Iberian Union. When these overtures failed, as did those made to two Italian princes, the provisional government turned to Leopold of Hohenzollern-Sigmaringen. The catholic Leopold was not of the same branch of the House of Hohenzollern as the King of Prussia and was, in fact, more closely related to the Bonapartes. Nevertheless, his ties to Prussia were such that he was universally considered a Prussian prince. His father held the title of Royal Highness and had served at one time as prime minister of Prussia; Leopold himself was an officer in the Prussian army.[2]

As might be expected, French protests against the placing of a Hohenzollern on the throne of Spain were vigorous. The story of the exchanges between the French, Spanish, and Prussian statesmen, the off-again, on-again candidacy of Leopold, the excessive French demands, and Bismarck's editing of the famous Ems telegram properly belongs to a study of the origins of the war which was finally declared on July 19, 1870. These complexities need not be discussed here. The implications of the Franco-German conflict for Belgium's neutrality were foreboding, particularly because the brevity of the contiguous French-German Confederation border and the nature of the terrain meant much of the fighting would take place within a short distance of Belgium. Thus, while the Belgians played a limited role in the diplomacy preceding the outbreak of the war, they were forced to take steps to assure that their neutrality would be respected.

It would be more precise to say King Leopold II acted, for at the time of the international crisis Belgium was involved in domestic difficulties which precluded any fruitful diplomacy by the minister of foreign affairs or the cabinet. A split in the Liberal party during and following the elections of March 30, 1870, had placed the Rogier - Frère-Orban cabinet in an untenable position and caused its resignation on July 2. To the dismay of the king, who had been warning that the country must be unified and prepared to defend itself in the coming crisis, the succeeding premier, the Catholic Baron d'Anethan, insisted on including the antimilitarist Victor Jacobs in his cabinet. The chambers were dissolved and elections scheduled for August 2. Thus, when war broke out between France and Prussia, the Belgian government was in the hands of a newly appointed and inexperienced minority ministry engaged in a sharp electoral campaign which reached its culmination at the same time the Belgian army was mobilizing. Whatever leadership was needed would have to come primarily from the king, who, to a certain extent, was at odds with the new cabinet.

At the secret request of Napoleon III, the king on July 9 wrote personally to Leopold of Hohenzollern (who was his brother Philip's brother-in-law), urging him to end his candidacy. Beyond this there was little Leopold II could do to prevent the outbreak of war, and he henceforth worked to confirm France and Prussia in their old promises to respect Belgium's neutrality. Although the Duke de Gramont, French minister of foreign affairs, had assured Beyens that French troops would not enter Belgium, and Nothomb had reported from Berlin his belief that Prussia and the German Confederation would respect Belgium, Leopold was nervous. On July 13, he wrote his cousin, Queen Victoria, that all he had obtained thus far was not enough. What was needed was a public declaration by each belligerent; a declaration which England alone could obtain as the price of her own neutrality.[3]

The king was anxious to involve the British in the defense of Belgium. Theoretically they were already involved by the treaties of 1839, which treaties also forbade any special agreements between Belgium and another power. Yet Leopold wished to strengthen his hand, and the arrangement he proposed was ideal for his purposes. Belgium and Britain would be making no alliance, yet Belgium would gain one important benefit of an alliance: She would have a fresh commitment from London to fight, not just oppose diplomatically, any invader of the little state. At the same time, proper attitudes in France and Prussia regarding Belgium would be reinforced. A firm statement of support extracted from England now would also be of special value in light of the recent tendencies of the foreign office. The British had, after all, been reluctant to take a hand in the Luxemburg and railway affairs and had shown hesitancies about guaranteeing the duchy. Non-involvement appeared to be the star by which the foreign office was guiding its course.

The reaction in London diplomatic circles to Leopold's proposal was indeed consonant with what had gone before. British Foreign Minister Lord Granville wrote his minister in Belgium, J. Savile Lumley:

All that can be done for Belgium seems to have been accomplished, whatever the worth of it may be. It is probably the best policy now to remain as quiet as possible. Not to ask unnecessary questions or to make complaints unless when absolutely necessary.
Calm for the present is the most dignified and expedient attitude for all neutral Powers great or small. It need not exclude vigilant observation.[4]

Edmund Hammond, the experienced and capable permanent undersecretary at the foreign office, was similarly opposed to any move which might stimulate accusations that Britain was organizing a league of neutrals. Moreover, 'if Prussia and France will not observe their engagements of 1839, neither would they observe any engagement of 1870'.[5] Only Queen Victoria and her knowledgeable secretary, Henry Ponsonby, favored taking action, and although their influence was considerable, Leopold's *démarche* seemed doomed to remain without effect.

On the same day, Victoria wrote Ponsonby she wished 'the government *would do* that about Belgium'. Leopold was writing her the news of the draft of a secret treaty which Bismarck had just shown Nothomb at Berlin.[6] The incriminating document, which dated from 1866, was in the hand of Vincent Benedetti, the French ambassador at Berlin. It seemed to prove conclusively the nature of French designs on Belgium, for Article Four stated that in return for French recognition of all that had occurred in the unification of Germany, the King of Prussia would not oppose Napoleon III if, after conquering Belgium, he were to incorporate that country into France. As Bismarck no doubt suspected when he allowed – perhaps it should be said encouraged – Benedetti to present the draft and then himself laid it aside for future use, its revelation caused anti-French stirs in Brussels and London. The secret draft was, in fact, what saved Leopold's proposal to the British. Shocked by its contents, William E. Gladstone, the British prime minister, became convinced his country could not stand idly by. As he later wrote the Belgian king, he believed 'that amidst many difficulties, the wisest course was to establish a fresh point of departure, and obtain from each belligerent a new and solemn pledge, at a critical moment, and with a practical application, on any violation of which the world would cry shame'.[7]

The British cabinet forthwith invited the belligerents to sign a treaty stating their intention to respect Belgium and which provided that Britain would declare war on whichever state should violate Belgium during the current struggle or in the year following its conclusion. Replies were tantalizingly slow in coming, but by August 9 the necessary signatures were obtained. The Belgian reaction was, as Lumley described it, 'great and genuine' satisfaction for the treaty 'universally considered to be a masterpiece of diplomacy'.[8] But the treaty was not all that Gladstone provided the small country. On July 28 Leopold had written the British prime minister explaining that while the Belgian national bank presently had sufficient reserves for its needs, a loan of a million pounds sterling from the Bank of England would provide still more security. Within a day, Gladstone had contacted the governor and director of the Bank of England, explained what an '*excellent* stroke' such a loan would be and had informed Leopold of both the cabinet's and the bank's favorable reaction.[9] Belgium and Britain were not in alliance, but chance and Leopold's insistence had apparently brought them into a closer relationship than had existed for some time.

The answers of France and Prussia to the British inquiry were not the only written affirmations these countries made of their intent not to invade Belgium. Shortly after the French foreign minister gave his verbal assurance to Leopold, the king received a letter to similar effect from Napoleon III. A written statement by Gramont followed, which asserted France would respect Belgium if Prussia did so also; it was balanced by a private note from Bismarck giving the same promise and making the same reservations. None of these communications had pleased Leopold completely. Only formal declarations made without reticence and based on the treaties of 1839 would be satisfactory. Until the conclusion of the protective treaty he continued to drive this point home to Granville.

Unlike some of his ministers, Leopold was convinced that reliance on diplomacy and the integrity of treaties could go only so far in protecting Belgium in an international scene characterized by open power struggles. He wrote to Victoria that in order Belgium's neutrality 'should continue to be taken seriously abroad, it should be vigorously affirmed at home. Our conduct should and will be such that no one will be tempted to pass our way'.[10] The Belgian army was mobilized; several thousand horses were bought, the fortress at Antwerp garrisoned, and by the end of August nearly 95,000 infantry were guarding the frontiers. Two days after the outbreak of war, Prime Minister d'Anethan telegraphed his representatives abroad that Belgium was guarding the routes from Prussia to France which passed through her territory, 'based by honor as we are not to permit their use by any of the belligerent forces'.[11] Foreign soldiers who crossed the border would immediately be arrested and interned until the end of the war. Though the possibility of difficulties arising in this connection were great, few in fact did develop. Following the Prussian victory at Sedan, the fleeing French were too demoralized to resist arrest (indeed many sought refuge in Belgium), and the Germans too confident of ultimate triumph in the war to make trouble. The figures of captured troops quoted by Leopold are no doubt exaggerated, but they do indicate how busy the frontier guards were. In the three days after the battle at Sedan, claimed the king, over ten thousand French and three or four hundred Prussians had been taken prisoners in Belgium.[12]

The Prussian success at Sedan was hailed by the Belgian sovereign as politically fortunate, for a French victory would have embodied grave danger for Belgium. But while the threat of French imperialism was diminished, a peace which did not threaten Belgium's territory was yet to be established and friendly, comfortable relations with the dominant Prussian state remained to be assured. A rumor from Paris that the Duchy of Luxemburg might be offered to the Germans brought a lengthy reply from the king's secretary, Jules Devaux. From the point of view of Belgium, all small neutral states, and also England, an offer of the duchy to Prussia would cause interminable difficulties. Prussian control of the Luxemburg railway with its connection through Spa and Pepinster would mean that 'at each movement of Prussian troops our territory would be violated for their passage'.[13] To grant Prussia Luxemburg now would undo all that had been achieved by the diplomacy of 1867. Moreover, Belgium's recent loyal fulfillment of her duties as a neutral caused her to believe that 'something ought to result from the present crisis which should be a profit rather than a loss for her'.

This hint that the Duchy of Luxemburg should be part of the Belgian kingdom was, as usual, ignored. More surprising was that the Belgians soon allowed Prussia the use of their railways to evacuate wounded troops. This was done despite d'Anethan's recent declaration that Belgium was bound to deny the use of her routes to either belligerent, and Leopold's use of the neutrality of Belgium's railroads as an argument against Prussian control of Luxemburg. The Belgian acquiescence was no doubt prompted by a desire to better relations with Prussia and to shorten the wounded's tortuous period of travel. Yet viewed from another angle, the decision reflected the government's lack of courage to maintain its previous position against a dominant army. True, the strain of the preceding weeks had been great, and a certain relaxation may have seemed in order. On September 21, Leopold confided to Lumley that the cavalier manner of the Prussians was disturbing. When they had asked if transit of wounded Germans would be considered a breach of Belgian neutrality, they had been answered in the affirmative. Despite this reply, and an earlier protest, the Germans had nevertheless transported their wounded through Belgium. The king now feared Prussia might next ask permission to use the railways for 'some still more compromising purpose assuming a military character and involving a Breach of Belgian neutrality'.[14] Were Belgium called upon to answer Germany before she had time to consult Britain, and were she required to use force, would England give military aid?

The king, who made his request on his own and was not speaking for his ministers, was attempting to extend into the future the special arrangement with Britain which had so successfully protected Belgium in the current war. Granville would have none of it. He notified the king that it was against British practices to give assurances regarding their course in future hypothetical cases. Moreover, the queen's government had

never affirmed that it was consistent with the neutrality of Belgium to allow the sick and wounded of either belligerent to be conveyed through the country as a measure the decision of which rested with Belgium alone; but have always held that the consent of both belligerents to their passage could alone exempt it from the imputation of being a breach of neutrality.[15]

Incidentally, such consent had been obtained when a Prussian general escorting the captured Napoleon III sought to transport his prisoner across Belgian territory. The fallen emperor himself requested permission to pass through Belgium, thus enabling the Brussels officials to hold that, since both belligerents had made the request, approval was consonant with Belgium's neutrality. The tone of Granville's rebuff was ominous, however, and it was softened only by a closing assurance that Britain would always fulfill her existing treaty engagements, which of course included those of 1839.

Leopold could hardly have been pleased by the communication. Queen Victoria herself was upset by its tenor and latent contradictions and chided Granville for them. Her foreign minister did not retreat before her criticism, defending his position and concluding that 'it is not desirable that the Queen's Government should be questioned on every possible hypothetical case and upon every rumor founded or unfounded'.[16] Leopold, not Britain, was weakening the latter's obligation to guarantee Belgium's neutrality by putting it in doubt so shortly after the recent treaty. The queen was mollified and in turn agreed that it was well 'to check the importunities of a not unnaturally nervous little State'.[17]

Throughout the summer months, Leopold II's lack of confidence in Belgium's ability under her own power to escape the crisis was patent. All too aware of his country's vulnerability, he could not maintain the calm aloofness that Granville, safe behind the Channel, could so easily recommend. Leopold was an activist; he could not sit by and do nothing. His appeals for support, however, did have a nagging, nervous quality which can only in part be explained by his newness in 1870 to the responsibilities of the throne. Even later, when Leopold was acting in the Congo as if the small size of Belgium could in no way hinder his diplomacy, he maintained a strain of fatalism in his attitude toward the other powers. The king's reaction was typical, in December 1870, when he learned of Bismarck's declaration that since the Duchy of Luxemburg had allowed France to violate its neutrality without protest, German armies would in their dealings with the duchy be concerned only for their own convenience. 'All that', Leopold wrote, 'is a repetition of the eternal fable of the wolf and the lamb. The lamb? It is Turkey, Denmark, Luxemburg, Belgium, Holland, Switzerland according to the appetite of the wolf.'[18] His words might well have been even more bitter had he known that while Gladstone devised his treaty in response to the news of the Benedetti secret draft, the British prime minister had confided to John Bright that 'single-handed defense of Belgium would be an enterprise which we incline to think Quixotic' if France and Prussia combined against the neutral state.[19]

The contrast between Leopold's anxiety during the crisis, and the attitude of the Belgian people and government following it, is marked. The episode had in some ways caused the nation to mature. Confidence in Belgium's ability to care for herself increased, as did the corollary belief she could be more independent of others – a development no doubt furthered by Granville's chilling response to Leopold's second approach. Though Leopold did not lose the fatalistic views which at times were shared by his ministers, on the whole the succeeding governments seemed convinced that Belgium was more than a puppet in the power struggle and could stand on her own, if she were prudent in her movements. The nation's intent to defend her territorial integrity and forbid passage of foreign troops had been given graphic demonstration which was clouded only by the peculiar acquiescence to Prussian use of the railways for evacuation of wounded troops. Despite this last wavering, the value of a course of strict neutrality was confirmed. For Belgium's later relations with her European neighbors, these results of her 1870 experience were to be of more than routine import.

6.2 PRELUDE TO CRISIS: THE MILITARY CONVERSATIONS

Successful weathering of the Franco-Prussian War and the British sponsored treaty led the Belgians to relax their guard in subsequent years and to take a rather complacent attitude toward the dangers which surrounded them. Concern was not warranted nor many preparations needed, for it was England's duty and interest to fight any of Belgium's attackers for her. It is understandable, then, that there were indignant outcries at an article which appeared on February 2, 1887, in the London *Standard*, a paper known to be close to the British government. The article's implications were all the more serious because the piece was obviously written in reference to the crisis occasioned by the rise of the French *revanchard*, General Boulanger, who by his bellicose behavior seemed to be provoking another Franco-German conflict. The theme of the article was that England should not allow herself to be drawn into a war over the issue of troop passage through a neutral country, which matter should be viewed as different from permanent occupation of a neutral state. The piece was signed *Diplomaticus* and was commonly attributed to Alfred Austin, a close friend of Lord Salisbury, the current prime minister. Although the foreign office declared that the article was not official and did not represent the views of the government, the Belgians could not help but be disturbed. They redoubled their efforts to assure Europe that a violation of Belgium's neutrality, or a failure to support Belgium if she were violated, was unthinkable.[20]

During the Boulanger affair, the Belgians had discussed in detail with the Germans the extent of their own military preparations. Leopold, apparently questioning the value in future wars of the fortresses upon which the Belgian army had heretofore heavily relied, even arranged with William II that information on new German improvements in explosives and arms be passed on to the Belgian army. Nevertheless, no decisive improvement in Belgium's military strength was achieved despite the admonitions of Leopold, the Kaiser, and others. As the years passed and no difficulties appeared, its necessity appeared to fade.[21]

The Moroccan crisis of 1905 thus found Belgium unprepared. Engulfed by war rumors, the Belgians recognized that there were many problems they had not yet resolved. Where was an attack most likely, and how should it be met? Should Belgium still rely upon her neutrality; if so, how should it be implemented? Should she appeal, as in 1870, to one or more guarantor states; which ones, at what stage of a crisis? Would it be best, as some military men suggested, to have a prior understanding with some power? True, it might infringe on Belgium's neutral status but it would assure effective and immediate aid. If guarantors did come, what sort of relationship could the Belgians establish with them, or would all control of Belgium be lost to her protectors?

The Brussels officials were not alone in their concern. In view of the international situation, the British and French had begun military talks toward the end of 1905. Since the previous year, the French had been aware of a German plan to attack France from the north by wheeling troops through Belgium.[22] The French did not know how seriously to take this information. Nevertheless, it was obvious the Entente would benefit if some previous arrangement could be put into effect whereby, as soon as Belgium were violated, French and British troops could be pumped into that country to stem the invasion. With the approval of Foreign Secretary Sir Edward Grey, Lt.-Gen. James M. Grierson, director of military operations in the British war office, made his move in the middle of January 1906. He instructed his attaché in Brussels to confer with Belgian military authorities 'as to the manner in which, in case of need, British assistance could be most effectually afforded to Belgium for the defense of her neutrality'.[23] This Lt.-Col. Nathanial W. Barnardiston did by meeting several times with Major General Ducarne, chief of the Belgian general staff.

The approach surprised the Belgians. Their war minister was gratified at the possibility of British support and quickly authorized Ducarne to enter discussions.[24] The latter had long held a favorable opinion of the English, and the memory of past British support combined with the suddenness of the Moroccan crisis influenced him not to rebuff the attaché. Recently, there had been rumors in London that Belgium would not resist a German request for right of passage; also, there had been a notable lack of evidence of English intention to aid Belgium were she attacked. Talks with the attaché would provide opportunity to emphasize that

Belgium would fulfill her obligations and expected England to do likewise; they might also shed light on British intentions. Furthermore, the French could not be trusted to spare Belgium; perhaps a hint might be gained as to how the wind was blowing in Paris.

The military conversations were detailed. Barnardiston informed Ducarne that in the event of war Britain would be prepared to field four cavalry brigades, two army corps, and one division of mounted infantry; together they would comprise over 100,000 men. These troops would be disembarked at French ports and later at Antwerp after command of the sea was ensured. Ducarne, in turn, answered British inquiries regarding the strength of the Belgian army and gave the attaché valuable maps. Various provisions for military cooperation, such as the definition of the area in which British soldiers would act and arrangements for logistic support of the troops, were worked out.[25]

The main difficulty, according to the reports of the men involved, was the time it would take for aid to arrive. The Belgians wanted the British beside the Belgian lines by the twelfth day of mobilization, instead of four or five days later than that as the British schedule planned. When Grierson met Ducarne and the French chief-of-staff, General Brun, at the French military maneuvers the following summer, additional discussions were held. Ducarne was cheered by the promise that, thanks to a reorganization of the British army, 150,000 English troops could be sent to Belgium in a shorter period of time than had hitherto been planned.

In subsequent years, Germany was repeatedly to charge that Belgium violated the treaty of 1839 by engaging in the military conversations. It is true that the British attaché gained information the Germans would have liked to obtain also. But it is clear that the Belgians had no intention of departing from neutrality.[26] The question for them was rather how the treaty of 1839 should be implemented, how Belgium should go about protecting her neutrality. At the time, Ducarne emphasized that Belgium was prepared to meet any attack, whether from Germany, France, or England, and that the discussions with the attaché were predicated upon the fact that 'entry of the English into Belgium would only take place after the violation of our neutrality by Germany'.[27] In duplicate dispatches sent to the Belgian ministers in Berlin and Paris early in January, 1906, Foreign Minister Baron Paul de Favereau had affirmed Belgium's intention of fulfilling her obligations and 'if peace were compromised, to make, from the military point of view, all the efforts that the resources of the country permit and that the defense of the land requires'.[28] Two weeks later, after Barnardiston had contacted Ducarne, Favereau wrote Count Charles de Lalaing in London that the best way to protect Belgium's neutrality and rights, should events worsen, would be to obtain formal declarations from the future belligerents before war broke out.

The foreign minister urged his representative to do all he could to better Belgium's relations with England, which had deteriorated as a result of differences over the Congo; all obstacles to the realization 'of their benevolent intentions in the manner most useful for us must be cleared away'.[29] Favereau was circumspect, however. Apparently unconvinced by Barnardiston's insistence that Belgium need not fear France, he warned Lalaing that the English might side with France and become belligerents. In such an event, Belgium should gain as much as she could from British good will, 'while avoiding with greatest care becoming engaged in a situation where the protection offered us would, as a consequence, bind us to one of the belligerent parties and expose us to being dragged into participation in the hostilities'.[30]

If Baron Favereau viewed Barnardiston's approach as an informal indication of the place Belgium held in the plans of the British general staff and did not take it amiss, there were others who did. Baron Jules Greindl, by now Belgium's leading and most respected diplomat, was disquieted at his station in Berlin by the news of Barnardiston's mission. If Britain wished merely to reaffirm her intention to uphold her obligations, why did Barnardiston not mention the possibility of an attack by France as well as by Germany? Military attachés have no power to make agreements; why were regular diplomatic channels not used? The whole affair sounded too much like what had happened at Paris a year earlier, when Delcassé had believed he had British military support but was then disappointed. Behind the attaché's language Greindl suspected 'there hides the thought of involving us in engagements which would force us to take the part of one of the belligerents'.[31] Perhaps it was a snare. Baron Paul Guillaume, Belgian minister at The Hague, also evinced concern over the devious ways of the British. The British minister in Brussels let Favereau know he was aware of Barnardiston's activities, yet made no similar *démarche* himself. This indicated the British were acting more out of self-interest than from sympathy for Belgium's plight.[32]

How long the military conversations continued is not known; in any case, they were soon outdated by changes in Anglo-French planning. A key feature of the British plan was the use of Belgian ports for the landing of troops; when the admiralty ruled that from the outbreak of hostilities the Channel would have to be closed north of the Dover-Cape Grisnez line, the work of Barnardiston and Ducarne lost much of its value. In 1909 Ducarne reported he was unclear as to the British position because the conversations of 1906 had not been continued. Thus the talks initiated by Barnardiston had short-lived military value. They did leave, however, a legacy of distrust in the minds of Belgian diplomats which grew perceptibly in succeeding years and by 1912 spelled the quick failure of British efforts to renew contacts. Doubt of British intentions in the decade preceding the war eventually took on such dimensions that it deeply affected Belgium's diplomacy and military planning.

There were several general reasons for a cooling of the Belgians' friendlines toward their English and French neighbors. Already piqued by English criticism of Leopold's government of the Congo, the Belgians were angered by Britain's failure to recognize the annexation of the Congo by the Belgian state in 1908.[33] News of military preparations to the south refreshed memories of French imperialism. The ruling Catholic party was offended by French policies regarding the Roman church. It also was rendered nervous by the freedom allowed socialists in France and pre-ferred the German system which granted socialists less leeway. But these were not the major reasons for the changing attitude of the Belgian officials. What most disturbed them was the solidification of the two vying European groups that occurred when England seemed to move completely into the French camp. After the Anglo-Russian agreement of 1907 the Belgians felt they had no one to whom they could turn, whereas before that accord they had viewed England as sufficiently detached to be dealt with as an uncommitted benevolent power.

How distrust of England increased is exemplified by Greindl's ref-erence, three years after the event, to Barnardiston's approach in terms markedly more suspicious than those previously used.

Colonel Barnardiston asked us, in substance, to associate ourselves with an English and French aggression against Germany...; to make the Belgian army completely available to combat the German army in their place, while the Eng-lish would have taken the scarcely perilous task of holding ... Antwerp, ... our fortress, which would permit England at the conclusion of peace...to dis-pose of us as it suited her.[34]

Greindl may have been oversympathetic toward Germany, as he has been accused of being, but his suspicion of England was shared by a number of men at the Rue de la loi, most notably by the influential Leon Arendt, who held the third-ranking post in the ministry, that of general director of policy. Upon learning in January 1911 of an impending visit by English Chief-of-Staff Henry Wilson, Arendt minuted a warning. Wilson was probably coming to arrange

the cooperation of the Belgian army in the plan, without doubt already drawn up between Paris and London, envisaging a campaign by the allied armies in our country under the pretext of guaranteeing Belgian neutrality in case of a Franco-German war.

It is a new indication, and one step more on the path to the envelopment of Belgium, which France and England follow ... to drag us insensibly into their orbit, so that at the psychological moment we will no longer be capable of disengaging ourselves from their embrace.[35]

Arendt suggested Wilson be told that it was up to Belgium to decide when guarantors of her neutrality should intervene; such a call could not be made until there were an actual violation, otherwise Belgium would be violating her neutrality herself. Should the English come to Belgium's aid, it would be best if they came by way of French ports, not Antwerp. Moreover, violation of the distant Belgium province of Luxemburg would not necessarily mean that Belgium would be the center of the next war, which might be the case if she asked for aid.

His penultimate comments were stimulated in part by the outcry raised in Britain and France against a defense bill then being debated in the Dutch States General. This bill provided for construction of a fort at Flushing at the mouth of the river Scheldt to replace the obsolete forts at Elleswoutsdyk and Terneuzen. Such a fortress could prevent the sending of warships and supplies up the Scheldt to Antwerp, the course Britain most likely would take in coming to the aid of Belgium. Rumors spread that the fortress was being built at Germany's request; protests were raised in the French chambers and a campaign was begun in the British press. The military correspondent of the London *Times*, Lt.-Col. Charles à Court Repington, led the attack. No one could question the right of the Dutch to build the fortress, he wrote, but the fort was 'a pistol aimed at England..., a slap in the face of Belgium'.[36]

In Repington's view, German interests alone would be served by the fort; he was sure Belgium would oppose its construction. Similar concern was expressed through official channels. In October 1910, the British minister at Brussels, Sir Arthur Hardinge, told Julien Davignon (Belgian foreign minister since 1908) that the Flushing fort would make it difficult to send aid if Belgium's neutrality should be menaced. His choice of words was unfortunate, for Davignon and Leon van der Elst (secretary-general of the ministry and second in position only to Davignon) immediately became concerned whether England contemplated a preventive occupation of Antwerp. This concern was shared by Albert de Bassompierre, division head within the *Direction politique*. In a dinner conversation several weeks later with the British military attaché, Col. Tom Bridges, De Bassompierre's suspicion that England planned to send a fleet to Antwerp if there were a war was confirmed by Bridges' comment that 'the Flushing fort would change our whole strategy'.[37] Shortly thereafter, De Bassompierre informed Davignon that the *Direction politique* remained convinced it was dangerous to let London believe that Belgium would turn to England in time of war, even if England were a belligerent. From Berlin, Greindl commented acidly that the Entente press was treating the matter far more heatedly than if it were inspired only by a solicitude for Belgium's neutrality.[38]

In this affair, as in the delayed reaction to the Barnardiston talks of 1906, Belgian official distrust of the English is evident. The foreign ministry believed there was reason to doubt the value of receiving aid from Britain through Antwerp. Arendt and others pointed out time and again that if British ships appeared at Antwerp under the pretext of bolstering Belgian neutrality, Germany would justifiably take offense and invade Belgium. Even should Germany have violated Belgium first by marching through the southeastern corner of the state, it would be unwise to receive aid through Antwerp. The presence of a belligerent there would attract the Germans, who would march across the entire country, turning it into a major battlefield.[39] It was for this reason that Baron Edmond Gaiffier d'Hestroy, after he had succeeded Arendt in 1912 as general director of policy, termed the possibility that an international conference might rule the Scheldt open to warships coming to the defense of Belgium's neutrality 'precisely the hypothesis we dread the most'.[40]

The possibility that England might offer aid not as a sympathetic neutral, as in 1870, but as a belligerent, caused the Belgians to do some hard thinking concerning their course of action should war break out. A sense of urgency was added to their debates by the occurrence of the Agadir crisis in July of 1911. On September 16, Davignon held a conference with Van der Elst, Arendt, De Bassompierre, Count Leo d'Ursel (head of Davignon's staff cabinet), and Greindl, who would be returning to his Berlin post in two days.

First discussed was the problem that any Belgian mobilization might be interpreted by Belgium's neighbors as an indication that the small country intended to take the part of one of the belligerents; failure to arm, on the other hand, might invite a preventive occupation. Following a suggestion made by Greindl as far back as 1906, a circular was agreed upon which clearly stated Belgium's intention to uphold her obligations and the precautionary nature of any mobilization Belgium might order. This circular was to be sent without date to the legations; should Belgium mobilize, her ministers would be instructed to deliver the circulars the same day. Attention was then turned, among other matters, to the strategy the army should follow were belligerent troops to pass through the most southeastern corner of Belgium, that sector won by such desperate negotiation in 1831 which was now known as the province of Luxemburg.[41]

The importance of this question, both for Belgium and for her neighbors, is obvious. In 1906, Grierson at the British war office had questioned whether Belgium would fight if only Luxemburg province were violated; he had been assured by Barnardiston that while some Belgians might advocate doing nothing, the army would want to fight. By 1909, however, the British foreign office was receiving reports that Belgium might 'throw in her lot with Germany'.[42] When the Committee of Imperial Defence met on August 23, 1911, General Wilson stated that Belgium might not fight over violation of her southern provinces; Winston Churchill, at the admiralty, and War Minister Sir John French believed the Germans did not need to fear a Belgian attack even if they advanced on a broad front.[43] The concern of the French was so great at this time that they were constructing various war plans to meet this possibility. Among them was Joffre's Plan XVII, which in one of its versions envisaged a preventive invasion of Belgium. The designer of the German war plan, General Alfred von Schlieffen, had indicated as early as 1905 that he expected little opposition from the Belgians, who would perhaps refrain from hostilities, choosing the advantages of being a disinterested third party. His famous plan envisaged a strong German right wing which would swing through Belgium and the Maastricht appendix, seize the channel ports and cut Paris off from British aid. By 1911, the notion that Belgium might not resist was so widespread that the first secretary of the German embassy in London could tell his Belgian counterpart that should Germany violate Belgium, it would be only by a quick passage. Belgium could fulfill all her duties by putting up a mere resistance of form. On the other hand, should English troops be on Belgian territory, then that land would become a battlefield.[44]

So the problem stood. If Belgian troops limited themselves to harassing the invaders, as Arendt proposed, then the other belligerents would insist on entering the country and Belgium would become the major theater of the war. If the small Belgian army engaged in full battle far from established fortifications, as Van der Elst suggested, it risked being decimated and leaving the remainder of the country without defense.

No decision was reached at the meeting, and the question was referred to the war minister. In November, using a detailed note recently received from Chief-of-Staff General Ceulemans as a guide, Arendt drew up a forty-four page memorandum entitled 'In case of war, what shall we do?' Very shortly this memorandum became the accepted basis for all subsequent planning. Both it and Ceulemans' note are of considerable interest for their prescriptions for Belgian action under various circumstances. In the event of an invasion of Luxemburg province, it was believed that the Belgian army was capable of opposing the Germans. (This was hardly the opinion of foreign observers.[45]) The generals had one reservation: The army should never allow itself to be cut off from its bases. Arendt agreed completely. The army should not be sacrificed for a principle; above the obligation of maintaining the geographic integrity of all of neutral Belgium was that of the national defense as a whole. If some land had to be abandoned to one belligerent, the Belgians should not complain if a second waged war there also. But:

An attack on the integrity of a fraction of the territory, which because of circumstances was not repulsed, would not authorize any of the belligerents to occupy other parts of the country under the pretext that neutrality was lost for the whole. Neutrality persists as long as the Government is standing and possesses the means of making neutrality respected, even if in a restricted sphere.[46]

The Belgians must remain masters of the heart of their country, Arendt argued. Should Luxemburg province be invaded, opposing forces should not be allowed to spread throughout the country. If the invasions were on a broader scale, then appeal to a guarantor might be necessary. But it was important that the aid brought by a guarantor be regulated by a convention. Under no circumstances should Belgian fortifications be occupied by a belligerent power. At the outbreak of hostilities, England might not yet be a declared belligerent, but such a situation would not last long. Should the English try to send warships to Antwerp, Belgium's national redoubt, it was to be hoped that the Dutch would close the Scheldt. Any aid received should not go beyond the goal of defending Belgium's neutrality; the nation should not simply become the ally of any state happening to assist it. Rather, Belgium should remain independent; for were she a belligerent, no matter whether victor or vanquished, she could expect either to be annexed to France or constrained into a close relationship with Germany.

The idea of such a convention had been in the air for some time, and earlier that year H. Costermans, director of the secretariat general and also a member of Davignon's staff cabinet, had recommended it to the foreign minister. Greindl, who was in agreement with the premises of Arendt's memorandum, was doubtful whether Belgium could persuade a guarantor to sign such a treaty as Arendt envisioned before sending troops into Belgium. Also, would the Belgians themselves be able to keep a neutral attitude in the non-invaded portion of their territory?[47] Despite these difficulties, after a year of additional debate, both a protest to be delivered at the capital of the violating country and a treaty to be concluded with an aiding guarantor were drawn up by De Bassompierre.

The closing phrases of the protest reserved Belgium's right to call upon a guarantor for aid and indicated that any intervention would be limited to making Belgium's neutrality respected; after this was achieved, Belgian troops would not participate in any ulterior operations undertaken by the guarantor.[48] The treaty stated that collaboration with a guarantor was intended to maintain Belgian independence and would be limited solely to repelling the invader; this goal achieved, Belgian soil was not to be used as a base for additional attacks upon the violator. The final clause asserted that in all events only Belgian troops would be permitted to occupy the Belgian fortresses.[49] These two documents demonstrated the conviction within the Belgian foreign ministry that there no longer existed a disinterested guarantor of Belgium's neutrality. In drawing them up, the diplomats made a valiant attempt to plan for its preservation despite this fact.

It is clear that, at the time of the Agadir crisis, the Belgians did not fear a direct attack by Britain, but rather the consequences of unasked-for aid zealously donated for selfish reasons. Within a few months, their estimation of English goodwill was lowered. Cause of the change was a *démarche* made by Lt.-Col. Tom Bridges to Belgian Chief-of-Staff Gen. H. Jungbluth on April 23, 1911. Bridges was acting upon the orders of British D.M.O. Gen. Henry H. Wilson, who had not bothered to clear his initiative with the foreign office. The attaché's account, written many years later, describes the discussion as routine and duly qualified. According to Van der Elst's report, however, Bridges stated that, if there were a war, English troops would be disembarked in Belgium even if aid had not yet been requested. Jungbluth protested that preliminary consent by Belgium was essential; the attaché answered that, while he realized this, the British would have to land in any case, as Belgium was not prepared to block the passage of German soldiers. Jungbluth replied that Belgium could defend herself against Germany.[50]

Bridges also visited War Minister Gen. Augustin Michel and told him there might be value in disembarking the English army before there was any violation of Belgian territory; in this case, what would Belgium do? Michel exploded, ending his retort by declaring that in any case the Belgians would receive the English with cannon. So vehement was Michel's language that Bridges informed the current British minister in Brussels, Sir Francis Villiers, of the disagreeable incident. Villiers quickly visited Davignon, assuring him that Britain planned no incorrectness toward Belgium and that Bridges' statement had no official quality.[51]

The Belgian foreign ministry's criticism of the British advance was stronger and more immediate than in 1906. The day after the Jungbluth interview the *Direction politique* warned Davignon that Belgian neutrality had no meaning to England. Had war broken out in 1911, England would have violated Belgium; now the policy, followed since 1905, of dragging Belgium in the wake of the Entente was being furthered. Gaiffier wrote Davignon that his office had long had information indicating England would not wait for a call or even a declaration of war before landing troops on Belgian soil. Jungbluth should make clear to Bridges that Belgium would not acquiesce in Britain's perfidious intentions.[52]

After considering the incident for over two weeks, Davignon informed Greindl. The oblique approach, the foreign minister thought, could only have been dictated by the war office at the instigation of the British foreign office. He assured Greindl that 'the general staff is studying means of meeting this new danger which comes precisely from the power we have always considered the best guarantor of our neutrality'.[53] Greindl's reply urged that everything possible be done to increase Belgium's military forces.

Arendt, although he had turned over his post of general director of policy to Gaiffier at the beginning of April, nevertheless was able to express his views in notes written from partial retirement. In a series of memoranda on relations with the neighboring great powers, he pointed out that the English conception of the guarantee of Belgium's neutrality was a sort of protectorate best realized by occupation of Antwerp, the key to Belgium's defense system. This was why the British had opposed the Flushing fort so vehemently. English occupation of Antwerp would mean German invasion and the destruction of the heart of the country. 'The hypothesis of a French or English invasion of western Belgium has not been envisaged until now. It is of the greatest urgency that our general staff study it and take the dispositions necessary to meet this danger.'[54] This last point Greindl had been advocating since the previous December.

Gaiffier's general conclusions were similar. Both France and Germany had plans for sending troops through Belgium. Any future protector of Belgium's neutral rights would continue to participate in hostilities even after those rights had been saved. This was fact, not hypothesis, for did not Barnardiston's and Bridges' propositions 'tend to make us accomplices of an English and French aggression against Germany'?[55] A corollary of any Franco–British entry into Belgium was German invasion; it was time for Belgium to open her eyes to the danger and make preparations.

Despite assurances by Grey and Villiers that England did not dream of sending troops to Belgium unless invited to do so, the Rue de la loi remained suspicious throughout the pre-war period. This attitude was strengthened by the inquiries of the secretary of the French legation in

Brussels in November 1912, which seemed too similar to those of Bridges.[56] To discourage Entente adventurousness, the Belgians let their distrust be known. In September 1912, War Minister Michel informed the British naval attaché that Belgium was capable of greatly hindering a British disembarkment. A month later he commented that should Germany invade first, Belgium might not ask for aid because 'it will perhaps be more difficult for us to get rid of our policemen than our aggressors'.[57] That same month Van der Elst told Villiers he did not believe Belgian neutrality would be violated, but 'if it were, it would *not* be by the German side'.[58] At the end of the year, the British permanent undersecretary of state, Arthur Nicolson, inquired whether Belgium would side with or against England and was told by Villiers that Belgium expected violation and was now making preparations against attack from any of three sides. To t he French minister in Brussels, Antony Klobukowski, it was obvious by the end of 1913 that 'official Belgium leans toward Germany'.[59]

The problem for the Belgian leaders was not which side to support, but how best to spare their country the ravages of war. They would be neutral, but did this necessitate letting themselves be fought over? The conclusion, as stated in Arendt's memorandum, was 'No'. This clearly was the *Direction politique*'s view in February 1914, when reports were received that the German army no longer planned to enter France by way of Liege but by cornering through the province of Luxemburg. As such a violation was impossible to halt, the province would have to be abandoned to the conflict; but the rest of Belgium would remain neutral. No mention was made of inviting in any guarantor.[60]

The Belgians feared that the ruin of their country would be the result of any 'rescue'. This fear caused a steady deterioration of relations with E ngland. In October 1913, Gaiffier noted that until 1905 Belgium had had g reat faith in Britain as a protector.

But as a result of England's entry into the Dual Entente, the declarations of Colonels Barnardiston and Bridges, and the emotion provoked in England by the plan to fortify Flushing, a complete reversal of opinion occurred in official Belgian circles concerning the opportuneness and efficacy of British assistance.[61]

There were definite national interests which led the Rue de la loi to take the stand it did regarding England. Yet British diplomacy only increased rather than lessened Belgian suspicions. Striking examples of this are the *démarches* of Barnardiston and particularly of Bridges. Although these were not official, and although Bridges may not have been authorized to use the language he did, it should have been realized in London that any such inquiries might be taken amiss, given the conditions under which the Belgians were operating. The circuitous route employed enabled the British to avoid committing themselves and provided a ready basis for a *dementi*; but this put the matter in a worse light from the Belgian viewpoint. The British foreign office's ambivalent attitude regarding Barnardiston's activities was a further irritation; just what was the connection between the war office's planning and Downing Street's intentions?

During the decade before the war, virtually every attempt the French and English made to assure Belgium of their concern for her increased the growing suspicion in Brussels. The French somewhat expected to be the object of Belgian distrust, and the choice of British rather than French attachés for the delicate approaches was indicative of this. The British, on the other hand, could not understand why Davignon did not oppose the Flushing fort, apparently failing to perceive that the Belgian foreign ministry actually wanted the fort constructed.[62] Thus, the net result of the fortress discussions, as of the attachés' activities, was to stimulate distrust and separate the two nations rather than bring them into a closer and friendlier relationship; surely this was the opposite of what was intended.

The British were not entirely to blame; in Brussels the nervous diplomats took alarm at the slightest slip, as when Hardinge mentioned that England might act if Belgium were menaced. Fear of France was of course by now almost a traditional habit in the northern capital, and each reassessment of the situation did show it to be a wise one. Yet far too drastic implications were read into the unofficial statements of Bridges and the Anglo-French protests over the Flushing fort. This was in part symptomatic of the tension of the period, but the Belgians' oversensitiveness was primarily due to their geographical location and neutral status. Well aware that there was little chance Belgium would not be invaded, they wished to avoid any gesture which might encourage the entry of belligerent forces or make matters worse, once violation occurred. In short, the Belgians were now hewing to the advice given by Granville in the similarly difficult situation of 1870 that the best policy was to remain quiet and not ask unnecessary questions or make complaints. To the particular dismay of the British, the Brussels officials seemed all too convinced that calm was 'the most dignified and expedient attitude for all neutral Powers...'

The Brussels officials were in an unfortunate position where any statement might be taken amiss by one party or another. Their fence straddling neutrality seemed to many observers as indicative of ambivalent intentions. Thus the distrust in Brussels was matched by distrust of Belgium in the other European capitals which hung on until the very outbreak of war. For example, on the same day the German ultimatum demanding free passage for German troops was delivered, Klobukowski twice telegraphed to Paris his suspicions that truth might lie behind the rumors of connivance between Belgium and Germany. A similar fear was aroused in the mind of Paul Cambon, the French ambassador at London, by Davignon's statement of July 31, 1914, that Belgium did not suspect any of her neighbors and was prepared to repel an attack if one should occur. Cambon wrote that 'this strange response [to the British inquiry], which arrived while I was with Sir Edward Grey, gave us the idea there was perhaps some secret arrangement between Germany and Belgium'.[63]

Throughout the years before the war, the Belgian diplomats had relied upon a mixture of friendly assertions to the powers that Belgium would actively protect her neutrality and an attitude cool enough to indicate overt advances might drive her into an enemy camp. From the Belgian point of view, the uncertainty this behavior created in the Entente camp was beneficial, for the fear that Belgium would resist a French advance forced the abandoning of plans for a preventive invasion of Belgium. Yet it is also true that doubt regarding Belgium's position stimulated the French to consider sending troops into Belgium and weakened the belief in other countries that Belgium would indeed defend herself. This was especially true in Germany. The Belgian minister in Berlin in 1914, Baron Napoleon Eugène Beyens, reported that in his last interview with the German secretary of state, Gottlieb von Jagow, the German gave the impression he expected Belgium not to reject abruptly the German ultimatum. Rather, he seemed to believe Brussels would propose that Belgian troops be allowed to put up a token resistance and then retreat to Antwerp. The possibility of such an arrangement was in Von Jagow's mind, for a day earlier he had suggested to the German minister at Brussels, Baron Claus von Below-Saleske, that in presenting the ultimatum he should 'propose to the Belgian Government that it might retire with its troops to Antwerp, and that we, if it should be so desired, could undertake the protection of Brussels against internal disturbances'.[64] There is no evidence Below carried out the suggestion.

General Von Schlieffen had drawn up his invasion plan and predicted little Belgian opposition in 1905 well before the Belgians had decided not to defend the province of Luxemburg. The younger Von Moltke, who replaced Von Schlieffen as chief-of-staff, did reduce the extent of the sweep through the Low Countries, but the Germany army remained committed to the essentials of Von Schlieffen's plan in the succeeding years. While there is nothing to indicate the Germans were aware of the Belgian decision regarding Luxemburg, it is clear that Belgian diplomacy did little to weaken the Germans' adherence to their war plan and, in fact, enhanced it.

The obviously lukewarm Anglo-Belgian relations encouraged this adherence, but even more so did the dilapidated state of the Belgian army. As late as 1909 that army had remained at a war effective of 100,000 men, but this was a paper figure only. This effective was to be supplemented by the *garde civique*, an organization tacitly admitted to have little military value. In that year the official effective was increased by 80,000 men and the system of bought substitutes ended; to mollify public opinion, however, the term of duty was shortened and it was promised that only one son per family would be taken for service. Von Moltke confidently wrote that the Belgian army would be easily scattered unless it withdrew to Antwerp, and the British repeatedly urged the Belgians to strengthen their forces. The gathering war clouds of 1913 stimulated the chambers to generalize military service; but the war effective was still only 330,000 men and would not be reached for another ten years. The lack of Belgian preparedness was thus of a nature to encourage the Germans and to feed Entente doubts of Belgium's intentions. As Bridges put it in 1911:

The very weakness of her national defence is a temptation to her government to play a double game, and though she is doubtlessly willing to carry out her treaty obligations, it is open to give doubt whether she is in a position to do so.[65]

'Doublegame' is too harsh a term for describing Belgian behavior in the years before the First World War. Yet there is some truth in it; the many statements of the Entente military and diplomatic officials leave no doubt of what their own views would have been had they known of the Belgian decision regarding Luxemburg province. The Belgians, on the other hand, saw themselves making important sacrifices to support the peace of Europe and maintain the principle of neutrality set forth in the 1839 treaty. Moreover, they believed they were keeping to a path of the most scrupulous neutrality possible, guided by impeccable legal interpretation. This was true, but the problem was that legalism, at the first essay, did not provide a satisfactory course. An attempt to defend every inch of Belgian territory might lead to the loss of all of Belgium. A new interpretation of the treaty of 1839 was required which would allow defense of only part of Belgium. Such an interpretation was acceptable only if it could be shown to be legally valid, placing it within the tradition of the past sixty years of Belgian diplomacy and making it a worthy alternative to the no-longer attractive first interpretation. Hence the insistence that the main interest of the drafters of the 1839 treaty was not the protection of the territory of Belgium from the grasping hands of all her neighbors but the establishment of a permanent state which had a value worth preserving unconnected with the guardianship of the disputed lands. By ascribing this spirit to the treaty, it could be argued the law and European peace would be best defended by not following what had heretofore been considered the letter of the law. Cast aside was d'Anethan's view of 1870 that Belgium was honor-bound absolutely to prevent the use of her routes by any belligerent.

It is not surprising the Belgians took the view they did. There was no particular reason why the patriots of an eighty year old nation should not see things differently than did the foreign diplomats who contrived the establishment of the state, or differently than did their own ministers of earlier decades. More important, the decision regarding Luxemburg province conformed to the awkward realities of the situation in which the Belgians found themselves. Yet while the realities of their weak power circumstances were the main determinant of the Belgians' position, the Brussels officials preferred publicly, and to a great extent even among themselves, to speak only in terms of their legal position. To diplomats in the other capitals, the Belgian reliance on words reflected either ignorance or a refusal to recognize the basis of a *Realpolitik*. It does seem that despite the existence of some concrete planning, the majority of the Belgian populace and government officials were carried by the logic of their verbal arguments to the point of believing these were sufficient substitutes for military preparedness. Even the military, whose duty it was to be concerned for such matters, was excessively overconfident of the effectiveness of the undermanned and unsatisfactorily equipped Belgian army.

To the end, the Belgians kept their guard against possible attacks by both the Entente and the Triple Alliance. Suspicion of England and France was countered by fears concerning Germany. In recent years, rumors of German designs on the Congo were legion, and the construction in Germany of more railroad lines to the Belgian border than would be used under normal conditions was obvious to all. In a 1913 visit to Berlin, King Albert was thoroughly alarmed by the Kaiser's talk of 'inevitable and imminent war' which reminded him of the emperor's warning to Leopold II in 1904 that in the next war Belgium would have to be either 'with us or against us'.[66]

An informal assurance of Germany's intention to respect Belgium's neutrality was therefore sought at the time Dutch fortification of the Scheldt brought new whisperings concerning German plans. When Van der Elst inquired of his friend Baron Wilhelm von Schön if a declaration in the *Reichstag* would calm the public, the German ambassador at Paris replied that a formal statement might not be possible, for it might imply that Germany had considered violating Belgium; however, he was sure Belgium had nothing to fear. German Chancellor Theobald von Bethmann-Hollweg gave the same assurance, but said a public declaration would weaken Germany's military position with respect to France. This reply satisfied the Belgians, and they were gratified when, in April 1913, Von Jagow stated in the *Reichstag*, in reply to an interpellation, that Germany would respect the conventions which established Belgium's neutrality. Three weeks earlier, in the same month, a similar promise was unofficially made by Sir Edward Grey, the British foreign minister.[67]

In a secret speech to the Belgian chamber during the debate on the military law of 1913, Premier Charles de Broqueville disclosed that he suspected Germany would be the first to violate Belgium but believed it necessary to prepare for all events.[68] Upon the outbreak of the Austro-Serbian war, troops were mobilized to meet attack from France and England as well as Germany. One division guarded the coast, one watched Germany, and two patrolled the long French border; Antwerp and Brussels were each garrisoned by one division, while the cavalry was stationed at Brussels. The soldiers were sent to their posts even earlier than the British thought the situation warranted, for the Belgians wished that their 'neighbors and guarantors should see in the decision our strong desire to uphold our neutrality ourselves'.[69]

6.3 AUGUST 1914

During the crisis of August 1914, the Belgians clung to their independent position. On August 1, they received formal assurance France would respect Belgian neutrality. Davignon quickly moved to obtain a similar statement from Germany. Shortly after noon De Bassompierre informed Von Below-Saleske that Belgium intended to publish the formal French declaration. The German thanked him for the information but made no formal statement himself. In private conversation he again expressed his opinion that Belgium had nothing to fear from Germany and that his government probably found it useless to repeat earlier declarations. This same language was used by Von Below-Saleske the following morning in a conversation with Davignon; the Belgian replied he did not doubt German correctness but would attach the greatest importance to a formal declaration. King Albert also sought reassurance from his cousin, Kaiser Wilhelm II; his request reached Berlin only at 5 p.m. on August 3, by which time the die had been cast.

Meanwhile Grey informed Brussels that British ambassadors had been instructed to inquire at Paris and Berlin if Belgian neutrality would be respected. No definite commitment was made, but the Belgians were convinced by Villiers' words that England would come to the rescue were

Belgium invaded.[70] When no reply had been received from Berlin by the morning of August 2, Villiers again got in touch with Davignon. The Belgian, however, put the British minister off:

There was no reason whatever to suspect that Germany intended to violate the neutrality of Belgium. The Government had consequently not even considered the question of an appeal to the guaranteeing Powers, more especially as they considered themselves in a position to resist aggression from whatever quarter it might come.[71]

At seven in the evening on August 2, Von Below–Saleske appeared at the Rue de la loi and presented a note which required an answer within twelve hours. The ultimatum stated that Germany had reason to suspect France would invade Belgium and that it was necessary for Germany to enter Belgium to anticipate the French attack. Berlin hoped passage could be arranged amicably; if it were opposed, Germany would be forced to consider Belgium as an enemy. There was no suggestion that the German demand was limited only to railway passage through the province of Luxemburg.

The Belgians responded quickly. Slightly after 8 o'clock, a council of ministers was held in the presence of the king; at ten it was joined by the ministers of state (ex-ministers, diplomats, and others nominated by the king). The sitting continued all night. Only after the Germans' morning deadline was met did Davignon inform the other powers of the ultimatum and of the Belgians' reply, which concluded with the words 'the Belgian government are firmly resolved to repel, by all the means in their power, every attack upon their rights'.[72] Later in the morning the council met again and decided to solicit the diplomatic but not the military support of the guaranteeing powers excepting Austria and Germany. Though the French immediately indicated they would respond to an appeal for military aid, it was not until the morning of August 4, when actual German violation of the border had been confirmed, that Davignon requested Great Britain, France, and Russia to cooperate in the military defense of Belgium.

The failure of the legalist position was a blow to the Brussels officials. Yet Albert de Bassompierre confessed that he felt a surge of relief when the ultimatum arrived. Granted the situation was one the Belgians had least expected, it nevertheless allowed no hesitations or interpretations. The tension caused by the reasoning which had led to the decision to abandon the province of Luxemburg now disappeared. No longer to be feared was 'the problem of conscience which had always, heretofore, seemed so formidable. . .'[73] The fate not just of a corner of territory but of the entire country was at stake. Since this was the case, the Belgians worried less about the advances of their overzealous defenders than about the initial violation; as De Bassompierre observed, the situation was finally clear. So clear, in fact, that after some discussion it was decided not to ask the British to sign, before their troops entered Belgium, the convention so carefully drafted two years earlier.[74]

6.4 NOTES

1. Gilbert, *Farewell Address*, pp. 17–18.
2. Lord, *Origins of the War of 1870*, p. 14. See also Steefel, *Bismarck*, and Bonnin, *Bismarck and the Hohenzollern Candidature*.
3. *Letters of Queen Victoria*, 2nd ser., vol. II, pp. 25–27: 'Leopold to Victoria, July 10, 1870'; pp. 30–32: 'Same to same, July 10, 1870'. Huisman, 'Juillet 1870', pp. 26–27. Beyens, *Le Second Empire*, vol. II, p. 427. Demoulin, 'Documents inédits', pp. 135–137, no. 5: 'Leopold to Granville, July 13, 1870'.
4. Demoulin, 'Documents inédits', p. 143, no. 10: 'Granville to Lumley, July 20, 1870'.
5. *Ibid.*, pp. 157–160, no. 23: 'Memorandum by Hammond'.
6. *Ibid.*, p. 149, no. 14: 'Victoria to Ponsonby, July 24, 1870'.
7. *Ibid.*, pp. 179–180, no. 41: 'Gladstone to Leopold, Aug. 11, 1870'.
8. *Ibid.*, pp. 177–178, no. 40: 'Lumley to Granville, Aug. 10, 1870'.
9. *Ibid.*, pp. 155–156, no. 21: 'Gladstone to R. W. Crawford, July 29, 1870'; pp. 156–157, no. 22: 'Gladstone to Leopold, July 29, 1870'.
10. *Ibid.*, pp. 139–141, no. 8: 'Leopold to Victoria, July 17, 1870'.
11. Quoted in Du Bois, 'La Belgique', p. 370.
12. *Letters of Queen Victoria*, 2nd ser., vol. II, pp. 56–58: 'Leopold to Victoria, Sept. 4, 1870'.
13. Demoulin, 'Documents inédits', pp. 191–193, no. 49: 'Devaux to Beaulieu, Sept. 14, 1870'.
14. *Ibid.*, pp. 195–197, no. 51: 'Lumley to Granville, Sept. 22, 1870'; pp. 199–201, no. 54: 'Same to same, Sept. 25, 1870'.
15. *Ibid.*, pp. 197–198, note: 'Granville to Lumley, Sept. 23, 1870'.
16. *Ibid.*, pp. 205–207, no. 58: 'Granville to Ponsonby, Sept. 28, 1870'.
17. *Ibid.*, pp. 208–209, no. 60: 'Ponsonby to Granville, Sept. 30, 1870'.
18. *Ibid.*, pp. 225–226, no. 74: 'Leopold to Victoria, Dec. 24, 1870'.
19. Morley, *The Life of Gladstone*, vol. II, p. 342: 'Gladstone to Bright, Aug. 4, 1970'.
20. See documents reproduced in Fernand Van Langenhove, *Le dossier diplomatique de la question belge*, pp. 7–10, which include the official British explanation of the affair given to *Le Temps* in February 1917. See also Schwertfeger (ed.), *Amtliche Aktenstücke*, second com. vol., *Der geistige Kampf*, pp. 70–73. This and the succeeding section of the chapter are adapted from the author's article 'Belgian concern over neutrality and British intentions, 1906–14', *Journal of Modern History*, XXXVI, no. 4 (Dec. 1964), 416–427.

I am indebted to the University of Chicago Press for permission to reprint portions of this article.

21. See Gottschalk, 'Die deutschen Dokumente', pp. 1033–1053.
22. Joffre, 'Le problème belge en 1912', pp. 721–722. There is some debate concerning the veracity of France's source of information, supposedly an informant known as *le Vengeur*. See Albertini, *The origins of the War of 1914*, vol. III, p. 418.
23. Great Britain, *British Documents on the Origins of the War (BD)*, vol. III, p. 179, no. 217 (b): 'Grierson to Barnardiston, Jan. 19, 1906'. See also Tyler, *The British Army* and Williamson, *The Politics*, pp. 86–88.
24. Beyens, *Germany before the War*, p. 317; Great Britain, *BD*, vol. III, pp. 187–188, no. 221 (c) (1): 'Barnardiston to Grierson, Jan. 19, 1906'; pp. 193–196, no. 221 (c) (7): 'Same to same, Mar. 17, 1906'.
25. For the Belgian account of the talks see Ducarne's report to the minister of war, Apr. 10, 1906, in *The Belgian Grey Book*, vol. I, Appendix, no. 4 (1) in *Collected Documents Relating to the Outbreak of the European War*, pp. 354–360. The British version may be found in Great Britain, *BD*, vol. III, pp. 187–200, no. 221 (c).
26. The detailed nature of the military talks is revealed by the charts published in Hosse, *Die english-belgischen Aufmarschpläne*. Hosse thinks Belgium completely and permanently abandoned neutrality. Albertini accuses Hosse and others of 'effrontery' in making such judgments and himself criticizes the Belgian government for having had too strong a preference for Germany (*The Origins of the War of 1914*, vol. III, pp. 420 note, 474). Schwertfeger in his second commentary volume, *Der geistige Kampf*, gives a well balanced discussion of the problem. There are many articles concerning Belgium's neutrality and the talks in *Die Kriegsschuldfrage* (after 1928 *Berliner Monatshefte*), ed. by Alfred von Wegerer. Numerous works, such as Emile Waxweiler's *Belgium, Neutral and Loyal*, defend Belgium's actions. No attempt will be made here to cite or evaluate the immense literature on Belgian neutrality before 1914.
27. This is the wording of a marginal note in Ducarne's report to the minister of war, April 10, 1906. The report was found by the Germans when they occupied Brussels and was published in the *Norddeutsche Allgemeine Zeitung* as proof of Belgian conspiracy without translation of the note or indication that it was part of the document. See also Belgium, M.A.E. Arch., INDM, VII: 'Favereau to Lalaing, Jan. 26, 1906'.
28. Belgium, M.A.E. Arch., INDM, VII: 'Favereau to Greindl, Leghait, Jan. 12, 1906'.
29. *Ibid.*, 'Favereau to Lalaing, Jan. 26, 1906'.
30. *Ibid.*, 'Van der Elst memorandum of private conversation with Barnardiston, Jan. 23, 1906'.
31. *Ibid.*, 'Greindl to Favereau, Feb. 12, 1906'. At this time, when Germany was already committed to the Schlieffen plan, Greindl confidently wrote, 'I do not suspect Germany of any evil designs in our regard...' (*Ibid.*, Feb. 13, 1906).

32. *Ibid.*, 'Favereau to Guillaume, Feb. 22, 1906'; 'Guillaume to Favereau, Feb. 25, 1906'.
33. See Thomas, 'Anglo-Belgian military relations and the Congo question, 1911–1913', pp. 157–165, and Louis, *Ruanda-Urundi 1884–1919*, pp. 52–92.
34. Belgium, M.A.E. Arch., INDM, VII: 'Greindl to Davignon, Jan. 16, 1909'.
35. *Ibid.*, IX: 'Arendt note for Davignon, Jan. 27, 1911'.
36. *Times* (London), Dec. 21, 1910; see also *Times*, Dec. 19, 1910.
37. Belgium, M.A.E. Arch., Classement B, 156, I, 'De Bassompierre note for Davignon, Nov. 4, 1910'.
38. *Ibid.*, 'Note by Davignon with Van der Elst minute, Oct. 20, 1910'; 'De Bassompierre note for Davignon, Nov. 12, 1910'; 'Greindl to Davignon, Jan. 26, 1911'. See also Thomas, 'The use of the Scheldt in British plans', pp. 449–470.
39. Belgium, M.A.E. Arch., Classement B: 'Note written by Arendt at the end of 1911'; 'Arendt note of Feb. 19, 1912'.
40. *Ibid.*, 'Gaiffier note of Sept. 5, 1912'.
41. Belgium, M.A.E. Arch., INDM, VII: 'Greindl to Favereau, Feb. 13, 1906'; IX: 'Pro-memoria of Meeting Sept. 16, 1911'. The settlement of the Moroccan crisis led Davignon not to dispatch the circular in 1911. The Balkan crisis brought its dispatch during February and March 1913 (XII: 'Gaiffier note for Davignon and minute, Jan. 28, 1913'). Davignon's circular of July 24, 1914, also enclosed the statement of Belgian intentions; on Aug. 1, 1914, the Belgian ministers were instructed to deliver it (*Grey Book*, vol. I, nos. 2, 16, *Coll. Doc.*, pp. 300, 308).
42. Great Britain, *BD*, vol. VIII, p. 380, no. 313: 'Chilton to Grey, Feb. 25, 1909'.
43. *Ibid.*, pp. 351–382, no. 314: 'Extracts from Minutes of Committee of Imperial Defence, Aug. 23, 1911'.
44. Ritter, *The Schlieffen Plan*, p. 146. Belgium, M.A.E. Arch., Corr. pol., Leg., G.B., Unbound Series, VII: 'Lalaing report, Feb. 15, 1911, of Von Kuhlmann conversation with Gaston de Remaix'.
45. See Great Britain, *BD*, vol. VIII, pp. 409–411, no. 331: 'Extract from 1913 Report for Belgium'. France, *Documents diplomatiques français (DDF) (1871–1914)*, 3rd ser., vol. IX, pp. 612–614, no. 472: 'Commandant Génie to Noulens, Mar. 16, 1914'.
46. Belgium, M.A.E. Arch., INDM, X, pp. 16–17, 'Arendt memorandum "En cas de guerre", Nov. 1911'. Annexed to it is a copy of Gen. Ceulemans' note of Sept. 24, 1911.
47. Belgium, M.A.E. Arch., INDM, Duplicate dossier: 'Costermans note for Davignon, Jan. 17, 1911'; X: 'Note by Arendt, Feb. 1, 1912'.
48. *Ibid.*, XI: 'De Bassompierre draft, initialed by Gaiffier, Dec. 12, 1912'. This draft corresponds closely to the protest made Aug. 5, 1914, and printed in the *Grey Book*, vol. I, no. 44, *Coll. Doc.*, p. 323, with one notable exception: the three sentences here summarized were omitted.
49. Belgium, M.A.E. Arch., INDM, XI: 'Project of treaty, Dec. 12, 1912'.

50. Maj.-Gen. Tom Bridges, *Alarms and Excursions: Reminiscences of a Soldier*, pp. 62–63. Belgium, M.A.E. Arch., Corr. pol., Leg., G.B., Unbound Series, VII: 'Van der Elst note, Apr. 24, 1912'. This is reproduced in the *Grey Book*, vol. I, Appendix, no. 4 (2), *Coll. Doc.*, pp. 360–361. Williamson, *Politics of Grand Strategy*, p. 215.

51. Belgium, M.A.E. Arch., INDM, Unbound dos. for 1930–31: 'Note by Alfred de Ridder, May 31, 1930'. Archivist De Ridder reproduces a memorandum written in May 1917 by Baron de Broqueville telling of the Michel-Bridges interview.

52. *Ibid.*, X: 'Apr. 24, 1912'; 'Gaiffier note to Davignon, Apr. 27, 1912'.

53. *Ibid.*, 'Davignon to Greindl, May 10, 1912'.

54. *Ibid.*, 'Arendt memorandum, "Relations politiques avec l'Angleterre"', Apr. 10, 1912'.

55. *Ibid.*, XI: 'Gaiffier note to Davignon, Aug. 6, 1912'.

56. Belgium, M.A.E. Arch., Corr. pol., Leg., F., Unbound Series, IX: 'Gaiffier note, Dec. 2, 1912'; see also Great Britain, *BD*, vol. VIII, pp. 404–405, no. 328: 'Villiers to Grey, Nov. 22, 1912'.

57. France, *DDF*, 3rd ser., vol. IV, pp. 288–291, no. 278: 'Capt. Génie to Millerand, Oct. 29, 1912'.

58. Great Britain, *BD*, vol. VIII, p. 400, no. 325: 'Villiers to Sir W. Langley, Oct. 5, 1912'.

59. France, *DDF*, 3rd ser., vol. VIII, pp. 850–853, no. 673: 'Klobukowski to Doumergue, Dec. 25, 1913'. Nicolson, *Portrait of a Diplomatist*, pp. 289–291.

60. Belgium, M.A.E. Arch., INDM, XIV: 'Unsigned note written in hand of Gaiffier, Feb. 28, 1914'.

61. *Ibid.*, XIII: 'Gaiffier note for Davignon, Oct. 9, 1913'.

62. Belgium, M.A.E. Arch., Corr. pol., Leg., G.B., Unbound Series, VII: 'Van der Elst account of interview with Villiers, Oct. 1, 1912'; INDM, X, pp. 36–37, '"En cas de guerre", Nov. 1911'. Grey made a sincere effort to regain Belgian trust. Cf. Great Britain, *BD*, vol. VIII, p. 409, no. 330: 'Grey to Villiers, Apr. 7, 1913'; Belgium, M.A.E. Arch., INDM, XII: 'Lalaing to Davignon, Apr. 8, 1913'.

63. France, *DDF*, 3rd ser., vol. XI, pp. 468–470, no. 612: 'Cambon to Viviani, Aug. 2, 1914'.

64. *The German Documents Relating to the Outbreak of the War*, p. 486, no. 648: 'Jagow to Below, Aug. 2, 1914'. *Grey Book*, vol. II, no. 51: 'Beyens to Davignon, Sept. 21, 1914'. *Diplomatic Documents Relating to the Outbreak of the European War* (ed.) James Brown Scott, Part I, pp. 472–475.

65. Great Britain, *BD*, vol. VIII, p. 390, no. 319: 'Bridges to Villiers, Oct. 19, 1911'.

66. Van der Elst, 'La préméditation de l'Allemagne', p. 531.

67. *Ibid.*, 525–527. *Grey Book*, vol. I, no. 12: 'Davignon to Belgian ministers at Berlin, London, and Paris, July 31, 1914', *Coll. Doc.*, pp. 305–306. Great Britain, *BD*, vol. VIII, p. 409, no. 330: 'Grey to Villiers, Apr. 7, 1913'.

68. Van Langenhove, *Le dossier diplomatique*, p. 15.

69. *Grey Book*, vol. I, no. 11: 'Davignon to Belgian ministers at Berlin, London, and Paris, July 31, 1914', *Coll. Doc.*, pp. 304–305.
70. *Ibid.*; see also De Bassompierre, 'La nuit du 2 au 3 août 1914 au ministère des affaires étrangères de Belgique', p. 889.
71. *Grey Book*, vol. I, no. 38: 'Davignon to Belgian ministers, Aug. 4, 1914', *Coll. Doc.*, pp. 319–321.
72. *Ibid.*, no. 22: 'Davignon to von Below-Saleske, Aug. 3, 1914', *Coll. Doc.*, pp. 311–312.
73. De Bassompierre, 'La nuit', pp. 887–888.
74. Jacques Davignon, Baron Léon van der Elst, and Jules van den Heuvel (former minister of justice who for a long time had given the ministry of foreign affairs the benefit of his legal acumen) argued for the convention at the crown council of the afternoon of Aug. 4, 1914. They were overruled by Paul Hymans, Emile Vandervelde, François Schollaert, Georges Helle- putte and other important political leaders who thought that when the Belgian house was burning, the firemen should not be delayed by negotia- tions which might be long and complicated. Hymans, *Mémoires*, vol. II, pp. 95–97.) Undoubtedly it was as a consequence of this decision that the phrases in De Bassompierre's protest note draft referring to a conven- tion limiting the role of a guarantor were omitted when protest was made to Germany on Aug. 5, 1914 (see note 48).

7. Dividing the spoils

The rapid advance of German troops left the Belgian ministry of foreign affairs time for little more than a brief discussion with the Dutch concerning buoying of the Scheldt before all activities had to be transferred to Antwerp. Many important documents had to be left behind, later to be seized by the Germans and exploited for propaganda purposes. The fall in October of the national redoubt, which few Belgians had believed Germany would bother to attack seriously, forced the government to flee to the French town of Sainte-Adresse, near Le Havre. King Albert stayed behind as a focus for the Belgian spirit of independence and resistance; his headquarters was at La Panne, one of the fifty or so of the small country's approximately 2636 communes still independent. When the front was stabilized following the battle on the Yser, the only unoccupied regions of Belgium were the thin strip between that river and the French frontier and the enclave of Bar-le-Duc, spared invasion by its envelopment by Dutch territories. Such a tiny region within almost instantaneous reach of German troops could not serve as a base for an independent government, and the cabinet resigned itself to remaining in Sainte-Adresse.

Separated from their countrymen and deprived, at least at first, of what seemed all meaningful activity, the Belgian ministers were soon threatened with the danger of sinking into a morass of political bickerings. Domestic issues were viciously debated, and in the area of foreign affairs there were arguments whether Belgium should cease her active participation in the war and how and what territorial demands should be put forward. As a gesture of unity in the face of national disaster, representatives of the parties of the left were invited to join the Catholic dominated cabinet. Among those who accepted were Emile Vandervelde of the Socialists and Paul Hymans, disciple and biographer of Frère-Orban and then leader of the Liberal party. The latter acquisition was a particularly important one, for Hymans was destined to defend Belgium's interests at the peace conference and to become a leading figure in Belgian diplomacy for the next two decades.

The exiled cabinet early began to contemplate what a peace treaty would hold for Belgium. Fairly confident that the Entente would be victorious, the ministers were initially reassured by the promises of their British and French friends that Belgium would be restored and her rights and desires respected. Yet, as months passed, the Belgians came to believe that their country deserved more than a return to the *status quo* established by the Conference of London of 1830; the inequities of that settlement and certain other matters should be adjusted in Belgium's favor. The French and British, while still possessing benevolent intentions regarding Belgium, were also becoming concerned that their own sacrifices be justly rewarded. Destruction of French villages, railroads, and factories, and the sinking of British shipping meant that Belgium no longer would have the major claim on any reparations Germany might pay. And it was of course possible that the allies, on the pretext they could not afford to leave the Belgian alley open again, would make such demands on the little country that Belgian sovereignty in foreign policy and defense matters would be illusory.

The Belgians therefore found themselves simultaneously practicing diplomacies of aggrandizement and of defense. Experience was to show these were not entirely contradictory but that they could conflict in an embarrassing manner. The prime question was how a small country could extract the most concessions from the great powers.

Thanks to some military successes in Central Africa, the Belgians considered straightforward territorial bargaining there. They soon faced difficulties and found the only effective leverage Belgium had on her rescuers was the prestige gained by the resistance to the unprovoked German aggression in Europe. Her representatives to the peace conference did all they could to invoke the influence of this prestige and Belgium's popularity among the peoples of France, England, and the United States upon the diplomatic negotiations; yet they eventually had to resort to blunt and obstinate behavior before any dividends were obtained. The pleading of the Belgian case at the Entente chancelleries and at the Paris peace negotiations was a good example of the classic contest between moral suasion and power politics.

7.1 ENDING NEUTRALITY IN THE CONGO

The Belgians' mixture of fear and ambition first became evident regarding the Congo. The Brussels diplomats had long worried over French, British, and German designs on their African possession. These dated from the Congo Free State's earliest years but did not officially become the problem of the Belgian government until a combination of foreign criticism of Leopold's rule and the king's peculiar financial arrangements led Belgium to annex the Congo as a colony. The transfer of sovereignty was undertaken in 1908 not without difficulty, for both the French and British posed economic and territorial conditions. Settlement was reached with France, but Great Britain continued to refuse recognition of the annexation. Though Downing Street defended its attitude in high-sounding phrases calling for assurances of the maintenance of free trade and improved treatment of the natives, the Belgian diplomats suspected the verbal finery was only meant to conceal crass territorial designs. This belief seemed to be borne out by the manner in which the British and Germans collaborated in challenging Belgian claims on the valuable area of Mfumbiro north of Lake Kivu. On the occasion of the 1911 Agadir crisis the Belgians discovered that the pre-emption right given France in 1884 was a subject of barter in Franco-German negotiations, certainly not reassuring news. More disconcerting were the rumors generated by English-German talks of the same year and during the Haldane mission of 1912 which indicated that Britain would not oppose territorial rearrangements in Central Africa if Britain herself were allowed to make good certain claims, perhaps on Katanga and along the eastern borders of the Belgian Congo.[1]

When war broke out in Europe in 1914, there was initially every reason for Belgium to preserve the neutrality of the Congo. War there would be difficult to wage and a financial drain; its outcome would surely not affect the decision in Europe and it would set back the civilizing mission in Africa severely. Most important, any contest in Central Africa would endanger the integrity of the Congo either during hostilities or at a subsequent peace conference. It was patent, however, that if fighting did break out in the region it would be unlikely that the neutrality of the Congo would be unscathed. Davignon therefore tried to persuade the great powers to take advantage of Article Eleven of the General Act of the Conference of Berlin. That article provided that if a power should find itself at war in Europe:

the territories belonging to this Power and comprised in the conventional zone of commercial liberty may be, with the common consent of this Power and of the other party or parties belligerent, placed for the duration of the war under the regime of neutrality and considered as belonging to a non-belligerent State; the belligerent parties may renounce, thenceforth, the extension of hostilities to the territories thus neutralised, as also their use as a base for the operations of war.[2]

In the last days of July 1914, as catastrophe appeared imminent in Europe, the Belgians took precautions to assure that no incident should occur in the Congo which would jeopardize Belgium's neutrality in Europe. Orders were issued that under normal circumstances warships of belligerent nations were not to be allowed to enter the Congo River. These instructions were made obsolete by Germany's invasion of Belgium. After the quick response of Britain and France to the little country's appeal for aid, it seemed 'impossible to proclaim and observe absolute *neutrality* in the Congo'.[3] Albert de Bassompierre argued that Belgium 'can not refuse the allied fleets access to our waters or French troops the use of our railroad...[in the colony]'.[4] On August 6, the governor general of the Congo was told not to apply the rules of neutrality to British, French, and Russian naval forces but rather to aid them.[5]

Though defensive measures were taken throughout the colony, more positive protective steps were needed. The following day, Davignon inquired of the powers if they would make use of the provision of the Act of Berlin and neutralize their colonies in the Congo basin. The immediate French reaction was encouraging. President Raymond Poincaré saw little difficulty in declaring the French Congo neutral. He nevertheless held his reply in reserve, ostensibly because of rumors that hostilities had already begun in the Ubangi region. Two days later, the Belgian minister reported that the French government was 'strongly inclined' to have neutrality proclaimed for all possessions in the conventional basin of the Congo and was inviting Spain to suggest this at Berlin.[6] The French had endeavored to take the initiative from the Belgians. More important, rather than neutralize their colony independently, as had the Belgians, the French indicated they would link such a step to similar actions by the other belligerent states, most particularly Great Britain. This is not surprising, for if the French proclaimed their colony neutral while British colonies challenged the Germans, France would have little claim for African spoils were Germany defeated. Also, if the British did want to wage war in Africa, France could not properly refuse them assistance. It is difficult to believe that any proposal whatever would have gone into effect unless Germany convinced the Entente that she would respect the declared neutrality of Central African colonies. After the invasion of Belgium, that would have been a difficult task.

A similar concern for the overall situation in the Congo basin was held by the British government, with which the French conferred upon receipt of the Belgian proposal. Although the Committee of Imperial Defence had studied the problem in the past, the British asked for time. Meanwhile, Spain did not broach the issue at Berlin, for the Madrid government would not accept the mission until the views of Great Britain were known.

Even though the London government did not reject neutralization outright, by the end of the second week of August the proposal was a dead letter. At the same time that the British were considering the neutrality of all the Congo basin, they were sounding out the French on the possibility of common action in the Cameroons. The French were agreeable for they were eager to regain territory which had been surrendered in 1911 as a result of the Agadir incident. The governor of Gabon thought success was virtually assured in such an enterprise. This was also the estimation of Pierre de Margerie, in the French foreign ministry, who believed 'that in view of the present situation Germany should be attacked wherever possible'.[7]

In light of these opinions, Klobukowski told the Belgians he believed it impossible for France to envisage neutralization of her Congo territory. Four days later, on August 17, the British government officially declined the Belgian proposal, asserting that Germans had already attacked the British Central African Protectorate. Also, British troops had destroyed the wireless station at Dar-es-Salaam in German East Africa, which, along with other stations, had been causing difficulties for British shipping. It was not until October of 1915 that Grey admitted that at the time England refused the Belgian proposal, Germany had not yet taken any hostile initiative against a British colony in Central Africa.

The Belgians' hope of saving the entire Congo basin from war was ended, but a chance remained that they might preserve the neutrality of their own colony. The morning following receipt of Klobukowski's message, Pierre Orts, diplomatic counselor in the ministry of colonies, proposed that Belgium inform the allies of her intention to keep the Congo neutral. France and England should be warned that their cruisers could not enter the river mouth or take on provisions; nor could the allies use the Matadi-Leopoldville railway for transmission of troops or munitions. Orts suggested further that the allies be asked whether the neutrality of the Congo under these conditions would be against their best interests. If the reply were affirmative, such neutrality would be 'impossible to maintain against the will of the allies'.[8] But if the colony were to make a sacrifice, something should be obtained in exchange. Perhaps France and England would guarantee Belgium the possession of her colony after peace had been established.

Orts' position involved a stricter interpretation of neutrality than that which had been recommended two days after the outbreak of war in Europe. This interpretation may have reflected annoyance at the Entente powers' refusal to declare their colonies neutral. It is more probable, however, that the Belgians merely wished not to provoke an attack by giving Germany grounds for a claim that the Congo was no longer neutral. Davignon, De Broqueville, and Minister of Colonies Jules Renkin quickly approved.

In discussing the new Belgian position with the French and British, Secretary-General Van der Elst met opposition, for these countries expected the Belgian Congo to offer privileges to allied navies and troop shipments. The preference of the Entente officials for a flexible interpretation of Congo neutrality became increasingly evident as the talks progressed. Given the circumstances in Europe, Van der Elst could not hold firm against French and English pressure. The Belgian position was therefore redefined. As the German government had already violated the neutrality of Belgium, it would certainly not respect that of the Congo, he wrote. The German ultimatum had stated that the territory of Belgium and her possessions would be guaranteed only if Belgium allowed German troops free passage. This Belgium had not done; according to the wording of the ultimatum, Germany must then consider Belgium an enemy in the Congo as well as in Europe. Convinced that the powers which had supported Belgium's integrity would also support that of her colony, Van der Elst proposed informing the Entente ministers that 'Belgium has decided to facilitate passage of their troops through her territory and to assure their ships refuge in the Congo mouth should need arise.'[9]

Davignon described this position to the British and French envoys on August 22. To avoid any misunderstanding, Villiers gave the Belgians a draft of his report to London, presumably for their approval. In this message, the readiness of the Belgians to allow France to ship troops and munitions on the Matadi-Stanley Pool railway was emphasized as was the access of allied ships to the Congo River mouth. Summing up the discussion, Villiers declared:

The result is that the Belgian Government are prepared to afford to their allies such facilities as they may require for military operations in West Africa, asking in return for assurances that Great Britain and France will support them in securing the independence and integrity of their colonial possessions.[10]

A statement of assurance was jointly given by the French and British on September 19, 1914. But well before then the Congo was at war. On the same day that Villiers and Davignon were agreeing on the extent to which the Belgian Congo's neutrality should be compromised in favor of the allies, a German gunboat fired on Albertville, the chief Congolese port on Lake Tanganyika. By the end of the first week of September several incidents involving the Belgian colony had occurred, although the major military conflict centered on the nearby Northern Rhodesian town of Abercorn.

The failure of Belgian efforts to persuade Britain and France to examine with Germany the possibility of neutralizing the Congo basin was all the more unfortunate because the Germans had also been attempting to initiate such a discussion through the good offices of the United States. Unfortunately, the request came too late. The day it was made, the German commander-in-chief for East Africa, Colonel Paul von Lettow-Vorbeck, eager to harrass the enemy and angered by the British shelling of Dar-es-Salaam, launched his attack on Albertville despite having been warned that any European war should not be carried to the colonies.[11] Once both sides had drawn blood, there was little hope peace could be maintained, and United States Secretary of State William Jennings Bryan's month-long delay in forwarding the proposal further assured its failure.

Throughout August and September, Belgian policy regarding the Congo was one of caution and fear. Belgian intentions were prudent and honorable, but they had little chance of success because of the position taken in London. It was the British government that essentially determined Entente policy in Central Africa at the start of the war, and the opportunity to seize German colonies was too great for the empire-minded British to forego. Thus it was that when a British naval captain arranged a truce with German East Africa following the raid on Dar-es-Salaam, his efforts were repudiated by the admiralty; plans instead were laid for capture of that German port, which occurred on September 4.[12] The French, who at first had been attracted to the Belgian proposal, appreciated the chance to harm Germany however possible, and by the end of August were deeply involved in the Ubangi.

The Belgians were left with the choice of alone remaining neutral in the Congo basin, perhaps seeing some of their stations spared destruction but risking loss of any voice in the arranging of Central African affairs at a peace conference should the Entente be victorious. Moreover, in view of Entente aid in Europe and the German raid on Albertville the choice really seemed to be one between a stationary defensive war or offensive action. The series of rapid defeats in Belgium stung the officials to take what active offensives they could; it is not surprising that Renkin's orders sent to the colony on August 28 were in that vein. Aid was promptly given French troops in the Cameroons. In the middle of September, the Germans attacked Abercorn, a town in Northern Rhodesia just fifteen miles from the southern tip of Lake Tanganyika. Caught unprepared, the British troops appealed for help; the Belgians were happy to respond. The request made by the local commander was soon countermanded by London; yet eventually the appeal was renewed by the British high commissioner in Rhodesia, and Belgian troops did participate in the freeing of Abercorn.[13]

Although German pressure on Abercorn was broken, English ambivalence regarding Belgian participation in the Central African war remained. At the heart of the problem was Britain's reluctance to see Belgian troops occupy territory in German East Africa, which she desired for herself at the end of the war. It was probably more for this reason than from desire to spare the Belgian Congo the difficulties of carrying out a military campaign that London continued to refer to the 'desirability of maintaining the partial neutrality of the Congo'.[14] Such comments annoyed De Bassompierre and Renkin; an inquiry brought a prompt apology from Sir Francis Villiers. The British government merely wished to indicate it still considered itself bound by the assurances given earlier that Britain would not draw on Congolese facilities except in dire necessity. 'His Majesty's Government take note, however, of the fact that the Belgian Government have definitively abandoned the policy of partial neutrality which occasion these assurances, and it will therefore in the future be unnecessary to recur to the subject.'[15]

The Belgians, who in the decade before the war had argued there was no such thing as partial neutrality, had indeed changed policies in Africa. Ambition was overcoming caution; plans were laid for a major attack on German East Africa, and a list of territorial goals was drawn up. In May 1915, shortly after Paul Hymans arrived in London as the new Belgian minister, he received from Davignon a list of Belgium's desiderata upon the conclusion of peace. They were vaguely phrased, except for Part V regarding the Congo. A short memorandum stated that a peace settlement should bring the Congo territorial and economic benefits. Better access to the ocean was needed and could be obtained by gaining control of part of the Cabinda enclave and of Portuguese land along the south bank of the Congo near the river's mouth. Portugal would be compensated for these cessions with territories taken from German South West Africa or East Africa. British support would be vital for such a transaction and could be demanded as the price of the aid Belgium had given in Rhodesia. Belgium might also capture Ruanda in the course of military operations; as England no doubt would want to annex German East Africa, the turning over of this territory to the English should warrant their intervention at Lisbon. Mention was also made of minor rectifications of the Congo-German East African border as established by a convention of 1910. Certain annoying clauses of the Berlin Act should be voided, though the ruling on freedom of trade should remain; also, conventions should be concluded which would improve access to the heart of the Congo, particularly from Dar-es-Salaam. It was added that the colony's claims should be kept distinct from those of the mother country, just as the basis of those claims (effective military aid as compared to being the innocent martyr of a Franco-German quarrel) were distinct.[16]

The Belgian claims on behalf of the Congo, though not extensive in terms of territory, were nevertheless considerable because of the complicated diplomacy required to consummate any arrangement with Portugal. At first glance, the Belgians' optimism appears naïve, but the manner in which they subsequently pursued their goals, both in Africa and in Europe, reveals that this optimism was countered by a strong streak of pessimism. Belgium's ambitious hopes were always presented to the allies in a cautious, hardly confident manner. The composition of her war aims was done upon a foundation of nagging fear that after all was over, Belgium's modest needs and wishes would be trampled in the great powers' rush to secure the spoils of war for themselves. It was to gaining assurances that this would not happen that the Belgians devoted their military efforts in Africa and their diplomatic skills in Europe and America.

7.2 War aims and diplomacy

During the first year of the war, Belgium's diplomacy was limited to tightening relations with her defenders and to promoting her cause among the populations of friendly states. Neither of these were difficult tasks, although one incident developed early in the war which brought some French complaint and was to take on added significance through its recurrence years later.

In the middle of August, following a sharp battle in which the Belgian army sustained heavy losses, it was decided to stage an orderly withdrawal to the defenses of Antwerp. This move was in accordance with the traditional defense plan established since 1859 and with the explicit recommendations made by General Ceulemans and other leading military figures in the years prior to the invasion. The Belgians wished to hold on, but the numerical preponderance of German troops was too great. While the Germans were marching on Louvain, French troops were still below Namur and British soldiers were just appearing in the West. It seemed clear that the juncture of allied forces would not take place before the Belgian army were cut off from Antwerp. Loss of the national redoubt and the 'island of independent Belgium' could not be contemplated. Though France begged the Belgians to maintain their lines in defense of Brussels for two more days, it was decided this was impossible; retreat was ordered on August 18. The annoyance among French military figures lingered, but upon learning the specifics of the Belgian army's difficult position the governments of both France and England acknowledged the necessity of the retreat and affirmed their continuing confidence in the Belgian defensive effort.

It was only a few days after the Belgian government moved to Antwerp that De Broqueville conceived of sending a special mission to the United States. Though Davignon considered this an irregular approach to diplomacy, its advantages were numerous. There was no telling what role the United States might yet play in the European contest, and where better could Belgium look for aid than a country similarly neutral and noted for its resources and its idealism? Armaments might not be forthcoming, but perhaps arrangements for food supplies could be made; at the peace the small country would need all the support it could get from world opinion.

On August 31, Minister of Justice Edmond Carton de Wiart left on his trip, accompanied by Emile Vandervelde (Socialist chief and minister of state), Baron Louis de Sadeleer (a leading Flemish Catholic and minister of state) and Paul Hymans (also a minister of state and head of the Liberal party); thus the most prominent sectors of Belgian political opinion were represented. Visits were paid to President Wilson and to Theodore Roosevelt, and speeches were given at every opportunity. It was evident from the first that the Belgians were well received, and the ultimate success of the tour was even more far reaching than was thought at the time.

The importance of American sympathy and friendship was quickly demonstrated. The devastation brought by the war had gravely disrupted the Belgian economy and the requisitions of the occupying troops made the situation worse. Each commune set up its own emergency committee to procure supplies; in Brussels the *Comité Central de Secours et d'Alimentation* was formed under the presidency of Ernest Solvay with the influential banker Emile Francqui serving as its prime mover. This private organization soon despaired of obtaining the necessary food supplies and turned, as did the committees of other cities, to London to purchase food. The British, though willing to sell, distrusted German promises not to requisition the supplies when they reached Belgium. The problem was brought to the attention of Herbert Hoover, who was head of the American Relief Committee in charge of the repatriation of Americans stranded in Europe at the beginning of the war. Hoover's suggested solution of consigning the goods to the American minister in Brussels, who would then oversee their distribution, proved successful. The American ministers in London and Brussels, Walter Hines Page and Brand Whitlock, threw their support to the project; the German governor general in Belgium, happy to be spared the task of feeding the civilian population, renewed his promise to permit the shipping of supplies to Belgian civilians. The aid of the Dutch and Spanish ministers was obtained and on October 22, 1914, the Commission for Relief in Belgium was established under the presidency of Hoover; in a corresponding move the *Comité Central* became the *Comité National*. The services these committees performed were immense both physically and in terms of morale. The over five million metric tons of supplies provided enabled the Belgian peoples to survive, and knowledge of American sympathy gave them hope for the future.[17]

The fate of the Belgian civilians was a constant concern of the government. The officials did what they could to aid the work of the C.R.B., but leadership of the movement necessarily fell to the Americans. One matter not directly within the scope of the commission was the supplying of raw material for Belgian factories. Unless these were kept in operation, there would be unemployment and a temptation to the Germans to dismantle the machines and ship them home. Paul Hymans took up the matter with Grey on several occasions. With the aid of Francqui and Hoover, a plan was made for importation of raw materials and the export of manufactured goods under the auspices of the C.R.B. The proposal was not acceptable to the Germans and fell by the wayside in 1916. Disappointed on this score, Hymans pressed the British to start considering the means by which Belgian industry might be re-established following the war. Concentrating on the battlefield, the British were only vaguely interested but did agree to the establishment of an interallied commission to study the problem. With the same concern in mind, Hymans took up the issue of Belgian economic relations with the British empire in the hope that Belgium might be granted preferential treatment in trading with the dominions after the war. The British were vague on this point also, and nothing came of Hymans' approach.

In broaching these issues, the Belgian minister was attempting to gain one of Belgium's main war aims. When the foreign ministry turned its attention to war aims in the spring of 1915, it had chosen to state its desires generally and not to formulate any specific territorial demands quite yet. Its six point program was simple. Belgium's independence was to be sacred; she was to be invited to participate in the peace talks and was to receive reparation for damages suffered. If Germany were unable to pay, then the allies should help Belgium rebuild her ruins. Point IV called for a revision of the treaties of 1839 which would allow Belgium to be neutral of her own choice; that is, she desired her independence to be guaranteed, but only in a manner compatible with full Belgian sovereignty, a principle which it was held the Conference of London had not followed in forcing Belgium to be neutral. The following point listed the territorial gains desired for the Congo, and the last cited long-term commercial treaties as a proper avenue by which the allies might repay Belgium for her service in the cause of civilization.[18]

The omission of territorial claims was surprising in light of the well-known desire of several members of the government to augment Belgian holdings in Flemish Zeeland, Limburg, and the region of the Duchy of Luxemburg. The reason was the disharmony which reigned in the exiled government. Numerous schisms had developed regarding foreign affairs, one of the most debilitating of which was between the annexationists and the 'little Belgians'. The former group believed that Belgium's economic future and political security would be enhanced by judicious territorial acquisitions. The others hewed to the policy established by Frère-Orban in 1867: territorial demands would damage the prestige earned by Belgium's self-sacrificing behavior over the years, draw the enmity of the powers, and in the long run weaken rather than strengthen Belgium's security. Moreover, was Belgium's security a sufficient motive for claiming the dismemberment of neutral Holland, particularly as the inhabitants of the region in question had shown no recent desires to join Belgium? Some Walloons feared annexation of Luxemburg (and of course also Limburg) would bring Germanic elements into the state which would combine with the Flemings in the battle for political power, exacerbate the linguistic controversy, and create a strong pro-German influence in the country.

For their part, many Flemings resisted the notion of seizing Dutch territory, asserting that such action would provoke a conflict with the neighboring kingdom which would seriously harm the development of Flemish culture and solidarity. Groupings on the political left feared that under the guise of patriotism the right might succeed in annexing sufficient amounts of Roman Catholics and conservatives to achieve firm control of the country in the next decade. To the Socialists, any talk of annexations was anathema to political doctrine; however, their chief, Emile Vandervelde, somehow managed to trim his sails in this issue sufficiently enough that he could, in good conscience, remain in a union cabinet that eventually did press for some territorial gains.

The arguments over the proper definition of the national interest which raged in the *salons* at Sainte-Adresse prevented any resolution of territorial claims for several years. It was bitter, debilitating, and had its casualties; in 1916, for example, the foreign minister had to force Baron Guillaume's resignation after the Belgian representative in Paris sent notes to King Albert, the French president and premier, and journalists protesting against current small-Belgium policy.[19] But this was not the only division among the Belgian officials on foreign policy; there was another dispute which to a certain extent cut across other factional groupings. It concerned Belgium's continuing official status as a neutral. On September 5, 1914, France, England, and Russia signed a convention at London in which they agreed not to conclude any separate peace or to propose peace conditions to the enemy without first obtaining each other's consent. The Belgian government was not invited to participate, and when it learned of the convention, fears began to mount. What if the war should drag on until a compromise peace were established? Would the compromise be made at the expense of Belgium? The memory of the Benedetti treaty was not reassuring. Many diplomats urged that Belgium protect herself by requesting admission to the September 5 convention; in December of 1915 the *Direction politique*, still headed by Gaiffier, recommended such a course lest the powers think they were authorized to speak in Belgium's name and to regulate her affairs. Napoleon Eugène Beyens, the former minister to Germany who had been substituting for the dying Julien Davignon since July 1915, thought otherwise. His authority may have been lessened by his *ad interim* status, but his arguments were lucid. The London pact was an alliance, and Belgium as a small state would be unable to influence her partners while being bound to execute their will by the terms of the alliance. She might be required to fight not just until her own lands were freed but also to take part in an offensive on German soil. Surely, too, the Germans would resent the Belgian action and abandon what little restraint they had shown in ruling occupied Belgium. Most important, Belgium would lose the prestigious position she possessed as a violated neutral; she would become just another belligerent and be deprived of her best argument for total reparation after the war.[20]

Despite the biting attack of those who said he was like a woman still insisting she was defending her virginity after she had been ravished by scores of soldiers, Beyens maintained his opinion. Both Klobukowski and Villiers indicated that Belgium had not been invited to sign because of her special status. Such a signature in September 1914 would have appeared to verify German claims that Belgium had not actually been neutral, and any signature in December 1915 would be tardy and superfluous. Beyens was ably supported by Van der Elst, and on December 20 the cabinet was brought around to the view that instead of signing the pact Beyens should quietly obtain declarations from the powers that would provide the necessary guarantees.

When he approached the English on the matter, Hymans was pleasantly surprised. The lord president of the council, Lord Crew, indicated his country's willingness to make a declaration which would renew the multiple promises made at the beginning of the war. He assured

Hymans, to whom the fear of isolation had become an obsession, that the allies would not settle Belgium's affairs without the concurrence of her representatives. When Crew inquired about Belgian territorial claims on Luxemburg, Hymans replied that if the powers decided the duchy could not subsist as an autonomous state it might be restored to Belgium. His main emphasis, however, was upon the achievement of full Belgian independence of territory and of any economic tutelage that Germany might want to impose in a negotiated peace.[21]

Although Beyens had also obtained favorable results in his talks at Paris, the drafting of an appropriate declaration by the French and British foreign ministers took some time. On February 14, 1916, the ministers of France, England, and Russia formally declared that:

the Belgian government will be called to participate in the peace negotiations and that they [the allied powers] will not end hostilities until Belgium is reestablished in her political and economic independence and is largely indemnified for the damages she has suffered. They will offer their aid to Belgium to assure her commercial and financial reconstruction.[22]

The Italian and Japanese ministers did not join in the statement but did indicate they had no objections to its contents.

This Declaration of Sainte-Adresse, as it was called, if criticized by some members of the Belgian government as minimal and vague, was nevertheless welcomed by Beyens and his supporters. All the Belgians had originally requested had been granted with but one exception. That was their call for mention of her 'just claims'. This reference to postwar territorial acquisitions had appeared to the British and French as unwise. Publication of territorial demands would only stiffen the fighting will of the German people; Paul Cambon, the French ambassador in London, suggested that such a vague statement would only raise questions and stimulate further debate within the Belgian government.[23]

The validity of these arguments could not be challenged. But the Belgians did realize that it was time a definite program were established regarding territorial claims. In the past months the 'big Belgium' advocates had gained supporters and Beyens himself had authorized tentative feelers regarding Luxemburg. Gaiffier urged Hymans to take up with Grey the question of Dutch control of the mouths of the Scheldt and thus of Antwerp's access to the sea; he hoped to work Beyens into a position where the foreign minister himself would voice official interest in the matter. If the policy director wished Belgium's security and economic position on the Scheldt improved, he did not demand annexation of Flemish Zeeland, as did some expansionists. Hymans explained this restraint to Paul Cambon. Belgium had need of friendly relations with Holland. She was a neighbor and at the fall of Antwerp had accommodated 600,000 Belgian refugees. It also occurred to Hymans that Holland was a neutral and that Belgium would not enhance her moral position by issuing claims on a non-combatant's territory. Moreover, it was the attitude of the allies, not of all the other countries, that would determine what Belgium would receive. Therefore Belgium should carefully consider her aims, formulate a precise program and present it, rather than a vague generality, to the allies.[24]

Hymans' views now carried more weight than earlier, for on January 18, 1916, he had become minister without portfolio in a newly constituted national union cabinet headed by De Broqueville. The establishment of the new ministry indicated that if the debates within the exiled government were not ended, a new effort would be made to resolve them. Nine days later, the cabinet traveled to meet with the king. Albert believed that only a compromise peace would be possible and that therefore Belgium should ask only for restoration of her pre-war boundaries. De Broqueville appears to have disagreed with him at this time, but in subsequent months he was won over to Albert's views. No decision was reached during the formal cabinet meeting on whether to broach the Scheldt question with England or not; afterwards Hymans did persuade the king that the proper course would be to discuss the matter with England without speaking of territorial gains; perhaps the British would take an initiative that Belgium herself could not. A week after the declaration of Sainte-Adresse was made public, another conference was held. Minister of Colonies Renkin attacked Beyens and the declaration and called for territorial annexations. After Beyens defended himself, Hymans took over. He insisted on the fixation of a definite program which should correspond to the actualities of the situation as well as to Belgian desires. Annexation of German territories was to be avoided, for it would stir desire for revenge in Germany and cause domestic dissension. Prudence would have to be shown regarding the Netherlands, for that country should not be alienated. Belgium's most reasonable program should, for the present, be limited to two points. First, the Duchy of Luxemburg should go to Belgium if the powers believed it could not lead an autonomous existence. Second, the problem of the Scheldt should be presented to England without any precise solution being proposed. Though Beyens believed it was up to Belgium to present her preferred solution and not ask England to settle the Scheldt problem for her, Hyman's recommendation was accepted.[25]

Hymans had shown himself the skilled politican and diplomat that he was. The differences within the cabinet were papered over and a program adopted which did not endanger Belgium's best propaganda weapon – her uncalculating self-sacrifice in the war. It was the only lever by which Belgium could hope to move the powers at a peace conference, and events were to prove the necessity of keeping it untarnished. The French, for example, were already showing themselves difficult on the Luxemburg issue. Despite the willingness of the French ambassador in London to consider Luxemburg and the left bank of the Scheldt as the proper objects of Belgian aspirations, at the Quai d'Orsay the attitude was different. At one point in 1915, French Minister of Foreign Affairs Théophile Delcassé had indicated that Luxemburg should go to Belgium, but more recently he had said nothing when efforts were made to obtain guarantees to that effect. At the end of January 1916, French adjoint political director Philippe Berthelot termed any consideration of the matter premature and indicated that France, because her capital was too near the German border, might 'take up the policy of Louis XIV'.[26] Alsace-Lorraine would not suffice; part of the Palatinate would have to be annexed; the case of the duchy had yet to be considered.

There was reason also to question whether Britain looked favorably on any Belgian aggrandizement. Warnings had been made about issuing claims, and the English attitude regarding Central Africa was scarcely encouraging. True, a declaration in addition to that of February was obtained stating that the allies would work 'to maintain the Belgian Congo in its present territorial state and to have a special indemnity attributed to that colony for the damages suffered in the course of the war'.[27] But the British did not appear willing to award the Congo the rich fruits of victory, as the wording 'present territorial state' intimated.

Shortly before the Congo declaration was made, Belgian-directed troops launched an effective campaign in German East Africa. Two days before it began, the English, who were also attacking in the same region, asked agreement that any occupation by British and Belgian troops be temporary and that final attribution of territory await the close of hostilities. They also said that 'to prevent confusion, to secure uniform action and to promote the communication of the Allies the British government are prepared to undertake the whole control and administration of occupied territory...'.[28] Though he accepted the first proposition, the second was not pleasing to Renkin, who a few weeks earlier had instructed the acting vice-governor of Katanga:

One of the goals of our military effort in Africa is, as you know, to assure possession of German territory for use as a pawn in negotiations. If when the peace negotiations open, changes in possession of African territories are envisaged, the retention of this pawn would be favorable to Belgian interests from every point of view. But it is indispensable that the conquered territories be occupied by us to the exclusion of foreign authority...[29]

The penchant for aggrandizement revealed by the colonial minister differed markedly from the attitude of Beyens, who since January 1916 had held the foreign ministry portfolio in his own right. A conflict was almost inevitable, and the result was one of the sorriest episodes of Belgium's wartime diplomacy.

The issue which brought it about was a British request for aid in capturing the town of Tabora. This the Belgians willingly gave, but they rejected a subsequent appeal to lend Congolese troops to the British; Belgium's colonial forces were to fight only under the Belgian flag and Belgian officers. In September 1916, just prior to the fall of Tabora, the Belgians informed the British that they were ready to turn the town over to them; Belgium now occupied Ruanda, Urundi, Udjiji, Karema, and part of Bukoba, more than enough pawns for future negotiation. There had been some dispute between the Belgians and English over the delimitations of the Belgian occupation zone; Renkin's desire was either to withdraw from Tabora to occupy more adequately the regions in dispute or to continue holding Tabora for the British in return for recognition of the Belgian version of the occupation boundaries.

The British, short of troops, admitted the need of Belgian assistance and inquired regarding the limits Belgium would accept for her provisional occupation and the permanent acquisitions she desired. For once the Belgians were not petitioners, but they allowed the tables to be turned on them. In his October 7 answer to the British, Beyens displayed his cards, and it became obvious he was bidding too high. He demanded both Tabora and the previously mentioned regions as occupation zones; he also set forth Belgium's designs on Portuguese Cabinda and the left bank of the Congo. The announcement of demands of such scope brought an understandable reply from London: England would control the Tabora region herself and considered any discussion of the future disposition of the German territories as premature.

The English in their annoyance went so far as to accuse Belgium of contemplating a separate peace. The embarrassed Belgians denounced the accusation but had no alternative than to evacuate Tabora. On December 14, Beyens informed Villiers that Belgium would cede the village. A few hours later he wrote again, this time saying that because so much had happened since September the Belgian offer of that month to turn Tabora over to the English could no longer be considered in effect. Were Belgium allowed to occupy the region, she would be glad to aid the English in their military campaign which was currently faltering for lack of troops. Such sharp bargaining was rejected, and the still further compromised Belgians eventually provided the English military support in Africa without even a compensatory recognition of the boundaries of the Belgian zone of occupation.[30]

The vacillations and *gaucheries* of Belgian diplomacy in this episode stemmed from the bitter conflict – which went beyond mere differences of opinion – between Renkin and Beyens. The Renkin entourage was influential and the Congo was the colonial minister's particular bailiwick; Beyens was not always able to withstand Renkin's demands. Exactly who was responsible for each step in the discussions is not yet known, but an estimate can be made with the knowledge that Renkin's appetite for colonial conquest grew continually throughout the war. The desire to gain the Portuguese territories had existed from the first stages of the conflict, but the intention had heretofore been that an exchange would be worked out with the aid of Britain. As Renkin wished to arrange the deal, it was to operate not by Britain's good offices but by a tightly driven bargain that Downing Street could well interpret as blackmail. This bargain was all the more distasteful because while England's soldiers were freely letting their blood for the restoration of the Belgian homeland, the Belgians were setting a price for their cooperation in Africa. The error committed was a serious one, for it brought into the open what had thus far been successfully repressed, though no doubt acknowledged by the various governments: that the Belgian campaigns in Africa were intended as much to obtain pawns for negotiations with Britain at the peace conference as they were to harm Germany or hold stakes against that empire. Moreover, the manner in which Belgium presented her aims in Africa turned her from a nation whose war performance there automatically merited reward to a greedy nation asking compensations which she apparently believed could be gained only by taking advantage of a current British weakness.

The results at the peace conference of all this were unfortunate, but Beyens, who was not the chief figure responsible, did not have to deal with them. Only one final quarrel and disappointment was reserved for him before he abandoned the foreign ministry portfolio in August 1917. Not a partisan of the theory of strategic frontiers, he believed a state of Belgium's size could be protected only with the aid of foreign powers. He had also had enough of the regime of neutrality, and so in July 1916 he informed the allies that any continuation of the 1839 arrangement would be a diminution of Belgium's sovereignty, a pretext for Germany to intervene in Belgian affairs, and an illusory protection. He added that while Belgium did not wish an alliance with her neighbors she hoped that as the independence of the small state and her colony were of such value to France and Britain the allies would guarantee it. Belgium would not be party to such a treaty but would agree to maintain her defenses at their necessary strength by general and obligatory service in the armed forces. The British reaction was somewhat favorable, but the project was let slide into limbo by the Belgian government. The cabinet objected to the promise made by Beyens regarding the armed forces, a promise that was needed if British assent were to be obtained and which was not overly rash, as such general and obligatory service had been prescribed by the law of 1913. Hymans was instructed to state that Belgium could not limit her sovereign power to organize her national defense as she wished. The British replied it seemed that Belgium was asking to be relieved of any responsibility to the power she was petitioning to guarantee her; they took care not to discuss the matter again.[31]

The division within the Belgian camp was complicated by a difference of attitude between the king at La Panne and the ministers at Sainte-Adresse. Albert, acutely aware of the sufferings of his soldiers and the Belgian populace, was determined not to ask his people to make addition-al sacrifices unless faced by absolute necessity. On several occasions he forced Beyens to tone down replies to German statements for fear of provoking occupation of the small remainder of independent Belgium. The commander-in-chief and his generals were convinced that allied military victory was improbable; only compromise could end the war. Territorial claims would only annoy Germany and make compromise more difficult. The foreign minister, who within the cabinet was considered to be the king's man, was sympathetic to this view; but it was he, rather than Albert, who had to find a *modus vivendi* with the patriotic ministers so confident of imminent French triumph.

In October of 1916, Beyens and Minister of Finance Aloys van de Vijvere traveled to La Panne to discuss the cabinet's criticism of the king's unwillingness to reject totally unofficial German peace feelers. The king was dismayed to learn of the manner in which De Broqueville was attacking Beyens and that ministerial hot-heads were using the word 'treason' in referring to the king's attitude. Albert agreed not to take up the German approach, for he believed it would be necessary to wait until the allies' Somme offensive failed (as he was sure it would) before Paris and London could be persuaded to negotiate. Meanwhile, he would not risk his men or his country. In December, he wrote in his diary:

Our war aim is not the same as England's; we are not in arms to destroy Ger-many. We will not march in unrealizable enterprises. Offensives will not succeed; experience has proved it.[32]

The cabinet came round to the king's view on this matter as soon as it was understood that the British were planning a spring offensive for Belgium which would undoubtedly lead to the destruction of a large sector of the country. During December three cabinet meetings were held in the king's presence to consider the effect of the planned offensive and whether to reply independently of the Anglo-French answer to President Wilson's inquiry regarding the war aims of the belligerents. To the assembled ministers Albert read a statement that the liberation of Belgium by arms would be equivalent to her destruction. 'She had been dragged in the wake of the great nations, confused and intermingled with the other small states which do not have the same rights. The moment is come to defend our point of view.'[33] Without asking for an impossible separate peace, Belgium should make her war aims known so that she could play a role in the preparation of peace.

The ministers agreed without dissent and a special note was drafted. It was never sent, for once returned to Sainte-Adresse and away from Albert's influence, the ministers allowed the French and British in the name of unity to push them into renouncing the separate note and incorporating their response with those of the great powers. The Quai d'Orsay was so disturbed by Albert's attitude that Berthelot was sent to La Panne, carrying also with him a sharp letter from Earl Curzon, President of the British House of Lords. The interview must have been difficult. Albert apparently did not back down; he wrote to Curzon that though he did not contemplate a separate peace, he could not share the allies' belief the enemy would be crushed.

I think there will be neither victors nor vanquished and the present situation will not be markedly modified... In all conscience, those who are responsible for the interests of the Belgian nation can not support a war policy which exposes Belgium to total destruction.[34]

The split between the king of the Belgians and his two great allies grew wider as weeks passed. In February, he was affronted to learn that the French and British wished to put the Belgian army under British Field Marshal Douglas Haig's command in a diversionary maneuver in Flanders. Such a thought was offensive to the country's pride. Moreover, the king noted in his diary, securing the entire Flemish coast would aid Britain more than Belgium and would lead to devastation of Belgian lands. And he had not even been consulted! 'One can clearly see that small countries should distrust the larger powers, even when the latter call themselves allies.'[35]

At Sainte-Adresse, the internecine quarrels over foreign affairs did not subside even after Prime Minister De Broqueville took over as foreign minister in August 1917. The war outlook at the time was grim. Revolution in Russia had climaxed the collapse of the eastern front. In the West, the Nivelle offensive on which the French had pinned so many hopes had failed miserably, and the British were bogged down at Passchendaele. As Albert had predicted, the war of attrition was producing nothing more than intense suffering. The Germans appeared to be holding on despite the allies' best efforts. The Americans were coming, of course, but would their aid be sufficient and prompt enough to forestall the necessity of a compromise peace? Many Entente supporters feared not; De Broqueville, perhaps influenced by King Albert, was among them. When approached by Baron Evence Coppeé, a Belgian industrialist who was in close rapport with Baron Oscar von der Lancken-Wakewitz, chief of the political section serving the German governor general in Belgium, the prime minister indicated he was willing to continue the conversations. To the cabinet his attitude smacked of defeatism and disloyalty; De Broqueville found himself without support even among his fellow Catholic party members. His position weakened, De Broqueville abandoned the foreign affairs portfolio immediately; five months later after nearly seven years in the office, he resigned as head of the cabinet.

De Broqueville paid dearly at the time for his lack of judgment, yet his political resurgence in later years indicates his sin was not irredeemable. Nor did the cabinet's criticism of his backdoor dealings reflect the opposition to any and all peace negotiations that had existed a few months earlier. Indeed, the exile government made a point, during the same period, of informing both the Vatican and the United States, independently of French and British notes, that Belgium's war aims were simply political, economic, and military independence, the integrity of Belgium and her colony, reparation, and guarantees against future invasion. The king for his part continued to resist involvement of Belgian troops in offensive action. Germany could make any action expensive, and it would be the soldiers, not the chauvinist diplomats, who would pay the cost. Only in the last months of the war, when the astute king recognized that the end was near, did he authorize the Belgian army to participate in an allied offensive freeing the country of the German occupation.[36]

De Broqueville's successor as foreign minister in January 1918 was Paul Hymans, who laid aside the post of minister of economic affairs accepted three months earlier. Hymans' first concern was the status Belgium would assume in postwar Europe. Beyens' initiative for an Anglo-French guarantee had died a quick death, but not before the Belgians realized that the British and French would not give something for nothing. Indeed, the French had earlier indicated that a departure by Belgium from neutrality might not be in their best interest and that they would expect to express an opinion were the issue formally raised. In October 1917, De Bassompierre, who had become *Directeur politique*, drafted a lengthy memorandum in which he gave particular attention to the attitude of France. His conclusion was that while the Belgian government desired to end the system of permanent neutrality, the French and British would agree to this only if such a change were to their advantage, that is, if they knew Belgium would fight against Germany in any future war. '*Military accords with France and England are the indispensable condition for our liberation from neutrality.*'[37]

While most of the current staff of the ministry of foreign affairs was critical of neutrality, there were some Belgians who were not. Former diplomats such as Arendt and Baron Van Eetvelde favored its continuance, as did Edmond Carton de Wiart, Count Charles Woeste (former chief of the Catholic conservatives), and a few other politicians. Hymans himself believed that while neutrality had been useful in the nineteenth century, in recent years it had led the country into passivity and an absence of a well-defined policy. Full sovereignty was needed to develop the nation's sense of dignity and responsibility. Such a scheme as Beyens had proposed was merely a disguised form of permanent neutrality. Full independence was necessary. The choice of whether to maintain a voluntary neutrality or to form alliances could be decided later; it would be premature to publish any preference on this issue until the general organization of postwar Europe was discernible.[38]

By September 1918, when this position was communicated to the foreign governments, it was clear the Entente would be victorious. In anticipation of the coming peace talks, Hymans pilgrimaged to Paris to seek support on three points: Belgium's desire to have Brussels chosen as the site of the peace conference, her annexationist hopes regarding the Duchy of Luxemburg and Flemish Zeeland, and her need for French aid in the economic reconstruction of the country. On the first point, a matter of prestige, the Belgian did not expect success, and indeed he was put off by French Minister of Foreign Affairs Stephen Pichon.

Over the past months, Hymans had become increasingly interested in territorial gains. He now carefully outlined his case regarding Luxemburg. It was impossible for the duchy to maintain an autonomous existence. Re-establishment of the duchy's status of 1914, including membership in the Zollverein and the German control of the duchy's railways exercised since 1871, would irrevocably make the duchy a German dependency. The roads of the duchy were a perfect path into Belgium for German troops and lack of control of the Luxemburg fortress prevented Belgium from defending adequately her own southeastern territories and the right bank of the Meuse. The dynasty of the duchy, which had passed to the house of Nassau-Weilburg upon the death of William III of the Netherlands without male heir in 1890, was pro-German. Grand Duchess Adelaide had been sympathetic to the Germans during the war, and her youngest sister was now engaged to the aging crown prince of Bavaria – clearly a political union. On the other hand, Belgium had historical and sentimental ties to the duchy; these had been callously ignored by the Conference of London and should now be rectified. The modalities of the reunion of the two regions Hymans suggested should be left to the freely expressed wishes of the populations; Belgium had long favored self-determination.[39]

Hymans expected French acquiescence to Belgium's wish, for despite Berthelot's reluctance to commit himself in 1916, in June of 1917 French Prime Minister Alexandre Ribot had assured Gaiffier that France did not wish to annex Luxemburg and acknowledged Belgian claims on the region.[40] Pichon, however, refused to give any additional assurances and said such issues should be reserved for the peace conference; regarding Hymans' request that Belgian troops participate in the allied relief and occupation of Luxemburg, he believed there would be no difficulty. When pressed Pichon did say he personally was convinced the duchy would go to Belgium but could not commit the French government. The new French Prime Minister Georges Clemenceau similarly acknowledged, but did not come out in official support of, Belgium's claims.

On the issue of the Scheldt Hymans had more success. A few years earlier, the Dutch government had complained of annexationist propaganda coming from Belgian writers, and France and England had pressured Beyens into giving the Dutch a special disavowal of annexationist intentions. This he could do because he personally had none, and the memorandum which he had communicated to the other governments in 1916 calling for a revision of the Scheldt regime had not asked for any transfer of territory. Since then the Belgians' ambitions had increased, although circumstances did not permit much action in their favor. Pichon now voluntarily stated he would support Belgium in any discussions with Holland regarding the Scheldt; Clemenceau did likewise. French President Raymond Poincaré went further, speaking as well of Belgian interests in the cantons of Eupen and Malmedy which had been attributed to Prussia in 1815. The French attitude thus seemed to be one of willingness to support Belgium against Holland combined with obvious reservations regarding Luxemburg. These last, Hymans expected, would disappear upon the conclusion of a military accord.[41]

That was substantially how matters stood when word arrived that armistice negotiations were under way. During discussion of the precise terms of the armistice, Hymans attempted to make some reservations concerning Belgium's right to preferential trade privileges for the next few years and to insert a specific list of restitutions that should be made to Belgium so that the small country's economy could start to re-establish itself immediately. The impatience of the diplomats of other nations to proceed was such that the Belgian foreign minister was forced to drop his detailed plans and succeeded only in inserting in the armistice note a clause requiring the immediate restitution of the treasury of the Banque Nationale de Belgique.

7.3 THE PEACE CONFERENCE

When the armistice went into effect at 11 a.m. on November 11, all Belgium rejoiced. Yet beneath the shouting and patriotic speeches were great worries. A tremendous task of reconstruction lay ahead, and now that the common enemy was vanquished the differences between Fleming and Walloon, so carefully nourished by the Germans, divided the country as never before. The outlook for the peace conference was encouraging, but there were indications that neither Britain nor France were truly interested in Belgium's expectations for the peace. The French, from the words of their diplomats and the actions of various private pro-French committees in Luxemburg, obviously had designs on the area. Neither they nor the British had convincingly stated that the treaties of 1839 should be revised in their entirety, and the British and Dutch had indicated opposition to any cession of territory by the Netherlands. The Belgian armies in Africa controlled favorable positions, yet the British did not want to allow the Congo regime, which they had criticized when it was under both Leopold II's and the Belgian parliament's direction, to extend its domain. There would be difficulties in opposing the aspirations of the English in Africa while simultaneously asking their support regarding Flemish Zeeland.

The Belgians did have some counts in their favor. World opinion was sympathetic, and they appeared to have some title to speak in the name of international morality; unfortunately any mention of territorial claims on neutral Holland would tarnish that title. Then, too, Belgium's armies in the Congo had earned a reward, and the Belgian defensive effort in Europe during the first weeks of August 1914 had done much to save Paris and alter the course of the war. These facts the great powers could not overlook. On the whole, however, the situation was such that the Belgian delegates approached the peace conference with foreboding.

They were aware that while they were undertaking their difficult diplomatic task they would not benefit from the full support and attention of their compatriots. It was to be expected that the first order of the day at home would be to re-establish business. Returning refugees and prisoners of war had to be settled, factories refurnished, and commerce restored. What was unexpected in its severity, at least by some members of the government in exile, was the extent to which the linguistic differences of the country had grown and become embittered during the German occupation.

The Germans did not anticipate a lengthy war and therefore initially did not establish a highly organized system and policy of occupation. As it became clear that the war would drag on and that Germany might have to use Belgium as a pawn in any peace, policies changed. General Von Bissing, governor-general of Belgium from the winter of 1914 to April of 1917, was influenced by pan-German views and held thoughts of eventual annexation. A number of officials in Berlin were also aware of this possibility and of the probability that support of the Flemish cause, propaganda regarding the Germanic ties between their peoples, and the weakening of the cohesion of Flemings and Walloons as a unified nation would serve German purposes. A policy was therefore developed of rigorously enforcing the letter of already existing Belgian linguistic laws, inevitably benefiting the Flemish. Use of Flemish in the administrative affairs of Flanders was required under an old law, and the 1914 law calling for children to receive elementary education in their native tongue was strictly applied. Most important, the long standing demand of Flemish leaders for a university of their own, with courses taught in Flemish, was granted in 1916 when the University of Ghent was reopened as a Flemish institution.

To many Flemings, these gifts were tainted because received from the hands of the enemy. Only five of the former members of the Ghent faculty agreed to teach in the reopened institution, and many foreign instructors had to be employed. The majority of Flemish leaders rejected the reforms provided by the Germans, protesting the actions of the occupation authorities at Ghent. For their attitude they came to be known as 'passivists' in comparison with the few 'activists' who readily collaborated with the Germans in the name of Flemish freedoms. The activities of the latter group were controversial and split the Flemish movement severely; the response of Walloons to all of this can be well imagined.

In early 1917 a group of activists led by August Borms and P. Tack organized a Council of Flanders. Its manifesto implied the creation of a separate Flemish state, and its organization was that of a shadow provisional government. The Council's activities were closely controlled by the occupation authorities with whom members of the Council met weekly. Their hopes were strenthened when, in March 1917, Von Bissing divided Belgium into two administrative districts, one Flemish with its capital in Brussels, the other Walloon with its administration in Namur. This arrangement assured that the Flemish section would take over most of the existing national offices in Brussels, while the Walloons would have to establish their own administrative structures and offices from practically nothing. Those officials who resigned in Brussels were replaced by Flemish activists; as a result of failure of their efforts to stimulate a corresponding Walloon activist movement, the Germans had to staff most of the Walloon administrative offices themselves. In December, the Council proclaimed the independence of Flanders, but the German occupation authorities forced a revision of this declaration to one of autonomy rather than independence.[42]

News of the activist movement was slow in reaching the front, but eventually Flemish soldiers, who made up a majority of the army, became aware of what was happening. Those who were sympathetic formed first a Flemish Study Club and, after its prohibition by army authorities, the political Front party.

The rapid collapse and retreat of the German army in late 1918 left the Flemish activists exposed to the wrath of both the passivists and the Walloons. Many fled to Holland, but others were captured and tried for treason in the fall of 1919; over forty were sentenced to death, but outcries and appeals eventually brought amnesty for all. Such a brief statement scarcely conveys the heat of the controversy and even the riots that tore the newly liberated Belgium on this matter. Many Walloons, angered by what they considered to be treason by the activists and Front party, grimly declared that post-war Belgium would be Latin or not exist at all. On the other hand, Flemings of all shades of opinion were determined that Flemish rights should be better respected in the future. King Albert wisely recognized that the clock could not be turned back, and in his first speech to the chambers in November 1918 promised a number of linguistic reforms. Yet the breach between Fleming and Walloon which had been growing slowly in the nineteenth century was opened wide by the German occupation; long standing bonds between the peoples had been struck asunder, and statesmanly speeches could not conceal the fact. For decades to come, the linguistic controversy was to anger and divide the Belgian people to the point that onlookers and Belgians alike would worry if there was, or is, indeed a Belgian nation.

The full seriousness of linguistic developments during the war may not yet have been evident in January 1919, but the danger that the great powers might overlook little Belgium's needs, unless she presented her case forcefully, was clear. Paul Hymans' fears seemed justified by the attitude revealed by the great powers in the first weeks of the conference in January 1919. Shortly before the initial meeting, he discovered that while the great powers, including Japan, and also Brazil, were granted seats for three delegates at the plenary sessions, Belgium was allowed only two. A quick protest rectified the matter, but a new insult was to come. At the first meeting and during the following week the procedural rules established by the Big Five were distributed. Britain, France, the United States, Italy, and Japan were to be considered the principal allied and associated powers and would have two or three representatives on the five commissions of the conference. The remaining twenty-two nations present were given the title of 'Powers with Special Interests' and the privilege of electing five delegates to the commissions to represent them all. The Belgians, who believed they had played a key role in the hostilities, resented being classified with Liberia, Panama, and other states which had done little more than issue declarations of war. Like the other small powers, Belgium resented being dictated to and considered as negligible. Thus, at the second plenary meeting Hymans protested. Though Belgium had been granted a special status in that she, Greece, Poland, Serbia, and Rumania were each granted two delegates to the commission studying reparation, Hymans stated Belgium deserved particular representation on the other commissions. Belgium's international stature and geographic position recommended she have two delegates on the commission preparing the constitution of the League of Nations; in the past she had been among the top industrial producers of the world and therefore merited inclusion in the group dealing with international labor legislation. Antwerp was reason enough to participate in the commission concerning ports, and it would be unthinkable that after four years of German occupation Belgium should not participate on the war crimes committee.

Surely Hymans' arguments were valid; but his case was not strengthened by the manner in which the representatives of other small states, emboldened by his declaration, began attacking the dictatorial ways of the Big Five. The annoyed Clemenceau bluntly replied that the big powers had lost many men in the war and that if the League of Nations were not to be discussed perhaps they would not have invited the small powers to the peace conference at all. Hymans itched to demonstrate the brutality of this declaration of the omnipotence of force and the inequality of states; its contradiction with the proclaimed intention of founding a society of nations based on law and equality of states was obvious. He said nothing because it would hurt his cause; sometimes 'it is necessary to have the courage to be silent'.[43]

His speech, in addition to creating a stir, did gain Hymans results. Belgium was granted one seat on the war crimes commission and two on that dealing with labor, as Serbia voluntarily abandoned her place. The small powers then promptly elected Belgian delegates to the remainder of the commissions. The demonstration was obvious; Belgium was now considered the champion of all the small nations against the greater powers. Though his country's prestige was augmented, Hymans later wondered if his speech had been worthwhile. Great powers, like high lords and financial potentates,

become easily irritated at pretentions of equality by the more modest or less strong. Small countries generally have little to offer to the big powers, and at the peace conference Belgium had everything to ask and nothing to offer. It was a congenital weakness.[44]

The need for intimate negotiations and for the accomplishment of a great deal in a short time required that most of the work of the conference be done in small groups. Yet it is worth noting that after Hymans' intervention no plenary session, at which the delegates of the small nations outnumbered those of the big powers, was held until the final days of the peace conference.

When the specific discussions began, the Belgians took as their prime goal the revision of the 1839 treaties in their entirety. Although they did not state the ramifications of their aim openly, they hoped such a revision would bring both a change in the Scheldt regime and an increase in territory. Hymans, who during the first years of the war had some sympathy with Beyens' viewpoint, was now an avowed annexationist, albeit with a realist's ability to recognize the difficulties involved. The development of his views had been much influenced by a memorandum regarding the Scheldt written for the ministry of foreign affairs years earlier by Charles Rogier's former protegé, Emile Banning. Among Hymans' closest collaborators were Pierre Orts, now *ad interim* secretary-general of the ministry, and Renkin, who was minister of interior in Leon Delacroix's second post-war cabinet. Both men were advocates of restoring to Belgium the lost territories of the 1830s and enlarging the African colony. The most surprising of Hymans' associates at this time, however, was Pierre Nothomb, a fervent expansionist and descendant of Jean-Baptiste Nothomb, the prominent revolutionary figure. Granted access to the foreign ministry, he conducted a virulent propaganda campaign and stimulated pro-Belgium demonstrations in Luxemburg as had Banning a half century earlier. The *Comité de Politique Nationale* which he led was at first of considerable help to Hymans in gaining support for a territorial policy at the peace conference, but it was later to cause the foreign minister some embarrassment because of its excesses and unwillingness to cede to the realities of the situation.

Belgian hopes of gaining Limburg and Luxemburg had been respectively bolsteredand dashed by a series of peculiar events in those regions following the armistice. On November 13, at the request of German authorities, the Dutch government allowed German troops evacuating Belgium to pass through Limburg. According to The Hague, the decision was motivated by a desire to aid Belgium in ridding herself of her occupants as soon as possible. Though the war was not formally over, the armistice had altered its character and the Dutch did not think it necessary to intern belligerent soldiers entering their territory. An equally pertinent reason, not mentioned but quickly recognized, was the inability of the Dutch to prohibit German passage; an attempt to block the border might cause incidents leading to pillage of the Limburg countryside. The decision was, strictly speaking, a violationof the Netherlands' neutrality and suggested that should Germany stage an invasion through Limburg in the future, she would not be opposed. The Belgians brought this to the attention of the powers (no mention was made of a similar permission granted by Belgium to victorious Prussian troops in 1870). Orts called for a diplomatic initiative. Belgium should reserve for herself the right to take whatever measures the situation warranted and forty-eight hours later send ships up the Scheldt transporting materials from the Belgian military base at Calais; finally Belgian troops should follow the Germans through the section of Limburg in question. Though French and British protests quickly went to The Hague, Pichon did not go along with Berthelot's suggestion of demanding reparation and guarantees from the Dutch; the Americans and British immediately rejected any action of force. Hymans, to Orts' dismay, therefore decided against sending Belgian troops into Limburg; the effect such action would have on Wilson and Lloyd George at the peace conference would be too deleterious. After obtaining King Albert's approval, he did follow the first two steps of Orts' proposal and military goods were transported on the Scheldt. By November 25, Pichon was ready to demand allied occupation of Limburg to halt the German passage. The British and Americans again demurred, but even so the Belgian position had been improved. The need for a proper defense of Limburg had been demonstrated, a breach had been made in the 1839 regime of the Scheldt, and a perfect opening had been provided for a declaration of Belgium's intent to revise the 1839 treaties.

Dreams of reunification with Luxemburg faded when, despite the promises of Pichon and Poincaré, Commander-in-Chief of the Allied Armies Marshal Ferdinand Foch did not allow Belgian troops to occupy the duchy. Instead, the French army took over from the Americans in December, as Foch established his own headquarters in Luxemburg. Near the end of the month, a small revolution broke out with apparent French blessing. But on January 10, after Grand Duchess Adelaide had abdicated in favor of her sister Charlotte, the French army put an end to the revolt. To the Belgians, it appeared that the French intended Luxemburg to become a republic so that it more easily might be joined to France; the heavy-handedness of the maneuver and the royalist sympathies of the commanding French general had led them to mitigate their course. Perhaps the French intention was to proceed by steps, obtaining economic control, a hold on the railways, and then annexation. Whatever the case, there was no intention of letting Belgian forces in to counteract the vigorous French propaganda. Foch's greatest concession was to allow Belgians in a small border town; Hymans declined it.

Hymans fought against French absorption of the duchy. French control of the Antwerp-Rhine trade and of the strategic places and railways of the duchy was almost as dangerous for Belgium now as it had been in the time of Napoleon III. Belgium might not need to fear annexation, but her independence of economic and political action was at stake. A thorn in Hyman's side was the state of public opinion in the duchy, where many inhabitants were saying it would be better to gain the advantages of attachment to a large power than to be exploited as another Belgian Congo. There was some comfort in the assurance given by the British that they recognized the danger posed to Belgium by a French Luxemburg and that the duchy would not be allowed to go to France. But that, of course, did not mean Belgium would get the duchy, and any support given by the British on the Luxemburg issue was balanced by their attitude regarding Holland and the Scheldt. The alignment of interests had become topsy-turvy. Despite the various hints received during the war, the Belgians had expected English support on the Scheldt and French support on Luxemburg. When the reverse proved to be the case, the Belgians were in an awkward bargaining position, for on both issues they had revealed their hands most fully not to their supporting power, but to their opponent.

Hymans had hoped to discuss revision of the 1839 treaties with France and Britain alone before approaching the Dutch. Fear of annoying the American president as well as the Italian and Japanese delegates militated against this; soon rumors that, if the matter were not taken up in its entirety only parts of the treaties would be examined by the various commissions, provoked Hymans to go before the Council of Ten (made up of two delegates from each of the five great powers). His exposé of Belgium's desires on February 11 was lucid and his approach sophisticated. For the most part it went over the same political, historical, and economic grounds covered by three detailed notes which had been presented to the allies at the beginning of the conference. The crucial point was raised by Wilson. Though Hymans had not specifically asked for annexation of the left bank of the Scheldt, that was the implied solution; how could neutral Holland be brought to consent? Hymans replied that he was merely presenting Belgium's defense problem and leaving the search for a solution to the conference. His only request was that the powers support him in negotiating with the Netherlands. The reason why Hymans wanted the issue discussed at the peace conference, rather than outside it, became clear when Hymans, in reply to a British question, suggested that if the Dutch relinquished territory to Belgium they should find compensation in East Frisia or Prussian Guelderland. The foreign minister then went on to ask that the powers invite the Luxemburg government to seek a *rapprochement* with Belgium. The cantons of Eupen, Saint-Vith, and Malmedy should be attached to Belgium as should also the small neutral territory of Moresnet.[45]

The result of Hymans' speech was the creation of a Commission on Belgian Affairs. Presided over by French statesman André Tardieu and containing as one of the American representatives Professor Charles H. Haskins, both friends of Hymans and supporters of the Belgians' cause, its reports made during the first weeks of March were favorable to Hymans' hopes. The treaties of 1839, it was held, had indeed hindered the defense of the country; they should be revised in collaboration with the Netherlands and Belgium freed of any limitation on her sovereignty. Eupen, Malmedy, and Moresnet were to go to Belgium, although a reverse sort of plebiscite should occur in the first two regions. In those places registers would be kept open to be signed by persons opposing annexation to Belgium; if a majority signed, the lands would remain Prussian. Such a system was patently not meant to work and was a mere gesture toward the principle of self-determination. Apparently also a favorable attitude was held toward granting the Netherlands compensation from the German regions of Borkum and Cleves if Belgium were given portions of Dutch territory.

The committee did not take up the question of Luxemburg; that was reserved for the Supreme Council. Though by now the increasing popularity of Grand Duchess Charlotte and the influence of Francophile groups in the duchy had led the Belgians to renounce any thoughts of annexation, they did have hopes of a close economic union which would strengthen their economy, increase their prestige, and perhaps lead to a closer relationship. But on February 19, a commission constituted in Luxemburg to consider the duchy's economic future had declared for economic union with France. Shortly thereafter the grand-ducal government announced it would seek economic union with both France and Belgium. A tripartite accord spelled French domination; Hymans therefore appealed to Colonel Edward House, Wilson's right-hand man, and British Foreign Secretary Arthur Balfour to approach Clemenceau. The Tiger agreed to order Foch and the French troops to withdraw from Luxemburg. But if the duchy voted for France in the referendum on economic affairs currently being contemplated, he could not turn down the offer. Meanwhile, throughout March Lloyd George ignored the recommendations of Balfour and Sir Eyre Crowe that British assent to French control of the Saar mines be contingent upon a pro-Belgian arrangement of the Luxemburg issue.[46]

While what appeared to be favorable progress in the treaty revision was being achieved at a painstakingly slow pace, the discussions concerning Germany's reparation payments were giving Hymans alternate fits of hope and despair. The Belgian treasury was empty, important loans had been made, and vast reconstruction was needed. In the Declaration of Sainte-Adresse and elsewhere, the powers had promised that Belgium would be restored; this was the theme of the seventh of Wilson's fourteen points. Yet the implementation at Paris of these promises was another matter. At the end of February, Hymans approached Colonel House concerning the necessity for Belgium of receiving reconstruction money as soon as possible, that is, of obtaining a priority on the first German payments. House was sympathetic and said he would arrange that Belgium receive a priority of two and a half billion gold francs (two billion gold marks or five hundred million United States dollars). The French, however, dragged their heels, for they believed their country merited a priority also.

The Belgians became impatient as the Big Four debated the future of Europe in secret. (The Japanese did not take an active part in those questions not bearing directly on their country's interests.) Though rumors were legion, little specific could be learned regarding the lot of Belgium. As time passed, it became evident that the powers were not paying much attention to Belgium's claims at all. This lack of concern was symbolized by French rejection of a Belgian loan request and insistence that Belgium formally recognize her already large debt to France for defense loans during the war. In reply, Hymans launched a campaign to reawaken the powers' sense of moral responsibility to fulfill their promises regarding Belgium.

Hardly had he begun when a note by the British naval section on the report of the Commission on Belgian Affairs was accidentally left at his office. Upon reading it, he discovered that the admiralty preferred that control of the Scheldt remain in Dutch hands; otherwise, should Belgium again fall to an invader, Antwerp would become a naval and submarine base especially threatening to Britain. This seemed as good an explanation as any of the absence of the expected British support for Belgian claims for sovereignty of the Scheldt. When the shocked Hymans confronted the British under secretary, Arthur Hardinge, with the memorandum, he received more assurances of sympathy but no denial of the viewpoint expressed by the admiralty.[47] Hymans apparently had little suspicion that Hardinge's attitude was such that he had scornfully commented to the Dutch minister that 'the Belgians are on the make and they want to grab where and whatever they can'; Britain would refuse to consider infringement on Dutch territorial integrity, although some discussion of the Scheldt problem seemed reasonable.[48]

Vague assurances of goodwill, mixed with disinterest, were the products of interviews with Pichon and Poincaré, although Italian Minister of Foreign Affairs Baron Sonnino was more solicitous. In Brussels, Delacroix informed the French ambassador that if the powers did not stand by their word his cabinet would not be able to fulfill its mandate of reconstructing the country; in such an event he would resign after publicizing why Belgium was not being reconstructed. After all this campaigning, Hymans was finally received by the Big Four on March 31. It was the opportunity he had long wanted, but it harmed more than aided his cause. A reproach for lack of support of Belgium's aims was interpreted by Lloyd George as an assertion that Britain had done nothing during the war for Belgium and had not suffered grievous losses. Hymans could not bear the Welshman's insulting attack and replied in kind. Barely able to shake hands at the end of the hearing, the two men were to harbor some enmity for each other throughout the remainder of their careers.

A similar incident occurred four days later when King Albert met with the Four (House was filling in for the ailing Wilson). Two days before his own audience, Hymans had conceived of a visit by the much respected king as a gesture which would focus attention on the Belgian cause. Albert's arrival by airplane did exactly that, and he was given marked attention in his interviews. When the issue of Luxemburg came up during the April 4 Supreme Council meeting which King Albert and Hymans attended, Clemenceau, who had remained silent during the Hymans-Lloyd George incident, now launched a vicious assault on Hymans and the Belgian government, which he said was guilty of leading an anti-French campaign in the duchy. The Tiger became so carried away that the meeting had to be brought to a halt.

There was, of course, truth to Clemenceau's charge, but the French pot was certainly as black as the Belgian kettle. It is strange that Hymans, who throughout his career was universally acknowledged as one of the politest and most skilled and well-liked of diplomats, was involved in two such unpleasant episodes. They were, no doubt, a result of the increasing tensions and overwork that burdened the Big Four. The imbroglios likely also stemmed from the recognition by the Big Four of obligations to Belgium previously acknowledged but which, because of the powers' own national interests, they no longer wished to fulfill. Then, too, the leaders were annoyed by the presentation, at a time when many more vast problems were to be settled, of what Queen Victoria had called 'the importunities of a not unnaturally nervous little State'. For the Belgians there was little choice but to risk annoying the powers by pesky prodding. The conference had been established on the principle of inequality of power, and if the small state did nothing, it was sure to receive next to nothing. It was not enough to rely on Clemenceau's promise that he would look after Belgium's interests. Obviously enough, the nature and validity of those interests would be understood and defended differently by a Belgian than a Frenchman, particularly a French premier whose first concern was to make sure France got a large wedge of the pie on which the British also had sizeable claims.

A prime example of how the Belgians were being kept from the table, indeed not even informed of the course being served, was the discussions over the future status of the Rhineland. To many observers a fifteen year occupation appeared meaningless; it would only be after the occupation ended that Germany would be militarily dangerous. Marshal Foch was therefore calling for an occupation of thirty to forty years' duration. Such an affair would be expensive and amount to French annexation of the region; Lloyd George opposed it. The Belgians had great interest in the future of the territory along their eastern border, but they were not consulted. In his talks at Paris, King Albert expressed his opinion that a fifteen year occupation was useless and his desire for a political and military buffer zone separating Germany from France and Belgium. The Belgians had still not been formally consulted when on April 13 Foch asked for their support. Delacroix rejected the Marshal's scheme, and Hymans suggested the creation of a disarmed autonomous Rhineland state in place of a long occupation. No effort was made by the powers to bring Belgium into the discussion, and Belgian approval was not asked prior to the decision in favor of a fifteen year occupation (in which Belgium would participate for the first ten years) combined with the establishment of a permanently demilitarized zone reaching fifty kilometers east of the Rhine. The solution was acceptable and no complaints were registered. Hymans and other Belgians nevertheless remained supporters of an autonomous Rhineland state and regretted that more advantage had not been taken of the brief movement that broke out at Cologne to that effect a few months earlier. In 1923, when a similar outbreak occurred, there would be Belgians who remembered what Hymans termed the 'great political enterprise which would have modified the entire aspect of the former German empire'.[49]

Because of Clemenceau's recent wrath, Hymans had little hope of resolving the Luxemburg issue. He was relieved to discover, however, that the outburst had cleared the air. Giving way to the pressure of Balfour and the Americans, the Frenchman agreed that the powers should recommend that the duchy postpone the referendum on its future form of government and the dynasty. An April 19 meeting with Clemenceau was filled with sweetness and light. Hymans left with the impression that Belgium could arrange her relations with the duchy as she wished. Talks were begun with Luxemburg delegates five days later.

Despite the amelioration of the Luxemburg situation, the attitudes of Lloyd George and Clemenceau, the lack of consultation on the Rhineland issue, and the rejection by Wilson of Hymans' request that the League of Nations be seated at Brussels all demonstrated that events were not proceeding well for the Belgian diplomats in March and April of 1919. On April 23, they learned that while Belgium would be the only non-great power member of the Reparation Commission, no decision had been reached on the partition of the first German payment due May 1, 1921, and no priority awarded beyond that of the costs of the occupation armies and food shipments to Germany. Hymans protested; he called for a priority of two and a half billion francs and full payment within ten years of Belgium's total damages, which should include the costs of war and of the redemption of the paper marks which Germany had forced upon Belgium during the occupation. In addition he demanded that Van Eyck and Dirk Bouts paintings stolen from Belgium and manuscripts equal in value to those burned at Louvain be turned over. Under pressure from Delacroix and Minister of Colonies Louis Franck to obtain all these goals, Hymans presented his case to the Big Three (Italy had by this time withdrawn from the conference). The allies appeared sympathetic but neither Wilson nor Lloyd George would allow a breach in the recently established principle that war costs would not be included in the reparations bill. Though granted a priority, Belgium's delegates insisted on payment of their war costs, arguing their country's involvement in the war was of a nature different from that of the allies and warranted Belgium special treatment. Hymans said such treatment was necessary if his country were to be reconstructed; he would not accept the responsibility of signing a treaty which did not accord it.

When, in answer to a question by the British prime minister, Hymans affirmed that Belgium might not be present eight days hence when the conference was to receive the German delegates, the meeting broke into feverish discussion groups.[50]

Hymans had staged his dramatic move at a propitious moment. Belgium no doubt would have gained little and probably have lost a great deal by a separate peace with the Germans, but the Big Three could not afford to let Belgium withdraw. The departure of the Italian delegates and the current difficult relations with the Japanese had embarrassed the other big powers and had revealed to the Germans dissent within the alliance. A well-publicized withdrawal by the Belgians would further tarnish the Big Three politicians' images among their constituents and deprive their claims on Germany of much of their moral authority.

After some time a final offer was made. Belgium's war expenses would not be reimbursed, but the powers would free Belgium of responsibility for all the loans contracted as a result of the violation of the treaties of 1839; these costs the allies would add to their own bills of damages which the Germans were to pay. Any payment for the marks circulated by the Germans during the occupation was left to Belgium to settle by direct negotiations, for if the conference dealt with this currency problem in regard to Belgium it would have to do likewise for the several other regions which experienced occupation. The Germans would, of course, be forced to return art works taken from Belgium. The solution was generous and equitable. Belgium gained her priority and was freed of war debts which amounted to over five billion francs, not including interest payments. The sizeable and immediate relief desired was thus provided. Since it was agreed that the exact total of the German payments, as well as the percentages by which it would be distributed among the victorious powers, would not be determined until after the peace treaty were signed, Hymans was more than satisfied. The Belgian cabinet was not; Renkin, Franck, and Minister of Economic Affairs Henri Jaspar traveled to Paris to emphasize that they would not allow signature of the treaty until reimbursement of the occupation marks was included. Hymans soon convinced them that under the circumstances Belgium had made a great gain, and all were in accord when Hymans telegraphed Delacroix that refusal to sign would isolate Belgium and that he and the two other Belgian delegates to the conference, Vandervelde and Jules van den Heuvel would resign if the cabinet persisted in its attitude. Delacroix visited Hymans, was converted, and subsequently called the foreign minister to Brussels for a crown council. Hymans pleaded his case well, the cabinet decision was changed, and Belgium agreed to sign the treaty.

The presentation of the document to the German delegates on May 7, 1919, did not mark the end of the Belgians' trials. The Paris discussions had proceeded at a furious pace for nearly four months, yet much remained to be settled, for example the disposition of the colonies seized from Germany. On the morning of May 8, while having a leisurely breakfast, Hymans read in a newspaper that the preceding afternoon the Big Three had decided that all of German East Africa was to go to England; nothing was reserved for Belgium.

Hymans had done his best to keep the powers aware of Belgium's African claims. The Belgians' first audition before the Council of Ten at the end of January had been to that purpose. It would have been foolish to present Belgium's aims on Portuguese territory to the conference without first obtaining assent from Portugal. Pierre Orts, who was presenting the Belgian case, therefore limited himself to defending the value and justice of allowing Belgium to maintain control of all the territories her troops had occupied and administered since 1916. The temporary arrangement of that year should become permanent. As the Belgians wanted to gain the regions outright, they had no use for the League of Nations mandate system Wilson was then proposing; to avoid irritating the president, however, Orts avoided the issue and merely indicated Belgian acceptance of Wilson's fifth point regarding the legitimate interests of the peoples of the colonies. The representatives of the powers heard him out impatiently; Lloyd George was openly hostile and it was clear the audience was only *pro forma.*[51]

Realizing that Belgium would have to solidify her position if it were to be recognized by the conference, Hymans had initiated bilateral talks with the English. Lord Milner, the British colonial secretary, and Orts had a stormy time of it. Orts refused to abandon Belgium's claims while Milner insisted England had to have a route west of Lake Victoria to connect her possessions in northern and southern Africa – the Cape to Cairo railway once again. In an effort to divert Belgian attention from Ruanda-Urundi he suggested Belgium find compensation in Cabinda and the Portuguese held left bank of the Congo. This, as both men knew, was Belgium's true goal. Orts agreed to such a deal if England could arrange it. Belgium would, however, have to have commercial access to Lake Victoria, free railway communications in the region, and port facilities at Kigoma and Dar-es-Salaam to benefit Congo trade moving to the Indian Ocean.

Milner said he would sound out the Portuguese, and little was learned of the issue until on May 8 Hymans received his rude surprise from the newspaper. He immediately insisted that Belgium would not recognize the settlement as announced. Clemenceau, Lloyd George, and Wilson were friendly but all seemed ignorant of Belgium's African conquests and the basis of her claims, though Lloyd George vaguely remembered Orts' January exposition to the Council of Ten. On May 12, Hymans asked Franck to instruct the Belgian command in German East Africa to 'oppose calmly and with discretion, but also firmly, any attempt to implement this decision [of the conference] on the spot'.[52] The same day, Milner arrived in Paris to negotiate with Orts. He tried to bluff the Belgian, but after two days of sparring offered Orts a choice: either Ruanda or a small piece of Portuguese land on the left bank of the Congo River for which Portugal would be compensated by considerable territory from England's East African mandate. In regard to the first alternative, Orts insisted that a cash indemnity be added and that Urundi should be joined to Ruanda, for otherwise the latter region would be without the necessary access to Lake Tanganyika. He did not require, however, that these territories reach as far east as the shores of Lake Victoria; space would thus be allowed for the British railway. As for the Portuguese territory, it was far too small to compensate for abandoning all the lands Belgium held in German East Africa. More was needed: Belgium should be allowed to keep approximately 7000 square kilometers of Ruanda, land which Germany with Britain's aid had forced from Belgium in 1910; facilities for Belgian trade to the East should be guaranteed, and a sizeable indemnity paid.

For the next several weeks the two men fenced. Milner's refusal to allow cash indemnity made the Portuguese alternative unacceptable to the Belgians. Milner, however, did cede on the question of Urundi, and Orts, in return, agreed to waive his demand for additional cash. Thus the Ruanda-Urundi solution prevailed. The main lines of the agreement were reached by the end of May, 1919, but it was not until March 15, 1921, and after brief difficulties with the United States that the treaty was signed which turned over to Belgium Great Britain's mandate in the region.[53]

English pride rankled at relinquishing more land to Belgian colonial rule, so often criticized in Britain. The Belgians were disappointed but could not complain of their lot. They had gained what were considered two of the richest and most heavily populated regions of Central Africa. Ruanda and Urundi were also important for trade communications, and because of their climate were considered among the best areas of Central Africa for white colonization. The Belgians would have preferred outright possession of the territories rather than a mandate, but at least they were being treated no differently than any other nation in this respect. Moreover, alteration was easily obtained of those clauses of the Act of Berlin and its supplement, the Act of Brussels of 1890, which limited the taxes that could be levied on merchandise entering the Congo. On September 10, 1919, at Saint-Germain-en-Laye a treaty revising the various earlier acts and establishing new accords on the sale of arms, ammunition, and liquor in Africa was signed by the numerous interested powers. Particularly pleasing to Belgium was the right then gained to establish tariffs and award monopolies in the Congo as she wished.

Frantic but obstinate negotiation in the last days of the Paris conference salvaged something of the Belgians' territorial aspirations in Africa. Such was not the case for their claims in Europe, and it may well be that the obstinacy with which they defended their demands on reparations and German East Africa was in part responsible for this. Though the Belgians saw each of the issues as separate and distinct, the representatives of the powers were more concerned with the total gains made by any one country. Thus Milner was able to argue, as he briefly did, that Belgium had done so well in the reparations negotiations that she did not need to receive any lands in Africa.

The Belgians' main concern was Luxemburg. At the end of April, it appeared Hymans would have his way in arranging a bilateral economic union with the duchy. But Clemenceau was not through. On May 28, Luxemburg's head of government and minister of foreign affairs, Emile Reuter, informed the powers that in accordance with their request a referendum on Luxemburg's economic future would be postponed. He also indicated that Luxemburg favored a tripartite economic union but that if a choice were to be made between France and Belgium, his country would opt for France. When Hymans mentioned that Belgo-Luxemburg talks had already begun, Clemenceau suddenly asked that France participate. The shocked Belgian protested, but his angry righteousness, though provoking denials of evil intentions, did not obtain a formal French declaration to Luxemburg rejecting a tripartite accord. Within the duchy pro-French sentiment was building rapidly, and the Belgo-Luxemburg conversations failed to progress. As the stalemate to the east continued, Hymans desperately searched for success elsewhere, particularly in the region of the Scheldt.

The Commission on Belgian Affairs had supported Belgium's call for revision of the 1839 treaties and had recommended that the Dutch participate with the five powers and Belgium in negotiations to that end. But the Dutch dragged their feet; no meeting was held until May 19. Dutch Foreign Minister Jonkheer Herman van Karnebeek chose the occasion to reiterate his view that while the Netherlands was willing to reconsider the Scheldt regime and recognize the end of Belgium's neutrality, any cession of territory was out of the question. He also insisted that the negotiations should be conducted bilaterally between Belgium and Holland.

This last suggestion was rejected by Hymans, who was still hoping for support from the powers. He asked how Belgium's territory could be adequately defended when the valleys of the Meuse and the Scheldt were not in her control. He demanded no cession of territory but requested for Belgium the attributes of sovereignty over the Scheldt, its western dependencies, and the Ghent-Terneuzen canal and railway. Holland should formally recognize Belgium's right to use the lower Scheldt at any time for defense and grant Belgium military privileges on the left bank. Also, the locks controlling the waters of Flanders should be in Belgian hands. As for Limburg, the foreign minister went on, Belgium did not want it but desired that steps be taken there which would increase Belgium's protection. Finally, there was need for a new arrangement for the enclave of Bar-le-Duc and for large Antwerp-Moerdijk and Rhine-Meuse-Scheldt canals.[54]

These proposals were rejected by Van Karnebeek on June 3; he could not allow any territories to be withdrawn from Dutch sovereignty so they could be placed under that of the Belgians. Matters concerning some aspects of Scheldt navigation and new canals he would discuss bilaterally. The differences between the two countries regarding both the contents and method of negotiation were complete, and the Supreme Council chose to settle those issues itself. The following day, it appointed a commission made up of representatives of the five powers plus Belgium and Holland to study revision of the 1839 treaties and to submit 'proposals implying neither transfer of territorial sovereignty nor creation of international servitudes'.[55] But it was not for this Commission of XIV, as it came to be known, to do the actual negotiating on matters regarding waterways. Rather, Belgium and Holland were to reach agreement between themselves and then present their recommendations to the fourteen.

Surprisingly, the Belgo-Dutch talks went smoothly at first. The Dutch, anxious to demonstrate to the powers that they were reasonable and recognized the legitimacy of some of Hymans' demands, acquiesced on several counts. Belgium was given permission to improve and enlarge the Scheldt waterway so it could accommodate the increasingly heavy traffic of ever larger vessels; Holland agreed to contribute to the cost and a joint commission was established to supervise the work. Two long canals from Antwerp to the Rhine were agreed upon, and numerous minor issues were settled. Finally, the Netherlands acknowledged the end of Belgium's neutrality.

The political issues being discussed before the fourteen did not progress as well. Orts set forth Belgium's need for protection to the east and for military use of the Scheldt. As territorial exchanges were not to be allowed, he asked that a Belgo-Dutch military accord establish a common defense of Limburg; in time of war, Belgium should be able to extend her defenses to the Scheldt and her allies able to send troops and munitions up the river. This last suggestion the Dutch rejected as an international servitude and were supported by the powers; the commission, on the other hand, agreed with the Belgian viewpoint on Limburg and sought to persuade the Dutch to make an agreement for a joint defense of the region. When the Dutch rejected such a solution as inimical to their sovereignty, the powers advised Belgium to appeal to the League of Nations.

A guarantee of armed support by the League was attractive, but what of the period of years before the League was in effective operation? This thought, joined with the failure to obtain good strategic boundaries and fear of any revival of Germany's strength, led the foreign minister to seek inclusion in any revision of the 1839 treaties of a clause by which France and Britain would continue to uphold their traditional obligations regarding Belgium, although no mention was to be made of neutrality. Beyens' views of 1916 were being rehabilitated. Hymans also wished the Dutch to put in writing their verbal promise to consider any violation of Limburg as a *casus belli*; he did not want the Germans to pass through unscathed as they had after the armistice. A French draft for such a treaty met Hymans' first request, but as he negotiated to obtain the second, he learned that Britain would not grant any guarantee unless Belgium would, in turn, be neutral. This was unacceptable, and the Belgian's formal statement to the commission on March 23, 1920, was a bitter denunciation of the powers' failure to fulfill their promises to strengthen Belgium's security. Hymans did, however, agree to accept a simple treaty suppressing Belgium's permanent neutrality in order to have established by law what was already determined by fact.[56]

Just before this treaty was to be signed, the Dutch put forward claims to the Wielingen Channel of the Scheldt, one of the most heavily used of the three entrances to the river. The lower Scheldt was, of course, under Dutch sovereignty, but by a quirk of nature the Wielingen Channel, upon reaching the North Sea, bent sharply south and for some length coursed within three miles of the Belgian coast, thus falling under Belgian control. Throughout the nineteenth century this channel had been sporadically disputed by the two small countries until an unwritten *modus vivendi* had been reached. Why the Dutch suddenly brought the matter forward at this time is not completely clear. Later negotiations showed they were using it as a counter-issue against Franco-Belgian pressures regarding Limburg, and this may have already been the case in the spring of 1920. Their arguments for control of the entire channel were weak, and Hymans promptly pointed out that the Dutch had not objected to German submarines making use of the channel during the war; he even possessed maps on which the Dutch themselves had indicated the channel was not within their territorial waters. Maintenance of sovereignty over the Wielingen was of great importance to the Belgians, for not only was it a lever to use on Holland, but it also provided the only access to Belgium's sole deep water port on the North Sea, Zeebrugge.

The Dutch claim on the Wielingen irritated Hymans immensely; he broke off economic negotiations and the proposed treaty fell by the wayside. Pierre van Zuylen of the Belgian foreign ministry later wrote that 'the Belgian government in refusing to sign acted primarily under the impulse of spite and anger after the repeated checks received in the revision negotiations'.[57] This was so, but as Van Zuylen himself admits, there was also the hope that if the treaty ending the neutrality were not signed, Belgium might be able to reopen the entire issue, including that of Limburg, under more favorable circumstances in a few months. (By this time the French were stating that if Belgium signed a military accord with them, they would force the Dutch to give way.) Then, too, there was the possibility that some sort of Limburg-Wielingen bargain might be arranged. Whatever the motivation for rupture of the negotiations, the Belgians were to regret they had not seized at least the economic advantages that had been granted them. Their major disappointment, however, was lack of privileged status in Limburg and Flemish Zeeland. Much of their diplomacy in the next years was to be devoted to obtaining the security which their efforts at the Paris peace conference had failed to assure.

7.4 WHAT SHALL THE MEEK INHERIT?

Indeed, nearly all of the Belgians' diplomacy in the next decade and even in the 1930s was a direct result of their successes and failures at the conference. Reparations and security were the chief concerns, but other matters lingered on for some time. For example, the treaty made no provision for German redemption of the occupation marks, and so these became the subject of endless Belgo-German negotiations. These were at first complicated by French objections to any arrangements by individual countries with Germany that might reduce the latter's payments to the Reparation Commission. Numerous schemes were discussed which all floundered because they involved payments so high that the German government could not or would not agree to pay them. Thus it was not until 1929 that a solution was reached which, though favorable to the Belgians, provided far less than they had originally demanded.

The regions of Eupen, Saint-Vith, and Malmedy, the sole acquisitions made by Belgium in Europe, proved a headache. The Germans did not fail to protest the method by which the populations were allowed to demonstrate their national preferences; the residents themselves were unfriendly, although only a few dared sign the registers. There were numerous unpleasant incidents up to 1921, when a less harsh regime was established. In 1926, Belgian civil and commercial law was introduced into the three regions, but pro-German sentiment remained strong in Eupen, where the Walloon percentage of the population was much smaller than in Malmedy. In 1920, impractical eastern boundaries, which forced trains to pass through customs three times in thirty-six kilometers, led the Belgians to persuade the conference of ambassadors to award them an additional strip of territory for which they paid Germany reasonable compensation.

The Weimar government did not abandon hope of regaining at least Eupen. In April 1925, Hjalmar Schacht, president of the Reichsbank, suggested that a settlement might be reached regarding the occupation marks were Belgium to retrocede the three cantons. German Foreign Minister Gustav Stresemann disavowed Schacht's approach but expressed hope that a solution of the mark issue might lead to negotiations over the territories. Though the Belgian response was chilly, Stresemann raised the issue on other occasions. The replies continued in the negative but became less forceful as the marks issue was dropped in favor of a cash settlement, not for all the regions, but just for the most predominantly German villages of Eupen. The matter reached its head following a meeting at Thoiry in September of 1926 between Stresemann and French Foreign Minister Aristide Briand at which it was rumored that the latter had not opposed Stresemann's soundings. At the time, Belgium was in the throes of an economic crisis; the influential financier Emile Francqui, who was also minister without portfolio, therefore encouraged a favorable reception of the German overtures. The predilections of the Socialist foreign minister, Emile Vandervelde, lay in the same direction for different reasons. Other members of the cabinet, including Minister of Justice Paul Hymans, would not agree. He was sure the cantons would eventually grow to be an integral part of Belgium and could not condone a gesture which seemed to repudiate the Versailles Treaty and imply the annexations of 1919 had been unjust. When consulted, the British intimated that sale of the lands would be a precedent that might cause trouble. The German offer was rebuffed, and Francqui's skill enabled Belgium to weather – or rather to postpone – the financial crisis.[58]

Additional diplomatic ink was also consumed in negotiations concerning the Grand Duchy of Luxemburg. Though the peace treaty required Germany to relinquish control of the duchy's railways and to acknowledge the departure of Luxemburg from the *Zollverein*, the Belgians were deeply dissatisfied by the lack of any provisions which would tie the area to Belgium. Talks with Clemenceau in August 1919 finally produced a clear renunciation of a tripartite accord, but only on the condition that France have control of the *Guillaume-Luxembourg* railway. Such a qualification would vitiate any Belgo-Luxemburg treaty and would give France a stranglehold on the economy and strategic communications of the area. It is not surprising that Hymans, the biographer of Frère-Orban, and his colleagues in the Belgian cabinet rejected the proposal.

On September 28, the long-postponed referendum was held in Luxemburg. The voters chose Grand Duchess Charlotte instead of a republic by a resounding margin; the vote on economic affairs was three to one in favor of union with France rather than Belgium. The annoyed Belgians, who had not recognized Charlotte in the hope of pressuring the Luxemburg government to be more amenable, ignored the demonstration in her favor and continued to withhold recognition. Hymans broke off the economic negotiations, and diplomatic relations between Luxemburg and Brussels came to a virtual halt. Thus at the end of the year, while the economic future of Luxemburg remained clouded, it was clear to all that the Belgian position had sharply deteriorated.

Over-arching the Belgians' disappointments on specific issues was a bitter one of a more general nature. That was the manner in which the great powers disregarded the wishes and susceptibilities of the small country. The Belgians had fought well in Europe and Africa and believed they deserved some reward. If their hatred were directed at the Germans, they were nevertheless aware that it was the Triple Alliance-Entente quarrels which had involved Belgium in the war. A strong feeling therefore existed that not only should Germany pay, but that Belgium was owed a sort of indemnity by Britain and France. While the Belgians wished this to be paid in concrete terms by the annexation of Luxemburg and favorable revision of the 1839 treaties, they also thought that Belgium's loyalty to those treaties should win her a special place among the councils of the powers.

Though much was made of Belgium's needs for economic reconstruction and military security, the country's main argument at the peace conference was that of moral right. It was a strong plea that made Clemenceau and Lloyd George nervous, particularly because the Belgians had such a good press in their countries. Had the war been shorter and the sufferings of the great powers less intense, the Belgians might have been more successful at the conference. As it was, the Belgian defense effort became lost in the memories of many observers or relegated to the category of just another incident in a greater slaughter.

Several years after the war Beyens continued to defend his policy at

Sainte-Adresse, arguing that it was the correct one at the time and that the unexpected duration of the war was what made it seem unsuccessful. Though this was true, his opponents must be given credit for recognizing that the war had temporarily voided many traditional concepts of international morality and that in a power conflict it was necessary to play power politics.

Davignon's maneuvers in the Congo during the first half of the war adroitly made virtue of necessity; Belgium's moral stature as an anti-war power was maintained at the same time neutrality was abandoned and additional territory was brought under her control. Just how far Davignon would later have gone in advocating Belgian conquests in East Africa can not be known, but he no doubt would not have done so with the unseemly greed that Renkin displayed in the Tabora negotiations. That unfortunate affair was revealing not only of the schizophrenia within the Belgian cabinet but also of the entire Belgian argument at the peace conference.

The Belgians wanted to be considered the personification of selfless loyalty and sacrifice. Yet at the same time they were asserting – and their maneuvers in Africa demonstrated their intent – that their unselfish sacrifice should be rewarded by gains beneficial to Belgium. These were, moreover, to be made primarily at the expense of neutrals. Offers of compensation in German territories were of course tendered, but the imposition of such exchanges upon neutrals was hardly in accord with the sort of legality and morality of which the Belgians were posing as champions. Had such exchanges been imposed on them, they would have been the first to protest. In the view of Clemenceau and Lloyd George, Belgium was attempting to turn moral suasion into power politics. One reason they felt no greater compulsion to give in to Belgian pleas was that they rightly believed that at Paris the Belgians were not acting solely for humanity and humanitarian principles but primarily for their own aggrandizement. Though Belgium's war aims and the arguments used to press her claims were not necessarily contradictory (after all, good performance does merit reward), they did clash somewhat, and this weakened the Belgian diplomats' effectiveness at the conference. Hymans managed to reduce the obviousness of this disharmony. Had he achieved revision of the 1839 treaties early in the peace talks, before the reparations and Ruanda-Urundi crises, he might have been more successful on that issue. Nevertheless, the thought that the African, reparations, and 1839 treaties problems could be discussed separately, and that awards made on one matter would not affect awards on another, was naïve.

Hymans' presentation of Belgium's case was also weakened by the lack of interest and support for the territorial claims among the Belgian populace as a whole. There was strong agreement at home on the need for reparation, but the territorial issue was divisive. In particular, many Flemings were critical of any effort to take territory from their friends, the Dutch. Though the foreign minister could assert that all Belgium joined in making the claims, his counterparts knew otherwise. They were further aware that the majority of the Belgian population was concentrating more on re-establishing the economy and on the linguistic struggle than on the peace conference. Indeed the government itself was for a long time unable to reach a clear statement of its war aims, and the vague manner in which Hymans was initially forced to put forward his suggestions during the war did not help him later.

The results of the Paris conference held a good deal of irony for the Belgians. Their most sizeable acquisition, Ruanda-Urundi, was the very one they did not originally intend to keep; the prize expected to fall to Belgium automatically, the Duchy of Luxemburg, was denied her by her supposedly strongest supporter, France; the English, instead of aiding the Belgian cause regarding Flemish Zeeland and the Scheldt, opposed it; finally, though Belgium was patently through with neutrality, the famous clause of 1839 was still on the books.

Though many Belgians at the time termed their performance at the peace conference a failure, this would not be a correct estimate. They had done well in the reparations negotiations and had retrieved an honorable settlement in Africa; had they wished, they could also have improved the economic regime of the Scheldt and inland waterways even if strategic boundaries were not obtained. It is further worth noting that the Belgian arguments were not without effect upon the powers as a group. In the reparation matter, as in the colony debate, when the powers were confronted by a resolute Belgian stand, they gave way not as much as Hymans hoped, but as much as probably was warranted. The embarrassment of a Belgian withdrawal from the conference could not be risked.

The conference was, after all, a great power conference; the Belgians had to make do as best they could. They did well, indeed better than other small states which, however, did not contribute to the war effort as Belgium had. Because power was the moving force, despite Wilson's idealism, the little country was doomed to disappointment, eloquent speeches and juridical arguments not withstanding. Much of the disappointment stemmed from a certain illusion which Lloyd George cruelly summarized in a comment regarding Hymans' diplomacy: 'When he dominated the conversation, he thought he dominated the situation.'[59]

The bitterest pangs were caused not by the lack of enough specific gains as by the manner in which the Belgians had been treated by the powers. Some bones were thrown to their pride, for example, the great power legations in Brussels were raised to the status of embassies and a place was given Belgium on the Reparation Commission; yet more often the Belgians were ignored or humiliated. Not allowed to participate in the decision-making of the conference, they were denied permission, except when matters directly pertaining to Belgium were under discussion, to join the conference of ambassadors which was to settle the many problems left untouched by the Big Five. Hymans' own interpretation was that the big powers were willing to grant the representatives of the small states much social politeness and honor but considered the desire of their lesser brethren to have a voice in the discussions as pure impertinence. Hymans did get his way on occasion, but it was a shame that he could not assure Belgium her rightful share of reparations without having to resort to the threat of leaving the conference.

For two decades or more, Wilson, Clemenceau, Lloyd George, and Orlando were scored for committing legions of errors and sins at the peace conference. More recently, historians have suggested that what the critics demanded of the statesmen was superhuman performance of an impossible task. This interpretation may be the more nearly correct, but it should not be allowed to hide the fact that the treatment of Belgium as a small power was one of the least glorious and honorable aspects of the affair. Memory of it was to rankle in minds of Belgian diplomats for years to come, confirm the distrust of large international gatherings that was a legacy of the 1830 Conference of London, and provoke them to an attempt to increase Belgium's status as a power in Europe.

7.5 NOTES

1. Van Zuylen, *L'Échiquier congolais*, pp. 352–425. Louis, *Ruanda-Urundi 1884–1919*, pp. 49–92. Willequet, *Le Congo belge*, pp. 277–326. Much of this section of this chapter originally appeared in the author's article 'The end of Congo neutrality, 1914', *Historian*, XXVIII, no. 4 (Aug. 1966), pp. 610–624, where the topic is discussed in more detail; the permission of that journal for re-use of these passages is appreciated.
2. United States Senate, *Miscellaneous Document No. 68*, 49th Congress, 1st session, Washington, 1886.
3. Belgium, M.A.E. Arch., Af., 1/2, 'De Bassompierre minute to draft of Davignon's instructions to Lalaing, Aug. 7, 1914'.
4. *Ibid.* The railroad referred to by-passed rapids on the lower Congo. Constructed on Belgian soil on the river's left bank, it provided communications with Brazzaville, in the French Congo, as well as with Leopoldville.
5. Van den Heuvel papers, 30: 'Copy of Renkin telegram to governor-general of Congo, Aug. 6, 1914'. The extract of this document printed in the

Ministry of Colonies' *Correspondance diplomatique et politique relative à la guerre en Afrique* (Brussels, 1919), no. 3, p. 9, omits this portion of the telegram.

6. Belgium, *The Belgian Grey Book*, vol. I, no. 61: 'Guillaume to Davignon, Aug. 9, 1914', in *Coll. Doc.*, p. 335.
7. *Ibid.*, vol. I, no. 74: 'Guillaume to Davignon, Aug. 16, 1914', in *Coll. Doc.*, p. 341.
8. Belgium, M.A.E. Arch., Af., 1/2, 'Orts note of Aug. 14, 1914'.
9. *Ibid.*, Van der Elst note (M.A.E., no. 6539), Aug. 1914.
10. *Ibid.*, Copy of Villiers note to Grey, Aug. 22, 1914.
11. See Gardner, *German East*, pp. 9–13.
12. Lt. Col. Hordern, *Military operations*, vol. I, pp. 20, 21, note.
13. Belgium, M.A.E. Arch., Af., 1/2, 'Tombeur to Renkin, Sept. 19, 1914'; 'Villiers *note verbale*, Oct. 8, 1914'; 'Renkin to Davignon, Oct. 28, 1914', and annexes.
14. *Ibid.*, 'Kidston to Davignon, Dec. 19, 1914'.
15. *Ibid.*, 'Villiers to Davignon, Jan. 14, 1915'.
16. Hymans papers, 79: 'Davignon to Hymans, May 23, 1915'.
17. The story of the C.R.B. may be traced in G. I. Day and H. H. Fisher (eds.), *Public Relations*.
18. Hymans papers, 79: 'Davignon to Hymans, May 23, 1915'.
19. The Netherlands, *Bescheiden betreffende de Buitenlandse Politiek van Nederland (BN)*, 3rd per., Part V, II, pp. 970–72, no. 973: 'De Stuers to Van Karnebeek, March 1919'. For a good review of the range of Belgian opinions on the territorial issue, see Robert Devleeshouwer, 'L'Opinion publique et les revendications territoriales belges à la fin de la première guerre mondiale 1918–1919', pp. 163–89.
20. Baron Napoléon Eugène Beyens, 'Deux politiques', *Le Flambeau*, V, no. 4 (Apr. 30, 1922), pp. 407–30; no. 5 (May 31, 1922), pp. 23–42.
21. Paul Hymans, *Mémoires*, vol. II, annex, pp. 883–87: 'Hymans to Beyens, Dec. 24, 1915'.
22. *Ibid.*, II, annex, p. 904.
23. *Ibid.*, II, annex, pp. 893–94: 'Hymans to Beyens, Jan. 15, 1916'; pp. 895–98: 'Same to same, Jan. 21, 1916'.
24. *Ibid.*, and also annex, pp. 889–90: 'Gaiffier to Hymans, Jan. 6, 1916'.
25. *Ibid.*, II, pp. 157–58.
26. Gaiffier's dispatch of Jan. 31, 1916 is quoted in *Ibid.*, I, 190.
27. *Ibid.*, II, annex, p. 905: 'Declaration of Apr. 29, 1916'.
28. Villiers *note verbale* of Apr. 17, 1916, is quoted in Louis, *Ruanda-Urundi*, p.216.
29. Renkin to Tombeur, Mar. 27, 1916, quoted in *Ibid.*, pp. 216–17.
30. Van Zuylen, *L'Échiquier congolais*, pp. 435–43.
31. Hymans, *Mémoires*, vol. I, p. 167. Pierre van Zuylen, *Les mains libres*, pp. 21–22.
32. *Les carnets de guerre d'Albert 1er, Roi des Belges*, ed. by General E. Raoul Van Overstraeten, p. 117: Diary entry of Dec. 5, 1916. See also entries of

April 17, July 2, July 22, and October 19, 1916. The editor of the letters was military advisor to both Albert and Leopold III. After the Second World War he was sharply criticized for his role in 1939 and 1940. Albert's letters, at least as presented here, indicate that Van Overstraeten's position then was similar to that held by the revered Albert in 1916 and 1917.

33. *Ibid.*, p. 123: Entry of Dec. 20, 1916.
34. *Ibid.*, pp. 129–30.
35. *Ibid.*, p. 141: Entry of Feb. 11, 1917.
36. *Ibid.*, p. 209. See also J. Wullus-Rudiger [Armand Wullus], *En marge de la politique belge 1914–1956*.
37. This memorandum of Oct. 11, 1917, is quoted in Hymans, *Mémoires*, vol. I, p. 170.
38. *Ibid.*, vol. I, p. 173. For a discussion of the last unofficial German effort to reach an agreement with Belgium, an effort quickly rebuffed by Hymans, see Jacques Willequet, 'Sondages de paix en 1918: la dernière mission du Comte Toerring', pp. 661–75.
39. The memorandum containing Hymans' arguments was transmitted to several capitals. See U.S.A., *Foreign Relations, 1919, Paris Peace Conference*, vol. II, pp. 436–40: 'Cartier to Lansing, Nov. 13, 1918.'
40. *Mémoires*, vol. I, pp. 190–92: 'Gaiffier to Beyens, June 9, 1917'.
41. Hymans' *comptes rendus* of his conversations with Clemenceau, J. Cambon, Ribot, and Poincaré are reproduced in *Ibid.*, vol. I, pp. 204–9.
42. Shepard B. Clough, *History of the Flemish Movement*, pp. 175–222. See also Henri Pirenne's essay 'La Belgique et la guerre mondiale' in his *Histoire de Belgique*, vol. IV, especially pp. 385–426.
43. *Ibid.*, vol. I, p. 322. The protocol of the Jan. 25, 1919, plenary session may be found in U.S.A., *Foreign Relations, 1919, Paris Peace Conference*, vol. III, pp. 176–201.
44. Hymans, *Mémoires*, vol. I, p. 328.
45. U.S.A., *Foreign Relations, 1919, Paris Peace Conference*, vol. III, pp. 957–69.
46. Hymans, *Mémoires*, vol. I, p. 378. Sally Marks, 'The Luxemburg Question at the Paris Peace Conference and After', pp. 10–11.
47. Hymans, *Mémoires*, vol. I, pp. 421–24. In a June 4, 1919, meeting of the foreign ministers of the great powers, Arthur Balfour stated that 'the British Admiralty as such did not desire any change in the status of the Scheldt...'. He did, however, make a weak plea for internationalizing the Scheldt regime (U.S.A., *Foreign Relations, 1919, Paris Peace Conference*, vol. IV, p. 798).
48. The Netherlands, *BN*, 3rd per., Part V, II, no. 826, pp. 808–9: 'Van Swinderen to Van Karnebeek, Dec. 18, 1918'.
49. Hymans, *Mémoires*, vol. I, p. 393.
50. U.S.A., *Foreign Relations, 1919, Paris Peace Conference*, vol. V, pp. 344–51: 'Notes of April 29, 1919, meeting'.
51. *Ibid.*, vol. III, pp. 797–817: 'Notes of conversation, Jan. 30, 1919.'

52. 'Hymans to Franck, May 12, 1919', is quoted in Louis, *Ruanda-Urundi*, p. 241.
53. *Ibid.*, pp. 234–54, and Van Zuylen, *L'Échiquier congolais*, pp. 451–59.
54. U.S.A., *Foreign Relations, 1919, Paris Peace Conference*, vol. IV, pp. 729–47: 'Notes of meetings, May 19 and 20, 1919'.
55. *Ibid.*, vol. IV, p. 801: 'Notes of meeting, June 4, 1919'.
56. Belgium, *Doc. diplomatiques belges*, vol. I, pp. 100–105, no. 27: 'Belgian declaration to Commission of XIV, Mar. 23, 1920'.
57. Van Zuylen, *Les mains libres*, p. 98.
58. *Ibid.*, pp. 226–27. *Documents diplomatiques belges*, vol. II, pp. 394–405, no. 138: 'Vandervelde to Gaiffier, Oct. 26, 1926, annex II, Oct. 23, 1926'. Hymans, *Mémoires*, vol. I, pp. 467–78. *Documents on British Foreign Policy*, ser. 1A, vol. II, pp. 93–94, no. 54: 'A. Chamberlain to Tyrrell, June 9, 1926'. For the most detailed account of these negotiations, see Klaus Pabst, 'Eupen-Malmedy in der belgischen Regierungs- und Parteienpolitik 1914–1940', pp. 206–315, 453–98.
59. Cited in Van Zuylen, *Les mains libres*, p. 100.

8. Diplomacy from a middle position: Security

At first glance, Belgium's position in post-war Europe appeared comfortable. Her suffering during the invasion had won her international respect and sympathy, Germany was defeated, intimate relations far different from those of 1906–14 were established with Britain and France, and general agreement to revision of the 1839 treaties promised Belgium a more prestigious and secure status. The disappointments of the peace conference indicated, however, that things were not as good as they seemed. Within months the Brussels officials were involved in some of the most difficult diplomacy of their country's history.

The key problem was the old, familiar one: Belgium's small size and lack of means to influence her larger neighbors. She counted on the prestige won by her noble efforts and suffering during the war to aid her diplomacy; but while these last were paid much lip service, their value in the marketplace of power politics had proven limited. Hurt by the treatment received at Paris, Belgium's pride demanded that her contributions and importance be recognized, and her diplomats subsequently followed a policy admittedly designed to augment the diplomatic as well as the moral prestige of their country. Their mood and conception of Belgium's proper role in international affairs was clearly put by Henri Jaspar, foreign minister from November 1920 to February 1924:

Belgium is not, in Europe, an out-of-the-way corner of land, whose scanty territory renders her negligible; she is an essential factor in the solution of many problems. As a result of her having been left out of account, as is seen more clearly every day, the Treaty of Versailles is incomplete and has not brought about a perfect peace... Belgium, whose fate is inevitably involved with that of Europe, will often be obliged to play a part in the great events of history. She must today prepare herself for this...[1]

Yet the arena in which the Belgians had to act was not accommodating. Until 1914 Belgium had survived the ambitions and antagonisms of the great powers not so much because she was guaranteed as because those ambitions and antagonisms had required the powers to respect Belgium's independence. But the international situation was different now and a stage was set to which the Belgian diplomats were neither accustomed nor prepared. Gone were the balances of power in which Belgium formerly moved and had her being. Given the defeat of Germany and the withdrawal of revolution-torn Russia from Western European affairs, there were no powers Belgium could wish to play off against each other unless she were to pit her two closest friends, Britain and France, in rivalry. In 1919 this was unthinkable, for Belgium's security was tied to both. Moreover, at the time, the two seemed too close to separate; if they did differ there was the danger that, as suggested by events at the peace conference, they might settle their problems at the expense of Belgium. Later, when the two great powers began to drift apart, their differences would threaten Belgium's security and economic development.

What, then, were the small country's alternatives? In view of the failure of the 1839 treaties, the strong sense of pride within the Belgian populace, and the absence of the traditional balance of power, enforced neutrality seemed meaningless. Close attachment to the policies of either France or Britain might bring some positive reward. Yet relations with David Lloyd George were strained and the British reluctance to make commitments was obvious; France, on the other hand, might be smothering. *Rapprochement* with the former enemy was unacceptable, as was reliance upon Soviet Russia. Belgium could chose to withdraw into herself; it was possible that such action would not weaken her security as neither Britain nor France could allow Belgium to be overrun again. But such a retreat would mean that many economic opportunities, such as economic union with the Duchy of Luxemburg, might be lost and that France would come to dominate the small country's economic affairs. Belgium's greatest strength lay in her commerce and industry; she had always been aggressive in these areas, and her post-war reconstruction required that she continue in this vein. Voluntary neutrality was more palatable than enforced neutrality, but did it have much to offer, and how would it help Belgium's security and economy? Of all the alternatives available, that of active involvement and close, but balanced, relations with Britain and France seemed most attractive, both in terms of the mood of the liberated country and its economic and security needs.

The problem was that Belgium's neighbors had their differences and their own aspirations. Each of the great powers had had enough of self-sacrifice during the war and was determined to experience as little more as possible. The byword of the 1920s was solidarity of the Entente, but this was more often a slogan than a reality. France, enjoying the greatest influence she had possessed in a century, was desirous of dominating the Continent. Belgium was naturally expected to fall in line; Hymans believed that Clemenceau 'could not tolerate Belgium daring to take the free tone of a sovereign and independent country'.[2] England, on the other hand, though somewhat preoccupied by domestic concerns and also desirous of maintaining the Entente, did not intend to abdicate her voice in continental affairs or let France move unchecked. At the heart of the several issues on which the two powers differed were their attitudes on the treatment of Germany. France insisted her enemy adhere to the letter of the Versailles treaty and fully pay every penalty contained therein no matter what the effect on Germany; the English favored a more flexible interpretation of the treaty and disliked French efforts to retard German recovery because they conflicted with Britain's wish to rehabilitate the German market for trade purposes.

The Belgians were caught between their great allies. They were faced by a task of rebuilding and were not in a financial position even to begin to meet the cost. As borrowing the necessary funds would be expensive and probably impossible, money and goods had to be taken from Germany. The Belgians believed they had a moral right to force their former occupiers to pay and also had a real fear of a quick German resurgence. Nevertheless, Belgium was a trading country and needed the development of the German market. And the establishment of French hegemony throughout Western Europe would not be beneficial to the little country. France could affect Belgium's commerce and the Rue de la loi would have difficulty exerting an independent diplomatic will. If the Brussels diplomats were to avoid becoming vassals to a Parisian suzerain, they would, as in the past, have to maintain close relations with Britain thus assuring continuing British interest in Belgium's fate. At the same time, they could not forget that in the matter of security they were dependent upon the immediate aid which only France could give in a crisis. The proper exchange for promises of such aid was, of course, cooperation with French policies.

Security, more than anything else, was the national goal, and even the issue of reparations took second place to it. As Paul Hymans wrote in his memoirs, 'the preoccupation which dominated Belgium at the close of the war and following the peace conference was that of security, necessarily united to that of independence'.[3] He and his colleagues were not prepared to define security simply as shelter from another German invasion. Security meant the ability of Belgium to shape her own course and develop her own economy as she wished in relative freedom. To be sure, protection from military threats received the initial emphasis; hence the concern for the establishment of appropriate treaties. Yet the broader concerns soon came to the fore, although the Belgians' tendency to speak of security matters solely in terms of national defense and to separate financial, commercial, reparations, and other matters under different headings often clouded the relationship. It is worth noting also that the interest of some leaders in establishing security treaties reflected the Belgians' preference for that course of action over one of paying the time, energy, and money necessary to bring Belgium's military strength to its full potential. Her munitions industries did flourish, thanks to the stimulation of international trade, but concerted efforts to compensate for Belgium's manpower limitations were not undertaken.

Sometimes the maneuvers required for the achievement of Belgian aims, for example in the Duchy of Luxemburg, forced the Brussels diplomats to waver from their middle position between France and Britain. Thus certain actions, while they gained Belgium advantages, also threatened the keystone of Belgium's security and independence of action: the preservation of equally close relations with England and France. What concessions had to be made were for the most part accepted by the Belgians without complaining as the price a small nation had to pay in a world of big power politics if it were to gain something more concrete than wordy promises. On the other hand, their indignation was great when the Netherlands failed to make concessions to Belgium in the same manner Belgium had to France. Though the Belgo-Dutch issues were not regulated entirely, that of commitments from the great powers eventually proceeded in a manner more to the liking of Brussels. A bilateral pact with London to balance the accord with Paris was not obtained, but the Locarno agreements did create a British guarantee of Belgium's eastern border and even involved a German pledge, for whatever it was worth. Aside from Dutch acquiescence to Belgian views on certain matters, this was all the Belgians at the time believed they wanted or needed.

8.1 LUXEMBURG, FRANKFORT, AND THE MILITARY ACCORD

Following completion of the peace negotiations at Paris, officials in Brussels confidently expected alliances would be promptly made to strengthen Belgium and other nations against any future German attack. The first set-back to these hopes was the United States Senate's rejection of the Versailles settlement and with it the Anglo-American guarantee of France which had been signed by Lloyd George, Wilson, and Clemenceau in Paris. Such a treaty implied the protection of Belgium; its loss was a disappointment. The Belgians had not planned to rely on it alone, however; they intended to contract their own agreements with Britain and

France to replace the obviously defunct guarantee clause of the 1839 treaties.

During the peace conference the possibility of a Franco-Belgian alliance was mentioned, and two days before the signing of the peace treaty Clemenceau personally broached the subject. In an August visit to Paris, Hymans indicated he favored the idea although his primary concern was a joint guarantee of Belgium's integrity given by both Britain and France.

The British did not wish to take on an unlimited obligation. They preferred an interim guarantee of not more than five years, pending the grant of one by the League of Nations, and insisted Belgium agree to be neutral for the duration of Britain's particular responsibility. The incensed Brussels officials replied that it would be 'absolutely impossible' to obtain the consent of the Belgian public to this condition. Despite the relatively sympathetic views of British Foreign Secretary Lord Curzon, Lloyd George would not give way. The Belgians were also discouraged by the French government's agreement with the five year limit and by the faith put in the League of Nations. Edmond de Gaiffier, now ambassador to France, wrote Hymans that either the League would abandon Belgium or take the role of arbiter and like the Conference of London in the 1830s impose decisions in the making of which the Belgians would have no voice. 'These methods by which small powers are sacrificed instead of diminishing are becoming worse. *A priori*, any decision of the League of Nations should to us be suspect. . .'[4] As Belgium was relatively safe for the duration of the Rhineland occupation anyway and to avoid a condition 'contrary to our dignity', on January 5, 1920, Hymans persuaded the coalition Belgian cabinet to drop the matter.

The intentions of the French in supporting the British proposed time limit become suspect in light of the alacrity with which the Quai d'Orsay rushed to fill the breach in Belgium's security arrangements. Three days after the cabinet discussion, French Ambassador Pierre de Margerie told Hymans that Belgium's failure to obtain the joint guarantee was cause to hasten negotiations with France lest Belgium's safety be longer unguarded. The foreign minister in turn suggested that the general staffs of the two countries make a preliminary study. But Hymans was well aware from Gaiffier's reports how eager the French were for a military convention and was not to be rushed. First, certain obstacles such as the Luxemburg dispute should be cleared away. Hymans told the ambassador, 'there was always a danger for a small country in being encircled by a larger one, that Belgium has need of air and her freedom of movement, that she does not want to be absorbed in any manner, dominated, or be morally and economically penetrated'.[5]

The Belgian cabinet supported the precedence of the Luxemburg issue over the military accord, and settlement suddenly appeared possible following a cabinet upheaval in Paris. Clemenceau was succeeded by Alexandre Millerand, who also took over the foreign ministry portfolio; the influence of men such as the former minister of munitions and then of the liberated regions Louis Loucheur was weakened, and at the Quai d'Orsay the replacement of Philippe Berthelot by Maurice Paléologue introduced a known friend of Belgium. At the end of the month, a top level meeting was held at Ypres in the railway car of French President Raymond Poincaré.

Belgian Prime Minister Léon Delacroix opened discussion by observing that consideration of a military entente dominated the agenda. He asked if such an entente would be of use unless the Netherlands could be persuaded to conclude a military agreement with Belgium or at least to fortify the Maastricht appendix. Marshal Foch replied that once agreements had been worked out between France, Belgium, and Great Britain, the Dutch could be brought around. After additional discussion, it was decided that the general staffs should prepare a document which could serve as a base for a military accord; the English were to be kept informed and invited to attend the staff conferences.[6]

The Belgian premier then observed that his government would be in a difficult position if it asked the chambers to ratify the accord without a favorable resolution of the Luxemburg problem. Foch countered that the two issues should not be confused; the military accord was necessary no matter what the fate of Luxemburg. Millerand trotted forth the argument that control of the *Guillaume-Luxembourg* railway belonged to France by virtue of the peace settlement which gave France Alsace-Lorraine, for that railway was an extension of the Alsace-Lorraine system. To this Hymans replied that the chapter of the treaty relating specifically to the duchy had, by common consent, left the problem unsettled. Discussion continued for several hours without concession on either side, and eventually attention was turned to commercial negotiations and other matters.

Hymans and his staff were dismayed that their premier, by taking up the military accord first, had implied that Belgium gave it priority over the railway question. When the foreign minister subsequently made clear that the latter issue took precedence, recriminations were exchanged between Paris and Brussels. The French were particularly annoyed because they had invited the British to send an observer to the staff conversations and Belgian insistence on progress in the Luxemburg matter had now not only prevented official talks from beginning but had led to the termination of unofficial discussions between Marshal Foch and General

Gillain.[7] Relations further deteriorated when Hymans learned that France had – in his view – pressured the duchy into a technical accord regarding the railroad. On March 5, De Margerie did admit that his government had not done all it could for Belgium, but said he could not understand the Belgians' desire to make the military accord part of a bargain and why they considered entrance into such an agreement a concession. Surely it served their own interest? In any case, Millerand would not make concessions; the ambassador therefore asked the Belgians to take some action which would make the premier more amenable.[8]

There is no doubt the Belgians wished to turn the military accord into a *quid pro quo* for control of the Luxemburg railways. It is also clear that they intended to reach some sort of defense agreement with France and that acceptance of a military tie was only in part the concession De Bassompierre had predicted in 1917. It was also part of a foreign policy which Hymans was soon describing as 'based on the principle of military arrangements'.[9] The Belgian foreign minister had delayed the military talks because he hoped to pry loose the French hold on the *Guillaume-Luxembourg*. Millerand, estimating the Belgians would eventually agree to the accord without that concession on the part of France, held firm. His one proposition was to set a date for talks regarding the railways, on the condition the Belgians would commence military talks shortly thereafter. To this Hymans agreed, although stipulating significant progress should first be made in the railway discussions. Hardly had he done so when Marshal Foch asked permission to ship French troops through Belgium if they were needed in the Rhineland.[10]

Foch's request, which he claimed was not intended to start military talks prematurely, was stimulated by disturbing events in Germany, events which provided Hymans another lever for shifting Millerand's position. At the beginning of April, the German government sent troops into the Ruhr district to quell leftist uprisings that had occurred there during and after the Kapp Putsch. France previously had opposed such a move unless the allies in turn extended their occupation. On the morning of April 6, French soldiers marched into Frankfort and Darmstadt; they later took control of the neighboring towns of Hanau, Homburg, and Duisburg. France was acting counter to the decision of the Supreme Allied Council, which two weeks earlier had disapproved such an entry; and she was doing so without prior notification to Great Britain.

The independent action of the French was a blow to the Entente. Lord Curzon protested fiercely and privately considered asking the Italian, American, and Belgian governments to join him in a statement of dissent.[11] His confidence was misplaced. On April 9, Belgium announced she would send troops to join the French in occupying Frankfort. New the French could claim it was not they but the British who were splitting the Entente.

When Millerand notified Hymans on April 4 of his intentions and requested Belgian cooperation, Hymans had replied it would be better first to send an ultimatum to Germany, but if all the allied governments favored common action, Belgium would participate. This answer was in accordance with his position of the previous several weeks, during which he had frequently called for allied unity. He had also been warning France that sending allied troops to the right bank of the Rhine would be unwise, provoking increased determination in Germany to disobey the peace treaty, causing riots which would slow production, and possibly stimulating the overthrow of the current German government which had shown at least partial willingness to fulfill the terms of Versailles. In March, when Britain and Italy had suggested the Weimar government be allowed to send more troops to establish order in the Rhineland, on the condition that allied officers observe their activities and encourage prompt withdrawal, Hymans had agreed.

Two days of thought now brought some changes. On April 6, when Hymans learned of the probable British reaction and the French desire for Belgian support, he had already discussed with the capable young chief of his personal cabinet, Jacques Davignon, whether Belgium should act if Britain refused. The foreign minister had achieved few successes in the past months; how could he hope to advance Belgium's negotiations in the future if the French request were disregarded now? A gesture of friendship might win French indebtedness and political concessions. 'Could we not let her understand, without concluding a bargain, that we hope she will take our support into account in the current discussions on other problems?'[12]

Hymans, Davignon, and De Bassompierre favored this course. Despite their arguments, a private meeting of several ministers in the home of Premier Delacroix on the evening of April 7 decided Belgium should not join the French. Confident the matter was settled, several ministers including Emile Vandervelde, head of the Socialist party and an opponent of the occupation, left Brussels the next morning. Later that day, probably on the insistence of Hymans, a cabinet meeting was called at which King Albert, just returned from Fontainebleau, was present. The foreign minister argued that Belgium would gain nothing by not supporting France and that Germany would rejoice at seeing France isolated and would strengthen her resistance to the Versailles Treaty. On the other hand, joining France would affirm the solidarity of the allies toward Germany, make France more sympathetic, and give Belgium more authority to reject any 'excessive demands' made by France in the military discussions. The objections of Delacroix and Minister of Economic Affairs Henri Jaspar were overcome, and it was voted to participate in the occupation.[13]

The announcement that a Belgian battalion would go to Frankfort brought effusive thanks from the French. Millerand informed Gaiffier that he would propose the nomination of a committee of Belgian and French experts to study the Luxemburg railway problem. By May, a partition of the railroads had been agreed upon except for technical details, and the French had advised Luxemburg to conclude an economic union with Belgium. With the deadlock in Franco-Belgian relations broken, the military conversations could be resumed.

The cost to Anglo-Belgian relations had not been slight, however. The English were provoked both by the turn in Belgian policy and by the lack of forewarning. Ignorant himself of the Belgian action, Belgian Ambassador Baron Ludovic Moncheur had a difficult time of it, first when he had no instructions for explaining his government's move to Curzon and later when he pleaded that the Belgians were 'promoting the solidarity of the allies by agreeing – in face of an apparent *fait accompli* – to a course to which they had previously demurred'.[14] Sir Eyre Crowe, the British assistant under-secretary, criticized Moncheur as failing properly to do his duty and the Belgians of deepening rather than healing the split among the allies. On April 19, at the Conference of San Remo when Hymans suggested England join in the Franco-Belgian alliance discussions, he was sharply rebuffed by Lord Curzon. The haughty British foreign secretary expressed his surprise at the presentation of the proposal at such a 'singularly unfavorable' moment. Granted the Belgians wanted to facilitate the Luxemburg discussions with France, Curzon

could not find in the transaction even if thus interpreted, any excuse for an independent action without even an intimation to us of what they proposed to do, and in open contradiction of the line which they had hitherto adopted.[15]

The Brussels officials brushed off the British reaction as one of hurt pride at the foreign office, taking comfort in reports of many influential Englishmen who approved of the Franco-Belgian action. That Hymans should broach an Anglo-Belgian entente so shortly after the episode nevertheless indicates a certain misjudgment on his part. In effect, his gesture of friendship appeared naïve and strengthened Curzon's opinion that the Belgians were not aware of the full import of their actions. It certainly did not lessen English fears of being dragged into unnecessary military adventures through an alliance with Belgium. But the British reluctance to make continental ties was deep rooted, and the absence of British officers at the military conversations, despite the urgings of the war office and the Imperial Defence Committee, can not be attributed to the incident.

Once the track was clear for Franco-Belgian negotiations, Marshal Foch lost no time in sending to Brussels a preliminary draft of a military entente designed to meet the danger of an unprovoked German attack. The first of its three articles concerned the actions France and Belgium should take during the allied occupation of the Rhineland (scheduled by the peace treaty to last fifteen years). The number of divisions each country would supply for the occupation and for an initial reinforcement of the occupation against any 'German aggression or threat, as well as a resistance on Germany's part to the peace treaty', were to be decided.[16] Should there be a 'general taking up of arms' in Germany, the nations were 'to mobilize the whole of their forces, proportionately to the population of each country'. The number of divisions, planes, armored trucks, and the amount of artillery each country would furnish was to be determined; their employment would be guided by plans established through the common accord of the two governments.

The second article provided that while the Rhineland occupation was being reduced, systems of defense should be established which would connect the Belgian frontier with those portions of the Rhineland still occupied. In preparation for the complete cessation of the occupation, France and Belgium would immediately begin organizing 'a coordinated system of defense at their frontiers, including the frontiers of Luxemburg'.[17] According to French Chief-of-Staff General Buat, the French would hope to rush troops into Germany before German soldiers could establish themselves in the demilitarized Rhineland zone. The importance of Maastricht and Luxemburg for such a plan was great; Buat told Gaiffier that France would take responsibility for the defense of the duchy and would study its borders minutely but would erect no fortifications there.[18] The remainder of the article stated that if mobilization were necessary, the defense system appropriate to the current status of the Rhineland occupation would serve as a base for the forces covering the junction of the French and Belgian armies. Mobilization of additional forces, should they be judged necessary in view of increases in Germany's military potential, was also envisaged. Article Three provided for annual staff conversations to regulate the technicalities embodied in the preceding articles.

The Brussels officials reacted cautiously to Foch's proposal. They knew any promise of keeping Belgian forces and equipment proportionate to those of France would raise 'very lively opposition' in Belgium, whose parliament would resent any apparent attempt by France to control Belgian military affairs. As far as equipment was concerned, such an amount of supplies was an impossibility anyway. More important, the statesmen did not want their political policy toward Germany to become too closely tied to that of France or for Belgium to be involved in frequent military adventures. Their interest in a military entente was that of security, not enforcement of the peace treaty. British participation was highly desirable, and 'once an Anglo-French-Belgian accord had been realized (if it were), common pressure should be put on Holland to lead her to consent to a concerted defense of Limburg'.[19]

Belgian Chief-of-Staff General Henri Maglinse easily persuaded Foch to omit the phrases regarding enforcement of the treaty and proportionate forces, and with these obstacles removed, a force level agreement was quickly reached covering the next five years. On the issue of Limburg, Foch was sympathetic; at Ypres he had even insisted that if the Netherlands refused a request to cooperate, 'we will tell her that southern Limburg with the passage of Maastricht is indispensable to us and that we will do with it what we wish.'[20] After the completion of the new draft, Millerand let it be known that once the accord was concluded, there would be occasion to study what should be done about Limburg; certainly it could not be left open to the enemy. By asking Brussels to proceed with the accord before the Limburg matter was settled, Millerand assumed some responsibility for the negotiation of an agreement with the Dutch. In September, when the accord was signed, Maglinse informed the British military attaché that Belgium counted on France and Britain 'coercing the Dutch in event of war' and that Belgium had no intention of discussing the matter with the Netherlands by herself.[21] The French Right, overconfident of its ability to stay in power, nevertheless did not hasten to exert any real pressure at The Hague; nor were the British active. The delay was unfortunate, for the succeeding governments were not as committed to solving the problem, and the lack of a defense plan involving both the Low Countries did much to vitiate the military pact and Belgian security.

The final version of the military accord signed by Foch, Maglinse, and Buat on September 7, 1920, did not vary greatly from that agreed upon in June. Some minor changes, mostly in wording, were made, and two additions appeared in the first article. Probably because of the difficulty Belgium would experience in the development and production of sufficient amounts of modern war materials, it was agreed the two armies would aid each other in this matter. It was further stated that France would supply 'the ships necessary for the protection, and, in case of war, the defense of the Belgian coast'.[22] By all indications, this was a late addition. Throughout the summer, the Belgians had tried in vain to bring Britain into the agreement. When it became clear that Belgium could not count on the British fleet to protect her ports, she had to turn to France.

The agreement signed by the military leaders was the only formal bilateral military understanding reached between Belgium and France in the interwar period. For several months, however, the Belgian foreign ministry considered the possibility of a separate protocol which would contain the political part of the accord. The technical body of the accord would be kept secret, but the protocol would be made public to satisfy curiosity and quiet suspicion. Hymans and De Bassompierre favored such a procedure, and on June 26 the political director gave a draft of the proposed act to Maglinse, who agreed to its contents. A more formal version was then drawn up, omitting at De Bassompierre's suggestion any specific reference to Germany which could embarrass relations with that country.[23] Its preamble stated the two countries were concluding the convention in the interest of strengthening the guarantees of peace provided by the League of Nations pact. According to Article One,

In case of an unprovoked aggression, directed at the same time against France and Belgium, the armed forces of the two countries will act in concert, according to a plan which will be established by the Belgian and French general staffs and approved by the two governments.[24]

This wording avoided naming Germany but hardly appears flattering to Great Britain. More important, the phrase 'at the same time' freed Belgium from the possibility of being dragged into war by way of French commitments to nations east of Germany; nor would France be involved should fighting occur in the bitter quarrel between the Netherlands and Belgium.

The second article indicated that the governments would independently decide whether the *casus foederis* existed; if it did, their forces would pursue common objectives to be proposed by the general staffs and approved by the governments. Article Three provided that after the occupation of the Rhineland was ended, and every five years thereafter, either of the governments could denounce the accord. The length of the notification period prior to cancellation was left to be determined. The next article allowed for regular reexamination of plans, and the final article stated that the convention would be ratified and the ratifications exchanged with the briefest delay possible.

Although much of what was contained in the convention was implicit in the technical accord, the convention went further. The military agreement was turned into a full-fledged political alliance. An avenue of escape was included; in time the Belgians, irritated by French reluctance to revise the provisions of the accord, regretted its absence in the technical document. It is true, as General Maglinse commented to the British military attaché, that Belgium could argue the accord should not take effect if she did not believe Germany guilty of aggression. But as the technical agreement committed Belgium to mobilization as soon as Germany took up arms and before any aggression occurred, how likely was Belgium to be spared combat? Furthermore, unlike the convention, the technical accord had no clause which limited its relevance solely to a German attack in the West on both Belgium and France.

Apparently the political convention drafted at the Belgian foreign ministry never came up for discussion with the French. In July, during the Conference of Spa, Millerand met with Delacroix, Hymans, and Jaspar. He inquired if Belgium were ready to sign a military entente which could either be an alliance or an accord. The Belgian premier replied that a treaty excluding Britain was not part of the Belgian program and would be unpopular with the chambers. It would be better to stick to having the general staffs work out concerted plans. Millerand believed it was for Belgium to decide the form the understanding took; but if it were to be a staff accord, the governments should approve and ratify it by exchanging letters.[25] This was the course followed. The technical accord was signed on September 7; within eight days Millerand and Delacroix exchanged letters stating the accord was purely defensive and that each nation retained its sovereign right to determine whether the agreement came into effect in any given circumstance. Copies of these letters were subsequently sent to the League of Nations to fulfill the covenant requirements concerning registration of treaties and agreements.

At the time the accord was signed, Delacroix was acting foreign minister as well as premier. Many aspects of Hymans' resignation are still unclear, but what is known of the story demonstrates the complications domestic politics posed for foreign policy. Discussions during the month of July showed that the members of the tripartite cabinet believed the government could remain in power until the end of October. At that time, three members of the cabinet would resign rather than support a bill in parliament providing for the fleminization of the University of Ghent; by then the king would have returned from his projected trip to Brazil and could appoint a new first minister.

When the French ambassador brought a request that Belgium ship arms to the Poles, who were resisting the encroachments of the Soviet Red Army, Hymans was so little interested that he turned the matter over to Delacroix and Minister of Defense Paul-Emile Janson and left on a trip. Pressured by the Socialist members of the cabinet, including Emile Vandervelde, not to do anything to harm the fortunes of the Russians, the Catholic Delacroix and the Liberal Janson forbade the shipment of arms; to mollify France they permitted two French munitions trains, which had already crossed the border, to proceed to Antwerp. Since the French could have shipped the arms from their own ports, it appears that the real aim in Paris was to involve Belgium in support of a French policy of which the British were critical.

Upon his return, Hymans approved the cabinet's action, but changed his views overnight following another appeal by the French ambassador. His resignation came shortly thereafter; it was hailed by most Liberals and especially by the militants who so strongly opposed what they considered the too pro-Fleming and Socialist policies of the cabinet. It was a skillful move, designed to strengthen Hymans' position with the militant Liberals and to avoid a resignation over the embarrassing linguistic issue. In order to prevent the resignation of the cabinet as a whole until the military accord was signed, Janson remained aboard.

The French were indeed angered by the Belgian decision not to ship arms. Relations worsened further when Delacroix hinted that an imperious French demand inconsonant with Belgian dignity had influenced the decision. According to Hymans, the rapid conclusion of the military accord, following a personal meeting of Delacroix and Millerand, was the compensation for the offense given France by these incidents.[26]

Announcement of the pact in Belgium brought instantaneous and strong reaction. It was praised by the majority of Walloons and cheered by the militant Liberals and those Catholics who admired France for her loyalty during the war and disliked the increasing influence of Flemish views in national politics. Many Flemings attacked the accord, fearing that it increased Walloon influence and adversely affected the campaign for Flemish rights at the same time it promised to involve Belgium in a Franco-German war. Each group suspected that the accord might lead to a strengthening of defense measures for Wallonia at the expense of Flanders. The more militant Socialists opposed the accord as a matter of principle, although experienced leaders such as Vandervelde were more flexible in their attitudes. The many politically-oriented newspapers flamed with pro and contra articles, and it soon became clear that the accord would remain an issue, both in itself and as a symbol in the linguistic controversy, for as long as it existed.

Had the terms of the agreement been made public, there is no doubt that the Flemish and Socialist diatribes would have been more venomous and more effective. In 1920, however, the majority of Belgian opinion was favorable toward France, and this attitude was strengthened by successful termination of the Frankfort occupation after little more than a month. On May 17, the Belgian and French soldiers left the Rhineland city since the German government had, following the cessation of disorders, reduced its own troops to the number permitted by the Rhineland demilitarization schedule.

The Belgians took particular joy in the prize obtained via the military accord: undisputed right to negotiate an economic union with the Duchy of Luxemburg. If there was any validity at all to the 1919 plebiscite in which the duchy opted, by a nearly three to one margin, for economic union with France, it may be questioned if that joy was mutually felt by the *Luxembourgeois*. They had little choice in the matter, however. After official French rejection in the second week of May of a Franco-Luxemburg customs union, the duchy had to follow Millerand's advice to deal with Belgium; its economic situation necessitated arrangements with some neighbor.

A small power itself, the duchy resented being pressured by relatively much larger Belgium. On the other hand, there was a tendency in Belgium to view economic control of the duchy as a legitimate reward for Belgium's efforts in the war. The negotiations which began after Hymans' resumption of diplomatic relations in June had a troubled course. A major difficulty was the fear of Luxemburg agriculturalists and Belgian industrialists of the competition they would face if tariffs were eliminated. The Belgians, afraid that if agreement were not reached Luxemburg interests would join cartels of French or German origin and thus provide even more dangerous competition, swallowed their objections. The *Luxembourgeois* did not. After determined negotiation they persuaded their counterparts to accept a system of tax rebates and subsidies controlled by a mixed commission which would protect the duchy's metallurgical and agrarian interests.

A second problem was that of the railways, the very one Hymans had believed solved in April 1920. In May of 1921, in return for Belgian support at a London conference on reparations, the French abandoned their claim on the railway, provided Belgium made certain economic concessions and that the railway were available for strategic use in wartime.[27] But the Brussels diplomats still had to contend with the duchy, which insisted on having a majority on the *Guillaume-Luxembourg*'s board of directors. The close tie between that line and those of the French Alsace-Lorraine railways suggests that the Luxemburg diplomats believed it best not to give way on this issue; perhaps support by French interests helped them stand firm. In any case, a provisional convention was rejected by Luxemburg in 1924, and while a commission of experts studied the matter further, the Alsace-Lorraine company took over temporary administration of the *Guillaume-Luxembourg*. It was not until 1934 that agreement was reached on the matter.[28]

The Belgium-Luxemburg Economic Union itself was signed on July

25, 1921, the railway question having been reserved for future discussions. Symbolic of the concessions made by the duchy was the replacement of its currency with that of Belgium. Yet the Luxemburg negotiators had won a few points: they had not abdicated control of their own railway, and they had gained preferential treatment for some of their commercial interests. Although the treaty was attacked in the Belgian parliament and bitterly so in the Luxemburg chamber, the outstanding success of the economic union in subsequent years indicates not only that the agreement was a viable one but also that it was particularly felicitous for the economic well-being of the countries involved.

8.2 THE SEARCH FOR WIDER SECURITY

While the Rue de la loi was pleased enough with the agreements with France and Luxemburg, these represented only half of Belgium's security goals. The treaties of 1839 still had to be revised and a settlement worked out with the Dutch; nor was a British guarantee yet assured. In all these matters the Belgians were to experience disappointment.

Throughout 1920, Hymans had kept the British informed of the Franco-Belgian military talks and had unofficially suggested that England join in. His reluctance to proceed with negotiations with France alone was real and was diminished only in part by French assurances that Britain would surely join any Franco-Belgian pact. The London war office did view such a course favorably, but when Delacroix broached the subject with Lloyd George at the Conference of Spa, the Welshman's reply was negative. Even though the Belgian did not propose a written treaty but just staff conversations similar to those undertaken by Barnardiston in 1906, Lloyd George thought the suggestion premature. There was nothing to fear from Germany for twenty years; what was to be feared were the effects of any allied intervention in Germany. Certain of the allied governments were more likely than others to take such action; it was therefore necessary to keep a free hand so that decisions could be reached independently.[29] In London, War Minister Winston Churchill told Moncheur that 'purely military accords can't exist, they are forced to take on a political character'.[30] If Britain agreed to defend such and such a sector, then she would be forcibly drawn into the next continental war because failure to participate would leave a portion of the front unguarded.

When Henri Jaspar, a Catholic, took over the foreign ministry portfolio in November 1920 in a coalition headed by Edmond Carton de Wiart, he had great hopes of winning not British membership in the

Franco-Belgian accord but a separate agreement. Lacking Hymans' experience he was not fully cognizant of the difficulties faced by a small power in bringing a larger country to acceptable terms. Yet he was determined Belgium's size should not make her a negligible quantity in Europe. Sir George Grahame, Villiers successor as British ambassador at Brussels, discouraged Jaspar politely, and Curzon commented, 'Jaspar must be very ill-informed if he thinks that he will succeed where M. Delacroix failed.'[31] Thirteen months later, however, Curzon and Jaspar had come close to final agreement on an Anglo-Belgian pact.

The pivotal point of the turn of events was the improvement in Anglo-French relations brought about following the rise of Aristide Briand to presidency of the French council of ministers. He was more amenable to British views on the treatment of Germany, and even when he differed with them he was often willing to negotiate. Though France by now had pacts with Poland, Czechoslovakia, Yugoslavia, and Rumania, as well as Belgium, her security could not be considered assured until the agreements with the secondary states were supplemented by one with Britain. At the end of 1921, Briand raised the issue with the foreign office, which agreed to consider a guarantee of France but not any accord which might involve Britain in Eastern Europe. Though Lloyd George subordinated the conclusion of such a treaty to settlement of other issues outstanding between France and England, preliminary drafts were drawn up at the Conference of Cannes in January 1920.

Jaspar and Georges Theunis, who had succeeded de Wiart as prime minister the preceding month, were present at Cannes and through an indiscretion learned of the Anglo-French negotiations. They immediately asked to be included; on second thought, they preferred to deal with England separately just as Belgium had with France, for that would be the more independent course. The proposed Anglo-French treaty, based as it was on drafts dating from 1919, referred to Belgium as a neutral. Jaspar protested against this; when Curzon stated he would do away with the word and might consider an Anglo-Belgian treaty if Belgium agreed to resist any German attack and prevent passage of German troops over her soil, the way seemed clear for an agreement.[32] A matter of special concern was whether completion of the accord was dependent upon the signing of the Anglo-French pact. Jaspar argued that Belgium's relations with England should not be conditioned by French policy; 'in the conduct of her foreign policy Belgium should appear independent and free of any other consideration than her self interest'.[33] He convinced Curzon and a few days later was informed that the London cabinet had decided the project would be signed no matter what the fate of the Anglo-French document.

The contents of the proposed treaty were straightforward. In the event of a direct and unprovoked attack by Germany against Belgium's territory, Britain would come to Belgium's aid with all her forces; Belgium in turn would employ all her forces to defend her frontiers in case of German attack. No obligation was to be placed by the treaty on the British dominions unless they themselves approved the accord. The duration of the treaty and the inclusion in the first article of the words 'direct' and 'territory', which somewhat narrowed the breadth of the British commitment, were to depend on the final wording of the French treaty then expected to be concluded shortly.[34]

The Anglo-Belgian discussions went smoothly and were disturbed only by one episode which revealed the Belgians' well developed pride and sense of national honor. Because the outlines of the treaty were orally established in relatively hurried discussions at Cannes, some confusion developed over whether Belgium was to defend herself against any foreign aggression or just German aggression. The British, partly because the French were demanding similarly broad terminology in their treaty, requested the more specific phrasing. This was acceptable to Jaspar. The touchy foreign minister insisted, however, that if this were done there should be omitted from the second article the sentence which stated Belgium would not make any engagements conflicting with the present treaty. To include it would be to imply Belgium considered permitting German troops to pass through her territories. In light of Belgium's performance in 1914, such an implication was offensive. The phrase requested by Curzon was a standard formula to be found in many treaties. Jaspar nevertheless became heated on the issue, which was finally resolved by omission of the debated sentence and rephrasing of the preamble so it included the promise desired by Britain but in a manner inoffensive to Belgium.[35]

The connection between the final Anglo-Belgian agreement and the proposed Anglo-French treaty is surprising in view of Jaspar's early campaign to have the two treaties concluded separately. It is surprising also because Jaspar had strongly repulsed a French effort to link conclusion of the two. Again the explanation is pride and Belgium's unwillingness to accept a treaty with Britain that might in any way be inferior to that concurrently being made by another power.

On the twentieth of January, De Margerie had intimated that the new French prime minister and minister of foreign affairs, Raymond Poincaré, desired that Belgium not confer with London until having reached agreement with Paris concerning what would be said. Jaspar replied diplomatically but categorically that 'never would I consent to being able to deal with England only as France intends and wishes'.[36]

In Paris, Poincaré asked Gaiffier to have signature of the Anglo-Belgian pact delayed ten days so that France and Belgium could jointly request military conventions as supplements to the guarantee treaties; conclusion of an Anglo-Belgian agreement without such a convention would weaken, he feared, the French attempt to gain one. Poincaré also desired the inclusion in the Belgian draft of an article committing Britain to defend the left bank of the Rhine were Germany to violate the Rhineland de-militarization articles of the peace treaty. The Belgian ambassador po-litely resisted, saying Anglo-Belgian discussions had gone too far to permit introduction of new demands. Poincaré proved amicable, admitted that Belgium would not be able to get a military convention from Britain, and accepted Jaspar's offer to conclude with France a treaty similar to any Belgium might sign with England. This last proposal was made in order to demonstrate Belgium's intent of maintaining equal relations with France and Britain.[37]

Having thus resisted French influence in his negotiations with Britain, Jaspar soon found himself relying on it. In their original proposal the Belgians had not set any time limit for the treaty. Curzon had countered by suggesting a ten year span and provision for renewal. The shortness of the period was a disappointment to the Belgians which became sharper when they learned France was asking for a treaty of thirty years' duration. Moncheur raised the issue with Curzon, who suggested that the French and Belgian treaties be identical in length and that Britain could envisage a twenty year term at the maximum. As for the word 'direct' (and presum-ably also 'territory'), its inclusion in the Anglo-French treaty was being debated, and Curzon did not wish to prejudice his case with France by ceding to Belgium on the issue. Jaspar agreed, and thus the link between the two treaties was formally acknowledged.

This was not a fatal mistake. But it was unfortunate, for Lloyd George was given a strong arguing point when he failed to uphold his cabinet's promise to conclude the Belgian accord without reference to the fate of that with France. The collapse of Anglo-French negotiations over Poincaré's insistence on a specific military convention and the concomi-tant loss of the Anglo-Belgian accord was a crushing blow to the diplo-mats of the small country. Many of them never really forgave the French. But they had perhaps been too sanguine all along in believing that Britain would sign before her discussions with France were completed. As Eyre Crowe explained in June, Britain would not sign with France until various differences were settled, particularly that concerning Tangiers; conclusion of a treaty with Belgium, to which country the French were already linked, would more or less assure them of British intervention in any war in Western Europe and make them less receptive to British demands in the negotiation of their own treaty. Jaspar protested, but he seemed to recognize he could not sway Lloyd George on the issue. It does appear that the Belgians were mistaken in their judgment of the attitude Poincaré would take. In January, the new premier had told the anxious Gaiffier that Belgium could be assured, 'I will conclude [the pact with Britain] even if I have to abandon many of my own demands'.[38] When Poincaré did not abandon enough of his demands, the Belgians asked him to be more amenable. But they had no good means of leverage on him. Belgium had already signed a military accord with France and in the negotiations for a pact with Britain had been explicit in her refusal to listen to French requests; now Poincaré could blame the failure of his demands on the lack of Belgian support.

Dependent as they were upon both Britain and France for their security, the Belgians' first desire following the war was a Franco-British guarantee. Eventually this proved the only way they could obtain a specific promise of British support, but the guarantee was far more collective and required more of Belgium than she had ever expected in 1919. Partially because of the postwar reversion against both the territorial and neutrality clauses of 1839, the Belgians generally viewed any collective engagement with distrust, suspecting that it might be both ineffectual and inconsiderate of the interests of small powers. The Belgians did not, therefore, greet the proposal in 1923 of a Mutual Assistance Pact under League of Nations auspices with much enthusiasm. They recognized the reasons that led England and other countries to reject it and were still hopeful of concluding a specific regional accord with their friends across the Channel.

More interest was shown in the 1924 Geneva Protocol for Pacific Settlement of International Disputes. Like the French, the Belgians were concerned with what recourse and support would be given those countries which, despite having abided by the terms of an arbitration settlement, were attacked by another power or in some other way were the victims of a violation of the arbitrator's decision. A further preoccupation was the necessity of an agreement on a general reduction of armament if the protocol were to go into effect. Hymans, who in March 1924 had succeeded Jaspar as foreign minister, lent his full support to the proposal but continued to talk of regional pacts as the most trustworthy form of insurance. Most of the Belgian press agreed the Protocol was a useful supplement to the League covenant and there was sincere disappointment over its defeat.[39]

The agreement on reparations achieved with the adoption of the Dawes Plan in 1924 and the plans for reduction of the Franco-Belgian occupation of the Ruhr which had begun in January 1923 eased European tensions markedly. Advantage was taken of the more promising atmosphere for discussion of mutual guarantees by German Foreign Minister Gustav Stresemann in February 1925. His suggestion of a pact between Britain, France, Italy, and Germany renouncing war for a given period and guaranteeing the *status quo* on the Rhine caused considerable stir. The Belgians noted the omission of their country from Stresemann's list of possible signators and obtained assurances from London and Paris that Belgium would be an equal partner in any negotiations concerning the Rhine frontier. In June, when Stresemann received representations from France and Britain to this effect, he promptly agreed. The foreign minister had not wished to make any agreement that would jeopardize his efforts to obtain Eupen and Malmedy. When Britain insisted Belgium's frontier be guaranteed, the German chargé at Brussels stated that Germany had never intended to exclude the small country from the pact.

The Belgians were receptive to the German proposal, not so much because they had faith in an agreement with Germany as because they valued a British commitment. In March, Hymans spoke in favor of 'special and regional agreements' which were 'the open door to possible solutions'. A treaty 'which would assure us of the guarantee of England would be the means of giving peace to the West. England's signature is the important thing to-day; without it real peace cannot be attained'.[40] When France insisted that a mutual guarantee treaty would be acceptable only if Germany joined the League of Nations and agreed to be bound by the terms of its covenant, Hymans approved. He nevertheless suggested that negotiations need not be delayed until Germany actually were admitted to the international body. The Belgian also sided with the French, against British and German objections, in opposing Stresemann's efforts to link a premature evacuation of the Rhineland to conclusion of the guarantee treaty.[41]

The Belgians separated with Briand, however, over the latter's attempt to stretch the proposed pact to cover the eastern as well as the western borders of Germany. They stated:

Belgium can in no way, by reason of her location and limited forces, engage herself in accords extending to regions distant from her and to interests which do not touch her directly. But she of course intends to uphold the obligations incumbent upon her as a member of the League of Nations regarding these questions.[42]

Belgium desperately wanted to be part of any accord on the Rhine but surely could not afford being dragged into war in the East. Granted the League covenant called for action against an aggressor; yet that general commitment was far less incumbent upon Belgium than would be a specific regional treaty. The Belgians did agree to support arbitration treaties between Germany and France's allies to the east, but their affirmative reply was qualified by the phrase 'in the measure of her [Belgium's] strength'. Brussels held firm against irritated French pleadings and there was no hiding of the relief when English pressure finally forced the French to admit that any guarantee would have to be limited to the West of Europe.

For Belgium, aid given under any guarantee would have to be immediate were it to be effective. Yet England was suggesting that before intervention should occur, all incidents should be submitted to the Council of the League which would decide if the accord were indeed violated and who was the aggressor. The French and Belgians easily persuaded Britain to renounce this plan and allow immediate intervention in the event of such a flagrant violation as that made by Germany in 1914. This was fine, but could not a decision by one power that it, or Belgium, was being attacked or threatened involve Belgium in action when she neither wished to be nor thought military action called for? What if the pact were prematurely invoked in connection with a minor violation or threat to the demilitarized Rhineland zone? When the diplomats of the little country indicated they wanted protection on this issue and to maintain the right to judge for themselves whether the treaty would go into effect, they found themselves in a controversy with France. The question did not so much regard the interpretation of the mutual security treaty as it did the extent and interpretation of the Franco-Belgian military accord.

On June 17, a joint Socialist-Catholic ministry took over in Belgium from the predominantly Catholic ministry, following notable Socialist gains in the April election. Emile Vandervelde became foreign minister in the new cabinet and did not hesitate to make clear that as far as he and Belgium were concerned, the new mutual guarantee pacts took precedence over and virtually replaced any earlier agreements. A compromise was reached on the issue of involvement in military action under the proposed treaty's terms. For while the Belgians admitted that 'armed violation of the Rhineland statute should be equated with the violation of French and Belgian territories', the final draft stated that the guarantee would take force only if there were agreement between the powers desiring to act and the state being attacked that there was a flagrant violation necessitating immediate action.[43]

Vandervelde was also concerned by the difficulties posed by the status of Luxemburg. Any French or Belgian action in support of the guarantee treaty would be keyed on use of the duchy's railways, yet it was possible that Luxemburg, a non-signatory, would deny passage unless the French and Belgians could also justify their request under terms of the League of Nations covenant. The French were unwilling to enter lengthy discussions on the matter, and as it was more directly connected with the military accord than with the mutual guarantee, it was left in abeyance.

With these issues now set aside, the proposed draft of the guarantee treaty was acceptable to the Belgians after one last alteration that was easily obtained. As Eupen and Malmedy had not been awarded to them directly at Versailles, it was necessary that the proposed treaty safeguard the frontiers established by or *in execution of* the peace treaty. The ground cleared of major obstacles, the Entente nations invited German representatives to meet with them at Locarno on October 5. Stresemann's reply contained a rude surprise; while accepting the invitation, Germany wished to be freed of the war guilt clause of the Versailles treaty. She also desired that terms for the evacuation of the Rhineland be drawn up before the conclusion of the treaty. France, Britain, and Belgium refused to discuss these requests; the shocked Belgians reminded Stresemann that German Chancellor Von Bethmann-Hollweg had himself admitted in the Reichstag on August 4, 1914, Germany's guilt in regard to Belgium.

The Belgians did not play a leading role in the meetings on the banks of Lake Maggiore, though Vandervelde used his influence as best he could to assure completion of the treaties. When Briand insisted that the Locarno pact should not prevent France from coming to the aid of her eastern European allies in the event of a German attack, the Belgians were sympathetic. They also took interest in the Germans' successful effort to obtain a wider interpretation of Article Sixteen of the covenant of the League, which Germany was to join as a result of the treaties. That article required members of the League to facilitate League actions taken against an aggressor. Stresemann argued that Germany's present military weakness made her vulnerable to any army granted passage through Germany under Article Sixteen; his concern regarding interpretation of the article was closely connected with his desire to maintain good relations with Soviet Russia. The issue, so pertinent to Belgium, was settled by the French, British, and German foreign ministers without Belgian participation. Article Sixteen was to apply to League members only, to the extent it was compatible with their military strength and geographic position.

After several additional difficult discussions, the Locarno conference came to a close on October 16 with the signing of five pacts. By the Rhenish convention Belgium, France, Germany, Italy, and Great Britain guaranteed the German-French and German-Belgian borders; the Germans further vowed to keep demilitarized those zones so established by the Treaty of Versailles. In addition, Germany, France, and Belgium agreed they would not war against each other except in self-defense or to fulfill League obligations. Arbitration procedures were established, and Germany signed arbitration treaties with France, Czechoslovakia, Poland, and Belgium.

The impossible had seemingly been achieved. Though there were many who did not take them at face value, the Locarno treaties appeared to mark the establishment of confidence and security in the west of Europe. The Belgian press, at first openly skeptical, cheered the success of the Locarno meeting. Jaspar and particularly Hymans, though far from sympathetic with many of Vandervelde's actions, warmly applauded his work at Locarno. Belgium had taken on additional responsibilities, but her security had been vastly strengthened by the gaining of the long-desired British guarantee.

8.3 NEGOTIATIONS WITH THE NETHERLANDS

In the symphony of joy raised over the Locarno achievement there was one outstanding sour note. While the preamble of the Rhine pact stated the abrogation of Belgian neutrality, the treaties of 1839 still had not, in fact, been officially revised. All depended on a Belgo-Dutch settlement regarding the Wielingen Channel and the defense of Limburg. Unfortunately, the conclusion of the Franco-Belgian military accord had only acerbated the internal tensions already existing at the break-off of negotiations in the spring of 1920. Flemish spokesmen loudly demanded an accord with Holland to counterbalance the French tie, and this led many Walloons to vow Belgium would make no undue concessions. Officials in Brussels, convinced the Netherlands would not give way unless under pressure by France and England, waited for Millerand to fulfill his promise of coercing the Dutch. In The Hague, suspicions were aroused regarding the military accord; some Greater Netherlands advocates viewed it as directed against Holland, while many diplomats feared a defense agreement with Belgium now would entangle the Netherlands in a Franco-German war in the West and perhaps also in any conflict in the East of Europe.

Even so, Dutch Foreign Minister Van Karnebeek desired to renew discussions. A far-sighted man, he recognized the value of a Belgo-Dutch understanding. In a future war, Holland could not expect to be spared by modification of some Schlieffen Plan. Moreover, the projected Juliana canal depended on waters drawn from the Meuse, a matter over which the Belgians could raise interminable difficulties if they wished.

His chief motivation, however, was fear of Anglo-French intervention which would aggravate Dutch public opinion.

When the Dutch brought forward their claim on the Wielingen Channel at the mouth of the Scheldt, Hymans had requested French and British support for his case. Curzon promptly suggested a joint representation indicating the allies' surprise at the unprecedented claim and their desire to see the revision of the 1839 treaties quickly achieved. At a French-English-Belgian Conference at Boulogne in June 1920, Hymans went a step further in asking Anglo-French representation supporting a Belgian-Dutch agreement concerning the defense of Limburg. Sir Eyre Crowe, the British permanent under-secretary, expressed doubt that such a move would affect the Dutch, who were determined to maintain their neutrality. Crowe did take it on himself, however, later to make clear to the Dutch ambassador in London that England maintained the traditional view that nations had sovereignty over a three mile belt of territorial waters. By the middle of July, Curzon was able to notify the Belgian ambassador that an Anglo-French note to The Hague was being drafted which expressed hope for rapid conclusion of an agreement granting Belgium sovereignty over the part of the Wielingen Channel situated in Belgian territorial waters.[44]

News of the impending *démarche* brought a Dutch appeal for its postponement. Curzon was inclined to grant this on the chance a direct Belgo-Dutch understanding might be achieved. The French, though assuring they did not mean to exert pressure on The Hague, were against delay. Before Paris took any action, however, Van Karnebeek let it be known that while he was not willing to renounce Dutch claims on the Wielingen Channel 'at the bidding of Belgium and under pressure from British and French governments without at least previous formal examination of Dutch arguments', he would accept the opinion, even if adverse, of a commission made up of Belgian, Dutch, French, and British experts.[45] This was clearly a face-saving maneuver to cover Dutch concession on the issue, for there was no doubt such a commission would decide in Belgium's favor. Yet the Brussels government refused to accept the proposal unless the British and French went ahead with their joint representation at The Hague. Though the French were willing to take further steps to influence Van Karnebeek, the Anglo-French representation did not take place, as Curzon saw no need of pursuing the matter once Van Karnebeek had shown himself so conciliatory.

The hardheadedness of the Belgians regarding the commission proposal is difficult to explain. As Curzon commented, the Dutch had to be given some bridge for retreat, and Belgium had nothing to lose and something to gain by accepting the proposal. The most likely answer is that the

Brussels diplomats feared that once the Wielingen issue were settled in Belgium's favor it would be difficult to resist Anglo-Dutch pressure to sign a new version of the 1839 treaties which would not incorporate an agreement for the defense of Limburg. On the other hand, delivery of the Anglo-French note would in no way affect the Limburg matter. Putting the issue before the experts would, of course, have amounted to arbitration on a matter of national sovereignty which Brussels would later insist could not be subject to arbitration; yet this was not the Belgian argument on this occasion. The conclusion must be that while Hymans wished the additional strengthening of the Belgian position an Anglo-French note would provide, his prime interest was in breaking the Dutch resistance as bluntly as possible, thus perhaps paving the way for an accord on Limburg. Minister of a small country which over the years had frequently complained of the crude manners of the great powers and had on numerous occasions taken advantage of face-saving compromises, he did not shrink from a power play in dealing with a country no stronger than his own.

The resignation of Hymans on August 25 led Van Karnebeek to renew his efforts to reach an amicable arrangement. In September, he invited Premier Delacroix to visit The Hague, at the same time indicating a willingness to renounce sovereignty over the Wielingen Channel. He only asked that Dutch warships be granted passage. Delacroix was eager to take a forward step and indicated interest in making the trip. The great powers had ruled that revision of the 1839 treaties should not involve cessions of territory or international servitudes. Delacroix's willingness to exchange such a servitude regarding Dutch warships for certain concessions on the Dutch side revealed that Belgium did indeed wish to link Limburg and the Wielingen and would therefore admit the latter as a negotiable issue. Delacroix in particular desired that Holland immediately sign an accord embodying the economic aspects of the treaty revision; repudiate the activists campaigning against Belgian unity; recognize Belgian sovereignty over the Wielingen; and agree to the simultaneous study of a concerted Belgo-Dutch defense plan for Limburg and the use of the Wielingen by Dutch warships. All points except that regarding Limburg were acceptable to Van Karnebeek, and over it the discussions were again broken off.

When Jaspar became Belgian foreign minister, he quickly destroyed hopes of an arrangement by publicly demanding a complete capitulation by Holland regarding the Wielingen. Lack of progress on the matter led him, however, to discussions with Van Karnebeek at Lausanne in August of 1921. The Dutch minister again rejected any defense accord on the grounds that Dutch opinion would not allow the abandonment of the neutral policy so successful in the last war. Jaspar immediately said that while he was willing to reserve the issue for future discussion, no political treaty could be signed until it was settled. Regarding the Wielingen dispute, both Jaspar and Van Karnebeek were willing to consider a division of sovereignty, with Holland controlling the right half of the channel, on the condition that Belgium be allowed to supply herself with food and arms by way of the Scheldt in time of war.[46]

Nothing came of these discussions, as the Belgian ministry of national defense took a dim view of the suggested division of sovereignty. The official rejection was given during the Conference of Genoa the following April and May. At that time, Jaspar made explicit the Belgian insistence on the connection between the Wielingen and Limburg issues:

The proposed solution could be envisaged only if there were compensation, only if the Belgian government could justify for the public opinion of the country the concession made on the Wielingen issue with a reciprocal advantage accorded by Holland. This would notably be the case if Holland did not show herself completely intransigent regarding measures assuring the defense of Limburg, a vital question for Belgium.[47]

Van Karnebeek would not capitulate. Instead, he proposed the Wielingen dispute be arbitrated. Again the Belgian verdict was negative. Belgium had too much to lose in regard to her sole deep ocean port of Zeebrugge to risk arbitration, which the Belgians believed too often resulted in transactional compromises satisfactory to no one. Another blunt rejection would have ruptured the negotiations, so the Brussels diplomats and jurists decided to resort to the pre-1914 status of the issue: *de facto* cooperation as far as the actual use of the channel was concerned and reciprocal reservations made by each state on the sovereignty issue. Belgian rights would thus be safeguarded in times of peace. In the event of war, Holland would probably refrain from contesting passage; if she did object, most likely Britain would aid Belgium.[48] Jaspar had committed himself so firmly to a Wielingen-Limburg bargain, however, that he could not change his ground, and it was Hymans who again took up the talks on this basis in 1924.

When the Brussels officials decided in 1922 to leave the Wielingen issue in abeyance, they came to the conclusion that the economic agreements reached at the end of the war no longer held great attraction. They would have to be renegotiated. The discussions between Pierre van Zuylen, the Belgian *Directeur politique*, and his Dutch counterpart, Beelaerts van Blokland, were lengthy and difficult. The Dutch readily recognized the end of Belgium's neutrality, although they fished for some compensation for their action. Regarding Limburg, Van Zuylen asked the Dutch to put in writing their long-standing verbal affirmation that they would interpret violation of that region as a *casus belli*. Using arguments remarkably similar to those employed by Jaspar in the discussions concerning the ill-fated Anglo-Belgian treaty, the Dutch objected that inclusion of such a phrase was an affront to their national honor. The indefatigable Van Zuylen continued to insist, on the chance the Dutch would lessen their economic demands to get him to give way. In the end, he obtained his *casus belli* statement and also all he hoped on the economic issues.

These last were many and complex, ranging from the Scheldt regime to the drainage of Flanders. The key to the Scheldt problem was the Dutch reluctance to do no more than maintain the navigability of the river as required by the 1839 treaty. An increasing percentage of the larger ocean vessels was therefore being forced to abandon Antwerp in favor of Rotterdam. After much fencing, the Dutch agreed to improve the navigability of the river under the supervision of a Belgo-Dutch commission. They also allowed construction of two new waterways connecting Antwerp and the Rhine, in compensation for dams placed in the intermediate waterways route by themselves as long before as 1846.

When these and other matters were settled, a treaty was signed on April 3, 1925. France and Britain, as signatories of the 1839 agreements, were notified of the treaty; after some brief difficulties accords were drawn up acknowledging the end of Belgium's neutrality. Germany and Austria were not consulted because of their earlier violation of Belgium's neutrality, nor was Russia, since the Soviet government was still not recognized. Most of the negotiations were in vain, however. Despite late concessions by Belgium regarding the sharing of expenses for the improvement of the Scheldt, the treaty was rejected by the Dutch States General. The Rotterdam merchants thought too much aid had been given Antwerp, and the pan-Netherlands groupings had successfully stirred sentiment against any deal with the Belgian government, which they believed was abusing their brother Flemings. Though the Belgian-Dutch treaty was abandoned, the great powers did go ahead on their own, and by a treaty of May 1926 cancelled the neutrality clauses of their 1839 treaty.[49]

This was as close as Belgium and the Netherlands were to come in the interwar period to resolving their differences. In 1928, negotiations were resumed but foundered over Beelaerts van Blokland's (he was now Dutch foreign minister) reluctance to allow the Rhine-Scheldt canal to be built east of the dangerous Hellegat pass, which the Belgians wished to bypass. The issue was referred to experts, but the offers from The Hague grew increasingly less attractive as far as the Belgians were concerned. By the end of the year, the Dutch were arguing that no Antwerp-Rhine canal was necessary and wanted permission for their own Juliana canal to pass through Belgian territory in return for Dutch recognition of the abrogation of the 1839 neutrality clause. Belgian Foreign Minister Hymans insisted that construction of the Rhine-Antwerp canal was a right accorded by the powers in the 1830s, not a favor extended to Belgium in the 1920s. Further discussions through 1932 proved fruitless. Belgium desired all she had gained in the proposed 1925 treaty, while the Dutch became increasingly sure, as the linguistic conflict in Belgium worsened, that they had no interest in dealing with the government to the south. It is perhaps ironic that while they could not reach an accord on these issues, the Belgians and Dutch along with the *Luxembourgeois* were able to agree at Ouchy in 1932 to a reduction of economic barriers between their countries. They were also able to join with the Scandinavian states in the Oslo Convention of the same year, which provided for modest, but important, economic cooperation among these small powers.

The basic problem associated with the revision of the treaties of 1839 was that while Belgium demanded concessions from Holland, the Dutch had little they wanted in return except complete control over the Wielingen Channel, and their case on that issue was so weak it could not overcome Belgian objections. Even if a Wielingen-Limburg defense bargain had been worked out, feelings on matters of national sovereignty were so high in both small countries that it is hard to imagine such a deal would work in practice. But without such an exchange the Dutch parliamentarians would not find sufficient equity and prestige in the proposed treaty to warrant its approval. Of course, the two countries did have many national interests in common, and it was his concern for these that led Van Karnebeek to negotiate the abortive treaty of 1925. But the embitterment of popular relations, combined with too sharp and stubborn bargaining on both sides, prevented the erection of a useful structure to shelter those common interests in the 1920s.

If an opportunity to improve relations were lost, neither country suffered great hardships as a result of the failure of the negotiations. In fact, the Belgians discovered they could do fairly well without the 1925 treaty. Antwerp's trade was stimulated by a decision to pay premiums making the cost of using Antwerp no greater for shipping interests than that involved in docking at Rotterdam. Since no satisfactory existing connections between Antwerp and Liege were available without Dutch cooperation, the Belgians constructed the Albert canal, greatly improving their communications and providing a valuable addition to their national defenses. Nevertheless, the fact remained that throughout the interwar period the antiquated Belgo-Dutch treaty of 1839 was not revised. This was embarrassing for the Belgian diplomats, and their pride was particularly pricked by the knowledge that they had been balked not by a great power but by another small country which had not even participated in the world war.

8.4 THE COST OF AMBITION

Though the Locarno accords eventually brought the sort of territorial guarantees which Belgium desired, the results of the small state's most active period of diplomacy, from 1920 to 1925, were disappointing. In their first fling at power diplomacy after a lifetime of neutrality, the Belgians were forced to make expensive bargains. Their willingness to do so, and the nature of the negotiations they undertook, revealed a radical departure in Belgium's attitude and behavior from the course followed before the war.

The negotiations regarding the Duchy of Luxemburg, a prize that had been renounced decades earlier, are an example of this. Hymans had originally believed that France would allow Belgium economic control of the duchy out of respect for Belgium's historical claims and loyalty during the war. In the end, he had to make important concessions to France – participation in the Frankfort occupation and a military accord, the terms of which were almost entirely dictated by Foch – before Belgium could establish economic union with the duchy. More concessions were drawn from Jaspar before France officially renounced claims on the *Guillaume-Luxembourg* railway, but even so full control of the railroad eluded the Brussels officials.

The importance of certain clauses of the military accord for Belgium's independence of action should also not be ignored. Although the Belgians never promised to go to war at the side of France unless they believed Germany were the aggressor, they did promise to mobilize if there were a general taking up of arms across the Rhine. It was possible that Germany might arm for conflict in the East and not for aggression in the West; or Germany might elect to invade France without crossing Belgian territory. A mobilization on Belgium's part, however, would be an open invitation to an attack, and should France call for a preventive strike, it would be hard for the Belgians to refuse participation. Then, too, France's right to defend the Belgian coast might create difficulties and might imply that Belgium envisaged the possibility of going to war without Britain's aid, an assumption the Brussels officials could scarcely wish the French to adopt.[50] The intended takeover of the defense of

Luxemburg without the duchy's approval was contrary to the independence of that sovereign state. Such planning may have seemed necessary for the security of France and Belgium, yet it did not harmonize well with the castigations the press and public of those countries directed against Germany for violation of Belgium's neutrality.

The same clause which referred to the Duchy of Luxemburg specified a coordinated defense system of the French and Belgian frontiers. In the 1930s, a bitter debate arose in Belgium over defense plans which centered on whether a frontier defense should be attempted or whether Belgian troops should begin their main effort at the Meuse and then retreat toward Antwerp if opposed by overwhelming forces. The Flemish deputies supported the latter plan as more practical; the Walloons, who saw a great sector of their territory being abandoned, opted for the frontier defense. Whether the wording of the accord meant a defense based at the frontier or only in its general neighborhood, it is clear from French statements that France expected Belgium to defend her geographic integrity and not abandon territory after minor skirmishes.[51]

Even if this issue had not arisen, the cooperation envisioned between Belgium and France in defense matters essentially meant that Belgium's defense was to be a function of that of France; on such matters the tail can not wag the dog. It has been suggested, also, that initially the staff conversations for which the accord provided went further in influencing the Belgian defense system than did the agreement itself. There can be no doubt that should the *casus foederis* come into effect, French troops would expect passage over Belgian soil; indeed in 1924, the chief-of-staff informed Hymans that, were hostilities to break out, Belgium would be responsible for handling French troop trains destined for Aachen.[52] Such arrangements were in violation of Article 421 of the Belgian constitution which stipulated that no foreign troops should traverse or occupy Belgian territory except by virtue of a specific law.

It should finally be noticed that the discarding of the political convention meant that no provision for terminating or limiting the duration of the military accord was provided. The Belgian government, which Hymans had insisted did not wish to become closely tied to France, was committed by the exchange of letters to an understanding from which, unless a lapse were agreed upon, it could free itself only by the rude tactic of unilateral abrogation. At the time this appeared of little consequence, but in later years the constant pressure of French demands made in the name of the accord caused many Belgians to fear that they had become too close friends of their powerful neighbor and had lost their freedom of action.

Freedom of action was what the Belgians sought in the postwar period. The strictures of neutrality had been comfortable because they set fairly recognizable limits to Belgium's relations with other powers, but they were strictures nonetheless. The exhilarating plunge into full-scale participation in power politics in 1920 was, in part, a reaction against the stifling tradition of neutrality. In their relations with the Netherlands and Luxemburg, the Belgians tried to perform aggressively as a big power dealing with a little power; they sometimes did not scorn using what were essentially bullying tactics. The Dutch called their bluff, and in Luxemburg resentment lingered for some time over the way the duchy was forced to join in economic union with Belgium rather than France – the blame was put on Belgium, not France.

In most instances Belgium's pressure alone was not enough to achieve her goals. The aid of the greater powers was needed, and this usually was not produced free of charge. Thus, in dealing with Luxemburg and with the Dutch, Belgium had to become increasingly subservient to French wishes if she were to achieve her goals. Ironically, the efforts to protect Belgium from the deleterious effects of French control of Luxemburg resulted in an expansion of French influence over Belgium's defense and tariff policies. If Belgium did not have to pay the price of her ambition one way, she did another. The ending of neutrality had in no way improved her power relationship with her neighbors and perhaps had weakened it; the feeling of new-found freedom of action was therefore in part illusory.

The frustrations the Belgians experienced in their efforts to establish a new basis for their security were many. None was greater than the failure to garner a British accord to balance that made with France. Lack of such an agreement could allow Belgium to be pulled into the French orbit completely, in contradiction to the whole purpose of the search for security. Hence the constant effort to maintain a middle position between France and England, even though the latter had not favored Belgium with a defense treaty. No doubt the British realized they could have better leverage on Belgium by withholding a treaty than by granting it. The full extent of the danger posed to Belgium's independence of action and the complexity of the small state's problem in maintaining control of its own policy was, however, presented most clearly not in security negotiations but in those concerning reparations.

8.5 Notes

1. Henri Jaspar, 'The Keystones of Belgium's Foreign Policy', pp. 1033, 1035.
2. Hymans papers, 4, contains several pages written in 1928 intended for Hymans' memoirs. The quotation comes from these pages, which are more harsh toward Clemenceau than those eventually published.

3. Hymans, *Mémoires*, vol. II, p. 551.
4. Belgium, *Doc. diplomatiques belges (DDB)*, vol. I, pp. 87–89, no. 19: 'Gaiffier to Hymans, Jan. 1, 1920'. One editor of this document series, Fernand van Langenhove, has summarized its thrust in his *La Belgique en quête de sécurité 1920–1940*.
5. Belgium, M.A.E. Arch, INDM, dossier for 1920, Hymans note Jan. 8, 1920. Much of the remainder of this section of this chapter originally appeared in the author's article 'The Negotiation of the Franco-Belgian Military Accord of 1920', *French Historical Studies*, III, no. 3 (Spring 1964), pp. 360–78; the permission of that journal for the re-use of these passages is appreciated.
6. *Ibid.*, dossier for 1920, *compte rendu* of Jan. 28, 1920, meeting drawn up by Gaiffier and checked by Hymans.
7. Hymans papers, 177: 'Hymans to Moncheur, Apr. 16, 1920'.
8. Belgium, M.A.E. Arch., INDM, dossier for 1920, Hymans memorandum of Mar. 5, 1920, interview with De Margerie.
9. Great Britain, *Documents on British Foreign Policy (DBP)*, 1st ser., vol. XII, pp. 34–35, no. 9: 'Villiers to Curzon, Mar. 25, 1920'.
10. Belgium, *DDB*, vol. I, pp. 196–97, no. 66: 'Gaiffier to Hymans, Mar. 31, 1920'; pp. 347–52, no. 142: 'Hymans to Gaiffier, Moncheur, De Cartier de Marchienne, Mar. 30, 1920'.
11. Great Britain, *DBP*, 1st ser., vol. IX, pp. 327–28: 'Curzon minute to no. 301, Crowe memorandum, Apr. 6, 1920'.
12. Hymans, *Mémoires*, vol. II, p. 545.
13. *Ibid.*; Great Britain, *DBP*, 1st ser., vol. VIII, pp. 805–8, no. 94: 'Note of conversation between Lloyd George, Vandervelde, and Huysmans, Nov. 4, 1920'; Belgium, *DDB*, pp. 241–42, no. 85: 'Hymans note, Apr. 4, 1920'.
14. Great Britain, *DBP*, 1st ser., vol. IX, pp. 374–75, no. 347: 'Record of Crowe-Moncheur conversation, Apr. 10, 1920'.
15. *Ibid.*, 1st ser., vol. IX, pp. 432–37, no. 416: 'Curzon to Villiers, Apr. 20, 1920'.
16. Hymans papers, 177: 'Project of accord annexed to Foch letter of May 5 (11?), 1920'.
17. The phrase read 'coordonné à leurs frontieres...'. Later drafts changed the preposition to *de*, slightly altering the meaning to 'defense of their frontiers'. The adjective *orientale* was also inserted to make clear that the reference was to the eastern border of the duchy.
18. Hymans papers, 177: 'Gaiffier to Hymans, May 18, 1920'.
19. *Ibid.*, 177: 'Pro-memoria of May 25, 1920, meeting'.
20. '...nous nous en disposerons'. Belgium, M.A.E. Arch., INDM, dossier for 1920, *compte rendu* of Jan. 28, 1920, meeting.
21. Great Britain, *DBP*, 1st ser., vol. XII, report of Brig.-Gen. F. Lyon to Parr, Sept. 6, 1920, enclosed in no. 38, pp. 67–69: 'Parr to Curzon, Sept. 14, 1920'.
22. Belgium, *DDB*, vol. I, pp. 405–8, no. 175: 'Accord Militaire défensif franco-belge'. The final version of the force level agreements was as follows.

During the next five years of the Rhineland occupation France would maintain one cavalry and six infantry divisions, an effective force of 85,000 men. Belgium would provide two infantry divisions, a force of 13,200 men. Force level agreements for later periods were to be worked out at the annual staff discussions, which would also take up matters regarding mobilization, concentration and transportation of troops, and the organization of a coordinated defense system. Should reinforcements be needed, France would send nine infantry divisions between the eighth and twenty-first day of mobilization (this was to be raised to fifteen divisions within a year and eventually to eighteen); Belgium would send two divisions by the twelfth day at the latest and if necessary two more on the fourteenth day. For the possibility of full mobilization France would prepare eighty divisions, promising fifty-five of these immediately and to organize twenty-five more as soon as possible. Belgium promised twelve currently available divisions and agreed to envisage the formation of six more in a reserve capacity. Every battalion was to be equipped with five or six pieces each of field artillery and armored trucks and five to seven of heavy artillery. Each division should possess four to six aviation squadrons.

23. Hymans papers, 177: 'De Bassompierre to Hymans, June 26, 1920'; the draft of the protocol is enclosed.
24. *Ibid.*, 177: 'Project of convention'.
25. Jaspar papers, 225: 'Hymans note of July 18, 1920', recounting meeting of July 16, 1920.
26. Hymans, *Mémoires*, vol. II, pp. 510–19, 570. For the best account of Hymans' resignation, see Henri Haag, 'La démission de Paul Hymans et la fin du second gouvernement Delacroix (juillet-novembre 1920)', pp. 393–419.
27. Jaspar papers, 214: 'Gaiffier to Jaspar, Dec. 8. 1921'.
28. Miller, *Belgian Foreign Policy*, pp. 178–81.
29. Belgium, *DDB*, vol. I, pp. 398–99, no. 172: 'Delacroix account of talk with Lloyd George, July 12, 1920'.
30. *Ibid.*, vol. I, pp. 402–4, no. 174: 'Moncheur to Hymans, July 23, 1920'.
31. Great Britain, *DBP*, lst ser., vol. XII, pp. 80–82: 'Graham to Curzon, Dec. 14, 1920', and 'Curzon minute of Dec. 22'.
32. Belgium, *DDB*, vol. I, pp. 451–53, no. 202: 'Memorandum of Theunis and Jaspar conversation with Lloyd George and Lord Curzon, Jan. 11, 1922'.
33. *Ibid.*, vol. I, pp. 456–57, no. 204: 'Jaspar memorandum of talk with Curzon, Jan. 13, 1922'.
34. *Ibid.*, vol. I, pp. 495–97, no. 224: 'Jaspar note, Feb. 13, 1922, and annex, text of prospective treaty'.
35. *Ibid.*, vol. I, pp. 481–85, no. 218: 'Jaspar to Moncheur, Jan. 25, 1922'; pp. 495–97, no. 224: 'Jaspar note, Feb. 13, 1922'.
36. *Ibid.*, vol. I, pp. 472–73, no. 213: 'Jaspar note of conversation with De Margerie, Jan. 20, 1922'.
37. *Ibid.*, vol. I, pp. 477–78, no. 216: 'Gaiffier to Jaspar, Jan. 21, 1922'.
38. *Ibid.*, vol. I, pp. 478–79, no. 217: 'Gaiffier to Jaspar, Jan. 23–24, 1922'.

39. Belgium, *DDB*, vol. II, pp. 31–36, no. 1: 'Hymans memorandum, Jan. 7, 1925'. Miller, *Belgian Foreign Policy*, p. 186.
40. *Survey of International Affairs*, ed. by A. J. Toynbee, vol. II, p. 26 quotes *Le Temps*, Mar. 18, 1925, report of interview with Hymans the preceding day.
41. Belgium, *DDB*, vol. II, pp. 164–68, no. 49: 'Hymans to Gaiffier, Mar. 31, 1925'.
42. *Ibid.*, vol. II, pp. 190–92, no. 57: 'Ruzette to Gaiffier, May 26, 1925'. Baron Albéric Ruzette was serving as *ad interim* minister of foreign affairs in a Catholic cabinet which endured only a few weeks.
43. *Ibid.*, vol. II, pp. 289–94, no. 92: 'Briand to Vandervelde, Aug. 6, 1925'.
44. Great Britain, *DBP*, 1st ser, vol. XII, pp. 51–52, no. 22: 'Curzon to Earl of Derby, June 7, 1920'; pp. 52–54, no. 23: 'Crowe memorandum of talk with Hymans, June 23, 1920'; p. 56, no. 25: 'Curzon to Moncheur, July 20, 1920'.
45. *Ibid.*, 1st ser., vol. XII, pp. 60–61, no. 30: 'Curzon to Derby, Villiers, Aug. 2, 1920'.
46. Jaspar papers, 246: 'Memorandum "Les negociations Hollando-Belges en 1921–1922–1923" '.
47. *Ibid.*
48. *Ibid.*, and Pierre van Zuylen, *Les mains libres*, p. 166.
49. For a more detailed account of the negotiations see Van Zuylen, *Les mains libres*, pp. 160–93. Great Britain, *DBP*, ser. 1A, vol. I, pp. 715–19, no. 499 and annex: 'C. Hurst memorandum, May 5, 1926'.
50. Although the navy clause was in Article I, which was supposed to expire with the end of the Rhineland occupation, the French considered it as continuing in effect. (Hymans papers, 256: 'Van Langenhove note, Jan. 1, 1934'.)
51. Hymans papers, 256: 'Hymans to Herry, Sept. 22, 1933'.
52. *Ibid.*, 157: 'Maglinse to Hymans, July 10, 1924'. See Van Overstraeten, *Albert 1er – Leopold III*, pp. 41–42.

9. Diplomacy from a middle position: Reparations

At the same time the Belgians were endeavoring to assure their military security, they were deeply involved in discussions regarding Germany's payment of reparations. Though there was an obvious effort to keep the two sets of negotiations separate, they often impinged upon each other.

Reparation negotiations became linked with such matters as occupation of select German cities and eventually of the entire Ruhr region, control of the Luxemburg railways, efforts to establish an autonomous Rhineland regime, and early cessation of the Rhineland occupation; these and other issues all had direct import for Belgium's military plans and protection. Surely too, the amount of reparations received under Belgium's priority and the rapid reconstruction of Belgian industry achieved with these funds had indirect significance for Belgium's security. Most important of all, differences over reparations were a prime factor in keeping Belgium's two most important protectors at odds during the postwar decade. Her diplomats' task throughout the reparation talks was therefore complicated by the need not only to protect Belgium's share of reparations but also to preserve the Entente as best they could. It is the story of how the Belgians attempted to fulfill this task, rather than the lengthy and complex history of reparation itself, that falls within the scope of this study.

The Belgians enjoyed mediating between their friends, for they were thus able to enhance their nation's position in European councils. It might even be said that for a brief period they were grateful for the divergence of views between their powerful neighbors, as it meant matters could be arranged more favorably for Belgian interests than if they were settled privately by France and Britain.

The Belgians intended to be both active and independent in their negotiating and described their role as that of a hyphen connecting the English and French. Much of the time between 1920 and 1923 they did successfully serve as such a link. They knew that a hyphen runs the risk of being crushed between the nouns it joins. They soon also found that it could be stretched until it became either invisible or broken to form an appendage to the leading noun. The essential difficulty was that Belgium, like a hyphen, did not carry enough weight to claim a diplomatic identity of her own. Thus, during the Ruhr occupation, the Belgians could not separate themselves from French policy without appearing to move completely into the British camp. The struggle to mediate Anglo-French differences therefore took on aspects of a battle to preserve Belgium's independence of thought and action.

Throughout the crucial years of the reparation negotiations, from 1920 to 1925, the Brussels officials insisted they followed a consistent policy, the cardinal points of which were Entente unity and obtaining the maximum payment reasonably possible from Germany. They did, in fact, hold to this policy. But if Belgium's interests in Anglo-French solidarity and in maximum reparations did not conflict in the views of her diplomats, the course of events and differing interpretations of Germany's ability to pay led them to conflict in practice. As a result, the manner in which the Belgians implemented the broad lines of their policy was on occasion altered so sharply that recriminations issued from Paris and London. Each alternative the Belgians explored – close collaboration with France, mediation between France and Britain, and support of Britain – had drawbacks. In the early twenties they were not prepared to try another alternative, that of taking a back seat and becoming less involved; only toward the end of the decade did that course begin to appear more attractive. Yet it should be said that despite imperfections, Belgium's reparations diplomacy from her so-called middle position (which was usually not so squarely in the middle as the Brussels diplomats claimed) revealed the important work a small power could perform during periods of fluidity in international affairs.

9.1 THE EARLY CONFERENCES: SUCCESSFUL MEDIATION

The Paris Peace Conference, although it decided what the Germans were to pay reparations for, had not established the total amount due or a schedule of payment. These tasks, along with enforcement of disarmament and settlement of remaining territorial and other issues, were left to subsequent meetings of allied experts and sessions of the Allied Supreme Council. In the conferences immediately following the signing of the treaty the Belgians played only a peripheral role, for the most part supporting French calls for a firm policy toward the vanquished enemy. Indeed, initially, the Belgians had to petition for invitation to the discussions, for at Paris they had not been part of the Supreme Council. Belgium's legitimate interest in many of the issues was so obvious that no objection was raised to her participation.

At San Remo in April of 1920, his relations with Britain already strained by the Frankfort occupation, Hymans supported Millerand against Lloyd George. Like his French counterpart, he believed the English prime minister was under the influence of Signor Nitti and the Italians, whom Hymans and others suspected were trying to make up to the Germans. Many of the matters considered at the Italian resort did not affect the Belgians directly, but there was one result which they greeted with much satisfaction – an agreement on the evacuation of Frankfort as soon as Germany withdrew her excess troops from the Rhineland (a small contingent was to be allowed to stay briefly to maintain order).

Much remained to be settled after the San Remo conference, and further meetings were scheduled. The Belgians' pride was gratified by the choice of Spa as the site for the next major gathering, yet they felt slighted by the absence of any invitation to join Anglo-French discussions at Hythe in May and June. Their concern was that the great powers should make some bargain that would reduce Belgium's share of Germany's reparation payments. This turned out to be the case, as the French and British agreed that their own shares would be in the proportion of 55 to 25. Though proportions rather than percentages were used, it was clear that since 6 per cent of Germany's payments was to be allotted to Serbia, only about 14 per cent would be available for division among Greece, Rumania, Italy, Portugal, Japan, and Belgium. The Belgians, Millerand told Gaiffier, could expect to receive only 8 per cent of the payments, not 15 per cent as they had hoped.[1]

News of the Hythe agreement brought bitter objections from the small powers which anticipated reparations, and the issue was referred to a top level conference to be held in Brussels. In a private meeting there in Lloyd George's room on July 2, the French and British prime ministers agreed their partition figures would have to be altered to meet Italian objections. Millerand recommended a drop of 3 per cent each for France and Britain and 1 per cent for Serbia; thus Belgium would have 8 per cent and Italy 9 per cent of the payments. Lloyd George insisted the Belgian figure was too high and the Italian figure too low. When Delacroix and Georges Theunis, a Belgian financial advisor, arrived, Lloyd George offered them 6 per cent. This the Belgian prime minister rejected and straightway informed King Albert of the situation. The Italian delegates who followed Delacroix into the room, however, were persuaded to accept 9.5 per cent so that Belgium could have 8 per cent; the other small nations were left to quarrel over their joint share of 3.5 per cent. Unaware of this development, the next day Delacroix rejected an alternative proposal involving abandonment of Belgium's priority on Germany's first payments. When discussions turned to percentages, Lloyd George again tried to hold the Belgians below 8 per cent, but Millerand came to their support.[2]

From Brussels the diplomats moved to Spa, where they were to meet with German representatives. By the conclusion of the conference the basic division of reparation allotments had been made; the Belgians were successful in defending both their priority and their 8 per cent. The major business of the conference was presentation to Germany of the allies' program for disarmament and coal deliveries. In contrast to their negligible role a few days earlier, at Spa the Belgian delegates took frequent and important parts in the discussion. The crisis of the conference came when, after the Germans had accepted the disarmament program, Ruhr magnate Hugo Stinnes shocked the allies by what was considered his insolent presentation of the German case regarding the proposed program of coal deliveries. On July 14, France pressed for occupation of the Ruhr basin as a method of coercing Germany into paying.

Earlier that morning, Millerand had asked Hymans and Delacroix for two divisions and extensive aid in supplying occupation troops. According to the operations plan French General Dégoutte submitted to Belgian Chief-of-Staff General Henri Maglinse, the Belgian divisions were to hold the center of the Ruhr basin while the French would defend their flanks. The most dangerous and difficult task had been allotted to Belgium. Maglinse rejected the plan, which was then modified on Foch's orders to meet his demands. Belgian troops would occupy the region of Lippstadt; to do more would require calling veterans back to arms. Somewhat later, Maglinse visited French General Rucquoy and offered a regiment each of infantry and cavalry, three artillery groups, and a battalion of cyclists. This limited contribution was acceptable to the French.[3]

Even Lloyd George had, by this time, become convinced that some coercion might be necessary; he, nevertheless, made clear his aversion to such action in his questioning of Marshal Foch. General Maglinse was then called on for his opinion. Placed on the spot and having had additional time to reflect, Maglinse now replied that an occupation could be practical but there were 'certain difficulties' which would have to be examined. The nature of the country would require a large number of troops, all mines and factories would have to be occupied if the move were to be successful, and an area surrounding the Ruhr should be occupied to seal off the district from the rest of Germany. German labor was sure to resist, forcing allied troops to maintain a continuous alert; therefore a large supply of reserves would be needed to replace the tired and nervous soldiers. Even the French diplomats were taken aback when the Belgian's statement forced Foch to admit the job would require a full seven divisions. At the end of the discussion Delacroix quietly mentioned that the Belgian working classes would not permit any recall of troops to the colors for such a purpose; Belgium could use only her existing divisions.[4]

The Belgians' obvious reluctance to march, combined with recognition of the financial expenditures an expedition of seven divisions would necessitate, was enough to cool the ardor of the French. The Belgians had avoided offending the French, while at the same time winning the appreciation of the British. Moreover, the threat of an occupation was enough to cause the Germans to acquiesce to the allied demands on July 16.

Though the Germans were kept in line, the Spa Conference did little to improve allied unity. In subsequent weeks, the British and Belgians became irritated at French reluctance to go ahead with the proposed high-level Geneva conference which was to discuss with the Germans the total reparations they would have to pay. Lloyd George feared that the French, taking advantage of their presidency of the Reparation Commission, wished to use that commission to establish a figure so huge that negotiations with Germany would be impossible. The French would then have an excuse for occupying the Ruhr as a sanction against Germany. In an October 1920 meeting at Downing Street, Delacroix assured Lloyd George that the Belgian commissioner would firmly side with the British representative to prevent such an occurrence. When the Welshman asked if Belgium could resist French pressure and refuse to enter the Ruhr if France demanded such action, Delacroix replied, 'The French will only enter the Ruhr Basin if they are certain of being accompanied by the Belgians; well, I give you my word we shall not agree to that.'[5]

A prompt fixing of the German debt was to Belgium's advantage, and so Delacroix proposed that the Reparation Commission be allowed to meet with the Germans but be accompanied by ministers of sufficient stature to protect larger political issues. The suggestion resulted in a gathering of German and allied financial experts at Brussels in December. The hope of the British and Belgians was to persuade Germany to accept a reparations figure of approximately 269 billion gold marks which had been tentatively agreed upon by experts meeting at Boulogne in June. First, however, numerous side issues had to be settled. The thorniest of these was the costs of the armies of occupation. When it became clear that the allies could not agree even on this matter, the conference adjourned;

its reassembly was prevented by the sudden decision to hold a plenary session of the Supreme Council.

By the time the Council met at Paris in January of 1921 the Belgians were irritated with both the French and the British. The insistence of the former on collecting complete figures on war damages suffered and the unwillingness of the latter to reach a sensible figure for the army of occupation costs were delaying establishment of any total reparations figure, and the Belgians were convinced Germany would pay little until a definite figure had been set. Moreover, the French had recently given Belgian requests small support. Twelve days before the conference opened, Georges Theunis, who was now minister of finance in a new cabinet, wrote Delacroix (currently the Belgian delegate to the Reparation Commission) that it was time 'once and for all to establish opposition [to the way the French were acting] and to show the French delegation how dangerous *for them* was the course which they appeared to want to follow'.[6]

When France presented an exorbitant list of demands, the Belgians quickly joined the British and Italians in urging that the agreement of Boulogne be affirmed. There followed more than a few sharp exchanges between Lloyd George and Aristide Briand, who had just become French premier for the seventh time. Jaspar quickly intervened. Though he desired immediate fixation of the total figure, that was obviously not possible. Perhaps German payment could be established in a manner which would take account of future amelioration of the German economy; experts could then examine possible bases for German export taxes and establish precise guarantees. The British and French leaders accepted the suggestion but soon differed over whether the export tax should be 10 or 15 per cent. Jaspar mediated frantically throughout the afternoon and evening of January 28, and finally obtained agreement to a compromise scheme.

Although the resulting proposal was rejected by the Germans on March 1, the Belgians nevertheless achieved some of their goals. Their mediation efforts had increased their prestige in the eyes of Briand and Lloyd George, who now frequently consulted Brussels regarding the best manner of dealing with each other on reparation matters. Belgium had also brought Britain and France close enough together so that when Germany's counter proposals proved unacceptable, agreement could be reached regarding sanctions. Briand abstained from demanding a full occupation of the Ruhr, and Jaspar supported the French suggestion of a limited move by proposing that the Rhine ports of Düsseldorf, Ruhrort, and Duisburg be occupied.[7] The compromise was accepted. French, British, and Belgian troops entered the cities, customs barriers were established on the Rhine, and the façade of allied unity remained intact.

To the dismay of the Belgians, the Germans only became more obstinate. So did the French, who announced they intended to occupy the Ruhr basin if by May 1 Germany had not made substantial payments on the twelve billion marks due that date. Though the Brussels officials were eager to see their priority filled, they shrank from such a measure. The labor unions and populace in general in Belgium would dislike any calling up of troops; Vandervelde would surely resign as minister of justice, and a cabinet crisis might well occur. Yet if France were allowed sole control in the Ruhr in addition to the widespread influence she had in the Rhineland, Belgium's economy would be at the mercy of France. Furthermore, France might establish a stranglehold on Germany's reparation payments and ignore Belgium's priority claim.

On April 23, 1921, Louis Loucheur, again French minister of liberated regions, visited Jaspar, who was now the Belgian foreign minister; the Frenchman assured Jaspar that Belgium need not fear being forced to call up extra classes. France would undertake the occupation without asking either Belgium or Italy for troops in addition to those sent to evidence their participation. It is more than likely that the Luxemburg railways came under discussion at this time. In any case, when the issue of reparations and sanctions arose at the Second Conference of London on the last day of April, it had been arranged that Jaspar would support the French thesis of immediate occupation in return for Briand and Berthelot's promise to withdraw all French claims for participation in the direction of the *Guillaume-Luxembourg* railway.[8]

Support Briand Jaspar did, to the extent that he, rather than the French premier, presented much of the French case. Lloyd George, who was ready to consider some sanctions but not occupation of the Ruhr, was furious. He believed that Germany should be allowed time to reply to the allies' message of April 28 which set the reparations total at 132 billion gold marks; moreover, the Germans had a right to know the modalities of payment to be used, and these the Reparation Commission had not yet determined. At the very moment the conference appeared at the point of rupture, Jaspar suggested that sanctions be voted immediately but that, as proper mobilization would require a few days, their implementation be briefly delayed. Thus the Reparation Commission and the Germans would have time to make their decisions. Neither Briand, who feared his cabinet would be overthrown for being 'soft on the boche', nor Lloyd George was easily amenable, but Jaspar eventually brought them together by careful drafting of the ultimatum.

At Brussels there was relief that the occupation was delayed. Prime Minister Edmond Carton de Wiart told American Ambassador Brand Whitlock that it 'was to be avoided if at all possible'.[9] The Belgians were

proud of their work as mediators; as Whitlock commented in his diary,
'the Belgians love that rôle, and always try to play it, or pretend to play
it, at their conferences...'[10] Much was made of how Belgium's prestige
was increased and how her diplomats had proved Belgium was an independent power not controlled by either France or England. But was this
the case? Briand knew well enough that Belgium had too many crucial
issues at stake with France to be truly independent of French influence.
Thus his formal, and no doubt sincere, thanks at the close of the conference for the Belgians' 'spirit of conciliation and of ingenuity' rang somewhat hollow. Lloyd George chose not to mention Jaspar's prominent role
at all in his closing remarks.

9.2 FAILURE OF MEDIATION AND ENTRY INTO THE RUHR

Germany did capitulate to the ultimatum and turned over a billion marks
of specie payment in June 1921. Unfortunately, this success did not lessen
divergences among the allies. The British now argued the sum should be
used to meet the absolute priority of the costs of the armies of occupation,
while the Belgians insisted their own priority should not be neglected.
The French claimed their country had experienced such extensive damages that even though the costs of their army of occupation were covered
by German deliveries in kind, France should receive some gold immediately. Slowly the Belgians became exasperated. Jaspar told Loucheur and
then Briand that Belgian business interests were suffering as a result of
the customs line on the Rhine, yet France showed no intention of evacuating the three Rhine ports, although it had been assumed that the occupation would be ended after Germany submitted to the allies' ultimatum.[11]
Jaspar's annoyance mounted when he learned that at the same time
Briand was asking his support on the issue of Upper Silesia, Loucheur was
drawing up a bilateral Franco-German agreement at Wiesbaden, an action scarcely in harmony with the frequently proclaimed principle of
allied unity in all dealings with the recent enemy.

The situation became more acute following rejection by the French
cabinet of an agreement worked out by the allies' finance ministers in
August. Theunis had prevailed upon the British to reduce their occupation army's share of the German payment to the benefit of the Belgian
priority; France was to receive nothing. The outcries from Paris and the
cabinet's repudiation of the agreement signed by the French finance
minister caused Jaspar to write at the beginning of September:

It is completely useless for the French government to persist in saying it does
not wish to infringe on our priority and to protest its friendship for us when,

in fact, without any possible error, it is our priority which is at stake and which is threatened.[12]

Toward the end of October, Gaiffier pleaded with Briand to revise his negative attitude; otherwise the Belgians would be forced to accept an Anglo-Italian invitation to solidarize their interests *à trois*. Briand, aware that any concession on his part might lead to his overthrow, testily replied that he knew Theunis and his British counterpart were conniving against him in August. 'You wished to stab France in the back, but she didn't let you.' 'Don't forget her loyal and disinterested attitude on the Luxemburg question...'[13] The refrain was one which Gaiffier was to hear time and again in the succeeding weeks, as was Briand's complaint that once Belgium's priority were filled she would lose all interest in reparations and cease to support the allies.

If the French attitude was not pleasing, neither was that of the British. Most of their suggestions for improving Germany's ability to pay implied reduction of the Belgian priority, and the City hardly appeared willing to float a loan which would enable Germany to get on her feet. Jaspar railed against the 'scandalous egotism' of the British who wished 'with gaity of heart to ruin Belgium and France for the greater glory of Anglo-Saxon commerce'.[14] Customs sanctions had been abolished at the end of September. A moratorium was unacceptable. Jaspar and Theunis openly wondered if they were wrong in opposing a Ruhr occupation and told the British that perhaps it was only with the support of French troops that any German government could bring men like Stinnes to bay. The British treasury representative who met with the Belgian officials on December 2 and 3 came away with the impression that Theunis' views were hardening rapidly in favor of the use of force, while the depressed Jaspar still hoped to play the role of mediator.[15]

Belgium's estrangement from her friends over reparations reached a high point at the Conference of Cannes in January 1922. Prior to the conference, Loucheur conferred with Sir Robert Horne of the British treasury. Though no binding accord was made, it was fairly well agreed that Germany's payment would be reduced and the brunt of the reduction taken out of payments on Belgium's priority. Theunis, now prime minister, and Jaspar knew Loucheur favored diminishing the priority; they protested vehemently and while on route to Cannes on January 4 Theunis repeated his arguments in Paris to the French president. Millerand indicated he supported the Belgian priority and disapproved of Loucheur's deal. He urged Theunis to oppose the French foreign minister and assured the Belgian that he was arranging for Briand's immediate overthrow.[16]

At Cannes, Theunis persuaded Briand and Lloyd George that Germany could pay more than Loucheur had suggested; nevertheless the priority remained threatened. The scenes with Loucheur were violent, but Theunis knew time was with him. On Monday, January 9, Gaiffier telegraphed that if Belgium held on until Saturday, all would be well.[17] On Wednesday, Briand was recalled by Millerand to defend his policies before the French chamber. The charges levied against the premier were legion, varying from 'softness on the Germans' and being too much under the influence of Lloyd George, to betraying the Belgian priority. Briand defended himself ably, but the result was a foregone conclusion. On January 12 he resigned without waiting for a vote of no confidence.

Though the Belgian diplomats were informed of the anti-Briand plot and indeed did all they could to embarrass the genial Frenchman at Cannes, it is doubtful they rejoiced at his overthrow. Briand's only possible successor was Raymond Poincaré, with whom the Belgians knew from past experience negotiation was difficult. Yet it is true that relations between Briand and the Belgian leaders had reached a state of mutual distrust; moreover, as hope of prompt German payment receded and the filling of the priority became more remote, Theunis and Jaspar began to think in terms of a firmer policy toward Germany. Theunis, a financial expert who took Belgium's leading role in reparation discussions, while Foreign Minister Jaspar specialized in security negotiations, realized Germany had to be given a chance to recover. He nevertheless was convinced Germany was not paying all that she could. Belgium needed the reparations money, and he was determined to take whatever reasonable measures were necessary to get it.

His attitude is probably sufficient explanation of why the Belgians, when they discovered at Cannes that Briand was making headway on a possible security treaty with the British, did not work to support the French minister rather than risk an interruption of the treaty negotiations by a fall of the French cabinet. The Belgians' stance had already been reached by the time they arrived at Cannes, and it was, of course, possible that the treaty negotiations would continue regardless of who was the French premier. It seems clear, however, that economic matters were gaining ascendancy in the priorities of the Brussels officials. The existence of the military accord, the criticism within Belgium of that accord, and the dire domestic need of economic revival were all pushing the cabinet in that direction.

The theme of necessary and reasonable measures was upheld by Jaspar and Theunis firmly throughout the succeeding months. In May, for example, they told the French that while the Belgian government might not in principle be against the taking of sanctions, before such steps were made the failure of all other methods of extracting payment had to be demonstrated. The crucial test of this attitude came in August during another conference at London. Germany had again requested a moratorium on payments; Poincaré, who was now French prime minister and minister of foreign affairs as well, refused such a concession and called for allied seizure of German state forests and mines. The usual division between Britain and France quickly appeared, more sharply this time thanks to the personal antipathy between Poincaré and Lloyd George.

Theunis called for unity, invoking the common sacrifices of the past eight years, and proceeded to mediate. His first effort was a modification of the French proposal in a manner intended to satisfy the French demand for guarantees while allowing the Germans, if they showed any goodwill at all, opportunity to avoid losing control of their mines and forests. Though the British saw possibilities in such an arrangement, Poincaré rejected it immediately. Convinced the German economy needed a breathing period, Theunis stated Belgium would renounce 210 million gold marks of her priority, the very amount Germany was supposed to pay from August 15 to November 15. Again Poincaré objected, ostensibly because he would not accept an arrangement made at Belgium's expense, but actually because he did not wish to give Germany a *de facto* moratorium without gaining new guarantees from Germany. The Belgians themselves soon thought better of their generosity and withdrew this proposal. In desperation, they next suggested accepting Series D reparation bonds in lieu of cash payment; Germany, in turn, would make radical economic reforms and agree to cooperate with a supervisor of her mines and forests who would be appointed by the Reparation Commission.[18]

Though the London conference collapsed in disharmony, out of this last proposal there developed a solution satisfactory to the Belgians and British which Poincaré had to accept against his will. Upon the suggestion of Sir John Bradbury, the British delegate to the Reparation Commission, Theunis proposed that Belgium accept 2 fifty-million gold mark treasury notes in place of cash or Series D bonds. These notes could be guaranteed by deposit of the equivalent amount of gold by Germany in the *Banque Nationale de Belgique*; there would be no need for sanctions on Germany's silver and other fiscal mines and on her forests. Difficult negotiations within the Reparation Commission and particularly with Germany ensued. For some time, the Wirth cabinet in Berlin insisted that a consortium of German bankers and industrialists be the only guarantee for the bonds, which would have to be renewable; Germany could not allow her gold reserves to be exported. Theunis and Delacroix held firm in their rejection of any prorogation of the six month bonds. Eventually the Reichsbank and the Bank of England (which was to issue the bonds signed by Germany) were pressured into withdrawing their requests that the bonds be renewable and reached an agreement between themselves. In return for this German concession, the Belgians ceased to demand the actual deposit of German gold abroad, a requirement that Jaspar admitted was used only for bargaining purposes.[19]

According to Camille Gutt, Theunis' *chef de cabinet*, the treasury note idea came as a brainstorm which caused the Belgian diplomats to drop all else and work with feverish hopes. Consummation of the deal came as a shock to their friends, a pleasant one for the British and an unpleasant one for Poincaré. The Frenchman did all he could to hinder the negotiations. He protested when the actual deposit of gold by Germany was waved and stated that 'if we are reduced to the necessity of taking immediately the necessary guarantees to assure the future, I estimate that we will not hesitate to do so, no matter what the decision of the Reparation Commission'.[20] Poincaré's fury at Theunis' action was obvious to all. The Belgian premier, for his part, interpreted that wrath as proof of what he had believed for several months: Poincaré intended to enter the Ruhr in the fall of 1922 and could hardly bear to be balked for lack of an excuse.

Jaspar's personal relations with the Quai d'Orsay were even worse than those of Theunis. This was, in part, because of a personal incident which had arisen with French Ambassador De Margerie in January 1921 and partly because of Jaspar's touchy, somewhat irascible and egotistical character. It was even more a result of Jaspar's frequent resistance to French pressures and of rumors that he was under the influence of Lloyd George and wished to treat the Germans less harshly than did Theunis. It is true that relations between the prime minister and Jaspar were a bit strained, but only because of Theunis' meteoric rise to the first position in the nation past the long aspiring Jaspar. The sole major policy difference on the reparations issue was with Delacroix, on the Reparation Commission, whose dislike of any possible Ruhr invasion led him to be more influenced by the British representative than Jaspar wished.[21]

So far as Jaspar and Theunis were concerned, the treasury note arrangement was the ultimate effort to persuade Germany to pay without military coercion. No alternative was left. It was clear that France would not let slip the next opportunity to march; in subsequent months Poincaré became all the more determined to enter the Ruhr because Belgium had prevented that action in September. The Brussels diplomats nevertheless were not deterred from a last effort to dissuade Poincaré. On November 22, Theunis and Jaspar visited the French prime minister; upon learning his plans they warned him of:

the difficulty of persuading the Belgian parliament and certain members of the cabinet to admit a Ruhr occupation. It would be necessary to do the impossible so that the [imminent interallied] conference would succeed in order to prove to the public that there is no longer any other alternative than a resort to force.[22]

By December, it was generally understood within the Belgian government and between Belgium and France that the Ruhr would be occupied. The only question was when.[23]

Opportunity was not long in coming. At a December conference in London, Poincaré and the new British prime minister, Andrew Bonar Law, broke sharply over what treatment should be accorded Germany. Their differences were such that even Delacroix thought maintenance of Belgium's mediatory role unwise. If Belgium did persuade Britain and France to meet each other halfway on the matter of guarantees, the outcome would be unsatisfactory:

The French, confronted with the probably insignificant result of the exploitation of the guarantee, would always reproach Belgium for having constrained the action; and the British, in view of the continuing collapse of [German] credit might hold Belgium responsible for the consequences of her initiative.[24]

In January 1923, the powers met again at Paris. Though it appears that neither the French nor the Belgians expected any agreement, they were taken totally aback by the 'impossibility' of Bonar Law's sweeping proposal: a four year moratorium on reparations and a reduction in German payments to be accomplished by ending the Belgian priority and cancelling interallied debts. Such a plan Theunis quickly opposed in favor of modification of the French scheme. Even after Bonar Law awkwardly suggested Belgium keep her priority, Theunis insisted on guarantees which would bear on the German industrial magnates. The conference dissolved, and on January 9 the Reparation Commission, over British objections, declared Germany in default on coal deliveries; on January 11, French and Belgian troops, accompanied by some Italian engineers, moved into the Ruhr basin.

It was the financial issue that above all convinced the Belgian cabinet to approve, on January 6, Theunis and Jaspar's decision to enter the Ruhr; the Belgian public for the most part was persuaded the country had no other choice than to join the occupation. By the end of 1922, Belgium was supposed to have received payments worth over 31.6 billion francs, yet she had received only 4.5 billion francs in cash, promissory notes, and payments in kind. As Theunis told the Chamber, Germany had fallen severely behind in deliveries in kind, particularly of the coal so important to Belgium, and no forced loan had been imposed on

Germany's rich entrepreneurs. Coercion, not goodwill, was all the allies could now rely upon. As for Bonar Law's proposal, it was absurd, for it threatened the priority and gave nothing to Belgium since her debts to the allies were to be paid by Germany anyway.[25]

There were other reasons why Belgium had to go along with her southern neighbor that were not so well publicized. One was the old necessity of preventing French encirclement; if Belgium were to protect her important Antwerp-Rhine trade she could not let France have a lone hand in the Ruhr. Another important factor was that Belgium was deeply involved in vital trade negotiations with France. The small country depended on exporting for her livelihood, and France was pursuing a protectionist course that was markedly harmful to Belgium's economy. In December 1919, the French had suppressed a surtax on goods destined for Strasbourg which were shipped through Antwerp, but that had been their only major concession. The situation was made more difficult for the Belgians because in the May 1921 agreement, which brought Belgian support for a French reparations scheme in return for the abandonment of French claims on the Luxemburg railways, they had promised certain economic concessions as well as support for the French reparations program. The economic matters involved marks of origin, the lowering of certain Belgian tariffs, and the providing of compensations to France for the loss of the Luxemburg market, particularly wines, automobiles, and chemical products. The specifics regarding these had yet to be worked out, and the Belgians hoped that in return for their concessions France might lower her tariffs for Belgian products as she had for Swiss. Surely any break with France over reparations would make the economic negotiations more difficult.[26]

This is not to say that a bargain was involved in Belgium's entry into the Ruhr, for there was none. In subsequent days, Belgian diplomats in London said the action was motivated solely out of a desire to maintain the Entente, while in Paris they asserted Belgium was heart and soul with France in that country's search for reparations. Actually, the Belgians were caught in a conflict between the two cardinal points of their foreign policy: Entente unity and obtaining the maximum payment possible from Germany. The Brussels diplomats had long endeavored to prove that these points were consistent with each other. When they could no longer do so, then the matter became simply one of self-interest. Belgium needed reparations. In September she had firmly opposed England's call for an unqualified two year moratorium on German payments. Then, too, she could not afford to be separated from France.

Poincaré realized this when he spoke with Theunis and Jaspar in Paris the afternoon of January 5. He planned for French troops to go into the

Ruhr as far as Essen and Bochum. He would then allow Stinnes opportunity to give France satisfaction. If the industrialist failed to do so,
Poincaré would ask the British if they wished to join him in executing
his plan. Should they refuse, he would limit himself to exploiting the
French sector of the Rhineland. It would take seven days for France to
be ready; he hoped Belgium would join France in the operation, '*but
asked nothing*'.[27] The ministers gave no direct reply, saying they wished
to confer with the rest of their cabinet. According to Gutt many years
later, the discussion at this or another meeting about the same time was
somewhat troubled because plans for entry into the basin did not appear
well established. When fears regarding possible confusion mounted,
Marshal Foch broke into the conversation to tell the Belgians not to
worry. The matter should be left to him; everything would work out all
right, for he had plans made.[28]

Events did not develop as hoped. The entry of French and Belgian
troops into the Ruhr on January 11, 1923, met widespread passive resistance by the population. Although Italy became a nominal participant
in the occupation, Britain refused to join and the rift within the Entente
became a chasm. The passive resistance prevented any serious profits
from being gained by M.I.C.U.M., the Interallied Mission of Control
of Factories and Mines established by the French and Belgians to exploit
the Ruhr. Sabotage and other difficulties forced an expansion of the original limits of the occupation and the introduction of additional French
and Belgian troops. What was initially proclaimed to be an economic
occupation became a full-scale military enterprise and there were, indeed,
many who asserted this was what France intended from the outset.
Meanwhile, the German economy plunged into a collapse that spelled
an even longer delay before it would be strong enough to support a full
load of reparation payments.

9.3 ESTRANGEMENT FROM FRANCE

The Belgians of course insisted they were not French puppets and would
not have participated in the occupation unless they wished to do so.
This was not quite the case; they acted because they had to, not because
they wanted to. Well before the disastrous effects of the occupation had
reached their peak it was evident from newspaper pieces and comments
by influential figures that the affair was not to the liking of the Belgian
government and that Theunis had some opinions which did not coincide
with those of Poincaré. At a heated meeting between the two on March 12
at Brussels, Theunis won a major point. Up to that time, the French

had asserted no evacuation would take place until Germany completed all payments. The official communiqué issued following the conversations stated, however, that evacuation would take place 'in proportion with the execution by Germany of her obligations in regard to reparations'.[29] In other words, French and Belgian troops would begin to leave the Ruhr as soon as Germany made proper arrangements for payment of reparations.

The attitude of the Belgians troubled Poincaré, who was unsure whether it was caused by British pressure or by the socialist opposition within the small country. Nevertheless, he resisted drawing up a list of terms according to which withdrawal from the Ruhr would be accomplished. Such a list was what Theunis and Jaspar desired, for they already feared that Poincaré planned an indefinitely long stay in the district. At the end of March, Jaspar met with Mussolini to assure the dictator that Belgium was in the Ruhr of her own volition, not under the tutelage of France. Agreement was reached upon an outline of withdrawal terms proposed by Mussolini, and the Italians lost no time in sounding out the British, who reacted favorably.[30]

Though Jaspar went along with the Italian proposals, while insisting they be given greater detail, his attention was chiefly attracted by rumors of plans being considered in Paris. On April 14, it had been formally agreed that the terms for withdrawal would be drafted jointly by the French and Belgians. Yet the French were obviously working on a set all their own. Poincaré said that only preliminary considerations were taking place and that Belgium would be consulted in due time, but the Belgians knew there was danger in being presented with a full set of terms. As Delacroix warned, once a draft were completed 'any suggestions Belgium might subsequently make in her own exclusive interest would not be accepted'.[31] The events of Hythe and Cannes had not been forgotten. Gaiffier wrote that Poincaré would allow evacuation of the Ruhr only on Draconian terms that Germany could not possibly meet: 'To the French draft we should oppose a Belgian draft; that will be the critical moment of the Ruhr operation for us'.[32]

On May 2, the Germans presented their own proposal. It was so obviously unacceptable that Jaspar suggested to Poincaré that a collective Anglo-French-Belgian reply be made; at the same time he sounded out the British. Curzon showed interest, but Poincaré thought the need for prompt rejection of the German plan did not allow time to concert wording with England. The Belgian cabinet was disturbed by the rupture of the Entente and the souring of Anglo-Belgian relations as a result of the Ruhr occupation; it pleaded with Poincaré to allow forty-eight hours to reach agreement with the British. The Frenchman would grant only a twenty-seven hour delay and thus destroyed hopes of a collective reply.

Poincaré's refusal of a small, but sincere, request by the government which had so strongly supported him the previous December and January did not pass Jaspar unnoticed. He was already piqued by Poincaré's cavalier treatment of their April agreement, and this new incident quickly brought into focus the foreign minister's objection to a continuance of the *status quo*. On May 11, he drew up a lengthy position paper. Germany's economic status was growing worse and reparations were not being paid despite the sanctions taken. In April, the Belgians had persuaded the French, particularly Foch, to abandon the velvet glove policy of occupation in favor of that of the iron hand advocated by French General Maxime Weygand. Though they initially had supported a gentle policy, the Belgians had been pushed to this decision by the passive resistance. But the firm hand was not successful either, and so Jaspar now warned that coercion was merely a means, not a goal. Until a lower reparations total was set and France indicated whether her goals in the Ruhr were economic, political, or both, no solution could be reached. Moreover, Franco-Belgian action alone could not bring Germany around. First, because the Germans would not cede as long as Britain and the United States were so evidently opposing the Franco-Belgian action. Second, because Germany could not pay without the political, financial, and economic aid of Great Britain and the United States.

But there was a motive more important than reparations causing Jaspar to demand an interallied program. Since the end of her neutrality, Belgium's policy was based on Anglo-French understanding. This was the only policy which Belgium's geographical location and ethnic and social make-up would permit. The Ruhr affair was a serious blow to the Entente and held a great danger for Belgium.

Each day it ties us more unilaterally to the policies of Paris at the same time it separates us from Britain. We try to keep our individuality, but it would be peurile to deceive ourselves concerning the power we possess. *That weakens day by day* and, if we don't succeed in unscrewing the nut, we will inevitably be bolted to our southern neighbors not only in the question of reparations... but especially in political affairs, which would be a matter of exceptional gravity.[33]

Poincaré's refusal to allow an interallied note forced Belgium to choose between her preferred policy of collectivity and France, Jaspar went on. Since Belgium dared not reveal a Franco-Belgian split to the Germans, she was forced to renounce the collective note. Thus Belgium's independence and prestige were impinged upon. French delay in drafting withdrawal plans was another proof of French repugnance for an interallied policy. It was time for Belgium to act. 'She alone can bring the understanding among the allies back to a solid base. ... only she is equipped to discuss a practical and financially realizable plan.'[34]

The Belgians did have a plan, and on May 24 Jaspar sent it to Paris. In brief, it required that German payments should be made at the rate of approximately three billion gold marks per year, which would be raised from the revenues of the German state railway and from taxes on such items as industrial profits, tobacco, beer, and salt, as well as from coal deliveries. The plan itself was entirely devoted to indicating sources of revenue from which reparation funds might be obtained. In his covering note, the Belgian minister suggested that as the British were advocating a reduction in the total the Germans should be required to pay, Belgium and France (who because of their devastated regions were in special circumstances) should fix the minimum amounts they would accept Britain could then decide the amount of reparation funds she desired to use in paying her debt to America and indicate any reduction she wished to make in her own claims. As the demands of the other countries were small, a revised and lower total for the German debt could thus be reached.[35]

An infection of Jaspar's left adenoid delayed discussion of the Belgian proposals until June 6. Gaiffier had earlier warned that the French, consciously or unconsciously, were hanging on to the Ruhr for security, rather than economic, reasons and were in no hurry for an economic settlement. Theunis therefore lost no time in emphasizing Belgium's desire for quick economic peace in Europe. Belgium's trade balance was worse in 1923 than in 1922, and since the entry into the Ruhr the Belgian franc had fallen rapidly; after the last of the German treasury bonds of the previous September was liquidated on June 15, the situation would become worse. Succumbing to the Belgians' pressure, Poincaré agreed the Brussels proposals should be communicated to Britain and Italy in hope of arranging a collective response to the new German proposals which were to be submitted the next day. The Frenchman refused to commit himself, however, regarding the request that Belgium's percentage share of reparations be increased if the war debts of the other powers were erased by annullment of the series C bonds.[36]

The German proposals, though making important concessions, were still unsatisfactory. On June 9, Jaspar submitted his plan to Curzon and suggested that the powers collectively demand the cessation of passive resistance as a prelude to any future negotiations with Germany. The British cabinet was not eager to associate itself with such a note, in part because it had disapproved all along the Franco-Belgian action which had provoked that resistance, but mainly because it disliked the formula of evacuation of the Ruhr in proportion to Germany's payment. Such a formula would allow French occupation of the right bank of the Rhine for at least fifteen years and perhaps longer, as the occupation would deprive Germany of her richest districts making it difficult for Germany ever to pay completely. Curzon therefore inquired what was meant by cessation of the resistance and continuance of the occupation, and what the minimum payments demanded were.

Jaspar let it be known that he expected Poincaré to consult with him regarding the first two of Curzon's questions, but it was not long before it was clear that Poincaré did not intend to be influenced by the Belgians and indeed expected soon to be in the Ruhr alone. Gaiffier suggested the French prime minister liked Belgium only 'on the condition that she be content with a secondary role and not wish to depart from it by any initiative'.[37] Yet if Poincaré recognized Belgian disaffection, Theunis had no use either for the British desire to reduce drastically Germany's reparations bill. The Belgian premier wrote Jaspar that Belgium should 'definitely convert our French allies to a practical policy which would oppose with as much efficacity as possible this British policy'.[38]

Jaspar disliked Poincaré's attitude and was furious when the French leader asked that Moncheur be instructed to speak to Curzon in exactly the same manner as Poincaré had instructed his own ambassador. This was derogatory not only of Belgium's independence but was also a rude rejection of Belgian suggestions regarding the replies to be made to Curzon's questions. As it was, both the French and Belgian answers displeased the English: the Belgian because it was too vague, and the French because it was too specific and took up the touchy issue of the justification of the Ruhr entry, a matter which Jaspar counselled should be left unmentioned.

The Belgian diplomatic corps was almost to a man convinced that no settlement could be reached with Germany until new reparation figures were established. But Poincaré refused even to discuss reparations with Britain, much less Germany, holding that the passive resistance first had to be halted; any concessions in return for cessation of the resistance might otherwise appear as an admission that the Ruhr occupation was illegal. Jaspar, despairing over the French attitude, instructed Gaiffier to warn Poincaré that Belgium 'would never accept that there should be no conversation with our English friends and no discussion in depth of reparations . . . until the end of the passive resistance'.[39] Belgium had avoided publicizing this decision so as not to embarrass the common action in the Ruhr, but she would not waver from her views no matter what eventual reverberations they might cause. Gaiffier's reply was solemn. The hegemony of Western Europe was being contested between Britain and France.

The French government does not admit that we should play a conciliator's role between France and England. According to that government, Belgium and France are engaged in the same enterprise, are on the same side of the barricade; they should, in consequence, unite to lead England to their point of view.[40]

There was a similarity between the last part of this statement and the view expressed by Theunis a few weeks earlier. But the difference was more important, for France was now insisting there was no reason to modify her policies or for Belgium to question them. At stake were both Belgium's diplomatic middle position and the freedom of her foreign policy from French dictation. Jaspar, whose personal pride made him initially more alert to the problem than Theunis, accepted the challenge. Disgusted with Poincaré's treatment of what they considered legitimate Belgian wishes and proposals, he and Theunis henceforth guided Belgium's policy slowly, but with ever increasing determination, away from that of France.

On July 20, Curzon replied to the French and Belgian requests for a collective note to Germany. He agreed to ask for termination of the passive resistance and suggested that a committee of experts, which should include an American, be established to discuss Germany's ability to pay. The Belgians were much heartened by the concessions contained in the message. As far as they were concerned, the main weakness in the British note was lack of provision regarding interallied debts and care for the war-devastated regions. Surely continued discussions could bring agreement on these matters? Poincaré, however, had no use for Curzon's effort and called upon the Belgians to stick by the side of France.

He did see the need to let the Belgians have their way somewhat, and therefore withdrew his first draft of a reply to Curzon in the face of a long list of modifications proposed by Jaspar. His second version met some of the Belgian objections but was still vulnerable to their major criticism: that instead of taking a positive approach and suggesting methods of reaching accord with Britain, it was negative and revealed little interest in any resolution of Anglo-French differences. Convinced Poincaré was delaying any solution until the passive resistance in Germany, reportedly on its last legs, was broken, Jaspar and Theunis attempted an initiative. When they proposed to visit Paris and London to discuss the Belgian reparations plan, Poincaré insisted he would not have time to see the Belgians until after his own note would be sent to London. (The French press, however, announced the prime minister was on a weekend vacation.)[41]

Though annoyed by the way they were handled by Poincaré, the Brussels diplomats did not protest too loudly. On May 12, the long-desired economic treaty with France had been signed, and with this accomplished the Belgians had dared express their criticism of French policies more openly. But the Belgian franc continued to fall sharply, and now Poincaré himself was working hard to provide a loan of 400,000,000 francs which Theunis had urgently requested to support the Belgian currency. Thus it was that superficially the separate notes delivered by the French and Belgian ambassadors at London of July 30 appeared similar and indicative of Franco-Belgian solidarity. Beneath their surfaces, however, were attitudes which differed importantly. Their divergence was reflected in Poincaré's rejection of a new investigation of Germany's ability to pay and his failure to mention the possibility of a collective note to Germany, as compared to Jaspar's warm support for such a note and his willingness to consider both a reduction in the amount Germany should pay and a new investigation of that country's financial capacity.

Annoyed by the Belgian and French messages, Curzon could hold his anger no longer. In his note of August 11, he criticized what he called excessive demands. The British government was 'reluctant to contemplate the possibility that separate action may be required....'[42] The threat stimulated Jaspar to write a lengthy reply restating Belgium's desire for interallied discussion and putting forward once again the Belgian experts' proposals. Jaspar intimated he was disappointed Curzon had not recognized sufficient difference between the French and Belgian positions to warrant separate answers. The tone of the August 27 dispatch was amicable and conciliatory, and it was obvious that Jaspar was going out of his way to emphasize his intention of finding practical solutions acceptable to all the allies. Considerable space was devoted to defense of the Belgian priority and to the suggestion that if Germany's payments were reduced by virtue of a cancellation of interallied debts, Belgium's share of reparation payments should be increased, as she had no debt to be cancelled. Most interesting was Jaspar's protest that Belgium had not, 'like France, categorically rejected the British government's suggestion that the Ruhr occupation cease when new guarantees more productive than the occupation had been found and put into operation'.[43] Belgium would be delighted to return to the system originally envisaged in January – a control mission of a few engineers to apply the programs determined by the Reparation Commission.

The Belgian effort, though reasonable and sincere, could do little to break the deadlock between Poincaré and Curzon; this was no doubt one reason Poincaré did not suggest any changes in the preliminary draft which Jaspar sent him. The Frenchman, determined to wait until the resistance were broken, was in no hurry to reply to the German message of June 7. News of the Belgian note and expert's plan did provide Gustav Stresemann, who had recently assumed the German chancellorship, an excuse to reopen negotiations. At the beginning of September, he proposed to the Belgian representative in Berlin that some reciprocal guarantee of present frontiers be concluded among the powers interested in the Rhine region. The agriculture, industry, and railroads of Germany might serve as guarantees for the payment of reparations. If agreement could be reached on these terms, the passive resistance might be stopped.[44]

Jaspar relayed Stresemann's proposal to London, much to Poincaré's annoyance. In the Belgian's opinion it was worth facilitating the task of the chancellor in ending the resistance; were he to fail, total chaos would reign in Germany. Jaspar was further encouraged by news of another Stresemann request. Several of the parties supporting his cabinet were reluctant to consider cessation of the resistance without any assurance that the Ruhr occupation would be reduced. Could he be allowed to state confidentially that unofficial talks had begun with the French ambassador to find a basis for official negotiations following the halt of the resistance? The Belgian foreign minister urged the Quai d'Orsay to acquiesce. The Franco-Belgian victory would be complete only if the German government willingly ended the resistance and was not forced to do so by conditions in the Ruhr. Stresemann's cabinet presented the last chance of a negotiated settlement; its fall would be disastrous. Poincaré refused any gesture and moved to Sampigny to avoid meeting with Jaspar. The opportunity was lost as Stresemann soon abandoned his request and brought forth a list of conditions for cessation of the resistance that even Jaspar would not accept. The Belgian, however, was drafting a statement he thought the chancellor could make concerning treatment of men expelled from the Ruhr by the occupation authorities when, on September 26, the exhausted German government halted the resistance.[45]

Poincaré's intransigence had won out at a terrible cost for both Germany and the allies. By the middle of 1923, Theunis and Jaspar had had enough of it. If their flurry of activity in September had no practical result, it did reveal the distance that had developed between the Belgian and French attitudes and a renewed determination on the Belgians' part to maintain an independent policy. Cessation of the resistance accelerated this trend, for Poincaré's refusal to start negotiations with Germany until deliveries in kind were resumed increased Belgian doubt of French intentions. Jaspar protested Poincaré's decision but was forced to back down. Gaiffier wrote that he feared exploitation of the occupied territories might become a disguise for annexation; there can be no doubt that the Belgians resented Poincaré's description of their experts' plan as superficial. Jaspar, in particular, was annoyed by Poincaré's unwillingness to make things easier for Stresemann, and wondered if Paris had determined to reject out of hand any Belgian proposition.[46]

Encouraged by a favorable German reaction to the Belgian plan, Jaspar prevailed upon the French, British, and Italians to allow the Reparation Commission to study it. The commission made no progress because of the opposition of the French delegate and the lack of support from the British, who believed the French were not yet ready to see reason and that should Britain accept the proposal, she might weaken her own case that the occupation was illegal. Among Belgian diplomats there was some suspicion Poincaré was avoiding a reparations settlement, since Germany could pay so little, and hoped to use the Ruhr and Rhineland occupations to enhance French security.[47] At the end of October events occurred which did much to strengthen this belief.

9.4 THE RHINELAND SEPARATIST REVOLT AT AACHEN

By the closing months of 1923, Germany was on the brink of disintegration. Economically exhausted and politically divided by the failure of passive resistance to the Ruhr occupation, the struggling Reich was further weakened by minor revolts and demonstrations from the left and right extremes. Saxony and Bavaria were disinterested in, or unwilling to cooperate with, the central government. The memory of the Kapp Putsch of March 1920 was still strong, and there were rumors of similar movements brewing in Munich. Riots occurred in Hamburg and elsewhere; inflation was rampant and food shortages were widely reported.

The most serious threat to the shaky German unity was the possibility of the separation of the Rhineland either as an autonomous state within a federated Germany or, worse yet, as an independent state under the protection of France and Belgium. An attempt at founding a Rhineland Republic had been made at Wiesbaden in 1919, with considerable support from the commander of the French Army of the Rhine, General Joseph Mangin. The opposition of his British and American counterparts, who refused to allow separatist forces into Cologne or Coblenz, combined with German government protests and the embarrassment Mangin's obvious actions caused officials in Paris, brought about his recall and temporary collapse of the movement. Yet there were those who continued to work for removal of the Rhineland from the rest of Germany.

Chief among the German separatists were Dr. H. A. Dorten, the leader of the abortive effort of 1919; Dr. Josef Smeets, a popular figure whose wounds from an assassination attempt in March effectively removed him from the center of events in 1923; Dr. Hugo von Metzen, a former Krupp engineer and member of an old Rhineland family; and Dr. Josef Matthes of Bonn. As Dorten was strongly suspect in the region of the Rhineland occupied by the Belgians as being too much under French influence, Leo Deckers was able to attract some following in that area. Approximately sixty years of age, Deckers was a native of Aachen and a prosperous chemical and cloth manufacturer.

These men received considerable advice and material aid from a number of sources in France, Belgium, and elsewhere, as well as from their supporters in the Rhineland. The extent of that aid and of the direct knowledge and involvement of French and Belgian government and military officials was carefully concealed at the time and can not be determined with precision even today. Accusations have been leveled in many directions, but as is so often the case, hindsight indicates that matters were not so clear-cut as were alleged. Even those officials most favorable to a separatist republic were cautious and ambivalent in their actions. Moreover, there was little communication among them. It has been traditionally argued that the collapse of the Rhineland Republic, established in October 1923, was primarily due to British opposition and German resistance. Certainly these were key factors, yet important also were the divisions within the movement and especially the rivalry and distrust which existed between the French and the Belgian-oriented supporters of the republic.

There was reason to suspect, in the fall of 1923, that a renewed separatist effort might be successful if given judicious aid from outside. The troubles within the Ruhr had particularly severe repercussions in the zones of the Rhineland occupied by the victorious armies in carrying out the Treaty of Versailles. The populace had been under economic stress, and by the middle of the year the industrialists of Aachen and Mainz were upset with the Cuno government in Berlin. There was growing agreement that the passive resistance to the Ruhr occupation was disastrous and being maintained too long. Businessmen feared they would be dragged down by the economic morass into which the rest of Germany was falling and at the same time were becoming increasingly aware of the prosperity which might be achieved through separation and closer relations with France. The miners, wine growers, and Roman Catholics of the old Rhine *Pfaffengasse* were anti-Prussian and desired to have more of their fellow Rhinelanders in key regional positions.[48] Moreover, the Americans who had so steadfastly resisted the separation movement had, at the end of January 1923, turned over their Coblenz occupation zone to France and shipped their soldiers home.

These developments were not lost on Dorten, who had reorganized his party in 1922 with the idea of creating an autonomous Rhineland federal state within the Reich which would eventually be transformed into a totally independent state having strong connections with France. His minimal initial program was unacceptable to maximalists such as Von Metzen and Matthes, who demanded immediate total separation.

. Negotiation of their differences took some time, but the brightening prospect for revolt spurred settlement. So, too, did rumors that the German government was discussing with Britain the possibility of granting the Rhineland status as a separate province within the Reich, under the governorship of the mayor of Cologne, Konrad Adenauer. The separatist republicans did not dare allow Berlin to steal the wind from their sails in such a manner. At a special meeting held April 15, 1923, at Coblenz, the various parties working for Rhenish independence formed one organization. Though technically headed by Dr. Dorten, it was the opinion of observers that the moving force in the new alignment was Von Metzen; later events were to show that Matthes would be equally important. Dorten's concept of a federal state was abandoned in favor of complete separation, and plans were laid for garnering further support. Propaganda attempts were made to link the idea of cessation of passive resistance in the Ruhr with the concept of Rhenish separatism.

September and early October witnessed scuffles in several cities between adherents and opponents of the separatist movement. Rumors regarding proclamation of a separate state were legion. On Friday, October 19, the general staff of the Belgian army of occupation reported that German leaders of the movement, after close consultation with the French, had completed their plans for seizure of Aachen in the Belgian zone and for the establishment of a Rhineland republic.[49]

During the evening hours of Saturday, October 20, several hundred hand-picked separatist storm troopers filtered their way from neighboring cities into Aachen. Shortly after midnight, joined with 2500 local separatists, they seized the town hall and other government buildings. Posters appeared proclaiming the establishment of the Rhineland Republic, and Leo Deckers and a certain Dr. Guthardt acted as spokesmen of its provisional government. No shots were fired and there was little resistance. The chief of the German police admitted that his forces were outnumbered; as he had no specific orders to resist, he obligingly sent all his men to their barracks. According to a *New York Times* account, all Belgian officers were confined to their barracks on Saturday, and Deckers confided to a French reporter that he had informed the Belgians in advance of his move.[50]

News of the *coup* at Aachen came as an apparent genuine surprise to officials in Paris. Indeed, proclamation of the republic brought forth expressions of sharp concern, not for the unity of Germany but that the action was premature and would discredit the entire separatist movement. Officials at the Quai d'Orsay intimated they had not expected action from Deckers but rather from Dorten, Smeets, and Matthes; of Guthardt they had never heard.[51]

The official Belgian position was one of strict neutrality. Henri Jaspar telegraphed the Belgian minister in Germany:

Belgian military authorities did not have to intervene, as order was not disturbed; they observed a strictly neutral attitude in conformance with our instructions. We lack information on the extent of this movement to which, it hardly needs to be said, we are totally foreign.[52]

Though the Belgian position was one of neutrality, it surely was of a benevolent nature. The lack of Belgian action during the *coup* and the subsequent preservation of the altered *status quo*, in the name of law and order, greatly aided the separatists. Moreover, the latter were allowed to carry arms (many of them had French revolvers reportedly purchased at low rates) and to drill in public despite the long standing prohibition of such activities by the high commission overseeing the occupation of the Rhineland.

The contrast between the readiness of the Belgians for the *coup* and the surprise of the French is at first puzzling. It actually represents well the problems of communication which plagued the separatist camp, and also the very different interests and attitudes of French and Belgian officials toward the *coup*.

The French surprise was due to a sudden shift of plans by Deckers. Dorten and Matthes had been intending to make their move throughout the Rhineland on Sunday, October 28. Deckers and Dorten had their differences, however; Deckers desired greater independence of action for himself than was acceptable to the other two, who by this time had also broken with Smeets. The preceding week, Deckers had agreed to accept the orders of Matthes but would have nothing to do with Dorten. This offer was flatly refused by Dorten and Matthes, who gave Deckers until Friday the 19th to declare his acceptance of their leadership. Instead of so doing, Deckers met with a group of his own supporters on the evening of the 19th and decided to steal a march on his rivals by acting a week early. Deckers later defended his precipitate move of October 21 on the grounds that the Berlin government planned to announce autonomous status for the Rhineland the following week, a step which would have fatally weakened the drive for total independence. The French attributed Deckers' hastiness to opportunism, egoism, and his desire to be acclaimed a hero.[53]

Yet there was more than just personal feelings involved. At stake was the entire status of the new republic. Neither Deckers nor his Belgian supporters wished a Rhineland state wholly dominated by France. Such a republic would provide only an insignificant position for Deckers and be a threat to Belgium. She wished to control her own railways, her own exports and imports, and her own economy. If France were to dominate the railways and resources of the Rhineland, nearly surrounding Belgium on three sides, then the little country would have a difficult time indeed maintaining any independence of policy.

Poincaré recognized the skittishness of the Belgians. Dubious himself of the success of a Rhineland revolt which got off to such a disorganized start, the French premier recommended a reserved, neutralist policy when Belgian officials telephoned to express concern regarding British reaction toward the proclamation of the Rhineland Republic. 'The occupation authorities should limit themselves to assuring the population of freedom to express their views and to protect them from eventual reprisals.'[54]

Such a posture would benefit the rebels and allow both Brussels and Paris to wait and see. Caught by surprise, Dorten and Matthes were now leading uprisings in several towns, hoping to strengthen their positions as leaders of the separation movement before Deckers became too well-established or, forewarned, Reich authorities might be able to rally support. Deckers pressed ahead and soon encountered popular opposition. It was clear, however, that he thought it would be to Belgium's advantage to support him, and to France's advantage to tolerate him, in his struggle for independence from both the Reich and the French-backed separatists.

He was encouraged in this view by several Belgians who had what were thought to be important connections. Their leader was Baron Pierre Nothomb, lawyer, nationalist, irredentist, and author of novels, poems, and political essays. A former collaborator of Paul Hymans during the Paris Peace Conference, Nothomb had occasionally embarrassed his mentor by his excesses. Founder of the expansionist *Comité de politique nationale* which had worked hard for territorial gains after the First World War, he also served as president of the *Action nationale*. In the weeks prior to the promulgation of the Rhineland Republic, this Belgian D'Annunzio had been busy consulting with the German separatist leaders and with the French. It may have been through him or one of his chief aides, a Lieutenant Peters of the Belgian *sureté* in Aachen, that word was leaked to Belgian occupation authorities of Deckers' decision (reached under how much influence from Nothomb?) the preceding Friday evening to split with Dorten and Matthes and to act a week early.

On the Monday morning following the *coup*, Nothomb delivered to Prime Minister Theunis' office a confidential program for a Rhineland Political Community. He did so by means of his friend Jules Renkin, who, as a member of several cabinets and as minister of colonies during the war, had advocated strongly nationalist and expansionist policies. The proposed community, which it was hoped would also incorporate the Ruhr basin, was to be independent of the Reich, was not to be neutral, and was to be protected by France and Belgium. Those territories south of Eifel were reserved for the exclusive control and influence of France, those to the north reserved for Belgium; the Ruhr would be subject to a special agreement to be worked out later. In return for its independence, this republic would either take on a portion of the Reich's reparation payments or part of the French and Belgian national debts. Should the movement fail, the delimitation of the French and Belgian zones of influence would remain secret.[55]

To all this Theunis commented derogatively, '*Comme c'est simple!*' A financial expert with no firm party connections, Theunis had more interest in technical economic matters than in political intrigue. Jaspar termed the affair foolish and disavowed Nothomb's activities.[56] Yet the Belgians continued to follow a policy of benevolent neutrality toward the separatists, and there were officials who hoped that something might be arranged to Belgium's benefit which would not offend the British. The initial thrust of the revolt seemed successful, and Paul Tirard, the French chairman of the Occupation High Commission, had indicated he would recognize the separatists as the *de facto* government in whatever localities they held control.

According to Pierre van Zuylen, then active in the *Direction politique*, at about this time a person of fairly high position in the British government suggested to the high commissioner of the Belgian occupation zone, Edouard Rolin Jaequemyns, that to avoid complete separation of the Rhineland from Germany, Britain would accept an autonomous status for the region. This had been Belgium's preference during the separatist outbreak in 1919, for an autonomous Rhineland within Germany had greater chances of being successfully established, would strengthen Franco-Belgian security, and would avoid the problem of French encirclement of Belgium. Van Zuylen immediately contacted Jaspar and together they called Paris. The French did not react, either this time or when a second call was placed a few days later. To Van Zuylen such silence was incomprehensible, for reports were now coming in that the separatist movement was failing rapidly; as much should be salvaged as possible.[57]

By Tuesday, the twenty-third, events were going poorly for Deckers in Aachen. Although his men had taken over several neighboring towns and he had declared Düren his capital, loyalists in Aachen had demonstrated and forced separatist evacuation of several buildings. Besieged in the *Rathaus*, Deckers sent a petulant declaration to the Belgian High Commissioner by way of Lt. Peters, calling for Belgian protection for his existing government against the Prussians. Elsewhere, Matthes' group was making progress, yet it was by now clear that the separatist forces were made up primarily of mercenary thugs and that they were resented by a majority of the Rhineland population. According to a London *Times* correspondent, a decision was therefore reached on Tuesday in Paris and Brussels to take more positive action in protecting the separatists. French General De Metz, commander of the French forces in the Palatinate, mediated busily between the Deckers and Matthes groups with some success; he demanded, however, that Matthes be given a significant role in the provisional government.[58]

That same day, Nothomb was in Brussels for a frantic interview with Jacques Davignon, Jaspar's *chef de cabinet*, as Theunis refused to see him personally and Jaspar was not available. The story Nothomb told was complex; the gist of it was that while he had persuaded many important Frenchmen to support French and Belgian zones of influence, there were others who intended to establish French hegemony over the entire Rhineland Republic. The only way to preserve Nothomb's confederative scheme, and to protect Belgium from being encircled by France, was to give financial aid to the separatist group led by Von Metzen and a certain Lt. Colonel Leopold Reul, who were currently at Aachen.[59]

The orders sent by the Belgian minister of defense late Tuesday or the following morning to the commandant of the Belgian forces in the occupation zone, simply urged him to observe strict neutrality.[60] While such neutrality still presumably benefited the separatists, it did not suggest the positive encouragement Deckers now needed. The Belgians were being cautious. There was no need to make a potentially embarrassing commitment solely to preserve the Aachen region for French influence.

The message sent about the same time to the French troops by General Jean-Marie Dégoutte, commander of the French occupation forces, contained significantly different phrasing. While he also called for neutrality, Dégoutte went on to state that such neutrality was not intended to discourage the revolutionaries or in any way indicate that their action was disapproved.

The military authority should under no pretext uphold with force the representatives of the Reich who are leading a persistent resistance against France in the matter of execution of the Treaty of Versailles.[61]

Events remained confused in the Belgian occupation zone in the northern Rhineland, and the limited progress experienced by the revolutionaries to the south was not duplicated. There were incidents of Belgian intervention in favor of Deckers' men, but for the most part the occupation forces maintained neutrality. The rebels therefore had to battle fiercely on the 25th to maintain themselves against loyal German police forces. At one point Deckers was driven from the besieged *Regierungsamt* in Aachen, but an attack by an overzealous German policeman on a bystanding Belgian soldier angered the authorities, who promptly arrested several German police and reinstalled Deckers in the government building.[62]

Deckers' situation was tenuous in face of the strong opposition of the Aachen populace. Matthes' forces were having better success, especially within the French occupation zone. Coblenz, Duisberg, and Ruhrort were all under the green, white, and red flag of the rebels. At the end of the week, Matthes announced the cabinet members of the provisional government. Matthes was premier and Von Metzen, foreign minister; neither Deckers nor Dorten held portfolios, though the latter was already announced to be the republic's ambassador to Paris.

Permanent establishment of a Belgium-oriented separatist regime in the northern Rhineland would require more positive Belgian support. Yet Theunis and Jaspar would not give way to Nothomb's pleadings, and on November 2 Jaspar refused to see the firebrand. In view of their differences with Poincaré and their desire to return to closer relations with the British, the Belgian diplomats no doubt were giving careful consideration to a stiff note sent by the British on October 31. The restrained language in which the foreign office indicated it could not view with equanimity the creation of separate states in Germany or the dismemberment of the country scarcely concealed the strength of the British opposition to the course of events. There was truth, too, in the British contention that such disintegration would leave no central power with whom the victorious states could deal on reparations, and Belgium needed her share badly.[63]

On Friday, November 2, events occurred in Aachen which settled the fate of independence for the northern Rhineland. Between fifteen hundred and two thousand separatists, under the leadership of Josef Matthes, arrived from Crefeld and Düsseldorf. They quickly seized the town hall and the district government building, from which Deckers fled in the midst of the fighting. Matthes hardly had time to enjoy his victory when he was informed by the Belgian military governor that he and all his followers must leave. The revolutionary had no choice but to obey. The separatists were gone by late afternoon, and loyalist German authorities replaced them in the local and federal government buildings.

Matthes and the Quai d'Orsay were surprised and upset by what they considered a sudden reversal of Belgian policy. Matthes insisted he had informed Belgian authorities of his plans to capture the Aachen *Rathaus* and had acted when he received no objection. It was no doubt on this point that Nothomb wished to see Jaspar and Theunis on the morning of November 2. He later complained to Renkin that all he had done for two weeks to maintain that region independent of France was lost because of Belgian inaction. 'Encirclement will be accomplished by those very people whose policy seems dominated by fear of that encirclement.'[64]

Unbeknown to Nothomb, the Brussels officials and their high commissioner had apparently already decided what to do in the event of action by Matthes. Indeed, no special orders had to be sent to Rolin Jaequemyns on November 2, for it was already understood that no aid for the insurgents from outside the Aachen area would be allowed. Jaspar declined to see French Ambassador Maurice Herbette on the morning of the third, and later that day answered Herbette's written note by stating that 'the invasion of the city and public buildings by 1500 men from the exterior ... had nothing to do with the separatist movement properly speaking'.[65] Therefore the French had no basis to claim that the Belgian police had violated their previous neutral policy when they routed the French-influenced insurgents from the town hall. Rolin Jaequemyns replied to Matthes' protest by explaining that it was impossible for the high commission to negotiate with the Rhineland Republic, for the commission had never formally granted the republic *de jure* or *de facto* recognition; the actions of Belgium's forces in Aachen were legal, for the first duty of the occupation authorities was to suppress violence.[66]

The action at Aachen broke the back of the separatist movement in the North, although Nothomb, to whom it came as a surprise, hoped it would teach the French-inspired groupings that in the Aachen region they would have to accept Belgian rather than French supervision. The full intent of the Brussels government in the affair is not entirely clear. There is no doubt that the Belgians foreswore any extensive positive action that would aid the separatists, yet under the circumstances strict neutrality was bound to benefit the revolutionary cause; there were also several instances of positive support in local crises. It appears that Theunis and Jaspar, unlike the French, had little interest in an independent Rhine state; on the other hand, several Belgians, including Hymans, Renkin, Van Zuylen, and the influential ambassador to France, Gaiffier, had long been extolling the virtues of an autonomous Rhineland within Germany. Delay in word of British opposition to this last possibility and reports that negotiations were under way at Berlin for the appointment of Konrad Adenauer or Herr Orion, chief of the Düsseldorf provincial administration, as head of the autonomous region may have encouraged Jaspar to wait and see. When it became clear that such a solution displeased both the British and the French for different reasons, and that the French-oriented conspirators wished to spread their influence into the Belgian zone of occupation, it was time to end what Jaspar considered foolishness throughout.

Nothomb's fear that Belgian inaction would turn the northern Rhineland over to French influence was not justified. His hopes for the Rhineland Republic were so high that he could not conceive of its failing totally. Yet the decisions made in Brussels had much to do with that eventual outcome. The ousting of Matthes' forces from Aachen meant that the movement would henceforth be crippled both by loss of the Belgian zone of the Rhineland and by the psychological impact of an important defeat.

On November 3rd, Deckers was called to account at Coblenz by Matthes and other separatist leaders. In a sort of court martial he succeeded in defending himself and his motives, but he was henceforth excluded from all leadership of the movement. The French were disgusted. Their high commissioner, Paul Tirard, put much of the blame for collapse of the surge for Rhenish independence on individuals who were either 'unknowns' or 'undesirables' who took premature action. The populace naturally met these men with a hostile indifference which those close to Poincaré indicated the premier saw as *très facheuse* for the entire effort.[67]

The Rhineland Republic struggled on only briefly under Matthes' leadership. A larger degree of success was experienced by French-supported separatists in the Palatinate, where an autonomous government was maintained for a number of weeks with the aid of General de Metz.

It is unlikely that the Rhineland Republic would have succeeded under any circumstances, given the residue of loyalty to the central government still possessed by many German citizens and the firm diplomatic opposition of Great Britain. Yet it was the events in the Belgian occupation zone which assured that there would be time for these opposition forces to take effect. Separatist propaganda was initially so effective that for several days the world press assumed that the revolt might indeed reflect the wishes of the Rhineland populace. The latter, taken by surprise, required time to recognize its own feelings and to organize demonstrations of opposition. The hesitations in the British foreign office over the matter of an autonomous Rhineland within the Reich have not yet been explained; the see-saw of events in Aachen, however, did allow the British opportunity to resolve their position. Had Deckers not acted prematurely and had he not split so sharply with his fellow conspirators, the *coup* would have occurred simultaneously throughout the Rhineland. The sudden impact, joined with strong initial support from France, would have made the rebels much more difficult to dislodge. The matters of an autonomous Rhineland and the fate of the Stresemann cabinet might have turned out quite differently. Nothomb and Deckers, Matthes and his French backers, all wanted too much and in their striving overreached. None of them fully realized the determination of Theunis and Jaspar to maintain Belgium's independence of policy and action.

The Belgians' decision was eminently in their self interest, for they could not afford to be surrounded by France. Nor was a splintering of Germany likely to hasten reparation payments, despite the promises of the Rhineland regime. Theunis' and Jaspar's policy becomes even more understandable when it is realized that simultaneously with the Aachen revolt the Brussels diplomats were making their break with France and supporting British efforts to resolve the reparations deadlock. Having done this, Theunis and Jaspar had to be careful not to cross the British so severely on the Rhineland matter that Belgium would be isolated.

On October 20, Great Britain indicated she would be willing to explore a proposal on reparations made by the United States the previous December and recently renewed. In brief, the Americans suggested that they would either participate in a reparations conference or send an American to take part in an inquiry to be made by an advisory body to the Reparation Commission. The value of American involvement could not be underestimated.

Though Curzon favored the first alternative, Jaspar led him reluctantly to accept the second because France would never allow the Reparation Commission to be superceded completely. When Poincaré tried to hamstring the proposed committee by limiting its inquiry to merely the present situation, Jaspar sided with Curzon and Hughes in rejecting the obvious move to prevent any progress. The French were vexed and taxed Jaspar with breaking faith; to this the Belgian testily replied that though he had closely cooperated with France in the Ruhr, the issues of reparation totals and the Rhineland separatist movement were not part of any Franco-Belgian accord.[68]

As weeks passed, it became increasingly evident that despite cessation of the passive resistance, Poincaré did not wish to make plans for leaving the Ruhr. On November 19 at an ambassadors conference in Paris, the French, angered by the return of the German crown prince to his homeland, declared that unless the allies took further sanctions in Germany, they would act on their own. Britain threatened in such event to withdraw from all interallied bodies and was backed by Italy; the Belgians, thoroughly exasperated with Poincaré's attitude, declined to support the

French. It was soon announced that Paris contemplated no further military moves. This retreat was subsequently followed by French acquiescence to establishment of two committees of experts: one to examine methods of stablizing the German currency and balancing the budget, the other to determine the amount of capital recently exported from Germany and means for forcing its return. Assent was given to American participation on the committees, and no time limits were put on the period which would be investigated. According to the American representatives at Paris, Delacroix had much to do with persuading the French to allow a broader definition of the duties of the Reparation Commission which was acceptable to the Americans and British and would facilitate the work of the experts.[69]

The return of the Belgian diplomats to a more nearly middle position in the Anglo-French quarrel was noticeable to all. It is certainly not excessive to say that the Belgian action was one of the key factors in ending Poincaré's resistance to the establishment of what came to be known as the Dawes Commission for its American chairman, Charles G. Dawes. This was not the only result of the reassertion of Belgium's independence of policy. On January 27, Jaspar had a long talk with Poincaré. His main concern was the continuance of the French-supported separatist movement in the Palatinate section of the Rhineland. The Belgian sincerely desired that nothing compromise the chances of success of the Dawes Commission. If the French persisted in advocating the promulgation of the ordinances of the autonomous Palatinate government, a breach with Curzon was sure to develop. Moreover, the movement was bound to fail and would only embarrass the French. He also believed, although he did not tell this to Poincaré, that the new MacDonald government in Britain considered the affair as a test of whether Belgium was capable of being neutral between France and Britain in matters which did not directly affect Belgian interests; thus Belgium's future relations with the British Labor government were at stake. Jaspar therefore stated he was instructing Rolin Jaequemyns to abstain when the high commissioners voted on the French proposal. As such abstention spelled defeat of the French proposal regarding the Palatinate government, Poincaré protested vigorously. In the end, perhaps inwardly acknowledging that the assassination of the president of the so-called Palatinate Republic earlier that month had struck the movement a fatal blow anyway, the French premier agreed to adjourn *sine die* the issue of official promulgation of the ordinances.[70]

If Poincaré gave way on this issue, he did not on the perennial matter of the Luxemburg railways. Despite the bargain of May 1921, France was still demanding representation on the board of directors and being difficult on issues relating to transit. Jaspar called for a prompt settlement: France was to accept Belgian views on these matters and in return Belgium would support the accord already worked out between Maglinse and Foch for the strategic use of the railways.

One reason the Belgian asked for French amenability was that the economic accord signed the previous May was finally coming before the Belgian chambers, which were proving more than hostile. Because of the demands of the Ruhr occupation, it had been necessary to increase the tour of service in the Belgian army to fourteen months. The Socialists and Flemish Catholics, who favored six-month service, had not forgotten the mysterious military accord and raised considerable cry against the 'French policy' of the cabinet. On February 27 the economic treaty, which was hardly examined on its merits, fell victim to the anti-French movement. The ministry resigned, a political and financial crisis ensued, and eventually Theunis was asked to form a new cabinet. Most of his former collaborators kept their posts, although some additional Christian Democrats were admitted to the coalition. The main change was the replacement by Hymans of Jaspar, who had negotiated the defeated treaty. The irony is obvious; the man who recently had been opposing Poincaré with increasing firmness was sacrificed as supposedly too pro-French and was replaced by the figure most responsible for the Franco-Belgian military accord.

9.5 THE DAWES AND YOUNG PLANS

Relations between Belgium and France were no longer what they were; in the following weeks they continued to worsen as Theunis became exasperated with France's refusal to support the Belgian call for a compensatory increase in her reparations percentage if the other countries were freed of their interallied debts. No effort was made to hide Belgium's intention to end the Ruhr adventure. In February, Minister of Economic Affairs Aloys van de Vijvere, who also was leader of the Catholic party, told Dawes 'that Belgium wanted to get out of the Ruhr – that its post there was a burden to Belgium – that they went into the Ruhr because of their dependence upon France. . . . at present Belgium would act upon the Committee's report independently and move out of the Ruhr'.[71] On April 24, the Belgians officially accepted the plan proposed a few weeks earlier and set to work to persuade Poincaré to do likewise.

In an April 28 meeting at Paris, Theunis explained that the position of the Belgian franc was rapidly growing worse. The public (and obviously Theunis as well) blamed the Ruhr adventure and believed it imperative to end the occupation as envisaged by the experts' plan. Poincaré still insisted that evacuation occur only in proportion to payment of reparations. The Belgians finally forced the French minister to admit that the formula agreed upon a year earlier did not contemplate actual payment but rather Germany's acceptance of the obligation to pay – i.e., while promises to pay would not be enough to allow evacuation, negotiable bonds would be. Poincaré also yielded on discontinuing Franco-Belgian fiscal administration of the basin, as the experts' plan called for the economic and fiscal integrity of the Reich. He similarly agreed to abandon administration of the railways, although he insisted on maintaining some control of the Aachen-Coblenz and Treves-Coblenz lines to protect occupation troops. There was no need to fear sabotage, he said; the local mayors would be held responsible and if necessary a few could be shot.[72]

Though Hymans failed to dissuade Poincaré from his demand for a military convention corollary to any Anglo-French security pact, the Belgian diplomat did succeed in moving the Frenchman a long way toward accepting a reparations agreement with Britain. He and Theunis next traveled to Chequers, where Ramsay MacDonald promised that should Germany default on any new reparations agreement, England would be at the side of France.[73] Plans were laid for an interallied meeting, and Hymans and Theunis relayed MacDonald's promise to Poincaré, who received it favorably. The explanation for the French premier's newly developed amenability was the growing discontent within France at the failure of his policy of coercing Germany. In the elections of May 11, Poincaré was defeated; cabinet negotiations lasted over a month before the Radical Socialist, Edouard Herriot, became prime minister on June 14 after forcing the replacement of French President Millerand by Gaston Doumergue.

The coming to power of the Labor party in Britain and particularly the overthrow of Poincaré in France did much to facilitate adoption of the Dawes Plan, and there can be no doubt that Theunis and Hymans were relieved by this turn of events. They continued their efforts by visiting Mussolini in the middle of May and gaining his approval of all that had so far been achieved. It was significant, however, that when Herriot inquired if he should come to Brussels before his first official trip to London, the Belgian cabinet unanimously decided to ask him to come after the London visit. Although Davignon feared a repetition of what happened at Hythe and before Cannes, the ministers did not. Rather, they believed that since Herriot's views were so close to their own, they could trust him; moreover, they leaped at the opportunity to gain more freedom for themselves in any future talks with the British.[74]

These were the chief and sufficient reasons for the decision, yet in ret-rospect it appears that the Belgian government was choosing to play a less prominent role in negotiations, now that these were on the right track after so many difficulties. If the French and English were willing to converse directly, then it was to Belgium's best interests to let them do so.

Herriot's discussion at Brussels, upon his return, revealed no unexpect-ed difficulties. Although a few hitches later did develop in Anglo-French communications, they did not delay the convening of the allied represent-atives in London on July 16. Of the several issues there raised, those of future declaration of default and of the ending of the Ruhr occupation were the stickiest. For the most part, the Belgians played a lesser role than they had in some earlier meetings, but on these matters they became deeply involved. The French were insistent that it was the Reparation Commission that should decide if and when Germany was defaulting on the new plan were it put into effect. The British distrusted the Reparation Commission, in which the French president had two votes to every other delegate's one, and wanted an independent experts committee to consider any questions of default. Theunis and Hymans, who agreed the Repara-tion Commission should not be deprived of such an important task, suggested that any default declaration be made as a result of consulta-tion between the Commission and the proposed Agent General for Repa-ration Payments. Though the diplomats accepted the compromise, the bankers protested it would not inspire sufficient confidence to allow the underwriting of the loan which was the heart of the Dawes Plan. Theunis strove to find a new formula without success and finally threw his sup-port to the proposal of the American observer, Colonel Logan, that the Reparation Commission and the German government negotiate with the bankers directly. The eventual result was agreement on an arbitration committee which would decide questions of default if the Reparation Commission were unable to reach a unanimous decision.

It was the tenuous position of Herriot's cabinet and his fear of the at-tacks of the vocal rightist groupings in the French parliament that made agreement on the schedule of the Ruhr evacuation difficult to reach. Though Herroit was willing to withdraw French troops from the region once Germany had given proof she was abiding by the payment terms of the Dawes Plan, he believed he could not justify to the chambers taking such action before at least a year had passed. Stresemann wanted the evac-uation to commence immediately so that the German people would see some benefit from acceptance of the Dawes Plan. The Belgian view was definite. Hymans noted that any unnecessary prolongation of the occu-pation could cause irritation and even war. The occupation had been undertaken for economic, not security, reasons. It was important to evacuate as soon as possible, for the true guarantee of peace was the Entente; were that again broken, peace and security would be severely compromised.[75]

On August 13, 1924, Theunis nevertheless urged Stresemann to accept the promise of evacuation in a year as an important concession. The German would not give way, and the following afternoon collapse of the conference seemed to be imminent. In what appeared the last Franco-German-Belgian meeting the next day, Theunis in desperation suggested that Herriot could allow partial evacuation before the lapse of a year. Under pressure from all sides, Herriot finally accepted such a possibility, and subsequently arrangements were made for evacuation of the towns of Offenburg and Appenweier.

Approval of the Dawes Plan by all the governments involved marked the beginning of the period of Germany's fulfillment of her reparation obligations and the end of Belgium's critical role in the diplomacy of the western entente. The Belgians, of course, continued actively to defend their rights, but as diplomatic traffic between Paris and London increased, the Brussels officials played a more and more peripheral role. The Dawes Plan was no ultimate solution of the financial difficulties; but it did bring about a great lessening of tensions, of which all the governments were willing to take advantage, and led directly to the Locarno security pacts. A foreign loan was floated for Germany's benefit, and that country began regular payments of reparation annuities which were to grow from a billion gold marks to two billion five hundred thousand by the end of five years. Reduction of the Ruhr occupation went at a quicker pace than expected; economic control was lessened immediately, and by the end of the year military withdrawal was well under way. The Belgian troops were among the first to depart, and on July 21, 1925, the last French soldiers left the industrial district. The three Rhine ports occupied in May 1921 were evacuated the following month.

In December of 1925, the Reparation Commission fixed the total receipts of every kind obtained from Germany during the twenty months between the beginning of the occupation and the commencement of the Dawes Plan on September 1, 1924, at 894,230,569 gold marks. Of these Belgium received approximately the value of 94 million gold marks in deliveries in kind and 355,781,489 gold marks in specie; payments of 6,766,213 gold marks were also made on the German treasury bonds. As 109 million marks were devoted to payment of the costs of the occupying forces, Belgium's net gain of about 347.5 million gold marks was disappointingly low; moreover the German economy was in such a state, thanks to the passive resistance, that a general reduction in reparation was unavoidable.[76] The Ruhr occupation was hardly a successful venture, though there were those who argued that without it Germany would never have been brought to terms. The occupation was not received well by world opinion, especially in the United States, and helped provide sympathy for Germany while weakening concern for France, Belgium, and Italy.

No arrangement had been made in the Dawes Plan for the distribution of future German payments, and so complex negotiations followed, culminating in a meeting of the ministers of finance of the main interested powers in January 1926. Theunis had to battle to protect the Belgian priority, which the British claimed was already filled. With some French support, he won out and then persuaded the powers that Belgium deserved 4.5 per cent and not 2.5 per cent of the future German payments. The retreat from the 8 per cent of Spa was considerable, but the condition of Germany was such that there was no alternative. Theunis did well to maintain the priority even at the expense of a reduction of the Spa percentage; immediate cash was far more important to Belgium's reconstruction than slightly larger payments in the distant future. An additional achievement was final settlement of the Belgian war debt issue. Though the peace conference had agreed the Belgian debt was to be paid by Germany, United States rejection of the treaty and insistence on direct, rather than indirect payment (to prevent any linking of debts and reparations) had left the issue in a confused state. It was now agreed that 5 per cent of all of Germany's payments would be alloted to payment of the Belgian debt; of this amount France was to receive 46 per cent and Britain 42 per cent; 12 per cent was to go to Belgium for payment to the United States.

The Belgian position had been felicitously established by the Dawes Plan, and the Belgians therefore had few issues to raise when its revision was considered in 1928. Arguments for revision were strong, however. Germany did not yet know the revised total she would have to pay, and additional provisions were necessary for coping with the difficulties of converting German payments from marks into foreign currency. The first soundings were made by Stresemann, who hoped that the occupation of the Rhineland might be ended before 1935, the date set by the Treaty of Versailles. The French reaction was that there could be no acceleration of evacuation unless new guarantees were found to replace that of the occupied Rhineland. A similar view was held by the Belgians, who were, however, firm in their desire to see the occupation ended immediately and relations between the allies and Germany finally regularized. Hymans urged Poincaré, again the French prime minister, to cash in the Rhineland stake while it still had bargaining value. He did not specify what he thought France should ask, but he made clear that Belgium wanted redemption by the Germans of the paper marks introduced into Belgium during the war; despite much negotiating, this touchy issue had still not been settled.[77]

In 1923, the German approach would have been rejected automatically, but by the end of the decade the situation was different. The Locarno pacts had produced a notable détente, Germany had entered the League, and her regular payment of the Dawes annuities had reestablished confidence in Germany's willingness to meet her obligations. There were also signs of growing economic instability in central Europe. The French and Germans were both eager to reach a permanent settlement, and Poincaré recognized the exchange value of the Rhineland occupation. But before any deal could be made with Germany, the allies had to reach agreement among themselves on the total amount and distribution of reparations. The allied experts came close to a deadlock during their meetings in the spring and summer of 1929. The problem was that the combined allied reparation demands called for annual payments of several million gold marks more than those made under the Dawes Plan. Germany would not agree to this, and it was not until the aid of the American expert Owen D. Young was solicited that accord was reached on a schedule of payments. Belgian acceptance of Young's plan nevertheless remained in doubt for some time as negotiations on the paper marks redemption hung fire. Eventually, the Germans gave way and agreed to pay annuities which by 1966 were supposed to amount to a total payment of 607,600,000 marks. It was agreed between Belgium and Luxemburg that of each annuity slightly more than 3 per cent would be turned over to the duchy.[78]

The Young Plan was officially approved by the Belgian government on July 24, 1929. Despite the resistance of Germany and the only grudging generosity of her friends, Belgium had managed to hold to a fair share of the reparation payments. Many details remained to be settled, and these were taken care of at a conference held at The Hague in August. Its chairman was Jaspar, now the Belgian prime minister. He had his work cut out for him, as Philip Snowden, the British chancellor of the exchequer, held to the position established by Arthur Balfour in 1923 that the combined sum of German and allied payments to Britain could not be less than the amount of Britain's payments on her debt to the United States. Jaspar mediated vigorously, winning the appreciation of the delegates. Eventually the British demands were met, primarily at the expense of the Germans, who accepted the terms reluctantly. A second session of the conference was held the following January, at which the last technical matters were settled. By then, the Germans had accepted the Young Plan in a national plebiscite (Dec. 22, 1929), despite the campaign of Adolf Hitler and Alfred Hugenberg against it.

As it was finally established, the Young Plan required Germany to pay gradually increasing annuities for thirty-seven years which would average about 1,988,800,000 gold marks exclusive of the costs of servicing the Dawes Plan loan; from 1966 to 1988 payments would be somewhat lower. Of these annuities, however, only 612 million marks were unconditionally payable; transfer of the remainder of any annuity could be postponed if this were warranted by the current economic conditions. The total sum Germany was to turn over was 113,907.7 million gold marks, of which Belgium would receive 16,948.8 million. Though the Belgians regained the 8 per cent share allotted them at Spa, as their priority had, by now, been met, they had to agree that their part of the Young Plan payments would come out of the conditional portions of the annuities. Because Jaspar feared Germany might not ever make the conditional payments, he arranged with France that in such an event France would grant Belgium 6 per cent of the proceeds of the Young Plan loan to Germany in which Belgium herself was not participating.[79]

The Young Plan was not enthusiastically greeted in Belgium, for the growing European depression indicated that the conditional payments would not be met. In 1931, the continuing economic collapse in both Europe and America caused U.S. President Herbert Hoover to call for a moratorium on all intergovernmental payments. The Belgians, who had gone through so much to protect their economy and remembered Wilson's promise of full reparation, disliked giving way at this point. As it was obvious that little would be forthcoming from Germany and that Belgium's payments to the United States would continue unless the moratorium were accepted, the Belgians had only one choice. They did succeed, however, in having payments under the occupation marks agreement exempted from the moratorium. At the Lausanne conference of 1932, which set forth a new system of reduced German payments, the Belgians again protected their mark agreement. Their efforts were to no avail, for the depression continued and the advent of Hitler to power in Berlin in January 1933 soon brought the final repudiation by Germany of her war debts.

9.6 BELGIUM'S MEASURE OF INFLUENCE

It is difficult, if not impossible, to settle on any figure as the exact total of reparations paid by Germany. Payment was made under too many different titles and in too many different ways; moreover, the value of deliveries in kind and confiscated German property was always the subject of debate. Only for the era of the Dawes and Young Plans are precise figures available. From September 1, 1924, to the entry into effect of the Young Plan, Belgium received 527.4 million marks; during the brief life of the latter agreement, the small country received 237.5 million marks, of which 43.1 million were paid under the occupation marks agreement.[80] If the Belgian claim is accepted that by October 1924 only approximately 1,745,000,000 gold marks of the priority had been paid, then a rough estimate of Belgium's total proceeds from the occupation marks agreement and reparations would be about 2,509 million gold marks, a far cry from Belgium's original hopes.

Any assessment of Belgium's reparations diplomacy should not be based solely on the amount of cash and deliveries in kind obtained. The Belgian diplomats did well to get what they did, for they were laboring under severe difficulties. At several crucial junctures, neither the French nor the English were seriously willing to take into account Belgian opinions and desires, and while all professed adherence to Wilson's seventh point and the principle of the Belgian priority, Lloyd George's behavior before Spa and Loucheur's deal prior to Cannes revealed just how much faithful support the Belgians could expect.

As the representatives of a small power, the Belgian diplomats had no way they could exert their will independently of the attitudes of their greater neighbors. This was realized from the start; hence the decision not to establish a position separate and distinct from those of France and England, but to serve as a hyphen between the two allies. The Belgians hoped that in recognition of their services the Entente members would support certain measures which were in Belgium's exclusive interest. It was a reasonable plan, and for the first three years it worked, as the Belgian priority was preserved despite Anglo-French desires to do away with it.

Unfortunately, as the French and British drifted farther and farther apart during 1922, it was increasingly difficult for Belgium to bridge the gap. Moreover, while the Belgians had thought mediation an honorable and rewarding task, they had found it painful and less than efficient in procuring Belgium's reparation goals. The decision to accompany France into the Ruhr spelled the substitution of partisanship for the previously held middle position. The danger of siding with France was obvious, yet doing so might produce more concrete results than had been obtained in recent months. Poincaré, at odds with the British, would surely show appreciation for Belgium's collaboration and listen to her counsel more willingly. Had this not, after all, been the result of the joint occupation of Frankfurt in 1920? In any case, the economic and political risks in staying behind when France acted were even greater than those of accompanying her.

It seems fair to say that while Jaspar and Theunis knew they had somewhat reduced the independence of Belgium's position on reparations, they did not expect Poincaré to take the extreme attitude he did. When Gaiffier explained that Belgian policy rested upon Anglo-French *rapprochement*, the Frenchman replied:

The axis of Belgian policy is where she has a military understanding. Detach yourselves from France, break the military accord, and count on England to defend you against Germany. She will send you three divisions three weeks after the declaration of war. You have done all you can to conclude a military entente with Britain and have failed.[81]

Poincaré, relying on his Ruhr policy to confirm French dominance of the Continent, considered Belgium his vassal already. Recognition of this forced Theunis and Jaspar consciously to break with the French premier. They had pledged to stick with the Ruhr operation and did not dare reveal any divergence of opinion to Germany on that issue for fear the passive resistance would only be prolonged. They therefore advocated their own experts' plan with increasing eagerness because it both offered a transactional solution and indicated that Belgium's voice was not an echo of Poincaré's. They nevertheless were unable to force the French prime minister into negotiating with Germany, and the abortive independent Rhineland movement must have come as a welcome opportunity to demonstrate Belgium's freedom of action. By the time the Dawes Plan was proposed, Belgium was again holding a middle position between England and France.

In September 1923, Gaiffier had summed up neatly the lessons of Belgium's Ruhr policy:

A little country can not be associated with a great military power in such an operation without running the risk of playing a contributory or even subordinate role. This was the injustice which was, in fact, reserved for Belgium. She was considered by the world as a satellite of France; her prestige suffered enormously especially during the first months of the occupation.[82]

There could be no doubt of the truth of what the ambassador said. But he described only part of Belgium's difficulties. Belgium's security depended upon the maintenance of friendship between France and Britain and she worked hard to further this. Yet were that friendship to become too close, it was more than possible that the two great powers would settle matters to their liking without taking Belgium's desires into any more than cursory consideration. Dependence on only one power threatened

Belgium's independence of action; the need of mediation between France and England implied a threat to her security; and lack of such a need deprived Belgium of her best lever for influencing international discussions and maintaining her political individuality. A hyphen must separate as well as connect.

At the time the proposals of the Dawes Committee were being examined, Hymans wrote Theunis that 'Belgium's role will depend, as always, to a great extent on the worth of her experts'.[83] This was indeed true, not only for the specific negotiations at hand, but for Belgium's relations as a whole. The small country's best hope for the preservation of her interests rested not on Belgium's strength but on the goodwill and respect of the neighboring powers. The search for the best means of collecting goodwill, which could be translated into specific economic or political advantages, was therefore at the heart of Belgium's diplomacy. Naturally, then, the success of the nation's efforts depended greatly upon the personality and character of its diplomats.

Despite notable differences among them, Hymans, Jaspar, and Theunis were all excellent defenders of their country's interests. The first was gracious, flexible, and famous for his personal charm. Hymans had an exceptional understanding of the English and spoke their language fluently. His personal relations were such that he was elected the first president of the League of Nations. While Hymans belonged to the Liberal party, Jaspar was a Catholic. He was wise enough to know he did not have his predecessor's ability to arrange matters on the basis of personal contacts and made up for this by ordering his affairs in a clear and precise manner. A man of tremendous energy and ability, he was always hampered by lack of an even temper and an excess of personal pride. Theunis, though nominally a Catholic, was primarily a non-partisan technician. His avoidance of political infighting enabled him, particularly in domestic affairs, to steer a course which would have been impossible for the leader of an political party. Lord D'Abernon termed him 'a businessman of proved capacity combining habitual bluntness with a facility for rhetoric when occasion demands it'.[84] Theunis' concentration on the financial aspects of foreign policy did disturb Jaspar, however, who set more store by political relations, as did Hymans.

Of the three, Hymans has retained the most fame, and rightly so. Yet despite his dramatic participation in the Frankfort occupation, the Luxemburg railway matter remained unsettled; as for the Franco-Belgian military accord, Hymans himself regretted it within a few years. Jaspar, on the other hand, because of his prominent ego and difficult personal relations, failed to receive the recognition he desired and deserved. His careful mediation several times did much to postpone the Ruhr occupation. He came closer to reaching a treaty with England than did any other Belgian of the period, and the fault of failure was not entirely his. The linking of the Anglo-French treaty with the Anglo-Belgian tie was unfortunate but could hardly be avoided.

The most important service Jaspar rendered Belgium was provided by his greatest weakness. It was Jaspar's pride which, during the Ruhr occupation, prevented him from letting Poincaré turn Belgium into a fiefdom. And it was his irascibility that forced the Frenchman occasionally to make concessions which, however, were mostly only of form. Perhaps a more flexible diplomat such as Hymans might have succeeded in establishing a close collaboration with Poincaré instead of Jaspar's cold war, but all indications are that the French premier would not have been willing to alter his position no matter who asked him to do so. Jaspar himself, notably on the issue of facilitating Stresemann's task, gave way to the man from Lorraine; yet his attempts to exert his own will were important. The foreign minister's caution at the time of the Rhineland revolt may have spared Belgium untold problems with a possibly French-controlled Rhineland; it certainly allowed time for the British to decide upon their own policy and for the inhabitants of the region to make their true views known.

Theunis, according to one report of Gaiffier's judgment, was afraid of the Frenchman and took flight at the least opportunity.[85] Few people, of course, opposed Poincaré successfully, and Theunis did bring him to admit important changes of policy shortly before his electoral defeat. The Belgian prime minister's greatest contribution was his brilliance at financial negotiation and his skill at managing Jaspar, smoothing over some of the foreign minister's rough edges, and helping him (indeed taking control) in many instances.

Hymans and Jaspar varied considerably in the sophistication of their diplomacy; they also differed in their concepts of the role Belgium should play in postwar Europe. Both men believed Belgium's words in European councils should carry more weight than her size and strength would normally warrant, thanks to her prestigious behavior during the war and peacetime mediation between France and Britain. Hymans, though he envisioned a larger role for his country than that of the pre-war years, was content to admit that Belgium, as a small power, should remain on the periphery of European affairs; she should become deeply involved only when issues directly affecting her were at stake. Jaspar, on the other hand, envisioned an even larger and more active part for his nation and wished to play as central a role as possible in all discussions. Here, if anywhere, the difference in the personalities of the two men is evident. Thus the change of ministers in March 1924 brought not a change in any specific policy, but a lowering in Belgium's level of activity which reflected an alteration in the Belgian foreign ministry's concept of its own undertakings. Thanks, also, to the even more important changes in London and Paris which occurred the same spring, the story of Belgian reparations diplomacy in subsequent months and years lost its dramatic quality and resumed a quieter course which seemed more consonant with Belgium's small power status. More active diplomacy no longer was needed, at least in the area of reparations. The payment of Belgium's priority was assured, and France and England were again cooperating; the necessity of, and the space for, a middle position had disappeared.

But if a distinctive period in Belgium's diplomatic history had drawn to a close, there could be no denying that the country had played an important role in European affairs and on the whole had done crucial service for the maintenance of the Franco-British-Belgian entente. In this respect Belgium's reparations diplomacy had considerable import for her military security. It is true her diplomats' opinions were seldom decisive in determining the victorious powers' strategy toward Germany, yet they did much to shape tactics in matters such as the timing, extent, intensity, and duration of coercive measures. On the issues of appointment of the Dawes committee, the independent Rhineland movement, and reduction of the Ruhr occupation in 1925 the Belgian voice was of even more significance. The reparation discussions were exhausting and frustrating, yet from them the Belgian diplomats learned, in a way they could not have learned during the decades of neutrality or from the isolated experience of the peace conference, the extent of a small state's influence upon the affairs of great powers. It was greater than the cynics imagined, but its limits, particularly for independent action, were very real.

9.7 NOTES

1. Hymans papers, 155: 'Gaiffier to Hymans, May 10, 1920'; 'Same to same, June 25, 1920'.
2. Great Britain, *Documents or British Foreign Policy (DBP)*, 1st ser., vol. VIII, pp. 400–09, nos. 39, 40, 41: Proceedings of the Conference of Brussels, July 2–3, 1920. Also, Hymans papers, 155: 'Hymans note on Brussels Conference'.
3. Hymans papers, 155: 'Hymans note on Spa Conference'.
4. Great Britain, *DBP*, 1st ser., vol. VIII, pp. 597–605, no. 71: 'Notes of meeting, July 14, 1920'. 'Minutes of the London Conference on Reparations, August, 1922', *House of Commons Sessional Papers*, London, 1924, XXVII, Cmd. 2258, p. 24.

5. Great Britain, *DBP*, 1st ser., vol. VIII, pp. 794–96, no. 91: 'Memorandum of conversation between Lloyd George and Delacroix, Oct. 11, 1920, note 8'.
6. Jaspar papers,. 204B: 'Theunis to Delacroix, Jan. 12, 1921'.
7. Henri Jaspar, 'Locarno et la Belgique', p. 162. Great Britain, *DBP*, 1st ser., vol. XV, pp. 225–38, no. 28: 'British notes of Allied Conference March 1'.
8. Jaspar papers, 214: 'Gaiffier to Jaspar, Dec. 8, |1921'; 241: 'Jaspar's note of talk with Poincaré, June 27, 1924'. The British thought the French were wooing Belgium cleverly at the beginning of April by abolishing the *surtaxe d'entrepôt* (Great Britain, *DBP*, 1st ser., vol. XVI, pp. 536–37, no. 501: 'Grahame to Crowe, Apr. 11, 1921').
9. Whitlock, *The Letters and Journal*, vol. II: *Journal*, p. 662: Entry of May 2, 1921.
10. *Ibid.*: Entry of May 1, 1921. Jaspar's role is outlined in Great Britain, *DBP*, 1st ser., vol. XV, ch. 4: 'Proceedings of the Fourth Conference of London', pp. 487–587.
11. Loucheur, *Carnet secrets 1908–1932*, p. 83. Jaspar papers, 208: '*Compte rendu* of Jaspar-Briand conference, June 7, 1921'. The foreign minister was exasperated by the slowness of French replies to his messages. These delays were in part explained by Gaiffier, who wrote on July 7 that top French officials were otherwise occupied. Millerand was at Le Havre, while the fifty-nine year old Briand had picked up a girl of fourteen and a half years, installed her in Montmartre, and was carrying out '*le plus parfait amour*' (Jaspar papers, 8).
12. Jaspar papers, 214: 'Jaspar to De Laubespin, Sept. 5, 1921'.
13. *Ibid.*, 214: 'Gaiffier to Jaspar, Oct. 27, 1921'.
14. *Ibid.*, 215: 'Minute of confidential note to Delacroix, Dec. 2, 1921'.
15. *Ibid.*, and also 214: 'Memorandum of Theunis and Jaspar talk with Fass, Dec. 2, 1921'. Great Britain, *DBP*, 1st ser., vol. XVI, pp. 829–32, 833–37, nos. 749 and 751: 'Record of Fass interviews with Belgian ministers, Dec. 2 and 3, 1921'.
16. Interview with M. Theunis, Mar. 23, 1962.
17. Jaspar papers, 197: 'Gaiffier to Jaspar, Jan. 9, 1922'.
18. *Ibid.*, 210: 'Jaspar note of Geneva conference, May 4, 1922'; 226: 'Two letters from Bemelmans to Theunis, Aug. 16'; 221A: 'Same to same, Aug. 19'; 221B: 'Belgian project, Aug. 28, 1922'.
19. *Ibid.*, 221A: 'Bemelmans to Theunis, Aug. 19'; 221B: '*Note verbale* to British, French, and American governments, Sept. 11'; 'Delacroix to Theunis, Sept. 12'; 'Jaspar notes of talks with Landsberg, Grahame, Sept. 15'; 'Jaspar to Obert de Thieusis, Sept. 19, 1922'.
20. *Ibid.*, 221B: 'Jaspar memorandum of talk with French Chargé Jaunez, Sept. 16, 1922'. The quotation is from a Poincaré telegram read to Jaspar by Jaunez.
21. *Ibid.*, 8: 'Gaiffier to Jaspar, Nov. 8, 1922'. Interviews with M. Theunis, Mar. 23, 1962, and M. Gutt, Apr. 10, 1962.
22. I am indebted for this quotation to M. Jacques Willequet, historical counselor to the Belgian ministry of foreign affairs, who quoted from the origi-

nal document in his letter to me of Oct. 23, 1962. The failure of Theunis, Jaspar, and Poincaré to reach an agreement was promptly noted by the Germans (*Akten der Reichskanzlei*: *Weimarer Republik. Das Kabinett Cuno 22. November 1922 bis 12. August 1923*, p. 8, no. 5: 'Bergmann to Reich finance minister').

23. Interviews with M. Theunis and M. Gutt.
24. Quoted by M. Willequet in letter of Oct. 23, 1962.
25. 'What Drove Belgium into the Ruhr', *Literary Digest*, 21. Belgium, *Documents diplomatiques aux réparations (DDR)*, no. 3: 'Theunis address to lower chamber, Jan. 9, 1923'. The specific accuracy of the figures cited is open to question although their general order of magnitude appears correct.
26. Jaspar papers, 8: 'Gaiffier to Jaspar, Nov. 6, 1922'.
27. *Ibid.*, 223: '*Aide mémoire* in Jacques Davignon's handwriting of meeting between Theunis, Jaspar, and Poincaré'. The note is dated Jan. 5, 1922, but its contents and the heading of Claridge's Hotel, Paris, indicate the writer made a not unnatural mistake in dating the year.
28. Interview with M. Gutt.
29. Belgium, *DDR*, no. 16: 'Official communication of Franco-Belgian conference held at Brussels Mar. 12, 1923'.
30. Loucheur, *Carnets*, p. 116. Jaspar papers, 216: 'Jaspar report of Mar. 27 meeting with Mussolini, note of Apr. 7, 1923'.
31. Jaspar papers, 225: 'Delacroix to Theunis, Apr. 5, 1923'.
32. *Ibid.*, 226: 'Gaiffier to Jaspar, Apr. 20'; see also dossier 8: 'Same to same, Apr. 19, 1923'.
33. *Ibid.*, 226: 'Jaspar note "Situation particulière de la Belgique", May 11, 1923'.
34. *Ibid.*
35. Belgium, *DDR*, no. 30: 'Jaspar to Moncheur, June 9, 1923', and Annex 1.
36. Jaspar papers, 226, '*Compte rendu* of June 6 meeting, June 8, 1923'; 'Note of Gaiffier telephone message for Jaspar, June 9, 1923'.
37. *Ibid.*, 8: 'Gaiffier to Jaspar, June 23'; see also dossier 226: 'Same to same, June 15, 1923'.
38. *Ibid.*, 226: 'Theunis to Jaspar, June 19, 1923'.
39. *Ibid.*, 226: 'Jaspar to Gaiffier, July 11, 1923'.
40. *Ibid.*, 226: 'Gaiffier to Jaspar, July 12, 1923'.
41. *Ibid.*, 228: 'Jaspar to Gaiffier, July 28, 1923'.
42. 'Correspondence with the Allied Governments respecting Reparation Payments by Germany', *House of Commons Sessional Papers*, 1923, XXV, Cmd. 1943, no. 10: 'Curzon to Saint Aulaire and Moncheur, Aug. 11, 1923'.
43. Quoted by M. Willequet in letter of Oct. 23, 1962.
44. Jaspar papers, 229A: 'Della Faille to Jaspar, Sept. 1, 1923'.
45. *Ibid.*, 229A: 'Jaspar to Obert de Thieusies, Sept. 6'; 'Same to same, Sept. 11'; 'Jaspar to Paris embassy, Sept. 13'; 'Faille to Jaspar, Sept. 17'; 'Jaspar to legation in Berlin, Sept. 18'; 'Jaspar to Gaiffier, Sept. 21, 1923'.
46. *Ibid.*, 229A: 'Gaiffier to Jaspar, Sept. 25'; 'Same to same, Sept. 26'; 229B: 'Jaspar to Gaiffier, Oct. 3'; 'Same to same, Oct. 12, 1923'.

47. *Ibid.*, 229B: 'Della Faille to Jaspar, Oct. 10, 1923'; 'Gaiffier to Jaspar, Oct. 12, 1923'.

48. *New York Times*, June 24, 1923.

49. Jaspar papers, 240: 'Note of 2nd bureau of general staff, Oct. 19, 1923'.

50. *New York Times*, Oct. 23, 1923.

51. *Ibid.*, Oct. 22, 1922.

52. Jaspar papers, 240: 'Jaspar to legation in Berlin, Oct. 21, 1923'.

53. *New York Times*, Oct. 22, 26, 29, 1923.

54. Laroche, *Au Quai d'Orsay*, p. 181. Laroche was *Directeur politique* at this time.

55. Jaspar papers, 240: 'Theunis to Jaspar, Oct. 22, 1923'; 'Jaspar to Gaiffier, Oct. 22, 1923'.

56. Jaspar papers, 240: 'Jaspar to Gaiffier, Oct. 22, 1923'.

57. Author's interview with M. van Zuylen, May 15, 1962. Also, Van Zuylen, *Les mains libres*, p. 156.

58. *New York Times*, Oct. 24, 29, 1923.

59. Jaspar papers, 240: 'Note by Davignon, Oct. 23, 1923'. Author's interview with Baron Nothomb, June 27, 1962.

60. *Ibid.*, 240: 'Forthomme to Lt. Gen. Constant, Oct. 23 or 24, 1923'.

61. *Ibid.*, 240: 'Constant to Forthomme, Oct. 23, 1923', enclosing copy of Dégoutte's orders.

62. *New York Times*, Oct. 26, 1923.

63. *Ibid.*, Nov. 1, 1923, and Laroche, *Au Quai d'Orsay*, p. 182.

64. Jaspar papers, 240: 'Nothomb to Renkin, Nov. 3, 1923'; *New York Times*, Nov. 4, 1923.

65. Jaspar papers, 240; 'Jaspar to Herbette, Nov. 3, 1923'; see also Petrement to Jaspar, c. Oct. 24, 1923. Schmidt, *Versailles and the Ruhr*, p. 151.

66. *New York Times*, Nov. 8, 1923.

67. Laroche, *Au Quai d'Orsay*, p. 182.

68. Jaspar papers, 219X: 'Jaspar to Gaiffier, Nov. 2, 1923'.

69. U.S.A., *Foreign Relations*, vol. II, pp. 102–04: 'Herrick to Hughes, Dec. 6, 1923'. D'Abernon, *The Diary of an Ambassador*, vol. II, pp. 296–97.

70. Jaspar papers, 241: 'Jaspar report of interview with Poincaré, Jan. 27, 1924'; 'Jaspar to Van de Vijvere, Jan. 29, 1924'.

71. Dawes, *A Journal of Reparations*, p. 121: Entry of Feb. 24, 1924.

72. Hymans papers, 171: '*Compte rendu* of Theunis, Hymans, and Poincaré meeting, Apr. 28, 1924'.

73. *Ibid.*, 171: 'Note of May 2–3 meeting with MacDonald'. The unsuccessful negotiations for an Anglo-French pact are briefly discussed above (Chapter 8).

74. *Ibid.*, 171: 'Davignon to Hymans, June 17, 1924'. Davignon was still the foreign minister's *chef de cabinet*.

75. *Ibid.*, 157: 'Hymans note, end of July 1924'.

76. *Le Temps*, Dec. 23, 1925. Other accountings vary; one committee reported the Belgian share as 393.9 million gold marks while the Belgian experts on

that committee claimed 317.2 million was a more accurate figure (Miller, *Belgian Foreign Policy*, p. 148, note).

77. Hymans papers: Dossier on Young Plan, 'Note of talk with Poincaré, Aug. 27, 1925'; 'Note of conversation with Chancellor Müller, Sept. 10, 1928'.
78. Moulton and Pasvolsky, *War Debts*, p. 476.
79. Myers, *The Reparations Settlement*, pp. 52–59, 75. Miller, *Belgian Foreign Policy*, p. 158, note.
80. Moulton and Pasvolsky, *War Debts*, pp. 266–67.
81. Jaspar papers, 226: 'Gaiffier to Jaspar, July 7, 1923'.
82. *Ibid.*, 229A: 'Gaiffier to Jaspar, Sept. 18, 1923'.
83. Hymans papers, 157: 'Hymans to Theunis, July 4, 1924'.
84. D'Abernon, *Diary*, vol. I, p. 259.
85. Loucheur, *Carnets*, p. 130: 'Diary entry of July 19, 1923'.

10. The limitation of commitments

The conclusion of the Locarno accords in 1925 and the resolution of many reparation issues gave the Belgians increased security and opportunity to be more free of the Quai d'Orsay. In the ensuing years, Franco-Belgian affairs were not as closely linked as they had been during the Ruhr occupation, yet many of the two nations' concerns still coincided. Thus the pulling and tugging characteristic of the reparation debates did reoccur when the countries chose differing approaches to mutual problems. Nowhere was this more evident than in the conflicting interpretations in Paris and Brussels of the role of the 1920 military accord in the defense of the West against German attack.

The Belgians sincerely believed the accord was made obsolete by the Locarno pacts; not so the French. When Flemish and Socialist opposition to a military bill provoked a parliamentary crisis in the mid-1930s, the accord was abrogated. The growing threat of totalitarian invasion soon stimulated other reductions in Belgium's international commitments and a marked shift from the activist diplomacy of the twenties.

During that decade, Belgium's range of alternative actions in protecting her economy and security was narrowed as Europe once again divided into two camps. Acutely aware of their own weakness, the Belgians had to decide between throwing their lot in with one camp which they hoped would be victorious or attempting a policy which just might spare them the impact of invasion. The trouble with the first course was that Belgium might lose her independence of action and be offered up as a battleground without truly receiving the sort of protection she needed. The second course, even were it successful, might leave her helpless before the eventual victor in any major European upheaval. Scant attention was given to a third course of action, that of arming Belgium to the hilt. Neither political nor military figure scould envision Belgium strengthening herself sufficiently to deter singlehandedly either the French or the Germans; and once one side invaded, the other was sure to do so also and the country would become the no-man's land of the war. Moreover, Belgian domestic politics precluded the passage of the extensive military bills such a course would require.

In subsequent months and years, the Belgians were accused of betraying democracy by their behavior. The events leading to the Belgian surrender to overwhelming German forces and the frantic evacuation from Dunkirk of the exposed British troops in 1940 have added fuel to the controversy. Judgment of Belgian policy and behavior in the thirties is a delicate matter. Polemics settle little and cloud much. If the furor of debate is set aside, it is possible to consider the rationale behind Belgian actions and to see that these were not inexplicable aberrations from the small country's past policies, as so many people thought at the time, but rather natural developments, considering the international and domestic situations and all that had gone before.

10.1 REVISION OF THE 1920 MILITARY ACCORD

There is ample evidence of growing Belgian weariness with French self-assuredness and unyielding ways in the years preceding and following the Locarno treaties. On reparation matters the Belgian minister in Berlin and his superiors in Brussels believed that concessions could and ought to be made to Stresemann and his successors; otherwise rightist elements would gain control in Germany. They were also concerned by the manner in which the French seemed to act as a law unto themselves in the Rhineland and elsewhere, paying little heed to Belgian views. The evolution of Belgian thought on this matter is evident in the report of Henri Rolin, chief of Vandervelde's personal cabinet, to the foreign minister in September 1925.

...it appears to me that, contrary to the thesis defended by the Belgian government at the time of the Ruhr occupation, Belgium would have the greatest interest, especially in the event of conclusion of a security pact, to avoid that France alone could prolong and at need extend by a unilateral decision her occupation in the Rhenish territories.[1]

The Belgians did indeed take a different view of the Rhineland occupation from the French. After the conclusion of the Locarno accords, the Belgian foreign office made clear its lack of interest in the occupation and its desire to see an end put to this irritant in relations with Germany. Hymans later emphasized his wish that the occupation be ended promptly, while the allies could gain compensation for their withdrawal. Jaspar, who was prime minister from May 1926 to May 1931, agreed; he believed the occupation was no longer an effective guarantee of security. The army chief-of-staff saw Belgian participation in the occupation of their third zone of the Rhineland, after the second zone was evacuated in 1933, as costly and detrimental to Belgium's military preparedness.[2] Thus the Belgians were pleased when the Young Plan brought accelerated withdrawal of occupation forces.

When in March of 1931 the ill-fated German-Austrian customs union was announced, the Belgians again parted company with the French. They disliked the union's violation of the Versailles Treaty but chose not to follow France in officially protesting the act. Rather, they accepted the lead of the British, who suggested the matter be submitted to legal inquiry. Hymans, who had succeeded Vandervelde as foreign minister in 1927, resisted a French request that the Belgian representative on the International Court oppose the union: political considerations should not interfere with judicial process. Legalism, so dear to the Belgians, was thus upheld; at the same time, the Belgians demonstrated they would conduct their relations with Germany independently of France.

The need of moving to the edge of the French current had been a topic of concern for some time. Though Vandervelde defended the military accord while he was foreign minister, his preference was for Locarno. Once out of office, he called for 'contacts, but no *contracts* which give the impression of a military tie between two countries to the exclusion of other nations or against other states'.[3] Hymans also had doubts, for he disliked the widespread interpretation of the military accord as a lien tying Belgium to French policies. King Albert shared his concern. In October 1930, Albert warned that war could soon break out on the Polish frontiers or in the Balkans. The French had alliances which could involve them in distant wars; Belgium should be careful not to become engaged in conflicts where her interests, honor, and security were not threatened. 'We cannot admit that they dispose of us, that against our will they throw us into the melée.'[4]

The French engagements to which Albert referred were those Paris had concluded with Eastern European nations during the previous nine years. Particularly prominant were the alliances of 1921 with Poland and of 1924 with Czechoslovakia; important also were the friendship agreements of 1926 and 1927 with Rumania and Yugoslavia. Because of these accords, there was a chance that France would come in conflict, not in the West but in the East, and then expect Belgium's aid or ask her to facilitate passage of French troops through Belgian territory. The possibility of such complications was discussed at a *Comité diplomatique* meeting in November. At that time, it was decided that Belgium would take arms only to defend her existence or to fulfill her obligations. Belgium should inform Britain of her policy of 'full independence' and thenceforth act in concert with England. In informing his representatives abroad of this decision, Hymans pointed out that if the council of the League were not in unanimous agreement with a French charge that Germany had violated the Versailles treaty, France would be free to act herself and to ask Belgian assistance only if France were directly attacked. Such an event would fall under the jurisdiction of the Locarno treaties. 'Belgium will take arms only if respect for her international engagements and the imperious exigencies of her independence and territorial integrity so command.'[5]

On December 22, King Albert sought clarification as to what policy should be taken regarding the Franco-Belgian military agreement. Hymans advised against repudiation, for that would arouse distrust and harm relations; instead, the accord should be made subordinate to the Rhineland pact. This was the same course recommended by Gaiffier, a few weeks later, when he wrote that any request for abolition of the accord would be interpreted in Paris 'as an abandonment or at least an indication of a change in our sentiments'.[6] Thus it was decided to make a statement in parliament that would make clear to Paris, and to the Flemish population in Belgium, the interpretation given the accord by the Brussels government.

There can be no doubt that Flemish opposition was an important stimulus to the government's efforts to reassess the value of the accord. Fighting for recognition of their linguistic rights, the Flemings were critical of any ties to France which might strengthen the hand of the Walloons. They objected to the accord, in particular, because they feared the secret clauses would make Flemings the canon fodder for French aspirations of continental dominance and because they suspected that it was, in part, aimed against their friends, the Dutch. When French Marshal Henri Philippe Pétain referred in 1927 to Belgium as the 'avant-garde of Latin civilization' the Flemish protests were vehement. Yet these were nothing compared to the outcry in February 1929 when a bogus version of the military accord was published in the *Utrechtsche Dagblad*. According to the forgery, England and Belgium planned to violate neutral Dutch territory in event of war with Germany; Belgium would send troops to aid France if she came to blows with Italy. No matter that the culprits were soon apprehended or that the newspaper document was demonstrably false; relations with the Netherlands took a turn for the worse, and Flemings had a new *cause célèbre*. The government, moreover, had difficulty explaining why, if the accord was as innocent as claimed, it could not be published minus the military technicalities which obviously had to be kept secret.

Public revelation of the agreement to use the territories of the Grand Duchy of Luxemburg without the duchy's consent, the plans for mobilization upon any general German rearmament which sounded so much like preventive war, the possibility of being forced into war when neither Belgium nor France were directly attacked, and the relinquishing of the Belgian coast to the protection of the French fleet would be too embarrassing to be considered. But the Belgian government was nevertheless embarrassed in private. Vandervelde had earlier informed the French that he would consider it an 'infinitely grave measure' to take disposition of Luxemburg territory without the approval of the grand ducal government.[7] There would be occasions when Article Sixteen of the League Covenant would require Luxemburg's cooperation, but this would not be the case if the council were divided in its judgment of a German action or if France wished to aid Poland or Czechoslovakia, which countries might be the victim of aggression committed without violation of arbitration treaties or the Covenant. His discomfort had increased when he was forced to turn aside a request by the duchy for a reaffirmation of the 1867 statute guaranteeing the duchy's neutrality.

Hymans was equally unhappy about some of the provisions of the accord and indicated that rather than leaning upon France, Belgium should look for opportunities to develop concerted policies with other small states, especially those of Scandinavia. This was one of the major conclusions he drew in an important survey of Belgium's international position which he completed in January of 1931. A second conclusion was that Belgium should hold herself aloof from quarreling groups of opponents. She should be a good neighbor to France, but if she were to have a special relationship with any nation, it should be Britain, which country possesses 'a fundamental and constant interest in the maintenance of our independence'.[8]

These recommendations all led to Hymans' main goal: 'The essential interest of Belgium is to avoid war. We have nothing to win and everything to lose in a war.'[9] The sentiment was, of course, no departure from the position held over the past decade, but the manner and connection in which Hymans expressed it shows that it marked the crystallization of a change in attitude that had begun with the Ruhr fiasco and the Locarno achievement. To avoid war, Belgium had to separate herself from France. She would remain loyal to her Locarno and League obligations, but she could not risk letting French adventurousness involve her in unnecessary conflict. (Just a few months before, Pétain had stated that in event of a Franco-German war French troops would enter Belgium without waiting for permission; Poincaré had asserted also that the military accord implied Belgium would join France in aiding an attacked Poland.[10]) Only if England went to war would Belgium also.

The difficult question was how could France be brought to admit the demise of the accord without harming relations? A unilateral statement in the Belgian parliament would soothe the Flemings and Socialists but would irritate the French. After recommending such a statement to King Albert, Hymans therefore endeavored to gain French approval of his wording. His first effort was rejected because it, in effect, declared that the 1920 agreement had been replaced by Article Four of the Locarno Mutual Guarantee Treaty. The French were determined to hold Belgium to mobilization in event of general German rearmament; to the clause regarding the Belgian coasts; and to the plans affecting Luxemburg. Fernand van Langenhove, the Belgian secretary-general, protested that as these provisions were in the portion of the accord dealing with the period of Rhineland occupation they were no longer valid. Yet he did not resist the French counter-proposal simply because all measures taken under the accord, including mobilization, were subject to the approval of the French and Belgian governments. The *Direction politique* did not take such a broad view, complaining the French wording maintained the embarrassing aspects of the accord and could 'perhaps serve to justify a premature entry of French troops into Belgium, following the conception of Marshal Pétain'.[11] Chief-of-Staff Lt.-General Emile Galet had little use for the French draft either. He questioned the value of Franco-Belgian military cooperation in time of peace and pointed out that it could force Germany to take measures regarding Belgium which might lead to war. 'It would give us an appearance of being allies of France which could, at the very moment our government would have need of all its liberty of action, limit that liberty or even annihiliate it.' Furthermore, Locarno implied that Germany had the right to ask for military talks if Belgium were having discussions with France.

Though he wished to bury the accord, that was not his chief purpose; nor did he wish to offend the French. His immediate aim was to mollify the Belgian chambers; enough modifications could be made in the French draft to achieve that end. So it was that the French version was accepted in an informal exchange of letters, and Hymans made use of it in a March fourth speech to the chambers:

...the arrangement...of September 7, 1920 has...no other object than to prepare aid to assure practically the technical conditions...for military cooperation between Belgium and France in the event of an unprovoked German aggression.
The obligation of that cooperation... is today determined in a more precise fashion by the dispositions of the Treaty of Guarantee concluded at Locarno...

which has defined the engagements which alone, alongside those of the Covenant of the League of Nations, bind the two governments in matters of mutual assistance.[12]

If, in some ways, this wording appeared to be just another rephrasing, it did have important implications. Reference could no longer be made solely to the mystical 1920 accord as cause for Belgian support of France in any conflict between that country and Germany. Henceforth, discussion of Belgian obligations would fall within the framework of Locarno and the League Covenant and be influenced by the opinions of the participants in those pacts. Direct confrontation with France would be lessened, as Italy and England would have a restraining influence on French actions. Other small powers would support Belgium's interpretation of Article Sixteen of the covenant which bound all states to give aid against an aggressor and affected Belgium particularly in regard to passage of troops; should war break out, Belgium would have more allies than just France.

The 1931 restatement might have served satisfactorily until the passage of time had quietly entombed the principal accord, but for two factors: the steady increase of Flemish discontent and the rise to power of Adolf Hitler in Germany. Both had impact upon Belgium's defense plans.

Cessation of the occupation of the Rhineland in 1930 and of the Duchy of Luxemburg had made protection of Belgium's eastern frontier immeasurably more difficult. No longer could Germany's attack be met on German territory; the battle would have to be fought in Belgium, and there was no good defensive boundary east of the Meuse. Moreover, any defense system based on the natural Liege-lower Meuse line would have two exposed flanks, of which the northern could easily be turned by way of poorly defended regions of Holland; the southern flank could be protected by French entry into the duchy. Another possibility was a line running from the lower Scheldt and Antwerp to Namur and the upper Meuse. Though this defense line did initially surrender more territory to an attacking German force, it was shorter than the first, had a left flank protected by the mouths of the Scheldt, could be easily supplied, and still shielded France.

The Belgian province of Luxemburg presented a special problem. According to plans established by the Belgian and French general staffs, the right flank of Belgium's army would extend only as far south as the point of the duchy; the French intended to defend the eastern frontier of the duchy and link up with the Belgian lines in the event of war. The withdrawal of the occupation troops and the extension of the Maginot line just to Longwy thus left Belgian Luxemburg without prepared defenses and open to any quick enemy attack which could penetrate the duchy before the arrival of French troops.

As late as 1928, the Belgian military had advocated the exclusion of any fighting from Belgian territory or, at worst, a frontier defense. By 1930, it was clear to many that such a program was no longer feasible. After extensive investigation, a parliamentary commission charged with examining national defense recommended, in agreement with the views of Chief-of-Staff Galet, that Liege and the new fortress of Eben-Emael be organized as an advanced position and that the Antwerp-Namur line be strengthened. The bridgehead at Ghent was to be fortified to provide a second line of defense should retreat be necessary.

This plan represented a victory for the new school of military thought in Belgium, represented by Galet, over the older views of such men as Maglinse. The latter, who had retired as chief-of-staff in 1927, put far more trust in the value of French military assistance in time of crisis, and thought in terms of a large army making use of many border fortifications. In contrast, the hallmarks of the new thinking were a small mobile army, skillful use of Belgium's rivers as defense barriers, and reliance on a few key fortresses and British aid.[13] It is possible that Galet's plan represented something of a victory for the views of King Albert. Galet and Colonel E. Raoul van Overstraeten had been among the king's closest advisors during the long months of the war spent at La Panne. The three had witnessed the impossibility of protecting not just the province of Luxemburg but even a larger section of the country against sudden German attack. They further believed in the value of what they had done in keeping a small section of Belgium free, remaining on national soil rather than leaving as had the ministers.

The new plan protected the army from any German flanking maneuver through Dutch Limburg and preserved the forces from total expenditure before French and British aid could arrive. But many Walloons of eastern Belgium saw themselves as sacrificed, and clamored for a frontier defense. They were told that such a defense was impossible and that they were asking Flanders to give its life-blood foolishly. On the other hand, there was a group of Flemings which insisted that while the Walloons would be spared the ravages of war, fortification of Antwerp meant the destruction of Flanders. Charges of treason and treachery were not uncommon.

Out of the heat of controversy there arose a significant faction, primarily Walloon, that demanded a frontier defense. Its leader was Albert Devèze, a Liberal leader of ability who in late 1932 had attained the post of minister of defense. Thanks to his influence, some fortifications were constructed in the Ardennes and the controversy continued. There is some evidence for belief that Devèze was encouraged in his views by the French. He had many French contacts, and one author suggests that in 1933 the French made the grant of a loan to Belgium, at that time in desperate financial difficulties, indirectly contingent upon revision of Belgian defense plans. Gaiffier reported, in October of that year, that the French minister of interior had indicated 'the determining element in the decision [of the French cabinet to grant Belgium a loan] was the effort undertaken by Belgium to fortify her eastern frontier'.[14]

The new effort to which the French referred involved both increased fortifications north of the Vesdre on the Herve plateau and a bolstering of the *Chasseurs ardennais*, an elite unit Devèze had created to defend Belgian Luxemburg. Though the *Chasseurs* would be unable to repulse any concentrated German attack, they could delay its progress. As their existence calmed Walloon agitation, King Albert and new Chief-of-Staff General P. A. Nuyten, a confirmed disciple of Galet, were willing to play along with the defense minister's pet project. The Belgians had always intended a defense in depth, and preparation of advanced positions was consonant both with this concept and with the need of a main defense position anchored to suitable terrain sufficiently removed from the border that it could be reinforced without being overrun in a surprise attack. Hymans was therefore able to protest critical articles in the French press by arguing that '. . . never has the general staff proposed to renounce the integral defense of territory, that is to say, defense starting from the frontier'.[15]

To many Flemings, the fussing about Belgian Luxemburg was one more proof of French intentions of involving Belgium in war with Germany and of French control of Belgian foreign policy through the 1920 secret agreement. Their resistance to government defense proposals increased accordingly. This resistance was all the more serious because of the continuing failure of disarmament talks among the great powers. Anxiety was great in Brussels. The Belgian officials distrusted Germany but recognized that she could not be humiliated forever; relaxation of Franco-German tensions was essential to any lasting peace. Nor were matters improved by the obvious differences between the king and the general staff on the one hand and the ministry of defense on the other; the strains of the peculiar constitutional arrangement which had been so marked in the decades before the great war were once again appearing.

The advent of Hitler brought concern but not alarm, for the Belgian diplomats did not believe the Führer planned any imminent aggression. Germany's abrupt withdrawal from the League was a shock, for it weakened the organization which embodied a chief principle of Belgium's diplomacy: international discussion and negotiation in which the voice of small as well as great powers could be heard. (It was this opportunity plus Hymans' election as first president of the League assembly that had lessened the jaundiced view of the organization expressed by Gaiffier and others at its inception.) Germany's act also threatened to destroy the cornerstone of Belgium's security, the Locarno treaties. Hymans promptly let it be known that maintenance of Anglo-Franco-Italian solidarity and the reaffirmation of the Locarno pact were necessities. The treaties did not require German membership in the League, and none of the provisions foreseeing the dissolution of the treaties had been met; the treaties could not be broken unilaterally and Germany had not asked for their demise. Nevertheless, declarations from Paris, London, and Rome in support of the treaties would be useful, if only to remind Germany of her obligations and to quiet British journalists who were suggesting that the treaties were now defunct.

Such a formal, public statement was discouraged by the other governments, although their private assurances of loyalty to the accord were warm. They did not wish to allow Germany any opportunity to question the validity of the treaties. The Belgians accepted this view and soon halted their somewhat panicky call for confirmations of Locarno.

Yet the Belgian position had been weakened. Continuation of the arms race could only increase the danger. In the realistic Belgian view, to use King Albert's words, 'reconstruction of the defeated power is in the nature of things. It is necessary to expect it and to accommodate oneself to it'.[16] Germany was racing toward total armament but still needed several more years. The Brussels officials therefore argued that Germany should not be forced to relinquish what had thus far been achieved but rather should be prevented from going further. A limit should be fixed and controls established. This was contrary to the position of the French, who were opposing German rearmament of any sort. At the end of 1933, Hymans traveled to Paris to ask the French to reconsider but had no lasting success. Disheartened at the lack of progress in disarmament and fearful that French stubbornness would let Hitler escape any limiting agreement whatsoever, Prime Minister Charles de Broqueville, after consultation with Albert, determined to issue a final public appeal and warning. The death of the king in a mountain climbing accident delayed De Broqueville's speech, but on March 6, 1934, he cautioned the chambers that the only means by which German armament could be halted was a preventive war, a cure worse than the current illness. Germany was no longer the defeated nation of 1918. The present question was not whether German rearmament would be tolerated, but whether there would be an armaments race leading to war.[17]

Instead of the speech having the effect intended, it brought the premier criticism; many parliamentarians refused to admit the situation was as serious as described. Some French interpreted the speech as another example of lack of support from the very quarter they believed ought to be the most faithful; in April, France rejected any negotiation regarding German armament.[18]

Disarmament or not, a bilateral pact with Great Britain was also a means of strengthening the Belgian position. Occasional inquiries since Locarno as to the possibility of staff talks had been coolly received in London. The search for an Anglo-Belgian accord at this time was suggested by the French, who earlier had appeared miffed over Belgian insistence on maintaining solidarity with England instead of relying solely on France. What France would gain was obvious: additional security for her northern border.[19]

Hymans knew he was playing the French game in attempting to secure British commitments on the Continent, but this was also to Belgium's interest. In April 1934, he sent Pierre van Zuylen to London to discuss disarmament and incidentally to mention a military accord. The *Directeur politique* linked the two issues by suggesting that should the northern border of France be further protected by joint Anglo-Belgian military planning, France might view a compromise regarding German armament less negatively. In reply to the argument that Locarno guaranteed Belgium's borders, he pointed out that something more was needed now, something similar to the British declaration of 1870 reaffirming the treaties of 1839. It was imperative there be no doubt in the German mind that Britain would fight should Belgium be attacked.

A month later, Hymans pursued the matter personally. During his London visit, he emphasized that a reinsurance pact would make actual British intervention on the Continent less, rather than more, likely. Even if a military accord failed as a deterrent, it was wise for Britain to be prepared to come to Belgium's aid, for if the Germans came any distance into Belgium, London would be within easy range of their air force. Reference was even made to the old barrier concept, once so disliked by the Belgians but now seen as a useful means of attracting increased British commitment. The text of the negotiated, but unsigned, Anglo-Belgian pact of 1922 was brought forward, and the British reaction was surprisingly favorable. No decision was reached as to whether the Belgian wishes should be met by a declaration or a convention. The matter was left to ripen, the British asking for secrecy lest the French request a similar accord.[20]

A crisis in domestic politics soon forced Hymans from his post. He was replaced by Jaspar, who eagerly hoped to bring to fruition his plan that had been stymied in 1922 by British insistence on obtaining, rather than avoiding, a similar pact with France. British interest was flagging, however. At several junctures, hints were dropped that the cabinet would take up the matter more quickly, and possibly with better result, if Belgium signed a non-aggression pact with Germany. Brussels quickly made clear such action was impossible: the chambers would resist it and the French would surely take umbrage. At the end of June, the Belgians were told that a convention was out of the question. But the British foreign and prime ministers soon made declarations in parliament affirming that Britain was, as always, much concerned with Belgium's security, especially so since the development of military aircraft.

During the discussions, Van Zuylen asserted that an Anglo-Belgian pact was the only means available for resisting possible French pressure to install French troops in Belgium to guard against German attack should Germany remilitarize the Rhineland; even the Belgian public might acquiesce to this unless British support could be counted on.[21] He may have been dredging up arguments, but his comment reflected a well-established distrust in Belgium of French planning. This distrust had not been allayed by the difficulties experienced in finding a suitable restatement of the military accord in 1931, and subsequent incidents had made matters worse.

One such was triggered by remarks of Marshal Pétain. His passing indication that, in the event of Franco-German war, French troops would enter Belgium even though the small country had not been attacked by Germany, caused a flurry. Polite inquiries brought denials and assurances that French troops would not enter Belgium unless she were under attack and that such action must follow a common decision of the two governments. Yet Hymans warned of the danger of French interpretations of Locarno. Belgium risked being pulled into a conflict where her interests were not involved and where she was not obliged to act by any pacts; premature entry of French troops could provoke a German attack; worst of all, England 'might use our imprudence or our weakness *vis-à-vis* France as an excuse to refuse us the assistance prescribed by the Treaty of Locarno'.[22]

Distrust for the Franco-Belgian accord of 1920 remained high within the Belgian foreign ministry as well as among the Flemish populace. To the diplomats, the Luxemburg clause was 'inadmissable'; the stipulations concerning the Rhineland occupation, obsolete; and those regarding the granting of immediate assistance 'ill-defined' and insufficiently in harmony with the Locarno treaties and the Kellogg-Briand Peace Pact which Belgium had signed in 1928. The choice appeared either to revise the accord, which involved the danger of becoming tied in some additional way, or simply to wait the events out.[23]

Rather than become embroiled in complex negotiations, Hymans informed the French ambassador that even the granting of immediate aid in the event of a sudden violation of Locarno, as provided by the security treaty, had to be subject to prior agreement between the guarantor and the country to be rescued. Though the French did not issue an immediate rebuttal, they were annoyed with what was considered to be the general attitude in Brussels. In May 1933, the secretary-general of the French foreign ministry, Alexis Saint-Léger-Léger, told the Belgian ambassador that Belgian interests should cause the small country to lean more toward France than England.

I understand that it is less out of lack of sympathy for France than from anxiety not to appear to be sailing in her wake that you act as you do. Nevertheless, you are doing her wrong, perhaps without wishing it, for you are uniting your efforts with those of the powers whose tendency is to diminish France. Therefore, do not be astonished if your policy has as counterpart a renunciation by France of her policy of partiality for you.[24]

When the French did express their views on the military aid issue in December, it was to acknowledge the Belgian position. But, at the same time, they argued that any German contravention of the Rhineland clauses of the peace treaty must be considered a hostile act against France as well as Belgium, thus obliging Belgium immediately to give assistance to France by opening her borders to French troops.

This last, in the Belgian view, seemed contrary to proper interpretation of the Versailles and Locarno treaties and opposed to Belgian sovereignty. The Brussels ministry became further disturbed when the British refused to uphold the Belgians' insistence that their approval be granted prior to French or British measures on Belgian soil against a sudden action by Germany, for example, in the demilitarized zone. The British feared the necessity of Belgian approval would paralyze any application of the Locarno guarantees.[25] With some sour thoughts of the Barnardiston episode of 1906, the Belgians clung to their position; the French did not pursue the matter.

One reason they did not was that they were gaining satisfaction in their request that a French officer survey the Belgian coast to facilitate French planning for its defense. Important opposition to this concession did exist in Brussels, for it was widely believed that Belgium's maritime defense was more properly a British than a French concern. It was argued that the French should not be given encouragement in thinking Belgium would go to war without Britain's support. Moreover, the clause regarding naval protection was in the section of the accord that dealt only with the period of allied occupation of the left bank of the Rhine. To acquiesce to the French request would be to strengthen the military accord and give it life it should no longer have. Finally, the Locarno treaties implied that Germany had as much right to plan as did France; if word of French reconnaissance leaked, the Germans might demand similar privileges.

Despite the opposition within his ministry, Hymans yielded to the importunities of his military advisors and granted authorization for a French officer in civilian garb to inspect the Belgian coasts. He insisted, however, that no joint studies could be undertaken without British participation and secretly informed the British of what was taking place. The latter declined to participate in discussions, on the grounds that talks among just two or three powers were contrary to the Locarno agreements; no doubt they also did not wish the French to believe Britain was bound to intervene in any Franco-German conflict.[26]

Having gained permission to inspect the Belgian coast, the French next made not overly subtle efforts to influence Belgian defense plans to the east. For some time Belgian officials had been indicating their hope that France would extend the Maginot defense line, constructed along the French border with Germany, to include the French border with Belgium. The French repeatedly pointed out that extensive fortification of their lengthy northern border was financially impossible and that such vital industrial centers as Lille were located so close to the border that they could only be protected in Belgium. Nevertheless, it seemed evident that the French expected the next German attack to come through Belgium and hoped to meet it there rather than exposing their own soil to the devastation of war.

In March 1934, French Ambassador Paul Claudel, alleging he was acting on his own initiative without instructions, attempted to persuade Hymans that should France build a northern Maginot line, France might feel so secure as not to aid Belgium. Would it not be better to make a great effort at Arlon, building a large fort, for construction of which France would give financial aid? Hymans rejected the overture; he could not accept money on a matter of national sovereignty. A week later, Gaiffier reported from Paris that Claudel's overture accurately reflected French thinking. 'The *Directeur politique* would like to make the erection of defense works in the environs of Arlon the counterpart of the cession to Belgium of the exploitation of the *Guillaume-Luxembourg* railway line.'[27] The continuing French desire to use that line to their advantage must have been pleasing to the shade of Napoleon III.

Hymans attributed Claudel's tentative to the proddings of Pétain, whose influence in French governmental circles was, however, waning. Yet Hymans was sufficiently disturbed to draft a position paper. French interests, he wrote, required that war be kept out of French territory, that Belgium's fate be linked closely to that of France, and that as brief a delay as possible occur in the sending of French divisions into Belgium. Belgium's interest was to avoid a war which threatened complete devastation,

to avoid being dragged into a conflict in which *the entire nation* would not have the desire to battle for its independence and which would determine the irremediable rupture of the national unity...[28]

Belgium should endeavor to show that she did not link her fate with that of any neighboring country. In the event of the threat of conflict, she should keep her freedom of decision to act only with England. Negotiations between French and Belgian military regarding action in support of Locarno should be so limited as not to bind the governments. 'Construction of fortifications justified more by a French than a Belgian interest should be out of the question.' This was the case for Arlon; to build there would invite the Germans to consider Belgium an enemy and would whet French desires in time of danger to request immediate entry of French troops into Arlon to aid the Belgian defenders.

Belgium in general should avoid any act which, in case of threat of conflict, would permit France to maintain that by common accord dispositions had been drawn up for the deployment of the French army in Belgium the modification of which...would gravely compromise military operations. Such dispositions... would dangerously weaken us in our resistance to tentatives which would be made to lead us prematurely to take a position in the conflict, contrary to our interests.

If this was the attitude within the ministry of foreign affairs, it was not shared at the ministry of defense, where Devèze was continuing his campaign for a frontier defense and closer ties with France. His views were not entirely acceptable either to King Leopold III, who shared many of his father's opinions and chose him as his model, or to Chief-of-Staff General Nuyten. The lack of harmony within the government on the defense issue could not be concealed. Devèze made trips to Paris against the wishes of the monarch. Leopold III, acutely aware of the financial crisis into which the country was plunging, repeatedly called on Prime Minister Charles de Broqueville to make economies, while the military demanded increased armaments and a longer term of service. In 1934, at the first minister's request and yielding to Flemish pressure, Nuyten submitted a list of possible reductions in military expenditures, most of which incurred upon Devèze's pet frontier projects. The defense minister was not consulted, and when he learned of the maneuver he forced the resignation of Nuyten, who was not protected by the premier. His successor, Lt.-General Cumont, promptly traveled to Paris, where he learned that actually the French were now more concerned for Belgian defense of Limburg than of the eastern frontier.[29]

Efforts to demonstrate Belgian interest in becoming less closely tied to France were also delayed by the international situation. Germany's withdrawal from the League and continuing armament was disturbing, as was the failure to obtain a specific defense agreement with England. And the Ethiopian affair only underlined the disarray that plagued the western entente despite the seeming unity briefly proclaimed at Stresa following Hitler's announcement in March 1935 of the reconstitution of the German air force and the establishment of conscription.

The Ethiopian crisis was precipitated by an incident at Wal-Wal in December 1934 which Mussolini quickly inflated into reason for an Italian attack on Ethiopia. After months of delay, the League, to whom Ethiopian Emperor Haile Selassie had appealed, condemned Italy as an aggressor and voted sanctions against her. Apart from the natural desire to avoid war, especially strong in England, a major reason for the League's failure to take stronger steps, or to enforce sufficiently those voted upon, was the fear that an annoyed Italy would fail to back France and Britain against Germany. The Belgians supported the League and obeyed its sanctions, for they had long upheld international law and emphasized the duty of larger countries to protect smaller ones; besides, it was essential to keep in the good graces of the British. But there were misgivings, and while the sanctions were enforced, feelers for an Italo-Belgian accord regarding German aggression were also current. According to Van Zuylen, there were prominent Belgians who saw the choice to be between Italy, a possible ally against Germany, and an uncivilized African country, and believed the wrong choice was made.[30]

The worsening of the international situation led only indirectly to the official rupture of the 1920 accord. The direct cause was the domestic political crisis within Belgium. Linguistic division was the chief problem, but there were other factors as well. The depression had sapped both the economy and the confidence of the country. The political parties were unable to cooperate with each other and no one party could obtain a majority of seats in the Chamber; coalition cabinets came and went with discouraging rapidity. Even within individual parties there were serious divisions along ideological, personal, and linguistic lines. The younger generation of politicians distrusted the worn ways of their elders and often called for the state to play a greater role in Belgium's economic and social affairs, a view that conflicted with the country's tradition of *laissez-fair*-ism and seemed unduly optimistic in view of the difficulty experienced in putting together any cabinet at all.

On the left was the Socialist party, split between old-line Marxists and modern revisionists. Although the hard Marxist line had been sufficiently abandoned to permit frequent participation in bourgeoise cabinets, the older generation still liked to quote Marxist slogans; men such as Vandervelde took care not to appear to be backsliding toward capitalism. The possibility of tension between nationalistic views and international solidarity always lay close beneath the surface of party affairs. Theoretically, there could be no enemy to the left; in 1935, the Socialists therefore finally forced Belgian recognition of the Soviet Union as the price for their participation in a coalition cabinet.

Views within the Catholic party were wide-ranging. Some young members advocated a social reform program while others, generally older, held a *laissez-faire* philosophy. A significant portion of the party acknowledged the need for a strong armaments program, yet the Christian Democrats took a different view based on Christian pacifism. The linguistic division overlay all the other differences, further preventing the success of any move toward party unity. In particular, the *Vlaams National Verbond* (the Flemish National Union or *VNV*), organized in 1933 by Flemish nationalists from the old Front party, made significant inroads among young Flemish Catholics who were sympathetic to the *VNV*'s talk of autonomy for Flanders or union with the Netherlands.

The Liberal party was better organized than its two chief rivals, but this was, in part, because it was smaller. As years had passed, the Liberals had come to be representatives of the conservative position within the country. This was not entirely fair, for there were progressive thinkers within the party. Yet its posture on electoral reform had begun to lose it votes before the turn of the century, and the crisis of the depression tarnished its *laissez-faire* views on the economy. Indeed, there were Catholics and Flemings who believed that the purpose of Devèze in proposing military legislation was to stir the issue of patriotism and win a new image and more votes for the party in the coming elections.

Increased armaments and a longer term of service appeared mandatory if Belgium were to convince Hitler it would be too costly to invade France by way of Belgium. Though service was compulsory, providing a large pool of men with some training, its brief term of eight months meant both that the training in use of modern equipment was not extensive and that for most of the winter months the Belgian frontier positions were undergarrisoned. But when Devèze put his proposals for an eighteen month term of service before the chambers at the beginning of 1936, he met widespread opposition. The Socialists distrusted him on personal grounds and many antimilitarists opposed lengthened service on principle; many Catholics were critical of the plans of a Liberal who favored

France, which country had recently signed a military pact with the godless Soviets. The most vocal opponents were Flemings, who raised a polemic against the 1920 accord, arguing that if it had no more meaning than that attributed to it by Hymans in 1931, it should be abolished. Its continuance obviously encouraged suspicion of secret clauses, and it soon became clear that if the military bill itself were to be discussed, the 1920 accord would have to be pronounced dead.

Although some French officials intimately acquainted with problems in Brussels, such as the military attaché, readily admitted the accord was obsolete, this was not the opinion of the Quai d'Orsay. There it was believed that any alteration of the existing arrangement would harm French military talks with the British, encourage Germany, and remove authorization for Franco-Belgian staff talks. By February 1936, continued Flemish opposition to the military bill forced Prime Minister Paul van Zeeland to Paris to talk with French Minister of Foreign Affairs etienne Flandin. The latter insisted on the *status quo* until the Belgian contended that without revision of the 1931 statement the chambers would not lengthen the tour of service, a massive anti-French demonstration scheduled for the end of March would occur in Brussels, and feelers for Belgian-Dutch military talks would be crippled.[31] Flandin then agreed to a joint statement indicating how completely the 1920 pact had been absorbed into the Rhineland treaties. His chief concern was maintenance of staff talks, which Van Zeeland assured him were authorized by the Locarno treaties.

Draft statements were exchanged and mutually criticized. The French negotiator refused to evaluate the 1920 arrangement in the depreciated currency of a military accord but rather in the more expensive terms of a political convention. After all, France had given something up for the convention:

...the 1920 plebiscite in the Grand Duchy had shown a clear majority favoring economic union of the Grand Duchy with France. We renounced to Belgium's profit that advantage because we considered signature of the convention of the Franco-Belgian military accord was worth more, in our opinion, from the point of security than the economic advantages which we could have been able to obtain through an economic union with the Grand Duchy.[32]

Progress in the negotiations was so halting that at the end of February the secretary-general of the Belgian foreign ministry, Fernand van Langenhove, traveled to Paris. He was blunt: a declaration which would end all polemics was needed; it would be either bilateral or unilateral, but it was going to be made promptly. Thus confronted, the French gave way on several points of wording. On March 6, 1936, formal approval was given a joint statement, the most important clause of which declared that the only currently viable remnant of the accord concerned the continuation of staff talks designed to uphold the Locarno treaties. The following morning the German army marched into the formerly demilitarized zone of the Rhineland.

10.2 ABROGATION

If Hitler's move came as a shock to the normal European citizen, it was a lesser surprise to the diplomats. For some time, a guessing game had been going on in the chancelleries as to when Hitler would act. Since the beginning of the year, the Belgians had become increasingly concerned regarding the reaction France, and especially Great Britain, would make to a remilitarization of the Rhineland, but they did not see the danger as imminent as it actually was. Like the French, they also expected that any German occupation would be symbolic rather than full-scale.

The first of February, Van Langenhove jotted down his thoughts. Any violation should be brought to the attention of the League. As many powers thought that Articles Forty-two and Forty-three of the Treaty of Versailles imposed a humiliating servitude on the Germans, it was doubtful that the Locarno powers would be supported if they used force. Moreover, were those powers strong enough to risk the threat of force? The unpreparedness of France and Britain and the weakness of the cabinets in the two countries were recurrent themes in Belgian dispatches of the ensuing weeks. The official Belgian position, as Prime Minister Paul van Zeeland expressed it, was to remain faithful to her engagements and to adapt her attitude to the circumstances of the moment. There was good reason for the small country not to be more specific than the great powers, especially as the British were appearing to consider the demilitarization of the Rhineland as a tool for bargaining rather than an absolute value to be maintained in its own right.[33]

When the Germans announced their action, the Belgians recalled troops on leave and, with the French, appealed to the League. At an emergency meeting of the Locarno powers minus Germany, Van Zeeland suggested the treaty violation affected Belgium more severely than the other states. She was small and depended on the sanctity of international law to protect her. Germany's excuse of the Franco-Soviet pact did not apply to Belgium, yet Belgium was more endangered than France if the ratio of her resources to the length of her joint border with Germany were taken into account. He went on to call for a common front against the enemy. 'The Belgian government is decided to take a complete part with no reservation in any collective action of the cosignatories of Locarno.'[34]

It became clear that the French and British were far from agreeing on whether negotiations for the reconstruction of the Locarno treaties, as Hitler had suggested, could begin until after German troops were compelled to withdraw from the remilitarized zone. When British Foreign Secretary Anthony Eden asked the opinion of his good friend, Van Zeeland, the latter replied: 'What dominates the situation is that one can not go to war to maintain the principle of the demilitarized zone.'[35] His statement was not significant in that Belgium's attitude would affect any military action undertaken but rather in that it summed up the inability of the powers to counter Hitler's strong-arm move with similar tactics of their own.

The premier suggested that the loss to Belgium's security represented by the remilitarization could be compensated for by a pact which would include Holland and by a firm British promise to intervene militarily should Germany attack. He did not agree with Flandin that evacuation of German troops had to precede any renegotiation of the Locarno treaties. Perhaps agreement could be reached on a symbolic occupation or on a distinction between the present full-scale occupation and the erection of permanent fortifications. 'What is essential is to avoid that any proposed solution should oblige Hitler to choose between his fall or war.'[36]

In private conversation with Eden, Van Zeeland suggested that all the compensations offered by Germany should be accepted: a non-aggression pact with France and Britain and similar pacts with nations to the east of Germany, an air pact, and German reentry into the League. The remilitarization should be reduced to a symbolic level and any fortification should be postponed until a definite settlement had been reached; Germany would have to accept condemnation of her methods, although continued militarization would be acknowledged by the other Locarno powers. If Germany rejected these bases of negotiation, the Locarno powers should use sanctions, including military measures if necessary. Belgium would help enforce any common decision; if France and England separated, she would try to bring them together.[37]

The Belgian prime minister was acting in the best tradition of Belgian diplomacy since the outbreak of the First World War. In retrospect, compromise with the Germans may not appear to have been the best course. Yet Van Zeeland's evaluation of the weakness of France and the lack of British will to take strong action was realistic. He was also aware of the disarray of his own country's military preparations and the lack of unity on foreign affairs.

Van Zeeland has been criticized for relying on the traditional role of mediator and injured innocent rather than taking a more belligerent stance and also for the fact that any mediation meant nudging the French from their hesitant thoughts of acting firmly toward the more cautious British position.[38] Yet both the French and Belgians knew little could be achieved without British aid; at the time it seemed to the Belgians far better to exact as high a price as possible in compromise negotiations with Germany than to talk in terms of all or nothing and achieve the latter. Eden, for one, thought Van Zeeland's advice sound.

French Chief-of-Staff General Maurice Gamelin, who favored immediate retaliation, has written that when he asked his Belgian counterpart to facilitate a French advance on Cologne through Belgian territory, he learned that 'the Belgian government had been terrorized by the idea of finding itself involved in a conflict...'[39] This may have been true in part, but the main fear was of acting without British support. The situation was far different from that of 1923, and it would have been foolhardy for the Belgians to have marched just with France. Nor were the French ready, as they later had to admit.

The disparity between the French desire to use sanctions even to the point of military action and the British unwillingness to prevent Germany from occupying 'her own back yard' prevented any immediate agreement at Paris. The British delegates indicated the need to confer with the cabinet as a whole and the talks were shifted to London, where a meeting of the League Council was concurrently held.

Continuation of the deadlock provided Van Zeeland an opportunity to resume his self-appointed task of mediator. On March 13 he intervened, much in the sense of his prior comments to Eden. The French were disappointed by his position and attributed the renewed reluctance of the British to take firm measures to the reticent attitude of the Belgians.[40] Eventually an agreement was reached that was embodied in a March 19 statement asserting the maintenance of the Locarno treaties and the promise of mutual assistance in the face of unprovoked aggression. The terms of the treaties were to be revised, but Germany was to accept limits on her forces in the Rhineland and was not to erect fortifications there; adherence to these stipulations would be overseen by an International Control Commission. Germany could submit the question of the compatibility of the Franco-Soviet pact with the Locarno treaties to the International Court of Justice. Belgian security was strengthened by British assent to an Anglo-Franco-Belgian agreement that until a new Locarno pact was signed the three powers would mutually consult and take action against aggression; staff talks were envisaged.

The League Council heard sympathetically Van Zeeland's plea of an innocent country wronged. It condemned Germany's action and left settlement of the matter to the Locarno powers. Of these, Italy abstained from ratifying the March 19 agreement. Hitler delayed his reply to provide more time to solidify his *fait accompli*. At the end of March he rejected the proposals, only agreeing not to increase his troops in the Rhineland and to let his promise be overseen by a control commission. His attitude forced the British to issue the guarantee provided for in the March 19 agreement and to authorize staff conversations.

It initially appeared that at long last Belgium had achieved her goal of joint military planning with both Britain and France; from the little country's point of view this was almost better than the Locarno accords themselves. But hopes were quickly dashed. British parliament members went out of their way to make clear to Prime Minister Stanley Baldwin that they distrusted involvement in staff talks similar to those which some suspected helped to precipitate war in 1914. In April, French and Belgian staff officers learned both of the restricted conception the British held of staff talks and of the meager and late-arriving aid Britain could provide in the event of German attack: two infantry divisions ready for battle probably no sooner than between the twentieth and thirtieth days of mobilization.

Though the staffs agreed to maintain contact via military attachés in the future, it was clear that France and Belgium would have to look to each other for immediate support. Their staff conversations were quickly resumed. In May, General Van den Bergen, the latest Belgian chief-of-staff, met with Gamelin. Plans were made for the arrival of the French First Army as an advance guard in the event of German attack and for an eventual linkage of French and Belgian troops in support of what would be Belgium's main line of defense, the Albert Canal running from Antwerp to Liege and the Meuse. Belgian plans for demolition of bridges and other preventive measures were discussed thoroughly. Although the military accord was supposedly buried in March 1936, in actuality Franco-Belgian military cooperation was now the closest it had been in nearly a decade. In July, following a meeting in Brussels, the French under chief-of-staff could report that whatever the tendencies of the Belgian political parties, the Belgian general staff 'is entirely won over to close collaboration with the French army'.[41]

Negotiations with Germany dragged. The election of the Popular Front government in France brought a reduction in French demands on Germany before any revision of the Locarno pacts would be considered. Van Zeeland, for his part, called upon his friends to lift sanctions taken against Italy and in other ways attempt to gain Italian support for the March 19 agreement. At a July meeting of Belgian, French, and

British representatives it was agreed to ask Germany and Italy to revise the Locarno pacts without setting any preliminary conditions.

With no diplomatic solution to the problems of Belgium's perilous international position visible within the framework of collective security, with growing dissension at home, and sensitive to the failure of Britain and France to take strong action against the remilitarization of the Rhineland, the Belgian diplomats began to reassess their policies. The secretary-general presented a carefully constructed position paper early in July. While rehearsing the collapse of collective security and the disruption of international agreements, Van Langenhove asserted Belgium's traditional role was that of a barrier between the powers; her security was based on an equilibrium among them. Belgium currently risked being caught in the middle of a great power war. She should strengthen her defenses, but it was also important that Belgium

practice a policy entirely independent and freed of any exclusive lien... Finally...we must be strong and united at home. For this purpose, it is necessary that our international status be simple and clear, that it cease to be an object of controversy and distrust among large sections of public opinion. Our obligations should be limited to what is strictly indispensable. They should permit us to conserve our liberty of decision until the last moment. Should we fight, it must be evident to all that we do so uniquely for the defense of the country.[42]

He concluded that maintenance of the responsibilities Belgium formerly held under the Locarno treaties was beyond her means and posed excessive risks. Many Belgian politicians were saying Belgium's duty was that of preventing the country from being the route of invasion. Yet Locarno called for more, and if a similar statute were now established, Belgium could be forced to oppose an aggressor even though her territory were not invaded. Such action would make Belgium the focus of a devastating military conflict and subject her to far-reaching internal division. The secretary-general therefore advocated a western pact under which Belgium would assume no obligations but which would guarantee her inviolability.

Van Langenhove's reference to internal division could not be taken lightly. The chambers were at an impasse regarding the military bill, and a survey of the political scene did not offer encouragement. The depression had not strengthened the existing parties while stirring discontent; new militant parties influenced by events in Germany and Italy were also appearing. The *Verbond van Dietsch Solidaristen*, which made its appearance in 1933, advocated a *Thiois* state based on corporative principles which would include all of Holland, Belgium, Luxemburg, and

Frisia. Though the group was not large, the parading of its greenshirts unsettled further the political scene. The *Verdinaso* also forced the larger *VNV*, which was formally organized in 1933, into a more fascist-like stance and stimulated Flemish nationalism.

More serious was the Rexist party. A splinter from the Catholic party, this organization took its name from *Christus Rex*, the Catholic party magazine; it rapidly gained attention through the flamboyance and oratory of its demagogic leader, Leon Degrelle. The party's program was ill-defined but had fascist tendencies. The Rexists were generally understood to stand for the reorganization of the state about a strong executive; this executive would be advised by a corporate council and a council of state which would assist in drafting legislation to be rubber stamped by a weak parliament. The red scare was advertised, as was distrust of all political and diplomatic combinations, particularly with corrupt France. The party's real drawing cards were the mystique of 'faith in the leader', Degrelle's attractive personality, and his ferocious campaign against communists and the 'banksters' and 'rotten garbage' in the government. While the *Verdinaso* and *VNV* had many Flemish supporters, Degrelle drew much of his strength from Wallonia and his native region of Belgian Luxemburg.

The events of past years in Germany, Austria, and France warned the old parties of the danger that could come from the Rex group, and they were dismayed by the outcome of the May 1936 elections. Despite an increase in the number of deputies to be elected, the result of a parliamentary reapportionment, the Catholics lost sixteen seats, the Liberals lost one seat, and the Socialists lost three seats. Meanwhile, the Flemish nationalists doubled their representation to a total of sixteen, and the Rexists won twenty-one seats; the Communists also gained. As in other European countries at this time, the extremist parties were experiencing an upsurge; too, the number of Walloon supporters had decreased while the Flemish representation grew. Most important was the alteration of the power balance which had existed in the chambers since 1919. Heretofore, as the Catholics and Socialists held nearly the same number of seats, the Liberals, although they possessed far fewer seats, controlled the outcome in any close vote following party lines. Now a Liberal-Catholic bloc represented only eighty-six out of two hundred and two votes, and a Liberal-Socialist coalition could count only ninety-three votes. Only an incongruous Catholic-Socialist combination could dominate the chambers after May. Indeed, Van Zeeland at first declined to form a cabinet. When Vandervelde failed, Van Zeeland agreed to try but was balked by inter-party squabbles. Economic crisis seized the country as a general strike, originating in France, spread quickly. King

Leopold III finally intervened, scolded the polticians for their squabbling, and Van Zeeland put together a shaky coalition in June.

The possibility of improved cooperation between any of the major parties was diminished by the rash of political fronts that were formed in the following month. First, a Popular Front made up of Communists, Socialists, Radical Liberals, and Democratic Christians appeared; most of the regular Liberals did not associate with this group. On July 19, the Flemish wing of the Catholic party set up its own front, and shortly thereafter a Walloon Front was organized. On October 8, Degrelle made his long-expected announcement. An agreement had been reached between the Rexists and the Flemish Nationalists. Its basis, according to the Flemish, was the two groups' mutual desire for an authoritarian state and a corporate society; their liking for National Socialist Germany and for Franco; and their distaste for France and the Belgian-French accord of 1920.

Domestic support of Belgian foreign policy also suffered from news of the signing of a Franco-Russian alliance in May of 1935. Although Belgium officially recognized Soviet Russia the following July, the distaste of many Belgians for communism and therefore for the Franco-Russian alliance remained strong. The slogan of 'Neither Rex nor Moscow, but Belgium', a parody of Degrelle's motto, was on the lips of heretofore complacent deputies. Relations with France were further ruffled by difficulties over treatment of Belgian workmen in French border zones and France's refusal to grant Belgium a reduction in tariffs. The strikes stimulated in France by the victory of the Popular Front in May 1936 and which spread rapidly to Belgian cities further disgruntled Belgian governmental circles.

It was the overwhelming need for a strong military bill and the necessary national support for the bill that caused the Belgians to take the final step of abrogating unilaterally the 1920 military accord, even though it had already been declared virtually dead. Disagreement with France over the interpretation of the accord had pushed Belgian thinking in this direction for some time, and disillusionment with the League and the feeble response of the Locarno powers to the Rhineland remilitarization had accelerated the process. It is difficult to establish who the first Brussels officials were to call for a purely independent policy, for many had been moving to this view during the first half of 1936 and indeed for some time before that. Van Langenhove's memorandum summarized the logic of the position and provided a basis on which to operate.

The May elections also had their impact, for they stimulated significant reconstruction of the cabinet. Van Zeeland replaced the controversial Devèze with Lt.-General H. Denis, a technician. The foreign ministry portfolio was relinquished by the premier to the rising star of the Socialist party, young and energetic Paul-Henri Spaak. Though considered a Young Turk with strongly leftist views, Spaak had not spoken out recently on foreign policy. If anything, Spaak had held to his initial neutralist inclinations and not followed the lead of party chief Vandervelde when he became more favorable toward military arrangements with France after the Popular Front had risen to power. Spaak's appointment allowed the Socialists to hold an important cabinet post without offending anti-French Flemish Catholics.

In a July 20 speech to foreign correspondents, which at the time received only limited notice, Spaak insisted that Belgian foreign policy be placed 'under the sign of realism' and that he 'desired only one thing: a foreign policy exclusively and wholly Belgian...'.[43] His participation in the fear of being pulled by France into a distant conflict was evident:

One cannot reasonably ask the nations of a continent to consider with the same realism and sincerity of judgment matters directly concerning them and events which may take place thousands of kilometers away, where the nations have neither interest nor influence.

If no specific decision as to Belgium's course of action was enunciated during the summer months, the trend away from the French connection was more firmly established. At the end of July, Belgium petitioned Eden for British aid in provisioning her army and requested that England take charge of the defense of Belgium's coast, a duty the French had considered as theirs since 1920. In Paris, according to the reports of the Belgian ambassador, there was full recognition of Belgium's drift away from alliance to neutrality and considerable discontent about it in official circles. The populace still thought of Belgium as it had during the Great War. With prophetic skill Kerchove warned that when the French people came to realize that twenty-two years had passed and Belgium had changed, it would 'reproach the Belgian disaffection all the more bitterly because it had let itself be lulled by dreams and illusions and will impute felony and treason to the simple adaptation of our country to modern necessities...'.[44] Spaak replied that the French were themselves the artisans of the Belgian disaffection. The cordial phrases of the French were too clearly contradicted by their actions in economic affairs.

It was not until the end of September that the Brussels diplomats began soundings regarding the sort of guarantee Van Langenhove had described. By this time, Van Zeeland had publicly called for a foreign policy that would reduce the chances of Belgian involvement in any future war. During the session of the League assembly that fall, Van Langenhove and the *Directeur politique*, Pierre van Zuylen, laid the groundwork; the task was appealing to the latter, who had always been suspicious of France and England and held strong preference for a neutral or, at least, an uncommitted Belgium. Talks with the British went smoothly, for good communications had kept Downing Street sympathetic to current Belgian views; indeed the British had already shown receptivity to Van Langenhove's concept of a renewed Locarno.

In meeting with the French, the Belgians stressed the need for national unity and did all they could to dispel rumors that Belgium would put up only a token resistance at her eastern frontiers before withdrawing to Antwerp. Unsatisfied, the French representative argued that a neutral Belgium would deprive Britain of needed air bases, a point that had not been raised by the British. It was asserted that continued and closer staff talks were needed; in this connection French Foreign Minister Yvon Delbos commented that if Belgium should alter her policy France might 'one day envisage the complete abandonment of Belgium to her fate'.[45] As for the Duchy of Luxemburg, its inviolability would be recognized with the proviso that if Germany occupied the duchy without its government appealing for aid, France would have the right to send in her own troops. Though this last point was only indirectly related to Belgium's situation, the French view obviously bore implications for the Belgians.

All this was by way of prelude, for the heart of French objections lay, first, in the view that any reduction of Belgian obligations would be a blow to the concept of collective security. Second, Article Sixteen of the League Covenant required countries to allow passage of troops sent to oppose an aggressor labeled as such by the League; refusal to allow passage would, in the French view, be a violation of Belgian obligations to the League. These arguments were inadmissable at the Rue de la loi. It was believed there that by defending their territory and acting as a barrier, the Belgians were contributing greatly to European security. The French interpretation of Article Sixteen was hotly denied.[46]

There were important figures in Belgium besides the chief ministers and diplomats who advocated a return to a free-hand policy. Foremost among them was the young king, who for some time had been fretting over the French connection and the lack of Belgian military preparedness. Disturbed by the precariousness of Belgium's domestic and international situations and by the threat of a cabinet crisis if Socialist and Flemish opposition defeated the languishing military bill, he sought for the secure political ground his nation had held during the Great War. There is little doubt that he was taking guidance from the policies of his father of twenty years earlier. His chief military advisor was his father's former aide-de-camp, E. Raoul van Overstraeten, a long time enemy of the military accord. Considered the *éminence grise* of Belgian affairs and resented by the ministers for his authority without responsibility to the public, the able colonel had considerable influence on King Leopold III – the full extent of which neither the officer nor the king dared admit at the time. It was Van Overstraeten who actually wrote the declaration abrogating what was left of the 1920 military accord.[47]

In preparation for an October 14 meeting of the cabinet with the king to discuss the military bill, Van Overstraeten drafted a lengthy memorandum emphasizing Belgium's military needs and the importance of national unity which could be gained only through a truly independent foreign policy. It was in the words of this memorandum, save for a few minor additions and the substitution of 'government' for 'sovereign', that Leopold III addressed his ministers, calling for them to unite patriotically to solve the military question. The king declared:

Our military policy, like our foreign policy on which it depends, should aim, not at preparing for a more or less successful war, following upon a coalition, but at keeping war from our territory.[48]

He went on to say that 'an alliance, even if it were purely defensive, would not lead to the desired object . . .'. Belgium would have to bear the brunt of invasion by herself, for help could not arrive in time. Therefore a policy 'solely and exclusively Belgian' was necessary. Public opinion should be convinced that Belgium's military system aimed only at preserving Belgium from war.

Emile Vandervelde, impressed by Leopold's discourse, thanked the king for his intervention and announced that the Socialist party would support a strengthening of the army, including lengthening of the term of service. Joined with Prime Minister Van Zeeland and supported by the cabinet, Vandervelde persuaded the king to publish the speech.

The address was greeted with appreciation but also puzzlement within Belgium. It was viewed as a renunciation of the tie with France, and this interpretation was substantiated by later comments by Spaak. A number of Walloons were offended, and a sizeable section of the Socialist party objected to what it saw as a breach of the collective security against fascism. Varied attempts to trim the cabinet's sails to meet the winds of discontent only led to further confusion. Just what was meant? Was there in fact a sudden change in policy? If not, why the fanfare? Amid accusations and questions, a preliminary vote on the military bill was lost. Further explanations by Spaak and Van Zeeland over succeeding weeks persuaded the doubters that the accord with France was no longer binding and that Belgium was following a truly independent foreign policy; at the same time, Belgium would remain a loyal member of the

League of Nations. The only important change was that Belgium would no longer provide a guarantee *à la* Locarno to France and Germany.

Public opinion shifted to support of a new military bill which set seventeen months as the longest possible term of service, and on December 2 it was passed in the Chamber by a vote of 137 to 43 with 8 abstentions. All the Flemish Nationalists voted against it, but only 16 Catholic votes were in the negative column. In the Senate the vote was 122 to 19 with 6 abstentions. The ministry's clear intent to abrogate the 1920 accord had won the confidence of a great number of Flemish Catholic deputies; their votes, combined with those of the Liberals and the Socialists, insured the safety of the bill.

The support of the Rexists for the bill was an extra dividend not entirely expected despite their calls for a greater army. Once the fear of being dragged by France toward Moscow was allayed, the Rexists had difficulty finding support. Three days after the king's speech, Spaak announced a drive which was described as being against extremists of all persuasions, but which was universally understood as an attack on the Rex party. The Rexists were forbidden to hold several rallies, and when they attempted demonstrations, they were arrested. Within a few months Degrelle was to lose to Van Zeeland by a disastrous margin in a Brussels by-election. His defeat marked a downward turn in the Rexists' fortunes; despite continued agitation, their strength waned in the following years.

The reaction abroad to the king's speech was as great as that at home. Most people had forgotten, or were unaware of, the March 6 Franco-Belgian statement that most of the military accord was no longer in effect, so greatly had Hitler's move into the Rhineland overshadowed other events. Leopold's statement therefore came as a shock and appeared stronger than it actually was. The Belgian emissaries had not been forewarned and were unable quickly to counter burgeoning rumors. Although sympathetic with Belgian views, the British were annoyed by the suddenness and strength of the declaration, which they feared might derail completely the faltering attempts to replace the Locarno treaties. The French complained that the Belgian action was favorable to Germany and weakened French influence in other countries, such as those of the Little Entente. The French press denounced Belgium; Pertinax (the sharp-tongued columnist for the *Écho de Paris*, André Géraud) went so far as to liken Belgium's action to Hitler's breach of the Locarno accords. The bitterness of the attacks was, as Kerchove, the Belgian minister in Paris, commented, the necessary result of the failure of the press to keep abreast of the evolution of Belgian opinion over the years. The French government protested the suddenness of the announcement and Belgium's apparent withdrawal from the League. Some mention was made of possible 'alteration of the political and military dispositions of France'.[49]

This last threat was not of great concern to the Belgians, for recently France had been anything but amenable in economic negotiations and they knew that should Germany attack Belgium it was imperative to their neighbors' self-interest to come to Belgium's aid. Moreover, the Brussels officials insisted that the king's speech did not mean an end to Anglo-Franco-Belgian staff talks occurring under the March 19 agreement. The French tried to force a formal commitment on this point, but Kerchove persuaded them not to worry about statements of principle but rather to allow the staffs to work out technical agreements; were official statements issued, public opinion in Belgium might be so aroused as to prevent even technical staff discussions. Such conversations were attempted; they did not go well, as the French became irritated at what they considered Belgian refusal to cooperate. The French believed that King Leopold III was against them and had directed the Belgian army staff and defense ministry not to divulge any information regarding Belgian plans. By the end of March 1937, French Minister of War General Maurice Gamelin was grumbling about withdrawing his military attaché from Brussels.[50]

It was the charge that Belgium was reneging on her commitments to the League, specifically regarding Article Sixteen, that was bothersome. The Belgians denied all rumors that would have them withdraw from the League and declared their policy of independence did not conflict with Article Sixteen. They refused to debate the interpretation of that article, saying that only the League itself was competent to make final definition. Spaak also avoided replying to a list of questions Delbos had formulated regarding Belgium's future defense, although Kerchove did informally provide some answers. The French were relieved when the ambassador stated:

...it is certain that we shall defend Belgium at the frontier or, if that is impossible, at the Meuse; there can be no question of our retiring to the Scheldt, leaving free passage to the enemy armies.[51]

But it was passage of French troops and accommodation of British airplanes that constituted the main issue. The Belgian attitude toward collective security was revealed in a note drafted by Van Langenhove at the end of October. There he indicated that Belgian views had shifted as a result of the check the League's weak efforts had received in the Ethiopian affair. One level of duty implied in Article Sixteen involved economic sanctions. These were inefficacious and would never save Belgium. A higher level involved warfare, but it could hardly be assumed that countries other than those immediately affected by the aggression and which participated in regional pacts would take that action. 'Even within that restrained limit, Belgium has decided, for her part, no longer to accept such a burden, which surpasses her means of action.'[52] In a similar tone, Spaak told the Belgian lower chamber that if collective security implied that all nations should take the same attitude and obligations, then it was a cloudy ideology unworkable because not based on realities. But if collective security meant that a country should do all it could within its means, then Belgium was supporting collective security.

The Belgians explained their views in talks with other European nations. Any decision of the League Council calling for troop passage had to be unanimous, including the vote of Belgium, whose representatives should, by right, participate in the deliberations. Thus Belgium would be controlling her own fate. From the legal viewpoint, the Belgians held that if allowing troop passage would force their country into war, then the sanction of troop passage was not obligatorily incumbent on Belgium, for all nations agreed that while economic sanctions were obligatory, military sanctions were not. Spaak suggested that further definition of the League Covenant should be made, but 'until such precisions have been given, notably in matters concerning Article Sixteen, we will accept no other interpretation than that which we ourselves will give it in the fullness of our sovereignty'.[53]

Although no agreement was reached regarding Article Sixteen, the dispute with the French soon cooled. The latter had nothing to gain by irritating Belgium further, and anyway the British had already accepted the premise of a guarantee of Belgium without a corresponding Belgian guarantee of Britain. So it was that with the aid of Eden, personally solicited by Van Zeeland, by the end of the year Franco-Belgian relations had improved to the point where France recognized Belgium's independent position and revision of Locarno could again be discussed.

Negotiations with Germany regarding the Locarno obligations made little progress, but in a January 1937 speech Hitler volunteered to recognize and guarantee Belgium and Holland as neutrals, which term was explained to mean independent and impartial. It is Van Zuylen's opinion that this gesture quickened British pressure on France for the two countries to reach a formal settlement with Belgium.[54] The initial document of guaranty suggested by Britain and France was unacceptable to Belgium because it implied a contractual agreement that Belgium would defend her own territory. As in 1922, such wording offended Belgian pride, and so a new formula was reached according to which France and Britain recognized Belgium's determination, so frequently affirmed, 'to defend with all her forces the frontiers of Belgium' and to prevent passage of

BELGIUM
1939

30 MI.

30 KM.

VOORNE

MAAS

SCHOUWEN

OVER FLAKKEE

N

EAST SCHELDT

THOLEN

WALCHEREN

SOUTH BEVELAND

WIELINGEN CHANNEL

Flushing

W. SCHELDT

Terneuzen

SCHELDT

Zeebrugge

Ostende

BRUGES

ANTWERP

A

Lier

La Panne

Nieuport

Koningshi

W E S T

E A S T

GHENT

Dunkirk

Thourout

Thielt

SCHELDT

Malines

FLANDERS

LYS

FLANDERS

MECHELIN

YSER

Alost

BRUSSELS

B R A B

Ypres

Courtrai

Audenarde

Lille

LYS

SCHELDT

H

Halle

Wavre

Tournai

Waterloo

Leuze

A

FLEMISH (DUTCH)

Rotterdam

Mons BERGEN

Soignies

WALLOON

I

Charleroi

GERMAN

NETHERLANDS

Quievrain

FRENCH

Bruges

Antwerp

SAMBRE

Dunkirk

Ghent

Beaumont

Ypres

BRUSSELS

Cologne

Philippeville

Lille

Maestricht

F R A N C E

Mons

Namur

Liege

Aachen

Eupen

GERMANY

Mari bou

Malmedy

Hirson

LUXEMBURG

F R A

Sedan

Longwy

PEOPLES
OF
BELGIUM
AND
LUXEMBURG
1939

50 MI.

50 KM.

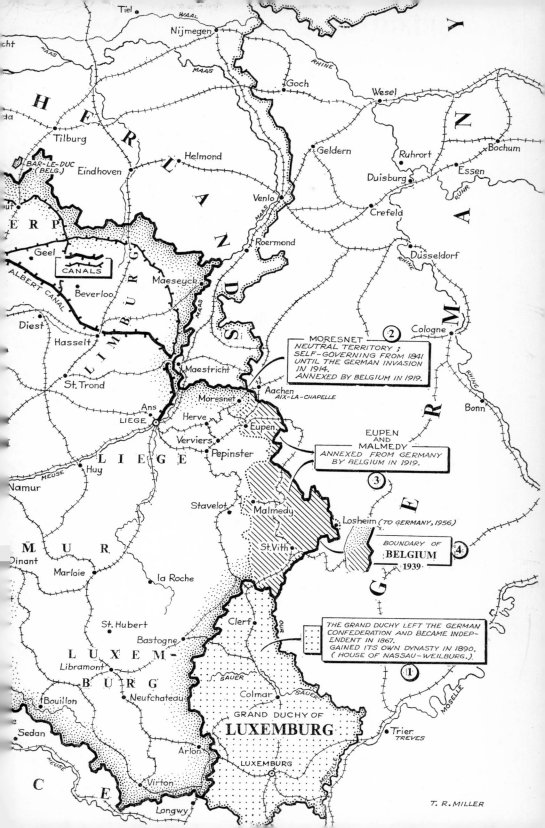

Tiel

WAAL

MAAS

Nijmegen

RHINE

N E T H E R L A N D S

Goch

Wesel

Bochum

Tilburg

Helmond

Geldern

Ruhrort

Essen

BAR-LE-DUC
(BELG.)

Eindhoven

Venlo

Duisburg

RUHR

A N T W E R P

Geel

Roermond

Crefeld

RHINE

Düsseldorf

CANALS

Beverloo

Maeseyck

ALBERT CANAL

L I M B U R G

Cologne

②

Diest

Hasselt

St. Trond

Maestricht

Moresnet

MORESNET
NEUTRAL TERRITORY;
SELF-GOVERNING FROM 1841
UNTIL THE GERMAN INVASION
IN 1914.
ANNEXED BY BELGIUM IN 1919.

G E R M A N Y

Bonn

Ans

LIEGE

Aachen
AIX-LA-CHAPELLE

Herve

Eupen

L I E G E

Verviers

Pepinster

EUPEN
AND
MALMEDY
ANNEXED FROM GERMANY
BY BELGIUM IN 1919.

③

Namur

MEUSE

Huy

Stavelot

Malmedy

M U R

Dinant

St. Vith

Losheim (TO GERMANY, 1956)

BOUNDARY OF
BELGIUM
1939

④

Marloie

la Roche

St. Hubert

Clerf

OUR

THE GRAND DUCHY LEFT THE GERMAN
CONFEDERATION AND BECAME INDEP-
ENDENT IN 1867.
GAINED ITS OWN DYNASTY IN 1890.
(HOUSE OF NASSAU-WEILBURG.)

①

L U X E M -

Bastogne

Libramont

B U R G

Neufchateau

SAUER

Colmar

SAUER

MOSELLE

Bouillon

GRAND DUCHY OF
LUXEMBURG

Sedan

Arlon

Trier
TREVES

MEUSE

C

E

Virton

LUXEMBURG

MOSELLE

Longwy

T. R. MILLER

troops of aggressing nations.[55] The powers maintained their own responsibilities toward Belgium while releasing the small state from the obligations she held under the Locarno treaties and the London accord of March 19, 1936.

If the Anglo-French declaration eased Belgium's position, the need for a renewed Locarno remained strong. During a visit by Eden to Brussels, Van Zeeland suggested that a first step to wider agreement with Germany might be a pact limited to guaranteeing Holland and Belgium. Eden was receptive and the Dutch interested, but Delbos rejected it for fear Germany would never be persuaded to go further. Indebted to the French for the April declaration, Spaak acquiesced to their desire for a treaty covering the Franco-German border. A proposal was launched but allowed to stagnate, as the Germans dragged their heels and the French became increasingly convinced that a treaty with Germany would serve little purpose and might embarrass French relations in the East of Europe.

Concurrent with these negotiations, the Belgians were discussing with Berlin the possibility of some German statement similar to the Anglo-French declaration. The initial suggestion had been German, and when the new Locarno negotiations appeared doomed, the Belgians indicated their interest. They had no desire to offend Hitler; moreover, if Hitler were eventually to break the promise or pact he made, Belgium's moral position and right to demand aid from others could only be strengthened. The drafting of the German statement was delicate. Germany, no longer a member of the League, wished no reference to that organization; the Belgians wanted their obligations to the Covenant acknowledged. The solution was a vague sentence to the effect that Germany 'has acknowledged the public declarations of the Belgian government defining the international position of Belgium'.[56] The declaration, formally issued on October 13, 1937, went on to mention Belgium's independence, determination to defend her territory, and Germany's recognition of Belgium's inviolability and willingness to aid Belgium against aggression. In Belgium, there was some criticism of the clause which exempted Germany from her promise should Belgium be engaged in military action against Germany; yet that point was hardly debatable. To those who criticized dealing with Germany at all, Spaak replied that the October declaration was a natural outgrowth of that of April and of the decision to follow a policy independent of any one group of countries.

10.3 THE THREAT OF AGGRESSION

The course of events in Europe in the years immediately following the king's speech strengthened the Belgians' conviction that their policy was the only viable one. The issues of the Spanish Civil War divided the country. The conservative and strongly Catholic element, if critical of Franco's methods, sympathized with his battle against the 'communist dominated' official government. The Socialists supported the Loyalists and argued that the Spanish government had legal right to purchase arms from Belgium. Spaak was caught between his party and the strong voice of the conservatives. Within the foreign ministry there was little sympathy for the Spanish government; even that little disappeared with the assassi-nation of the young Baron de Borchgrave, an attaché at the Belgian mission in Madrid. Although no final proof was established, the circumstances surrounding the assassination and the desultoriness with which the Spanish government inspected the affair pointed to Loyalist complicity. In response to Spaak's demands, Madrid offered condolences and military honors at the funeral. The government refused to accept responsibility, however, and suggested the matter be submitted to the International Tribunal at The Hague. The case was never heard, for Spain eventually paid an indemnity and Belgium dropped charges.

Throughout the war, Spaak pursued a firm policy of non-intervention, arguing that it was the most efficacious policy for maintaining European peace and stating correctly that any other course would divide Belgian opinion too bitterly to be considered. At the end of 1937, pressure arose from commercial and financial circles for the establishment of official relations with Franco's government, which now controlled a large por-tion of Spain as well as Morocco. Socialist opposition prevented such action, and it was only later that Belgium officially recognized Franco's regime.

A neutral attitude was even more strongly approved by the Belgian chambers in regard to Hitler's annexation of Austria in March 1938. If France and England were to take no action, then it was hardly incumbent upon the Belgians to expose themselves, they thought. Moreover, as Spaak admitted regarding his own views, there was sympathy for the Austrians' economic plight and some belief that *Anschluss* was necessary. The majority of criticism was directed at Hitler's methods, and not too great a point was made of his violation of the Versailles treaty.[57] The Socialists, who might have supported Austria the most strongly, were relatively silent, for they could not forgive the Vienna government its treatment of their political brethren.

No sooner had the *Anschluss* been accomplished than concern began to mount for Czechoslovakia. Obligated by a treaty signed at Locarno to aid that country in the event of German attack, France searched for support in England, Prussia, and then Belgium. After recent statements by Spaak terming collective security in 'full decadence' and indicating he would consider France and Britain invaders if they tried to aid Czechoslovakia by attacking Germany through Belgium, a direct request for permit of troop passage was impossible.[58] The French ambassador therefore approached the leaders of the three main Belgian political parties, suggesting that the 1937 French guarantee of Belgium might be withdrawn if troop passage were refused. Vandervelde, Hymans, and Moeyersoen all indicated they would take the risk and opposed granting the facility.

The Belgian attitude was fortified by word that the Dutch no longer considered themselves bound to accept a League decision to apply Article Sixteen, but only by their own government's views in each case. Sentiment remained strong for reducing Belgian chances of being involved in any way; when the Duchy of Luxemburg suggested the possibility of a Belgian guarantee, Van Zuylen scotched the idea.[59] July brought participation, at the invitation of the regular members, in the meeting of the Scandinavian states in Copenhagen. The communiqué issued at the end of the conference called for a convention on armaments and declared that League sanctions, as a result of existing conditions and recent practices, could not be called obligatory. The French protested the setting of this example for other states, and their secretary-general, Léger, exclaimed that 'Collective security is certainly sick, but is it necessary to take away what little is left?'[60]

During the tense September days of the Czechoslovakian crisis, Spaak held firmly to his policy of independence, convinced that it contributed to the maintenance of peace and was the best chance of keeping Belgium out of war. Reports were frequent to the effect that neither France nor Britain were prepared for a military showdown with Germany, and this had been the Belgian opinion for some time. Spaak, though not consulted by his neighbors regarding the crisis, therefore supported British Prime Minister Neville Chamberlain's actions at Munich.[61] Some concern did develop, as a result of an article in the London *Times* on the internationalization of colonies, that some bargain would be reached with Germany at the expense of the Congo. In reply to a Belgian query, the British indicated they would aid Belgium, should the small nation be attacked in Europe by Germany, in hopes of winning the colony in a peace settlement; but a guarantee of the colony was expressly avoided. It was only after the war that Van Zuylen, in his history of the Congo state, was able to demonstrate that earlier in 1938 the British had indeed been talking about a redistribution of African colonies as part of an overall arrangement with Germany. At the time it was wondered if the British were merely trying to frighten Belgium back into the Anglo-French defense system.[62]

In the succeeding weeks, much of the attention of the Rue de la loi was focused on the questions of aiding the Netherlands in the event they were attacked, and of policy toward overflight of Belgium by foreign aicraft. When, at the end of January 1939, the British urged that Franco-Belgian staff talks be taken up again, their main plea was the need to aid Holland efficaciously should she be attacked. This effort to bring Belgium into the allied camp, as Van Zuylen termed it, was sidestepped by a renewed declaration of Belgium's independence of policy. Paul Emile Janson, Spaak's uncle and replacement as foreign minister in the cabinet now headed by Spaak, emphasized that were the Netherlands invaded, which he doubted would happen, Belgium would defend her own frontiers. The Dutch government, for its part, steadily indicated its wish not to become involved in staff talks.[63]

The Belgian policy toward foreign overflights in time of war was established in a Van Zuylen note of September 1938.[64] Antiaircraft artillery fire and pursuit planes should be employed within reason to prevent their passage. A more efficacious act would be to warn Belgium's neighbors of the passage of planes; but how could this be done if Belgium were officially neutral? He adopted the Dutch solution. As observers would not be certain if the planes were merely in passage or intended to bomb the country, warnings to the local population should be broadcast. Radio monitors in neighboring countries would pick up the domestic broadcast and know what to do. In the days preceding the Polish crisis of September 1939, both Germany and Britain inquired regarding Belgian policy on overflights and were assured that if Belgium were aware of the flights, action would be taken against the planes. The Germans were also assured that should France attempt to march through the Belgian province of Luxemburg, Belgium would resist.

There was no ignoring the steady deterioration of the international situation as 1939 wore on. German seizure of Prague and the tension over the Polish corridor pointed all too clearly toward Armageddon. It was impossible for the Belgians not to make some gesture, futile though it might be, to halt the slippage toward war. On August 21, Leopold called to Brussels representatives of the signatory states of the Oslo Convention for economic cooperation. Speaking for the group, two days later, he issued an appeal to the powers in favor of peace.

Some schizophrenia regarding the extent Belgium should expose herself remained, however. On August 27, Van Zuylen, Van Langenhove, and Prime Minister Hubert Pierlot (Spaak's Catholic successor in February 1939) declined to act on an urgent French request that Belgium intervene at Rome to indicate France was prepared to arrange differences with Italy if the latter could achieve peace. The idea had originated with Pierlot; but while there was opportunity to obtain prestige, especially if King Leopold III acted as arbitrator as the French suggested, the lack of strong British support and the size of the risks involved were discouraging factors.[65] The king, on the other hand, willingly joined with Queen Wilhelmina of the Netherlands in a final effort to achieve peace by volunteering their good offices to those nations quarreling over the fate of Danzig.

On August 27, Pierlot sent out the formal statement of Belgian neutrality in any conflict over Poland to his representatives abroad. The next day, he informed the French and British that Belgium intended to be neutral, but that if attacked she would appeal to them for aid; there is no evidence of a similar note sent to Germany. Assurances had previously been received from all three great powers that a declaration of neutrality would be respected. After the German attack on Poland September 1, Pierlot ordered his emissaries to deliver the prepared declarations; stage C of a five-stage mobilization begun on August 25 was also ordered. On September 3, Britain and France declared war on Germany.

Military preparedness had not been neglected in the months since the passage of the military bill. The seventeen months service meant that Belgian fortifications could be adequately covered throughout the year. Plans for full mobilization called for twenty infantry divisions in addition to troops stationed at established fortresses, plus one cavalry corps – a total of about 650,000 men.[66]

A key problem was the furnishing of munitions. Although a highly industrialized country, Belgium had not paid great attention to her munitions industry since the war. Her immediate reconstruction needs had not included munitions, and the limited level of Belgium's military effort had provided little stimulation in later years. Spaak was aware of the problem and in 1936 asked Britain for aid, pointing out that Belgian factories could produce only a twentieth of her powder needs, no major explosives, and only a small amount of cartridges and aviation fuel. Though the foreign office was inclined to help, the matter became ensnarled in committee discussions; Belgium received a reply only two years later, one which was not overly encouraging. It has been suggested that delay such as this could only confirm the Belgian diplomats' confidence in an independent policy, since close relations with Britain would stimulate domestic debate and apparently would be only small military assistance.[67] It is worth noting, however, that no crash armament program was begun in Belgium. Given the domestic turmoil, the Belgian dislike for military affairs, the fear of attracting invasion with desirable munitions factories, and the small country's tradition of investment in commerce, finance, and other forms of manufacturing, this is not surprising; yet the choice had significance for the entire Belgian war effort.

Military alerts were signalled on several occasions, and at the times of the *Anschluss* and the Czechoslo vakiancrises partial mobilization had been declared. Plans for the distribution of troops had been thoroughly overhauled. At the urging of the king, in turn stimulated by Van Overstraeten, dispositions had been made against possible attack from the South. Indeed, Van Overstraeten had insisted in 1938 that the greatest danger lay in that direction.[68] He was not alone in his fears that France might attempt a preventive invasion, as Van Zuylen's account and many documents demonstrate, although suspicions never mounted to the level held before the first war. It was, of course, true that there were advocates of such action in France. More pertinent to Belgium's stance of neutral independence was the necessity of appearing not to arm solely against Germany. That country had protested on several occasions the imbalance of Belgian defenses; some preparations to the South were therefore diplomatic.

The plan of operations for the East, based on the 1936 military bill, bore the influence of Van Overstraeten and put an end to the program of frontier defense. Difficult under any circumstances, the latter was impossible after the Rhineland remilitarization. It would also have required a penetration of French troops farther into Belgium than time could be allowed for by the French mobilization schedule. The new plan established a forward line along the Meuse from Namur to Liege and thence along the Albert Canal to Antwerp. Ahead of it, only outposts and skirmishers such as the *Chasseurs Ardennais* would be deployed. It was expected that the French would plug the small gap south of Namur. But though based on good terrain and the strong fortifications of Liege, this line was so extended and so distant from French and British reinforcements that in 1939 the main defense line was prepared between Antwerp and Namur. Its heart lay between Koningshoyckt (near Antwerp) and Wavre (to the northwest of Namur), and therefore came to be known as the K.-W. line. Although abandoning half of Belgium to the enemy, it was the most advanced position the generals and the king believed could be defended on a long-term basis. The new plan, then, did not constitute a full scale defense *at* the frontier but rather a defense in depth *from* the frontier; as such it did not contradict the Belgians' promises not to leave their frontier uncovered.

During the crisis in September 1939, Belgian troops were sent to the South and West as well as to positions along the Meuse and toward the eastern frontier. But after the rapid fall of Poland and the shift of masses of German troops to the Rhineland, the Belgians became nervous. Without the knowledge of the ministers, but probably with permission of the palace, Chief-of-Staff General Van den Bergen had been talking discreetly with the French military attaché since early 1938. Little precise had been accomplished, however. In June, the Senate foreign affairs commission indicated it did not believe staff talks conflicted with the policy of independence. Now, at the end of October, in response to an approach by British Admiral Sir Roger Keyes, the king agreed to have Van Overstraeten meet with the British military attaché. The talks were not extensive but did reveal the Belgian defense plan. In the light of future events, Van Overstraeten's answer to a query whether any Belgian retreat would be to the West or South is significant: 'We will pivot about Antwerp, maintaining our left on the Scheldt, no matter what happens.'[69] Beginning in the latter part of November, limited communication also took place with the French military; as little as possible was put in writing for fear of German discovery. Though urged by the foreign ministry, these talks were carried out by the king's office; their end result was a rough, rather than a detailed, undertaking of the nature and speed of allied reinforcement of an attacked Belgium. Throughout, the diplomats were troubled; many believed that the allies might arrange a leak to provoke a German invasion, thus providing justification for France to march through Belgium.

In subsequent weeks there were numerous alarms. One of the most severe was the second week of November. German troop moves, overflights, and passing comments by her diplomats had steadily increased Belgian uneasiness. On November 6, the Dutch queen sent an urgent appeal based, she said, on new information: would King Leopold III join her in a call for peace? The text of the proposed appeal was disapproved by Van Langenhove, Van Zuylen, and Spaak as so neutral as to offend the allies, although Van Overstraeten liked it. A Belgian version was rejected by Queen Wilhelmina, so at Leopold's suggestion, Spaak, the king, and Van Overstraeten traveled to The Hague that night. A new note edited there by the foreign ministers of the two countries was rejected by the king and his general, which two then proposed another version that was eventually accepted and published on the seventh.[70] During the next days, Leopold personally sought the support of other sovereigns.

Reports soon came from Berlin that the German press was suddenly denouncing neutrals. Thought was given in Brussels to shifting to full mobilization; the evening of the eighth the Belgian ambassador in Berlin,

Jacques Davignon, sent word that the papers had gone to print before the arrival of the royal appeal. He advised prudence, and decision was made against full mobilization. On the eleventh, the British requested additional military talks. The Belgians indicated willingness and important conversations were held over the next few days. On the twelfth, the British and French replies to the monarch's note were made public. Fearful that the denunciations of German actions would irritate Hitler, perhaps against Belgium, Van Overstraeten and the king arranged a new royal *démarche* indicating that the monarchs did not consider their mediation task ended.

Though tensions remained high, within a few days it became clear that if Hitler had indeed planned an attack, it had been postponed. But the crisis had brought home the possibility of a German offensive against Holland alone. Surely the allies would demand troop passage and Belgium would be forced out of her neutrality. Despite much worrying, no change in policy was announced. The importance of military preparedness was underlined, and additional effort was directed to it. Since the first mobilization, the king had taken active charge of the military as commander-in-chief. As such, his role had increased, as had that of Van Overstraeten. There is no doubt this was pleasing to both men, who made studious efforts to act in a manner similar to that of Albert in the first war. As aide to the former king, and far more experienced than Leopold, Van Overstraeten exercised much influence, and there is ample evidence that his advice extended beyond the military realm to foreign affairs. The disagreements that arose in the November crisis between the king and his aide on the one hand, and the civil ministers on the other, were minor, but with the benefit of hindsight they appear as preludes of trouble to come.

At the close of the crisis, Van Overstraeten suggested that it was time to revise the appeal to guarantors that had been prepared in the event of need. Prior to the first war there had been much talk of guarantees of Belgian territory before troops were admitted to Belgium. But the German attack had come so abruptly that the matter was not settled in 1914 and required difficult negotiation prior to the declaration of Saint-Adresse. To avoid a similar problem, some promise to maintain the *status quo* of the territorial integrity of both mother country and colony was needed immediately. The king sent his aide to the foreign ministry and a note was worked out. Spaak did not wish to send it for fear the allies would in return ask obligations from Belgium. The difference of opinion had not been resolved when another crisis occurred.[71]

On January 10, 1940, a German light plane made an emergency landing at Mechelin-sur-Meuse. Lost in fog, the military aviators had mistaken the Meuse for the Rhine and then run out of fuel. Taken prisoner, one of them twice attempted to burn documents he was carrying; when their remnants were seized, he attempted suicide. Upon examination, the documents proved to be instructions to *Luftflotte 2* regarding the actions of the Sixth German Army and Seventh Air Division in an offensive across Belgium. Belgian intelligence called Van Overstraeten, who ordered that news of the discovery be revealed only to the chief-of-staff. He informed the king and upon the latter's instructions alerted Defense Minister Denis and the French, British, and Dutch chiefs-of-staff. Military precautions were taken, and the text of possible appeals for aid were approved by the foreign ministry; yet the military refused to reveal to the ministry the reason for sudden concern.

After being kept in ignorance for nearly thirty-six hours, Spaak asked to see the king and was given full information on the twelfth.[72] By this time, the chief question was whether the documents had fallen into Belgian hands by mistake, as was later proven at the Nuremburg trials, or whether Germany was laying a trap. Perhaps Hitler wanted to know how Belgium would respond to attack and would then plan accordingly. Or perhaps he wished to lure French and British troops into Belgium so he would have an excuse for attack. The decision was that the documents were real plans, not decoys.

Van Overstraeten favored secrecy regarding the discovery. But on the thirteenth, Van Zuylen persuaded him that after sufficient military measures had been taken, the wisest course would be to leak the news to the Germans. Belgium's goal was not merely to meet a German attack squarely but to avoid invasion entirely. Though there was reason to fear Hitler might react in anger to the news, more likely he would postpone any attack because the element of surprise was lost. Spaak and Pierlot approved the idea and appropriate plans were made.

That same evening, Van Overstraeten met with Keyes and the British attaché. After discussing the importance of British air support, Keyes left to make soundings for the three guarantees Leopold desired in the event of war: a promise not to make a separate peace; a guarantee to re-establish the territorial integrity of Belgium and her colony at the war's end; and financial aid for restoring the country.[73] Prevented by bad weather from flying the Channel, Keyes telephoned the first lord of the admiralty, Winston Churchill. Somehow the weight and intent of the king's inquiry became confused, and Churchill understood King Leopold to be indicating that Belgium might invite immediate entry of French and British troops if the guarantees were given.

The reply Keyes received on the fifteenth was unsatisfactory. The British argued they could not make promises they might not be able to uphold at the war's end; moreover, the promises demanded exceeded those given France. Britain could only inform Belgium of any peace negotiations, do its best regarding Belgium's territory, and include her in financial plans. Such vagueness, in light of Belgium's experience after the first war and rumors of British willingness to bargain away the Belgians' Congo, was discouraging. What infuriated the Brussels officials, however, was the closing paragraph in which the British made clear that entrance into Belgium prior to any German attack was necessary if their aid were to be of value. When Belgium was doing all she could to avoid war, the British asked for a privilege that would surely invite German invasion. And in return for making Belgium the host of the holocaust, the English equivocated regarding guarantees. Keyes himself was embarrassed and agreed to draft a notice of rejection.

The early afternoon brought an urgent message from Paris. The French, informed by London that Belgium might soon invite aid, had moved troops to the Belgian border the previous night. But in the morning the border was still closed. Now Prime Minister Edouard Deladier had told the Belgian ambassador that the troops could not be kept in the snow and cold of the forward positions for long; they must either move immediately into Belgium or withdraw to the prepared French positions. If Belgium declined to call now, in the future French troops would not move until the Germans had actually invaded Belgium. The shocked Spaak, who was unaware of Keyes' message to Churchill, contacted Pierlot and Denis, and the three demanded a meeting with the king; there it was decided that admission of French and British troops was unthinkable. Keyes' completed draft of the rejection of his government's proposal was approved with minor changes by Leopold. It explained the king was not a dictator and could not impose upon his country the task of serving as a battlefield for others; he had undertaken to circumvent the Belgian civil government in his initial approach only out of a desire to save time. The reply to France was left to Spaak. He telephoned a 'No', and in his following note pointed out that preventive invasion would provoke German attack, destroy the moral force Belgium had gained by her rectitude, harm Belgo-Dutch solidarity, and be ill-timed, as the Germans were probably postponing any action now that they knew their plans were discovered.[74]

By that time, the Germans did indeed know, for Van Zuylen had forced his plan through in a furious debate ending in the early hours of January 16. The cabinet had approved rejection of the French offer but opposed any inquiry of Germany regarding the meaning of apparent plans for an offensive. Within the foreign ministry itself, some officials argued that revelation of the capture of the documents would provoke a hastened attack (which indeed was Hitler's initial reaction). The king and Spaak supported Van Zuylen, and the appropriate orders were sent to Davignon in Berlin. The words of the German reply meant little; far more significant was the lack of action and the news from the habitually reliable contact of the Dutch military attaché that the offensive against Belgium had been postponed.[75]

Another crisis had been survived, but it took its toll. Belgian relations with her two most important supporters had not been improved. British Chief-of-Staff General Edmund Ironside was angry with the Belgians for refusing to make detailed plans in advance and then 'screaming' for help; he cabled his French counterpart to pressure the Belgians and recorded that Prime Minister Chamberlain believed 'the Belgians had no right to put such conditions [as the guarantees requested by Leopold] under the stress of attack'.[76] Both the French and British military were under the impression that the Belgian king had asked for preventive occupation. Although the debate continues, the weight of evidence indicates this was the result of faulty communications, wishful thinking, and some over-anxious hints by the Belgian military, rather than of action by the Belgian king or government.

The French felt betrayed, and in their awkward position soon found it easy to mutter that if the war went wrong, it was all Belgium's fault. The conduct of the crisis within Belgium revealed the growing desire of the military and especially of the king and his chief advisor to take over direction of the country from the ministers, whom they apparently believed could not act decisively enough and were ignorant in affairs involving military defense. This trend was not missed by Spaak, and friction between the ministers and the king began to build. There was disarray, also, within the military. Rumors were rife that the night of January 13 Chief-of-Staff General Van den Bergen had ordered the barricades on certain roads leading into Belgium from France to be raised and that Belgian troops and railway companies had been told not to oppose the entrance into Belgium of French soldiers on trains. Such actions were counter to Belgium's professed neutrality, virtually inviting preventive French invasion, and meant that Belgium's entry into hostilities at that time no longer depended on her wishes but those of France. Van den Bergen argued that Van Overstraeten had approved these orders; this was denied. Minister of Defense Denis therefore sacked his chief-of-staff and replaced him with General Michiels.[77]

The January crisis did provoke increasingly specific discussions between British and French military representatives and Van Overstraeten regarding the disposition of French and British troops should Germany invade Belgium. One result was that Brussels, originally in the British zone of defense, was shifted to that of the Belgians. Attention was also focused on the possibility of a German attack through Holland and on the necessity of military cooperation with the Dutch. Such cooperation proved difficult, for the Dutch plans for troop deployment did not complement those of Belgium and some controversy arose regarding the manner and extent to which the Dutch should commit themselves to defense of the region of the Peel marshes. King Leopold III pressured his sister monarch not to allow her troops to be withdrawn into Fortress Holland, isolated from any Anglo-Franco-Belgian forces. The Dutch insisted that if they were to defend the southern portion of their state, Belgium would have to lend support in front of the Albert Canal. Yet the French were indicating they could probably aid Belgium immediately only at the less advanced K.-W. line. In the first part of April, the Dutch announced they were moving their forces northward.

During the February and March talks it had been decided that in the event of German attack French and British troops would be able to establish themselves only as far forward as the main defense line of Antwerp-Namur. The Belgians were therefore surprised and suspicious of a proposition put before them by the Allies following Hitler's April 9 attack on Denmark and Norway.

About midnight on April 9, the French ambassador and the British chargé woke Spaak to tell him that disturbing information had been received from The Hague. 'It is indispensable for Belgium's security that her Government immediately ask the allied forces to occupy positions... [best suited to the defense of the country].'[78] In answer to Spaak's query, French Ambassador Paul Bargeton indicated these positions would be on the K.-W. line, not farther forward at the Albert Canal. At a 1:30 a.m. meeting which included Spaak, Pierlot, Denis, and the king's secretary, it was decided there was little sense in allowing a preventive occupation which would disrupt Belgium's moral posture, divide domestic opinion, and might provoke German attack; this was especially true if French reinforcements would not be sufficiently advanced to prevent surrender of half the country to the enemy. The decision to reject the proposal was upheld by the cabinet which met later in the morning. To quell rumors in the press, a public reaffirmation of Belgium's policy of independence was released.

On the eleventh, Bargeton informed Spaak, in reply to the foreign minister's questions, that the proposal was not an all or nothing matter – should Belgium later call for aid, the Allies would come – and that the positions referred to were those already agreed upon by the allied commander-in-chief, General Gamelin. Spaak, who held no desire to see the heart of Belgium become the battleground of Europe, thereupon indicated that the cabinet's public statement of the tenth should be considered as the official reply to the Franco-British *démarche*. A little later, the king received a message from Gamelin suggesting that while plans called for French troops to advance only as far as the Antwerp-Namur line, France would do all she could to send troops farther on to the Albert Canal. A similar promise was made by the English on the twelfth to Spaak, on the condition that Belgium open her frontier immediately. The different approaches used by the allies reflected their awareness of the duality of control existing in Belgium. Neither approach worked. As an added precaution in the event the allies should decide on a preventive occupation and in face of reports of French troops at the border near Arlon, on the thirteenth Van Overstraeten made plans for a possible about-face by a few corps should attack come from the South. In despair, he saw Belgium '*in the vice* [*dans l'étau*] of two colossi ready to rush together and pulverize us by their shock'.[79]

Knowledge that French and British troops along the Belgian border were in a state of alert, although no reinforcement of German troops along Belgium's eastern border had been noticed, spurred Spaak to request a reaffirmation of Anglo-French intentions not to enter Belgium unless called. The foreign office complied, although vaguely; the French did so also, but there was no mistaking the annoyance of French Premier Paul Reynaud both over the Belgian decision and the publication of the Brussels cabinet's statement.[80]

The Belgians were irritated also. More than a few believed that Hitler was trying to provoke the allies into entering Belgium to provide an excuse for his own invasion, and that the allies were searching for some propaganda victory to counter Hitler's Scandinavian successes at the expense of involving Belgium in the war prematurely. As one diplomat pointed out, this would be disastrous, for were an affirmative response given to the allied request, 'at the end of the war an important portion of the populace, not necessarily Flemish nor Walloon, could accuse the government of having plunged the country into war; that would be the end of our national unity'.[81]

10.4 WAR AND SURRENDER

The actual outbreak of war was almost anti-climactic after the series of preceding crises. During the last days of April and the first week of May, rumors of attack and indications of German preparation increased. On the ninth, the informer passed word the attack would be on the morrow; in Brussels the German embassy was burning papers. During the early hours of the night German overflights of the Netherlands and the Grand Duchy were detected. Thirty minutes after midnight, communications with Berlin were cut. A few minutes after five, news came of attacks on Eben-Emael and of the bombing of Jemelle; a quarter hour later, Brussels was under bombardment. The ministers, who during the night had agreed not to call for allied help until an attack had actually occurred, now launched their appeal. In Berlin, Davignon was awakened at 5:45 a.m. and summoned to the office of the German foreign minister. Von Ribbentrop presented a twelve page document justifying a preventive German occupation of Belgium and the Netherlands because Germany had reason to believe a Franco-British attack on the Low Countries was imminent and that the little states were not sufficiently decided to oppose it. The Belgian ambassador, throwing caution to the winds, denounced the accusation as a fabric of abominable lies; in his vehement protest there was all the anger of two generations of family effort for peace twice frustrated. In the Belgian capital, when German Ambassador Von Bülow-Schwante requested audience at 8:30 a.m., Spaak interrupted him first to condemn the unprovoked and unannounced attack on neutral Belgium and then to spare Von Bülow-Schwante the task of reading the German announcement of necessity to 'ensure the neutrality' of Belgium, the Netherlands, and Luxemburg by means of arms. The German guarantee of Belgium, the Congo, and the dynasty if no resistance arose, was, of course, not accepted.

The general pattern of German aggression, the trumped-up nature of the German charges, the failure to announce the attack, and the circumstances surrounding earlier crises obviates the need of any discussion of the validity of the German charges. It is interesting to note, however, that while Belgium's neutral independence was maintained officially throughout 1939 and early 1940, far more discussion and planning was undertaken with the French and British than the Germans apparently realized, and certainly more than occurred in the four years prior to the first war.

The planning did have some positive effect in the face of the *Blitzkrieg*'s onrush, but not enough. The rapid fall of Eben-Emael to German paratroopers stimulated Belgian withdrawal from forward positions far earlier than expected; the order for retreat to the K.-W. line was given the night of May 11. Despite communication difficulties, that line appeared well reinforced when on the 14th and 15th the Germans broke through French positions stretching from Namur to Sedan, forcing the allies to abandon the well organized K.-W. line, the flank of which the Germans were turning, in favor of make-shift positions behind the Scheldt.

During the first days of the campaign, the Belgians pressed the French for explicit guarantees of Belgium and the Congo, but despite the personal efforts of Spaak at Paris, the French government avoided any commitment.[82] As the situation grew more serious, tensions between the allies and Belgium and between the king and his cabinet worsened. On the 18th, Pierlot, Spaak, and Denis, who had already shifted many government affairs to Sainte-Adresse, urged that part of the Belgian army be sent south; the king disagreed. Unbeknown to the Belgians, by the 19th the British chief-of-staff and cabinet were prepared to order the British Expeditionary Force to draw south, virtually abandoning the Belgians; Lord Gort, the British commander in the field, however, could not agree to this because of his current troop dispositions and the location of advancing German columns.[83]

On the 20th, General Maxime Weygand succeeded Gamelin as commander-in-chief of the allied armies. By this time, the crushing superiority of Germany in tanks and especially in the air was obvious to all. The necessity of reuniting the allied front led Weygand to propose a double counter-attack at a meeting of the several army leaders at Ypres. Belgian troops were to extend their front to free certain British groups to participate in the offensive. News of the change of plans for the Belgian army irritated the civilian ministers, already annoyed by what they considered the king's pursuit of a personal policy foreign to that of the government.[84]

Failure of the proposed counter-attacks the next two days demonstrated the closeness of defeat. Despite pressure from his ministers to flee, the king chose to remain with his troops. Disheartened by the defection of certain units and by the flight of his ministers, the king reaffirmed his decision to fight until exhaustion at the positions then held on the Lys River. To retreat would only further disrupt the army, already in chaos as a result of forced marches and the decimation of key units, without inflicting damage on the enemy.

By the 27th, the position of the Belgian army was desperate. Exhausted, disorganized, short of supplies, encumbered by thousands of refugees, spread too thin over an extended front, and without access to a railway, it was unable to hold out much longer against the superior German forces. A German breakthrough was imminent and likely to take a great toll in lives of both soldiers and refugees. At approximately 3 p.m. the king informed Van Overstraeten that he had asked Chief-of-Staff Michiels to prepare to send an envoy to the Germans. Citing Albert's delay at the battle of the Yser, the aide suggested waiting until evening. According to the general's memoirs, the king was displeased at the thought of what he considered additional fruitless losses. Van Overstraeten asserts he relaxed his own opposition in the belief that negotiations would take most of the night, thus allowing the allies time to take precautions. To protect this possibility he reworded the note to be sent to the Germans so that it indicated the messenger was not prepared to end hostilities but simply to inquire about conditions for surrender.[85]

When the demand for unconditional surrender was learned at eleven that evening, the king decided it had to be accepted. Already disturbed by the ominous presence next to the king of Henri de Man, a Belgian Socialist of increasing pro-Nazi leanings, Van Overstraeten was shocked when Michiels suggested a ceasefire for four or five the next morning. What of the allies? Should not Belgium hold out a bit longer? The king interrupted his aide to announce surrender would be at 4 a.m. In retrospect, Van Overstraeten wrote:

I was crushed. I no longer recognized the king. For the first time in seven years, he had disregarded my opinion on an important question.[86]

Perhaps in writing this, the officer was trying to enhance his standing with future generations; his reputation is such that his sentences must be taken with a grain of salt. Yet it is interesting that he admitted the *éminence grise* role which he earlier many times denied. As for the king, it was perhaps natural that he turned to new men and relied more on his own decisions after the advice of his former consultants had led to rapid defeat.

To inquiries about the French and British, the king replied that the allies were well informed of the desperateness of the situation; that noon he had sent word to Lord Gort that the Belgian army would have to capitulate to avoid complete disaster. A little later the French had also been warned that the Belgian front was on the verge of collapse.

At four o'clock on the morning of May 28 firing ceased along all but one sector of the Belgian front. The protocol of surrender granted Belgian officers permission to retain their weapons, placed the Chateau of Laeken at the disposal of the king, and declared that all Belgian territory would be immediately occupied.

Then the controversy began.

The Belgian surrender left the British and French in vulnerable positions, from which the British Expeditionary Force was extracted only by the miracle of Dunkirk. Yet the charges of treachery and betrayal levied by the French carried more emotion than truth. Frustrated by repeated failure to stem the German string of victories and guilty of allowing the most serious breakthrough near Sedan, the French were venting their petulance on Belgium not only for the recent defeats but also for failing to fall totally in line with French policies throughout the interwar period.

As the Belgian ambassador at Paris had warned, the French public was all the more angry that events had not gone their way precisely because they had earlier been misled to believe that everything suited their nation's plans.

A detailed analysis of the eighteen day campaign is the task of a military affairs monograph, yet some observations are possible on a more general level. Surrender on the twenty-eighth, given the Belgians' situation, was inevitable. The matter of timing is debatable, but only in terms of hours. If hours could be equated with lives later at Dunkirk, they could also at the Belgian front, where a debacle would have cost many lives among both the disorganized military and the three million civilians crowded into the 1,700 square kilometers of space still unoccupied by German troops. It also should be noted that by the evening of the twenty-seventh the Germans had developed their Menin-Courtrai breakthrough and were threatening the British left; the defeated Belgian army was already unable to shield its retreating allies.

In terms of strategy, the decision to abandon the K.-W. line is significant, for it marked a breach in the planning, based on the pattern of events of the first war, that saw the maintenance of a Belgian national redoubt as essential. That the Belgians did not pivot about Antwerp, as Van Overstraeten said they would, but rather extended their lines to keep contact with the British was in part the result of the nature of the German attack, which pressed from the north as well as from the east; it was also a function of the Belgians' desire to support their allies. Earlier in the crisis they had asked the Dutch not to take a selfish course but to maintain contact with the allies; the Belgians did the best they could to heed their own advice. Perhaps Belgian troops could have held out a bit longer before surrender, and possibly the allies could have been more promptly and fully informed of the decision. On the other hand, serious breakthroughs were occurring at the time, the allies knew the precariousness of the Belgian position, and communications were difficult. No doubt Leopold had also had enough with the orders and advice of allies who were fighting no better than his own troops. His nation had sacrificed much to the war gods of the great powers; in the ultimate extremity the king believed his decision had to be made for Belgium, not others.

In retrospect, it appears that as the thirties progressed, the Brussels leadership came to regard pre-1914 Belgian policy as the proper model for a little country in a vice formed by opposing powers. The Belgians acknowledged more quickly than did the French or British the change from the situation of the twenties. They were not so perceptive in recognizing the differences between 1939 and 1913. Yet most of their decisions made sense. A frontier defense, no matter how much the French wanted it, was impossible; the designation, after the abrogation of the military accord, of less extensive defense lines which the French and British had a chance of reinforcing before the Germans arrived was a necessity. Refusal to allow preventive occupation was consonant with Belgium's tradition of independence and the only course possible if Belgium hoped to exclude war from her borders. Belgium was the only country in Western Europe to have experienced nearly full and lengthy foreign occupation in recent decades. Her population had little desire for a repeat performance, whether her occupants were nominally friends or enemies.

The purely military issue was important. Equally so was the longer-range political issue of Belgium's independent position, and it provided the second focus about which the elliptical controversy regarding Belgian conduct turns. In 1914 and the years immediately following, Belgium's moral status in international affairs could not have been higher, simply because she had been a scrupulous neutral unfairly violated. In 1940 she was criticized for a similar, if not as strictly enforced, neutrality, and her moral position was questioned.

As during the years before the First World War, the Belgians argued they were doing all that could be asked of them in preparing to forbid the use of their land to any invader. But given the nature of Hitler's military machine, all encompassing aggression pattern, and totalitarian ways, how realistic a view was this? Surely a triumphant Hitler would not permit a truly independent Belgium. Nor was Belgium any longer required by international law to be neutral. Was it in her best interest to look no farther than her own defenses, or did her responsibility to western democratic traditions require more? As Léger plaintively put it, collective security was weak enough without Belgium weakening it further.

The Belgians believed they were realistic in viewing collective security as dead. It was the great powers which allowed it to die; there was no reason Belgium should be bound to the corpse just to give it appearance of life. Faced by the threat of imminent war, the Belgians saw their interests as limited. They wished to simplify and to regulate their position in Europe. The French ambassador at Brussels commented in November 1932 that, although participation in international conferences and Hymans' role in the League were flattering, he noticed:

as much in the masses as among the leaders there is a tendency, stronger each day, in favor of a more narrow conception of Belgium's interests. They prefer to let the great powers disentangle the snarl of international difficulties and to confine themselves to the role, perhaps less glorious but more calm, of a power of limited interests.[87]

Belgium's greatest complication, especially compromising because subject to so many interpretations and obviously directed against Germany, was the first eliminated. Other loose ends which could get caught in the war machine of the powers were cut off or transformed so as to be pulled from danger – the Locarno promises, the tentative London agreements, and the commitment to Article Sixteen of the League Covenant. The chief steps were taken not after careful diplomatic preparation but presented as *faits accomplis* in public declarations and thus not so susceptible to revision under the pressure of the allies.

Unfortunately, while the Belgians proclaimed neutrality, many of them did not really believe in it. Their confidence had been permanently shattered by the invasion of 1914; despite their public declarations, Belgian leaders expected far more certainly than they ever had in 1914 a German invasion should general European war break out. The result was only a half-hearted neutrality; the Germans were not fooled, and relations with the French military were promiscuous. The comments of Belgian officials at varying levels, the lowering of the border barriers on the night of January 13, and the sporadic correspondence of Gamelin with Leopold all encouraged the French to believe that in a crisis Belgium would invite entry of French troops before any actual German invasion.

Had the French and British been better prepared and able quickly to reach Belgium's easternmost defenses instead of lines in the heart of the country, it is possible the Belgians might have given more thought to changing their policy. As it was, their friendly neutrality in the face of obvious and total threat to Belgium and her friends only frustrated the French and raised the issue of morality in a different light than the Belgians anticipated.

Early entry of French troops would both have failed to protect all of Belgium, despite French willingness to 'try' to move ahead of the K.-W. line, and would have divided the domestic population against itself. The domestic issue was a legitimate cause for the Belgian leaders to switch to a stance which, they argued, could serve the West in the event of German attack as well as, or perhaps better than, could a Belgium torn by civil strife. Yet out of desire to maintain the impression abroad that they were still controlling events and not wishing to display their country's division and weakness, the Brussels officials failed at the time to make clear to their friends the true nature of the domestic crisis which pushed the king and cabinet to their action; thus they opened themselves to criticism which might have been avoided. As David Kieft has pointed out:

Because Belgian statesmen tended to give their new foreign policy a halo of sanctity by representing it in the most euphemistic language, it was easy to overlook or forget that this policy was a harassed government's response to an intolerable and dangerous situation.[88]

There was another reason besides the domestic crisis for the shift of policy that also received little public discussion. In a time of ultimate crisis, when the military power of states was at play, Belgium could not perform as she had during the peaceable twenties. The path of mediator was, by late 1939, almost completely closed; with the stakes as high as they were, the small country could not demand as much indulgence of the great powers or enjoy as much range of action as a decade earlier. Belgium had either completely to enter the French orbit or to declare her full independence. Given this choice and the nature of Belgian pride it is not surprising that the Brussels officials took the road they did.

Van Zuylen's judgment regarding the initial course of the war is clear, if oversimplified:

The responsibility for the catastrophies which developed falls on France and England, which countries in neglecting to arm themselves in time made the German aggressions possible. A strong France and a strong England would have found us at their sides.[89]

Although Belgium did not switch to the support of Germany, such a statement lends validity to Annette Baker Fox's theorem that small states act to strengthen rather than counter any imbalance of power.[90] But what more could the Brussels officials have done except to turn the country over to preventive occupation and to certain destruction as the site of Europe's Armageddon? Belgium's alternatives were limited and one by one her courses of action were blocked by domestic problems or the attitudes of the powers. Kieft has cogently argued that Belgium 'had no practical alternative' to her policy of independence, especially after it became clear Britain was not yet able nor willing to counter Germany. In his eyes, Britain's failure to strengthen Belgium's hand contributed both to the small country's international crisis and to her domestic crisis, which might have been reduced by the existence of a British arrangement to balance the French connection.[91]

By 1939, probably the only alternative besides preventive occupation and strict neutrality *à la* 1914 was surreptitious planning. The inadequacy of what planning was done and the conflicts it stimulated between the allies and Belgium and between the king and his civil ministers reflected a general weakness of Europe at the time, a lack of far-sighted, skilled leaders.

Leadership in Belgium in the thirties was difficult. The death of King

Albert deprived the state of the one man who could unite all factions. Moreover, the heroic aura that surrounded him almost guaranteed that he could not be replaced. Young Leopold did try to lead, for he carried the blood of his family. Ironically, it was the decisive steps he took which earned him the most opposition: internationally for his 1936 speech and 1940 surrender, and domestically for his decision to remain in the country after surrender. Paul-Henri Spaak showed flashes of his future leadership ability; at the time, he was very young for a politician and did not have the experience or following that additional years would give him. The inability of the chambers to vote military bills and the indecisiveness of many ministers all lead to the conclusion that in the 1930s the Belgian populace really did not want to make decisions.

If the indecisiveness of the great powers, the international and domestic economic crises, and the rise of splinter parties demanding extreme programs unattractive to many Belgians contributed to this atmosphere, it was the linguistic problem that was the dominant factor. It paralyzed any plan of real action; little could be done until it was solved, and there was no way of solving it without splitting the nation further. Thus the 1936 speech, if not some of the later decisions taken regarding Article Sixteen of the League Covenant, served not only Belgium proper but the allied cause as well. Without it and the abrogation of the 1920 accord, Belgium's defenses would have been unmanned and the other democracies that much more vulnerable.

It nevertheless seems true that the preoccupation of Belgian politicans with internal politics was so great that foreign policy and its public discussion sometimes came to be used as instruments in domestic politics rather than as concerns possessing intrinsic importance in themselves. There are few better examples of the connection between internal and foreign affairs than the history of the 1920 military accord. The Belgians' failure to acknowledge this link when the accord was first entered into, and the break in the chain of communication when the decision to abrogate was reached, only point this out more clearly. And if the Belgian diplomats should not have been caught by surprise by the king's speech, so too should the neighboring countries have been better prepared for the change of policy by those diplomats. The fact they were not reflects of course also on their own diplomatic corps; it further demonstrates that for some time in the early thirties the Belgians were successfully carrying water on both shoulders, desiring in part to be active and influential in the allied camp and in part to reduce their commitments. That the most important turn of policy was announced without careful warning and with Belgian attention fixed more on its domestic than its foreign effect, suggests that, by 1936, the Belgians felt a certain separation from international affairs and did indeed hold a more limited interpretation of the role of a small power than thirteen years earlier. As a German diplomat commented in August 1938, '...the desire to keep out of all quarrels dominates Belgian foreign policy...'.[92]

It is evident, too, from the negotiations regarding the revision of the military accord that during the pre-war period relations with France were far less cordial than they appeared on the surface. Part of the trouble lay in the faulty drafting of the original agreement, which with its unsavory clauses and lack of an overall time-limit should never have been approved as it stood. But the chief problem was that of the attitude of France, which nation ever since the time of Talleyrand had insisted that Belgium should lean toward her. The grudging manner with which the French listened to Belgian wishes and their continued insistence on loading the accord with obligations it was not intended to bear, at least in Belgian eyes, meant the agreement separated the two states rather than drew them together. Belgian pride in independence was too strong for any other reaction.

It is often forgotten that for fifteen years France and Belgium also had increasingly sharp differences, as well as agreements, on reparations, economic, and other security negotiations. Moreover, the military accord never represented more than half of what the Brussels statesmen saw as necessary for Belgium's safety. Thus, while the declaration of a policy of independence was due primarily to domestic considerations and secondarily to an international scene that required the small country to pursue a less active diplomatic style, the ending of the military accord reflected also a growing distaste for France, and French attitudes on, purely diplomatic grounds. The policy was not intended as a betrayal of France and Britain but paradoxically to strengthen Belgium's ability to aid those powers in resisting Hitler. Yet the aid France most needed was the right of preventive invasion, and the whole thrust of Belgian policy was not to win the war, but to avoid it.

10.5 Notes

1. Belgium, *Documents diplomatiques belges (DDB)*, vol. II, p. 324, no. 104: 'Rolin report, c. Sept. 4, 1925'.
2. Belgium, *DDB*, vol. II, pp. 511–16, no. 182: 'Hymans note, Aug. 7, 1928', and annex.
3. Terlinden, 'La politique de la Belgique', p. 495. See also Vandervelde, 'Belgian Foreign Policy and the Nationalities Question', p. 669.
4. Hymans, *Mémoires*, vol. II, p. 602.

5. Belgium, *DDB*, vol. II, p. 622, no. 217: 'Hymans to Cartier, *et al.*, Nov. 10, 1930'.
6. *Ibid.*, vol. II, p. 637, no. 223: 'Gaiffier to Hymans, Dec. 27, 1930'.
7. *Ibid.*, vol. II, p. 367, no. 126: 'Vandervelde to Herbette, Nov. 24, 1925'.
8. *Ibid.*, vol. II, p. 647–75, no. 230: 'Hymans note, Jan. 14, 1931'.
9. *Ibid.*
10. *Ibid.*, vol. II, pp. 616–17, no. 215: 'Gaiffier to Hymans, Oct. 17, 1930'.
11. This and following quotation are from *Ibid.*, vol. II, p. 691, no. 236: 'Van Langenhove note, March 1931'.
12. *Ibid.*, p. 695, no. 236, annex: 'Hymans to French ambassador, Feb. 20, 1931'.
13. Kieft, *Belgium's Return to Neutrality*, pp. 41–44. Kieft's review of domestic affairs in Belgium in the 1930s is incisive and was useful in the final preparation of this account.
14. Jaspar papers, 1: 'Gaiffier to Jaspar, Oct. 25, 1933'. Van Overstraeten, *Au Service*, vol. I, *Dans l'étau*, p. 33.
15. Hymans papers, 256: 'Hymans to Herry, Sept. 16, 1933'.
16. Van Overstraeten quotes the king, *Au Service*, vol. I, *Étau*, p. 37.
17. De Broqueville, 'Pourquoi j'ai parlé en mars 1934', pp. 289–298.
18. Belgium, *DDB*, vol. III, pp. 335–38, no. 121: 'Note of Barthou-Hymans interview, March 27, 1934'.
19. *Ibid.*, vol. III, pp. 333–34, no. 120: 'Note of Van Langenhove-Brugère conversation, March 24, 1934'; pp. 342–45, no. 124: 'Hymans-Claudel conversation, April 9, 1934'. Hymans *Mémoires*, vol. II, p. 679. Great Britain, *DBP*, ser. 1A, vol. III, pp. 330–31, no. 211: 'A. Chamberlain to Grahame, May 24, 1927'.
20. Hymans, *Mémoires*, vol. II, p. 680. Van Zuylen, *Les mains libres*, pp. 295–309. Belgium, *DDB*, vol. III, pp. 366–76, no. 130: 'Hymans note, May 23, 1934'.
21. Belgium, *DDB*, vol. III, pp. 366–76, no. 130: 'Hymans note, May 23, 1934'.
22. *Ibid.*, vol. III, pp. 39–48, no. 6: 'Hymans to Gaiffier, Feb. 17, 1933'; pp. 35–36, no. 4: 'Gaiffier to Hymans, Jan. 5, 1933'; pp. 37–39, no. 5: 'Same to same, Jan. 13, 1933'.
23. Belgium, M.A.E. Arch., INDM, loose folder 1918–1940, memorandum in hand of Hymans, dated 1933.
24. Belgium, *DDB*, vol. III, pp. 113–15, no. 29: 'Gaiffier to Hymans, May 8, 1933'.
25. *Ibid.*, vol. III, pp. 269–74, no. 96: 'Van Zuylen to Hymans, Dec. 18, 1933'.
26. Hymans papers, 256: 'Hymans to Minister of Defense, Feb. 12, 1934'. Belgium, *DDB*, vol. III, pp. 297–98, no. 106: 'Van Langenhove note, Jan. 9, 1934'; pp. 326–30, no. 118: 'Cartier to Hymans, March 6, 1934'.
27. Hymans papers, 256: 'Gaiffier to Hymans, March 27, 1934'.
28. This and the following two quotations are from *Ibid.*, no. 256: 'Memorandum entitled "Cooperation Eventuelle de la Belgique et de la France en Cas d'Agression Allemande", March 22, 1934'.

29. Van Overstraeten, *Au Service*, vol. I, *Étau*, pp. 45–49. *Les relations militaires franco-belges de mars 1936 au 10 mai 1940*. p. 22.
30. Van Zuylen, *Mains libres*, pp. 327–30.
31. Belgium, *DDB*, vol. III, pp. 456–60, no. 163: 'Excerpt from *compte rendu* of Van Zeeland-Flandin meeting, Feb. 15, 1936'.
32. *Ibid.*, vol. III, pp. 474–79, no. 169: 'Kerchove to Van Zeeland, Feb. 26, 1936'.
33. *Ibid.*, vol. IV, pp. 67–70, no. 12: 'Van Langenhove note, Feb. 1, 1936'; pp. 76–83, no. 15: 'Lantsheere conversation with Sargent, Feb. 24, 1936'.
34. *Ibid.*, vol. IV, pp. 132–38, no. 41: '*Compte rendu* of March 10, 1936 meeting'.
35. *Ibid.*, vol. IV, pp. 139–40, no. 43: '*Compte rendu* of March 10, 1936 meeting, cont.'.
36. *Ibid.*
37. *Ibid.*, vol. IV, pp. 141–43, no. 44: 'Note of Van Zeeland-Eden conversation, March 10, 1936'. See also Eden, *Memoirs, Facing the Dictators*, pp. 390–94.
38. Rothstein, *Alliances and Small Powers*, p. 110. Kieft, *Belgium's Return to Neutrality*, p. 82.
39. Gamelin, *Servir*, vol. II, p. 215. Paul-Henri Spaak, Belgian minister of communications at the time, doubts any such request was made during the crisis, at least in this manner (author's interview Nov. 1, 1967). This too is the opinion of Van Langenhove (Fernand van Langenhove, 'La crise fatidique du 7 mars 1936', pp. 31–32).
40. Belgium, *DDB*, vol. IV, pp. 147–51, no. 46: 'Kerchove to Van Zeeland, Mar. 14, 1936'.
41. France, *DDF, 1932–1939*, 2nd ser., vol. II, pp. 730–31, no. 480: 'Account of mission of General Schweisguth to Brussels, July 18, 1936'. See also pp. 155–56, no. 97: 'Schweisguth to Maurin, Apr. 20, 1936', and pp. 322–29, no. 217: '*Procès-verbal* of Franco-Belgian meeting of May 15, 1936'.
42. Belgium, *DDB*, vol. IV, pp. 233–37, no. 88: 'Van Langenhove memorandum, July 7, 1936'.
43. This and the following quotation are taken from Spaak's speech as printed in J. A. Wullus-Rudiger [Armand Wullus], *Les origines internationales*, pp. 341–44, appendix IX. At the time, his phrasing was interpreted to refer to relations with France. In his memoirs, Spaak indicates his words were meant to demonstrate to his own party and others that as foreign minister he would not be bound by the views and policy of the Second International (Paul-Henri Spaak, *Combats inachevés*, vol. I, p. 45).
44. Belgium, *DDB*, vol. IV, pp. 257–61, no. 104: 'Kerchove to Spaak, Aug. 25, 1936'.
45. *Ibid.*, vol. IV, pp. 313–20, no. 126: 'Kerchove to Spaak, Oct. 13, 1936'.
46. *Ibid.*; also, pp. 294–96, no. 120: 'Van Langenhove and Van Zuylen interview with Malkin, Sept. 22, 1936'; pp. 297–305, no. 121: 'Same with Massigli, Sept. 24, 1936'; pp. 305–7, no. 122: 'Van Langenhove talk with Massigli, Oct. 1, 1936'; pp. 307–8, no. 123: 'Same with same, October 3, 1936'. Also Van Zuylen, *Mains libres*, pp. 365–68.

47. It is interesting to note that Gamelin in his memoirs termed the Belgian aide 'all powerful' (*Servir*, vol. III, p. 160), while British Chief-of-Staff General Edmund Ironside made the mistake in 1940 of believing Van Overstraeten to be his counterpart (Ironside, *Time Unguarded*, p. 241: 'Diary entry of Apr. 1, 1940').

48. The official English translation of the speech may be found in *Belgium: The Official Account of What Happened 1939–40*, pp. 53–56, appendix I. The French text as found in Belgium, *DDB*, vol. IV, pp. 323–29, no. 128: 'Oct. 15, 1936', should be compared with Van Overstraeten's memorandum in his *Au Service*, vol. I, *Étau*, pp. 65–67.

49. Belgium, *DDB*, vol. IV, pp. 331–34, no. 131: 'Kerchove to Spaak, Oct. 15, 1936'; see also pp. 341–43, no. 137: 'Same to same, Oct. 16, 1936', and pp. 335–36, no. 132: 'Cartier to Spaak, Oct. 15, 1936'. Also Fernand van Langenhove, 'À propos des relations militaires franco-belges, 1936–1940', *Revue belge de philologie et d'histoire* (1969), pp. 1211–13. The apparent suddenness of the announcement has also led some historians, both at the time, and later, to interpret Belgium's actions in 1936 as reflecting almost solely the king's view. *Cf.* Binion, 'Repeat Performance: A Psychological Study of Leopold III and Belgian Neutrality', *History and Theory*, VIII, no. 2 (1969), pp. 213–59. Binion's argument that Belgium's policy 1936–40 was the result of a neurotic king's desire to relive and alter the tragedy of Küssnacht, where Queen Astrid was killed in a car accident while the king was driving, does not give sufficient weight to the circumstances of the military accord's creation, the efforts of the foreign ministry over several years, and the domestic situation in Belgium.

50. France, *DDF, 1932–1939*, 2nd ser., vol. IV, pp. 427–30, no. 255: 'Laroche to Delbos'. Belgium, *DDB*, vol. IV, pp. 402–7, no. 160: 'Kerchove to Van Langenhove, Oct. 30, 1936'; pp. 518–23, no. 206: 'Kerchove to Spaak, Mar. 6, 1937'. The decrease in frequency and detail of Franco-Belgian staff contacts from 1935 through 1938 is outlined in *Les relations militaires*, pp. 28–35.

51. Belgium, *DDB*, vol. IV, pp. 408–14, no. 161: 'Kerchove to Spaak, Oct. 31, 1936'.

52. *Ibid.*

53. Belgium, *Annales parlementaires*, Chambre des representatives, p. 318, Dec. 2, 1936.

54. Van Zuylen, *Mains libres*, p. 383.

55. Belgium, *DDB*, vol. IV, pp. 564–65, no. 227: 'Laroche to Spaak, Apr. 23, 1937'.

56. *Ibid.*, vol. IV, pp. 604–5, no. 247: 'Von Neurath to Davignon, Oct. 13, 1937'. See also: Davignon, *Berlin 1936–1940*, p. 65; U.S.A, *DGP*, ser. D, vol. V (1953), pp. 631–32, no. 473: 'State secretary to embassies, Sept. 24, 1937'.

57. U.S.A., *DGP*, ser. D, vol. V, pp. 647–69, no. 490: 'Richthofen to foreign ministry, Mar. 18, 1938'.

58. Miller, *Belgian Foreign Policy*, p. 255.

59. Belgium, *DDB*, vol. V, pp. 68–70, no. 15: 'Van Zuylen note, Apr. 11, 1938'.
60. *Ibid.*, vol. V, pp. 93–97, no. 26: 'Le Tellier to Spaak, Sept. 10, 1938'.
61. Interview with M. Spaak, Nov. 1, 1967.
62. Belgium, *DDB*, vol. V, pp. 130–36, no. 43: 'Cartier to Spaak, enclosing note of Lantsheere-Strang interview, Dec. 12, 1938'. Van Zuylen, *L'Échiquier congolais*, pp. 498–503.
63. *Les relations militaires*, pp. 64, 90.
64. Belgium, *DDB*, vol. V, pp. 102–4, no. 30: 'Sept. 13, 1938'.
65. *Ibid.*, vol. V, p. 308, no. 128: 'Le Tellier to Pierlot, Aug. 27, 1939'; p. 309, no. 129: 'Van Zuylen note, Aug. 27, 1939'.
66. *Belgium: The Official Account*, p. 11.
67. Kieft, *Belgium's Return to Neutrality*, pp. 165–6.
68. Van Overstraeten, *Au Service*, vol. I, *Étau*, p. 82.
69. *Ibid.*, p. 133. Despite frequent Belgian statements of this nature, in fact orders issued to the III Corps called for three divisions to retreat, if necessary, in a line which provided for a link-up with French reinforcement coming from the South and East, rather than withdrawing directly toward Antwerp. This reveals that what brief contacts there were had made the Belgian military sensitive to French fears of Belgian withdrawal north-east to Antwerp (Marnay, 'La politique militaire de la Belgique en 1939–1940', *Revue générale belge* [May 1960], p. 15 and *Les relations militaires*, pp. 34–35, 86–87).
70. Van Overstraeten, *Au Service*, vol. I, *Étau*, pp. 144–47. Spaak, *Combats*, vol. I, pp. 69–70.
71. Van Overstraeten, *Au Service*, vol. I, *Étau*, p. 162. A well balanced account of the January 10, 1940, crisis may be found in *Les relations militaires*, pp. 102–14.
72. Van Zuylen, *Mains libres*, p. 523. The annoyance this secrecy caused within the foreign ministry and the hindering effect it had on diplomatic work is revealed in Davignon, *Berlin*, pp. 199–205.
73. Van Zuylen, *Mains libres*, pp. 525–28. Van Overstraeten, *Au Service*, vol. I, *Étau*, pp. 175–77.
74. Belgium, *DDB*, vol. V, pp. 459–61, no. 214: 'Le Tellier to Spaak, Jan. 15, 1940'; pp. 465–67, no. 220: 'Le Tellier to Daladier, annex, Jan. 17, 1940'. Van Overstraeten reproduces the king's note in *Au Service*, vol. I, *Étau*, p. 181. On the sixteenth, the embarrassed king asked Spaak to 'cover' him by obtaining a written statement from Keyes to the effect that the king had not asked for the entry into Belgium of British or French troops (Spaak, *Combats*, vol. I, 75–77).
75. Throughout this period, the Dutch attaché in Berlin had contact with an informer whose identity remained unknown to the Belgians until the war's end. He was General Oster, of the German *Abwehr* (counter intelligence). His information was nearly impeccable, but because the West was not aware of how frequently Hitler changed his mind regarding the day of attack, Oster's information was not considered as reliable as it actually was (Davignon, *Berlin*, p. 232).

76. Ironside, *Time Unguarded*, pp. 206–7: 'Diary entry of Jan. 14, 1940'.
77. Van Overstraeten, *Au Service*, vol. I, *Étau*, pp. 191–92. Capelle, *Au service du roi*, vol. I, p. 151.
78. Belgium, *DDB*, vol. V, pp. 478–82, no. 228: 'Spaak memorandum of talks with Bargeton and Avelin, Apr. 11, 1940'. *Les relations militaires*, pp. 124–29.
79. Van Overstraeten, *Au Service*, vol. I, *Étau*, p. 228. See also Van Zuylen, *Mains libres*, p. 542.
80. Belgium, *DDB*, vol. V, pp. 482–83, no. 229: 'Spaak to Le Tellier and Cartier, Apr. 13, 1940'; pp. 483–84, no. 230: 'Le Tellier to Spaak, Apr. 13, 1940'; pp. 485–88, no. 231: 'Cartier to Spaak, Apr. 14, 1940'.
81. *Ibid.*, vol. V, p. 493, no. 233: 'Lantsheere-Strang interview, Apr. 17, 1940'. The revelations contained in Gamelin's memoirs concerning the decision made by the Anglo-French Supreme Council on April 9 to search for a preventive occupation of Belgium, joined with documents located in Germany, indicate that Belgian suspicions were founded (Gamelin, *Servir*, vol. III, pp. 317–19). British Chief-of-Staff Ironside had for some time insisted that should Belgium be invaded, Britain should bomb the advancing columns without awaiting Belgian permission (Ironside, *Time Unguarded*, p. 109: 'Diary entry of Sept. 18, 1939').
82. Van Overstraeten, *Au Service*, vol. I, *Étau*, pp. 265, 27.
83. Ironside, *Time Unguarded*, p. 320: 'Diary entry of May 19 and editor's note'. See also Kennedy and Landis, *The Surrender of King Leopold*, pp. 13–15.
84. Van Overstraeten, *Au Service*, vol. I, *Étau*, p. 296.
85. *Ibid.*, pp. 341–44.
86. *Ibid.*, p. 349.
87. France, *DDF, 1932–1939*, 1st ser., vol. I, pp. 650–51, no. 293: 'Corbin to Herriot, Nov. 3, 1932'.
88. Kieft, *Belgium's Return to Neutrality*, p. 187.
89. Van Zuylen, *Mains libres*, p. 393.
90. Fox, *The Power of Small States*, p. 187.
91. Kieft, *Belgium's Return to Neutrality*, p. 187.
92. U.S.A., *DGP*, ser. D, vol. V, p. 656, no. 496: 'Von Bargen to foreign ministry, Aug. 31, 1938'.

11. Nationalism and internationalism

The collapse of Belgium's defensive effort in 1940 and the internecine feuding during the long years of occupation severely scarred Belgium's national unity. Few people realized the true depth of the wound until the battle of the royal question unfolded in all its agony. The eventual closing of debate on that issue did nothing to soothe lacerated sensitivities and to reunite the severed tendons of Belgian society. Rather, Flemish-Walloon enmity was reinforced and, despite agreement on state support for church schools, a wide breach remained between conservatives and radicals.

It was against this background of continuing national discord that the Belgian diplomats launched upon a policy of far-reaching internationalism. It was a wise course, for it corresponded to the existing state of international affairs and was perhaps the only path that could arouse sympathy rather than controversy among the Belgian populace. Moreover, it provided Belgium a position of importance as a leader of an Europeanization movement at the time when polarization of the world power struggle between the United States and Soviet Russia had finally removed Belgium from the geographical center of conflict. It was ironic that just as Belgium's policies began to bear fruit the crisis of granting independence to the Congo shocked and awakened nationalistic susceptibilities, causing a revulsion from Belgium's previously favorable attitude toward the United Nations. The emergence of Gaullist France and the ensuing weakening of the North Atlantic Treaty Organization and of the Europeanization movement further strengthened the arguments of those Belgians favoring a more nationally-oriented policy. Yet because the best national course still remained that of European cooperation, if not as close alignment with the United States and the United Nations as heretofore, no serious division of opinion resulted. By backing the European integration movement and, at the same time, being critical of certain American and United Nations actions, the Belgians managed to implement their pro-Western sympathies while demonstrating their intention of maintaining a Belgian policy independent of both France and the United States.

Interesting as are the problems of the post Second World War era, it is impossible to examine them in quite the same manner as those of earlier years. Good documentary material is still scarce; indeed, it may be wondered how much will ever be available, for in this age of jet and electronic communication more and more affairs are settled orally. On the other hand, the press, official communiqués, and United Nations publications present an insuperable mountain of verbiage which, though at times enlightening, is often confusing and is nearly always characterized by that hallmark of a politician's skill, the capacity to tell little while saying much. Then there is the matter of perspective. In several instances, for example the Congo crisis and Charles de Gaulle's policies in France, not enough time has passed to allow anything more than merely preliminary evaluations of the Belgian response. In other instances, such as judgment of royal and ministerial policies during the war, the issues are so complex and so clouded by the Fleming-Walloon controversy that again the historian finds himself on uncertain ground. A detailed analysis thus seems fraught with difficulties. But one can attempt to find a path through the maze of events, to link the high spots, and perhaps to provide some pattern of order that will satisfactorily set Belgium's post-war policies in the context of her previous diplomatic history.

11.1 WARTIME POLICY AND LEOPOLD III

The controversy roused by Leopold III's surrender was acerbated by his decision to stay in the occupied country and by his actions there during the remainder of the war. The nuances of the conflicts between the cabinet and the king and within the cabinet itself are still not clear and perhaps never will be. Yet a rough outline can be sketched. The latent differences between the parliamentarily responsible ministers and the king, which came into the open after the French defeat at Sedan, turned both upon the military issue of which direction the retreat should take and upon the political implications of the king's possible capture. It was something of a shock to the ministers, still hoping for a relatively prompt allied victory, to discover that the king was contemplating remaining in Belgium. Such a course raised serious constitutional questions, for did not government responsibility rest with the elected ministers and not with the king? How could he act without being 'covered' by ministerial approval? Would this be treason? As valid as was the first issue, the second was more the result of an emotionally supercharged situation. In retrospect, it appears that Leopold was, correctly, not as convinced as his ministers as to the eventual outcome of the war and was sure that if the allies did win, it would not be immediately. There was more than a little similarity between his attitude and that of King Albert in 1916. While the war continued, Belgium would need whatever shield she could get from the full weight of the oppressor's heel. But this argument probably took the fore only later. At the time, the young king was obsessed with his responsibility as commander-in-chief and as the symbol of national spirit. German propaganda had incessantly suggested that while Belgium was bleeding to death, the national leaders were flying to irresponsible security in England. To counter the mounting effects of these charges, King Leopold III declared on May 25 that 'Officers and Soldiers, whatever happens, my fate shall be yours.'[1] The king may have believed that his presence during the occupation might help counter the expected efforts of the Germans to destroy national unity by pitting Fleming against Walloon through revival of the policies which had this effect during the earlier occupation. Yet Leopold's main concern was to show that he was one with the peoples of his realm. No doubt, too, the memory was strong in his mind of his father's stay with the troops while the ministers squabbled at Sainte-Adresse.

On May 24, 1940, Prime Minister Pierlot, Foreign Minister Spaak, and the other cabinet members decided to leave the country and begged Leopold to join them. According to Pierlot's account of the meeting, Leopold believed that if he left Belgium, he would never return. France would soon surrender; continued Belgian resistance could in no way help the British who would not be continuing the war on the Continent but rather on the seas. Belgium would have limited independence for many years, and it was his duty to help her maintain some form of national life. When the ministers questioned the constitutionality of the king's role if the ministers should maintain their government in exile and continue the war effort in contradiction to the king's views, Leopold had no answer.[2] Constitutional experts were later to argue for years whether Leopold's surrender was that of head of state and bound the country as a whole or whether it was as commander-in-chief and affected only the armies. Certainly the document was not countersigned by a minister, but if the king were acting solely as commander, was a counter-signature necessary? The ambiguities of the constitution and the conflict between monarch and ministers over defense matters, which had flared sporadically over the past century, thus again came to the fore at a time of utmost crisis.

Spaak later announced that the ministers 'found the King's arguments foolish, crazy, worse, criminal ... because we were appalled to see that his moral sense had collapsed, because we found ourselves in the presence of a case of physical and moral failure'.[3] Spaak and Pierlot's vilification of the king reached its height a few hours after French Premier Reynaud's announcement and denunciation of the Belgian surrender. Reynaud painted Belgium so black that in order to spare their country the odium being heaped upon it, to assure the support of the allies at a peace conference were they rapidly to gain victory, and to preserve the sympathies of the host nations to thousands of Belgian exiles, the ministers had to go far to demonstrate that the king was a maverick and that the Belgian nation itself continued to oppose the enemy. The word treason passed the lips of many; a rump parliament meeting at Limoges on May 31 repudiated the surrender made without ministerial approval and passed a decree stating that the occupation placed the king in a situation in which it was impossible for him to reign. This was close to an act of deposition, and it probably would have been, had there been enough members of parliament present to make the session legal.

Ironically, by the time the parliamentarians had a chance officially to voice their disapproval of the king's act, the ministers who had stirred them to this demonstration were having second thoughts. Though Leopold had implied he would treat with the enemy, thus far he had not. Perhaps dissuaded by the ministers' opposition, the advice of jurists, or the German demand for unconditional surrender, he instead sealed himself off as a prisoner of war in his palace at Laeken. As such, he became the focus of national spirit and even a symbol of resistance. Within the shattered country it was openly acknowledged that surrender had been the only viable course. The crucial factor in the ministers' shift of opinion was the sudden collapse of France. Spaak and Pierlot had refused to consider such a possibility; the king, always better informed in military affairs, had grasped the significance of the German *Blitzkrieg* more quickly than the civilians.

Spaak and Pierlot had pinned their hopes on France; they had little confidence in Britain's chances for a conquest of the Continent. Following Petain's accession the ministers started to flee to North Africa. When it became clear that French resistance would not continue there, the Belgians returned to Bordeaux to debate whether or not to go to England. After a lengthy discussion, Spaak and Pierlot declared that the Belgian government should, like that of France, abandon the struggle. On June 18 and 19 the exiles asked the Argentine legation in Switzerland and also the Vatican to convey to Brussels their view. They had come to France to continue the war, but as France had ceased to fight,

Belgians within that country should cease also. The government believed:

that the fate of the Belgian officers and soldiers should be identical to that of the French officers and soldiers,...that the Government will resign as soon as the fate of the Belgian soldiers and refugees in France shall have been settled in order to facilitate probable peace negotiations between Germany and Belgium.[4]

On June 26, Pierlot wrote Leopold saying that the government thought the return of Belgians now in France and the conditions of an armistice or convention regarding Belgium should be negotiated with Germany. He asked the king's advice and volunteered to resign his post.

Not all the cabinet agreed with its leaders. Minister of Finance Camille Gutt and Minister of Colonies Albert de Vleeschauwer had their doubts. The latter was sent to London to act, not as colonial minister, but as administrator-general of the Belgian Congo and Ruanda-Urundi – an obvious step in excluding the African territories from any metropolitan surrender. The leading opponent of the cabinet's decision was Minister of Health Marcel-Henri Jaspar, who was true to his name in being fiercely independent. He quickly traveled to London and on his own attempted to continue the Belgian war effort, despite the repudiation of his colleagues who declared him no longer part of the government.

Leopold, when he received the minister's approach, gave it a cold shoulder. 'The King takes part in no political act and does not receive politicians.'[5] The Germans for their part announced that members of the exile government could not return to Belgium. These developments, joined with time in which to regain their spirits, the pleas of De Vleeschauwer and Gutt, and the needling speeches of M.-H. Jaspar led Spaak and Pierlot to change their minds. Life at Vichy became intolerable. An attempt to flee to America miscarried; after a painful sojourn in Spain Spaak and Pierlot struggled to London in October 1940.

They had been preceded by Gutt, who worked ardently at reunifying the Belgian exile camp behind the noble and symbolic figure of the prisoner of Laeken. Haste was made to win the sympathy of the Unites States, and Gutt and Pierlot soon traveled to Washington. Georges Theunis, serving as a special ambassador, in 1941 persuaded the New York State Supreme Court to issue an attachment against the over two million dollars worth of gold held in that state by the Bank of France. This sum was approximately equivalent to the amount sent for safe keeping to France by Belgium before the invasion. Contravening Belgian instructions that in an emergency the funds should be transferred to London, the French had sent them to Dakar, from whence the Germans had transmitted them to German banks under the legal fiction of a Belgian account.[6]

The gain of this sizeable amount of gold enabled the exile government to finance the creation of Belgian military and naval units which fought alongside British forces. These units were manned by refugees and by Belgian nationals drafted from their domiciles in unoccupied countries. Nearly three dozen Belgian merchant ships were also donated to the allied war effort.

The greatest Belgian contribution came from the Congo. Large supplies of gold, cobalt, uranium, copper, tungsten, palm oil, and rubber were provided the allies. Some difficulties did develop because the United States was willing to pay higher rates than the British Commonwealth, and the Congo industrialists became disturbed at the difficulties they met in purchasing the machinery necessary for expansion of production. In June of 1942, an Anglo-Congo trade agreement was renewed for three months with the view that it would be superseded by an American-British-Congolese treaty. The tripartite agreement never got beyond the drafting stage, and efforts were abandoned in 1943 when it appeared that the various problems had been met by existing arrangements. To facilitate matters, however, an informal Tripartite Supply Committee was established. An important secret accord was additionally reached in December 1944 for the sale of Congo uranium to the United States.

The Congo's contribution to the war effort was not solely economic. Despite advice from Leopold to be cautious, Pierre Ryckmans, the governor-general, agreed with the aggressive views of Renkin during the first war. Though there was no danger of attack, the *Force publique* was mobilized and at the beginning of 1941 it marched across the Sudan to attack the new Italian colony of Abyssinia, although Belgium was not formally at war with Italy. There was little thought of reviving Leopold II's dream of a Belgian belt across the continent (in the late 1890s he had come close to winning nominal control of Ethiopia), but decisive Congolese victories at Asosa, Gambela, and Saio did much to break the Italian hold on the area. Subsequently, a second army was formed to operate against French colonies under the control of the Vichy government; the change in loyalties of these areas after the allied landings in North Africa made Congolese action unnecessary.[8]

Despite the Belgians' success in persuading the United States to turn over French gold, they could not cajole the British and Americans into taking another greatly desired step: relaxation of the continental blockade to permit the feeding of the hungry peoples in the conquered country. The issue was difficult, as Gutt admitted in a speech at the Hotel Astor:

Naturally the English blockade is a combat arm and we would not want to weaken it; but we would explore and test what can be done, without weakening it, in the way of feeding our children and our sick.[9]

Some relief was obtained thanks to Herbert Hoover's National Committee on Food for the Five Small Democracies. Yet this aid was limited and in no way comparable to that provided by the C.R.B. during the first war. There were many reasons for this; some of the most important were the negative attitude of German authorities, the early involvement of the United States in the conflict, the lack of shipping and the threat of German U-boats, and the loss of sympathy resulting from the circumstances of Belgium's surrender.

Throughout the war, Spaak endeavored to maintain the operations of the foreign ministry as best he could. For the most part he had to be content to sit below the salt at the Anglo-American table and be grateful for what titbits of information and consultation he could glean. There was a tiff with the Russians in May of 1941 when Stalin, in an effort to improve his relations with Hitler, withdrew his recognition of the *émigré* government. Ties were renewed a few weeks later after Hitler's attack on the Soviet state. Another incident developed in the first weeks of 1944 when the Americans were slow to join the British in discussing with Spaak and Pierlot plans for control of Belgian civil affairs after the projected allied invasion. Apparently the delay was connected in some way with U.S. President Franklin D. Roosevelt's reluctance to grant supreme authority in France to General Charles de Gaulle, whom the Belgian ministers had early recognized. Such irritations were the predictable lot of an exile government; Spaak endured them well and even found opportunity to build imaginatively for the future.

While the foreign minister was working in collaboration with the allies, the king was playing a more clouded role. To his current and future critics, Leopold's actions appeared treasonable; for his supporters they constituted a reasonable course of behavior. Leaving polemics aside, it may be said that the king's performance can best be understood as that of a man who, as he publicly stated, saw his duty to be that of safeguarding the unity and interests of his country no matter what the outcome of the war.

In the later debate over Leopold's attitude much was made of a note sent by the king's *chef de cabinet*, Louis Frédéricq, to Belgian ministers in Switzerland and France. The message, intended to be relayed to De Vleeschauwer, was written in response to the administrator's announcement that Congolese forces would participate in allied attacks against Italian possessions. The gist of the royal view was that the Congo risked much in becoming involved, particularly regarding Italy, with which country Belgium was not and never had been at war. A defensive attitude was more proper; troops should not be sent into foreign territory. A circular telegram sent out by the Belgian minister at Berne a week later appeared even more concerned with restricting the activity of Congolese troops so as not to offend the axis. Once more the king seems to have been drawing guidance from the past; in any case the similarity of the king's cautious advice to the views defended by Davignon and Beyens during the previous war invalidates the charge of collaboration if not that of appeasement. It is significant that the king, despite his statement that he would not take a political role, did decide to give this political advice at the time the Belgian exile government was at its worst disarray.[10]

Far greater controversy revolved about the king's visit to Hitler at Berchtesgaden on November 19, 1940. Some accused Leopold of soliciting the interview by way of his sister, Princess Marie-José of Piedmont; this the king denied. According to German documents published in 1961, the Führer in an interview with the princess made the initial suggestion of a meeting. Marie-José, however, admitted she was primed to bring up the matter; she said her brother was willing to traval incognito to any location Hitler suggested. The princess spoke from notes concerning her brother's views regarding the Congo, and she expressed her own desire for the early release of Belgian prisoners of war. The dictator for his part agreed to set an interview and said Leopold 'had acted in a very manly way and very wisely by remaining with the Army and in the country'.[11]

There are several conflicting accounts of the famous meeting. It began in a strained atmosphere which deteriorated rapidly. To Hitler's inquiry, Leopold replied he had no personal requests. The implication was that he wished to discuss national political matters, but it was Hitler who first brought up the status of German-Belgian relations. The king promptly inquired if Germany would guarantee Belgium's independence in the coming period of peace. Hitler refused to be precise, but he did imply that while Belgium could not have independent foreign and military policies, some measure of domestic independence might be granted. The Führer resisted Leopold's prodding and irritably rebuffed the king's requests concerning provisions and Belgian prisoners of war.[12] Following the conversation, an awkward tea was held, at which the discouraged king was so withdrawn that he failed to reply to Hitler's statement that after the war Belgium might be granted the territory of Calais and Dunkirk (this perhaps to compensate for the regions of Eupen, Malmedy, and Saint-Vith, which Hitler had reattached to Germany).[13]

The implications of the interview for subsequent debates over Leopold's right to remain on the throne after the war were far reaching. They would have been even more so were it known that Leopold had asked (and been denied) permission to form 'a small army of from 10 to 15 thousand men who would be armed with rifles only, so that it would be available to the Belgian Government as a ready instrument at the conclusion of peace'.[14] To what purpose did Leopold intend to put these troops, and to what government did he refer? Whatever interpretation is made, it is clear both that Leopold in no way sold out or made concessions to Hitler and that he did undertake to discuss political matters without the approval of his ministers.

In the following months, Leopold did what he could to alleviate the Belgian food problem. The next April he drafted an appeal to President Roosevelt which the representative of the German foreign ministry in Belgium, Werner von Bargen, recommended the king be allowed to send; Berlin ruled, however, that this could not be permitted. Though Leopold frequently tried to persuade the Germans to improve Belgium's provisioning, he kept aloof to such an extent that Von Bargen wrote in May 1941 that he was unsure of whether even a modest form of active cooperation could be obtained from the king.[15]

Leopold's critics nevertheless assert that the king was not aloof enough and should never have sent congratulations to Hitler on his birthday in 1941 or condolences to the Italian king in 1942 upon the death of his son. Nor should he have traveled to Austria, an action hardly befitting a prisoner-king. Suspicions also surrounded the king's deportation to Germany shortly before the allied invasion. The king insisted, backing his case with sound arguments, that the move was made against his will; the opposition, however, charged the trip was made at his request, and it too produced documents and powerful reasoning.

The constitutionality of the king's behavior – and there were hotly debated points that have not been mentioned, such as his second marriage without the required ministerial approval – is open to question. Judgment on that issue is not the goal here. But two rather basic conclusions do seem apparent regarding the king's activities in the area of foreign relations. First, his post-surrender efforts to ameliorate Belgium's wartime lot met with little success. Second, if some of Leopold's actions might not have indicated as adamant opposition to the Germans as some Belgians would have liked, he avoided even the most modest forms of active collaboration.

Be this as it may, Leopold's behavior was not acceptable to many Belgians. While the king remained in Austria, first as a prisoner and then as a voluntary exile, the debate over whether he should return became entangled with the linguistic controversy. For the most part, Walloons and Socialists opposed Leopold; the king's support was among the Flemings and Catholics. Leopold resisted the cabinet's pressure for his abdication, and in turn on July 19, 1945, the chambers upheld the May 1940 declaration of the king's 'impossibility to reign' although the enemy was by now defeated. The king's brother Charles therefore continued to serve as regent, as he had since his election September 20, 1944, shortly after Belgium's liberation.

The royal question soon became the dominant issue in the press and in political discussions at all levels of society. Criticism of the king's behavior had already been rife in France before the war, and the sharp attacks by Reynaud, Spaak, and Pierlot at the time of Leopold's surrender only increased the ardor with which writers from a variety of nations commented on Leopold's behavior. Robert Goffin's *Le roi des belges, a-t-il trahi?* (New York, 1940), which concluded Leopold was more betrayed than betrayer, started the counter-attack. In Great Britain, Emile Cammaerts, an author of Belgian heritage who had become the chief interpreter of the small nation to the English speaking world, defended the king in *The Prisoner of Laeken, Fact and Legend* (London, 1941).

The government's official statement of 1941, *Belgium: The Official Account of What Happened* appeared to support the king's actions. But upon their return to Brussels at the close of the war, members of the former government in exile expressed their criticism of the king's acts and made certain demands upon him. In his political testament of January 1944, and in later statements, Leopold refused to compromise his power or admit any error. Instead, he appointed a commission of nine scholars from several geographic regions of Belgium to study all but his private papers. *The Report of the Commission of Information Instituted by His Majesty King Leopold III, July 14, 1946* (Luxemburg, 1947) which appeared in March of 1947 upheld the constitutionality of Leopold's acts and criticized the performance of the government in exile. The *Report* in turn stimulated a series of articles in the Belgian daily *Le Soir* by former premier Hubert Pierlot. The twelve installments, which began on July 5, 1947, expectedly defended the ministers' actions and supported the parties of the left in their position on the royal question. Beginning on September 23, 1948, Victor Larock, a Walloon Socialist member of the Chamber, published fifteen articles entitled '*A quand la lumière*', in *Le Peuple*, the Belgian Socialist daily. Larock attacked the king's behavior both directly and via innuendo. Meanwhile, the Flemish Catholic press carried numerous articles commending Leopold for his courage and devotion to country. In Brussels, the non-partisan *Groupement national belge* published collections of documents intended to clarify the issues and which on occasion seemed to reflect some sympathy for the king's position.

Polemics appeared on either side, but there were also a number of serious studies, both by parliamentary task forces and by individual scholars, on the broader issue of the proper constitutional role of the king. Among the best of these were two by W. J. Ganshof van der Meersch *Le commandement de l'armée et la responsibilité ministerielle en droit constitutionnel belge* (Brussels, 1949), and *Des rapports entre le chef de l'état et le gouvernement en droit constitutionnel belge* (Brussels, 1950). The scholars were divided in their opinions but generally recognized that henceforth it would be well if the sovereign did not take over actual command of forces in the field, an event which would be unlikely in the future in any case with the development of large coalition commands of mixed nationalities.

Besides being a theoretical constitutional issue, the royal question very quickly became a point of strong political conflict among the established Belgian political parties. The Catholic groupings, more than ever identified with the desires of Flanders, called for the king to resume his full powers. The Socialists and the Communists, who until 1947 participated in the government, demanded abdication. Their strongholds were the industrial and mining regions of Wallonia. The Liberals were split, but on the whole were sympathetic toward the king until the turmoil within the country persuaded party leaders that there should be an *effacement* of the royal question – a polite way of suggesting abdication. The political deadlock remained despite new elections and grew more bitter as time passed. Eventually the Catholics proposed a popular 'consultation' on whether Leopold should resume exercise of his constitutional powers. The king acquisced to the idea while asserting that no plebiscite could be binding. When the Liberals also were won over, a Catholic-Liberal ministry was formed in 1949 and plans made for the plebiscite.

Held the following March, the plebiscite gave 57.68 per cent of the vote to Leopold, with a majority expressing against the king only in the Walloon provinces of Liege and Hainaut. The political parties and the chambers remained severely split, however. On July 22, 1950, Leopold III returned to Brussels. Plans for wide-spread strikes were immediately formulated, and on July 27, Paul-Henri Spaak led a massive demonstration before the royal palace. By the last days of the month, the country appeared on the verge of civil war. On August 1, announcement was made of the king's decision of the previous evening to delegate all royal powers to his son, Prince Baudouin, who was to become king in his own right on his twenty-first birthday on September 7, 1951. The change of power took place on August 11, 1950, and official abdication came a bit ahead of schedule on July 16, 1951.

11.2 INTERNATIONAL COOPERATION

Diplomacy from both within and without Belgium had only slight effect upon the country's fortunes during the war, instead having its greatest implications for the domestic issue of the royal question. Yet an important part of any wartime diplomacy is concerned not with immediate matters, but with the future state of affairs after the war's end. That consideration had much to do with Leopold's wait-and-see policies, and it was in this connection that the exile government made its most important contribution to Belgium's post-war well-being: participation in the formation of the United Nations and the creation of the Belgium-Netherlands-Luxemburg (Benelux) economic union.

In September of 1941, the Belgian exiles endorsed the Atlantic Charter statement of peace aims drawn up the previous month by President Roosevelt of the United States and Prime Minister Winston Churchill of Great Britain. Territorial changes against the will of the populations involved and other forms of aggrandizement were renounced; the right of peoples to choose their own forms of government, equality of economic opportunity, disarmament of aggressor nations, freedom of the seas, and the value of international collaboration were all affirmed. In January 1942 the Belgians signed the Washington Declaration establishing the antiaxis coalition.

These were the first steps on the path which eventually led to membership in the United Nations. The Belgian ministers were too engrossed in the problems of liberating their homeland to take an active part in the negotiations leading to the Dumbarton Oaks Conference of October 1944, nor did the great powers go out of their way to consult the exiled government. It was generally known that Belgians both in London and at home favored the formation of a new international society. They held a strong concern, however, that any new body should not be the puppet of dominating great powers. Van Zeeland and Spaak admitted that though small states would legitimately have to accept secondary roles, just the same those states should have an influencing voice. To protect their interests, they should be allowed to join regional ententes designed not to rival the international organization but to supplement the collective security. Above all, there should be no rule of unanimity in the international organization which would permit one great power to veto the wishes of the rest of the world.

The decision of Churchill, Roosevelt, and Stalin at Yalta that the great nation permanent members of the United Nations Security Council should have veto powers therefore caused dismay in Brussels. At the famous San Francisco Conference of April-June 1945 which took as its task the drafting of a charter for the new organization, the Belgians fought doggedly, but without success, to abolish this veto. Disappointed as they were, the diplomats of the small country did agree to accept the charter as it stood, for they recognized that some form of an international organization was better than none. The government was in no hurry to present the matter to the Belgian chambers, and it was only several months after the conclusion of the conference that the chambers gave their approval to the country's membership in the United Nations. But there was no doubt of the genuine pride felt within Belgium when Spaak, like Paul Hymans years before, was elected the first president of an international assembly upon which so many hopes were based.

The willingness of Spaak, the chief architect of Belgium's 'lone hand' pre-war policy, to support the United Nations despite reservations regarding some articles of the charter was indicative of the movement toward international cooperation which characterized Belgium's postwar diplomacy. The readiness of Belgium and her neighbors, at the end of the war, to settle long-standing differences and irritation was evidenced by the convention of 1946 which arranged for the Luxemburg railways to be controlled by a Franco-Belgian-Luxemburg corporation. Fifty-one per cent of the shares of this corporation were to be controlled by the duchy, while the remainder were divided between Belgium and France. The Luxemburg government was also granted the right to name a majority of the corporation's board of directors.

The event which most clearly marked Belgium's commitment to international cooperation, however, was the creation of an economic union with the Netherlands. This required more than profession of ideals and tacit acceptance of vague commitments which, because they had so little relation to the reality of Belgium's power position, most observers considered Belgium would usually be obliged only nominally to honor. This required specific and occasionally powerful concessions that would immediately affect the entire life of the country.

The idea was an old one. Bitterness stemming from the revolution, economic differences which had helped stimulate the Belgian revolt, and neutrality prevented any true cooperation in the nineteenth century. The rivalry between Antwerp and Rotterdam joined with quarrels over the defense of Maastricht, Dutch distrust of what was believed to be a

Paris-directed Belgian foreign policy, and tensions produced by the linguistic controversy and Dutch sheltering of Flemish leaders after the first war vitiated all efforts in the twenties and thirties. By the fall of 1943, however, the joint suffering of invasion and defeat had erased older memories, and the two countries' governments in exile in London signed a bilateral payments agreement. Eleven months later, on September 5, 1944, a customs convention was signed by the governments of Belgium, the Netherlands, and Luxemburg: the Benelux agreements. The terms were vague, but it appears that the steps to economic union were envisaged to be an initial adoption of common tariffs, reduction of duties between the countries, and then agreement upon uniform laws for the application of a single tariff; finally, economic union would be reached with the removal of all obstacles to commerce among the partner countries, the coordination of domestic, financial, economic, and social policies, and the achievement of unity in dealing with other nations.[16]

The problems involved were many. One of the most serious was the disparity between the economies of the Netherlands and the Belgian-Luxemburg Economic Union (B.L.E.U.) following the war. It had been expected that the two groups would be starting out together and fairly evenly, but the fortunes of war dictated that the economy of Belgium should be the strongest in Europe while that of the Netherlands was in chaos. The allied liberation of Belgium in September 1944 had not been immediately followed by a freeing of the Netherlands; for eight months, while Antwerp served as a center for allied shipping, Holland's factories had been stripped by German troops and her farmlands flooded.

The Belgian-Luxemburg Union could therefore enjoy what might be termed a neo-liberalist economy, while the Netherlands perforce adopted an austerity program. Hard currency, self-regulation, free enterprise, and high prices and wages prevailed in the South, while soft currency, easy credit, government control, and low prices and wages characterized the Dutch economy.

The failure of another assumption, although foreseen by knowledgeable authorities, posed serious problems also. Prior to the war, it was often asserted that the economies of the B.L.E.U. and the Netherlands were complementary. This was not always the case, and the combination of low wages and government stimulation of Dutch industries following the war created severe industrial competition in many areas. Even under the B.L.E.U. agreements, Luxemburg's agriculture had received some protection; farmers in both Belgium and the duchy now demanded protection from the competition of Dutch agriculture.

In addition to these structural problems, there were many of a functional nature. It is one thing to agree in principle to the abolition of tariffs and another to determine which goods should first experience tariff reduction and in what stages. Then, too, some coordination of fiscal systems was necessary. Direct taxation was sufficiently similar in both the B.L.E.U. and the Netherlands not to pose any great problem. Indirect taxation, on the other hand, was a serious issue. For example, the beer-loving Belgians taxed spirits severely, while the Dutch, who prefer spirits, placed large excise duties on beer. Transmission taxes provided much state revenue in Belgium and were one-third higher than in the Netherlands and the duchy. Reduction of the Belgian turn-over tax might improve the position of Belgian industrial goods in price competition, but the Brussels government was loathe to accept such a change because of its implication for state finances. Other difficulties included restrictions on the movement of private capital between Belgium and the Netherlands.

Despite their inability to meet all these issues head-on, negotiators on all sides kept hope. Numerous agreements were reached, among them arrangements for the protection of Belgium's and Luxemburg's agriculture, although this was contrary to the ultimate goal of free trade within the community. The union itself was ratified in October 1947 and the tariff community inaugurated on January 1, 1948. A conference at the Chateau d'Ardenne in June of 1948 projected full economic union by January 1950, but it was soon realized that this could not be achieved so quickly. Some form of pre-union did seem possible, and agreement to that effect was reached October 15, 1949. By a year later, nearly ninety per cent of the trade among the three member countries was free of all controls.[17]

Other progressive steps followed. A certain amount of unification of excise taxes was settled upon in February 1950 and approved by the appropriate legislative bodies twenty-one months later; the issue of duties on many goods remained unsettled, however. Less success was obtained in the agricultural sector. An agreement reached in October of 1950 called for an international commission to establish minimum prices on agricultural goods, although the individual countries could take whatever steps they deemed necessary to protect their produce if the commission were not in unanimous agreement; the exporting country could appeal any action to an arbitration board. Certain products were freed of import quotas, and others were to be the object of compensatory taxes. Innocuous as it was, this proposal so aroused Belgian farmers that at the end of the year it was watered down; specific authorization was granted to the imposition of import quotas and the arbitration clause was omitted.

If the weakness of Dutch industry and the Netherlands' trade deficit threatened to destroy the Benelux in the organization's initial years, in the 1950s the reversal of these conditions as a result of the Dutch government's 'pump-priming' activities posed an almost equally dangerous threat. Perturbed by the increasing quantities of imported Dutch goods, produced at lower wage rates and selling below the prices of Belgian-manufactured goods, Belgian industrialists banded together to protest 'dumping' and to call for compensatory taxes on Dutch imports. Negotiations led to voluntary restriction by certain Dutch industries of exports to Belgium. In July 1953, these protection measures were approved in a more general manner and it was agreed that emergency steps, including the banning of all imports, might be taken to protect 'sick' industries.

Additional adjustments and concessions were made, as the negotiators attempted to reduce the issues dividing the Netherlands and the B.L.E.U. The Benelux itself prospered. By 1956, it was tied with Canada as the fourth largest trading power in the world. The Benelux ports handled nearly the same volume of goods as the three other major port areas in Europe combined, and internal trade within the Benelux rapidly increased.[18] The final creation of complete economic union was postponed several times until on February 5, 1958, the agreement was signed; it became effective November 1, 1960. Some quotas and a few scattered tariffs remained, but these were of minor significance in comparison with the overall reduction of trade obstacles and the numerous accords that had been reached in the areas of finance, wage policies, and social legislation.

Not only did the Union provide its members with great economic gains, but it also enhanced the political stature of Belgium and the Netherlands at a time when the reconstruction struggles of the other European nations and the confrontation of the United States and the U.S.S.R. threatened to overshadow the importance and legitimate desires of small nations. The economic achievements of the Benelux won the respect of the European powers; many statesmen were persuaded to the views of Paul van Zeeland, foreign minister from 1949 to 1955, who commented that any retreat from such international cooperation would be fatal. Benelux had shown the way toward increased European economic integration. Advice and cooperation concerning similar projects for the integration of the European economy were frequently sought of its members and particularly of Belgium, which country had assumed the foreign policy lead within the bloc during the years the Dutch were struggling to strengthen their economy and to solve the crises in their Indonesian colonies.

From the very end of the war, both Spaak and Van Zeeland had been advocates of a better united, indeed an integrated, Europe. Spaak called for unification to meet the Soviet threat and Van Zeeland served as head of a Belgian Independent League for European Cooperation. In 1948, this league joined with Winston Churchill's United Europe Movement and other similar organizations in creating a Council of Europe. Though the Council's duties were ill-defined and it was forbidden to deal with defense problems, it did manage to carve out the areas of social legislation and cultural agreements as its special field of concentration. Spaak served as its president for several years, cajoling, praising, and scolding the foreign ministers of Western European countries into closer relations. In December 1951, he resigned his post because he did not believe enough action was being taken. Nevertheless, he had done much to set the Council on its feet and give direction to the good intentions of its participants.

The Brussels government and the Belgian chambers themselves were somewhat hesitant to follow Spaak headlong into European integration. Yet they did view some tightening of bonds as essential for the maintenance of peace and security, economic welfare, and Europe as a force in world affairs. Nuclear weapons, the expensive means required to deliver them, and the division of the world into opposing camps had, it was believed, rendered the older, national systems of defense inadequate. In March of 1948, Spaak, who was then both prime and foreign minister, warned the chambers that 'a political treaty only has value – and especially for a country like ours – if military accords are involved… It seems to me absolutely impossible today to conceive of a national Belgian defense exclusively within the body of Belgium'.[19] The contrast of this with his own prewar statements, and Henri Jaspar's criticism of French demands on Britain in 1922, is striking. Spaak went on to say that political and military agreements do not have great value unless upheld and supplemented by pacts for economic collaboration. 'And, aside from the still too insufficient example of the Benelux countries, the other countries of Western Europe – and by that I mean Belgium equally well – have all practiced too individualistic a policy.'

What Spaak was speaking for was a system of alliances with other European nations which would have a broader scope than any agreement Belgium had ever made before. The emphasis put upon the inclusion of economic clauses was typical of the approach used by the Belgians in the following years. Economic cooperation was viewed as mandatory for European recovery, and in the Belgians' eyes it was also one of the best, if not the best, ways to promote European integration; moreover, economic cooperation among the members of an alliance in peacetime would improve the possibilities of true military cooperation in time of war. The Benelux, the Organization for European Economic Cooperation, the

European Payments Union, and later such organizations as the Common Market and Euratom were all part of Belgium's approach to the security problems of the post-war era.

Two weeks after Spaak made his speech, Belgium signed the Treaty of Brussels with England, France, and the other Benelux nations. While the economic cooperation envisaged in this pact never amounted to much, the Brussels Treaty represented a significant step forward in the uniting of Europe for common defense. Though in favor of the United Nations and hopeful that it would preserve peace, many Belgian parliamentarians had for some time felt compelled to point out the need of regional alliances. Belgium had traditionally avoided commitments that might involve her far from her borders. A hierarchy of obligations within the international organization was therefore necessary. Though both Belgium and the United States could make pledges of responsibility for world peace, it should be incumbent only upon the latter to take on world-wide obligations; those of Belgium should be limited to the regions of Europe and the North Atlantic. Another argument for regional accords was the necessity of immediate action. Twice the victims of sudden invasion, the Belgians were wary lest endless debates delay the international body in taking effective action. Failure of the campaign to abolish the great power veto in the Security Council made the problem more acute and put into sharp relief the utility of regional ententes which could act quickly to protect the legitimate self-interests of their members.

Existing close relations with Britain and France and talk of the American nuclear shield had not brought a prompt entry of Belgium into regional partnerships. In part, this was due to the presence, until the end of March 1947, of communists within the governing coalition who opposed any agreement which might be directed against Russia. In the main, the Belgian position can be attributed to a reluctance to take any step that might sharpen the division between East and West. Spaak strongly supported the maintenance of the victorious wartime coalition, and many were the times that he referred, as had Hymans following the first war, to Belgium's role as that of a hyphen between the great powers. Thus, when the French and British signed the Pact of Dunkirk of March 4, 1947, Spaak privately expressed his view to them that the pact should be expanded to include other Western European countries; at the same time he approached the Soviet government. His suggestion that some sort of Belgo-Russian accord might serve the interests of peace apparently had little virtue in the eyes of the Soviets, for they declined even to reply.[20]

Such rebuffs were discouraging, and the Rue de la Loi was not blind to the steady expansion of Russian hegemony in eastern Europe. Continuing use of the veto by the Soviets in the Security Council led the

Belgians further to distrust the Russians' assertions of true desire for international cooperation. With increasing frequency, opinions were expressed in the Belgian chambers that it was time, though no animosities were held toward anyone, that in the interests of her own legitimate self-defense and to secure international peace, Belgium should choose her allies. At the end of January 1948, British Foreign Minister Ernest Bevin, in an important policy statement in the Commons, announced that in view of increasing Soviet activities in Eastern Europe, it was time that Western European nations should draw closer together. To that effect, he was sending emissaries to the Benelux nations inviting them to establish a closer relationship with the member nations of the Dunkirk pact.

The Belgian reaction was favorable, and the drafting of a reply was promptly begun with the Dutch. Brussels and The Hague were in general agreement, but enough differences arose to prevent the response being sent until February 19, the very day the French and British ministers delivered their proposals. If there were some debate between the Dutch and the Belgians as to how close they should allow themselves to be drawn into the Franco-British camp, they were firm in their insistence that what was needed was a regional arrangement rather than a series of bilateral treaties. Then, too, if the Benelux countries were to take on new obligations in Europe, they should be granted more of a voice in deciding the future of Germany, a matter which the great powers had reserved for themselves. Although the Dutch protested against any phrasing that would direct the accord against any one power, they were overruled, as reference was made to prevention of future German aggression.[21]

The negotiations were speeded, and their course directed in a manner desired by the small countries, by news of the communist putsch in Czechoslovakia on February 24. Within three weeks, on March 17, 1948, the Treaty of Brussels was signed by Britain, France, Belgium, the Netherlands, and Luxemburg. Defensive in character, the accord did not violate the United Nations charter. On the other hand, while Spaak insisted that the pact 'in no manner can be considered as an act of aggression against the U.S.S.R.'[22] it surely marked a shift in the Belgian stance and the end to one phase of Belgium's postwar diplomacy.

The implications of the Brussels pact were fulfilled with Belgium's participation in the North Atlantic Treaty Organization created thirteen months later. According to its terms twelve nations, including those of the Brussels treaty, promised to aid each other in opposing aggression in the North Atlantic area and to collaborate in the maintenance of modern military arms and planning under the direction of a North

Atlantic Council. Some Belgians were fearful that the N.A.T.O. would ride roughshod over their little country's wishes but Spaak, who was to serve as its secretary-general from 1957 to 1961, strove to strengthen it. His arguments were powerful:

Let us end our timid efforts, which at best show vague good will more than a closer awareness of realities, and let us accept the consequences of the plain fact that the fate of all of us in the West is inextricably linked. The atom bomb leaves no room for neutrality or separate national policies. The West is condemned not only to wage war together but to create policy together... The Atlantic Alliance is a great thing. But with its present imperfections it cannot survive. Either it will be complete or it will not be.[23]

It was no doubt with this spirit and point of view already in mind that the Belgian government in 1950 decided in favor of participation of Belgian volunteer troops in the Korean War. The force sent was not as large as those of several other nations, but it was token of an important development in Belgian thinking regarding the small country's responsibilities in world politics and to her N.A.T.O. allies.

The N.A.T.O. however, did not meet the need for a solely European defense group which could act without requiring the massive assistance of the United States. At this time it also did not make provision for West Germany, despite American hints that Bonn should become a N.A.T.O. capital. Neither the Germans nor their neighbors desired a rebirth of German militarism, yet many persons thought it foolish not to utilize the resources of West Germany in any future conflict, for without German troops the allies would find themselves fighting a defensive battle in France rather than on the Elbe.

Thus it was that in the early 1950s, the Brussels statesmen supported a proposal put forward by René Pleven of France for the creation of an integrated European army and a European Defense Community (E.D.C.). Under this arrangement, West German troops could be added to a European common army without creating a German national army. There was some difference of opinion in Belgium concerning the inclusion of Germany in the defense community, but both the conservative Van Zeeland and the more radical Spaak saw the European army as a step forward; Van Zeeland described its creation as a first step in bringing about political integration.[24] Objections to the slight surrender of national sovereignty were overcome and a start was made in the fall of 1953 at the necessary revision of the clauses of the constitution contrary to the terms of an E.D.C., such as those stating that only the king could be commander-in-chief of Belgian forces and that solely volunteers could be recruited from the colonies. About the same time, British and Canadian troops arrived to man the British military base in the Flemish Campine created by an Anglo-British accord ratified earlier in the year to facilitate supply of British troops in Germany.

Despite the progress of its planning and approval of an E.D.C. by all its other members, in August 1954 France failed to ratify the arrangement, and the European Political Union, a companion organization to an E.D.C. which envisaged a directly-elected European assembly and a common market, also had to be dropped because of the French attitude. In the place of an E.D.C. was established a Western European Union that was looser and narrower in scope. Its members were the five nations of the Brussels pact, Italy, and West Germany, which was admitted on special terms. This expansion of the Brussels treaty membership caused the treaty's preamble to be altered so that it was directed not against future German aggression but toward the promotion of the unity and integration of Europe.

If hopes for a European Defense Community were destroyed, success was obtained in another area of integration, coal and steel production. In the formation of the Coal and Steel Community, as in the planning for various other European institutions, Belgium insisted she was not the leader – she was too small to dream of taking on such a role – but only a good follower. Yet the constant Belgian prodding, the behind-the-scenes diplomacy, and especially the persistent eloquence of Van Zeeland and Spaak did much to bring about the implementation of the Schuman Plan.

It was realized in Belgium that the plan put forward by the French premier in 1950 would bring difficulties as well as benefits to Belgium's industries. Especially hard-hit would be the Borinage coal mines which, because of a lack of modern machinery and a decreasing supply of easily accessible coal, would not be able to meet the competition provided by the mines of the Saar, Ruhr, and Alsace-Lorraine if free trade in coal were introduced. Some Belgians, including Frans van Cauwelaert, leader of the Christian Social party and president of the Chamber (he had also objected to the E.D.C.), disapproved of granting certain powers to the High Authority envisioned in the Schuman Plan: 'We don't have the right to sell our sovereignty just like that.'[25] Despite the opposition of the mine owners and some constitutional problems, the plan was accepted in the Senate by a vote of 102–4 with the Socialists abstaining because they believed the plan would cause unemployment in the Borinage. In the Chamber, Spaak rallied the support of his party, declaring: 'Europe will only survive in unity! The period of small markets has ended and it is necessary to create a common market in Europe. No European country is able to assure its liberty and existence alone; together we can do it, but it is necessary to begin today.'[26] The Chamber approved the plan by a vote of 165 to 13.

As usual, the Belgians did not allow their interest in an integrated European economy and their wish to cooperate to cause them to forget their own concerns. Numerous safeguards were arranged to protect the coal industry for a period of years while steps were taken to modernize the mines or to ease the most marginal Belgian producers out of the industry. Yet while clearly desiring that events should not move too fast, the Belgian diplomats did not heed those politicans who interpreted the creation of a coal and steel community as a miracle and cried that integration should not be carried any further or disaster would result. The official Belgian view was made explicit by the Belgian representative to a special meeting of the Community's Council of Ministers just after France rejected the E.D.C. He declared that for his government the Community was not an end, but a beginning. It was the best possible body for bringing about the unity of Europe by overcoming the recent nationalist manifestations.[27]

This official view reflected accurately popular opinion within Belgium. Although Flemings and Walloons opposed each other on many issues, they were in general agreement on the matter of further economic integration within Europe. A public opinion poll conducted in 1951 revealed that sixty-five per cent of the Belgian populace favored close cooperation with other states. On the whole, industrial and professional groups were the most interested in European integration. The Flemings, long advocates of closer ties with the Netherlands, favored the idea more warmly than did Walloons; forty-six per cent of the voters in the Flemish provinces saw membership in the European Economic Community as beneficial to Belgium, while the comparable figure for the Walloon provinces was thirty-two per cent. In 1964, a similar poll revealed that about two-thirds of those replying supported further integration, a clear indication that recent progressive steps had not weakened the desire to push on.[28]

The efforts at European cooperation created an atmosphere favorable to political as well as economic negotiation. In September 1956, when West German Chancellor Konrad Adenauer and his foreign minister, Heinrich von Brentano, were visiting Brussels, agreements were signed altering the Belgo-German border. Though Eupen, Malmedy, and Saint-Vith had been returned to Belgium at the end of the war, some minor territorial problems had continued to exist. Now the four villages of Bildchen, Leykoul, Losheim, and Hemmeres, totaling a population of slightly less than seven hundred people, along with the forests of Freyen and Bullingen were turned over to Germany. These approximately eight square miles of land had been placed under Belgian control by the Council of Foreign Ministers in 1949. The West Germans, for their part, agreed to pay 15,600,000 Belgian francs ($ 312,000) reimbursement for Belgian investments in the area; they also ceded to Belgium two square miles of the forests of Wahlenscheid and Losheimergraben. The arrangement was said to facilitate local traffic and administration. Its greatest significance was the improvement that it marked in Belgo-German relations that had for so long been based solely on distrust.

Equally noteworthy were the efforts of the Belgians and Dutch to end long-standing differences. Ever since the frontier agreement of 1843, the Belgians had claimed sovereignty over the slightly more than thirty acres of the enclave of Bar-le-Duc; this claim the Dutch challenged. An attempt to resolve the issue in 1892 had fallen short; thirty years later, when the defense of Limburg and control of the Wielingen were being debated, the Dutch asserted the Belgian claim to the enclave was based on a mistaken document. Negotiations were not resumed until 1955; renewed deadlock did not stifle the desire to settle the matter, and so it was agreed in 1957 to submit the case to the International Court of Justice. On June 20, 1959, that body ruled in favor of the Belgian claim. Even more important, economically for Belgium and as a symbol of the growing Belgo-Dutch frindship, was the long-needed waterway agreement of 1963. According to its terms, existing Antwerp-Rhine connections were to be improved and also shortened by some twenty-five miles. Belgium was to pay eighty-five per cent of the construction costs of the ten year project; the Netherlands would pay the remainder as well as those for upkeep.

During the 1950s, the Belgians worked hard at building ties with other nations. In February of 1955 a treaty of 'friendship, establishment, and navigation' was signed with the United States, the first new treaty between the two countries since 1875. Relations with the Soviets were also improved, and in October of 1956, while on a visit to Moscow, Spaak signed a cultural accord providing for the exchange of professors, students and scientists. Throughout the period, King Baudouin maintained an exhausting schedule; there were few major capitals of the western powers where he was not a formal guest. By the end of the decade, Belgium had established warm friendships and a position of respect and leadership in Europe which was far superior to any she had held before. Then the Congo Crisis broke.

11.3 THE CONGO CRISIS

It is fair to say that the possibility of revolt in the Congo was far from the minds of most Belgians, including the public officials, in the postwar years. Some persons suggested that independence might be granted eventually, but the colony was manifestly in no way yet ready for it. To prevent premature agitation such as that disrupting British and French colonies, Belgian colonial administrators opted for a training and education program which would not cram a handful of leaders with embarrassing and irrealizable European notions of independence. Rather, an effort would be made slowly to raise the educational level of a broad sector of the populace so that when independence was granted there would exist a citizenry capable of using it properly. Besides, there were few Belgians, bankers or street cleaners, who were in any hurry to renounce the riches of the colony or the pride of its possession.

Only limited attention was given to the reforms and independence movements appearing in such British colonies as the Gold Coast in the early 1950s, nor to similar developments occurring somewhat later in neighboring French colonies. Thus Charles de Gaulle's Brazzaville speech in 1958, in which he offered French colonies the choice of membership in the French Community or immediate independence, startled some Belgian authorities, who angrily protested what they considered gratuitous provocation of trouble by the French president. Others recognized that the minor reforms begun in the Congo in 1956 and 1957 would have to be accelerated. Yet there was scant meeting of minds on this point, and so it was that little planning for prompt independence had occurred when serious rioting at Leopoldville in January of 1959 forced the Belgians to acquiesce to the creation of a Congolese government. Despite the riots' warning, the pace of the mother country's planning remained so slow that Minister of Colonies Maurice van Hemelrijck resigned in frustration. His successor, Auguste de Schryver, met the demands of increasingly influential Congolese nationalists by agreeing to formation of a Congolese parliament; independence would be granted in four years.

This would have been a hasty enough change of status, but the succession of events was to accelerate further. Fear of involvement in a struggle similar to that of the French in Algeria swept the small country. Socialists led an effective campaign against the sending of Belgian troops to the Congo (the constitution already stated that only volunteers could be used in colonies). Caught between the nationalists in the Congo and the Socialists at home, the Belgian cabinet uttered vague statements about some form of self-government for the colony in 1960 and was constrained to allow a Round Table Conference in January of that year to discuss the Congo's future.

There was little expectation in Brussels that the conference would cause serious difficulties; the Congolese were too inexperienced and divided among themselves effectively to oppose Belgian diplomats. Anyhow, the conference was only consultative and the Belgian ministers would be free to interpret its conclusions as they wished after its adjournment. Such proved not to be the case. Despite their other differences, the nationalists presented a united front in demanding immediate independence. The Congolese had not recognized that De Schryver's speech of the previous December had signalled a change in government policy on the matter of prompt independence. They therefore did not dissolve into factions but remained united and highly aggressive on this issue. The Belgian populace was similarly unaware of its government's change of stance, for De Schryver had purposely understated its significance in order to avoid political backlash; in so doing, he unwittingly assured that when the backlash came, it would be doubly harsh.

When the Belgian cabinet examined the possible replies it could make to Congolese demands for immediate independence, it was dismayed by the paucity of choice. Outright refusal and the use of force was impossible in view of world opinion, the attitude of the Belgian electorate, and the dangers of an interminable war. National pride would not allow turning the problem over to the United Nations; to do so would be to admit having made serious mistakes and to give credence to ancient French, German, and English charges that the small country never was fit to rule a colony. A temporary delay in granting independence might have been arranged, but only at the risk of a guerilla conflict. Reeling from a rapid succession of shocks, the government accepted the Congolese demand, set the date of independence for June 30, and fervently hoped that a decade's worth of preparation could be achieved in the next few months, both before and after the official declaration of independence. As Catherine Hoskyns has commented, 'it was clear that the promise of independence had been won by Belgian weakness rather than by Congolese, strength...'.[29]

The Belgian hopes were in vain. On the third day of the official life of the Republic of the Congo, serious outbreaks of violence occurred in Luluabourg and the capital, Leopoldville. Shortly thereafter, on July 5, members of the former *Force publique* in Thysville and the capital revolted against their Belgian officers. The ensuing days and months were ones of panic and terror for Europeans living in nearly every region of the former colony. The Belgian government could not stand idle while its nationals were threatened and despoiled. Despite the protests of the Congolese prime minister, Patrice Lumumba, Belgian troops were sent to bases at Kitona and Kamina, held by Belgium by a treaty of friendship signed the day before the colony became independent. It was not until July 10, after rioting had spread widely, that the troops left the bases and restored order in the proximate areas.

The following day Moise Tshombe, President of Katanga, proclaimed the independence of his province from the central government, requesting Belgian aid and asserting that Lumumba was under communist influence. It is questionable how much public support Tshombe initially possessed, for the people of Katanga were not consulted and those of the northern region were vocally opposed to secession. On the other hand, Tshombe appeared to have informal Belgian support, both secret and not-so-secret. As one knowledgeable observer wrote:

From the beginning, secession was a political stratagem designed to preserve the comparative wealth of Katanga and to advance the interests of Tshombe and his political supporters, the Belgian residents in the province, and the foreign investors in Union Minière du Haut-Katanga and other economic enterprises in Katanga.[20]

Faced with disintegration on all sides, Lumumba first called for United Nations' intervention to restore the rioting Congolese army to order. The following day, July 12, he was joined by the Republic's president, Joseph Kasavubu, in requesting United Nations' military aid to combat Belgian 'aggression' and Belgian support of the rebel Tshombe regime. On the fourteenth of July Lumumba, learning that his cabinet had also requested American aid during his own absence from Leopoldville, appealed to the Soviets, asserting that the Congo was being illegally occupied by Belgium and that his own life was in danger. The United Nations did intervene, although the future extent of its involvement was not foreseen. There was little or no opposition from the United States or Soviet Russia to the initial proposal of sending a United Nations' peace-keeping force which would not include troops of the great powers. The Americans feared that otherwise the Soviets would become involved by way of such countries as Ghana, and the Russians wished to check any Belgian effort to retard decolonization. In accordance with the intentions of numerous emerging nation members of the international organization and with the desires of Lumumba, the United Nations passed a resolution on July 14 calling for the withdrawal of Belgian troops from the Congo. Subsequent resolutions of July 22 and August 9 asked Belgium to 'implement speedily' that withdrawal and to remove her troops from Katanga. By July 23, Belgian troops had been transported from Leopoldville, and although

Belgian compliance with the United Nations was scarcely eager, increasing international pressure brought the evacuation of major Belgian
military contingents from the Congo during the first week of September.
Nine tons of munitions did, however, find their way to Katanga. Well
before September, the Belgian ambassador was expelled from Leopoldville by Lumumba.

Belgian behavior throughout all of this reflected annoyance, ambivalence, and the same difficulty that had led to the decision to grant immediate independence: weakness. It was clear from the start that the Brussels
government was guilty of mis-estimating the situation in the Congo and
of poorly judging the effect of its own policies. Traditionally more concerned with European than global affairs and disposed toward the peaceful settlement of all disputes, the Belgian populace was genuinely opposed
to use of force in the Congo. On the other hand, there was resentment of
what was considered the interfering and bullying ways of the foreign
powers; at no time in this century, except during the invasions of 1914
and 1940, did Belgian nationalism come so obviously to the fore. Then,
too, there was a growing lack of confidence in the United Nations.
There, despite her superior economic development and years of political
independence, Belgium had been put on a par with the backward African
and Asian nations enjoying premature and irresponsible (so said many
Belgians) independence. Many influential citizens of the small country
disbelieved the resoluteness or capacity of the United Nations and
African nationalists and assumed that with a little tenacity and maneuvering behind the scenes they could have things pretty much their own
way. This meant, in effect, that Belgian commercial interests would
maintain control of certain economic enterprises, particularly the prof-
itable ones of Katanga; the onerous task of political government would
be left to the Congolese, who would soon see the wisdom of continued
Belgian participation in the economic development of their country at
terms exceptionally favorable to Belgian businessmen. The attempt of
Foreign Minister Pierre Wigny to bluff his way in opposition to numerous
reprimands from the United Nations' Security Council and secretary-
general was scarcely veiled in a November 14 press conference in which
he called the United Nations efforts a failure and stated, 'We cannot
remain a member of the United Nations in the future, if officials of the
United Nations do not show the proper restraint and do not conduct
themselves in a proper manner.'[31]

The various divisions of opinion in Belgium found expression in the
weak coalition cabinet of Gaston Eyskens. The foreign minister repeatedly indicated that he viewed the Katanga secession with misgivings;
at the same time, his concern for the welfare of Belgian nationals and

Europeans of all countries residing in the Congo caused him to argue for additional action by Belgian troops, particularly in Katanga, where they were to maintain peace and order. But if Wigny, in his general statements regarding the Congo crisis, appeared willing to cooperate with the United Nations, this was not the case for many of his subordinates and particularly for Belgian diplomatic officials on the scene in Katanga, who were obviously lending their support to Tshombe. Both the defense and African affairs ministries frankly and openly backed Tshombe and used all their strength, which on the local level was more influential than the foreign ministry's, to keep Katanga in business no matter what this meant for the Republic as a whole. If a totally independent Katanga were impossible, then the rich region should have autonomy within a loose federation; apparently the deleterious effects for Katanga implicit in a collapse of the central Congo government were discounted. Conflicting pressures from Leopoldville, Elisabethville (the capital of Katanga) and within Belgium herself kept the Belgian cabinet and ministries divided against themselves and thus precluded any decisive action or positive resolution of the fluctuating course of Belgian policy.

Indeed, the only continuing theme in Belgium's foreign relations at this time was increasing animosity and difficulties with the United Nations and various nations in Africa. At the beginning of December, for example, the United Arab Republic seized all Belgian assets in Egypt because the Congolese had demanded the departure of U.A.R. diplomats from Leopoldville. A few days later, Belgium rejected a United Nations' report decrying the return of Belgian nationals to the Congo and insisted she had the right of aid the Congolese government (which since the deposition of Lumumba in September had improved relations with Brussels). On January 1, 1961, United Nations' Secretary-General Dag Hammarskjöld denounced Belgian assistance to the Congolese national army in contravention of a United Nations' resolution of September. A little over a week later, Ceylon, Liberia, and the U.A.R. presented to the Security Council a resolution condemning the behavior of the Belgian administration of Ruanda-Urundi in regard to the conflict in the Congo. Though it was defeated, it was clear that Belgium's ill-concealed but only half-hearted actions to aid certain Congolese factions were winning her much distrust. At the end of January, Hammerskjöld publicly opposed rumored Belgian attempts to turn over to the Congolese government those air bases formerly in the hands of Belgium but which since July had been controlled by the United Nations. Anti-Belgian feeling within the international organization culminated with the resolution of February 21 which, among other points, urged 'the immediate withdrawal and evacuation from the Congo of all Belgian and other foreign military and para-military personnel and political advisers not under the United Nations Command, and mercenaries'.[32]

The day before the resolution was passed, the Belgian government which it reprimanded fell due to opposition within Belgium to the austerity program instituted by Eyskens to compensate for the recent loss of revenues. The cabinet continued to fulfill caretaker functions until the elections scheduled by King Baudouin for March 26; but henceforth it was even less able to resolve its internal differences or take a firm stand either of cooperation with the United Nations or of truly efficacious support for the Congolese figures who had overthrown and allegedly murdered Lumumba. The elections showed increased support for the Socialists and particularly for Belgium's leading diplomat, Paul-Henri Spaak, who had resigned as secretary-general of the N.A.T.O. to run for political office. Yet the wanderings in the wilderness were not yet over, for it would take nearly a month for a new cabinet to be formed. Meanwhile the annoyance of the African, Asian, and Soviet Bloc nations continued to mount against what were considered to be renewed colonialist machinations by the Belgians. The result was a sharp censure of Belgium for failing to cooperate with the United Nations' voted by the general assembly on April 15 by the resounding score of sixty-one to five, with thirty-three nations abstaining.

On April 21, a new Belgian government was put together, with Théo Lefèvre as premier and Spaak as foreign minister and vice-premier. The new coalition did not mean that there would be any sudden meeting of minds between the statesmen in Brussels and New York, but it did spell better cooperation for the future. Spaak was more committed to the principle of the United Nations than his predecessor, and as a Socialist he did not hold excessive sympathy for the directors of the *Union Minière* and the *Société Générale de Belgique*, one of the largest finance houses in Europe and possessor of important holdings in Katanga. But above all, Spaak was a Belgian; though he held high concern for the United Nations, he would not let what he considered to be Belgium's legitimate rights be trampled in the name of international cooperation. The path toward Belgian-United Nations' cooperation in the Congo was far from straight.

It would be tedious and perhaps irrelevant to attempt, particularly with the limited documentation as yet available, a detailed narration of the continuing complexities of the Congo affair. Many of them involved purely tribal rivalries and political squabbles within the Congo, and others were primarily a result of the fencing of the great powers at the United Nations and elsewhere. The main issue involving Belgium was the Katangan secession. Though Belgian troops had officially been withdrawn from the region in September of 1960, over two hundred Belgian officers had been seconded to Tshombe's forces to advise them in their training. These were supplemented by many Belgians who returned to Katanga only weeks after their supposedly definitive departure. Equally important were the numbers of white mercenaries who bolstered the Katangan gendarmerie. The mercenaries were of diverse origin – former French Foreign Legion officers, German soldiers of fortune, and so forth. There was no doubt many Belgians were among them, and though the Belgian government officially denied that it was permitting the enlistment of mercenaries there were several locations, including a prominent one in the center of Brussels, where youths could make arrangements to get to Katanga.

The leaders of the United Nations' Congo operation were adamant in their insistence that the Katangan secession be ended, for in their view the continued life of the central regime depended upon its access to Katangan revenues. The clamor for an end to the mercenaries' activities became such that at the end of October Spaak stated the Belgian government would withdraw the passports of Belgian nationals who continued to serve in Tshombe's army. Although a number of Belgians did return home, Tshombe continued his resistance thanks to Katanga's considerable wealth, the training already provided to his gendarmerie by Belgian soldiers, and the continued presence of a number of mercenaries. By the time of Spaak's announcement, U Thant, acting secretary-general of the United Nations who had succeeded to the post following Hammarskjöld's death in September, had already determined that United Nations' troops should stage a drive to disarm the mercenaries and end Tshombe's secession. In all, three efforts were undertaken; one at the beginning of September, another during the first days of December, and the third – which assured partial achievement of the United Nations' goals – at the turn of the year.

The military actions of the United Nations were deeply resented in Belgium. Spaak, for his part, was under pressure from the domestic right as well as from the domestic left. On the tenth of December 1961, a Brussels crowd made a brief effort to stone the American embassy but was quickly dispersed by police. Posters described United States' President John F. Kennedy, because of his support of the United Nations' actions, as being in league with Soviet Premier Nikita Khrushchev to destroy Katanga. The cries that Katanga was the only bastion of the West in Central Africa were, for the most part, a veil for the truer feelings of hurt pride and wrath at the possible loss of great financial investments. It was hard enough for Spaak as foreign minister to abide the blow being dealt to his country's morale and economy, but what concerned him most was the manner in which the United Nations appeared to be militarily interfering with the internal affairs of small, independent Katanga at the behest of the great powers. On December 8, he cabled U Thant that:

it is with the greatest distress and with total disapproval that the Belgian Government finds that the United Nations has come to engage in an action so far removed from the principles of the Charter whereby it was established.[33]

Spaak worked diligently to improve Belgium's tarnished international image and to mitigate the impact of the United Nations' actions upon Katanga and his own country. His attempts eventually met with some success. Major United Nations' military actions were halted, and after much difficulty Tshombe was brought to the bargaining table with delegates of the central government. Spaak himself conferred repeatedly with representatives of the United Nations, and on October 1, 1962, publicly declared to the General Assembly his support of a plan for the ending of the Katangan secession produced by U Thant the preceding August; on November 27, Spaak and Kennedy issued a joint communiqué in favor of the plan. Tshombe remained obstinate. The failure of U Thant's plan successfully to be implemented, joined with the ever-growing cost of the United Nations' mission, prompted the leaders of that body to apply sanctions against Katanga during the last weeks of 1962. When United Nations' troops again took up action in Katanga, Spaak protested, saying that the governments, including his own, which supported U Thant's plan had 'never wished anything of this kind'.[34]

The mildness of this statement compared to that of a year earlier revealed the extent to which the Belgian government, if not the Belgians privately working in Katanga, had acclimated itself to the possible cessation of Katangan independence. Tshombe had been given numerous opportunities to accept favorable compromises; his refusal to carry through on any of them finally cost him his bargaining position. During the last weeks of December 1962, United Nations' troops occupied much of Katanga against only spotty opposition; Tshombe himself fled briefly to Rhodesia. By the end of January, Joseph Ileo had assumed the post of minister resident of the central government in Elisabethville. The Katangan secession was over.

The affair had been, and would continue to be, costly to Belgium in terms of the lives and welfare of her nationals, her finances, and her international reputation. Though the sufferings of individuals who had been brutalized by various troops in the Congo could not be washed away, the financial crisis could be weathered, and Spaak himself did much to rehabilitate Belgium's diplomatic position. Within the United Nations, the abiding hostility of most members of the Afro-Asian bloc prevented

Belgium from regaining the prestigious position she had formerly held in that body. But in Europe, Belgium's voice soon acquired more authority.

Following the war, the Belgians had felt somewhat annoyed that just as their country had begun to win increased prestige in international councils, those councils had expanded and the preponderant influence of Europe in world affairs was reduced by events in widely separated areas of the globe. Actually this was not mere coincidence, for the turning of the great powers' attention to Africa, Asia, and South America invited and made it easier for Belgium to take a greater part in European affairs. After one bitter experience at playing power politics on a global scale, Belgium was eager to return to an arena that was of more comfortable size where she held a more respected position. Under Spaak's guidance, Belgium began again to play a role of low-keyed leadership on the Continent.

Efforts to persuade De Gaulle not to veto Great Britain's bid to enter the Common Market failed when the French president announced his formal opposition in January 1963; but Spaak won the lasting appreciation of the British, Dutch, and others for the skill of his attempt. In accordance with the policy he followed immediately after the war, the foreign minister did all he could to improve East-West communications. 'Let us show boldness', he told the United Nations' General Assembly in October 1963. 'Let us take risks, if need be, to defend the cause of peace.'[35] Peaceful coexistence should be strengthened; observation points should be established in both East and West to guard against surprise attacks. Perhaps a nonaggression pact would be feasible. Spaak, if anyone, knew the doubtful value of promises written on scraps of paper, but every possible avenue to an East-West entente should be explored.

Despite his somewhat idealistic talk of European union, Spaak was a realist at heart. He was also aware that the conservative groups in Belgium favored De Gaulle's limited European integration proposals to those which were more supranational. Thus, after eighteen months of stagnation following De Gaulle's initial veto of Britain's entry into the Common Market, the Belgian was among the first of the non-French members of that economic organization to shift support from his original proposals of a federated Europe to the French scheme for a weaker confederation. Better to have some progress down the path of unification, imperfect though it be, than none at all; for either progress were continually to be made or the entire project would wither on the vine.

Relations within the N.A.T.O. were strained by the Congo crisis, but the portly minister was willing to let time heal the wounds. During the first part of the 1960s he worked hard to deprive of foundation rumors that the alliance itself was in crisis; nevertheless, he looked after his own country's concerns and avoided commitments that might be embarrassing or contrary to his nation's traditional emphasis on defense rather than offense. Thus he did not hesitate to announce that should a mixed-manned nuclear N.A.T.O. fleet be established, Belgium would not participate. On the other hand, it was not as great a surprise as it would have been earlier when Belgium agreed to host the headquarters of the N.A.T.O., so necessary to her defense, after De Gaulle had removed France from the alliance. Differences with his own party over various matters had, however, brought Spaak's resignation in 1966, and he was no longer a member of the government or the chambers when the N.A.T.O. headquarters were opened south of Brussels in 1967.

Troubles with Africa did not disappear overnight; in 1964 they caused Spaak what he called some of the most difficult days and decisions of his life. The former mandates of Ruanda and Urundi were established as independent states on July 1, 1962, with domestic upheavals less dangerous than those that had plagued the Congo, though nevertheless serious. The larger republic, however, remained riven by civil war, as a group of rebels – primarily the political heirs of Lumumba, scantily supplied with communist arms – terrorized the northeastern region about Stanleyville. On November 24, 1964, Belgian paratroopers flown to the region in American planes rescued approximately 1,700 whites held by the rebels. This was not accomplished without bloodshed; approximately eighty hostages were killed in the panic and far more of the rebels were destroyed by Belgian bullets. Spaak insisted that the mission was intended only as a humanitarian rescue and pointed out that it was authorized by the central Congo government, now headed by Tshombe (such was the serpentine path of Congolese politics). The Belgian troopers were withdrawn promptly after order had been restored in Stanleyville. Their action, though directed primarily to the rescue of white prisoners, had succeeded in breaking the back of the insurrection; white mercenaries, joined with the Congolese army, killed or dispersed the remaining rebels.

The censure poured upon Spaak by various African nations for his deed was sharp, but not nearly as universal or severe as it had been a few years earlier. Some statesmen were perhaps secretly relieved that this latest Congo rebellion had been quieted, and none dared appear rascist in criticizing the rescue of whites from the acknowledged brutality of the rebels. Spaak skillfully defended Belgium's actions by portraying them as a virtuous necessity. The storm passed.

Respected for her successful European role and criticized for her performance in Africa, Belgium in the post-war period had more difficulty adjusting to the demands of a new world order than she did to the changes wrought by the war in Europe. On the northern continent a good deal of imagination and foresight was used. On the southern, there was a notable lack of proper planning. In Europe there was a predilection for trying new things. Spurred by the divisiveness of the linguistic issue at home, the Belgians also began to search for unity in terms of participation in a larger European entity that would incorporate the aspirations of several lands and tongues. Yet in Africa, the pattern was one of obstinate adherence to traditional colonialist ways until far too late. Nor did the Belgians initially hesitate to defy the United Nations in this area and by so doing help create the circumstances which may ultimately be considered to have permanently lamed the organization.

There were those who suggested at the time that the broadened view Belgium displayed in her diplomacy immediately after the war was an aberration from her more traditional self-centered ways. The Congo crisis seemed at first to substantiate this argument, yet in the long run its effect was just the opposite. The catastrophe enabled Spaak and scores of other Belgians to see that it was necessary to adjust to new conditions not only in Europe but in the world; the United Nations and the emergent countries had to be taken into account. Like Metternich a hundred and thirty years before, Spaak disliked the presumption of the new states and of certain politicians in the Congo; like Metternich also, he realized that both the interests of his own country and of the world in general were to be best served by not undermining the independent sovereignty of the new republic, once that sovereignty had been granted. Though the interests of Belgian nationals still had to be protected, the attitude with which this was done could be, and was, altered. After the Congo crisis, Belgium was smaller in size than she had been for decades, but her diplomatic view was larger.

11.4 NOTES

1. Order of the day, May 25, 1940, reproduced in *Belgium: The Official Account*, p. 104.
2. Arango, *Leopold III*, pp. 64–69.
3. Huizinga, *Mr. Europe*, p. 109.
4. *Recueil de documents et supplément établie par le Secrétariat du Roi concernant la période 1936–1950* is quoted in Arango, *Leopold III*, p. 80.
5. *Recueil*, as quoted in Arango, *Leopold III*, p. 82.
6. *New York Times*, Mar. 23, 1941.
7. U.S.A., *Foreign Relations*, 1942, vol. II, pp. 2–3: 'Matthews to Hull'; pp. 9–11: 'Hull to Biddle'. Spaak, *Combats inachéves*, vol. I, pp. 175–78.

8. Martelli, *Leopold to Lumumba*, pp. 200–201. Terlinden, *Histoire militaire*, vol. II, pp. 523–26.

9. *New York Times*, Apr. 28, 1941.

10. Arango, *Leopold III*, pp. 114–120. See also the second volume of Robert Capelle's *Au service du roi*.

11. U.S.A., *DGP*, ser. D, vol. XI, pp. 312–15, no. 183: 'Memorandum by Paul Schmidt, Oct. 18, 1940, of Hitler's conversation with Princess Marie José, Oct. 17, 1940'. This report, published in 1960, is in contradiction with Schmidt's personal narrative, *Hitler's Interpreter*, which first appeared in its German edition in 1949. In his book, upon which many of the accusations against Leopold were based, Schmidt states that it was the princess who initially raised the matter of an interview. He further suggests that she did so without her brother's knowledge. Whichever version is accepted, it should be noted that General Wilhelm Keitel reported to the commander-in-chief of the occupying army on July 4, 1940, that Leopold had already repeatedly asked for interviews with the Führer (U.S.A., *DGP*, ser. D, vol. X, p. 212, no. 167).

12. U.S.A., *DGP*, ser. D, vol. XI, pp. 612–19, no. 356: 'Memorandum of Hitler-Leopold conversation of Nov. 19, 1940, Nov. 21, 1940'.

13. Schmidt, *Hitler's Interpreter*, p. 204.

14. U.S.A., *DGP*, ser. D, vol. XI, pp. 612–19, no. 356.

15. *Ibid.*, ser. D, vol. XII, pp. 568–69, no. 359: 'Bargen to foreign ministry, Apr. 16, 1941', and editor's note: pp. 918–23, no. 569: 'Same to same, May 29, 1941'.

16. Material on the economic union is voluminous, most of it dealing with the economic aspects rather than with the politics of the union's formation. One resumé particularly useful on the latter area is Meade, *Negotiations for Benelux: An Annotated Chronicle 1943–1956*.

17. Eyck, 'Benelux in the Balance', p. 77.

18. *What is the Significance of Benelux*? (Brussels: Benelux Secretariat-General, n.d.).

19. This and the following quotation are from Spaak's declaration to the chamber on Mar. 3, 1948, Belgium, *Annales parlementaires*, Chambre des représentatives, p. 11.

20. Institut Royal des Relations Internationales (Brussels), *La Belgique et les Nations Unies*, p. 180.

21. Van Campen, *The Quest for Security*, pp. 61–66; the text of the Brussels pact is given on pp. 248–51. See also Van Langenhove, *La sécurité de la Belgique*, pp. 205–15.

22. Spaak's speech to the Belgian chamber is quoted in Institut royal, *La Belgique et les Nations Unies*, p. 15.

23. Spaak, 'The Atomic Bomb and NATO', pp. 353–59.

24. Belgian Government Information Center, *Belgium and Current World Problems*, pp. 25–34.

25. As quoted in Mason, *The European Coal and Steel Community*, p. 15.

26. As quoted in Haas, *The Uniting of Europe*, p. 147.

27. Communauté européene du charbon et de l'acier, *Compte rendu analytique des débats de la seance du mardi 30 novembre 1954*, p. 17. See Laurent, 'Paul-Henry Spaak and the Diplomatic Origins of the Common Market, 1955–56', pp. 373–96.
28. Eyck, 'Benelux in the Common Market', p. 296, and 'The Benelux Countries', p. 358.
29. Hoskyns, *The Congo since Independence*, p. 41. See also Anstey, *King Leopold's Legacy*, pp. 235–40.
30. Lefever, *Crisis in the Congo*, pp. 12–13.
31. Mezerik, *Congo and the United Nations*, vol. I, p. 23.
32. *Ibid.*, vol. II, p. 84.
33. *Ibid.*, vol. III, p. 59.
34. *Ibid.*, vol. III, p. 88.
35. *New York Times*, Oct. 9, 1963.

12. Epilogue

> Our intervention is often exercised with a certain efficaciousness in view of facilitating the entente among the powers; we can thus contribute to the maintenance of peace in Europe, for us a vital interest. It is nevertheless not necessary to exaggerate the influence that a small state can exercise on the politics of the great powers. Without doubt, it can soften the clashes or propose conciliatory formulas; but whatever the talents of its statesmen, the determinism to which the politics of the great powers is obedient escapes its range of action.[1]

So wrote Fernand van Langenhove on July 9, 1936, while serving as secretary-general of the ministry of foreign affairs. His statement is interesting not only because it reflects the dismay and fatalism with which the Belgians saw the development of the second great world conflict, but also because it represents a certain evolution in Belgian diplomacy.

Certainly Barthelemy de Theux and Felix de Meulenaere would not have written thus in the 1830s. The Belgian revolution far from contributed to peace; indeed, in the flush of rebellion Belgian leaders launched excessive demands and promoted the possibility of further conflict as an appropriate means to achieve their end. A period of maturation was necessary before they realized that continuing peace was their best safeguard. Central to that realization was recognition that it was the powers' desire to act in their own self-interest to avoid general war and not the actions of the Belgians that initially had assured the continuing existence of the small state.

The concentration of the Belgians on domestic affairs and their reluctance to become involved on the international scene during the following decades indicated a perhaps excessive discounting of the effectiveness of actions undertaken by Belgium alone rather than sponsored by the guaranteeing powers; at least so would appear to witness the slowness of Brussels officials to act in the Luxemburg and railways affairs. Only when the horizon was already black with war clouds did Belgium attempt to strengthen her defenses sufficiently enough to discourage a great power from attacking her. Even then, there were plans to avoid total opposition to peripheral infringement of Belgian territory.

The moral prestige gained during the First World War encouraged Belgians such as Paul Hymans and Henri Jaspar to believe that, freed of the constrictions of enforced neutrality, Belgian diplomats could play a larger part in world politics. Their experience, including the disillusionments over reparations and the Franco-Belgian military accord, must have been in Van Langenhove's mind as he wrote his statement. Yet if his views contributed to the decision to reduce Belgian commitments in the 1930s, they were also a factor in the important role, in which he participated, undertaken by Belgium in bringing Western Europe together following the Second World War.

The audacity and stridency of the small power's diplomacy immediately following the 1830 revolution, so similar to the nature of the diplomacy of emerging nations in the twentieth century, soon disappeared. Having gained acceptance into the established order, the Belgians worked to preserve rather than alter that order. Certain characteristics of the early period remained, for they were reflections not so much of the revolutionary situation as of the state's lack of military might. Without the use of Hans Morgenthau's third option in diplomacy, the threat of force, the Belgians had to concentrate on the first two: persuasion and compromise. Often these were applied to themselves, as the Belgian leaders learned not to be ambitious in foreign affairs (this is one reason for the steady intensity of debate on domestic issues since the founding of the country). Yet when external negotiations were seriously undertaken, they were pursued with a tenacity of spirit marked by all observers.

During an extended period of negotiation with the British in 1910 over the Kivu and Mfumbiro regions of Africa, Julian Davignon remarked to the British undersecretary for foreign affairs, Sir Arthur Hardinge:

Ours is...a small country, but this makes it all the more important for us if we are to justify the confidence of Parliament to show that we are jealous and tenacious of our independence, our dignity, and our rights.[2]

Belgian persistence in negotiation was related to her pride. There were occasions, as in the scuffles with the Second French Empire, that the little nation did not stand firmly on its dignity; but in general the Belgians have tended to be unyielding, especially if they interpret a concession as infringing on their sovereignty and reputation. Such an attitude was behind their actions in the fortress and lumbering affairs of the 1830s and in De Theux's rupture of relations with Vienna after Metternich withdrew the Austrian ambassador from Brussels. It was evident in the reply to Entente efforts in 1911 to influence Belgium's military planning.

Hymans' criticism of the Paris Peace Conference was based in part on the great powers' failure to allow Belgium a larger voice; his views were resurrected by others following the Second World War, when Belgium opposed the arrangement granting the great powers veto privileges in the United Nations Security Council. Pride prodded Jaspar in his reluctance to bob in the wake of French policy between the wars; it is visible, too, in Belgium's insistence that guarantee treaties take as an assumption, rather than as a matter to be explicitly stated, that Belgium would fully defend herself against foreign attack.

The Belgians' great sensitivity for their sovereignty is quickened not so much by the possession of imperial interests far flung over the globe, although Belgian business does range widely, as by suspicion born of the country's size. A larger nation can make compromises or accept a minor setback without seeing its dignity, power, and influence in future affairs seriously threatened; simultaneous triumphs in other affairs can also offer compensation. But this is not true for Belgium. Setbacks or losses can not be interpreted as demonstrating the magnanimity of Belgium but rather as confirming her limitations.

The Belgians have been especially aware of small matters that appear either to strengthen or lessen their status in international circles, for it is on prestige rather than on the threat of force that Belgium's diplomacy of persuasion and compromise must rest. Efforts have been made to establish a reputation of high quality in Belgian diplomacy in order to compensate for Belgium's lack of military strength and narrow scope of affairs. A slight or insult such as the British delay in recognizing the annexation of the Congo by Belgium in 1908 is not forgotten quickly; United Nations' criticism of Belgium's performance in the Congo in 1960 still rankles and affects Belgian attitudes toward the United Nations and the United States, which supported the U.N.'s Congo actions. On the other hand, such gestures as that made by the Entente powers after the First World War in promoting their representatives at Brussels to the rank of ambassador are appreciated (since the middle of the nineteenth century the diplomats of the major powers had not carried that title at Brussels). Jaspar's pleasure at being a close consultant of his French and British counterparts is everywhere evident in his private correspondence. Following the German invasion of 1914 the Belgians did much to gain world sympathy and enhance their prestige by parading the scrupulous care with which they had conducted their diplomacy as neutrals over the preceding years.

The Belgians' watchword after they became accepted members of the European polity was reliability. Their policies and statements were designed to emphasize this feature of their diplomacy. Perhaps even more useful, however, was the sense of continuity established within the foreign service and ministry. This was achieved even when cabinet changes were more frequent than usual. Indeed these often amounted only to musical chairs, for coalition politics frequently held sway. In the interwar period, when cabinet alterations almost became a way of life, the familiar faces of De Broqueville, Hymans, Jaspar, and Theunis could nevertheless usually be found in at least several of the top positions. If few Belgian diplomats matched Van de Weyer's thirty-six years at the Court of Saint James, their lengthy sojourns at their posts strengthened continuity and helped to convey an impression of reliability to the powers to which they were accredited.

A similar effect was produced by the frequency with which several members and generations of leading Belgian families entered public careers. Not all combinations were as notable as the father-son careers of the Beyens and Davignon families, but there are many that come to mind, ranging from the Rogiers, Orbans, Griendls, and De Borchgraves to the Van der Elsts, Jaspars, and the Janson-Spaak relationship. This last example points out further that many of the leading public families of Belgium were linked by marriage or by the marriages of relatives, as in the case of the Hymans, Jaequemyns, and Borchgrave families. This pattern of close relationships existed through all levels of the Belgian civil service. Not unique to Belgium, it was more extensive than in many other states and had more effect because of the limited size of the small nation's foreign service. Thus it was that representatives of other countries when dealing with Belgian diplomats often discovered they were conversing either with long-time acquaintances or close friends or relatives of such acquaintances.

The effort to enhance the Belgians' moral prestige and thus their efforts to negotiate from a weak-power basis is partly keyed to emphasis on legality. Unable to wage a major war in defense of her rights and fearful that a victorious power might infringe on those rights even if Belgium were not involved in a conflict, Belgium is dependent upon international law and diplomacy to maintain her integrity. Making a virtue out of a necessity is good diplomacy, and the Belgians have not hesitated to suggest that Belgium's reliance on legal, rather than extra-legal, means to further her wishes is a reflection of a special quality that warrants the respect, protection, and occasionally the deference of great powers. Sometimes the emphasis on strict legalism led to a circumscribed outlook that sharply limited the range of Belgian diplomacy, as during the last half of the nineteenth century. At other times it was used as a tool to avoid undesirable commitments, as Spaak used it to escape the vague strictures of Article Sixteen of the League of Nations Covenant.

Even when so doing, he commented that:' Small countries, more than others, should have a concern to respect scrupulously and to apply rigorously all the engagements they take.'[3]

This legalism, though a key factor in gaining the world's sympathy in 1914 and on other occasions, has less frequently worked to the disadvantage of the small state. In particular, it won the wrath of many in the late 1930s who questioned not Belgium's legal right to her independent stance but rather her moral right to separate herself from French policy. To the Belgians, it was unthinkable that legal and moral right could be opposed to each other, and in the case in point they argued that it was only by exercising their legal right to an independent policy that they could properly pursue the moral necessity of armament against Hitler. It was similar thinking that led to the decision prior to the first German invasion that it was both legally and morally right not to oppose a minor incursion over Belgium's borders. Had such a policy actually been followed, the fate of Belgium at the hands of the victorious powers might have been less attractive than it actually was.

Just as the Belgians have made a virtue out of the necessity of their dependence on international law, so too have they worked to turn liabilities into assets. If Belgium's location has proved a source of danger, it has also been used to oblige neighboring powers to be friendly or to stay away for fear of provoking an attack by some other state. The Belgians have also attempted to turn their small size into an asset, associating virtue with the weakness so much a necessary condition of being a small power. Their success in doing so has won them support and occasionally real bargaining power. Neither Lloyd George nor Clemenceau dared, for example, to risk appearing as despoilers of Belgium's rightful reparations no matter how much they desired to increase the shares of their own nations. There is no question, too, that public support, both at home and abroad, of British diplomacy in 1870, 1914 and on several other occasions was strengthened by the moral prestige acquired through promising protection to a little country.

Yet while it was often to the advantage of the great powers to support the image the Belgians so carefully propagated of a small power possessing unusual qualities of virtue, at times this image has for them been a source of irritation. It aided King Leopold II in masking his Congo schemes until the time was past for his plans safely to be undone by the great powers, and it was the image that Lloyd George so carefully advertised during the war that partially curbed his reparations demands later. Lord Curzon, for his part, denounced the image as a sham during Belgium's participation in the Ruhr occupation, and there were many other great power representatives that grumbled about it over the years. Surely some of Belgium's relations with Holland, the 1920 military accord's secret plan to make use of the Duchy of Luxemburg, and the Katanga secession reveal that small size does not necessarily preclude a nation's participation in questionable behavior. On the whole, however, the Belgians have successfully equated inability to use force with unwillingness to use force and thence with purity of motive; and on the whole, this has been true.

This is not to say Belgium has not used force. She has, for example in the 1830s and during the great wars. In the latter instances, any truly successful result was precluded not only by Belgium's lack of resources but also by her lack of commitment fostered by the knowledge that no matter how great an effort was made, Belgium's military alone could not protect the country.

If only partially successful at using their own force, the Belgians have been adept at using the force of others to their own advantage. This is a theme that runs through nearly every episode of Belgium's diplomatic life from the royal diplomacy of the nineteenth century through secret ministerial diplomacy to the more public negotiation of the post World War II era. It consists simply of the playing off of the powers one against another: Britain against France, France against the Netherlands, England against France or Germany, Germany against England and France, and so on again through the cycle. As Arthur Hardinge commented in 1907, the confrontation of the great powers is almost a necessity for the safe continuation of Belgium:

So long as the political situation in Western Europe is dominated by a latent antagonism between France and Germany, strong enough to prevent their cooperation, but not acute enough to produce actual war, Belgium feels secure from the alternative perils of partition between her two powerful neighbors, or invasion by one or the other.[4]

This was indeed true for much of Belgium's history. On some occasions, as in 1870, it was as a direct result of Belgium's efforts that the powers balanced each other; at other times, the powers automatically balanced without Belgium taking action. Even after the triumph of the Entente over the Central Powers, Belgium managed to find a middle position, mediating between Britain and France; and although Germany was still seen as the enemy, the Belgians did occasionally mediate between her and the Entente. When Germany became the dominant power of Europe, although the Belgians kept up their balancing efforts, they knew a balance no longer existed; the potential of their own diplomacy was reduced and they began to limit their commitments. Since the First World War, the Belgians have been absorbed in domestic and colonial troubles; yet these have not prevented Belgium from being an important mediator of international differences in working toward a United Europe and a reduction of conflicts between Gaullist France and Britain and the United States. The Western camp is big enough and incorporates sufficient differences of opinion that Belgium can assert herself without flirting with the Communist East, a region that has traditionally been beyond the primary scope of Belgian diplomacy.

It is the pairing of the concept of mediation with that of balance that partially reconciles Hardinge's observation with Spaak's famous declaration that:

Never, in the policy of the Belgian government, will there be born the idea of playing the card of one great nation against that of another. On the contrary, in every measure of the possibilities, in every matter in which we have a role to play, we shall try to be a hyphen between the great powers.[5]

A quick review of Belgium's diplomatic history would give judgment to Hardinge. Yet the British diplomat himself pointed out that an important concern to the Belgians was not to let the great powers drift too far apart. It is the emphasis placed upon mediation and cooperation by Spaak that perhaps best indicates the direction taken in the evolution of Belgian diplomacy in the twentieth century.

If over the years the presence of flux in the international scene has been to Belgium's advantage, her national interests generally called for the maintenance of peace. Only in the 1830s was war and revolution an obvious instrument of policy. This is noteworthy, for it would seem that certain territorial aspirations such as the annexation of Dutch Limburg and Zeeland and of the Grand Duchy of Luxemburg could be obtained only as a result of general European upheaval. Moreover, as the linguistic division has grown in recent decades, there have been both Flemings and Walloons who see disruption of international peace as providing the best opportunity for furthering their aspirations for administrative division of their country. Yet the fact remains that any upheaval sufficient enough to permit a rearrangement of Belgium's borders could also devour the country entirely. Thus in each crisis her diplomats have asked first for guarantees of Belgium's territorial integrity and only later inquired about annexations.

The economic dimensions of Belgium's diplomacy and national interests must also be taken into account. Since the early stages of the industrial revolution, Belgium has thrived on the production of her mines and industries. Her location and thorough development of her railways and the port of Antwerp have made transit trade an important source of national income.

The motto of the 1830s, *enrichez-vous*, has not been lost on Belgian entrepreneurs in the decades after their nation's birth. Extensive investments were made throughout the globe; the interlocking of personnel between such huge corporations as the *Société Générale* and the government was not by accident. Highly dependent upon imports to meet basic population needs and upon exports and transit trade for income, Belgium has always had interest in maintaining a peaceful international scene conducive to trade and to bettering her competitive economic position. Nor is it surprising that a state with so many foreign investments often included among its chief national interests the duty of protecting and fostering those investments.

In a critique of Belgium's performance in the Congo, Roger Anstey has written:

Belgium consistently failed to see that a whole series of separate achievements, principally material and mostly related to an unreflecting economic purpose, was not enough...

It may also be that the people of Belgium, a country which is not a nation (because riven by at least three conflicts: the Roman Catholic Church versus anti-clericals, monarchy versus republicanism and, above all, Walloon versus Fleming), shut themselves up in a conception of the state which is seen only as the arbiter of divergent interests, and which therefore lacks the sense of homogeniety which is a condition of nationhood. If this is so, there would be no disposition to wish upon the Congolese a nationalism which Belgians did not themselves possess... Rather concern oneself with the day-to-day business of making a living.[6]

While it is possible to differ with Anstey's view of Belgian nationalism, particularly for the years prior to 1930, his comments regarding the concentration on business activities and the special difficulty Belgium now experiences in defining her national interests must be acknowledged.

They may in part explain the strong emphasis Belgium has placed on pragmatic economic cooperation and on internationalism in recent years. Her statesmen are familiar with the problems of holding divergent factions together, and for more than half a century Belgium has dealt with conflicts between socialists and conservatives, Flemings and Walloons, with specific steps and compromises that must be revised every few years. With Belgium's widespread trade and financial involvements, linguistic diversity, the proximity of other countries, and the increasing tendency of the populace to travel, the people of Belgium are far more international in their outlook than those of France, Germany, or Britain. The difficulty of reaching long standing solutions to the divisions within their own country may cause them to be more tolerant of the differences which exist within the various systems of European cooperation and to find more identity and fulfillment in the success of those institutions than otherwise might be expected. At her beginnings, Belgium's national interests were strongly affected by the level of cooperation of the powers within the concert of Europe. From 1850 to 1950, her concerns were economic growth and the maintenance of a proper balance among the powers so that Belgium would have some maneuvering room without being threatened. Since 1950, the two governing interests are economic growth and European integration, for the compromises to Belgium's sovereignty involved in integration will strengthen more than weaken the small state. Military security has always been a central concern, but in a nuclear age of superpowers Belgium's security more than ever seems dependent upon the preparations of others and particularly upon the Western world's willingness to cooperate.

There have been suggestions that the best measure of success of the diplomacy of small states is not how many of their own ambitions they have satisfied but how well they have resisted the demands of greater powers.[7] The Belgians have done well on these terms, although military defeats have marked two occasions when their diplomacy failed to overcome the almost insuperable problems posed by Belgium's size and location. In following their policy of persuasion, compromise, and prestige, the Belgians have shown that if the diplomacy of a small power must at times be static and legalistic, it can also be creative.

Diplomacy has been called the art of the possible. For Belgium, the possible has often been limited by her size. Many of the methods and approaches her diplomats have used are such as might be employed by large and small nations alike; yet Belgium has put them together and applied them in a style which is inextricably linked with her diminutive size.

Equally important for Belgian behavior in international affairs as the physical limitations imposed by the nation's size is the manner in which her diplomats have viewed the smallness of the country and judged of what the possible actually consists for Belgium. It has been argued that an appropriate definition of small powers must take into account a psychological as well as a military and material difference between them and great powers. According to Robert Rothstein, small powers 'earn their title not only by being weak but by recognizing the implications of that condition'.[8]

Certainly it is true that over the decades, Belgium's smallness has been treated as an asset and as a liability, as a reason for activity or for disengagement in foreign affairs. It has conditioned her diplomats' sense of pride, proportion, and responsibility. It has been seen as an all-dominating factor and merely as one among many which must be dealt with in everyday diplomacy and which should not, through timidity or self conscious-ness, be granted more weight than its due. Thus it is the attitude Belgian leaders have themselves taken toward Belgium's size that has shaped their behavior in regard to particular problems and has been at the very heart of the nation's diplomacy.

NOTES

1. Belgium, *DDB*, vol. IV, p. 241, no. 92: 'Van Langenhove note, July 9, 1936'.
2. Quoted in Louis, *Ruanda-Urundi 1884–1919*, p. 88.
3. Belgium, *Annales parlementaires*, Chambre des représentatives, p. 318 Dec. 2, 1939.
4. Great Britain, *BD*, vol. III, p. 202: Editor's note printing excerpts from the General Report on Belgium for 1906, enclosed in Hardinge's dispatch of April 10, 1907.
5. Quoted in Institut Royal des Relations Internationales (Brussels), *La Belgique et les Nations Unies*, p. 170.
6. Anstey, *King Leopold's Legacy*, pp. 260, 263–64.
7. Fox, *The Power of Small States*, p. 3.
8. Robert L. Rothstein, *Alliances and Small Powers*, p. 29.

Bibliography

The following list indicates only those works which have been most directly useful in the preparation of this account. The books written on Belgium's neutrality, especially from the point of view of international law, are legion. Numerous also are the general accounts of European diplomacy since 1815 and the multicolored document collections that have been issued by the European governments during the same period. Many of these have been helpful to me but have not been included here for reasons of space.

1. UNPUBLISHED SOURCES

Belgium, Archives générales du Royaume (Arch. gén.):

  Jules van den Heuvel papers
  Paul Hymans papers
  Henri Jaspar papers
  Charles Rogier papers
  Sylvain van de Weyer papers

Belgium, Ministère des Affaires étrangères, Service des Archives (M.A.E. Arch.):

  Correspondance politique:

    Incident Franco-Belge, 1869–1870
    Legations, France
    Legations, Great Britain

  Classement:

    Afrique
    B
    Indépendence, Neutralité, Defense militaire de la Belgique (INDM)
  Fonds Lambermont

  Volumes noirs:

    Question du Gr.-Duché de Luxembourg

Craig, Gordon A. 'Britain and Europe (1866–1869): A Study in the Application of Non-Intervention.' Unpublished Ph.D. dissertation, Princeton University, 1941.

2. DOCUMENTS AND OFFICIAL PUBLICATIONS

Belgium

Annales parlementaires. Brussels.
Belgian Government Information Center. *Belgium and Current World Problems*. New York: 1953.
The Belgian Grey Book. 2 vols. London: Belgian Ministry of Foreign Affairs, 1914–15.
Also in *Collected Documents Relating to the Outbreak of the European War*. London, Foreign Office, 1915.
Belgium: The Official Account of What Happened 1939–40.
London: Evans for the Belgian Ministry of Foreign Affairs, 1941.
Biographie nationale. Brussels: Académie royale des sciences, des lettres et des beaux-arts de Belgique, 1866–   .
Correspondance diplomatique et politique relative à la guerre en Afrique. Brussels: Ministère des Colonies, 1919.
Discailles, Ernest. 'Un diplomate belge à Paris de 1830 à 1864', Académie royale de Belgique, Classe des lettres et des sciences morales et politiques et classe des beaux-arts, *Mémoires*, in 4°, 2nd ser., III (Dec. 1908). Reproduces 525 documents.
Documents diplomatiques belges: La politique de securité extérieure, ed. by Charles de Visscher, and F. Vanlangenhove. 5 vols. Brussels: Académie royale de Belgique, Commission royale d'histoire, 1964–66. (*DDB*.)
Documents diplomatiques aux réparations (du décembre 1922 au 27 août 1923). Brussels: Ministère des Affaires étrangères, 1923. (*DDR*.)
'Documents inédits sur la crise internationale de 1870', ed. by R. Demoulin, Académie royale de Belgique, Commission royale d'histoire, *Bulletin*, CXXII, no. 2 (Apr. 1957), 127–238. (*DI*.)
Histoire parlementaire du traité de paix de 19 avril 1839 entre la Belgique et la Hollande. 2 vols. Brussels: Librarie Universelle de Mary-Müller, 1839. Reproduces many documents and speeches.
Langenhove, Fernand van. *Le dossier diplomatique de la question belge*. Brussels: Van Oest, 1917.
Ridder, Alfred de.*La crise de la neutralité belge de 1848: Le dossier diplomatique*. 2 vols. Brussels: Kiessling, 1928. Compiled by the long-time director general and historical counselor of the Belgian Ministry of Foreign Affairs.
Ridder, Alfred de. 'Un diplomate autrichien à Bruxelles en 1848. Lettres du comte de Woyna', Académie royale de Belgique, Commission royale d'histoire, *Bulletin*, LXXXIX, no. 2 (Apr. 1925), 128–236.
Schwertfeger, Bernhard (ed.). *Amtliche Aktenstücke zur Geschichte der Europäischen Politik 1885–1914 (Die belgischen Dokumente zur Vorgeschichte des Weltkrieges)*. 5 vols. with 2 supplementary vols. and 2 commentary vols., Berlin: Deutsche Verlagsgesellschaft für Politik und Geschichte, 1925. The first five volumes are a reissue of Schwertfeger's *Zur Europäischen Politik 1897–1914*. *Unveröffentliche Dokumente*. 5 vols. Berlin, 1919. The

first supplementary volume reissues the *Belgische Aktenstücke 1905–1914*, edited at the German foreign office and published in Berlin in 1915 following the capture of the documents by German troops. The second supplementary volume *Der geistige Kampf um die Verletzung der belgischen Neutralität*, contains the first Belgian grey book and the first part of the second grey book.

France

Documents diplomatiques français, 1871–1914. 41 vols. Paris: Ministère des Affaires étrangères, 1929–59. (*DDF, 1871–1914.*)

Documents diplomatiques français, 1932–1939. Paris: Ministère des Affaires étrangères, 1964– . (*DDF, 1932–1939.*)

Documents diplomatiques, Livres jaunes: Affaires du Congo et de l'afrique occidentale. Paris: Ministère des Affaires étrangères, 1884. (*LJ, Congo, 1884.*)

–Affaires du Congo et de l'Afrique occidentale. Paris, Ministère des Affaires étrangères, 1885. (*LJ, Congo, 1885.*)

Journal official de la République française. (*JORF.*)

Les Origines diplomatiques de la guerre de 1870–71. 29 vols. Paris: Ministère des Affaires étrangères, Lavauzelle, 1910–32.

Germany

Akten der Reichskanzlei: Weimarer Republik. Boppard am Rhein: Boldt, 1968– .

Documents on German Foreign Policy, 1918–1945. Washington: United States Department of State, 1949. (*DGP.*)

Gottschalk, Egon. 'Die deutschen Dokumente des Jahres 1887 zur belgischen Frage', *Berliner Monatshefte* (Nov. 1931), 1033–53.

Kautsky, Karl; Max Montgelas, and Walther Schucking (eds.). *The German Documents Relating to the Outbreak of the War.* Translated by the Carnegie Endowment for International Peace, Division of International Law. New York: Oxford University. Press, 1924.

Lepsius, Johannes; Albrecht Mendelssohn Bartholdy, and Friedrich Thimme (eds.). *Die Grosse Politik der Europäischen Kabinette 1871–1914.* 40 vols. Berlin, 1927.

Great Britain

British Documents on the Origins of the War 1898–1914, ed. by G. P. Gooch, and H. Temperley. 11 vols. London, 1926–36. (*BD.*)

'Correspondence with the Allied Governments respecting Reparation Payments by Germany', *House of Commons Sessional Papers.* London, 1923, XXV, Cmd. 1943.

Documents on British Foreign Policy, ed. by E. L. Woodward and Rohan
    Butler. London, 1946–   . (*DBP*.)
'Documents Exchanged between His Majesty's Government in the United
    Kingdom and the French Government, and the Belgian Government,
    concerning the International Position of Belgium', *House of Commons
    Sessional Papers*. London, 1936–37, XXIX, Cmd. 5437.
'Inter-allied Conferences on Reparations and Inter-allied Debts held in Lon-
    don and Paris, December 1922 and January 1923', *House of Commons
    Sessional Papers*, London, 1923, XXIV, Cmd. 1812.
'Minutes of the London Conference on Reparations, August, 1922', *House of
    Commons Sessional Papers*. London, 1924, XXVII, Cmd. 2258.
The Parliamentary Debates

The Netherlands

Bescheiden betreffende de Buitenlandse Politiek van Nederland, 1848–1919.
    (Rijksgeschiedkundige Publicatiën.) The Hague: Nijhoff. 1964. (*BN.*)

United States

Senate. *Executive Document No. 196.* 49th Congress, 1st session. Washington‹
    1886.
Senate. *Miscellaneous Document No. 68.* 49th Congress, 1st session. Washing-
    ton, 1886.
Senate. *Senate Report No. 393.* 48th Congress, 1st session. Washington, 1884.
Papers Relating to the Foreign Relations of the United States. Washington:
    Department of State.

Miscellaneous

Collected Documents Relating to the Outbreak of the European War. London:
    Foreign Office, 1915.
Communauté européene du charbon et de l'acier. *Compte rendu analytique des
    debats de la seance du mardi 30 novembre 1954.*
*Das Staatsarchiv: Sammlung der official Aktenstücke zur Geschichte der Gegen-
    wart.* Ed. by L. K. Aegidi and A. Klauhold (Hamburg). A periodical.
Day, George I. and H. H. Fisher (eds.). *Public Relations of the Commission for
    Relief in Belgium. Documents.* 2 vols. (Hoover War Library Publications
    no. 7.) Stanford: Stanford University Press, 1929.
Diplomatic Documents Relating to the Outbreak of the European War, ed. by
    James Brown Scott. 2 parts. New York: Oxford University Press, 1916.
Documents on International Affairs. London: Oxford University Press, 1929– .
What is the Significance of Benelux? Brussels: Benelux Secretariat-General,
    n.d.

3. Memoirs and letters

Allen, Maj.-Gen. Henry T. *The Rhineland Occupation*. Indianapolis: Bobbs-Merrill, 1927. By the commander of the American troops.

Banning, Emile. *Mémoires politiques et diplomatiques. Comment fut fondé le Congo belge*. Paris-Brussels: Renaissance du Livre, 1927. Written shortly after the Berlin Conference but not released for publication until after First World War. Not as complete as might be wished but contains several detailed passages of much value.

Bassompierre, Albert de. 'La nuit du 2 au 3 août 1914 au ministère des affaires étrangères de Belgique,' *Revue des deux mondes*, 7th ser., XXXI (Feb. 15, 1916), 884–906. An eyewitness account by the foreign minister's secretary.

Beyens, Baron Napoléon Eugène. 'Deux politiques', *Le Flambeau*, V, no. 4 (Apr. 30, 1922), 407–30; no. 5 (May 31, 1922), 23–42. A defense of his policies as foreign minister during the First World War.

– *Germany before the War*. Translated by P. V. Cohn. London, 1961. Recalls his experience as Belgian minister in Berlin.

Bridges, Maj.-Gen. Tom. *Alarms and Excursions: Reminiscences of a Soldier*. London: Longmans, Green, 1938.

Broqueville, Count Charles de. 'Pourquoi j'ai parlé en mars 1934', *Revue générale*, 72nd yr., CXLI, March 15, 1939, 289–98.

Bülow, Prince Bernhard von. *Memoirs of Prince von Bülow*. 4 vols. Translated by G. Dunlop. Boston: Little, Brown, 1931–1932.

Capelle, Robert. *Au service du roi*. 2 vols. Brussels: Dessart, n.d.

D'Abernon, Viscount. *The Diary of an Ambassador*. 3 vols. Garden City: Doubleday, Doran, 1929–1930.

Davignon, Jacques. *Berlin 1936–1940: Souvenirs d'une Mission*. Brussels: Éditions Universitaires, 1951.

Dawes, Charles G. *A Journal of Reparations*. London: Macmillan, 1929.

Dorlodot, Baron René de. *Souvenirs*. Brussels: Goemaere, 1947. Primarily a critique of the Belgian government's policies during the 1930s.

Eden, Anthony. *The Memoirs of Anthony Eden, Earl of Avon*. 2 vols. Boston: Houghton-Mifflin, 1960–1962.

Gamelin, Maurice L. *Servir*. 3 vols. Paris: Plon, 1946–1947.

Goblet d'Alviella, Lt.-General Count. *Mémoires historiques: Dix-huit mois de politique et de négociations se rattachant à la première atteinte portée aux traités de 1815*. 2 vols. Paris: Librairie internationale, 1864–1865.

Hymans, Paul. *Mémoires*. Edited by Frans van Kalken with the collaboration of John Bartier. 2 vols. Brussels: Institut de Sociologie Solvay, 1958.

Ironside, Edmund. *Time Unguarded: The Ironside Diaries 1937–1940*. Edited by R. Macleod and D. Kelly. New York: McKay, 1962.

Joffre, Marshal Joseph J. C. *The Personal Memoirs of Joffre, Field Marshal of the French Army*. 2 vols. Translated by T. B. Mott. New York: Harper, 1932.

— 'Le problème belge en 1912', *Revue des deux mondes*, 8th ser., X (Aug. 15, 1932), 721–33.

Juste, Theodore. *Memoirs of Leopold I, King of the Belgians.* 2 vols. Translated by Robert Black. London: Sampson Low, Son, and Marston, 1868. An historian's skilful linking of many of the king's public utterances and letters.

Langenhove, Fernand van. *La sécurité de la Belgique: Contribution à l'histoire de la période 1940–1950.* Brussels: Univ. libre de Bruxelles, 1971.

Laroche, Jules. *Au Quai d'Orsay avec Briand et Poincaré 1913–1926.* Paris: Hachette, 1957.

Lebeau, Joseph. *Souvenirs personnels (1824–1841) et correspondance diplomatique de Joseph Lebeau.* Edited by Armand Freson. Brussels: Office de Publicité, 1883.

Letters of Queen Victoria, The. First series edited by A. C. Benson and Viscount Esher. 3 vols. New York: Longmans, Green, 1907.

Second series edited by G. E. Buckle. 3 vols. New York: Longmans, Green, 1926–1928.

Third Series edited by G. E. Buckle. 3 vols. New York: Longmans, Green, 1930–1932.

Loucheur, Louis. *Carnet secrets 1908–1932.* Edited by Jacques Launay. Brussels: Brepols, 1962. Sketchy.

Metternich, Prince Clemens von. *Memoirs of Prince Metternich.* 5 vols. Edited by Prince Richard Metternich; transl. G.W. Smith. New York: Scribner's, 1880–1882.

Miller, David Hunter. *My Diary at the Conference of Paris, with Documents.* 21 vols. New York: Appeal Printing Co., 1924. Only forty sets published.

Noville, Jean Albert. *Paul van Zeeland au service de son temps.* Brussels: Lucien de Meyer, 1954. A collection of Van Zeeland's speeches.

Overstraeten, General E. Raoul van. *Albert Ier – Leopold III: Vingt ans de politique militaire belge (1920–1940).* Paris: Desclée de Brouwer, 1949.

— *Au Service de la Belgique. I, Dans l'étau.* No subsequent vols. published. Paris: Plon, 1960.

— (ed.). *Les carnets de guerre d'Albert Ier, Roi des Belges.* Brussels: Dessart, 1953.

Reynaud, Paul. *In the Thick of the Fight 1930–1945.* Translated by J. D. Lambert. New York: Simon and Schuster, 1955.

Schmidt, Paul. *Hitler's Interpreter.* Edited by R.H.C. Steed. London: Heinemann, 1951.

Spaak, Paul-Henri. *Combats inachevés.* 2 vols. Paris: Fayard, 1969.

Stanley, Henry M. *The Congo and the Founding of the Free State.* 2 vols. New York: Harper, 1885.

Stengers, Jean. 'Textes inédits d'Emile Banning', Académie royale des sciences coloniales, Classe des sciences morales et politiques, *Mémoires,* new ser., II, no. 3 (1955).

Talleyrand, Prince. *Memoirs of the Prince de Talleyrand.* 5 vols. Edited by the Duc de Broglie. Translated by Mrs. Angus Hall. New York: Putnam's, 1891–1892.

Weygand, General Maxime. *Mémoires*. 3 vols. Paris: Flammarion, 1950–1957.
Whitlock, Brand. *The Letters and Journal of Brand Whitlock*. Edited by Allen Nevins. 2 vols. New York: Appleton-Century, 1936.

4. ARTICLES, PERIODICALS AND NEWSPAPERS

Anagoste. 'La paix par l'Entente', *Le Flambeau*, VI, no. 7 (July 31, 1923), 488–509.
'Aus den Archiven des belgischen Kolonialministeriums. Zur Entstehungsgeschichte des Kongostaates', *Deutsches Kolonialblatt* (Berlin: Reichs-Kolonialamt), XXIX, nos. 3/4 (Feb. 15, 1918), 18–33. This series of articles is based on documents found in Brussels by the invading Germans.
'Aus den Archiven des belgischen Kolonialministeriums. L'État Indépendant du Congo et la France. 1885–1892', *Deutsches Kolonialblatt* (Berlin: Reiches-Kolonialamt), XXVII, nos. 6/7 (Apr. 1, 1916), 59–91.
'Aus den Archiven des belgischen Kolonialministeriums. Das Lado- und Bahr el Ghazel-Pachtgebiet des Kongostaates', *Deutsches Kolonialblatt* (Berlin: Reichs-Kolonialamt), XXVII, nos. 10/11 (June 1, 1916), 135–61.
'Aus den Archiven des belgischen Kolonialministeriums. Zwei bisher unbekannte Dokumente zur Vorgeschichte des Kongostaats aus den Jahren 1878 und 1879, das Comité d'études du Haut-Congo betreffend', *Deutsches Kolonialblatt* (Berlin: Reichs-Kolonialamt), XXVIII, no. 24 (Dec. 15, 1917), 297–307.
Binion, Rudolph. 'Repeat Performance: A Psychological Study of Leopold III and Belgian Neutrality', *History and Theory*, VIII, no. 2 (1969), 213–59.
Blanchard, Marcel. 'Françaises et Belges sur l'Oubanghi (1890–1896)', *Revue d'histoire des colonies*, XXXVII, no. 1 (1950), 1–36.
Buchet, General Charles. 'Le rôle de la Belgique dans la défense des frontieres de la France', *La revue de France*, Fourteenth year, VI, no. 21 (Nov. 1934), 27–47.
Buttgenbach, André. 'Le mouvement rexiste et la situation politique de la Belgique', *Revue des sciences politiques*, LIX, no. 4 (Oct.-Dec. 1936), 511–54.
Calmes, Christian. 'Malaise et annexionisme belge en 1867', *Hemecht*, XXI (1969), 373–96.
Cammaerts, Emile. 'The Belgian Military Conversations of 1912', *Contemporary Review*, CXLIV, no. 811 (July 1933), 47–55. By a noted interpreter of Belgium to the English-speaking world.
— 'Belgium and the Entente', *Edinburgh Review*, CCXXXVIII (July 1923), 183–97.
— 'The Belgian Problem', *Contemporary Review*, CLI, no. 858 (June 1937), 658–66.
Craig, Gordon A. 'Great Britain and the Belgian Railways Dispute of 1869', *American Historical Review*, L, no. 4 (July 1945), 738–61.

Demoulin, Robert. 'Léopold II et la Grand-Duché de Luxembourg au prin-
temps de 1867', *Mélanges offerts à G. Jacquemyns* (Brussels: Univ. libre
de Bruxelles, Editions de l'Institut de Sociologie, 1968), 163–89. The best
account of royal diplomacy in this affair.

Devleeshouwer, Robert. 'L'Opinion publique et les revendications territoriales
belges à la fin de la première guerre mondiale 1918–1919', *Mélanges offerts
à G. Jacquemyns* (Brussels: Univ. libre de Bruxelles, Editions de l'Institut
de Sociologie, 1968), 207–38.

Discailles, Ernest. 'Trois dates de l'histoire du grand-duché de Luxembourg,
1839, 1851, 1867', Académie royale de Belgique, Classe des lettres et des
sciences morales et politiques et classe des beaux-arts, *Bulletin* (1907),
298–337.

Du Bois, Albert. 'La Belgique pendant la guerre franco-allemande 1870–1871',
Revue de Belgique, 2nd ser., VI, no. 3 (1892), 366–85.

Elst, Baron Léon van der. 'La préméditation de l'Allemagne', *La revue de
Paris*, XXX, no. 2 (Mar.-Apr. 1923), 521–31.

Eyck, F. Gunther. 'Benelux in the Balance', *Political Science Quarterly*, LXIX,
no. 1 (March 1954), 65–91.

— 'Benelux in the Common Market', *Current History*, VL, no. 267 (Nov.
1963), 295–301.

— 'The Benelux Countries', *Current History*, XXXXVII, no. 280 (Dec. 1964),
355–61.

Foot, M.R.D. 'Great Britain and Luxembourg 1867', *English Historical
Review*, LXVII, no. 264 (July 1952), 352–79.

Glasgow, George. 'Foreign Affairs, Franco-Belgian Friction over the Ruhr',
Contemporary Review, CXXIII (Apr. 1923), 509–17.

Grieken, E. van. 'H. M. Stanley au Congo (1879–1884) d'après le manuscrit
de Ch. Notte', Institut royale colonial belge, *Bulletin des séances*, XXV
(1954), no. 3, 1124–79; no. 5, 1428–61. Reviews a list of documents on the
Congo that Leopold II is believed to have ordered destroyed.

Haag, Henri, 'La démission de Paul Hymans et la fin du second gouvernement Delacroix (juilliet-novembre 1920)', *Mélanges offerts à G. Jacquemyns* (Brussels: Univ. libre de Bruxelles, Éditions de l'Institut de Sociologie, 1968), 393–419.

Helmreich, Jonathan E. 'The Negotiation of the Franco-Belgian Military
Accord of 1920', *French Historical Studies*, III, no. 3 (Spring 1964),
360–78.

— 'Belgian Concern over Neutrality and British Intentions, 1906–14', *Journal
of Modern History*, XXXVI, no. 4 (Dec. 1964), 416–27.

— 'The End of Congo Neutrality, 1914', *Historian*, XXVIII, no. 4 (Aug.
1966), 610–24.

Huisman, Michel. 'Juillet 1870', *Le Flambeau* (Jan. 1932), 26–27.

Jaspar, Henri. 'The Keystones of Belgium's Foreign Policy', *Current History*,
XIX, no. 6 (Mar. 1924), 1032–37.

— 'Locarno et la Belgique', *La revue belge*, 6th yr., IV (Nov. 15, 1925), 154–
169.

— 'Les directives de la politique extérieure de la Belgique', *L'Esprit International*, Seventh year (Jan. 1933), 3–22.

Kurgan-van Hentenrijk, G. 'Une étape mouvementée de la réorganisation des chemins de fer belges: Le rachat du Grand-Duché de Luxembourg par l'état (1872–1873)', *Revue belge de philologie et d'histoire*, L, no. 2 (1972), 395–446.

Langenhove, Fernand van. 'L'accord militaire franco-belge de 1920 à la lumière des Documents Diplomatiques Belges', Académie royale de Belgique, Classe des lettres et des sciences morales et politiques, *Bulletin*, no. 11 (1967), 520–35.

— 'La crise fatidique du 7 mars 1936', Académie royale de Belgique, Classe des lettres et des sciences morales et politiques, *Bulletin*, no. 1 (1967), 17–39.

— 'A propos des relations militaires franco-belges, 1936–1940', *Revue belge de philologie et d'histoire* (1969), 1198–1215.

Laurent, P.-H. 'Commerce, Colonies and Claims: King Leopold I and Belgian-American Statecraft, 1832–1846', *Expansion belge 1831–1865: Recueil d'études*. Brussels: Académie Royale des Sciences d'Outre-mer, 1965, 550–66.

— 'Paul-Henry Spaak and the Diplomatic Origins of the Common Market, 1955–1956', *Political Science Quarterly*, LXXXV, no. 3 (Sept. 1970), 373–96.

Leroy-Beaulieu, Paul. 'La politique continentale et la politique coloniale; à propos de la necessité de l'annexion totale de la Tunisie', *L'Économiste française* (May 7), 1881.

Lingelbach, William E. 'Neutrality *versus* Alliances. Belgium and the Revolution in International Politics', *Proceedings of the American Philosophical Society*, LXXIX, no. 4 (Nov. 15, 1938, 607–38, Defends Belgium's abrogation of the 1920 Franco-Belgian Military Accord.

Lorette, J. 'Problèmes de politique étrangère sous Léopold Ier: A propos d'éventuelles participations belges à la guerre de Crimée (1854–1856)', *Expansion belge 1831–1965: Recueil d'études*. Brussels: Académie Royale des Sciences d'Outre-mer, 1965, 568–71.

Loridan, Walter. Belgium and the United Nations', *Annals of the American Academy of Political and Social Sciences*, CCXLVII (Sept. 1946), 165–70.

Marks, Sally. 'The Luxemburg Question at the Paris Peace Conference and After', *Revue belge d'histoire contemporaine* (1970), 1–20.

Marnay, Philippe. 'La politique militaire de la Belgique en 1939–1940', *Revue générale belge* (May 1960), 3–60.

Pabst, Klaus. 'Eupen-Malmedy in der belgischen Regierungs- und Partienpolitik 1914–1940', *Zeitschrift des Aachener Geschichtsvereins*, LXXVI (1964), 206–515.

Pacificus. 'Faillait-il aller dans la Ruhr?', *Le Flambeau*, VI, no. 1 (Jan. 31, 1923), 71–5. Yes, says an eminent statesman.

Rheindorf, Kurt. 'Der belgische-französiche Eisenbahnkonflikt und die grossen Mächte 1868/69', *Deutsche Rundschau*, CXCV (Apr.–June 1923), 113–36.

Roeykens, F. A. 'Les débuts de l'œuvre africaine de Leopold II (1875–1879)', Académie royale des sciences coloniales, Classe des sciences morales et politiques, *Mémoires*, new ser., I, no. 1 (1955).

Simar, Théophile. 'Léopold II et le Soudan', *Congo, Revue générale de la colonie belge*, Fifth year, II, no. 4 (Nov. 1924), 506–28.

Spaak, Paul-Henri. 'The Atomic Bomb and NATO', *Foreign Affairs*, XXXIII, no. 3 (Apr. 1958), 353–59.

Stengers, Jean. 'Léopold II et la rivalité franco-anglaise en Afrique, 1882–1884', *Revue belge de philologie et d'histoire* (1969), 425–79.

Terlinden, Viscount Charles. 'La politique de la Belgique', *Nouvelle revue de Hongrie*, LV (Dec. 1936), 489–99. Supports Flemish views criticizing the frontier defense plan.

Thomas, Daniel H. 'The Use of the Scheldt in British Plans for the Defence of Belgian Neutrality 1831–1914', *Revue belge de philologie et d'histoire*, XLI, no. 2 (1963), 449–70.

— 'English Investors and the Franco-Belgium Railway Crisis of 1869', *Historian*, XXVI, no. 2 (Feb. 1964), 228–43.

Thomas, Mary E. 'Anglo-Belgian Military Relations and the Congo Question, 1911–1913', *Journal of Modern History*, XXV, no. 2 (June 1953), 157–65.

Vandenbosch, Amry. 'Small States in International Politics and Organization', *Journal of Politics*, XVI, no. 2 (May 1964), 293–312.

Vandeplas, A. 'Quelques measures de precaution de Léopold II en 1883', *Revue d'histoire des colonies*, XLIII, no. 1 (1956), 5–13.

Vandervelde, Emile. 'Belgian Foreign Policy and the Nationalities Question', *Foreign Affairs*, XI, no. 4 (July 1933), 657–70.

Waddington, A. 'L'Insurrection belge. Le Royaume de Belgique', *Histoire générale du IVe siècle à nos jours*. Edited by E. Lavisse and A. Rambaud. (2nd ed.) 12 vols. Paris: Colin, 1909, X, 334–67.

Weyer, Sylvain Van de. 'Histoire des relations extérieures depuis 1830', in *Patria Belgica*, edited by Eugène van Bemmel. 2 vols. Brussels: Bruylant-Christophe, 1873.

'What drove Belgium into the Ruhr', *Literary Digest*, LXXXVI, no. 7 (Feb. 17, 1923), 20–21.

Willequet, Jacques. 'Sondages de paix en 1918: la dernière mission du Comte Toerring', *Mélanges offerts à G. Jacquemyns* (Brussels: Univ. libre de Bruxelles, Éditions de l'Institut de Sociologie, 1968), 661–75.

Zeeland, Paul van. 'Aims of Recent Belgian Foreign Policy', *Foreign Affairs*, XVIII, no. 1 (Oct. 1939), 140–47.

Bulletin périodique de la presse belge. Edited by the French Ministry of Foreign Affairs.

Chronique de politique étrangère (Brussels).

Economist (London).

Le Flambeau (Brussels).

Mitteilungen der Afrikanischen Gesellschaft in Deutschland.

L'Indépendance belge (Brussels).

New York Times.
Le Soir (Brussels).
Le Temps (Paris).
Times (London).

5. MONOGRAPHS AND GENERAL HISTORICAL WORKS

Albertini, Luigi. *The Origins of the War of 1914.* Translated and edited by
I. M. Massey. 3 vols. London: Oxford University Press, 1952–1957.

Anstey, Roger. *Britain and the Congo in the Nineteenth Century.* Oxford: Clarendon, 1962.

— *King Leopold's Legacy: The Congo under Belgian Rule 1908–1960.* London:
Oxford University Press, 1966.

Arango, E. Ramón. *Leopold III and the Belgian Royal Question.* Baltimore:
Johns Hopkins Press, 1961. A balanced account of a still hotly-debated
issue.

Aron, Raymond. *Paix et guerre entre les nations.* Paris: Calmann-Lévy, 1962.

Banning, Emile. *Les origines et les phases de la neutralité belge.* Edited by Alfred
de Ridder. Brussels: Dewit, 1927.

Bemmel, Eugène van (ed.). *Patria Belgica.* 2 vols. Brussels: Bruylant-Christophe, 1873.

Betley, J.A. *Belgium and Poland in International Relations 1830–1831.* The
Hague: Mouton, 1960.

Beyens, Baron Napoléon Eugène. *Le Second Empire vu par un diplomate belge.*
2 vols. Paris: 1924. Based to a large extent upon the papers of the author's
father, who was Belgian minister to the court of Napoleon III.

Bindoff, Stanley T. *The Scheldt Question to 1839.* London: Allen and Unwin,
1945.

Bonnin, Georges. *Bismarck and the Hohenzollern Candidature for the Spanish
Throne. The Documents in the German Diplomatic Archives.* Translated
by I. M. Massey. New York: Humanitas Press, 1957.

Boulger, Demetrius C. *The History of Belgium, Part II, 1815–1865.* London,
1909.

— *The Reign of Leopold II, 1865–1909.* 2 vols. London: Ardenne, 1925.

Bulwer, H. Lytton. *The Life of Henry John Temple, Viscount Palmerston.* 2 vols.
Philadelphia: Lippincott, 1871.

Cammaerts, Emile. *The Prisoner of Laeken, Fact and Legend.* London: Cresset,
1941.

Campen, S.I.P. *The Quest for Security: Some Aspects of Netherlands Foreign
Policy 1945–1950.* The Hague: Nijhoff, 1958.

Carcan-Chanel, Nicole, and Martine Delsemme. *Agents diplomatiques belges
et étrangers aux XIXe et XXe siècles. Deux études economico-sociales.*
Brussels: Univ. libre de Bruxelles, 1968.

Churchill, Winston S. *The Second World War.* 6 vols. Boston: Houghton Mifflin,
1948–1953.

Clough, Shepard B. *A History of the Flemish Movement in Belgium*: *A Study in Nationalism*. Reprint of 1930 edition; New York: Octagon Books, 1968.

Collins, Robert O. *King Leopold, England, and the Upper Nile, 1899–1909*. New Haven: Yale University Press, 1968.

Crowe, S. E. *The Berlin West African Conference, 1884–1885*. London: Longmans, Green, 1942.

Deschamps, Henry-Thierry. *La Belgique devant la France de Juillet, l'opinion et l'attitude françaises de 1839 à 1848*. Paris: Société d'Édition 'Les Belles Lettres', 1956.

Discailles, Ernest. *Charles Rogier (1800–1885)*. 4 vols. Brussels: Lebègue, 1892–5.

Edmundson, George. 'The Low Countries', *The Cambridge Modern History* 14 vols. Edited by A. W. Ward, G. W. Prothero, and S. Leathes. New York: Macmillan, 1902–12, X, 517–44.

Expansion belge 1831–1865: Recueil d'études. Brussels: Académie Royale des Princeton: Sciences d'Outre-mer, 1965.

Fenaux, Robert. *Paul Hymans: Un homme, un temps, 1865–1941*. Brussels: Office de Publicité, 1946.

Fitzmaurice, E. *Life of Lord Granville*. 2 vols. London: Longmans, Green, 1905.

Fox, Annette Baker. *The Power of Small States: Diplomacy in World War II*. Chicago: University of Chicago Press, 1959.

Ganshof van der Meersch, W. J. *Le commandement de l'armée et la responsabilité ministerielle en droit constitutionnel belge*. Brussels, 1949.

— *Des rapports entre le chef de l'État et le gouvernement en droit constitutionnel belge*. Brussels: Bruylant, 1950.

Gardner, Brian. *German East: The Story of the First World War in East Africa*. London: Cassell, 1963.

Gilbert, Felix. *To the Farewell Address: Ideas of Early American Foreign Policy*. Princeton: Princeton University Press, 1961.

Goffin, Robert. *Le roi des belges, a-t-il trahi*? New York: Maison française, 1940.

Gooch, Brison D. *Belgium and the February Revolution*. The Hague: Nijhoff, 1963.

Haas, Ernst B. *The Uniting of Europe: Political, Social, and Economic Forces 1950–1957*. Stanford: Stanford University Press, 1958.

Herre, Paul. *Die kleinen Staaten europas und die Entstehung des Weltkrieges*. Munich: Beck, 1937.

Hordern, Lt.-Col. Charles. *Military Operations in East Africa*. 2 vols. London, 1941– .

Hoskyns, Cathrine. *The Congo since Independence: January 1960–December 1961*. London: Oxford University Press, 1965.

Hosse, Carl. *Die english-belgischen Aufmarschpläne gegen Deutschland vor dem Weltkrieg*. Vienna: Amalthea-Verlag, 1930. The most detailed monograph of those attempting to prove Belgium ended her neutrality by dealing with England. Most of the book is devoted to the 1905 talks; relatively little is said of the 1911 conversations.

Huizinga, James H. *Mr. Europe*: *A Political Biography of Paul-Henri Spaak*. New York: Praeger, 1961.

Hymans, Paul. *Frère-Orban*. 2 vols. Brussels: Lebègue, 1905–1910.

Impe, Herman van.*Le régime parlementaire en Belgique*. Brussels: Bruylant, 1968.

Institut Royal des Relations Internationales (Brussels).*La Belgique et les Nations Unies*. (Prepared by a commission of the institute for the Carnegie Endowment for International Peace.) New York: Manhattan, 1958.

Jordan, W. M. *Great Britain, France and the German Problem, 1918–1939*. London, 1943.

Juste, Théodore. *Histoire du congrès national de Belgique, ou de la fondation de la monarchie belge*. 2 vols. Brussels, 1850.

Kalken, Frans van. *Entre deux guerres*: *Esquisse de la vie politique en Belgique de 1918 à 1940*. (Actualités sociales, new series) Second ed. Brussels: Institut de Sociologie Solvay, 1945.

Keith, Arthur B. *The Belgian Congo and the Berlin Act*. Oxford: Oxford University Press, 1919.

Kennedy, Joseph P., and James M. Landis. *The Surrender of King Leopold*. New York: Joseph P. Kennedy Memorial Foundation, 1950. The clearest short account of Belgium's relations with the allies during the brief period of active Belgian participation in the Second World War. An appendix publishes correspondence between Admiral Keyes and Lord Gort.

Kieft, David O. *Belgium's Return to Neutrality*: *An Essay in the Frustrations of Small Power Diplomacy*. London: Oxford University Press, 1972. The best account of Belgian policy in the 1930–1936 period.

Klauw, C. A. van der. *Politieke Betrekkingen tussen Nederland en België 1919–1939*. (Leidse Historische Reeks, II) Leiden: Leiden University Press, 1953.

Lademacher, Horst. *Die belgische Neutralität als Problem der europäischen Politik, 1830–1914*. Bonn: Ludwig Röhrscheid Verlag, 1971.

Langenhove, Fernand van. *La Belgique en quête de securité 1920–1940*. Brussels: Renaissance du Livre, 1969.

Langer, William L. *The Diplomacy of Imperialism 1890–1902*. 2 vols. New York: Knopf, 1935.

Lannoy, Fleury de. *Histoire diplomatique de l'indépendance belge (1830–1839)*. Brussels: Office de Publicite, 1948.

— *Les origines diplomatiques de l'indépendance belge*: *La Conference de Londres (1830–1831)*. Louvain: Peeters, 1903.

Lefever, Ernest W. *Crisis in the Congo*: *A United Nations Force in Action*. (Studies of U.S. Policy and the U.N.) Washington: The Brookings Institution, 1965.

Les relations militaires franco-belges de mars 1936 au 10 mai 1940. Travaux d'un colloque d'historiens belges et français. Paris: Centre National de la Recherche Scientifique, 1968.

Lichtervelde, Count Louis de. *Leopold of the Belgians*. Translated by T. H. and H. R. Reed. New York: Century, 1929.

Lord, Robert H. *The Origins of the War of 1870*. Cambridge: Harvard University Press, 1924.

Louis, W. R. *Ruanda-Urundi 1884–1919*. Oxford: Clarendon Press, 1963.

Luykx, Theo. *Politieke Geschiedenis van België van 1789 tot heden*. Amsterdam: Elsevier, 1969.

Martelli, George. *Leopold to Lumumba: A History of the Belgian Congo 1877–1960*. London: Chapman and Hall, 1962.

Martin, Theodore. *Life of the Prince Consort*. 4 vols. New York, 1875–1879.

Masoin, Fritz. *Histoire de l'État Indépendant du Congo*. 2 vols. Namur: Picard-Balon, 1912.

Mason, Henry L. *The European Coal and Steel Community, Experiment in Supranationalism*. The Hague: Nijhoff, 1955.

Meade, James E. *Negotiations for Benelux: An Annotated Chronicle 1943–1956*. (Princeton Studies in International Finance No. 6.) Princeton: Departement of Economics and Sociology, Princeton University, 1957.

Mezerik, A. G. (ed.). *Congo and the United Nations*. 3 vols. New York: International Review Service, 1960–3.

Michael, Horst. *Bismarck, England und Europa*. Munich: Verlag der Münchner Drucke, 1930.

Miller, Jane K. *Belgian Foreign Policy between Two Wars 1919–1940*. New York: Bookman, 1951.

Morgenthau, Hans J. *Politics Among Nations: The Struggle for Power and Peace*. (3rd ed.) New York: Knopf, 1960.

Morley, John. *The Life of William Ewart Gladstone*. 3 vols. London: Macmillan, 1903.

Moulton, Harold G., and Leo Pasvolsky. *War Debts and World Prosperity*. (Institute of Economics of the Brookings Institution, Publication no. 45.) New York: Century, 1932.

Murphy, Agnes. *The Ideology of French Imperialism*. Washington: Catholic University of American Press, 1948.

Myers, Denys P. *The Reparations Settlement*. Boston: World Peace Foundation, 1930.

Nicolson, Harold. *Portrait of a Diplomatist, Being the Life of Sir Arthur Nicolson First Lord Carnock, and a Study of the Origins of the Great War*. Boston: Houghton Mifflin, 1930.

Nothomb, Jean-Baptiste. *Essai historique et politique sur la révolution belge*. (4th ed.) 2 vols. Brussels: Muquardt, 1876.

Ollivier, Emile. *L'Empire libéral*. 17 vols. Paris: Garnier, 1895–1915.

Omond, G. W. T. *Belgium and Luxembourg*. (The Nations of Today Series, edited by John Buchan.) London: Hodder Staughton, 1923.

Oncken, Mermann. *Die Rheinpolitik Kaiser Napoleons III. von 1863 bis 1870 und der Ursprung des Krieges von 1870/71*. 3 vols. Stuttgart: Deutsche Verlags-Anstalt, 1926.

Pirenne, Henri. *Histoire de Belgique des origines à nos jours*. 4 vols. Edited by F. Schauwers and J. Paquet. Brussels: Renaissance du Livre, 1963.

Power, Thomas F., Jr. *Jules Ferry and the Renaissance of French Imperialism*. New York: King's Crown Press, 1944.

Raeymaeker, Omar de. *Belgie's Internationaal Beleid 1919–1939*. Brussels, 1945.

Ridder, Alfred de. *La Belgique et la Prusse en Conflit, 1834–1838*. Paris: Vromant, 1919. Although written to demonstrate that Prussia has always dealt unfairly with Belgium, the book is well balanced; it includes many quotations from archival sources.

— *Histoire diplomatique du traité de 1839 (19 avril 1839)*. Brussels: Vromant, 1920. Reproduces portions of many documents.

— *Le mariage du roi Léopold II, d'après des documents inédits*. Brussels: Dewit, 1925.

— *Les projets d'union douanière franco-belge et les puissances européennes (1836–1843)*. Brussels: Lamertin, 1933. Concentrates on the attitudes of England, Austria, and Prussia; reproduces many hitherto unpublished documents.

Ritter, Gerhard. *The Schlieffen Plan: Critique of a Myth*. Translated by Andrew and Eva Wilson. New York: Praeger, 1958.

Robertson, A. H. *European Institutions, Co-operation: Integration: Unification*. New York: Praeger, 1959.

Rothstein, Robert L. *Alliances and Small Powers*. New York: Columbia University Press, 1968.

Schmidt, Royal J. *Versailles and the Ruhr: Seedbed of World War II*. The Hague: Nijhoff, 1968.

Seton-Watson, Robert W. *Britain in Europe 1789–1914*. Cambridge, England: Cambridge University Press, 1955.

Steefel, Lawrence D. *Bismarck, the Hohenzollern Candidacy, and the Origins of the Franco-German War of 1870*. Cambridge: Harvard University Press, 1962.

Terlinden, Viscount Charles. *Histoire militaire des belges*. 2 vols. Brussels: Renaissance du Livre, 1966.

Thomson, Robert Stanley. *Fondation de l'État Indépendant du Congo*. Brussels: Office de Publicité, 1933.

Toynbee, A. J. (ed.). *Survey of International Affairs*. 2 vols. London: Oxford University Press, 1928.

Tyler, J. E. *The British Army and the Continent 1904–1914*. London: Arnold, 1938.

Vandenbosch, Amry. *Dutch Foreign Policy since 1815: A Study in Small Power Politics*. The Hague: Nijhoff, 1959.

Wampach, Gaspard. *Le Luxembourg neutre: Étude d'histoire diplomatique et de droit international public*. Paris: Rousseau, 1900.

Waxweiler, Emile. *Belgium, Neutral and Loyal: The War of 1914*. New York: Putnam, 1915.

Webster, C. K. *The Foreign Policy of Palmerston 1830–1841*. 2 vols. London: Bell, 1951.

Willequet, Jacques. *Le Congo belge et la Weltpolitik (1894–1914)*. Brussels: Presses Universitaires, 1962. By the historical counsellor of the Belgian Ministry of Foreign Affairs.

Williamson, Samuel R., Jr. *The Politics of Grand Strategy: Britain and France Prepare for War, 1904–1914*. Cambridge, Mass.: Harvard University Press, 1969.

Wullus-Rudiger, J. A. [Armand Wullus]. *La Belgique et l'équilibre européen, documents inédits*. Paris: Berger-Levrault, 1935.

— *La Belgique et la crise européene 1914–1945*. 2 vols. Paris: Berger-Levrault, 1945.

— *Les origines internationales du drame belge de 1940*. Brussels: Vanderlinden, 1950.

— *En marge de la politique belge 1914–1956*. Paris: Berger Levrault, 1957.

Zuylen, Pierre van. *Les mains libres: Politique extérieure de la Belgique 1914–1940.* Paris: Desclée de Brouwer, 1950.

— *L'Échiquier congolais, ou le secret du roi*. Brussels: Dessart, 1959.

Index

Aachen, 14, 256, 296: in Rhineland separatist revolt, 284–85, 289–92
Abercorn, 181–83
ABERDEEN, Lord, 66–67
Abyssinia, 374
Action nationale, 287
ADELAIDE, grand duchess of Luxemburg, 198, 205
ADELAIDE, Princess Eugénie Louise, 36
ADENAUER, Konrad, 285, 292, 390
Admiralty, British, 156, 182, 207–08, 224 n. 47
Africa: and Congo crisis (1960–64), 396, 400–402; discussed at Paris Peace Conference, 212–14; during First World War, 180–81, 183, 191, 193; and founding of Congo Free State, 118, 120–21, 139; *see also* Congo, Belgian; Congo Free State; Congo, Republic of
Agnates of House of Nassau, 33
Agreement of November 1882 (regarding Congo), 127
ALBERT I, king of Belgium, 6, 145, 201, 238, 263, 356, 362; and Belgian defense planning after First World War, 233, 313–14, 318–20; and Belgian policy during the First World War, 187, 190 194–96, 371; at the Paris

Peace Conference, 208–09; and William II of Germany, 168–69
Albert Canal, 254, 332, 347, 353–54
Albertville, 181–82
Alima River, 125
Alsace-Lorraine, 191, 231, 389
ANCILLON, Johann, 45–46
ANETHAN, Baron Jules J. d', 147, 150–51, 168
Angra-Pequena, 130
Ans, 72
Anschluss, 343, 347
ANSTEY, Roger, 412
Antwerp, 1, 68, 72–73, 110, 189–90, 202, 205, 208, 215, 239, 253–54, 256, 274, 348, 358, 381–82, 391; and capitalization of Scheldt tolls, 94–95; fortification of, 44, 93, 143, 150, 166–67, 169, 176, 184, 317–18, 332, 337, 347; struggle for control of (1830–39), 13, 16–17, 26 30–32, 34, 36, 40–41, 58
Appenweier, 298
ARENDT, Leon, 197; and Belgian planning in the event of war (1900–14), 157–64
Aristocracy, 5, 72
Arlon, 324–25
Armistice: in 1830, 15–16; in 1918, 198–99, 204